CRIMINOLOGY
An Interdisciplinary Approach

C. Ray Jeffery

Professor of Criminology
School of Criminology
Florida State University
Tallahassee, Florida

Prentice Hall, Englewood Cliffs, New Jersey 07632

Library of Congress Cataloging-in-Publication Data

JEFFERY, C. RAY (Clarence Ray) (date)
  Criminology: an interdisciplinary approach / C. Ray Jeffery.
  p. cm.
  Bibliography: p.
  Includes index.
ISBN 0-13-193591-7
  1. Crime and criminals. I. Title.
HV6025.J38 1990
364—dc20   89-33956
                               CIP

Editorial/production supervision and
  interior design: Mary Anne Shahidi
Cover design: Ben Santora
Manufacturing buyer: Laura Crossland

ACKNOWLEDGMENTS
Figures 11–2, 11–4, and 11–8. *Brain, Mind, and Behavior,* 2nd ed. by Floyd E. Bloom and Arlyne Lazerson. Copyright © 1985, 1988 by Educational Broadcasting Company. Reprinted with permission of W. H. Freeman and Company. **Figures 11–3 and 11–5.** *The Brain,* By Richard Restak, M.D. Copyright © 1984 by Educational Broadcasting Corporation and Richard M. Restak. Reprinted by permission of Bantam Books, a division of Bantam, Doubleday, Dell Publishing Group, Inc. **Figure 11–6 .** *Fundamentals of Neuropsychology,* 2nd ed. by Brian Kolb and Ian Whishaw. Copyright © 1980, 1985 by W. H. Freeman and Company. Reprinted with permission. **Figure 13–1.** *Biological Psychology,* 2nd ed. by James W. Kalat. Copyright © 1981, 1984 by Wadsworth, Inc. Reprinted by permission of the publisher.

 © 1990 by Prentice-Hall, Inc.
A Division of Simon & Schuster
Englewood Cliffs, New Jersey 07632

Printed in the United States of America
10 9 8 7 6 5 4 3 2 1

ISBN 0-13-193591-7

Prentice-Hall International (UK) Limited, *London*
Prentice-Hall of Australia Pty. Limited, *Sydney*
Prentice-Hall Canada Inc., *Toronto*
Prentice-Hall Hispanoamericana, S.A., *Mexico*
Prentice-Hall of India Private Limited, *New Delhi*
Prentice-Hall of Japan, Inc., *Tokyo*
Simon & Schuster Asia Pte. Ltd., *Singapore*
Editora Prentice-Hall do Brasil, Ltda. *Rio de Janeiro*

This book is dedicated to those willing to consider a new approach to criminology and criminal justice. This includes especially my graduate and former graduate students who have made my life a little bit easier by their involvement in the thinking and learning process.

Contents

Contents

Preface

This book is designed as a different approach to criminology, based on a systems approach and an interdisciplinary approach to human behavior. The text contrasts criminology as a behavioral science with criminal justice as the application of political processes to criminals. I argue for a criminology based on a syntheses of biology, psychology, sociology, and other behavioral sciences. A theory of criminal behavior must involve an interdisciplinary effort. Most criminology texts are sociological texts which minimize or ignore biology and psychology. The text uses an Organism × Environment interaction model of behavior, from genes to brain function to learning to society, as a basis for behavioral analysis, and it draws on the recent developments in genetics, neurology, biochemistry, and psychobiology, as well as the more traditional materials from psychology and sociology.

Criminology textbooks are devoted to sociological criminology, not interdisciplinary criminology. Most criminology textbooks are also criminal justice textbooks. We do not need another textbook in sociological criminology, as several good textbooks are now available. We do not need another textbook in criminal justice, as several good textbooks are on the market. What is needed is a textbook devoted to criminology as an interdisciplinary science. This textbook is a behavioral science textbook, and it discusses the usual criminal justice topics (criminal law, police, courts, and prison systems) from a behavioral science context in an effort to integrate criminology and criminal justice.

Criminology/criminal justice texts are usually committed to retribution, deterrence, and rehabilitation as the models of crime control, whereas in this book emphasis is placed on crime prevention. Recent developments in the behavioral sciences are used to prevent crime before it occurs. Emphasis is placed on both environmental design and bioenvironmental theory as ways of preventing crime.

The text is designed for undergraduate classes in criminology, and for prelaw and law students as well as psychology and biology students interested in human behavior and deviancy. The book can also be used in a beginning class for graduate students in criminology/criminal justice, as well as a supplementary source of readings for graduate seminars in criminology, psychology, and biology.

Organization of the Textbook

Part 1 of the book deals with *philosophical and historical* issues in criminology: the nature and structure of criminology; systems theory, science, and criminology; the evolution of human beings and of society; the evolution of criminal law; classical legal criminology; and positivism, science, and criminology.

Part 2 deals with *criminology and law:* criminal law, ethics, and jurisprudence; law, science, and society; and the criminal justice system.

Part 3 deals with *criminology: the biological and psychological sciences:* criminology and genetics; criminology and the brain; criminology and Freudian psychoanalysis, and criminology and learning theory.

Part 4 deals with criminology: the social sciences: sociological criminology, sociology, law, and social control; biosocial and demographic variables in crime; and economic and political crimes.

Part 5 deals with *criminology and the future:* crime prevention and the individual offender; crime prevention, ecology, and the physical environemnt; and crime prevention: scientific versus legalistic models.

I wish to thank G. O. W. Mueller for reading some preliminary chapters and for his support for an interdisciplinary approach to criminology. His criticisms and comments were of great value. Simon Dinitz reviewed the manuscript and also supported the thrust of the book. Mueller and Dinitz were a major force in the creation of the book.

My colleague Frederic Faust read the manuscript in its early raw form and acted as a sounding board for me throughout the writing process. We met at the Steak and Egg on a regular basis for coffee and an exchange of ideas and for this I thank him.

My thanks to Edwina Ivory and Deborah Orth for their typing of the manuscript.

I also wish to acknowledge the help of the Prentice Hall staff, including especially Paul F. Corey and Mary Anne Shahidi.

C. Ray Jeffery

PART 1: PHILOSOPHICAL AND HISTORICAL ISSUES IN CRIMINOLOGY

The Nature and Structure of Criminology

1

WHAT IS CRIMINOLOGY?

Definition of Criminology

Criminology is the scientific study of crime and criminals. Sutherland and Cressey (1970:3) defined criminology as the study of (1) the making of laws, (2) the breaking of laws, and (3) the reaction to the breaking of laws. The breaking of laws defines the criminal, the study of whose behavior has been a major aspect of criminology. The making of laws and the reaction to the breaking of laws are the defining components of crime within a political process. Criminal law is basic to the definition of crime.

Wolfgang and Ferracuti (1967) defined criminology as the scientific study of crime, criminals, and criminal behavior. Here the emphasis is placed on the scientific study of human behavior, which makes the criminologist a behavioral scientist. Conrad (Conrad and Myren, 1979) combined the Sutherland and the Wolfgang–Ferracuti definitions by defining criminology as ''the application of scientific method to the explanation of the phenomena generated by the interactions of the process of lawmaking, lawbreaking, and the reactions to these processes.''

Because of the nature of crime and criminals, criminology must be an interdisciplinary science involving the biological and behavioral sciences (biology, psychology, psychiatry, sociology, political science, economics, and anthropology) and the policy sciences (criminal law, public administration, philosophy, ethics, and history). *Human behavior* is the focus of criminology as an interdisciplinary behavioral science devoted to the scientific study and understanding of crime and criminals. Criminology is thus considered to be the scientific study of human behavior.

Criminology and the Criminal

Criminology as the study of the criminal involves the behavioral sciences in asking and answering questions concerning why human beings behave as they do. Why do people commit murder, rape, assault, robbery, and burglary? These are behaviors that can most meaningfully and usefully be understood in terms of knowledge and research from biology, psychology, sociology, and other behavioral sciences. Thus, by definition, criminology is the study of human behavior.

Criminology and Crime

The study of the behavior of criminals is only one aspect of criminology. Human behavior is not criminal unless it is designated as such by the legal system. The processes by which behavior is made criminal is called the criminal law, and the term *crime* is used to designate the legal definition of behavior imposed on the criminal by the criminal justice system—police, prosecutors, courts, and prisons.

Criminology involves the scientific study of law known as the sociology of law or sociological jurisprudence, and the sociology of social control. The objective is to study the human behavior of the police, lawyers, judges, prosecutors, probation and parole officers, and prison officers. Crime and criminal law are as much a product of human behavior as are criminals. Basic behavioral principles as found in genetics, the brain sciences, psychology, psychiatry, sociology, economics, and political science must apply. We must first have a fundamental theory of human behavior before we can develop a theory of criminal behavior or a theory of crime. That which unites criminals and crime is the concept of behavior.

Criminology and Criminal Law

Not only must we differentiate the study of crime from the study of criminals, but we must differentiate criminology from criminal law. Criminal law had its origin in the evolution of human societies and the emergence of the nation-state system, and it is based on political power and authority. Criminal law developed in the prescientific era, and as such is not subject to the criteria of scientific verification. Scientific questions and answers are always subject to refutation and revision. There are major differences between science and law, as will be discussed throughout this book.

In this textbook we will refer to the scientific study of crime and criminals as *scientific criminology,* whereas the political and legal aspects of crime, as found in the criminal law, will be labeled *legal criminology.* These two systems have developed as separate and independent systems for most of history; however, we will argue that there can be scientific studies of law, as indicated above, in the sociology of law and sociological jurisprudence, and law and science can form an interactive system.

Criminology and Criminal Justice

The term "criminal justice" refers to the agencies of social control which define and react to those behaviors falling within the purview of the criminal law. The criminal justice system is composed of the police–prosecutor–courts–prison system. The personnel of the system include police officers, lawyers, judges, probation and parole officers, and prison officials, as well as the executive and legislative branches of government. Inciardi (1987:v) defined criminal justice as "the structure, functions, and decision processes of agencies that deal with the management and control of crime and criminal offenders—the police, courts, and corrections departments. It is often confused with the academic disciplines of criminology and police science."

Myren (Conrad and Myren, 1979) objects to the narrow definition of criminology as sociology and the study of the criminal, and looks toward Radzinowicz's concept of criminology as including crime, criminal justice, punishment, prisons, police practices, and criminal law. Myren puts forth an interdisciplinary approach to criminal justice which includes criminology plus the police–courts–prison system.

The criminal justice system can be viewed as the interaction of science and law. While operating within the framework of criminal law, the criminal justice employee might apply scientific principles from the behavioral sciences. A judge might use a neurological examination in his/her evaluation of a defendant, or a probation officer might use psychological theory in his/her evaluation of a probationer. They are generally not scientists in the narrow sense of the word as used by Wolfgang and Ferracuti as contributors to a body of scientific knowledge. A criminal justice practitioner may contribute to the advancement of knowledge as well as to the application of knowledge to practical problems. The major issue then becomes one of determining how law and science should mix, that is, how they can be integrated within a total system so as to avoid the science versus law controversy or the criminology versus criminal justice controversy. (This idea was suggested by my colleague Frederic Faust.)

Nettler (1979) has written that criminal justice involves basic moral issues concerning what behaviors should be labeled as criminal and how such behavior should be dealt with. The critical concept here is "justice," as we shall see in our later discussions of criminal law and criminal justice.

Conflicts within the Behavioral Sciences

In this book we regard criminology as an interdisciplinary study of human behavior. As such, criminology must integrate knowledge about behavior from several disciplines. No single discipline or field has a monopoly on knowledge about human behavior and social institutions which is needed by criminologists for the development and advancement of the field. Yet, universities are typically organized into separate departments and schools, thereby discouraging the development of criminology as an interdisciplinary field.

There has been little integration of biology, psychology, and sociology into a unified field of behavior. Rather, we have a biology of behavior, a psychology of behavior, and a sociology of behavior; in fact, as we shall see, there are several biologies of behavior, several psychologies of behavior, and several sociologies of behavior, each claiming to be the correct explanation of behavior. Each academic discipline does different types of research at different levels of analysis, based on different basic assumptions concerning *human nature,* and as a result each comes to a different conclusion as to why people behave as criminals or noncriminals or what should be done with our criminal population. There has been no integrated theory of behavior which unites criminology as a behavioral science.

Biology and psychology are typically ignored or underplayed in most current criminology textbooks. Most texts are written by sociologists from a sociologist's point of view. In recent years, there have been major advances in biology, psychiatry, and psychology which have major ramifications for criminology and criminal law. Mental diseases such as schizophrenia and depression are now interpreted as diseases of the brain or neurological and biochemical problems rather than mental problems. Such psychobiological conditions as hypoglycemia, nutritional deficiencies, sociopathy, episodic brain dysfunction, premenstrual syndrome, post-traumatic stress disorder, and other neurological conditions have been related to criminal behavior.

People trained in law, medicine, sociology, and psychology work in physical and intellectual isolation from one another. In the absence of knowledge of what the behavioral sciences are doing in the way of research and treatment of behavioral disorders, lawyers convict and put into prisons or execution chambers people who have major medical and behavioral problems. The medical profession is not aware of the legal problems involved in the treatment of people with biomedical problems. Sociologists do not know biology and psychology, and psychologists and biologists do not know sociology or criminal law, although efforts are under way to integrate disciplines.

Conflicts within the Criminal Justice System

In addition to conflicting viewpoints concerning behavior within the behavioral sciences, there are conflicts within the criminal justice system. Each of the major components works as an isolated unit in conflict with one another. What the police do about crime conflicts with what lawyers or probation officers do. Courts often upset the work of the police or probation officers, and prison officials work for different goals than do the police or court officials. There is no general integrated system of criminal justice by which the activities of police, prosecutors, courts, and prison agencies are interrelated in terms of common purposes and strategies, although efforts at integration are two decades old. Such basic conflicts within the system must be recognized.

Conflicts between Criminology and Criminal Law

Not only are there many conflicts within criminology and within criminal justice; there are also major conflicts between criminology and criminal law. There is no integration of science and law. What the behavioral scientist says about human nature is seldom made a part of the criminal law. The lawyer makes very different and very unscientific assumptions about human nature, views of behavior which are at great odds with those put forth in biology, psychology, sociology, and other behavioral sciences.

This conflict is based on the overall objectives of scientific criminology and legal criminology. Scientific criminology has as its goal the study and understanding of human behavior in order that crime and criminal behavior can be prevented or eliminated through treatment. The goal of legal criminology is to find moral guilt and a criminal mind and to punish the behavior within the system of criminal law and prisons. Retribution and revenge are the traditional objectives of criminal law.

Scientific criminology leads to a medical model of crime control, with research and the hospital at the beginning and end of the process; legal criminology leads to a punitive model of crime control, with the prison and electric chair at the end of the process. One crime control model views criminals as sick people whose behavior is caused by events beyond their control; the other crime control model views criminals as evil people who must be punished in order for retributive justice to prevail. The differences between the scientific and legal approaches to crime and criminals may be gleaned from questions raised about problems basic to the field of criminology.

Should we focus our resources on building prisons and convicting criminals or on doing research? It costs $25,000 to $40,000 to put a person in prison, and while the person is incarcerated, the cost is another $20,000 to $30,000 per year (see Chapter 9). When released, the criminal may come out of prison more dangerous and criminalistic than when admitted. From a long-range perspective, would an investment in behavioral science research yield less expensive and more efficient and humane responses to criminal behavior?

Are we allowed to treat criminals or only to punish them? If we treat them, is compulsory treatment allowable under the law? May we stick a needle in the arm of a criminal to take blood as part of a medical examination to determine if the criminal has hypoglycemia or a brain disorder, or may we stick a needle in the criminal's arm only to execute him/her by a lethal injection, as is done in the state of Texas?

Should we use legal laws or scientific laws in dealing with our crime problem and criminal population? Should lawyers decide the fate of our criminals, or should psychologists, psychiatrists, and criminologists also play a role in the criminal justice process? If behavioral scientists are to be included, in what capacity should they be involved?

Are people who suffer from brain disease, hypoglycemia, premenstrual syndrome, or alcoholism insane, mentally ill, medically ill, or criminals? Do they belong in prisons or hospitals? Do we execute them or treat them? If we opt for treatment, what means are to be used to select and evaluate different treatment modalities?

Should everyone who commits murder, rape, or robbery be given the same sentence to the same type of institution, or should our sentencing practices be based on individual differences and needs? Who should determine the disposition of those found guilty of crimes—the criminologist, the psychiatrist, or the lawyer?

Does the brain of the criminal differ from the brain of the noncriminal, and, if so, in what ways? Can we detect abnormal and antisocial behaviors of potential criminals through the use of such diagnostic tools as CAT and PETT scans and biochemical analyses of the brain? Are we able to treat antisocial behaviors through nutrition, drug therapies, and modern medical techniques?

Why are a majority of criminals young adult males? What is there about being adolescent and male that predisposes one to a criminal career? Is it due to biological, psychological, or social factors, or to an interaction of all three?

Is criminal behavior a product of heredity or environment, or both? Do contemporary research findings in human genetics have implications for the study of human behavior, specifically for criminal behavior? Should we wait until a crime has occurred, as is now the practice of the police–courts–prison system, or should we attempt to prevent crime before it occurs through crime prevention programs?

Criminology involves many issues that are political in nature and are most controversial. Disagreement among criminologists on fundamental issues and orientations is reflected in the absence of a systematic, scientific basis for analyzing crime and criminal behavior, and in the failure to control the crime problem. Crime is one of the major domestic problems of our times, yet we have few successful programs for dealing with crime and criminals. We continue to rely on methods used for hundreds of years which have proven to be costly and unsuccessful. We have more men and women in prisons today than ever before, and we have a very high crime rate despite the fact that we are now spending millions of dollars on law enforcement, criminal trials, and punishment.

What Is Crime?

Crime is defined in different ways by lawyers and by criminologists. Lawyers define crime in legal terms as the violation of a criminal law and a response from the criminal justice system. Without a law, there is no crime. Sociologists/criminologists define crime as the violation of a conduct code or social norm. The sociologist is interested in the process of social control and the ways in which legal norms are part of the social control system. This argument is developed in Chapter 15, in which we discuss sociology and social control, and Chapter 7, in which we discuss criminology and criminal law. For the purposes of this book, crime is a legal concept created by the criminal justice system. The full meaning of the term ''crime'' is developed in subsequent chapters.

Who Is the Criminal?

The lawyer defines the criminal as one who has been convicted of a crime in a court of law. The legal process of arrest, prosecution, and conviction is essential in order that the label ''criminal'' be applied to an individual. The sociologist/criminologist defines the criminal as one who behaves in a given manner, whether or not an arrest and conviction result from the behavior. If one behaves as a murderer or rapist, then one is a criminal, whether or not he/she is arrested, convicted, and sentenced to prison.

The issue is: Do we study people who have been convicted of murder, or those who behave as murderers, even if not convicted? The critical issue is whether we are interested in studying the behavior of those who commit certain antisocial acts, or the behavior of the police, lawyers, prosecutors, and judges. As we shall see in Chapters 7 and 8, this is no small issue, since in many situations fewer than 1 percent of those committing crimes are ever arrested and/or convicted.

Who Is the Criminologist?

Wolfgang and Ferracuti (1967) defined the criminologist as one who engaged in the scientific study of crime and criminals [see Morris (1975)]. Such a definition excluded the police, probation officers, lawyers, judges, social workers, and others who administer the criminal justice system. The term ''criminologist'' thus becomes an extension of our definition of the term ''criminology.''

Criminologists are most often in a university setting, teaching and doing research in terms of their training in biology, psychology, medicine, sociology, and other behavioral science disciplines. The law practitioner, who is also involved in teaching and research in the area of criminal law and the behavioral sciences, would also be included in our definition of the criminologist. The lawyer who practices criminal law as a prosecutor or defense attorney or judge is not a criminologist within the meaning of this definition. Neither is the private detective a criminologist, although the term ''criminologist'' is often used on television to describe such practitioners.

By definition the criminologist is rooted in the behavioral sciences, not in the criminal justice system. The criminologist is a creator of knowledge; the criminal justice practitioner is a consumer or an applier of knowledge, although it is recognized that some people may do both.

ACADEMIC PROGRAMS

Criminology Programs

Criminology as a behavioral science has been associated with university educational programs in biology, psychology, psychiatry, and sociology. Early writing and research in crime and criminal behavior was done by biologists and psychologists. In 1924 a criminology textbook appeared by a sociologist, Edwin H. Sutherland, and it was followed by other textbooks by sociologists, including Gillin in 1926, Parsons in 1926, Haynes in 1930, Cantor in 1932, and Morris in 1934 (Reckless, 1970).

From 1930 to 1950, criminology developed as an academic discipline closely identified with sociology departments (Gibbons, 1979). Many prominent sociological criminologists emerged at that time, including Reckless, Sellin, Barnes, Shaw, McKay, and others. Psychiatrists were also developing studies of criminal behavior, but in isolation from sociological criminologists. Psychiatrists receive little or no training in sociology; sociologists receive little or no training in psychology, psychiatry, or criminal law; and lawyers receive little or no training in sociology, psychology, or psychiatry. The behavioral sciences developed a psychiatric criminology and a sociological criminology, whereas the lawyers developed a legalistic criminology related to the criminal justice system.

Sociologists are trained in sociology departments and receive a Ph.D. degree in sociology. Psychiatrists are trained in medical schools and receive an M.D. degree. Psychologists are trained in psychology departments and receive a Ph.D. degree in psychology. Criminology thus developed as a speciality within sociology, psychiatry, and psychology rather than as an interdependent, integrated scientific discipline.

By 1933, a school of police science was established at the University of California at Berkeley under the leadership of August Vollmer, a former chief of police in Berkeley. Vollmer felt that police performance could be upgraded if the educational requirements of police officers were increased from a high school diploma or less to a college education leading to a B.A. degree. This was a police science training program, not a behavioral science program. This program became a school of criminology in 1950 and a graduate school in 1959. Vollmer was instrumental in organizing the National Association of College Police Training Officials in 1941, and in 1946 the National Association was reorganized into the Society for the Advancement of Criminology. In 1957, it became the present American Society of Criminology (ASC), the official organization for sociological criminologists, with a few psychiatrists, lawyers, and psychologists also holding membership (Morn, 1980; Morris, 1975). The role of the sociologist in the life of ASC may be seen in the training and orientation of those who served as president of ASC.

The shift in orientation of the ASC from police training, as found in the Berkeley program, to sociology, as found in sociology departments, caused a rebellion within the ASC by police educators who advocated a return to the

President	Year(s)	Training/Orientation
Donald MacNamara	1960–1963	Police administration
Walter Reckless	1964–1966	Sociology
Marvin Wolfgang	1967	Sociology
G. O. W. Mueller	1968	Law, sociology
Bruno Cormier	1969	Psychiatry
Albert Morris	1970	Sociology
Simon Dinitz	1971	Sociology
Charles Newman	1972	Public administration
John Ball	1973	Sociology
Edward Sagarin	1974	Sociology
Nicholas Kittrie	1975	Law, political science
Gilbert Geis	1976	Sociology
William Amos	1977	Human development and psychology
C. R. Jeffery	1978	Sociology, psychobiology
Ronald Akers	1979	Sociology
Daniel Glaser	1980	Sociology
Frank Scarpetti	1981	Sociology
Harry Allen	1982	Sociology
Travis Hirschi	1983	Sociology
Albert Reiss	1984	Sociology
Austin Turk	1985	Sociology
Lloyd Ohlin	1986	Sociology
Don Gottfredson	1987	Psychology
William Chambliss	1988	Sociology

Vollmer tradition. This group of police educators left the ASC in 1963 to form the International Association of Police Professors, claiming that the ASC was too academic and too sociological. The International Association became the present Academy of Criminal Justice Sciences (ACJS) in 1970 (Morn, 1980). As a result of this split, we now have one professional organization for criminologists, one for criminal justice educators, and others for correctional specialists, lawyers, court administrators, and police chiefs. People in criminology on the one hand, and people in criminal justice on the other hand, ordinarily do not attend the same meetings or belong to the same professional organizations. Although the founders of ACJS claim that theirs was a move toward an interdisciplinary science, the result was to further divide the behavioral scientists from the practitioners. Most of the ACJS presidents came from criminal justice backgrounds, especially police backgrounds, not from the behavioral sciences. We have reviewed the claims that criminology and criminal justice are united as one field, or at least should be united, but the evidence indicates that we have separate professional organizations, separate journals, separate educational systems, and separate theoretical systems. The resolution of this division is yet to be accomplished.

Sagarin (1977), in his article "The Egghead, the Screw, and the Flatfoot," observed the differences between the egghead (professor), the screw (prison guard), and the flatfoot (police officer), and he pointed to the need for the criminologist, the police officer, and the prison guard to work together rather than separately, having separate journals and separate professional organizations.

Not only do criminologists and criminal justice educators go to different meetings, but they also read different journals. In 1910, the American Institute of Criminal Law and Criminology established a journal entitled the *Journal of the American Institute of Criminal Law and Criminology*. The name of the journal was changed in 1931 to the *Journal of Criminal Law and Criminology*. In 1951 the journal became the *Journal of Criminal Law, Criminology, and Police Science* and was published out of the Northwestern University School of Law in Chicago. In 1973, the journal once again became the *Journal of Criminal Law and Criminology*, and a separate publication called the *Journal of Police Science and Administration* was established.

In 1963, ASC started the newsletter *Criminologica*. While C. R. Jeffery was editor of *Criminologica*, a contract was entered into with Sage Publications in 1970 to publish a new journal, *Criminology: An Interdisciplinary Journal*, with Jeffery as its founding editor. This journal is now the official journal of ASC (Morris, 1975). In 1983, ACJS formed its own journal, *Justice Quarterly*, under the editorship of Rita James Simon.

Criminal Justice Programs

Education in criminal justice was originally limited to police science programs, usually at a junior college or at a police academy. Lawyers are trained in law schools and receive an LL.B degree, or, as it is now known, a J.D. degree in law. Law school education is quite separate from training in criminology and the behavioral sciences. Criminology and law are not integrated into a systematic approach to the crime problem. Schools of social work produce social workers who serve as probation and parole officers attached to courts, especially juvenile courts.

The school of criminology at Berkeley founded by Vollmer, discussed above, was the first major attempt to place police training at the college level. Other programs were established, including those at San Jose State University, Michigan State University, the University of Maryland, Indiana University, the University of Southern California, and Florida State University (Morn, 1980; Ward and Webb, 1984). Such programs emphasized police administration and, to some extent, correctional administration. They were criminal justice as opposed to criminology programs.

In the 1970s an explosion occurred in criminal justice programs due to the President's Commission on Law Enforcement and the Administration of Justice, and the establishment of the Law Enforcement Assistance Administration (LEAA) in 1969. Part of the LEAA program was LEEP (Law Enforcement Educational Programs), which paid students to go to college to prepare for careers in law enforcement. The federal government expended millions of dollars on law enforcement education, which was then expanded to include the courts and the prison system, now called "criminal justice." Criminal justice programs grew from 40 or 50 to over 1300 by 1978 as a result of federal policy which endorsed a hard-line "law and order" approach to crime control through the police–courts–prison system. Because of the rapid growth of criminal justice programs during the 1970s, the Joint Commission on Criminology and Criminal Justice Education and Standards was formed under the direction of Richard Ward, with members from the ASC and ACJS (Ward and Webb, 1984; Morn, 1980; Conrad and Myren, 1979; Zalman, 1981).

Several major educational programs emerged as a result of this new emphasis on law and order. John Jay College of Criminal Justice is part of the City University of New York system. The John Jay program is essentially an undergraduate training academy for police officers and correctional officials and offers a graduate program in criminal justice for administrators. The SUNY/Albany School of Criminal Justice was established in 1965 along the lines proposed by Myren, discussed above. Both the John Jay and the Albany programs served as models for criminal justice education during the 1970 period of growth and development, and both were very much committed to a criminal justice model with less emphasis on the behavioral sciences (Conrad and Myren, 1979).

Another major criminal justice program was established in 1965 at Sam Houston State University in Texas. The program was established by George Killinger, the former chair of the U.S. Parole Commission. The college of criminal justice at Sam Houston is devoted primarily to corrections. The facilities were built in Huntsville, where the department of corrections for the state of Texas is located, and are adjacent to and physically part of the Texas State Prison. Again, the emergence of Sam Houston State University in criminal justice education emphasizes the close ties between criminal justice education and the criminal justice system.

The University of California at Berkeley program became the school of criminology in 1950. The school of criminology added a graduate program, including the first and only doctorate in criminology, called the D. Crim. degree. The school of criminology at Berkeley was an interdisciplinary program, involving police administration, corrections, law, sociology, and psychiatry. However, the school was under the influence of former police officers, A. Vollmer, O. W. Wilson, and Joseph Lohman, a sociologist who became sheriff of Cook County, Illinois. When Lohman died suddenly he was replaced by Leslie Wilkins, a sociologist, followed shortly by Sheldon Messinger, another sociologist. Conflict between criminal justice and criminology was very obvious in the Berkeley program, as was conflict between the criminology faculty and the behavioral science faculty (Morris, 1975; Ward and Webb, 1984). The University of California program came to an end in 1975 when the board of regents disbanded the program due to internal strife and external political conflict. The criminology program had become very radical and political during the 1960s, the era of student protests at Berkeley. Radical or conflict or Marxian criminology emerged at this time as a result of social protests and the Vietnam war.

We can illustrate the basic structure of a criminal justice program through a discussion of the program at Florida State University. The program was established in the mid-1950s by Vernon Fox, a prison administrator and psychologist. The program consisted of corrections, which was offered in the school of social welfare. A police component was later added, followed by a joint doctorate in criminology and sociology in the 1960s. In 1970, the school of criminology was created separate from the school of social work, with its own dean. The new dean came from criminal justice and probation, and many faculty members were also from criminal justice, not the behavioral sciences.

Today the faculty is multidisciplinary (not interdisciplinary), consisting of sociologists, psychologists, political scientists, lawyers, and public administrators. Some exchange of ideas occurs, but for the most part each discipline maintains purity within this setup. Three of the faculty members are actively engaged in police work, popularly known as the ''professor cops.''

The school of criminology at Florida State University has four basic required undergraduate courses, one in criminology, one in law enforcement, one in courts, and one in corrections. Beyond that, a student may take a number of courses in these fields, but very few courses are offered on the behavioral science side of criminology/criminal justice. Most of the undergraduate majors seek employment as police or correctional officers. The employment aspect of the criminal justice system determines, to a large extent, the nature of college education in criminal justice and criminology. Our system does not hire psychologists or urban planners or crime prevention experts, and most students will not pursue a course of study that does not have high visibility for career possibilities. Criminology and criminal justice have been attractive college majors because of the number of jobs in criminal justice created by LEAA and other such political programs.

The graduate program at Florida State University has one required course in social theories and one in biological and psychological theories, in addition to several required statistics and research courses. But two courses and whatever else is elected does not educate one in the behavioral sciences. The Florida State University criminology program is probably the most behavioral of all in orientation, but this only reemphasizes the neglect of the behavioral sciences in our criminal justice programs. Although the Florida State University program is called ''criminology,'' it is based on the same type of program found elsewhere under the title ''criminal justice.'' In addition, however, Florida State University offers a substantive area in criminology and psychobiology wherein doctoral students may take courses in psychobiology to supplement their program. There is also a substantive area in crime analysis and computer mapping wherein doctoral students may take courses in urban geography and computer mapping to supplement their criminology graduate work.

The following universities offer some type of program in criminology and/or criminal justice at the doctoral level, as cited by Nemeth (1986).

Arizona State University, Criminal Justice, Ph.D.

Claremont Graduate School, Criminal Justice, Ph.D.

University of California at Irvine, Social Ecology/Criminal Justice, Ph.D.

University of California at Berkeley, Jurisprudence and Social Policy, Law School, Ph.D.

University of Southern California, School of Public Administration, Ph.D.

Florida State University, Criminology, Ph.D.

University of Maryland, Institute of Criminal Justice and Criminology, Ph.D.

Northeastern University, College of Criminal Justice, Forensic Sciences, Ph.D.

Rutgers University, School of Criminal Justice, Ph.D.

John Jay College of Criminal Justice, Ph.D.

State University of New York at Albany, Criminal Justice, Ph.D. in several areas

Pennsylvania State University, Administration of Justice, Ph.D.

Sam Houston State University, College of Criminal Justice, Ph.D.

Washington State University, Criminal Justice in Department of Political Science, Ph.D.

Not included in this list are three major programs in criminology and criminal justice. The program at the University of Pennsylvania under Marvin Wolfgang is entitled the Center for Studies in Criminal Law and Criminology. It does not offer a degree, but students do take a Ph.D. in sociology. Michigan State University has been a major university in police science and criminal justice education, and the degree is offered in the college of social science with an emphasis on criminal justice. Ohio State University has been a major center for criminology for years under the direction of Walter Reckless and Simon Dinitz. Reckless has been retired for a number of years and Dinitz will be retiring in a few years, and at this point criminology is being moved outside the sociology department at Ohio State University. There are courses in social deviancy in the sociology department, and the school of public administration offers a Ph.D. in public administration with a concentration in criminal justice. Indiana University, when Sutherland was alive, was also a school involved in criminology. However, criminology was always sociology, and Indiana University never took advantage of an outstanding opportunity to integrate sociology, psychology, biology, and criminal law into one approach to criminology.

A doctoral degree is recommended for those teaching in baccalaureate or graduate programs. Thirty-three percent of the criminal justice faculties hold a Ph.D. degree, and of these, 40 percent are in sociology. The predominance of sociology is due to the fact that few degrees are offered in criminology, and most of the people working in criminal justice have degrees in public administration, history, political science, and other fields related in some manner to criminal justice (Ward and Webb, 1984). People are not usually educated in criminal justice, except for those now graduating from criminal justice programs. Similarly, sociological criminology has shifted from studies of human behavior to studies of the criminal justice system, as seen in studies of deterrence, diversionary programs, juvenile justice system, police performance, and other aspects of the police–courts–prison system.

The orientation of graduate programs in criminal justice is clearly revealed in what the graduates of such programs perceive as areas of specialization and competency (Felkenes, 1980). Seventy-seven percent of the Michigan State University graduates indicate an expertise in law enforcement, whereas 78 percent of those from Florida State University and 75 percent of those from Sam Houston State University indicate an expertise in corrections. Florida State University had 79 percent of its graduates report an expertise in crime causation (behavioral aspects of crime) compared to 33 percent from Sam Houston State University and 36 percent from SUNY/Albany. This low percent of criminal justice graduates who indicate knowledge of crime prevention and crime causation reinforces the belief that the behavioral sciences are slighted in criminal justice programs. Experience with the graduates of such programs, plus personal involvement in the Florida State University program, supports such a view. The high rating for Florida State is based on one course in sociology, one course in psychology and biology, and perhaps one course in criminal careers, ecology, or female criminality.

From his survey of police education, Sherman (1978) concluded that police education is of poor quality and emphasizes vocational rather than basic liberal arts training. Sherman found that the dramatic increase in police education has not been matched by an increase in police performance. Although we assume that a Ph.D. in criminal justice will make for better police performance, we cannot even identify good police performance nor say that policing is a successful way to combat crime. Sherman recommends a general liberal arts education leading to a baccalaureate degree, with less emphasis on vocational and technical skills. Often, police training courses are offered by other police officers on the assumption that the experience of being a police officer will give one skills which can then be communicated. A survey of police education by the *Law Enforcement News* (John Jay College of Criminal Justice, 1987) revealed that no major changes have occurred in the educational levels or proficiency levels of police officers as a result of LEEP programs in the 1970s. The high school diploma is still the basic entrance requirement for police officers. Joseph McNamara, the police chief at San Jose, noted that both the quality and quantity of law enforcement is declining (John Jay College of Criminal Justice, 1987:7).

The typical educational background of criminal justice personnel includes the following:

Personnel	Degree	Educational background
Police	A.A.	Law enforcement
	B.A.	Criminal justice
	M.A.	Criminal justice
	D. Crim.	Criminal justice
Courts	B.A.	Criminal justice
		Political science
	M.A.	Criminal justice
		Political science
	Ph.D.	Political science
	J.D.	Law
	D. Crim.	Criminal justice
	D.P.A.	Criminal justice/public administration
	M.S.W.	Social work/case worker
Corrections	A.A.	Law enforcement, corrections
	B.A.	Criminal justice, corrections
	M.A.	Criminal justice
	D. Crim.	Criminal justice, corrections

Criminology and/or Criminal Justice as a Major

A report of the Association of American Colleges (1985) noted a crisis in undergraduate education, with its emphasis on vocationalism and absence of academic depth or breadth. A return to liberal arts education was recommended, with less emphasis on majors and more emphasis on interdisciplinary curricula that focus on the interrelationships of fields of knowledge.

In recent years we have witnessed a shift away from vocationalism toward liberal arts, with emphasis on langauges and communication, mathematics, natural science, and behavioral science. Students are encouraged to receive a well-rounded and well-integrated education which prepares them for life and not for a specific job. Since 50 percent of the jobs that will be available in twenty years do not exist today, it is hard if not impossible to design a curriculum for those jobs. Some medical schools have moved to a med-flex program, which allows an undergraduate student to take a broad general curriculum in preparation for a career in medicine. A more extensive liberal arts background is now deemed desirable for scientific as well as humanistic career development.

Criminology is not a major in most universities, but rather is part of a general sociology program. Where criminal justice exists as a major, criminology is made part of the criminal justice program, which emphasizes police, courts, and corrections. Criminal justice is a popular major, as noted above. Many students receive an A.A. degree in criminal justice from a community college and then transfer to a university for a B.A. degree in criminal justice, without having the benefits of a liberal arts education. They repeat essentially the same curriculum at the junior and senior level until they receive the baccalaureate degree, although they have had little exposure to psychology, sociology, biology, economics, political science, philosophy, history, or anthropology. In some academic areas no courses are taken, and in others only one or two courses are taken, at most.

A broad-based liberal arts education is essential to criminology and criminal justice as a major. The issues found in criminology must be integrated into a general liberal arts program. What is happening in biology or psychology or political science is critical to criminology and criminal justice. Also, the criminal justice system should be totally changed so that new careers based on the behavioral sciences can emerge in place of the present prison-court-corrections career patterns that now dominate our crime control model.

PLAN OF THIS TEXTBOOK

How This Textbook Differs from Other Textbooks

When I took a criminology course from E. H. Sutherland, he used the first thirteen chapters of his text covering essentially the sociological theories of criminal behavior. He used the last sixteen chapters during the second semester in a course called penology, now referred to as "corrections" or "the criminal justice system." Today we have many textbooks covering the criminal justice system, or the police–courts–corrections system. Among these are:

Introduction to Criminal Justice, Senna and Siegel
Introduction to the Criminal Justice System, Kerper
Criminal Justice in America, Vetter and Simonson
The American System of Criminal Justice, Cole
Criminal Justice, Kaplan and Skolnick
Criminal Justice, Newman
Criminal Justice, Blumberg

These books do not cover criminology, as such, or as in the case of the Cole text, criminology is covered in four pages. The Vetter and Simonson book devotes one short chapter to criminology or theories of crime causation.

Textbooks labeled "criminology" are written by sociologists and they are a combination of criminology, law, and criminal justice, styled after the Sutherland textbook.

Criminology, Sutherland and Cressey
Crime and Criminology, Reid

Criminology, Conklin
Criminology, Siegel
Criminology, Quinney
Crime and Punishment, Allen, Friday, Roebuck, and Sagarin
Society, Crime, and Criminal Behavior, Gibbons
Introduction to Criminology, Fox
Explaining Crime, Nettler

These textbooks offer more sociology than the criminal justice texts, and since Reid is both a sociologist and a lawyer, her textbook is much more legalistic than the others. However, Reid dropped the use of "criminology" from the first chapter of the fourth edition of her book. These texts offer very little, if any, discussion of modern biology, genetics, and psychology, although the Fox and Siegal texts both introduce an interdisciplinary bioenvironmental approach to criminal behavior.

There are also specialized textbooks in police practices and law enforcement, as well as in the courts and correctional systems. There are specialized texts on probation and parole, police effectiveness, and other aspects of criminal justice administration. Such books tend to take one part of the criminal justice system and look at it in great detail.

This text differs from the foregoing publications in several respects. (1) It is interdisciplinary. (2) It does not accept the legalistic approach as found in the criminal justice system, where the goals of the system are retribution, deterrence, or rehabilitation of criminals within a legal model. Rather, this text puts forth crime prevention as the crime control model to be pursued scientifically and legally. (3) It is based on a systems theory of science.

Criminology as an Interdisciplinary Science

Criminology was originally identified with biology and psychology, and then with sociology. But rather than an interdisciplinary criminology as an outgrowth, we have three separate criminologies: biological criminology, psychological criminology, and sociological criminology. Wolfgang and Ferracuti (1967:40) observed: "It is possible to trace the development of criminology along traditional lines of biology, psychology, and sociology without much overlapping or integration of these approaches."

The call for an interdisciplinary criminology goes back to Enrico Ferri and the scientific school, which advocated an interaction of criminal law and the behavioral sciences as basic to penal philosophy. In more recent times, Wolfgang and Ferracuti (1967) put forth a plea for interdisciplinary criminology based on biology, psychology, psychiatry, sociology, and law. Despite this plea, criminology has yet to develop a genuinely interdisciplinary approach to crime and criminal behavior.

But there is reason for optimism. Some criminologists are currently designing an increasingly interdisciplinary approach to crime and criminal behavior, based on modern biological psychiatry, behavior genetics, psychobiology, and bioenvironmental learning theory. Jeffery (1977, 1978; Morn, 1980) has called for an interdisciplinary approach to crime and criminal behavior, with a revival of interest in research of an interdisciplinary nature. My own interest in interdisciplinary criminology started when I was a student at Indiana University. I had Sutherland, a sociologist, for a criminology course, and Jerome Hall, a professor of criminal law and jurisprudence, for those areas. At the same time, B. F. Skinner, the behavioral psychologist, was chairman of the department of psychology at Indiana University. Although I did not take psychology at that time, I was at least exposed to a theory of behavior that was in contradiction to the symbolic interactionism of the department of sociology. I did return to behavioral psychology at a later date in my career (see Chapter 13). After I finished my Ph.D. at Indiana University, I received a postdoctoral fellowship to the University of Chicago Law School, where I had contact with several law professors, notably Francis A. Allen, Max Rheinstein, and Karl Llewellyn, all of whom were interested in law and society or the sociology of law. Later, while in Washington, D.C. on a research project, I met Nicholas Kittrie, a law professor and former dean of the American University School of Law and became interested in the ideas he presented in *The Right to Be Different* (Kittrie, 1971). I then joined the faculty of New York University, where I taught criminology courses in the law school in a program entitled Criminal Law Education and Research Center, directed by Gerhard O. W. Mueller, a lawyer/criminologist. Thus, from the beginning of my career I have viewed criminology as an interdisciplinary mixture of sociology, psychology, and law.

Criminal justice developed in isolation from criminology and the behavioral sciences, and as a result the philosophical assumptions are often in direct conflict with those of criminology. One of the goals of an interdisciplinary orientation is to bridge paradigmatic differences.

Radzinowicz (1962) recommended a graduate-level program devoted to the study of criminology, and he commented: ''As long as there is no separate course of study, there will be no flow of trained criminologists to discharge the functions of teaching and research. . . . As long as criminology is not being adequately taught, much that is being written upon the subject cannot fail to be vague, repetitive, superficial, and indeed useless.'' Radzinowicz (1965) advocated the estasblishment of an institute for the study of criminology, comparable to a West Point for criminology. An institute would be interdisciplinary in nature and would be devoted to advancement of research into crime and criminal law.

In his introduction to the Radzinowicz book, Breitel stated:

There has been no continuing, permanent organization or institution for the study of crime in all its phases in this country. Instead there have been only isolated curricula associated with university or professional schools, largely subordinated to vocational training in the field of criminal law administration, ranging from police science to administration to the education of lawyers in criminal prosecution and defense . . . there has been a frustrating falling short of achieving a place for the development of fundamental criminology in this country. This failure is a paradox because many experts throughout the world agree and even marvel that in this country there is a great concern and involvement with the problems of crime and criminology. (Radzinowicz, 1965)

The program in criminal justice established at the State University of New York at Albany was based on the ideas expressed by Radzinowicz in his book. However, as was noted above, the SUNY at Albany program was headed by Richard Myren, a police lawyer, who did not see the behavioral sciences as a core aspect of criminology, and in its place he developed a program in criminal justice. Myren led the group of police educators who broke from the ASC and established the ACJS.

As early as 1933, Michael and Adler (1933) recommended the establishment of an institute of criminology and criminal justice wherein criminal law and the behavioral sciences would be integrated in an interdisciplinary effort. Hall (1982) also recommended the establishment of a national institute of criminal law and criminology.

Sheldon Glueck (Glueck and Glueck, 1974:345 ff.) in 1963 at Harvard University recommended the establishment of a national academy of criminal justice. On the basis of his effort the U.S. Congress passed a bill to establish the Roscoe Pound Academy of Criminal Justice at Harvard Law School. The Congress also recommended the establishment of other academies at other locations.

The major defect in the whole proposal was that the members of the board of regents of the academy were all lawyers. Like the president's commission that followed it, the academy did not have a single member from the behavioral sciences.

In his discussion of criminal justice education, Peter Lejins (1983) stated that in the United States sociology dominated criminology, and he noted that there is a "tendency of the behavioral science disciplines to colonize the study of crime primarily in their own interests. . . . In their 'empire building' endeavors, scholars in these fields opposed the development of an independent field of criminology." He discussed the fact that law schools, schools of social work, and sociology departments offered course work in criminology and criminal justice without any interaction. "The teaching of law, sociological criminology, and social work was not integrated, nor was it linked with the operational agencies." Lejins emphasized the fact that behavioral scientists have little or no access to political figures or others making policy decisions concerning the criminal justice system. Not only do criminologists not have access to the political power bases of society, but criminologists are not employable by the operational agencies. One of the major problems for criminology at the present time is that the criminal justice agencies employ police officers, probation officers, correctional officers, lawyers, and court personnel, not experts in the behavior of criminals and deviants. Students do not want courses dealing with the behavioral sciences since such courses do not lead to employment upon graduation.

We do not educate lawyers in psychology or psychiatry, and we do not educate psychiatrists and psychologists in law or criminology. An interdisciplinary approach must be established within the framework of a research institute where lawyers could observe CAT and PETT scans and studies of the human brain, and psychiatrists and criminologists could study such concepts from the criminal law as intent, guilt, insanity, punishment, and retribution (Jeffery, 1985).

One of the problems facing criminology is the lack of sophisticated research. Michael and Adler (1933) noted that there is no science of criminology and no scientific method in criminology. They found that criminology depends on sociology and psychology, neither of which has adequately developed a science of human behavior. Wootton (1959) noted that there are no causal statements in criminology, and in 1967 the President's Commission on Law Enforcement and the Administration of Justice (1967a:8) noted that "until a science of behavior matures far beyond its present confines, an understanding of those kinds of behavior we call delinquency is not likely to be forthcoming." The President's Commission (1967b:273) also noted that "there is probably no subject [crime] to which the nation has devoted so many resources and so much effort with so little knowledge of what it is doing. . . . Knowledge about crime must await a better understanding of social behavior." The President's Commission (1967b:x) also found that "a small fraction of one percent of the criminal justice system's total budget is spent on research."

Ohlin and Mueller (1969) surveyed the research centers that had received funding from the Ford Foundation, including the Vera Institute, the University of Pennsylvania, Georgetown University, Florida State University, the University of Chicago, the University of California at Davis, the University of Toronto, and the University of Montreal. They (Ohlin and Mueller, 1969:120–122) concluded that "the projects of the centers have been much more concerned with studies of the organization and operation of the criminal justice system than with the study of crimes and criminals." More attention, they felt, must be paid to criminals and the basic processes of social control.

Mueller (1969:199) ends his discussion of interdisciplinary criminology with the following: "A blind criminal justice, a deaf forensic psychiatry, and a dumb sociological criminology stand a good chance not only of survival—if they stand together—but also of bettering humanity's plight."

Research in criminology and criminal justice has been neglected, and when undertaken, it has been sloppy and weak. Much of the training effort in criminal justice has been devoted to services rather than research. This type of training assumes that a research body of knowledge already exists which can be applied in the service areas. A major interdisciplinary research center must be established to study crime and criminals scientifically.

Such an interdisciplinary research and training center would have on its staff lawyers, biologists, psychologists, psychiatrists, sociologists, economists, philosophers, urban planners, mathematicians, and computer systems analysts. This team would be involved in interdisciplinary research on problems concerning crime and criminals, and would educate young, aspiring researchers in the new interdisciplinary science of criminology. A degree program offering a diploma or doctorate in criminology could be established for those already possessing the J.D., Ph.D. in a behavioral science, M.D., or M.S.W. degree. These people could then be employed as lawyers, psychiatrists, psychologists, sociologists, economists, or urban planners with an interdisciplinary background in law and the behavioral sciences. As things now stand, a sociologist cannot be employed as a criminologist, only as a sociologist with an interest in crime. He/she is not employed by a medical school or a law school. The same is true for lawyers and physicians. The lawyer who is employed by a law school or who works as a private or public lawyer is trained only as a lawyer. A psychiatrist is trained to act only as a psychiatrist. We need lawyers who know biology, psychology, and psychiatry and who can work within the area of criminal law. We need physicians who know law, psychology, and criminology and who can work within the area of criminal law. We need sociologists who know criminal law, psychiatry, and psychology and who can do research and teaching in criminology.

Prevention as a Crime Control Model

Not only must the behavioral sciences be integrated into one science of human behavior, but the behavioral sciences and the law must be integrated into a common approach to the problem of crime and criminals. The criminal justice system is justified in terms of punishment, retribution, deterrence, and rehabilitation of offenders within a legalistic model. The legal model is based on a theory of human nature that is mentalistic and nonphysical in nature, a theory that is out of touch with modern scientific views of human nature. Modern biological psychiatry and psychobiology are based on physicalism and the study of the brain as the organ of behavior.

We can use our new scientific knowledge to bridge the gap between science and law, but to do so we must alter the goals of the criminal justice system. Most criminology and criminal justice texts accept the police–courts–corrections system and start with the assumption that the system works if only we would tinker with it a little more. As Garland and Young (1983:5) stated, we consider criminology and criminal justice only within the present system. We do not consider alternatives to the present criminal justice system because we are bound by legal realism. The perspective of this book is that major conflicts exist between science, criminal law, and criminal justice, and such conflicts call for resolution if we are to create a feasible crime control model.

To prevent crime, we must utilize knowledge from biology, neurology, psychiatry, psychology, encology, sociology, and urban design. We cannot do this, however, as long as the current perspective of the criminal law based on retribution and deterrence dominates our thinking. Rather than presenting a justification for criminology or criminal justice, we argue that both criminology and criminal justice must be altered radically if we are to develop effective crime control policies.

This book is also research oriented. If science and law are to interact, and if new techniques for the prevention of crime are to be developed, we must first have the ability to diagnose and treat behavioral disorders. If we propose prevention and treatment, we must first have the means to prevent and to treat. We do not set up clinics for the prevention of cancer until we have done the research necessary to diagnose and treat cancer. The same thing is true for heart disease. In the case of crime, however, we do not attempt to prevent or treat the behavior, or if we do, we do so with techniques that are not scientific and that do not have a predictable outcome of success. Research is the first priority of such a commitment to crime prevention.

Issues in Criminology

We can now note three major problems or issues present in criminology which hamper the development of criminology as an interdisciplinary science. One issue is that of *mentalism,* or the mind–body dualism found in Western philosophy and in psychology and sociology as well as in criminology. The belief that behavior involves mental states and mental illnesses has made a science of human behavior impossible.

A second issue is that of *environmentalism,* the belief that behavior is caused by experiences with the environment, especially the social environment. Both behavioral psychology and sociology are based on environmentalism, the former on experiences with the physical environment, the latter on experiences with the social environment.

A third issue is that of *legalism,* the doctrines found in the criminal law. This view assumes a nonscientific, nondeterministic view of human nature as found in concepts of *mens rea* and moral guilt, as well as the view that immoral behavior must be punished by courts and prisons. The scientific view of human nature is ignored by the legal view of crime and criminals. Today we find criminal law in great conflict with modern biology and psychology, especially as to explanations of criminal behavior and to the use of punishment versus rehabilitation and prevention as a crime control model (see Chapters 15, 16, and 21).

Legalism has led to the police–courts–corrections system, the criminal justice system as a model of crime control. The scientific model has led to the medical model based on the prevention and treatment of antisocial behaviors through scientific means. Our purpose is to explore and establish the medical model and to integrate the legal model and the medical model as a basis for scientific criminology.

FURTHER STUDIES

Since criminology is an interdisciplinary science, it is necessary to realize that academic departments other than criminology or criminal justice offer work in areas important to criminologists. At the end of each chapter, starting with

Chapter 2, I include a short statement as to where a student may go for further study in the subject matter discussed in the chapter.

REFERENCES

ASSOCIATION OF AMERICAN COLLEGES (1985). *Integrity in the College Curriculum.* Washington, D.C.: Association of American Colleges.

CONRAD, J. P., and R. A. MYREN (1979). *Two Views of Criminology and Criminal Justice: Definitions, Trends, and the Future.* Chicago: Joint Commission on Criminology and Criminal Justice Education and Standards.

FELKENES, G. (1980). *The Criminal Justice Doctorate: A Study of Historical Programs in the United States.* Chicago: Joint Commission on Criminology and Criminal Justice Education and Standards.

GARLAND, D., and P. YOUNG (1983). *The Power to Punish.* London: Heinemann.

GIBBONS, D. C. (1979). *The Criminological Enterprise.* Englewood Cliffs, N.J.: Prentice-Hall.

GLUECK, S., and E. GLUECK (1974). *Of Delinquency and Crime.* Springfield, Ill.: Charles C Thomas.

HALL, J. (1982). *Law, Social Science, and Criminal Theory.* Littleton, Colo.: Fred B. Rothman & Co.

INCIARDI, J. (1987). *Criminal Justice.* San Diego, Calif.: Harcourt Brace Jovanovich.

JEFFERY, C. R. (1977). *Crime Prevention through Environmental Design,* rev. ed. Beverly Hills, Calif.: Sage.

JEFFERY, C. R. (1978). "Criminology as an Interdisciplinary Science." *Criminology,* 16(2):149–170.

JEFFERY, C. R. (1985). *Attacks on the Insanity Defense: Biological Psychiatry and New Perspectives on Criminal Behavior.* Springfield, Ill.: Charles C Thomas.

JOHN JAY COLLEGE OF CRIMINAL JUSTICE (1987). *Law Enforcement News,* February 24.

KITTRIE, N. (1971). *The Right to Be Different.* Baltimore, Md.: Johns Hopkins University Press.

LEJINS, P. (1983). "Educational Programs in Criminal Justice." In *Encyclopedia of Crime and Justice,* ed. S. H. Kadish. New York: Free Press.

MICHAEL, J., and M. ADLER (1933). *Crime, Law and Social Science.* New York: Harcourt, Brace.

MORN, F. (1980). *Academic Disciplines and Debates: An Essay on Criminal Justice and Criminology as Professions in Higher Education.* Chicago: Joint Commission on Criminology and Criminal Justice Education and Standards.

MORRIS, A. (1975). "The American Society of Criminology: A History." *Criminology,* 13(2):123–167.

MUELLER, G. O. W. (1969). *Crime, Law and the Scholars.* Seattle: University of Washington Press.

NEMETH, C. (1986). *Guide to Criminal Justice Education.* Cincinnati, Ohio: Anderson Publishing Co.

NETTLER, G. (1979). "Criminal Justice." In *Annual Review of Sociology,* Vol. 5. Palo Alto, Calif.: Annual Reviews, pp. 27–52.

OHLIN, L., and G. O. W. MUELLER (1969). *Some Speculative Investments in American Criminology and Their Chances of Return,* special report to the Ford Foundation.

PRESIDENT'S COMMISSION ON LAW ENFORCEMENT AND THE ADMINISTRATION OF JUSTICE (1967a). *Juvenile Delinquency and Youth Crime.* Washington, D.C.: U.S. Government Printing Office.

PRESIDENT'S COMMISSION ON LAW ENFORCEMENT AND THE ADMINISTRATION OF JUSTICE (1967b). *The Challenge of Crime in a Free Society.* Washington, D.C.: U.S. Government Printing Office.

RADZINOWICZ, L. (1962). *In Search of Criminology.* Cambridge, Mass.: Harvard University Press.

RADZINOWICZ, L. (1965). *The Need for Criminology.* London: Heinemann.

RECKLESS, W. (1970). "American Criminology." *Criminology,* 8(1):4–20.

SAGARIN, E. (1977). "The Egghead, the Screw, and the Flatfoot: Some Reflections and Some Problems Concerning the Future of the American Society of Criminology." Paper presented at the annual meeting of the American Society of Criminology, Atlanta, Ga., November.

SHERMAN, L. (1978). *The Quality of Police Education.* San Francisco: Jossey-Bass.

SUTHERLAND, E. H. and D. R. CRESSEY (1970). *Principles of Criminology,* 8th ed. Philadelphia: J. B. Lippincott.

WARD, R., and V. J. WEBB (1984). *Quest for Quality.* New York: University Publications.

WOLFGANG, M. A., and F. FERRACUTI (1967). *The Subculture of Violence.* London: Tavistock.

WOOTTON, B. (1959). *Social Science and Social Pathology.* London: Allen & Unwin.

ZALMAN, M. (1981). *A Heuristic Model of Criminology and Criminal Justice.* Chicago: Joint Commission on Criminology and Criminal Justice Education and Standards.

QUESTIONS

1. What are the major distinctions between criminology and criminal justice?
2. What major academic disciplines are associated with criminology? With criminal justice?
3. What basic vocational and professional opportunities exist for people with a background and training in criminology? In criminal justice?
4. What relationships exist between criminology and science? Among criminal justice, political policy, and criminal law?
5. What crime control policy is advocated by criminologists? By criminal justicians?
6. What is the history of education in criminology? In criminal justice?
7. What is meant by "criminology is an interdisciplinary science"?

Systems Theory, Science, and Criminology 2

OVERVIEW

The Nature of Systems Theory

Systems theory is an approach to knowledge and the analysis of data which is holistic in nature. It is rooted in the interrelationship of parts with the whole and with the flow of energy and information from one subsystem to another subsystem (Klir, 1972; Miller, 1978; Buckley, 1968; Kuhn, 1974, 1975; Boulding, 1978). Systems theory is closely related to organizational theory and the study of bureaucracies and social structures as interrelated systems of interaction.

The critical concept in systems theory is that of "interaction." Systems theory forces the investigator to think in terms of the mutual interdependence of variables rather than in terms of linear causation and influence.

The Hierarchical Nature of Systems

Systems emerge in a hierarchical nature; that is, one system emerges as a new system from a subsystem. Basic to systems analysis is the ability of a subsystem to interact with systems above and below it. Energy, organization, and information flow are key elements in this interaction of subsystems.

There is no agreement as to the smallest system or largest system within scientific analysis. The *atom* is a system, but in turn it is composed of elements such as hydrogen, oxygen, nitrogen, and carbon, which in a given combination form living systems composed of cells. *Cells* are systems interacting with one another to form organ systems. *Organs* (heart, liver, kidney, lung) are made up of cells, but they are more than cells; they are cells in a distinct kind of organization and communication system distinct from other cells. A brain is made up of cells, but cells in a specific type of organization with specific patterns of energy and information flow.

Individual *organisms* such as dogs, cats, or human beings are made up of individual organs in interaction. An organism is many organ systems in interaction. The organism, in turn, interacts with the environment and with other living and nonliving systems. In interaction, organisms form *groups, communities, populations,* and *societies.* Thus systems theory looks at the evolution from biochemical elements to cells to organs to organisms to groups, communities, and societies.

The Evolution of Systems

As we move from cells to society, we move from the smallest to the largest units, and from the earliest to the latest units to evolve. The following table (Miller, 1978) depicts the evolutionary history of the living system:

Size	Unit	Age
Smallest	Cell	3 billion years
	Organ	500 million years
	Organism	500 million years
	Group	500 million years
	Organization	9000 B.C.
Largest	Society	5000 B.C.

It should be noted from this chart that organs, organisms, and groups emerged at approximately the same time in history, and considerably earlier than organizations and societies. Organs and organisms probably evolved together in a common process. This suggests that in terms of biological interdependency, organs, organisms, and groups formed a necessary system for survival. Human beings can survive without formal organizations and societies, but they cannot survive without groups. Humans have belonged to groups since their earliest history, basically for the need for a mating dyad, for reproduction and child care, and for groups for food gathering and food sharing.

Systems Analysis and Human Behavior

As we noted in Chapter 1, the object of study of criminology is human behavior. In criminology, we are interested in the study of biosocial or bioenvironmental systems, which are living systems. A living system is one capable of reproducing and perpetuating itself through interaction with other systems in its environment. An open system is a system capable of interaction with its environment. In this book, we shall be most concerned with the behavioral aspects of the living human system.

A living system is an input–output system involving the taking in, processing of, and utilization of energy and information from the environment. A major example of a living system is the ecosystem, whereby the energy of the sun in the form of light is transformed by green plants into chemical energy in the form of carbohydrates (sugars), a process called photosynthesis. Another aspect of photosynthesis involves the cycling of chemicals, whereby oxygen is released and carbon dioxide is taken in by green plants.

The ecosystem includes people and their interaction with the environment. Person-environment interaction—the ecological process—may be characterized as an input–output system, whereby the organism takes in energy and information from the environment; transforms, stores, and utilizes the energy and information to adapt to and survive in a given environment. The living human system has been characterized as a detector–selector–effector system (Kuhn, 1975). In the living human system, the detector system is the sensory system—eyes, ears, nose, mouth, and skin. Information is taken into the organism through the sensory system. Food and liquids are taken in and changed biochemically in the cells into energy.

The selector system is the brain and nervous system. The brain is capable of receiving information from the environment by means of the sensory system, storing, coding, transforming, and using the information to guide and govern the major processes of the organism. The brain controls the other organs of the body, such as the heart, liver, and lungs, as well as the muscles and glands. The brain, as the organ of behavior, will be discussed in a later chapter. The brain activates the effector system or glands, organs, and muscles, resulting in that which we call *behavior.*

The model of behavior used in this book involves the organism interaction with the environment, or an O × E model of human behavior. Behavior is one of the basic ways in which human beings adapt to environmental conditions. This may be diagrammed as follows:

Environment ⟶ Brain ⟶ Behavior ⟶ Environment
⟵ Feedback loop ⟵

Behavior is one way in which the organism adapts to the environment. Adaptation is necessary for survival and it can occur in two ways, biological and cultural. A person can adapt to cold weather by shivering and pulling blood into the protected parts of the body, which is an unlearned autonomic response. Or the person can put on clothing and build central heating systems, which is learned behavior and cultural adaption. Higher brain functions, learning, and cultural adaption are critical here. This model of behavior is discussed in detail in Chapters 10 to 14.

Systems Theory and Control Mechanisms

Systems involve control mechanisms often called cybernetic systems. Through feedback from the environment to the organism, the organism is able to guide its behavior. An example of a mechanical feedback system is a thermostat designed to respond to changes in the air temperature by regulating the output of hot or cold air. If it is too cold, the hot-air system is turned on; if it is too hot, the air conditioning is turned on. The human body contains its own thermostatic system in the brain, which governs the temperature of the body.

Many examples exist of feedback loops from the environment to the organism by which human behavior is governed. A person pulls his/her hand away from a hot stove. A pilot controls the ascent or descent of a plane. A driver controls the speed and direction of a car. A marksman adjusts the aim of the rifle so as to correct the impact of the last shot. Each response leads to new information which is processed by the brain and used to guide and direct the next response. This ability of the organism to guide and direct its behavior based on past experience and future expectations is a basic control system for human behavior that is critical for future planning and direction of behavior. Systems theory is thus goal oriented, that is, living systems seek an adaptation to a broader environment. This might involve the concepts of purpose and maturation, such as an acorn becoming an oak tree, or a tadpole becoming a frog, or an embryo becoming a human being. Human beings are also goal directed, using past experience and present circumstances to plan for future events and goals. It is through the brain that past experience and present circumstances are used to govern behavior in anticipation of future events. This is discussed in more detail in Chapter 11.

Systems Theory and Causation

The nineteenth-century view of science was based on the linear causal model of Newtonian physics, that is, A causes B and B causes C. Within systems theory functional relationships and interaction replace causation. Hydrogen and oxygen interact so as to form water; hydrogen does not cause oxygen to become water. Only when you join hydrogen and oxygen do you get water. In the relationship, oxygen plays as active a role as does hydrogen. This is sometimes referred to as "reciprocal causation," where A influences B and B influences A (Koestler and Smythies, 1969; Mercer, 1981). As Dubin (1969:94) has stated, the behavioral sciences are built on the notion of relationship and interaction rather than on the notion of causality.

We may illustrate the use of the concept of interaction in criminology. In contrast to the usual interpretation of criminal behavior, which states that criminal behavior is caused by the family or the peer group or the school system or the genes or the brain, we can say that the family interacts with the school system, which interacts with the peer group, which interacts with the genes and the brain. Behavior is a product of many subsystems in interaction, which in turn create sequential and contingent relationships. This issue is discussed in greater detail in later chapters.

Criminology and Systems Analysis

The term "system" is often used in criminology to refer to the criminal justice "system." However, the criminal justice system is not actually a system because the several parts—police–prosecution–courts–corrections—do not interact with one another as a system. It is a poor system at best (Chapters 8 and 9).

More important for our purposes is the fact that the criminal justice system is not based on a systems approach. A systems approach to criminology would be a "cell to society" model, devoting attention to each level of analysis and to the interaction of the several levels (Bonner, 1955; Miller, 1978; Meyer, 1957). The following table illustrates how criminology could use a systems approach:

System	Concepts	Disciplines
Society	Transnational organizations, nation–state, political processes, criminal law, courts, prisons	Sociology Criminal law Criminology Political science
Population	Age, sex, ethnic groups, urban, rural	Geography Demography
Organizations	Religious, ethnic, social, political	Sociology Political science
Groups	Peer groups, family, schools	Sociology Education
Organism	Learning, personality, criminal behavior	Psychology Social psychology
Organ	Brain, neurotransmitters	Neurology Biopsychiatry Psychobiology Psychopharmacology Biochemistry
Cell	Genes	Genetics Biology

When applied to the study of crime and criminals, a systems approach would look like this:

1. Crime — Transnational organizations, nation–state, political processes, criminal law, courts, prisons
2. Criminals
   (a) Social level: age, sex, ethnic groups, peer groups, families, schools
   (b) Psychological level: learning, personality development, group processes, age and sex

(c) Biological level: human genetics, neurosciences, biochemistry

It must be kept in mind that these levels of analysis are constantly in
interaction; the genes influence the brain, which influences learning, personality development, and age and sex variables, which influence family, peer
group, and school variables, which influence political processes and the criminal justice system. Similarly, the social and political levels influence the genes,
the brain, learning, and personality development.

THE NATURE OF SCIENCE

Rationalism versus Empiricism

In the history of Western philosophy two different approaches to human nature
and knowledge have been taken. One view, put forth by the early Greeks (Plato
and Aristotle), holds that through logic and reason one can know truth, which
is eternal and external to oneself. By the proper logic and reason human beings
can discover the eternal truths. The material world, which is known through
sensation and experience, is an imperfect copy and can never give us truth.
This philosophy is based on a *dualism* of mind and matter, or mental and physical. The way in which ideas and truths are known is not the same as the way
in which we have sensations and experiences. This position is known as *rationalism* or *idealism.*

The second position is that of *materialism* or *empiricism*, which holds that
ideas and truth come from human nature and from sensations and experiences.
Ideas are not separate from experience of the physical environment. This view
denies the dualism of mind and matter and is based on a more holistic view of
individuals interacting with their environments.

Empiricism is associated with the British empiricists. Thomas Hobbes
(1588–1679) held that ideas are neurons in action, or motions in the brain
caused by sensations. This comes close to what is taught today as neurology
and biological psychology. John Locke (1632–1704) taught that the human
being is a *tabula rasa* at birth, that is, an empty tablet. The individual is born
without knowledge, and all knowledge is acquired through experience after
birth. David Hume (1711–1776) taught that we have no truth or ideas, only a
succession of sensory experiences.

Many attempts have been made to resolve the contradictions between
empiricism and idealism. Descartes (1596–1650) viewed mind and matter as
distinct, a matter of dualism. The issue of dualism will be a major one in the
coming chapters. Kant (1724–1804) attempted to join rationalism and empiricism. For Kant, empiricism was the experience of real phenomena. Knowledge
comes from the mind with its universal categories and necessary truth, which
Kant called noumena. The mind is a priori to experience and organized our

raw sensations into categories of truth. Understanding is imposed on reality by the perceiving individual. Again, with Kant as with Descartes, we are left with a dualism of mind and body, of reason and experience.

Mortimer Adler (1985), the eminent philosopher, in his *Ten Philosophical Mistakes* argues that true knowledge is not based on experience but on intellect and reason. Thus, Adler leaves us with rationalism versus empiricism. To quote Adler (1985:149–150), the senses, the imagination, and the passions operate according "to the same laws that govern all the other phenomena of the physical world, but the intellect and the will, being immaterial, do not act in accordance with these principles and laws [of science]." Thus Adler concludes that philosophy is based on ancient wisdoms which are as true today as they were 3000 years ago.

An early figure in scientific method, Francis Bacon (1561–1626), put forth a method of inductive reasoning based on observation and hypothesis testing. Inductive reasoning goes from observation of facts to general conclusions and principles, whereas deductive reasoning goes from universal principles to individual cases. According to Bacon, one must free oneself from prejudices and a priori logic based on deductive reasoning if one is to discover truth by the scientific method.

Science is an extension of positivism and empiricism. Basic to science is experience and physical observations of variables. Scientific method is based on observing, gathering, and classifying data; designing hypotheses and propositions concerning the relationships among variables; building theories based on testable hypotheses; and ultimately, predicting and controlling future events. Prediction and control are central to science, and scientific propositions and conclusions are always public and are subject to testing and evaluation. Such propositions must be stated such that they can be falsified. Science lives by the rule that there are no universal or external truths, for the winner of this year's prize in science will have disproven a theoretical system of ten years ago. Science is as interested in the questions raised as in the answers found.

Science differs from philosophy in denying that there are external truths that can be known by reason rather than by experience. Religion and philosophy put forth propositions that cannot be disproven, whereas science must limit its activities to what is knowable and provable. Science is also accumulative; that is, new theories are generated from old ones. In philosophy, the ideas of the early philosophers are still with us as the truth. No scientist would argue that chemistry or biology or physics of 300 or even 100 years ago was as predictive as it is today. In fact, science is only as valuable as its last experiment; what one believed yesterday may not be true today.

This conflict between philosophy and science is a major issue for criminology since the legal system has its historical foundations in philosophy and religion. When we discuss criminal law we will discuss the mentalistic foundations of the law and the nonscientific basis for legal action. This conflict between science and law has been mentioned above, and it is a topic we will return to many times in the course of our discussions of crimes and criminals, and criminal behavior.

Science and Politics

The history of science is the history of opposition and charges of heresy. New ideas challenge the old established order, and the history of science is filled with examples of people who were attacked for their scientific work. Michael Servetus (1509–1553), who discovered the pulmonary circulation of blood, was burned at the stake by John Calvin in 1553 (Talbott, 1970). In 1543, Copernicus announced the proposition that the sun, not the earth, was the center of the universe, and that the earth revolved around the sun. Galileo was an early genius in science who was interested in gravity, motion, the telescope, and astronomy. He supported the revolutionary ideas of Copernicus concerning the sun and earth, for which he was persecuted by the Catholic Church and was forced to recant his scientific views before his death in 1642. The year Galileo died, Isaac Newton (1642–1727) was born in England. The scientific revolution shifted from Italy to England, to be followed by the industrial revolution, a process not unrelated to the scientific revolution.

Charles Darwin emerged in England in the nineteenth century as the father of a new theory of biological systems. Darwin's ideas concerning evolution were most controversial and were opposed by the religious powers of the time. This controversy is reviewed in more detail in Chapter 10.

Isaac Newton gave us a new mathematics, a new theory of light, and new theories of motion and gravitation. Newton was not an outstanding student while at Cambridge, and was violently opposed by his colleagues for his radical ideas. It is a characteristic of scholars that often they are not good students by our traditional standards, and they are not accepted or recognized by their colleagues.

August Comte, the father of sociology, was forced into a very marginal and lowly academic life by university administrators who were his intellectual inferiors. Coser (1977) writes that his forced isolation allowed Comte to do some daring and bold intellectual work, but his freedom to plow the lonely furrow cost him dearly in the long run.

Ignas Semmelweiss, a Hungarian obstetrician, was able to reduce dramatically deaths resulting from puerperal fever (childbirth infections) by having the delivery room attendants wash their hands before handling a new patient. The fever, he contended, was passed from patient to patient on the hands of doctors and nurses. For this medical advancement Semmelweiss was driven from Vienna by his medical colleagues, only to die from an infection in an asylum for the insane (Talbott, 1970).

Marie Curie, the famous scientist who discovered radium, was awarded the Nobel Prize for her efforts, but she was also scorned by her fellow scientists. Eleven of the recent Nobel Prize winners in science were Jewish refugees from Nazi Germany. Nuclear physics and space exploration became established in the United States primarily through the efforts of scientists who were political refugees from Germany. Einstein's theory of relativity and his work in physics were referred to in Hitler's Germany as "Jewish physics" and ignored and condemned (Sagan, 1974). The development of genetics was condemned in the Soviet Union (see Chapter 10 for a discussion of the politics of genetics).

Gregor Mendel, the father of modern genetics, was refused admission to a university because of the ''unscientific nature'' of his work, and his paper on genetics was ignored for many years until rediscovered in the 1920s. At his death most all of Mendel's papers were burned by people who thought that his research was useless. Just before his death Mendel is reported to have said: ''Even though I will not be here, my time will come.''

The motto of the scientist who is a pioneer is:

Do not walk the trails
Where others have gone before
But cut a new path
Into the wilderness

In his very influential book *The Structure of Scientific Revolutions*, Kuhn (1962; Ritzer, 1975) challenges the idea that science is the quiet accumulation of knowledge by rational and well-intentioned human beings. Rather, science involves contrasting paradigms made up of major assumptions concerning the nature of the individual and the universe. New paradigms challenge old ones, and political revolutions occur. Political power—not scientific accuracy—determines the scientific dogma of the day. Science has been filled with revolutions, as when we moved from Newton to Einstein and from Darwin to Mendel to Watson and Crick.

The history of science is filled with accounts of extreme competition among scientists to publish a research report first. This type of competition was found in the search for DNA and RNA (Watson, 1968), for the hormones controlling the pituitary gland (Wade, 1981), and for the search for the natural opiates or endorphins within the human body (Levinthal, 1988). Scientific battles often become political and personal battles involving all of the dishonesties and frauds involved in other aspects of life.

Since its early history, criminology has been involved in paradigmatic struggles. As indicated above, one dimension of the problem has been the rejection of science by the legal profession. Another dimension has been the denial of biology and psychology by sociological criminologists. Throughout its history, attempts have been made in criminology to push certain ideas while keeping others out of circulation. At the 1978 meeting of the American Society of Criminology, the biological panels were greeted with scorn and criticism, and the organizer of the meeting was referred to as a ''neo-Lombrosian'' (Jeffery, 1979, 1980). Scientists who discuss genetics or sociobiology have been insulted, attacked physically, and threatened with physical abuse.

Within criminology there are constant bitter battles among biologists, psychologists, sociologists, lawyers, and politicians as to the nature of human nature and the purpose of criminal law. These different theoretical and philosophical approaches are discussed in detail below as a major aspect of this book. The controversies and politics surrounding criminological theory are highlighted in these discussions.

The Evolution of Science

As discussed above, living systems emerge in an evolutionary and hierarchical manner from cells to societies. It is interesting to note that the sciences evolved in the same order as the living systems hierarchies emerged in history, from the study of cells to the study of societies. We can illustrate this evolution in the following manner:

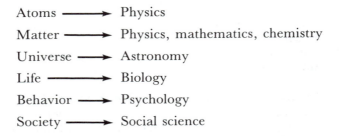

Atoms ⟶	Physics
Matter ⟶	Physics, mathematics, chemistry
Universe ⟶	Astronomy
Life ⟶	Biology
Behavior ⟶	Psychology
Society ⟶	Social science

August Comte discussed this development as the "hierarchy of the sciences," with sociology at the end of the process. Comte also developed the law of the three stages of development of knowledge, from the theological to the metaphysical to the *positivistic* or scientific. Positivism is based on empiricism, scientific method, and the use of science to solve human social problems. It should be noted that Comte ignored psychology in his hierarchy of the sciences, thus making sociology dependent on biology, the discipline immediately before it, or below it, in our hierarchical scheme. You cannot have chemistry without physics; you cannot have biology without chemistry; you cannot have psychology without biology; and you cannot have the social sciences without psychology. Each level of the hierarchy depends on the prior development of the level below it. Each new level incorporates the structure and function of the level below it.

The Unity of Science

Each scientific discipline developed historically as a separate body of knowledge and research with minimal interaction with other scientific disciplines. However, an interdisciplinary approach has emerged during the past twenty years, starting with the publication of a paper by Watson and Crick in 1954 on the biochemical basis of genetics in DNA and RNA molecules. We have seen the emergence of such interdisciplinary fields as biophysics, biochemistry, biological psychiatry, psychobiology, sociobiology, bioanthropology, and biopolitics.

A systems approach requires a unity of science, or the integration of scientific theory and research into a holistic body of knowledge (Koestler and Smythies, 1969; Mercer, 1981). The mind–body dualism of philosophy divided the mind from the body, the individual from the environment, and there is no integration of mind, body, and environment in one system (Capra, 1975).

INTERDISCIPLINARY CRIMINOLOGY

In Chapter 1 we argued that criminology must become an interdisciplinary science based on systems theory which would integrate the several disciplines into a single theoretical perspective on crime and criminals. This approach can be illustrated as follows:

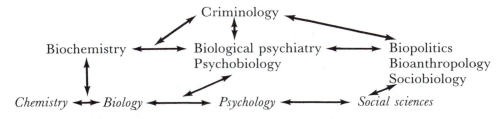

How Not to Study Human Behavior

Universities are traditionally organized along departmental and school lines based on historical and philosophical traditions. Contact by one academic discipline with others is very rare. In the evolution of science each discipline emerged as a separate aspect of academic life with its own faculties and professional membership.

The study of human behavior suffers because of the lack of an interdisciplinary approach to problems. In the organization of academic departments involved in the behavioral sciences, we see the influence of rationalism and empiricism. Anthropology has been divided into cultural, physical, and archeological. Cultural anthropology is devoted to the soft sciences as found in concepts of culture and society. It is based on introspection, field surveys, interviews, informants, oral histories, and other indirect measures of human behavior. On the other hand, physical anthropology is close to the hard sciences: biology, genetics, geology, and neurology. Physical remains are examined by scientific means such as radiation dating. Physical anthropology is closely related to paleontology and to the theory of evolution as found in biology, and human evolution from prehuman forms to modern human beings is central to physical anthropology. Archeology, the study of fossils and artifacts, is closely related to physical anthropology as a scientific approach to human evolution and human origins.

Psychology is split between humanistic psychology, clinical psychology, and experimental psychology. Humanistic psychology is based on the humanistic view of humankind with free will and a moral soul. Determinism and science are denied or are minimized. Scientific psychology is based on biological concepts and laboratory experimentation. Clinical psychology is divided between humanism and scientificism, as it is based on introspection, mentalism, verbal interviews, written tests, and other nonscientific and indirect measures of behavior. A science of behavior is not central to humanism or clinical psychology. Experimental psychology is involved in scientific research as found in behaviorism and in psychobiology, and the major object of experimental psychology is the establishment of a science of behavior. Major advances have been made in experimental psychology in recent years in psychobiology and learning theory. Most psychology departments are seriously divided between the humanistic, clinical, and experimental aspects of psychology, or as it is often phrased, those interested in humankind and those interested in rat psychology. The student can take a Ph.D. in clinical psychology or in experimental psychology with very little interaction between the two programs (Kendler, 1982:303).

Sociology has been divided between the micro/mentalistic approach as found in symbolic interactionism, ethnomethodology, and phenomenology, and the macro approach as found in structural-functionalism and social systems. The methodology varies from mentalistic introspection and subjective analysis of data to quantitative data and computer analysis. Most of the sociologist's data are of an indirect nature, gathered from case records, interviews, surveys, and questionnaires (Chapter 14).

Social psychology, which theoretically should bridge psychology and sociology, has developed into two schools of thought, psychological social psychology and sociological social psychology, each with its own theories, methodologies, advocates, and journals (Chapter 14).

Sociology lacks real integration with biology and psychology, although in recent years psychobiology and sociobiology have challenged basic sociological ideas. A beautiful example of lack of interaction among the behavioral sciences is found in the establishment of the Department of Social Relations at Harvard University in 1950 by Talcott Parsons (Mullins, 1973:50; Kendler, 1982:303). Into this department Parsons brought clinical psychology, social psychology, social anthropology, and sociology—all the nonscientific and nonphysical aspects of anthropology, psychology, and sociology. The scientific physical side of psychology was placed in a department of psychology. B. F. Skinner, the great behaviorist, was in the department of psychology, not in social relations. The department of social relations is no longer in existence, being replaced by a more traditional department of sociology at Harvard University, but the basic problem involved in the study of human behavior is well illustrated by this example from academic history, and the problem is still very much with us today.

Science, Technology, and the Industrial Revolution

The evolution of science has involved the development of technological systems by which a person extends his/her control over the environment. Some examples of this technology would include the microscope, the telescope, the camera, the X-ray machine, the compass, and the clock. The scientific revolution is very much related to the industrial revolution and the urban revolution, both of which have had a major impact on crime patterns and crime rates (Chapter 19).

Science and technology have resulted in major changes in the environment, referred to by Toffler as *Future Shock* (Toffler, 1970) and *The Third Wave*

(Toffler, 1980). Pollution of the environment with lead, cadmium, mercury, and other pollutants is related to abnormal and criminal behavior since the brain absorbs these heavy metals, which can result in serious brain damage. Similarly, population growth results in a large number of young adult males, the population usually involved in criminal activity. Ecology, population, and demography are very critical topics for criminological discussion, and these topics will be discussed in later chapters.

Science, Reductionism, and Holism

Systems analysis involves one in an argument known as reductionism versus holism. When we move downward from psychology to biology to chemistry we are using reductionism. Critics of systems theory argue that you cannot reduce psychology to biology or sociology to psychology, a mistake referred to as "biologizing" or "psychologizing." The critics are in error, however. Rather than reducing psychology to biology and chemistry, we view psychology as the integration of lower levels of analysis as found in chemistry and biology. A new level called psychology emerges which is based on, but different from, biology and chemistry. The genes interact with the environment to produce the brain, which then in interaction with the environment produces behavior, learning, and the basic system involved in psychology. Not only do the various hierarchical systems interact, but new systems emerge from such interaction. The individual organism emerges from cells in interaction, but the individual is more than cells in interaction, as is the brain.

A systems approach to science and knowledge emphasizes the need to move from cells to society to cells. To understand human nature and human behavior, we must integrate the levels of analysis, which can be illustrated as follows:

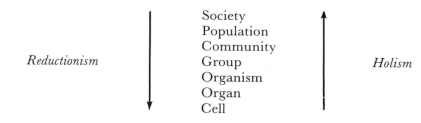

Sagan (1980) cites some outstanding examples of reductionism and holism as related to levels of analysis. The physicist reduces atoms to protons, neutrons, and electrons. To the scientist the atom is not a small hard particle that is irreducible, but is an empty space for the most part. In theoretical physics the distance between the nucleus of the atom and the electrons is like the distance between Miami and Seattle for the geographer or sociologist. At the same time the atoms in a room make up the chairs, tables, and individuals in the room. The same atoms also make up the cosmos, or as Sagan said, the human body is the "stuff of the stars" since the stars contain the same atomic materials as our bodies. We can reduce the galaxies to atoms, but then we must understand that atoms interact as a universe, or a galaxy, or the cosmos.

A dramatic illustration of reductionism and holism is the photograph of a young girl on a swing in a backyard. Then the camera moves to the yard, to the house, to the neighborhood, to the community, to the region, to the nation state, and finally to the earth from a photo taken from a satellite or space flight. The movement from reductionism to holism is well illustrated in the book *The Tao of Physics* (Capra, 1975), where a theoretical physicist shows how modern physics at the atomic level must be integrated at higher levels of meaning which he compared to eastern mystical religion. Eastern religions are holistic in nature, looking for the oneness of human beings and nature, and the indivisibility of reality based on the interaction of subsystems into one holistic system.

In criminology we often ask if crime and criminality are located in the genes of criminals, in the brain of criminals, in learning processes, in social structure, in political systems, or in the criminal justice system. The answer is: in all of these subsystems in interaction. Each level of analysis is involved, and to develop an interdisciplinary criminology we must first be aware of the value of a systems approach to the study of crime and criminal behavior.

Criminology as a Science

Criminology is not at present a science in the sense that the word is used to describe the hard sciences (physics, chemistry, mathematics, biology). Criminology is dependent on psychology, sociology, and law, and to the extent that these disciplines are not sciences, criminology is not a science. Michael and Adler (1933) and Wootton (1959) made these observations concerning criminology years ago (see Chapter 1 for a discussion of these comments).

Criminology has been dependent on official reports, verbal behaviors, indirect observations of behavior, and nonexperimental approaches to human behavior. As we stated in Chapter 1, knowledge about human behavior and research into human behavior have been wanting in criminology.

We also noted the need for a science of criminology through the establishment of an institute of crime and criminology. Biology has become a major hard science during the past thirty years with the emergence of human genetics and the brain sciences. Psychology has developed psychobiology and learning theory based on scientific principles and experimental research. Similarly, biological psychiatry has emerged in medicine. To the extent that criminology becomes an interdisciplinary science based on biology, psychology, and sociology, and to the extent that law and the criminal justice system are integrated within scientific criminology, a science of criminology may emerge in the future. We hope that will be the case.

FURTHER STUDIES

Systems theory is often associated with engineering and business as well as public administration. Scholars from biology, psychology, psychiatry, sociology, and economics also write in the area of systems theory. It is an overall concept of knowledge and science which transcends disciplinary boundaries as found in university structures. The history of science is to be found in history departments or in philosophy departments. Specialized history course are often found in medical schools or in other divisions of the university devoted to science and technology.

REFERENCES

ADLER, M. (1985). *Ten Philosophical Mistakes.* New York: Macmillan.

BONNER, J. T. (1955). *Cells and Society.* Princeton, N.J.: Princeton University Press.

BOULDING, K. (1978). *Ecodynamics: A New Theory of Societal Evolution.* Beverly Hills, Calif.: Sage.

BUCKLEY, W. (1968). *Modern Systems Research for the Behavioral Scientist.* Chicago: Aldine.

CAPRA, F. (1975). *The Tao of Physics.* New York: Bantam Books.

COSER, L. A. (1977). *Masters of Sociological Thought,* 2nd ed. New York: Harcourt Brace Jovanovich.

DUBIN, R. (1969). *Theory Building.* New York: Free Press.

JEFFERY, C. R. (1979). *Biology and Crime.* Beverly Hills, Calif.: Sage.

JEFFERY, C. R. (1980). "Sociobiology and Criminology: The Long Lean Years." In *Taboos in Criminology,* ed. E. Sagarin. Beverly Hills, Calif.: Sage.

KENDLER, H. K. (1981). *Psychology: A Science in Conflict.* New York: Oxford University Press.

KLIR, G. (1972). *Trends in General Systems Theory.* New York: Wiley.

KOESTLER, A., and A. SMYTHIES (1969). *Beyond Reductionism.* London: Hutchinson.

KUHN, T. (1962). *The Structure of Scientific Revolutions.* Chicago: University of Chicago Press.

KUHN, A. (1974). *The Logic of Social Systems.* San Francisco: Jossey-Bass.

KUHN, A. (1975). *Unified Social Science: A System-Based Introduction.* Homewood, Ill.: Dorsey Press.

LEVINTHAL, C. F. (1988). *Messengers of Paradise.* New York: Doubleday.

MERCER, E. H. (1981). *The Foundation of Biological Theory.* New York: Wiley.

MEYER, A. (1957). *Psychobiology: A Science of Man.* Springfield, Ill.: Charles C Thomas.

MICHAEL, J., and M. ADLER (1933). *Crime, Law and Social Science.* New York: Harcourt, Brace.

MILLER, J. G. (1978). *The Living System.* New York: McGraw-Hill.

MULLINS, N. C. (1973). *Theories and Theory Groups in Contemporary American Sociology.* New York: Harper & Row.

RITZER, G. (1975). *Sociology: A Multiparadigm Science.* Boston: Allyn and Bacon.

SAGAN, C. (1980). *Cosmos.* New York: Random House.

TALBOTT, J. H. (1970). *A Biographical History of Medicine.* New York: Grune & Stratton.

TOFFLER, A. (1970). *Future Shock.* New York: Bantam Books.

TOFFLER, A. (1980). *The Third Wave.* New York: Bantam Books.

WADE, N. (1981). *The Nobel Duel.* New York: Doubleday.

WATSON, J. D. (1968). *Double Helix.* New York: Antheneum.

WOOTTON, B. (1959). *Social Science and Social Pathology.* London: Allen & Unwin.

QUESTIONS

1. What are the major conceptual issues involved in systems theory?
2. How would a university organized along the lines of systems theory differ from the present organization around departments of psychology and sociology and schools of law and social work?
3. What is meant by "the hierarchical nature of behavioral systems"?
4. How does systems theory explain human behavior?
5. What level of analysis does criminology use when it uses a systems approach to knowledge?
6. What critical differences exist between rationalism and empiricism?
7. Science is pure and therefore is never involved in political controversy. Comment.
8. What is meant by "the unity of science"?
9. Psychology and sociology as academic disciplines represent integrated systems of theory and knowledge. Comment.
10. Does science of necessity involve reductionism?

Evolution, Human Beings, Society, and Criminal Law 3

HUMAN AND SOCIETAL EVOLUTION

Before we can have crime and criminals we must have the human species in its present form and we must have politically organized societies. Human evolution and the evolution of society have in common the fact that both evolved from simple forms of organization to more complex forms. In terms of systems theory, as outlined in Chapter 2, for humans this meant that genetic and cellular systems formed more complex organs, which in turn formed more complex organisms. These complex organisms, which we know as *Homo sapiens* or the human species, then formed bands, groups, and societies based on cultural systems. We are thus looking at human evolution beginning with the simplest organisms, and the evolution of social systems unique to human beings. We use systems theory and the ''genes to society'' concept of science as it is applied to criminology. The purpose of the present chapter is to discuss human evolution and that of society in preparation for later discussions of crime, criminal law, and criminal behavior.

Human Evolution

Human evolution is a part of a general evolutionary process which started with the basic biochemistry of hydrogen, nitrogen, oxygen, and carbon. From single-celled organisms, evolution progressed to multicelled organisms—worms, insects, fish, amphibians, reptiles, birds, mammals, and primates. Each species is differentiated from earlier species in terms of the complexity of organization.

Human beings are members of the class of mammals, the order of primates, and the species of *Homo sapiens.* The primates include lemurs, monkeys, apes, and humans. The ape family includes gibbons, orangutans, gorillas, and chimpanzees. Students of primate behavior, called ethologists and primatologists, study the behavior of apes to gain insight into the behavior of the human species since humans share many biological and genetic characteristics with apes. Closely related to ethology is the study of ecology, or the interaction of animals with their physical environments and with each other.

Primates have several biological features that are critical for understanding the behavior of the human species. Primates bear their young within the female, making for a long period of dependency between female and offspring. Primates, with the exception of humans, have a very definite mating cycle called the estrus, when the female is ready to mate and to conceive.

Apes are tree dwellers and have several means of locomotion: leaping, swinging by their arms (brachiation), or walking on their knuckles. Progression is from swinging in trees to walking on the knuckles to walking upright on two feet (bipedalism) (Lewin, 1984; Napier, 1972; Gerstein et al., 1988).

Apes survive primarily by eating berries, fruits, and insects, although they will eat meat if and when it is available. They are not usually predators or hunters, as is a lion or cheetah, for example.

Human Biological Aspects

Humankind evolved from early hominid forms called *Homo habilis* and *Homo erectus.* Modern humans, *Homo sapiens,* appeared on earth about 100,000 years ago.

The human species differs from chimpanzees and gorillas in several critical respects. Humans left the trees for the savannas (plains and grasslands near a forest area). Except for the baboon, humans are the only primate to have moved into the grasslands. Humans had an upright posture and walked on two legs (bipedalism), together with having a thumb and opposing fingers, and this made it possible to use tools and to develop a technology. Human beings could look over the grass for prey and could use a club or rock to attack a deer or rabbit. Humans became hunters and meat eaters, as witnessed by the development of a jaw and teeth suitable for grinding berries and nuts as well as for chewing meat and breaking bones.

The most important development in human evolutionary history was the development of the human brain, whose size is around 1250 cubic centimeters (cc), compared to 600 cc for the gorilla and chimpanzee. The human brain has a large neocortex, which provides the capacity for language, symbolism, complex learning, memory, purposive behavior, and cultural systems (the importance of the brain for behavior is discussed in Chapter 11). Because of the capacity to develop language and culture, humans could develop cultural systems which included the use of fire and the development of stone tools.

The Evolution of Groups

Many primates form primary groups of 15 to 50 individuals, including males, females, and offspring. The usual pattern is a multimale group, as found among monkeys, gorillas, and chimpanzees. These groups are dominated by adult males, who are much larger than the females (sexual dimorphism). The males protect the females and young from danger and predators.

Basic to society is the family unit of the female and her children. The male may have little to do with the rearing of the young, and he will associate with the female only during estrus, or the mating cycle. There is a prolonged period of dependency on the part of the infant on the female.

Males fight among themselves for positions of dominance and access to the females during the mating season, although kinship and personality also play a role in the male hierarchical system. Juvenile males must challenge the adult males when they are ready to enter the adult social system (Campbell, 1979; Lawick-Goodall, 1971).

The primitive human group was very similar to that of the gorilla and chimpanzee, that is, male, female, and infants. Several major differences are to be found, however. The human female is the only primate without a definite mating cycle or estrus. The human species is the only one that mates twelve months out of the year. This is regarded by sociobiologists as critical to the bonding of males to females on a more-or-less permanent basis. Monogamous nuclear families are thus created as the basic social unit of human societies, comparable to the atom in physics or the cell in biology. The biological and sexual basis of the family is then reinforced by social and legal institutions and norms (Gerstein et al., 1988).

From basic biological differences, different social roles evolved for males and females. Males were hunters, women were food gatherers and agriculturalists. Women were much more involved in homemaking and child rearing, a role that has been seriously challenged in most recent years as a result of the industrial revolution (Friedl, 1975).

Specialization of sex roles occurred at this time, and a simple division of labor based on age and sex role was basic to the social organization of primitive humans. Food sharing is regarded as a major step in the development of human societies, since it required the cooperation of males and females in feeding the group. The process of food sharing and cooperative hunting is regarded as an important factor in the development of language and symbolic communication, which in turn was involved in the evolution of a larger and more complex brain for the human species.

The basic organizing principle of primitive societies is kinship, or the nuclear family of male, female, and children. As such family units multiplied in number they joined together into bands or wandering hunting groups. Clans were bands of people who identified with a common ancestor, often a mythical animal such as a bear or eagle. As population growth continued, the kinship or blood relationship was no longer available as a basis for social groupings since individuals no longer shared close biological ties. At this point the tribe replaced the band and the clan. The tribe was a social unit based on a common language and a common cultural heritage. The tribe was the beginning of the transition from social order based on kinship to social control based on legal and political systems (Campbell, 1979; Lenski and Lenski, 1982).

The Evolution of Society

As stated above, the original types of human organization were the family and band, which were hunting and fishing units (Service, 1979). Since the human species had upright posture, a large brain, and the use of language, it adapted to the environment through cultural technological developments, the first of which was the agricultural revolution.

The agricultural revolution, which started around 10,000 B.C., was based on the domestication of plants and animals. This took place in India, China, and Mesopotamia with the domestication of wheat. When humans domesticated plants and animals they were no longer dependent on the cyclical nature of their food supply as was the case for hunting and fishing.

The agricultural revolution meant that human groups could remain in one spot and not have to roam as nomadic bands in search of game. Humans could establish permanent villages and permanent social groupings not based on kinship. With the agricultural revolution there was a tremendous increase in population, since an agriculturally based society can support a larger population than can a hunting and fishing economy. Human ecological adaptation to the environment and the ecological system was totally different as a result of the agricultural revolution (Pfeiffer, 1977; Lenski and Lenski, 1982).

The shift from hunting and fishing to agriculture gave females new status and power in society since they occupied important positions within the agricultural system. Whereas males were the hunters, females were the agriculturalists. Within the agricultural system the equality of the hunting and fishing economy gave way to social stratification and social inequalities. Elitism replaced equality. A more complex division of labor based on inequality and private property emerged as an important part of the agricultural revolution (Friedl, 1975).

The next major change was the industrial revolution from 1760 through 1880. The industrial revolution was a product of the new sources of power and energy in the form of coal, steam, gas, and electricity, which now also includes nuclear energy. Production changed from farming and rural economies to factories and manufacturing. Populations moved from rural to urban areas, creating large centers of population around the factories and industrial areas. New population growth accompanied the industrial revolution, which in turn created new pressures for urban growth.

The new urban centers became centers of trade, commerce, transportation, communication, production, and distribution. Recreation, entertainment, education, government, and related activities were also a part of the new urban system. Rural areas were now connected to and dependent on the nearest large urban centers, and urban centers were connected with other urban centers and with rural area by means of railroads, highways, and airports. The development of the automobile replaced the horse as a means of transportation, and the railroad and the airplane added to the complexity of the interaction of people living in these new urban areas. New means of communication replaced the smoke signal and the tom-tom. The printing press, invented around 1456, made books, newspapers, and magazines available on a mass scale. In the nineteenth and twentieth centuries came the radio, telegraph, telephone, and television.

The communication revolution has resulted in the development of huge libraries, and with the coming of computers we can now store, process, and retrieve information in microseconds. As Sagan (1977) has noted in his account of the evolution of the brain, the processing and storage of information has evolved from the gene to the human brain to libraries and computers.

As noted in Chapter 2, any system is dependent on the exchange of energy and information. All ecological systems involve the exchange of energy and information. In the case of the human social system the use of natural energy, including nuclear energy, and the use of information exchange and storage in the form of television, communication satellites, and computers have totally transformed the person–environment relationship as found in human ecology (i.e., the interaction of organisms with the environment).

The Evolution of the State

When we discuss the state we mean a society governed and controlled by a centralized authority arranged in a hierarchical manner with a monopoly over the use of force and coercion. State systems are based on a bureaucratic structure of authority with a chain of command that is hierarchical in nature.

The development of the state is very much related to the social and ecological changes discussed above, that is, population growth, the development of agriculture, and the beginnings of village life. The original source of social control was the kinship system based on blood ties, but population growth brought together groups of people without common blood ties so that the kinship system of control was no longer adequate as a social control agency. Power passed from kinship to those who controlled land and natural resources. As humans moved from a hunting and fishing economy to an agricultural economy, the owernship of land and other resources such as water became important to survival of the population (Lewellen, 1983; Cohen and Service, 1978; Service, 1975; Haas, 1982; Wright, 1977).

During the hunting and fishing period, control over communal hunts was necessary, and the distribution and sharing of food made some centralized control measures necessary. As humankind moved from hunting to agriculture, there was an increased need for centralized control of water supplies and irrigation practices, as well as food distribution and ownership of land. The origins of the state system occurred in China, India, and Egypt, where agricultural civilizations developed in connection with river valleys along the Nile, Ganges, Indus, Hwang Ho, and Yangtze rivers (Cohen and Service, 1978; Lewellen, 1983).

According to the anthropologist, Marvin Harris (1977) the state originated in the agricultural revolution. Harris talks about "cultural materialism" to refer to the material and technological means by which the human species adapted to its physical environment. Harris notes, for example, that the cultural taboo against eating pork on the part of some cultures, or the eating of the holy cows in India, was derived from the need to preserve the breeding stock. Pork production and consumption was high in the United States when farmers in the midwest raised corn, which could then be used to produce pork. When farming moved farther west, to the grasslands, herding cows on these lands was more profitable than raising corn for pigs, so production and consumption moved from pork to beef. The critical aspect of Harris's work is his view that the cultural system, based on material technology, and the ecological system are interdependent. Culture becomes not a symbolic superorganic system as Kroeber and others had viewed culture, but becomes a very physical and materialistic system of environmental and biological adaptation.

Two different theoretical positions are used to explain the origins of the state in political anthropology (Cohen and Service, 1978; Lewellen, 1983; Haas, 1982). One theory is based on social conflict, social inequalities, and the struggle that exists between different social classes. This view maintains that social inequalities existed before the state came into existence, and the state is a means of perpetuating existing social inequalities.

The conflict view is found in the evolutionary theory of Darwin and others, in the social contract theorists (Hobbes, Locke, and Rousseau), and in the works of Marx, Engels, and Morgan. Morton Fried represents this position among present-day anthropologists.

The second position maintains that the state grew out of cooperation and integration rather than conflict and struggle. The state evolved as a means of coordinating and controlling tribal hunts, the distribution of food and resources, and the use of land for agricultural purposes. The centralization of power, the concept of private property, and the hierarchy of authority became necessary because of the increase in population and the new complexity of the division of labor.

The integrative model is found in the sociological structural functionalists from Durkheim to Spencer to Parsons, and is found today in the writings of Elmer Service, a political anthropologist. The conflict view and the integrative view of political power are discussed in greater detail in Chapter 15.

Recent authors have emphasized that both conflict and integration are involved in the evolution of the state. Social inequalities, population growth, the agricultural revolution, and urbanization all interact with one another to influence the development of the state, and in turn the state has influenced the development of social inequalities, population growth, and urbanization.

These variables are interactive as part of the living system, and they mutually influence each other (see Chapter 2).

The Evolution of Society: Summary

The evolution of society can be summarized in the following manner:

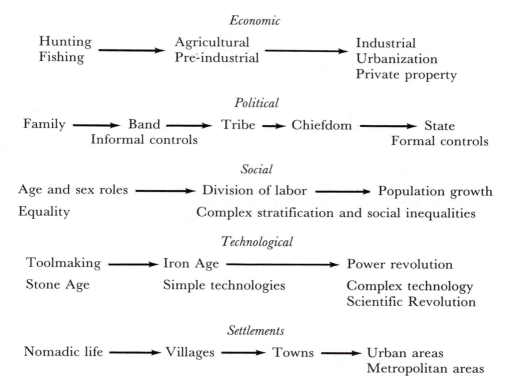

Economic

Hunting   ⟶   Agricultural   ⟶   Industrial
Fishing   Pre-industrial   Urbanization
                                                        Private property

Political

Family ⟶ Band ⟶ Tribe ⟶ Chiefdom ⟶ State
         Informal controls   Formal controls

Social

Age and sex roles ⟶ Division of labor ⟶ Population growth
Equality   Complex stratification and social inequalities

Technological

Toolmaking ⟶ Iron Age ⟶ Power revolution
Stone Age   Simple technologies   Complex technology
                                      Scientific Revolution

Settlements

Nomadic life ⟶ Villages ⟶ Towns ⟶ Urban areas
                                                Metropolitan areas

Another way to represent the transition from primitive to modern societies is thus:

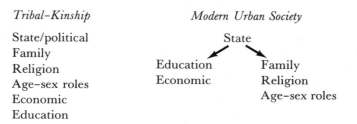

Tribal–Kinship   *Modern Urban Society*

State/political   State
Family
Religion   Education   Family
Age–sex roles   Economic   Religion
Economic   Age–sex roles
Education

In the tribal system all functions were performed by the tribal group—political, economic, family, and educational. In modern society the state system is the dominant institution controlling and governing in different ways the other institutions, such as the family, religion, educational, and economic. For example, the state establishes public educational systems; controls marriage, divorce, and the treatment of children; regulates business activities; and has replaced the church as the source of law and authority.

Biological Change, Social Change, Crime, and Criminals

In this chapter we have discussed the basic nature of humans and society, and human evolution from primates and the evolution of society from family kinship groupings. These biological and social changes are fundamental and necessary to an understanding of crime and criminal behavior.

The evolution of the brain resulted in a brain that has centers for both violence and aggression and rationality and purposiveness. Certain areas of the brain when stimulated result in violent behavior. The hormonal and biochemical nature of the brain must be understood if we are to understand criminal behavior and the struggle between the violence centers and the rational centers of the brain.

The evolution of sexual differences between males and females resulted in differences in physical and social development between males and females. Males have different genes, different brains, different hormones, and different body types than females. Males are also eight to ten times as criminalistic as females.

Both nature and nurture are involved in human development. The brain is the center of control for behavior, and the brain is a product of genes and environment in interaction. The human brain is pliable, which makes complex learning possible, which in turn makes cultural and social systems possible. We will discuss genetics, the brain and behavior, and learning theory in later chapters.

The development of human societies makes possible the concept of private property and theft. Technological changes in transportation systems were from the horse or oxen to the train to the automobile to the airplane. As such technological changes occurred, theft changed from horse theft to train robberies to auto theft to airplane hijackings.

The industrial revolution created urban centers and population growth, and crime rates are very much related to the ecological development of urban areas (see Chapter 19). Certain areas of the city have very high crime rates, other areas have very low crime rates. The coming of the automobile not only changed the nature of urban form, but it also changed the nature of sexual relationships, the family, marriage, recreation and entertainment, and most other aspects of social life.

Science and technology developed new means of controlling energy, communications, and transportation. Human biological capabilities were altered and extended by the scientific revolution, as the following diagram illustrates:

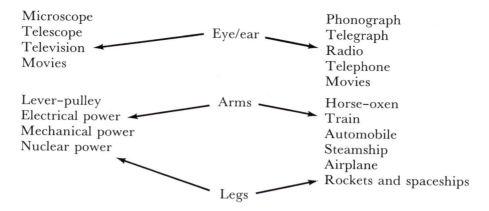

Human technology has also created knives, guns, and bombs, which are a part of criminal behavior. Technology and urban growth also created air and water pollution, which in turn damages the genetic structure and the structure of the brain. Lead and cadmium poisoning is a major factor in behavioral disorders and antisocial behaviors (see Chapters 11 and 18).

THE EVOLUTION OF CRIMINAL LAW

Tribal Law

As was noted above, the transition in social organization was from tribal to state, from simple to complex, and from hunting and fishing to agricultural to industrial and urban. Law as we know it emerged from this transition from a tribal society to a state society.

Primitive tribes are governed by custom, tradition, magic, and witchcraft. Anthropologists have taken two different approaches to the nature of primitive law. One view maintains that all custom is law, and therefore primitives have a legal system. Malinowski argued, for example, that primitive social systems are governed by custom, which is enforced by reciprocity or "a body of binding obligations . . . kept in force by specific mechanisms of reciprocity and publicity inherent in the structure of their society" (Malinowski, 1926:58).

The problem with the definition of law as custom is that it equates law with all social norms. All laws are social norms, not all social norms are laws. Custom is enforced by ridicule, tradition, social pressure, public opinion, and threats of ostracism from the group. Law is enforced by the use of force and coercion. Seagle (1941:7) wrote that "it is the fact that the sanction is applied exclusively by organized political government that distinguishes law from religion, morals, and custom." Hoebel (1954:28) stated that "a social norm is legal if its neglect or infraction is regularly met by the application of physical force by an individual or group possessing the socially recognized privilege of so acting.'' In commenting on the sociological and anthropological usages of the term ''law,'' Roscoe Pound (1945:300) said: ''This broader usage (law as custom) is common with sociologists. But certainly for jurists, and I suspect for sociologists, it is expedient to avoid adding to the burden of the term of too many meanings, and to use 'law' for social control through the systematic application of the force of politically organized society.''

Primitive people had little or no law because they are controlled by custom, religion, magic, and witchcraft, and the basic unit of society is the kinship group, not the political state (Redfield, 1967; Bohannon, 1967b; Seagle, 1941; Radcliffe-Brown, 1935, Llewellyn and Hoebel, 1941). The shift from *tribal law to state law* is one of the basic changes in institutional structure that occurred in the history of human social organization.

The Nature of Tribal Law

Primitive law is based on the principle of *self-help*. Primitive law is private law and it is enforced by the tribal group. In most primitive societies the *feud* is carried on by groups related to one another by blood or by social obligation. An injury to a member of tribe *A* by a member of tribe *B* led to a retaliatory strike against a member of tribe *B* (Barton, 1949; Llewellyn and Hoebel, 1941; Popisil, 1967; 1971).

Early Egyptian and Greek law was organized along tribal principles, based on a doctrine of ''lex talionis,'' or an eye for an eye, a tooth for a tooth. This principle is found in the Code of Hammurabi (2400 B.C.) (Koschaker, 1935), which placed a limitation on revenge since the offended party could take no more than an eye for an eye. Out of early tribal law we find the historical beginnings of a major justification for punishment: that revenge is justice and that punishment must fit the crime. We discuss retribution and revenge in later chapters.

The feud was very costly in terms of lives and injuries, so limitations were placed on the conditions under which the feud could be carried out. The feud was limited in many societies by the use of ridicule and the singing duel, in which the litigants insulted one another until satisfaction was obtained (Bohannan, 1967b).

A common way to limit the blood feud was through a system of compensation, or payment of damages to the injured party. The amount of the payment depended on the extent and nature of the injuries (Barton, 1949). Among the Comanche Indians restitution often took place in the form of horses. The military societies of the Cheyenne Indians performed police functions, especially during the communal buffalo hunts, and these military societies were an important step toward the development of the state system (Hoebel, 1954; Llewellyn and Hoebel, 1941).

The Teutonic tribes of northern Europe had a system of self-help and the blood feud. A system of compensation for injuries developed to assure peace between the conflicting parties (von Bar, 1916; Huebner, 1918). The Teutonic tribes who settled England (Angles, Saxons, Danes) brought with them the Germanic system of tribal law. The Anglo-Saxons developed a detailed system of compensation, called the *wergild,* money paid for the death of a tribal member. The payment schedule corresponds to our modern insurance contract, whereby a person is paid so much for the loss of an eye or an arm or a life (Thorpe, 1840; Attenborough, 1922; Rightmire, 1932; Kemble, 1879; Pollack and Maitland, 1899; Robertson, 1925; Seebohn, 1902).

From Tribal to State Law

As discussed above, the pattern of social evolution was from a hunting and fishing economy to an agricultural economy. Villages, population growth, and a more complex division of labor resulted in the decay of the tribal groups. Territorial groups replaced kinship groups. These territorial groups took the form of feudal kingdoms governed by lords, and eventually by a unification of kingdoms under a lord, which became the modern nation-state system (Stubbs, 1891; Traill, 1899; Rightmire, 1932; Kemble, 1879). *Land* replaced *blood* as the basis for social control. Individuals now owed allegiance not to the kinship group but to the land. The person who owned the land judged the person who had no land. Under a feudal system this was the lord–serf relationship, and anyone who lived on the land owed the lord services and allegiance. Under the state system the citizen owed the king services and allegiance.

In his *Ancient Law,* Sir Henry Maine (1906) referred to this shift from tribalism to state sovereignty as a shift from "status to contract." Under a status system rights are determined by one's membership in a family; under a contract system one's rights are determined by individual contractual relationships worked out within the framework of the political state. In his *Ancient Society,* Lewis Henry Morgan (1878) called this movement one of "savagery to civilization." "A tremendous change takes place when the tribal tie gives way to the territorial tie" (Kocourek and Wigmore, 1915). "Legal controls came to be associated with locality rather than with bloodstock or descent" [Goebel (1937a); see also Barton (1949) and Titiev (1954)]. Simpson and Stone (1948) summarize this movement as follows: "The cardinal characteristics of an emergent political society is that kinship is no longer the main bond of social cohesion. Stated affirmatively, this means that political organization has been superimposed upon kin organization." Mueller and Besharov (1986) have traced the growth of the criminal law from the family to the clan to the nation-state and finally to international bodies such as the United Nations.

THE EMERGENCE OF STATE LAW

The Unification of England

The political unification of the feudalistic settlements in England came about as a result of feudal warfare and conquests by one lord of another lord. The emergence of Christianity in England was also a unifying force. The conquest of England by the Normans under William the Conqueror (A.D. 1066) united the kingdoms of England under one king for the first time in history (Traill, 1899; Rightmire, 1932; Stubbs, 1891; Kemble, 1879).

The King's Peace

After the conquest William the Conqueror became the source of law and authority. The concept of the "king's peace" emerged; that is, any violations of the peace, such as fighting or thievery, were punished by the king as violations of the rights and authority of the king. The guilty party had to pay compensation to the king for these violations (Pollack and Maitland, 1932; Seagle, 1941).

By the time of Henry II (1154–1189) the Court of the King's Bench was open to citizens who had the proper legal writ, known as Pleas of the Crown. The Court of Common Pleas was established for pleas not involving the king directly (Maitland, 1931).

The king appointed local judges to represent him in local courts, and these judges made decisions that were recorded on the Pipe Rolls. In time these many judicial decisions came to be known as the common law of England. Common law is judge-made law with the authority of the king behind it; it is not customary law or tribal law.

Trial Procedures

The doctrine of self-help was based on the *appeal* of the injured party, where an accusation was made against the accused by the injured party. This was a private procedure that was replaced by a trial procedure by which the innocence or guilt of the accused party was determined. These trials originally involved trial by *ordeal*, a physical test involving the hot iron ordeal, the cold water ordeal, or the dry cereal ordeal. If the accused did not suffer injury from the ordeal, it was assumed that he was innocent. The ordeal depended on divine intervention, and clergy played an important part in the ordeal until the Fourth Latern Council of A.D. 1215 forbade clerical participation in the ordeal.

The Normans introduced the trial by *battle*, whereby the two litigants fought one another until one was killed or injured. The trial by battle also took the form of the *duel*, by which men of honor settled their differences (Radin, 1936; Attenborough, 1922).

The *indictment* came into existence at this time also, whereby local officials would take testimony from witnesses as to the type of crimes committed in the county. This led to the modern grand jury and became a means of public prosecution of criminal cases. The indictment led to a *trial by jury* in place of the ordeal, and such trials were held in the king's court (Holdsworth, 1923).

Compensation to the King

The old system of compensation to the victim or his/her family was replaced by compensation to the king. Crimes were no longer family or tribal affairs, but were offenses against the king. "The very core of the revolution in finance and law that took place in Henry II's reign was the transfer of the initiative in criminal matters from the kindred of the injured man to the king as public prosecutor'' (Jeudwine, 1917:84; Pollock and Maitland, 1899). The payment made to the king as part of the king's peace was called an *amercement.*

Gradually, the law of wrongs was differentiated into the law of torts and the law of crimes. Tort law involves compensation for injuries done to another party for which private responsibility exists; criminal law involves punishment done for injuries done to the general public or to the state. A distinction was now made between those offenses for which compensation was made and those for which compensation was not made. For those guilty of a criminal offense who could not pay the compensation to the king, a different kind of punishment had to be used, such as mutilation, outlawry, transportation, and death. The inability of a defendant to pay for the crime was a basis for the development of criminal sanctions (Potter, 1943). Pollock and Maitland (1899) wrote: ''Gradually more and more offenses became emendable; outlawry remained for those could not or would not pay.'' They cite the case of a forger who was saved from the gallows by the payment of the amercement to the king. A murderer could buy back his life, although a thief without the means of restitution was hanged. There can be no tort law for a judgment-proof population [Pike (1873); see also von Bar)1916)]. The fact that the compensation went to the king and not the victim discouraged victims from pursuing criminal cases in the court system, and the initiative to prosecute criminal cases was left to the king and his agents.

Punishment

As was noted above, the death penalty developed for those who were unable to pay the compensation due to the king. Executions were carried out for a great variety of offenses and they were public affairs attended by huge crowds in a holiday spirit. Cruel and ingenious methods of torture and death were used at these executions. By the time of Henry VIII there were over 200 capital offenses, and children, women, and animals were executed as well as men (Holdsworth, 1923; Plucknett, 1948; Radzinowicz, 1948–1957; Stephens, 1883).

Although many capital offenses and many executions occurred, the number of executions to the number of eligible offenders was small. Criminous clerks (priests) were exempted from the criminal law of the king under the benefit of clergy doctrine. Sanctuary was granted to a fleeing criminal by the monasteries, and a criminal who reached the safety of the church could leave the country, usually at Dover, for a foreign land (Plucknett, 1948; Holdsworth, 1923).

In capital cases the judges would interpret the statutes narrowly, or fail to apply the death penalty. Juries would return verdicts which required less than the death penalty, or they would find the defendant not guilty. Prosecutors would reduce charges through plea bargaining. All of these practices are still to be found in the criminal justice system. Such legal practices made the use of capital punishment most capricious and uncertain (Hall, 1952).

Transportation as a punishment was introduced in the late seventeenth century. Inmates were shipped to colonies, such as Botany Bay in Australia. Alexander Moconochi, a British penal reformer, made his reputation at the penal colony in Australia (Mannheim, 1970). In the nineteenth century imprisonment and the growth of our present prison system replaced the use of capital punishment and transportation as a major means of dealing with the crime problem. The development of the modern prison system, probation and parole, and treatment techniques are the subject matter of corrections and the criminal justice system (see Chapters 8 and 9).

The Police System

The disintegration of the tribal system left the community without a means of enforcing law and order. A system of local control developed caled the *hundred*, 100 men designated as responsible for the good behavior of the people in the community. A body of armed citizens, called the *posse comitatus,* pursued the criminal, and local political units were responsible for police protection, which was in the hands of private citizens (Pike, 1873; Pollack and Maitland, 1899).

As the crown gained power it extended this power into each local county government. The king's reeve or shire reeve (a shire is a county) watched over the king's financial and legal affairs in each shire, and he presided over the county court. The shire reeve came to be known as the sheriff, who is still the police officer at the county level in most states (Stubbs, 1891; Jeudwine, 1917).

From 1300 to 1900 there was no strong public police force in England. Pike, Stephens, Radzinowicz, and other legal historians described this period as one of lawlessness and violence. Local merchants organized private police forces to combat crime. John and Henry Fielding and Patrick Colquhoun led a movement to establish a strong centralized police force in England. John Fielding established the Bow Street Runners as a police unit in London, and in 1829 Sir Robert Peel organized a centralized police force for England, which at this time was limited to the city of London. Scotland Yard was also established during this period (Radzinowicz, 1948–1957).

The police system, like the court system, shifted from private to public during this period. Today we still depend on public police agencies—but with an increase in the usage of private police forces since public resources are not adequate to deal with the crime problem.

Later Developments in the Criminal Law

The enclosure movement, by which land was taken by the lords from the peasants and enclosed for herding sheep rather than for growing crops, led to a shift in population from rural to urban areas. Peasants moved from farms to towns and villages, and a new class of vagrants was created, forming the basis for some major social problems. A growing population and industrialization also contributed to this rural-to-urban shift. The Statutes of Labourers of 1349 ordered men to remain on their jobs and in the township. The Elizabethan

Poor Laws of 1598 and 1601 attempted to provide relief for a population of poor and destitute people. Workhouses and houses of correction were established, one to provide work for the able bodied, the other to provide punishment for those who would not work. However, in practice the two institutions were never clearly distinguished. The Settlement Act of 1662 made each parish responsible for the welfare of those residing in the parish, which meant residence by birth. Crowded slum areas were characterized by vagrancy, begging, gambling, drunkenness, prostitution, and theft (Pike, 1873; Stephens, 1883).

At this time a number of criminal laws were passed aimed at controlling vagrancy, theft, poverty, drinking, and gambling. Eighty percent of the executions of the day were for property offenses. "Sending paupers to Bridewell" was a common expression. The Waltham Black Act made it a capital offense for anyone to have a face blacked while doing injury to person or property. This act was aimed at the highwaymen and robbers of that time, and it extended the death penalty to many new areas of theft (Radzinowicz, 1948–1957). The Gin Act of 1736 was an attempt to control the public gin houses, and it caused so much popular resentment that rioting occurred as a result. Many rebellions and riots involving political and religious groups, such as the Lollards and Anabaptists, occurred at this time (Radzinowicz, 1948–1957; Pike, 1873). The criminal law was shaped to handle the many social problems created by urbanization and industrialization.

In *Theft, Law and Society,* Jerome Hall (1952) traces the changes that occurred in the law of theft due to the impact of urbanization and industrialization. His study begins with the *Carrier's Case* of 1473. In this case the defendant had been hired to carry goods to Southhampton. During the course of the journey he broke the bales and took the content. The concept of larceny as it developed in common law included the element of trespass. A person who is a bailee is in legal possession of goods; therefore, he cannot be held to be guilty of larceny. In the *Carrier's Case* the court found that the breaking of the bales constituted the trespass, and the defendant was convicted of larceny by bailee. The common law was thus extended into a new area, a move made necessary by the development of trade and commerce and the use of bailments in modern industrial societies. Hall (1952:10) states that the "door was opened to admit into the law of larceny a whole series of acts which had up to that time been purely civil wrongs."

Receiving stolen property was a major criminal problem at this time. Jonathan Wild organized a trade in stolen property which extended overseas as well as in England. He had a well-organized and effective criminal syndicate for the purpose of trading in stolen goods. By 1827 a series of statutory changes and judicial interpretations of the law placed receiving stolen property in the category of a felony (Hall, 1952).

The development of banking, a money economy with its use of credit, and the violation of the trust placed in persons dealing with money made it necessary to extend the criminal law to cover new areas of business and commerce. In the eighteenth century criminal law came to be the means by which offenses involving the business system were controlled. Civil offenses were made criminal offenses when servants, bailees, bank tellers, and clerks came into possession of money and property legally, which they then converted to illegal use. Civil actions against such persons were not adequate since these people were for the most part judgment-proof.

TYPES OF LAW

Common Law

The first type of state law was common law, the law found in the decisions of judges. The doctrine of *stare decisis* developed, that is, following the precedent of earlier case law. Lawyers cite earlier decisions similar in fact and argue that the precedent in that case should govern in the present case. Since judges make contradictory decisions in similar cases, the new case may be resolved in several different ways, thus setting more precedent. Some decisions are overturned by appellate courts, and in many instances the minority opinion in one case will become a majority opinion in a later case.

Since judges are constantly making and changing the law, it is hard to argue that the law embodies eternal and absolute values. The best explanations of the power of judges to make law are to be found in the positive law doctrine, where law is the command of the sovereign, and the legal realist doctrine, where law is viewed as the behavior of the judges.

Statutory Law

The second type of law is statutory law, law made by state and federal legislatures. Most states have gone to a statutory form of law. This means that another source of state power makes the law, namely, the legislators. This raises the question of the power of politics and the fact that legislators vote to support certain private interest groups. Governors and legislators support the death penalty because of public support and votes.

In the final analysis judges decide on the legality of legislation according to the doctrine of judicial review and the separation of executive, legislative, and judicial functions. The courts also review the activities of the executive branch of government.

Constitutional Law

The third type of law is constitutional law, including the law used to create a new government. Basic to the U.S. Constitution is the Declaration of Independence (1776), which states: "We hold these Truths to be self-evident, that all Men are created equal, that they are endowed by their Creator with certain inalienable Rights, that among these are Life, Liberty, and the Pursuit of Happiness." In this statement is the idea of natural and inalienable rights, or rights to be found in natural law. These rights were originally expressed in the writings of John Locke. Constitutional law is thought of as "higher law," not positive or human-made law. Corwin (1929) argued that constitutional law contained the idea of a higher law. Constitutional law is higher law in another sense. The law applied in any given case can be appealed to the Supreme Court, which will determine whether it is constitutional. Thus the Constitution ranks higher than common law or statutory law.

Some political scientists and lawyers view the Constitution as natural law embodying higher moral principles, but we can also regard such law as positive law or human-made law. U.S. Supreme Court judges are appointed by the president through a political process. The president selects men and women who are politically conservative or liberal, depending on the president's own political views. When a new justice is appointed, there is speculation as to how the Court will vote on critical issues, such as the death penalty, or abortion, or school desegration. This is especially true in those cases where the Court in the past has voted 5–4 or 6–3 on the issue. When a new president is elected, the future of the Supreme Court may be at stake.

Rather than being an apolitical body, the Supreme Court is as political a body as exists in our form of government. Behavioral scientists study the behavior of Supreme Court justices as they do the behavior of other political figures (Dye and Zeigler, 1978; Schubert, 1965; Glick, 1983).

The Evolution of Criminal Law: Summary

The evolution of criminal law was from tribal law to feudal law to state law. Law emerged from private vengeance and the blood feud to criminal law in which the king was the offended party. Crimes became offenses against the king; the king prosecuted the case, and the king gained compensation or revenge from the criminal. The victim no longer benefited from the conviction of the criminal.

If the criminal could not pay the compensation, he/she was usually executed. In later history transportation and imprisonment replaced the death penalty as the major means of controlling criminal behavior. The modern criminal justice system is a product of the growth of the state system, along with the agricultural–industrial–urban complex which now characterized western European nation-states. Criminal law moved from restitution and compensation to punishment and justice. This is a basic characteristic of modern criminal law.

FURTHER STUDIES

Human evolution is usually dealt with in anthorpology departments. The evolution of society is dealt with in anthropology and sociology departments. The evolution of the state system is discussed by anthropologists, lawyers, and political scientists.

REFERENCES

ATTENBOROUGH, F. L. (1922). *The Laws of the Earliest English Kings.* Cambridge: Cambridge University Press.

BARTON, R. F. (1949). *The Kalingas.* Chicago: University of Chicago Press.

BOHANNAN, P. (1967a). "The Differing Realms of the Law." In *Law and Warfare,* ed. Paul Bohannan. New York: Natural History Press.

BOHANNAN, P. (1967b). *Law and Warfare.* New York: Natural History Press.

CAMPBELL, B. G. (1979). *Humankind Emerging.* Boston: Little, Brown.

COHEN, R. and E. R. SERVICE (1978). *Origins of the States: The Anthropology of Political Evolution.* Philadelphia: Institute for the Study of Human Issues.

CORWIN, E. S. (1929). *The "Higher Law" Background of American Constitutional Law.* Ithaca, N.Y.: Great Seal Books.

DYE, T. R., and L. E. ZEIGLER (1978). *The Irony of Democracy,* 4th ed. North Scituate, Mass.: Duxbury Press.

FRIEDL, E. (1975). *Women and Men.* New York: Holt, Rinehart and Winston.

GERSTEIN, D. R., ET AL. (1988). *The Behavioral and Social Sciences.* Washington, D.C.: National Academy Press.

GLICK H. (1983). *Courts, Politics, and Justice.* New York: McGraw-Hill.

GOEBEL, J., JR., ed. (1937a). *Cases and Materials on the Development of Legal Institutions.* New York: Columbia Law Review.

GOEBEL, J. (1937b). *Felony and Misdemeanor.* New York: Commonwealth Fund.

HAAS, J. (1982). *The Evolution of the Prehistoric State.* New York: Columbia University Press.

HALL, J. (1952). *Theft, Law and Society,* 3rd ed. Indianapolis, Ind.: Bobbs-Merrill.

HARRIS, M. (1977). *Cannibals and Kings: The Origins of Culture.* New York: Vintage.

HOEBEL, E. A. (1954). *The Law of Primitive Man.* Cambridge, Mass.: Harvard University Press.

HOLDSWORTH, W. S. (1923). *A History of English Law,* Vols. 1–7. Boston: Little, Brown.

HUEBNER, R. (1918). *A History of Germanic Private Law.* Boston: Little, Brown.

JEUDWINE, J. W. (1917). *Tort, Crime and the Police in Medieval Britain.* London: Williams & Norgate.

KEMBLE, J. M. (1879). *The Saxons in England.* London: Bernard Quartich.

KOCOUREK, A., and J. H. WIGMORE (1915). *Primitive and Ancient Legal Institutions.* Boston: Little, Brown.

KOSCHAKER, P. (1935). "Law: Cuneiform." In *Encyclopedia of the Social Sciences,* Vol. 9. New York: Macmillan.

LAWICK-GOODALL, J. (1971). *In the Shadow of Man.* Boston: Houghton Mifflin.

LENSKI, G., and J. LENSKI (1982). *Human Societies,* 4th ed. New York: McGraw-Hill.

LEWELLEN, T. (1983). *Political Anthropology.* South Hadley, Mass: Bergin and Garvey.

LEWIN, R. (1984). *Human Evolution.* San Francisco: W. H. Freeman.

LLEWELLYN, K. N., and E. A. HOEBEL (1941). *The Cheyenne Way.* Norman: University of Oklahoma Press.

MAINE, HENRY (1906). *Ancient Law,* 10th ed. London: J. Murray.

MAITLAND, F. W. (1931). *The Constitutional History of England.* Cambridge: Cambridge University Press.

MALINOWSKI, B. (1926). *Crime and Custom in Savage Society.* London: Kegan Paul, Trench, Trubner & Co.

MANNHEIM, H., ed. (1970). *Pioneers in Criminology.* Montclair, N.J.: Patterson Smith.

MORGAN, L. H. (1878). *Ancient Society.* New York: Holt.

MUELLER, G. O. W., and D. J. BESHAROV (1986). "Evolution and Enforcement of International Criminal Law." In *International Criminal Law,* Vol. 1: *Crimes,* ed. M. C. Bassiouni. Ardsley-on-Hudson, N.Y.: Transnational Publishers.

NAPIER, P. (1972). *Monkeys and Apes.* New York: Bantam Books.

PFEIFFER, J. (1977). *The Emergence of Society.* New York: McGraw-Hill.

PIKE, L. O. (1873). *A History of Crime in England,* Vol. 1. London: Smith, Elder, and Co.

PLUCKNETT, F. T. (1948). *A Concise History of the Common Law.* London: Butterworth.

POLLOCK, F., and F. W. MAITLAND (1899). *The History of English Law before the Time of Edward I,* Vols. 1–2. Cambridge: Cambridge University Press.

POSPISIL, L. (1967). "The Attributes of Law." In *Law and Warfare,* ed. P. Bohannan. New York: Natural History Press.

POSPISIL, L. (1971). *Anthropology of Law.* New York: Harper & Row.

POTTER, H. (1943). *An Historical Introduction to English Law.* London: Sweet & Maxwell.

POUND, R. (1945). "Sociology of Law." In *Twentieth Century Sociology,* ed. G. Gurvich and W. E. Moore. New York: Philosophical Library.

RADCLIFFE-BROWN, A. R. (1935). "Law, Primitive." In *Encyclopedia of the Social Sciences,* Vol. 9. New York: Macmillan.

RADIN, M. (1936) *Handbook of Anglo-American Legal History.* St. Paul, Minn.: West Publishing Co.

RADIZINOWICZ, L. (1948–1957). *A History of English Criminal Law*, Vols. 1–4. London: Stevens & Sons.

REDFIELD, R. (1967). "Primitive Law." In *Law and Warfare* ed. Paul Bohannan. New York: Natural History Press.

RIGHTMIRE, G. (1932). *The Law of England at the Norman Conquest.* Columbus, Ohio: Heer Publishing Co.

ROBERTSON, A. J. (1925). *The Laws of the Kings of England from Edmund to Henry I.* Cambridge: Cambridge University Press.

SAGAN, C. (1977). *The Dragons of Eden.* New York: Ballentine.

SCHUBERT, G. (1965). *Judicial Policy Making.* Glenview, Ill.: Scott, Foresman.

SEAGLE, W. (1941). *Quest for Law.* New York: Alfred A. Knopf.

SEEBOHM, F. (1902). *Tribal Custom in Anglo Saxon Law.* London: Longmans, Green & Co.

SERVICE, E. R. (1975). *The Origin of the State and Civilization.* New York: W. W. Norton.

SERVICE, E. R. (1979). *The Hunters.* Englewood Cliffs, N.J.: Prentice-Hall.

SIMPSON, S. P., and J. STONE (1948). *Law and Society,* Vol. 1. St. Paul, Minn.: West Publishing Co.

STEPHEN, J. F. (1883). *A History of the Criminal Law of England*, Vols. 1–3. London: Macmillan.

STUBBS, W. (1891). *The Constitutional History of England*, Vol. 1. Oxford: Clarendon Press.

THORPE, B., ed. (1840). *Ancient Laws and Institutes of England.* London: Royal Commission of Public Records.

TITIEV, M. (1954). *The Science of Man.* New York: Holt.

TRAILL, H. D. (1899). *Social England.* Vols. 1–6. New York: Putnam.

VON BAR, C. L. (1916). *A History of Continental Criminal Law.* Boston: Little, Brown.

WRIGHT, H. T. (1977). ''Recent Research on the Origin of the State.'' In *Annual Review of Anthropology*, Vol. 6. Palo Alto, Calif.: Annual Reviews.

QUESTIONS

1. What is meant by the concept ''evolution''?
2. What physical and social traits differentiate the human species from primates in general?
3. What are the major stages in the evolution of human societies?
4. How are the evolutionary changes in humankind's physical and social systems related to crime and criminal behavior?
5. What is the nature of tribal law?
6. What differentiates tribal law from state law?
7. What are the differences among common law, statutuory law, and constitutional law?

Classical Legal Criminology   4

CRIMINAL LAW, REVENGE, AND JUSTICE

Revenge and the Prelegal System

As we discussed in Chapter 3, tribal law was based on revenge and the blood feud. The offended group carried out revenge against the offending group until some form of restitution was made by the offending group. This revenge system is based on blood relative groups, and violence and aggression are found in the behavior of the most primitive human groups.

The revenge/retribution response is found not only in the earliest history of primitive human beings, but also in the behavior of primates. Goodall (1971, 1979) has reported that chimpanzees are killers and will attack other primates or their own species even to the extent that one chimp colony was exterminated by another colony. Goodall (1979:620) concludes that ''chimpanzee violence compels us to acknowledge that these ape cousins of ours are even more similar to humans that we thought before.'' Ghiglieri (1983, 1987) interprets male chimpanzee aggression in terms of competition among males for mating rights with females. To compete for females, the males must compete among themselves not only for females but for territorial rights. Territorial rights are critical because of the need for a food supply for the females. Within this setting the males become very aggressive and kill members of other chimpanzee groups, but they do not kill members of their own group. Thus, such aggression takes care of both mating and food needs for the group, while keeping the aggression outside the group.

Chimpanzees eat berries and roots, and meat is not a major part of their diet; however, they will eat meat whenever it is available. As noted in Chapter

3, the transition from chimpanzee to *Homo sapiens* involved the transition from forest dwellers and a herbivorous diet to a mixed vegetarian and meat omnivorous diet. The structure of the brain changed in response to this adaptation to the environment. Early peoples were hunters and formed groups to carry out these survival activities (a discussion of violence and the brain will be found in Chapter 11). Humans have survived by violence and aggression since their earliest days. Not only is hunting and a meat diet dependent on violence, but the sexual behavior of mammals and primates often involves violent behavior and aggression (aggression and sexual behavior will be discussed in a later chapter). Whatever the historical roots, violence and aggression are very much a part of the evolutionary history of humankind.

Early legal systems reflect humans' violent nature. In her book *Wild Justice,* Jacoby (1983) traces the origins of revenge and restitution to early human history. The Bible is quoted as saying: "Revenge is mine, sayeth the Lord." Jacoby notes that the idea of revenge developed among the Jews and Greeks and other tribal societies, as well as with the early Christians. The Catholic Church itself resorted to extensive violence exemplified in the crusades and in the use of torture during the Inquisition of the sixteenth and seventeenth centuries.

Legal systems emerged, as we saw in Chapter 3, to control the blood feud and private vengeance. The law said "you cannot kill another person in retaliation for an injury to you or your tribe." However, the political state proceeded to establish criminal law on the basis of public vengeance; that is, the state arrested, convicted, and killed the offender through legal procedures. Although the victim or his family is not allowed to kill the offender, the state is. Public vengeance replaced private vengeance.

The movement from private revenge to public revenge is related to the development of the brain (see Chapter 11). The primitive brain is an emotional brain devoted to violence and aggression. With the development of the modern primate brain the rational centers of the brain came into existence. The raw savagery of primitive emotions were then encased in a rational system. The emotions of hatred and revenge were placed outside of the individual and into a rational structure of a legal system which said in effect "you can hate the criminal, but you must do so through the formality of the legal system and the legal profession."

Retribution, Justice, and Punishment

Political and legal philosophers did not justify punishment and the criminal law in terms of retribution and revenge since such motives for human behavior are considered debasing and vulgar. Since punishment and the killing of individuals by the state, as part of criminal law, are evils that require great justification, the use of punishment to carry out revenge was justified philosophically as "just deserts" or "justice" (Jacoby, 1983). Aristotle taught that justice was the quality of treating equals equally and unequals unequally (Benn, 1967a).

Justice involves equality and reciprocity between the offense and the punishment.

The great German philosopher Immanuel Kant (1724–1804) treated punishment as a virtuous end in itself, since the guilty should suffer, and by suffering the guilty were themselves made more moral. Kantian ethics required that before the world came to an end the last murderer must be punished in order that the moral order be restored to a proper balance. The guilty must suffer for their immoral acts, and only the guilty can be punished. According to Kant, we can never punish one person to deter or rehabilitate another. Reform and deterrence are not possible goals of the criminal justice system according to Kantian ethics; only behavior that is morally wrong is criminal and can be punished, and such behavior must be punished (Benn, 1967b; Michael and Adler, 1933):346–350; Jenkins, 1984; Jones, 1986).

The German philosopher G. W. F Hegel (1770–1831) held a position similar to that of his countryman Kant, teaching that the moral order required the punishment of criminals in order to right a wrong (Benn, 1967b; Michael and Adler, 1933).

Support for the retributive/revenge model of criminal law is contained in the writings of the famous British legal historian Sir James F. Stephens. In his *History of the Criminal Law of England* (Stephens, 1883:75 ff.) he stated that the purpose of criminal law is to allow the community to hate the criminal and to get revenge against the criminal.

On the other hand, O. W. Holmes in *The Common Law* (Holmes, 1881:45) stated that pure vengenance is not the proper foundation for criminal law, and he advocated deterrence and reform as purposes for the criminal law. In a scholarly discussion of the purposes of the criminal law, G. O. W. Mueller states that vindication, retribution, and penitence are theories of criminal justice not espoused or discussed today in the field of corrections, and "when these theories are mentioned at all, they are usually dismissed as archaic and irrational" (Mueller, 1966:66). It should be noted that Mueller wrote this article in 1966, just prior to the end of rehabilitation and the beginning of the new era of retribution and just deserts.

The retributive model of criminal law is referred to today as the "justice" or "just deserts" model, by which the criminal gets "his due" or "pays for his crime with his life" or "settles his debt to society." Several features of the justice model must be highlighted since this is the main structure of the criminal justice system.

1. Retribution is a philosophical and historical approach to behavior, not a scientific one.
2. Retribution is a backward-looking response to crime, not a forward-looking one. It does not look to the future behavior of the criminal but rather to what the criminal has done in the past. It denies reform, treatment, and prevention, and it denies the value of behavioral science research. It does not attempt to prevent crime or to reduce the crime rate.

3. Retribution perpetuates the human urge for revenge, and it brutalizes societies and individuals by its use. The symbols of retribution and justice are the hangman's noose and the electric chair.

4. Although retribution is justified as a moral position, it is an immoral, vulgar, and self-defeating response to human behavior. The humanness of human nature, as found in love, mercy, forgiveness, and helping one's fellow man, is lacking in the revenge response to human failings.

The theme of just deserts is still with us. In 1968, H. L. A. Hart (1968), the British legal philosopher, wrote a justification for retribution while denying the utilitarian view of deterrence and punishment. Hart (1968:231) stated that "a person may be punished if, and only if, he has voluntarily done something morally wrong; secondly, his punishment must match, or be the equivalent of, the wickedness of his offense; thirdly, the justification for punishing men under such conditions is that the return of suffering for moral evil voluntarily done, is itself just or morally good."

Hart (1968:4) defined punishment as:

1. The infliction of pain
2. For offenses against legal rules
3. Applied to the actual offender
4. That is intentionally administered
5. By a legal authority

According to this philosophical position, pain that is accidental, as in a football game or an accidental cutting of one's hand, is not punishment, nor is pain administered to a nonoffender punishment. Punishment involves intentional pain for morally wrong acts which are intentionally committed.

This view as expressed by one of our foremost legal philosophers is the core of the retributionists' position. The reemergence of retributive justice in the 1970s will be discussed in more detail in Chapter 8.

THE CLASSICAL SCHOOL OF CRIMINOLOGY

Legal Reform and the Nature of the Nation-State

The classical, or legal, school of criminology is based on the legal and political theories of sixteenth- and seventeenth-century philosophers. According to these legal reformers, the law under the revenge and retribution motive was harsh, arbitrary, and ineffective. These reformers saw the purpose of the law as social control and the betterment of humankind through effective social control, rather than justice and revenge [for the historical development of criminology, see Mannheim (1970), Rennie (1978), Vold and Bernard (1979), Radzinowicz (1966), Phillipson (1923), Hall (1945), Faust and Brantingham (1979), Jenkins (1984), and Jones (1986)].

Classicism contains three major philosophical components: social contract theory, hedonistic psychology, and utilitarianism. Social contract theory is found in the works of two major political philosophers, Thomas Hobbes and John Locke. Hobbes (1588–1679) was a physicalist/materialist who believed that matter, including mental activities, is made up of atoms in motion (this is a view close to that held today in neurology; see Chapter 11). In *The Leviathan* Hobbes posited a state of nature in which self-preservation was the only law, and a "war of all against all" existed. In such a society life was poor, nasty, brutish, and short. To escape from this state of nature, people created a society based on the political state. Such a politically organized society was brought into existence through a social contract wherein individuals sacrificed certain personal rights and freedoms in exchange for protection by the state from murder, rape, and robbery by others. Thus, the state restricts certain human freedoms and liberties while at the same time guaranteeing other freedoms and liberties. The right of the state to the police power by which it can punish criminals is created by the mystical social contract by which each person consents to being governed in exchange for the right to leave the state of nature for the state of society.

John Locke (1632–1704) was an early empiricist who taught that human knowledge comes from sensations and experience, not from innate ideas or reasons. He influenced the development of empiricism, science, and associational psychology (see Chapter 13 for this discussion).

Locke, in his *Two Treatises on Civil Government,* also posited a state of nature, a state before the political state in which human beings were viewed as equal with natural inalienable rights to life, liberty, and property. To preserve and maintain these rights, humankind created the political state by means of a social contract. This basic purpose of the state and of the police power of the state is to protect life, liberty, and property for individual citizens (this Lockean notion was written into our Declaration of Independence in the form of "Life, Liberty, and the Pursuit of Happiness") (Sabine, 1963; Friedman, 1967; Jenkins, 1984; Jones, 1986).

Hedonistic psychology is based on the principles of pain and pleasure. This is a physicalistic view based on the survival value of pain and pleasure in human adaptation to the environment. This philosophy sees humankind as composed of selfish, self-seeking, rational individuals seeking to maximize pleasure and minimize pain. Through such self-seeking behavior the greatest happiness for the greatest number would take place.

Utilitarianism is the third aspect of the legal school of criminology, based on the pleasure/pain principle as a means to maximize the greatest happiness for the greatest number. That is, if each person maximized his or her own self-interests, the greatest happiness for the greatest number would be achieved. By placing emphasis on the collective good, individual rights can be sacrificed to the greater good of society, as seen in the principle of criminal law which allows one person to be punished in order that others would be deterred from committing crimes. This is in contrast to the Kantian idea as found in retributive justice that no person may be used as a means to an end in order to reform or deter another person from crime (Jenkins, 1984; Jones, 1986).

Cesare Beccaria (1738–1794)

The foundations of the classical/legal school of criminology are to be found in the works of legal reformers, especially Beccaria and Bentham (Monachesi, 1970; Jenkins, 1984; Jones, 1986). In 1774, Beccaria, an Italian by birth, wrote a small book entitled *Dei Delittie Dele Pene* (An Essay on Crime and Punishment), which totally changed the justification for criminal law. Beccaria and his supporters opposed the harsh, cruel, and arbitrary nature of the criminal code of the times which, as has been mentioned, was based on executions without regard for judicial process or human rights.

Becarria accepted the social contract theory as found in the works of Hobbes and Locke. Humans were basically selfish and motivated to act out of self-interests. To protect selfish individuals from one another, humankind had to surrender freedoms to the state in return for protection from criminals and wrongdoers. The state had a right and a duty to punish criminals, but this must be done in a very legal way. Crime and punishment must be legally defined and not left to the arbitrariness of the judge. Crime cannot be defined ex post facto, that is, after the crime had been committed, but rather, the crime must be part of the judicial process before the behavior defined as criminal has occurred. This is referred to as the principle of legality, or *nullum crimen sine lege* (no crime without a law) and *nulla poena sine lege* (no punishment without a law).

Crimes must be defined in terms that are clear and precise. Punishment must be fixed in very specific terms. Moreover, punishment must be based not on revenge but on deterrence; that is, the pain of punishment must just exceed the pleasure of the crime and no more in order to deter the potential criminal. ''Let the punishment fit the crime'' was the motto (as stated in Gilbert and Sullivan's opera *The Mikado*).

Beccaria would do away with capital punishment and cruelty, and in their place substitute public education and crime prevention. Punishment must be certain and swift, but not severe. There must be no more restriction of individual rights than is absolutely necessary for the protection of society.

Jeremy Bentham (1748–1832)

Bentham, a British political theorist, is the second cornerstone to legalistic criminology. Bentham has the unique distinction of having his body preserved in Westminister Abbey, and to this day each year on the anniversary of his death the body is wheeled out for public display (Geis, 1970; Jenkins, 1984; Jones, 1986). Crime, not the criminal, was the focus of Bentham's work. In his *An Introduction to the Principles of Morals and Legislation* (1789), Bentham started with the statement ''nature has placed mankind under the governance of two soverign masters, pain and pleasure.'' Since by nature humans pursue pleasure and avoid pain, the criminal law must be established as a social control measure to ensure the greatest happiness for the greatest number. This is the basis for utilitarian doctrines concerning political policy.

The purpose of law is social control and the prevention of crime, not the pursuit of revenge and justice. Legislators, not God or nature, are the source of positive law. The legislator, through a calculus of pleasure and pain, establishes how much punishment must be attached to criminal behavior to deter such behavior. Criminal law is justified on the basis of deterrence and a reduction in the crime rate in the future. The classical school looked to the future and not the past in evaluating the purpose of criminal law.

Like Beccaria, Bentham was most interested in protecting the rights of the accused from abuses of state power, while at the same time keeping at a minimum the punishments used for crime. He would restrict capital punishment to murder cases only.

Sir Samuel Romilly and William Paley

An illustration of the nature of the political debates that went on in Parliament as a part of the legal reform movement can be found in the Romilly–Paley debates. Romilly was opposed to the death penalty, as were most of the legal reformers of the time, and he argued in Parliament that the number of offenses for which capital punishment was to be used should be reduced to a minimum, while the certainty of execution must be retained for a few cases in order that capital punishment act as a general deterrent to crime. On the other hand, Paley argued that capital punishment should apply to many offenses, but only in a few cases should it be used as an example (Rennie, 1978:15; Radzinowicz, 1948:248 ff.; Phillipson, 1923).

Classicism, Free Will, and Moral Responsibility

The criminal law posits the existence of free will, intent, and moral responsibility. The nature of human beings according to this legal position is based on rationalism and mind–body dualism (see the discussion in Chapter 12). According to this view the body is physical and therefore subject to the scientific laws of determinism, whereas the mind is nonphysical and is not subject to the scientific laws of determinism.

Both Beccaria and Bentham lived during and after the beginnings of positivism and the scientific revolution, that is, after the time of Copernicus, Galileo, Newton, Bacon, and Mill (see the discussion of positivism in Chapters 2 and 5). Therefore, both of these men had knowledge of the emerging scientific revolution that was coming into existence at that time in history. Also, they were influenced by the hedonistic psychology and utilitarianism of Hobbes and Locke, based on the belief of the power of pleasure and pain to determine human behavior. The tenets of the classical school have been used by legal scholars to justify law as a deterrent to behavior. This school contains a quasi-scientific element in its approach to human nature, in contrast to the nonscientific approach on the part of other lawyers, who use legal theory on free will and moral responsibility.

There is a basic unresolved conflict between the doctrine of free will as found in the criminal law and social control through pleasure and pain as found in the works of Beccaria and Bentham. The purpose of criminal law, according to the school of retribution and revenge, is to right a moral wrong and to establish a moral principle, whereas according to Beccaria and Bentham the purpose of criminal law is to punish some so that others will be deterred from criminal conduct in the future. Kant argued, for example, that no person can be punished in order that another person be deterred from crime. The joining of intentional wrong-doing and intentional punishment is the hallmark of the retributive school, but it is not the core of classical deterrence theory (Jenkins, 1984; Jones, 1986).

Although classicism and retribution have been joined as justifications of criminal law and punishment, they are totally different in nature.

1. Classicism contains the beginnings of a scientific approach to human behavior, and it rejects revenge as a motive for criminal law and justice.
2. Classicism is a forward-looking response, not a backward-looking response, to human behavior. It uses law as an agent of social control and social reform, and it expects greater utility and greater happiness as a result of law.
3. Classicism contains elements of mercy, kindness, and the betterment of humankind through reform of the law and the goal of deterrence.

Classical Criminology Theory Today

There has been a return to retributive criminology in the 1970s with a rejection of the rehabilitation model and the return to a law-and-order model of criminal justice (Sheliff, 1981; Glaser, 1979). This means longer prison sentences, mandatory prison sentences, a return to a high rate of executions, and other harsh and arbitrary actions taken against criminals. Although this is often thought of as classical criminology, it is much more a return to the retribution and just deserts positions. The reemergence of the punishment model will be discussed in Chapter 8.

Summary of Classicism

1. Classical legal criminology emphasized crime, not the individual offender.
2. The classical school wanted to limit or eliminate the bloody aspects of criminal law as found in revenge and retribution. The purpose of law is to reduce the crime rate by means of deterrence.
3. The classical school wanted a legalistic approach to crime, based on the principle of legality, with legal definitions of crime and punishment. This meant no crime or punishment without a law; equality of all before the law; a presumption of innocence for the accused; a minimal use of

criminal sanctions; fair criminal procedures without duress, torture, or secret procedures; speedy trials; humane treatment of offenders; and other substantive and procedural safeguards for defendants against the abuse of power by the state.

The classical school is found today in legal procedures and legal definitions of crime. This is what is taught to law students and criminal justice students in criminal law courses. This is what judges and lawyers practice in the courtroom. This is due process and the bill of rights. This, in other words, is the basis for the criminal justice model of crime control, the police–courts–prison system as defined by lawyers and legal procedures.

The problem with the legal reforms made by the classical school, as we shall see, is that these legal niceties are attached to a retributive system of justice. The defendant is given a fair trial, is provided with legal counsel, is protected from self-incrimination and torture, is given a speedy jury trial, and then is hanged. As the Irishman said: "First we give you justice and a fair trial, and then we hang you."

THE LEGAL ASPECTS OF CRIME

Criminal law establishes the boundaries of criminology since crime is defined in terms of criminal law. This statement establishes the political nature of crime; it does not explain why we use criminal law to control human behavior. In Chapter 3 we traced the origins of criminal law from revenge and retribution, and the evolution of law from tribal law to state law.

In this section we deal with some of the technical aspects of criminal law, such as the requirements for a crime, the nature of the political state, and the elements of a crime. However, we will not go into much detail in these discussions since these topics are discussed in criminal law courses in law schools or criminal justice programs. We attempt to relate criminal law issues to psychological and social issues and to look at the assumptions made by lawyers concerning criminal behavior and human nature.

The purpose of the state is to establish and maintain social order. In later chapters we discuss other aspects of law and social order, such as sociology, law, and social control (Chapter 15), and criminology, criminal law, and the behavioral sciences (Chapter 7).

The Nature of Crime: Definition of Criminal Law

Law involves the use of force and coercion by the political state. Law also involves the concept of territoriality, or jurisdiction based on land. A person can commit a crime only if he/she is physically present on the land (there are a few exceptions, such as mail fraud, which need not concern us here). I can violate the speed laws of the state of Florida only if I am in Florida. Alabama law or Georgia law does not apply, nor do the Alabama or Georgia courts have jurisdiction over such cases.

Criminal law involves offenses against the king or the state; crimes are public and not private offenses (Chapter 3). Criminal law is differentiated from contract law in that contract law covers personal and private obligations arising out of private agreements. If a contract is violated, the injured party is compensated for loss or injury. Tort law involves personal liabilities for injuries and damages done to others without the obligation of a contract, and the injured party is paid compensation for such damages. Criminal law may occasionally involve restitution or compensation, but such practices are not common and the threat of punishment or the use of restitution as punishment differentiates criminal law from contract and tort law.

In the case of contract or tort law, people hire lawyers and pursue the case in court on their own behalf. In the case of criminal law, the state, through a state attorney, or prosecuting attorney, or county attorney, prosecutes the case. The injured party to a criminal offense does not and cannot pursue the case in a personal capacity, but must depend on the actions of the prosecuting attorney to pursue such a case.

In contract or tort law the case is listed by the names of the parties involved, such as *Smith* v. *Jones.* In a criminal case the case is listed in the name of the state as the *State of Florida* v. *Jones* or the *State of Arizona* v. *Jones.* Since the state is the victim, the outcome of the case is one of punishing the defendant.

Since the state prosecutes and punishes offenders, the injured party is not allowed to retaliate against an attacker. The use of the feud to resolve personal injuries was outlawed by the growth of state law (see Chapter 3). In a recent case a female who had been raped killed her rapist several days later and was charged with murder. A father killed a truck driver who had earlier killed his son in a vehicular accident, and the father was found guilty of murder. Here we see limitations placed on private revenge where the victim is left without recourse if the prosecutor does not act or if the defendant is found not guilty.

The right of citizens to defend themselves against crime extends only to the right of self-defense where deadly force and danger to one's life is involved. The recent case of Bernhard Goetz in New York City attracted national attention when Goetz shot several black youths who demanded $5 from him (Rubin, 1986). A grand jury rejected an attempted murder charge in this case, thus allowing public sentiment to say that a man has a right to carry a gun and shoot criminals. More recently (October 1986) a Miami storeowner set up an electrified wire grid to protect his store from burglary, and the grand jury refused to indict the storeowner on a murder charge after a burglar who entered the premises was electrocuted. A female clerk in a convenience store shot and killed a youth who was stealing a pack of beer, and she was sentenced to a one-year prison term, which is now under appeal and under great public attack.

The right to self-defense is usually stated in terms of a reasonable belief that one's life is in danger and that no reasonable means of retreat are available. In recent years, with the return to a law-and-order philosophy of criminal justice, we have witnessed a return to "vigilantism" where private citizens take the law into their own hands, in effect acting as judge, jury, and executioner. The problems associated with private justice were the reasons for the creation of law in the first place (see Chapter 3), but the failure of the criminal justice system to protect citizens has led to the growth of private justice and retribution. Private justice is very dangerous, as it documents the failure of public justice. The answer must be found in crime prevention rather than in either private or public justice (see Chapters 18, 19, and 20).

Substantive Criminal Law: Seven Elements of a Crime

There are seven elements to a crime (Kerper, 1979; Hall, 1947; Hall and Mueller, 1965):

1. Legality
2. Actus reus
3. Mens rea
4. Concurrence of mind and body
5. Harm
6. Causation
7. Punishment

Principle of legality. The principle of legality provides that legal definitions of crimes and punishments must exist prior to the behavior. This is stated as *nullum crimen sine lege* (no crime without a law), and *nulla poena sine lege* (no punishment without a law) (Hall, 1947; Kerper, 1979; Low, Jeffries, and Bonnie, 1986). This rule is based on the principle that no one is expected to behave in a given manner, or to be blamed for so behaving, unless the law existed before the behavior occured.

This principle also protects the citizen from harsh and arbitrary actions on the part of the state (see Chapter 6). Legal rules do two things: (1) they allow the state to arrest, convict, and punish people, and (2) they limit the conditions under which the state punishes individuals, or they limit the use of coercive force by the state.

The principle of legality forbids *ex post facto* laws, laws passed after the behavior made criminal has occurred. The principle also makes null and void all laws that are vague and unclear.

Actus Reus. Actus reus means the "act" or behavior. It is physical and observable. The criminal law does not punish people for their thoughts only. The behavioral requirement can be either the commission or omission of an act. An omission of an act is considered to be a crime only if there is a legal duty on the part of the person behaving to act in these circumstances. The concept of actus reus is sometimes extended to include the circumstances of the act and the results produced by the act.

Mens rea.   The principle of mens rea is the most difficult and controversial in the criminal law. Mens rea means "intent" or "mind" or "mental element." This is the mind–body dualism found in Western philosophy (see Chapters 11 and 12 for discussions of this issue). I shall discuss the legal view of the "mind" and go on to state the problems inherent in this view in light of modern biology and psychology.In this respect this book differs from others [e.g., Low, Jeffries, and Bonnie (1986) and Klotter (1983)] which discuss mens rea as if it really existed. Mens rea is seriously questioned by modern science.

The crimiinal law excludes from criminal responsibility all involuntary acts such as coerced movements, reflex movements, convulsions, somnambulism, or unconsciousness [see the Model Penal Code, Appendix A, in Low, Jeffries, and Bonnie (1986)].

The Model Penal Code (section 2.02) defines mens rea as basic to voluntary behavior, that is, behavior involving a mental element. The person must have acted purposely, knowingly, recklessly, or negligently. The law requires that the physical element of each crime be judged separately in terms of the requirement of voluntariness.

Each crime has its own requirements for criminal intent or mens rea. Crimes such as murder and rape and robbery are divided into several categories depending on the nature of the mental element involved,and the punishment for each mental element is different.

The criminal intent or state of mind is never known through empirical observation. In Chapter 12 we discuss the mentalistic view of human nature: environment–mind–behavior—in which the mind is inferred from the behavior. We never observe mentalistic concepts such as purposely, knowingly, recklessly, or negligently. We observe people committing murder or rape, and from the behavior we say that they acted purposely or knowingly or recklessly or negligently.

The law assumes that people intend the natural consequences of their acts unless the defense can prove that the act was not voluntary. All behavior is voluntary as far as the law is concerned. From there we go to the defenses of infancy, coercion, duress, mistake, and insanity. The law states "the intention with which a man did something can usually be determined by a jury only by inference from the surrounding circumstances, including the presumption of the law that a man intend the natural and probable consequences of his acts" (Low, Jeffries, and Bonnie, 1986:205). The criminal law does not prove intent; it only proves a lack of intent, or an absence of intent, or a diminition of intent.

The basic assumption of the criminal law is that a nonphysical mind causes a physical body to move. As we discuss in Chapter 12, and discuss further in other chapters, mind–body dualism is in direct conflict with a science of behavior as found in modern behaviorism and bioenvironmentalism, where no assumptions are made about internal mental states.

The law is not entirely unaware of this problem, as seen in the fact that the law uses different terms to describe mens rea, such as corruptly, willfully, maliciously, wantonly, feloniously, negligently, and recklessly. In fact, 78 different terms are used. "In summary, the National Commission on Reform of Federal Criminal Laws stated, 'unsurprisingly, the courts have been unable to find substantive correlates for all of these varied descriptions of mental states' " (Low, Jeffries, and Bonnie, 1986:199).

The basic assumption of mens rea and intent is in turn based on the assumption of free will and moral responsibility. In essence, mens rea always amounts to the awareness on the part of the perpetrator that what he/she proposes to do is wrong. Mens rea is an evil mind. The perpetrator's decision to go ahead with the act despite this awareness of the wrongfulness of the act render the act criminal and blameworthy. "In the long-standing debate over criminal responsibility there has always been a strong conviction in our jurisprudence that to hold a man criminally responsible, his acts must have been voluntary, the product of 'free will.' In deciding responsibility the law postulates a 'free will' and then recognizes deviations" [Salzman v. U.S., 405 F.2d 358 (D.C. Cir. 1968), in Kerper (1979:68)].

In Durham v. U.S., 214 F.2d 862 (D.C. Cir. 1954) the court said: "The legal and moral traditions of the Western world require that those who of their own free will and evil intent or mens rea commit acts which violate the law, shall be criminally responsible for those acts." The concept of intent or mens rea along with free will is critical to criminal law and to the philosophy of punishment and is in conflict with the scientific view of human nature (see Chapters 5 and 12). This conflict between law and science (see Chapter 1) runs throughout criminology and criminal law, and we shall deal with it in great detail in later chapters.

Concurrence of Mind and Body.   The criminal law also requires that there be a concurrence between mind and body, or behavior and intent (Hall, 1947). This means that a person must intend to commit the act and commit the act at the same time in order to be guilty of a crime. If I decided to kill you next week, but by accident kill you today, there is no joining of mens rea and actus reus.

Harm.   The criminal law requires a harm, usually defined in terms of the object of the actus reus (Hall, 1947; Kerper, 1979). Such harms include harms to persons, to property, to the state, and to public morality. The usual classification of crime is crimes against the person, crimes against property, crimes against the state, and crimes against morality. The harm in homicide is the killing of another human being. In reckless driving the harm is the danger that this conduct creates for other human beings. The harm element involves public policy and public ethics as to what potential harms should be labeled by the criminal law as crimes. This issue is discussed in Chapter 6.

Causation.   The law also requires a causal relationship between the actus reus and the harm (Klotter, 1983; Hall, 1947; Model Penal Code). There must be a traceable relationship between the act and the intended harm. If the behavior is assault and battery, and the victim dies, the crime is murder if the defendant intended to kill, but if the victim lives, it is assault and battery or attempted homicide.

Punishment. The defining element of criminal law is the use of punishment as the sanction (Hall, 1947; Kerper, 1979). The transition historically was from compensation and restitution to punishment (Chapter 3). Because of these distinctions between civil law, criminal law, and science we punish those convicted of crimes, compensate the victims of civil violations, and treat those who are ill. The unemployed are given job training. The mentally ill are put in hospitals. The ''right to punishment'' concept contains within it the idea that those who voluntarily and of their own free will violate the criminal law are to be punished in order that justice be done. Punishment must match the wickedness of the act, or ''punishment must fit the crime,'' and this position is called retributive justice or the justice model. H. L. A. Hart stated that punishment involves pain intentionally administered by the state to a morally guilty offender. The criminal law is based on the assumption of voluntary actions and free will, as discussed above, and punishment flows from this view of human nature.

The scientific or positive school of criminology (Chapter 5) denied all the basic tenets of classical criminology when it emphasized science, determinism, research, and the treatment and prevention of criminal behavior. The motto of the scientific school was ''let the treatment fit the criminal.''

The legal school of criminology resulted in a system of punishment fixed by statutory law, such as a life or death sentence for murder and a ten-year sentence for robbery. On the other hand, the scientific school created the indeterminate sentence of one day to life within which time-span treatment could be provided as long as the defendant was deemed dangerous (Kerper, 1979: 93 ff.). The scientific model of criminology is discussed in Part 3.

Punishment is justified in terms of revenge, retribution, deterrence, and incapacitation. As was noted, revenge and just retribution are the basic justifications for criminal justice. The reemergence of the retributive justice model during the 1970s in the United States is discussed in Chapter 8.

Procedural Criminal Law

Procedural criminal law goes to the issue of ''how is the crime proven.'' Substantive criminal law defines what a crime is, whereas procedural criminal law defines the procedures to be used to prove that the crime was committed (Kerper, 1979).

Procedural criminal law pits the rights of the defendant against the power of the state, whereas substantive criminal law represents the power of the state against the individual citizen. The Constitution provides for the right of the state to establish justice (the police power), ensure domestic tranquility (police power), and promote the general welfare.

The rights of citizens against the state are expressed in the first ten amendments to the Constitution, known popularly as the Bill of Rights. From the beginning we see that the state is viewed as both a necessary evil and a source of goodness and justice. The constitutional amendments most involved in the rights of criminals are:

First Amendment Right to freedom of religion, speech, and press.

Second Amendment Right to keep and bear arms.

Fourth Amendment Right to be secure against unreasonable searches and seizures, as well as unreasonable warrants.

Fifth Amendment Right to indictment by a grand jury, as well as prohibitions against double jeopardy, bearing witness against oneself, and being deprived of life, liberty, and property without due process.

Sixth Amendment Right to a speedy and public trial by a jury, as well as the right to know the nature of the charges, the right to obtain witnesses, and the right to have an attorney.

Eighth Amendment Prohibitions against excessive bails and cruel and unusual punishment.

Fourteenth Amendment No state shall make or enforce any law which shall abridge the privileges of citizens of the United States, nor shall any state deprive any person of life, liberty, and property without due process of law, nor deny any person the equal protection of the law.

It must be noted that the Fourteenth Amendment has been used in the United States to apply the first ten amendments to the individual states, since the original Bill of Rights applied only to the federal government. The extension of the first ten amendments has been by means of the Fourteenth Amendment.

Summary

In this section of the chapter we discussed the nature of the political state, which involves the use of coercion and force, and territoriality. We also discussed the nature of crime as the violation of a criminal law, which means a public wrong prosecuted and punished by the state. The elements of a crime include the principle of legality, actus reus, mens rea, concurrence of act and intent, harm, causation, and punishment. Procedural criminal law, the process by which one is charged and convicted of a crime, is presented in terms of those features of the Bill of Rights that protect the citizen from the power of the state.

FURTHER STUDIES

The history of classical criminology is often presented in criminology courses devoted to criminological theory and/or the history of criminological thought. Law schools offer courses in criminal law and criminal procedure which cover the substantive and procedural aspects of crime and criminal law. The criminal law is a combination of retribution and revenge on the one hand and classicism on the other hand. What is taught in criminal law courses consists of the basic legal procedures for defining crime and punishment, and for determining the guilt or innocence of those charged with crimes. Lawyers are responsible for the operation of the criminal justice model of crime control.

REFERENCES

BENN, S. L. (1967a). "Justice." In *Encyclopedia of Philosophy,* Vol. 4, ed. P. Edwards. New York: Macmillan, pp. 298–301.

BENN, S. L. (1967b). "Punishment." In *Encyclopedia of Philosophy,* Vol. 7, ed. P. Edwards. New York: Macmillan, pp. 29–35.

FAUST, F., and P. J. BRANTINGHAM (1979). *Juvenile Justice Philosophy.* St. Paul, Minn.: West Publishing Co.

FRIEDMAN, W. (1967). *Legal Theory,* 5th ed. New York: Columbia University Press.

GEIS, G. (1970). "Jeremy Bentham." In *Pioneers in Criminology,* ed. H. Mannheim. Montclair, N.J.: Patterson Smith.

GHIGLIERI, M. (1983). *The Chimpanzees of the Kibale Forest.* New York: Columbia University Press.

GHIGLIERI, M. (1987). *East of the Mountains of the Moon: Chimpanzee Society in the African Jungle.* New York: Free Press.

GLASER, D. (1979). "The Counterproductivity of Conservative Thinking about Crime." In *Criminology: New Concerns,* ed. E. Sagarin. Beverly Hills, Calif.: Sage.

GOODALL, J. (1971). *In the Shadow of Man.* Boston: Houghton Mifflin.

GOODALL, J. (1979). "Life and Death at Gombe." *National Geographic,* 594–620, May.

HALL, J. (1945). "Criminology." In *Twentieth Century Sociology,* ed. G. Gurvitch and W. E. Moore. New York: Philosophical Library.

HALL, J. (1947). *General Principles of Criminal Law,* 2nd ed. Indianapolis, Ind.: Bobbs-Merrill.

HALL, J., and G. O. W. MUELLER (1965). *Criminal Law and Procedure,* 2nd ed. Indianapolis, Ind.: Bobbs-Merrill.

HART, H. L. A. (1968). *Punishment and Responsibility.* New York: Oxford University Press.

HOLMES, O. W. (1881). *The Common Law.* Boston: Little, Brown.

JACOBY, S. (1983). *Wild Justice.* New York: Harper & Row.

JENKINS, P. (1984). *Crime and Justice.* Monterey, Calif.: Brooks/Cole.

JONES, D. A. (1986). *History of Criminology.* Westport, Conn.: Greenwood Press.

KERPER, H. (1979). *Introduction to the Criminal Justice System,* 2nd ed. St. Paul, Minn.: West Publishing Co.

KLOTTER, J. C. (1983). *Criminal Law.* Cincinnati, Ohio: Anderson Publishing Co.

LOW, P., J. C. JEFFRIES, and R. J. BONNIE (1986). *Criminal Law: Cases and Materials.* Mineola, N.Y.: Foundation Press.

MANNHEIM, H., ed. (1970). *Pioneers in Criminology.* Montclair, N.J.: Patterson Smith.

MICHAEL, J., and M. ADLER (1933). *Crime, Law and Social Science.* New York: Harcourt, Brace.

MONACHESI, E. (1970). "Casare Beccaria." In *Pioneers in Criminology,* ed. H. Mannheim. Montclair, N.J.: Patterson Smith

MUELLER, G. O. W. (1966). "Punishment, Corrections, and the Law." *Nebraska Law Review,* January pp. 58–95.

PHILLIPSON, C. (1923). *Three Criminal Law Reformers: Beccaria, Bentham, Romilly.* New York: E.P. Dutton.

RADZINOWICZ, L. (1948). *A History of English Criminal Law,* Vol. 1. London: Stevens & Sons.

RADZINOWICZ, L. (1966). *Ideology and Crime.* New York: Columbia University Press.

RENNIE, Y. (1978). *The Search for Criminal Man.* Lexington, Mass.: Lexington Books.

RUBIN, L. B. (1986). *Quiet Rage: Bernhard Goetz in a Time of Madness.* New York: Farrar, Straus & Giroux.

SABINE, G. H. (1963). *A History of Political Theory,* 3rd ed. London: Harrap.

SHELIFF, L. S. (1981). "The Relevance of Classical Criminology Today." In *The Mad, the Bad, and the Different,* ed. I. L. Barak-Glantz and R. Huff. Lexington, Mass.: Lexington Books.

STEPHENS, J. S. (1883). *History of Criminal Law of England,* Vol. 2. London: Macmillan.

VOLD, G. B., and T. J. BERNARD (1979). *Theoretical Criminology.* New York: Oxford University Press.

QUESTIONS

1. How do legal and political philosophers justify the use of criminal law for revenge and just retribution?
2. What are the major components of classical legal criminology?
3. What contribution did Jeremy Bentham make to classical legal philosophy?
4. What view of human nature is maintained by classical legal philosophy?
5. How does criminal law differ from tort law?
6. What is meant by the principle of legality? Mens rea? Concurrence of mens rea and actus reus?
7. What is the basis for procedural criminal law?

Positivism, Science, and Criminology 5

INTRODUCTION

The second major school of criminology, to be contrasted to the legalistic or classical school, is the scientific or positive school of criminology. Scientific criminology developed out of the scientific movement of the eighteenth and nineteenth centuries, and it involves primarily the work and research of biologists, psychologists, psychiatrists, geographers, urban planners, and sociologists. Scientific criminology is found most often related to teaching and research in a university setting, in contrast to classical criminology, which is most often found in the applied world of the police, courts, and correctional system.

THE POSITIVE SCHOOL OF CRIMINOLOGY

The Growth of Science

In Chapter 2 we contrasted rationalism and empiricism, and we noted that whereas rationalism was based on the truth of innate ideas as found by reason, empiricism was based on sensory experiences. Empiricism, and knowledge through observation, led to systematic observations, prediction and control, and inductive methodology as basic to scientific methods and procedures.

Copernicus (1473–1543) put forth the theory in astronomy that the earth revolves around the sun, rather than the sun revolving around the earth, which had been the popular belief of the day. Galileo (1564–1642) followed Copernicus in the scientific approach to physics and astronomy, and for his scientific beliefs Galileo was condemned by the Catholic Church and forced to deny his theory. Other scientific scholars of the time were condemned and executed or exiled for beliefs contrary to religious dogma. The conflict between science and religion was mentioned in Chapter 2, and this conflict will be discussed in later chapters as well.

Isaac Newton (1642–1727) made critical contributions to the growth of physics and astronomy as sciences. Bacon (1561–1626) viewed experience as the key to knowledge, and he placed great emphasis on inductive reasoning (going from observed facts to general theoretical statements), in contrast to rationalism and logic, which placed emphasis on deductive reasoning (going from general statements to specific facts). J. S. Mill (1806–1873) perfected the inductive methods of science, and along with Bentham, was a major contributor to utilitarianism (Jones, 1986).

These thinkers contributed to the establishment of modern mathematics, physics, chemistry, and biology. Charles Darwin (1809–1882) totally changed our concepts of human nature and biology in his theory of evolution. (Darwin is discussed in Chapter 10.) Out of empiricism and science developed the philosophy of positivism. August Comte (1798–1857), the father of positivism and sociology, believed in the evolution of thought through theological and metaphysical states to the positive state where societies are governed by scientific principles. The betterment of humankind is dependent on the application of science to the solution of social problems. Comte thus established the tradition for the scientific study of human societies and social problems.

Out of this scientific revolution emerged the scientific study of mankind and human nature. Darwin made humankind a part of biology. Freud made humankind a part of psychology and psychic determinism. Marx made humankind a part of economic determinism. Comte made humankind a part of social determinism. The motto of the positivist was "through science human progress will be achieved." The contributions of Darwin, Freud, Marx, Comte, and other behavioral and social scientists will be discussed in detail in subsequent chapters devoted to the biological, psychological, and social foundations of criminal behavior.

Positivism and Criminology

Whereas the classical school represented the work of legal scholars in their attempts to reform criminal law, the positive school represented the work of scientists in their attempts to study and understand and reform the criminal. The focus shifted from crime to criminals, or as the British legal and criminological historian Sir Leon Radzinowicz stated: "The classical school exhorts men to study justice; the positive school exhorts justice to study men" (Radzinowicz, 1966:56). [For discussions of the historical development of criminology, see Mannheim (1970), Radzinowicz (1966), Rennie, (1978), Vold and Bernard (1979), Faust and Brantingham (1979), Jones (1986), and Jenkins (1984).]

The early history of criminology is to be found in the works of three Italian scholars, Lombroso, Garofalo, and Ferri, sometimes referred to as the "Italian school of criminology." The application of the methods of empiricism and science to the study of criminals and not crime was the focus of positivistic or scientific criminology. As Radzinowicz (1962; 3–4) noted: "Virtually every element of value in contemporary criminological knowledge owes its formulation to the very remarkable school of Italian criminologists who took pride in describing themselves as positivists. . . . The main weakness of the positivists lie in their failure to grasp the bewildering complexity of crime."

Cesare Lombroso (1835–1909)

Lombroso was born and educated in Italy. He was a biologist, a medical doctor, and an army physician. In his approach to criminal behavior, Lombroso was influenced by Comte and the positivists, by the German materialists, by Darwin and evolutionism, and by Gall and the phrenologists (Wolfgang, 1970; Rennie, 1978; Jones, 1986; Jenkins, 1984).

Lombroso became interested in psychiatry and the study of abnormal behaviors. As an army physician he had occasion to observe physical abnormalities among the soldiers he studied, including pellagra (a disorder of the central nervous system due to a dietary deficiency of niacin and protein) and cretinism (physical and mental stunting caused by a thyroid deficiency). He was also interested in disorders of the brain such as epilepsy.

At this point in history the Italian scholars were looking for physical causes of abnormal behavior in body build and brain abnormalities. A new physical anthropology was under way, based on measurement of the body and cranium of individual subjects, and biology served as a basic foundation for human behavior. Lombroso took from Darwin's evolutionary theory the idea of atavism: that is, a throwback to an earlier and more primitive state of development. He believed that criminals differed from noncriminals in the presence of atavistic traits in criminal populations, and he used the science of his time to measure the arms, legs, bodies, and skulls of criminals.

In 1876, Lombroso published *L'Uomo Delinquente* (Criminal Man), in which he distinguished the following types of criminals: the criminal epileptic, the moral imbecile, the born criminal, the occasional criminal, and the criminal by reason of passion. Lombroso placed emphasis on epilepsy, lack of a moral sense, and left-handedness as traits of criminals, all of which are today regarded as important in the understanding of the brain of criminals (see the discussion of the brain and behavior in Chapter 11).

In his book *Crime: Its Causes and Remedies* (1906, 1912) Lombroso added such social variables as poverty, migration, alcoholism, police corruption, criminal gangs, race, and urban growth to the list of variables that influenced crime rates.

Lombroso's work and ideas were received critically in some areas. Charles Goring (1870–1919), a British statistician, in his book *The English Con-*

vict (1913) argued that statistics, not body measurements, should be used to study the criminal. Goring studied British criminals and compared them to a control group of noncriminals, and he concluded that criminals did not exhibit the atavistic traits that Lombroso had found, although they were inferior to noncriminals in both physical and mental characteristics (Driver, 1970).

Lombroso has been criticized for his research methodology, especially his failure to use a noncriminal control group with which to compare his criminal population. According to Wolfgang (1970:266), Lombroso was aware of the importance of control groups, and G. O. W. Mueller told me that he had notes from a lecture given by Joe Lohman in a class in criminology at the University of Chicago in which Lohman referred to control groups in the study of skulls. Lombroso was especially attacked by sociological criminologists, although as Thorsten Sellin pointed out, sociologists have also used sloppy research procedures (Wolfgang, 1970:265). Lindesmith and Levin stated that Lombroso's work was ''in no way a contribution to criminology,'' a statement Wolfgang called an unwarranted denouncement of Lombroso. In their textbook on criminology, Sutherland and Cressey stated that ''Lombroso delayed for fifty years the work in progress at the time of its origin and in addition made no lasting contribution of its own'' (Wolfgang, 1970:288). Wolfgang (1970:288) responded: ''Lombroso illuminated the scientific study of criminal behavior with many provocative ideas and deserves a place of honor in his own field.''

Lombroso established the scientific study of the individual offender, and his work had a great impact and wide influence on scholars who followed him, such as Kretschmer, Sheldon, Hooton, and the Gluecks, as well as many in the field of psychiatry. His influence is still to be found, especially in Italy, Germany, England, and South America. His work was introduced into the United States by Drahms, MacDonald, Parsons, and Schlapp and Smith in the early twentieth century. In 1912, Lombroso's *Crime: Its Causes and Remedies* was published in English by the American Institute of Criminal Law and Criminology.

The rejection of Lombroso extended to the 1978 meeting of the American Society of Criminology, where the presence of geneticists, neurologists, and psychiatrists, was characterized as ''neo-Lombrosian'' foolishness (Jeffery, 1979:2–18). Recent developments in biochemistry of the brain and in the brain sciences substantiates a great deal of Lombroso's work in spirit if not in fact. It is interesting to note that as early as 1881 a book was published on the abnormalities found in the brains of criminals (Benedikt, 1881). This type of evidence was ignored for over seventy years while criminologists searched for the social causes of criminality.

Raffaele Garofalo (1852–1934)

Garofalo was the second important member of the Italian positivist school. Born in Naples, he was trained in law. His contribution to positivistic criminology was that of spelling out the implications of a science of behavior for criminal law and for lawyers (Allen, 1970; Jones, 1986; Jenkins, 1984; Rennie, 1978).

Garofalo published his major work *Criminology* in 1885. In this book he defined crime, not in legal terms as the classical school had done, but in terms of the moral sense of the community as found in the sentiments of "pity and probity." Thus crime is defined in behavioral and social terms rather than in legal terms. The scientist defines the behavior to be studied in terms of scientific needs rather than in terms of legal definitions established in order to punish the criminal. Thus the scientist escapes the unscientific definitions imposed on him by lawyers and legal codes. The goal of criminology is to categorize behavior in such a way that social defense (the defense of society) measures can be established. As we shall see in this and later chapters, the legal versus the scientific definition of behavior is a major controversy in criminology even today.

Garofalo differed from Lombroso in his evaluation of the causes of criminal behavior. He found the criminal to be deficient in moral sensibilities, a hereditary condition that leads to criminality and antisocial behavior; murderers lacking in both pity and probity; and thieves possibly a product of the social environment as well as moral degeneracy.

Garofalo added a curious twist to the idea of social defense, in that he thought the way to defend society against the criminal was through elimination of such unfit individuals, an idea he thought he found in Darwin's work on evolution. He would eliminate criminals through executions and transportation. He was not an advocate of reform or deterrence, and he rejected the classical school's view of free will and moral responsibility as aspects of criminal law. He also rejected the idea of just deserts or revenge, and in its place he used social defense. Garofalo rejected deterrence on the basis of the fact that each offender will respond to punishment in a different way, and therefore no measure of punishment that fits the crime can be established.

Garofalo also differed from the classical school in his definition of individual rights. Beccaria and the classical school had emphasized the doctrine of individual rights as opposed to the power of the state to punish. Garofalo placed social defense first, and he considered the right of the state to punish the criminal to override any innate rights the individual might have. In Garofalo we find the criminal justice system turned over to the scientific community without legal restraints. Garofalo placed emphasis on science, not law or concepts of justice. The state is of importance, not the individual. This issue also emerged in the work of Ferri.

Enrico Ferri (1856–1929)

Ferri was the third member of the Italian school of criminology. He was born in Italy and educated in criminal law and jurisprudence. In his early career he was influenced by the positivists and by scientists such as Lombroso. While at the university he opposed the legal notions of free will and moral responsibility (Sellin, 1970; Jenkins, 1984; Jones, 1986; Rennie, 1978).

Ferri was a true positivist and a believer in the scientific method. He accepted an appointment at the University of Turin in order to work with Lombroso. But believing that Lombroso was too narrow in his approach to criminal behavior, he expanded the discussion of criminal behavior to anthropological, physical, and social variables.

The goal of criminology, as far as Ferri was concerned, was to produce a scientific explanation and classification of criminals. Determinism replaced free will. Ferri completed the transformation of classical criminology by making the law subservient to scientific findings and principles.

In 1884, Ferri published *Criminal Sociology,* which went to a fifth edition and which replaced the classical school with the scientific school in every respect. In this book Ferri argued that classical criminology was based on the idea that:

1. Criminals are the same as noncriminals.
2. Punishment will control the crime rate.
3. Humans have free will and freedom.

In contrast, the positive school was based on the idea that:

1. Criminals differ from noncriminals.
2. Crime rates depend on variables other than punishment.
3. Free will is an illusion in the light of scientific determinism.

According to Ferri, the purpose of criminal law is to study and classify the criminal in order that treatment can be given. The role of the judge in the criminal trial is to see that the defendant is assigned the right classification and sent to a hospital rather than a prison, not to fix guilt and determine punishment. The hospital replaced the prison.

Ferri attended international conferences on criminology from 1878 to 1898 in which biology, neurology, and science were discussed in relation to brain diseases found in criminal populations. Ferri is responsible for taking Lombroso's ideas and transforming them into a theory of treatment of criminals through science. Garofalo had denied the role of treatment for criminals when he settled for the elimination of criminals in the name of social defense. It is to Ferri that we owe one of the basic characteristics of scientific criminology, that is, the treatment of offenders. This is often known as the "medical model" or "rehabilitative ideal" approach to crime control, and it is found in the juvenile court movement, probation and parole, and the indeterminate sentence, to be discussed in later chapters.

One aspect of Ferri's work is critical to the development of scientific criminology during the twentieth century. He followed Garofalo in the rejection of legal definitions and legal procedures, and he supported the treatment of offender without legal limitations or legal definitions. The type or length of treatment was in the hands of therapists and not lawyers and judges, and therefore the defendant/patient came to be subject to the abuses of therapists rather than lawyers. This is a major problem for scientific criminology, as pointed out by Kittrie (1971) in his book *The Right to Be Different*. This issue is discussed in detail in Chapter 20.

Ferri, like Garofalo, placed supremacy in the power of the state, not in the rights of individuals as Hobbes and Locke had done. State rights took precedence over individual rights. This is reflected in the fact that Ferri gave up socialism after World War I and turned to Mussolini and fascism (Hall, 1945:348).

Scientific Criminology Today

There have been major developments in genetics, biology, neurology, and psychology during the 1950–1980 era which have real implications for criminology (Jeffery, 1979, 1985; Fishman, 1981). These developments will be discussed in later chapters devoted to the biological and psychological aspects of criminal behavior.

The movement back to a retribution/justice model has delayed the use of new scientific findings to prevent and control criminal behavior, but hopefully in the future we will find better and more productive ways to integrate science and law than is now the case. A major argument of this book is for the need of an integrated interdisciplinary approach to the crime problem, and this includes the integration of criminal law and the behavioral sciences.

SUMMARY OF POSITIVISTIC CRIMINOLOGY

1. Positivism was an outgrowth of the use of science to study and understand human behavior. Positivism was a scientific, as opposed to legalistic, approach to the crime problem. Positivism involves the behavioral sciences: biology, genetics, neurology, anthropology, psychology, psychiatry, sociology, economics, political science, and urban planning.

2. Positivism supported the doctrine of reforming the criminal rather than the criminal law. By scientific methods the offender would be made whole. They are patients and not criminals. Hospitals replace prisons and electric chairs, and the medical model replaces the punishment model.

3. Positivism denied the legal approach to crime, including the definitions of crimes and punishments. For this reason there were no restrictions placed on the type or length of treatment as there had been on prison sentences. The classical school insisted on a definite fixed sentence, whereas the positive school wanted an indeterminate sentence of one day to life. As a result, the offender came to be at the mercy of the therapist, as opposed to the state and lawyers. This is a major problem in twentieth-century criminology that is dealt with in later chapters.

FURTHER STUDIES

Positivistic or scientific criminology is a basic part of criminology, usually taught from a sociological perspective. Courses are offered in criminology and criminal justice programs on the individual offender and his biological, psychological, and social characteristics. Courses are also offered in biology and psychology departments on human behavior, which have a direct bearing on our scientific understanding of behavior.

In Chapters 10 to 13 we discuss the major developments in biology, psychology, and sociology as applied to criminology. Chapters 7 and 15 are concerned with the integration of biology, psychology, sociology, and law.

REFERENCES

ALLEN, F. (1970). "Raffaele Garofalo." In *Pioneers in Criminology*, ed. H. Mannheim. Montclair, N.J.: Patterson Smith.

BENEDIKT, M. (1881, reprinted in 1981). *Anatomical Studies upon Brains of Criminals*. New York: Da Capo Press.

DRIVER, E. (1970). "Charles Buckman Goring." In *Pioneers in Criminology*, ed. H. Mannheim. Montclair, N.J.: Patterson Smith.

FAUST, F., and P. J. BRANTINGHAM (1979). *Juvenile Justice Philosophy*. St. Paul, Minn.: West Publishing Co.

FISHMAN, G. (1981). "Positivism and Neo-Lombrosianism." In *The Mad, the Bad, and the Different*, ed. I. L. Barak-Glantz and R. Huff. Lexington, Mass: Lexington Books.

HALL, J. (1945). "Criminology." In *Twentieth Century Sociology* ed. G. Gurvitch and W. E. Moore. New York: Philosophical Library.

JEFFERY, C. R., ed. (1979). *Biology and Crime*. Beverly Hills, Calif.: Sage.

JEFFERY, C. R. (1985). *Attacks on the Insanity Defense*. Springfield, Ill.: Charles C. Thomas.

JENKINS, P. (1984). *Crime and Justice*. Monterey, Calif: Brooks/Cole.

JONES, D. A. (1986). *History of Criminology*. Westport, Conn.: Greenwood Press.

KITTRIE, N. (1971). *The Right to Be Different*. Baltimore: Johns Hopkins University Press.

MANNHEIM, H. (1970). *Pioneers in Criminology*. Montclair, N.J.: Patterson Smith.

RADZINOWICZ, L. (1962). *In Search of Criminology*. Cambridge, Mass.: Harvard University Press.

RADZINOWICZ, L. (1966). *Ideology and Crime*. New York: Columbia University Press.

RENNIE, Y. (1978). *The Search for Criminal Man*. Lexington, Mass.: Lexington Books.

SELLIN, T. (1970). "Enrico Ferri." In *Pioneers in Criminology*, ed. H. Mannheim. Montclair, N.J.: Patterson Smith.

VOLD, G. B., and T. J. BERNARD (1979). *Theoretical Criminology*. New York: Oxford University Press.

WOLFGANG, M. (1970). "Cesare Lombroso." In *Pioneers in Criminology*, ed. H. Mann-heim. Montclair, N.J.: Patterson Smith.

QUESTIONS

1. What is meant by "positivism"?
2. What model of crime control did Enrico Ferri put forth for criminology?
3. Why did the view of human nature put forth by Cesare Lombroso receive such a critical reception in American criminology?
4. What are the essential elements of positivistic or scientific criminology?
5. Why has it been argued that scientific or positivistic criminology contained within its theoretical framework dangers for the individual offender?

Criminal Law, Ethics, and Jurisprudence

6

INTRODUCTION

The philosophy of law—jurisprudence as it is known—is concerned with the relationship between the law and other aspects of knowledge. The four major schools of jurisprudence are:

1. *Law and philosophy:* the relationship of law to morality, natural law doctrine, reason, God, religion, and ethics.
2. *Law and power:* the relationship of law to the state system and to the command of the king, and the ability of the state to enforce its codes by coercion and force. This is known as positive law or human-made law.
3. *Law and society:* the relationship of law to major social and historical changes and to major social institutions. This is known as sociological jurisprudence or the sociology of law.
4. *Law and science:* the relationship of law to biology, psychology, sociology, and other behavioral sciences. This is called legal realism or legal behaviorism. The most critical issues and the weakest ties are found in the relation of law to science, as we shall see as we discuss the conflict between law and science in future chapters.

In the philosophy of law we see once again the two major schools of Western philosophy at war with one another (Chapters 2 and 12). The philosophy of idealism or abstract universal value systems is found in the natural law doctrine that law embodies eternal and absolute values. The philosophy of positivism is expressed in sociological jurisprudence, in positive law and the analytic school, and in legal realism, where emphasis is placed on experience, history, society, causation, political power, social structure, and human behavior.

THEORETICAL ISSUES

Law, Philosophy, and Ethics

The basic doctrine found in the history of law is that of natural law—law that exists above and apart from human-made law or positive law. Natural law has been interpreted as coming from God; or from God's representative, the Pope; or from a platonic idealism where the mind is separate from the body and is thus able to arrive at absolute and external truths.

Rationalism taught that humans can comprehend truth and justice through the use of reason. Christian theology turned to God, who revealed to us the nature of truth and justice. St. Thomas Aquinas (1222–1274), the great Catholic theologian, taught in his *Summa Theologica* that there was natural law revealed to us by God, and positive law which we created to conform as nearly as possible to natural law (Feinberg and Gross, 1980; Arthur and Shaw, 1984; Golding, 1967).

The natural law doctrine posits the development of law independent of human actions. Such a view of law assumes a moral code that we must follow and which all people can find through faith. This view is in great conflict with the position that law is related to the power of the state, to society, and to science.

Legal philosophers are still talking about natural law doctrine. Modern versions of natural law have been put forth by Lon Fuller, Ronald Dworkin, John Rawls, and Jerome Hall. Lon Fuller, in his *The Morality of Law* (1964), argued against positivism and the separation of the Is and the Ought in law. He argues for a basic morality underlying the law (Hart, 1983; Feinberg and Gross, 1980).

Ronald Dworkin, in his *Taking Rights Seriously* (1967) stated that the purpose of the judge in a trial is to find the basic human rights involved in each case. There are legal principles that lie behind legal rules and which are basic to the fundamental concept of law (Hart, 1983; Feinberg and Gross, 1980).

John Rawls, in his *Theory of Justice* (1971), proposed that individuals have inalienable rights which free and rational people can find if they agree to enter into a social contact (from Locke) based on ignorance of their own social status in such a society. In this way liberty is assured to all unless such liberty interferes with the rights of others (from J. S. Mill) (Hart, 1983; Feinberg and Gross, 1980).

Jerome Hall, a criminal law scholar and a professor of jurisprudence also believes that the Is and the Ought should not be separated in the law, since the law represents basic moral values. Hall discusses law as based on ethics, free will and volition, and moral responsibility (see Chapter 4). In his writing on jurisprudence, Hall is opposed to positivism and legal realism (Hall, 1947, 1958, 1982).

The doctrine of natural law posits a system of natural rights and values which are eternal, absolute, and valid for all times regardless of biological, psychological, or social settings within which law occurs. Natural law is a "higher law" emulating from God and/or reason (Cowan, 1956:70). Positive law is distinguished from natural law, since positive law is made by humankind and is based on natural law. This doctrine of natural law gives the law a mystical and supernatural quality, because this law embodies a higher morality which extends beyond how people behave.

The separation of natural law and positive law, or the Ought and the Is, has created a dichotomy in legal thinking much like that of mind–matter dualism, and in fact it can be suggested that natural law represents the mind or nonmaterial aspects of reality, whereas positive law represents the body or the physical and behavioral aspects of reality. The term "natural" is used by scientists to refer to the law of thermodynamics, or the law of gravity, or the law of relativity, or the law of magnetism that are discovered through scientific effort. I shall argue that scientific natural laws are independent of the efforts of scientists, that is, gravity and relativity and magnetism exist separate from human behavior. On the other hand, natural law in a legal sense exists only as a part of human behavior, human social institutions, and human history. Law is not separate from the biological, psychological, and social nature of human beings. If people do not behave, law does not exist. This view of law is discussed below in terms of positivism, legal history and legal institutions, the sociology of law, and legal realism.

Law and Morality: The Hart–Devlin Debates

In his book *On Liberty* (1859) Mill took the position that crime and punishment had to be defined in terms of a harm to others. In *Liberty, Equality, Fraternity,* Stephen (1874) denied the position taken by Mill, and in its place he argued that criminal law should be used to enforce the morality of the community. In 1954 the report of the Wolfenden Commission recommended that law not be used to enforce morality, and it specifically stated that sex offenses that were private, consensual, and between adults were not to be regarded as crimes and subject to punishment (Report of the Committee on Homosexual Offenses and Prostitution, 1963).

In *The Enforcement of Morals,* Lord Patrick Devlin (1959) attacked the position taken by Mill and the Wolfenden Commission and supported the views of Stephen that criminal penalties were to be used to enforce morality. An English case, *Shaw* v. *the Director of Public Prosecutions* (1961), held that Shaw was guilty of corrupting public morality by the distribution of his *Ladies Directory,* a list of names and addresses of London prostitutes. In response to the Shaw case, and in a rebuttal to the Lord Devlin statement, H. L. A. Hart (1963) in *Law, Liberty, and Morality* defended the position taken by Mill. Hart argued that law and ethics are separated, and law should be used only to prevent harm to others and not to enforce morality. Hart noted that paternalism or the protection of an individual harm to him/herself was contrary to Mill's understanding of the meaning of liberty.

The issue of what behavior should be made a public wrong and a crime goes to the very foundations of criminal law. We shall not explore the issue further here, but return to it in great detail in Chapters 15, 17, and 18. In Chapter 18 we discuss sexual and drug crimes and there raise the issue of whether or not such behaviors are or should be criminal behaviors.

Legal Positivism and the Power of the State

In Chapters 3 and 4 we emphasized the concept of power and coercion as distinctive characteristics of the state system. The positive school of law, or the analytic school or Austinian school as it is sometimes known, made the concept of power central to the analysis of law.

There emerged in political theory the doctrine of the Divine Right of Kings, a doctrine that the king, not the Pope, had authority given by God to govern over humankind. This view of law as the command of the sovereign is found in the writings of Robert Filmer and Jean Bodin, and later in legal positivism. The idea that the king ruled by divine right was later rejected by John Locke when he put forth a theory of the social contract; that is, humankind entered into a social contract in order to protect common interests in life, liberty, and property (Laslett, 1967).

Thomas Hobbes (1580–1679) defined the state of nature as short, brutish, and nasty, and humankind entered into a social contract in order to create a state system that possessed the power to control this "war of all against all." Jeremy Bentham (1742–1832) believed that human beings were governed by pleasure and pain and that nations used pleasure and pain to control human behavior. Legislators, not God or nature, were the source of law. Legislators calculated pleasure and pain in order to establish criminal laws. Utilitarian motives and power, not ethics and natural law, governed the development of positive or human-made law. The important characteristic of positive law is that it is made by human beings.

John Austin (1790–1859) was a leading figure in the positive school of jurisprudence. He taught that law was the command of the sovereign, and the sovereign was one who possessed the power and might to enforce rules.

In Hobbes, Bentham, and Austin we witness a separation of the Is and the Ought, or law as it is and law as it ought to be. Attention is paid to what the law actually is, in contrast to finding eternal and absolute moral values in the law as the natural law people attempted to do. Law is made by human beings, based on power, and it changes in time and space as human behavior and human social institutions change.

A modern version of positivism is found in the work of H. L. A. Hart (1963, 1983). Hart argues for an Austinian position of the separation of law and morality, and he has been most critical of the natural law doctrine which joins law and morality.

The power of the police to arrest and to kill if necessary, and the power of a judge to sentence a person to execution or to prison, are based on the power of the state to enforce its rules. This power becomes vested in police officers, prosecutors, and judges. The critical point about law is not legal precedent or natural law, but the power of judges to control human life because of their place in a bureaucratic structure.

Law, History, and Social Institutions

Law has also been interpreted as originating not only in morality or power but in the history and social institutions of people. In Chapter 3 we discussed human evolution in terms of the evolution of society and criminal law. It was noted that the important transition was from primitive or tribal law to state law. Sir Henry Maine (1822–1888) described this evolution as being from "status to contract." Henry Morgan (1818–1881) viewed this transition as being from "barbarism to civilization" (see Chapter 3).

The German historical school led by Friedrich von Savigny (1779–1861) looked to the history of a people for the origins of law. Eugene Ehrlich (1862–1922) placed emphasis on "living law," the customary and social aspects of law which developed as a part of cultural and social history.

Roscoe Pound (1870–1964) was a major figure in sociological jurisprudence. Pound viewed law as a system of social control and social engineering, and he placed the study of law in a sociological rather than an ethical and philosophical context. Pound found society to be made up of conflicting social interests which through law and social engineering could be integrated into a consensus necessary for social policy. For Pound, as for the other historical/sociological figures, law was a social institution and a means of social control rather than the embodiment of moral principles. Law is a part of the broader social and historical aspects of society.

Major sociological theorists such as Comte, Durkheim, Spencer, Weber, and Marx have made contributions to sociological jurisprudence or what the sociologist calls the sociology of law. They are all very much a part of sociological jurisprudence as discussed herein, but we cover sociological jurisprudence and the sociology of law in Chapter 15, where we discuss sociology, law, and social control.

Law and Science

The most recent development in legal philosophy has been that of the relationship between law and science. This movement is based on British empiricism and the growth of science that occurred in the eighteenth and nineteenth centuries (Chapters 2 and 12). The emphasis is on human experience, not morality or power, and it has been called "legal realism" because the scholars who put forth this view wanted to see "the law in action" rather than "the law on the books."

Legal realism went beyond legal positivism which studied the law in the books. The legal realist liked to point out that law was not what was on the books, but what governmental officials did in the way of actual behavior. Behavior was the critical element. As we mentioned in Chapter 1, behavior is the basic concern of criminology, and it is for this reason that legal realism can be made a part of criminology, that is, the study of the behavior of those who make and enforce the laws.

For example, it can be pointed out that the speed limit on highways is 55 mph, but police do not arrest drivers going 57. They may arrest a driver going 62 or 65 or 70 mph; there is a great deal of discretion involved here. Courts may convict only those going 70 mph or better. A person kills another person, but because of the circumstances of the case and public sentiment, the jury finds the person not guilty, although it is obvious to everyone that he committed a murder. The criminal code can define speeding or murder, but what happens if the police do not arrest or the prosecutor does not prosecute or the jury does not convict? We must focus on the behavior of the police, judges, lawyers, witnesses, and jurors, as well as on the behavior of criminals, if we are to understand crime and criminal behavior.

O. W. Holmes (1841–1935), a great jurist and a justice of the U.S. Supreme Court, said that the "life of the law is experience and not logic." Holmes also noted that the purpose of the law was to predict the behavior of judges in any given case (Holmes, 1881).

Karl Llewellyn (1893–1962) used anthropology as his base for relating law to science. In *The Cheyenne Way* (Llewellyn and Hoebel, 1941), Llewellyn, a lawyer, and Hoebel, an anthropologist, discuss how primitive law worked in a primitive society (see Chapter 3).

Judge Jerome Frank (1889–1957) used Freudian psychiatry to understand why judges behaved as they did when they made law. Frank started his analysis with the myth that the law is certain, and he found the source of this myth in the fact that lawyers seek certainty and security. Lawyers seek a father figure in the law (Frank, 1930, 1950). Frank regarded the law as located in the deep emotional aspects of behavior rather than in the rational aspects. However, lawyers phrase their work in verbalisms and absolutisms in order to feel secure with their behavior and profession. Frank also noted how weak the court system is, especially as a fact-finding body (Frank, 1950).

Thurman Arnold (1881–1965) relied on political science for his legal realism. He concentrated on the symbols that governmental officials use to manipulate the behavior of citizens and to control their behavior. This is a basic theme of that part of political science which is devoted to the study of propaganda, public opinion, political parties, and election processes.

Underhill Moore and Harry Oliphant used experimental psychology and other operant conditioning to understand behavior. They applied the science of behavior and the laws of stimulus–response psychology to the behavior of lawyers and judges.

Fred Beutel published a book on experimental jurisprudence wherein he attempted to apply scientific principles to the study of the law. Similarly, Cohen, Robeson, and Bates tried to ascertain the moral sentiments of the community so that the law could be guided in defining crimes and setting punishments.

Realism was never popular with legal scholars. It had its heyday in the 1920–1930 era, and since has been lost in the arguments between the legal positivists and the natural law people. Several major projects of an interdisciplinary nature were undertaken, however (Mueller, 1969). The University of Chicago Law School in the 1960s had a research project to study the functioning of the jury system involving sociologists and lawyers. The University of Chicago Law School started a law and behavioral science project wherein social and behavioral scientists were brought in for a year to study at the law school. Yale University has had an interest in law and psychiatry, as seen in the book *Psychoanalysis, Psychiatry, and the Law* (Katz, Goldstein, and Dershowitz, 1967). The lawyer has always shown an interest in psychiatry as part of the insanity defense; however, psychoanalysis is not highly regarded in scientific circles today, and the law is working with the wrong type of psychology (see Chapters 12, 13, and 20).

Mueller (1969) has reviewed interdisciplinary scholarship in law. Mueller has always supported interdisciplinary programs in law and the behavioral sciences. He established the Criminal Law Education and Research Center at New York University School of Law, which included criminologists as well as criminal lawyers.

Michael and Wechsler (1940) published *Criminal Law and Its Administration*, in which they used social science materials and integrated them with legal materials. In a review of the book, David Riesman (1941) noted that this book was an excellent example of social engineering through law and a model for legal realism. Jerome Hall has been mentioned several times as a legal scholar who combined law, social science, and philosophy in his work in criminology and criminal law (Hall, 1958, 1982). Monahan and Walker (1984) have published a book on social science in law.

As stated in Chapter 1, there are few attempts to bring science into legal education or the legal process. Lawyers study law without the benefit of scientific findings. Hall, Radzinowicz, and Michael and Adler have all advocated an institute for criminology and criminal law (see Chapter 1). Such an institute would serve as a teaching and research center for interdisciplinary studies in criminology and criminal law. This must be done if we are to resolve the conflicts between law and science (see Chapter 1).

There is a basic need for more cooperative research between lawyers and behavioral scientists on the behaviors of lawyers, judges, legislators, and politicians in order that we may understand the judicial process as a behavioral process. The following can be cited as examples of such research: Glick (1983), Dye and Zeigler (1978), Atkins and Pogrebin (1982), and Schubert (1965). Some of these issues are discussed in Chapter 21. An unfortunate aspect of the classical school (Chapter 4) versus the positive school argument (Chapter 5) is that law is left to the philosophers and moralists, who make no effort to make law scientific, whereas human behavior is the concern of scientists.

The major assumption of this book is that human behavior is the subject matter of criminology (Chapter 1). This is usually interpreted to mean the behavior of criminals (Chapter 5). However, the behaviors of those involved in legal processes (e.g., legislators, governors, judges and witnesses) can also be studied scientifically. These issues are usually left to the criminal justice system and to criminal law, which describes them but does not attempt to explain them scientifically. Descriptive statements do not explain the behavior of these people. Science moves from description to classification, explanation, control, and prediction, none of which is to be found in the law.

Criminology can include law as a part of a science of behavior by incorporating into criminology the study of the power of the state, sociological jurisprudence, and the sociology of law (Chapters 14 and 15), and other studies of the behaviors of those making and enforcing the laws. Law and the behavioral sciences must be an integral part of an interdisciplinary criminology.

What Is a Crime, Who Is a Criminal?

Legal realism helps us to answer a question raised in Chapter 1: What is a crime, and who is a criminal? If we define crime, as we have done, as the violation of a criminal law, do we mean the way the law defines a crime ''on the books,'' or do we mean the ''law in action''? What if a person robs a store but is not apprehended; is he a criminal? What if he is apprehended but not prosecuted? What if he is prosecuted but not convicted? Is this person a criminal? Behaviorally, yes; legally, no. We need conviction and sentencing for a crime to exist legally. As we shall see in Chapter 8, there are a large number of ''unreported crimes'' or ''unofficial crimes'' which are not part of the legal process. To have a crime, we must have the behavior of the criminal and the behavior of the legal system in interaction. Both are necessary.

SUMMARY

Legal jurisprudence contains four essential schools or positions: (1) natural law embodying absolute truth and external values; (2) the power of the state to make law and to enforce law through power and coercion; (3) the development of law out of the history and sociological experiences of a people; and (4) law as human behavior, or law as related to sciences. The natural law doctrine is idealistic in nature. The other three are based on empiricism, science, and human experience. There are major contradictions and conflicts between the natural law school and the other three schools of thought, as there are between idealism and empiricism.

FURTHER STUDIES

Courses in jurisprudence are taught in law schools and in some political science departments as part of the history of political theory. Sociology departments sometimes have a course in the sociology of law. Some criminology or criminal justice programs will have a course on the history of criminological thought which will include some of the issues discussed in this chapter.

REFERENCES

ARTHUR, J., and W. H. SHAW (1984). *Readings in the Philosophy of Law*. Englewood Cliffs, N.J.: Prentice Hall.

ATKINS, B., and M. PORGREBIN (1982). *The Invisible Justice System*. Cincinnati, Ohio: Anderson Publishing Co.

*COWAN, T. A. (1956). *American Jurisprudence Reader*. Dobbs Ferry, N.Y.: Oceana.

DEVLIN, P. (1959). *The Enforcement of Morals*. Oxford: Oxford University Press.

DWORKIN, R. (1977). *Taking Rights Seriously*. Cambridge, Mass.: Harvard University Press.

DYE, T. R., and L. H. ZEIGLER (1978). *The Irony of Democracy*, 4th ed. North Scituate, Mass.: Duxbury Press.

FEINBERG, J., and H. GROSS (1980). *Philosophy of Law*, 2nd ed. Belmont, Calif.: Wadsworth.

FRANK, J. (1930). *Law and the Modern Mind*. New York: Brentano.

FRANK, J. (1950). *Courts on Trials: Myth and Reality in American Justice*. Princeton, N.J.: Princeton University Press.

*FRIEDMANN, W. (1967). *Legal History*, 5th ed. New York: Columbia University Press.

*FRIEDRICH, C. J. (1958). *The Philosophy of Law in Historical Perspective*. Chicago: University of Chicago Press.

FULLER, L. (1964). *The Morality of Law*. New Haven, Conn.: Yale University Press.

GLICK, H. R. (1983). *Courts, Politics, and Justice*. New York: McGraw-Hill.

*GOLDING, M. P. (1967). "History of the Philosophy of Law." In *Encyclopedia of Philosophy*, Vol. 5, ed. P. Edwards. New York: Macmillan.

HALL, J. (1947). *General Principles of Criminal Law*, 2nd ed. Indianapolis, Ind.: Bobbs-Merrill.

HALL, J. (1958). *Studies in Jurisprudence and Criminal Theory*. Dobbs Ferry, N.Y.: Oceana.

HALL, J. (1982). *Law, Social Science and Criminal Theory*. Littleton, Colo.: Fred B. Rothman & Co.

HART, H. L. A. (1963). *Law, Liberty, and Morality*. Stanford, Calif.: Stanford University Press.

HART, H. L. A. (1983). *Essays in Jurisprudence and Philosophy*. Oxford: Clarendon Press.

HOLMES, O. W. (1881). *The Common Law*. Boston: Little, Brown.

KATZ, J., J. GOLDSTEIN, and A. N. DERSHOWITZ (1967). *Psychoanalysis, Psychiatry, and the Law*. New York: Free Press.

*Source of particular importance in the preparation of this chapter.

LASLETT, P. (1967). "Robert Filmer." In *Encyclopedia of Philosophy*, Vol. 3, ed. P. Edwards. New York: Macmillan.

LLEWELLYN, K., and E. A. HOEBEL (1941). *Cheyenne Way*. Norman: University of Oklahoma Press.

MICHAEL, J., and H. WECHSLER (1940). *Criminal Law and Its Administration*. Chicago: Foundation Press.

MILL, J. S. (1859/1912). *On Liberty*. London: Oxford University Press.

MONAHAN J., and L. WALKER (1984). *Social Science in Law: Cases and Materials*. Mineola, N.Y.: Foundation Press.

*MORAWETZ, T. (1960). *Philosophy of Law*. New York: Macmillan.

MUELLER, G. O. W. (1969). *Crime, Law and the Scholars*. Seattle: University of Washington Press.

*PATTERSON, E. E. W. (1953). *Jurisprudence*. Brooklyn: Foundation Press.

RAWLS, J. (1971). *Theory of Justice*. Cambridge, Mass.: Harvard University Press.

REPORT OF THE COMMITTEE ON HOMOSEXUAL OFFENSES AND PROSTITUTION (1963). *The Wolfenden Report*. New York: Stein & Day.

RIESMAN, D. (1941). "Law and Social Science: A Report on Michael and Wechsler's Casebook on Criminal Law and Its Administration." *Yale Law Journal*, Vol. 50:4, 636–53.

SCHUBERT, G. (1965). *Judicial Policy Making*. Glenview, Ill.: Scott, Foresman.

STEPHEN, J. F. (1874/1967). *Liberty, Equality, Fraternity*. London: Cambridge University Press.

QUESTIONS

1. What is the meaning of law for philosophers interested in natural law doctrine and ethics?
2. What are the basic issues of the Hart–Devlin debates?
3. What is the basic principle of law as found in legal positivism?
4. What explanations of law are used by sociological jurisprudence and the sociology of law?
5. What law emerges from science and legal realism?

*Source of particular importance in the preparation of this chapter.

Law, Science, and Society　　　7

CRIMINAL LAW, CRIMINOLOGY, AND THE BEHAVIORAL SCIENCES

Classicism versus Positivism in American Criminology

Classicism is based on reforming the criminal law and the definitions of crime (Chapter 4). The classicists emphasized legal definitions of crime based on a philosophy of mind–matter dualism, intent, and criminal responsibility.

The positive school was an outgrowth of the scientific revolution, and it studied the individual offender by means of biology, psychology, and sociology. Positivists believed in determinism rather than free will. Whereas the object of the classical school is to punish the individual and thereby deter him/her from crime, the positive school studies criminals in order that they can be rehabilitated. Hospitals, not prisons, are the major means of crime control (Chapter 5).

As we have seen throughout this book, the basic conflicts between positivism and classicism still exist in criminology and criminal justice. The criminal justice system is based on the classical legal approach, whereas criminology is based on science and positivism. Hall (1945:346) has commented on the classical/positivist conflict in this manner: "The most serious criticism of twentieth century criminology is that it has hardly become aware of this major problem; far from trying to arise above the inhibiting restrictions of the schools, it has gone whole-hog positivistic." Jeffery (1956, 1970) expressed concern over lack of theoretical integration in criminology as a result of the legal/scientific conflict found in criminology. This conflict is far from resolved in 1989, and in this chapter I discuss some of the implications of this conflict for criminology and criminal law.

American criminology is a product of positivism and the work of Lombrosco, Garofalo, and Ferri. Vold (1958:39) stated that "all contemporary scientific criminology is positivistic in method and in basic formulations." Matza (1964:13) wrote: "The most explicit assumption of positive criminology is the primacy of the criminal actor rather than the criminal law as a major point of departure in the construction of etiological theories. The explanation of crime, according to the positive school, may be found in the motivational and behavioral systems of criminals." Lopez-Rey (1961:13) stated that "the repeated assertion is made that it is not the crime committed by the personality of the author that matters in the treatment of offenders. Such persistence has led to what we could call a criminological cult of the personality." Radzinowicz (1962:3–5) stated that "virtually every element of value in contemporary criminological knowledge owes its formulation to the very remarkable school of Italian criminologists who took pride in describing themselves as the positivists and who, in contradistinction to the classicists, regarded criminal law as a changing social institution and crime as a product of . . . the make-up of offenders, physical, mental and social. . . . The main weakness of the positivists lies not so much in the inadequacy of several of their individual hypotheses and conclusions, as in their failure to grasp the bewildering complexity of the phenomenon of crime."

Under the leadership of John Wigmore (Millar, 1970), dean of the Northwestern University School of Law, the National Council on Criminal Law and Criminology was held in 1909. From this conference came the American Institute of Criminal Law and Criminology, whose purpose was to unite the efforts of lawyers, sociologists, and psychologists in the study of crime and criminals. One of the results of the institute was the publication of the *Journal of the American Institute of Criminal Law and Criminology,* which later came to be the *Journal of Criminal Law, Criminology, and Police Science,* published by the Northwestern University Law School (Mueller, 1968).

The first editor of the journal was Robert Gault, a psychologist at Northwestern University. Since his editorship the editors have been predominately lawyers, with a few sociologists. The *Journal of Criminal Law, Criminology, and Police Science* has been under the control of a law school and lawyers, whereas the journal *Criminology: An Interdisciplinary Journal* has been under the control of sociologists (Mueller, 1968).

The institute also published the *Modern Criminal Science Series,* consisting of pioneering books written by foreign scholars and not readily available to American audiences. The books published in the series included:

C. B. DE QUIROS, *Modern Theories of Criminality*

HANS GROSS, *Criminal Psychology*

C. LOMBROSO, *Crime, Its Causes and Remedies*

R. SALEILLES, *The Individualization of Punishment*

G. Tarde, *Penal Philosophy*

G. Aschffenburg, *Crime and Its Repression*

R. Garofalo, *Criminology*

W. Bonger, *Criminality and Economic Conditions*

E. Ferri, *Criminal Sociology*

The publication of this series of foreign books on criminology in English, under the general editorship of John Wigmore (Millar, 1970) from 1910 through 1915, introduced to the American reader a positivistic background in criminological theory. The American sociologist or psychologist now had access to a series of the most critical books in criminology. It is no wonder that criminology turned positivistic during this period of history. A series of articles written on other pioneers in criminology was published by the journal in the 1950s and later published in a collection entitled *Pioneers in Criminology* (Mannheim, 1970).

Classicism and positivism are in conflict over:

1. The definition of crimes (legal versus scientific)
2. The nature of crime control (punishment versus treatment and prevention)
3. The nature of human nature (free will and moral responsibility versus determinism and scientific causation)

Scientific criminology (positivism) led to the development of the juvenile court, probation and parole, and the indeterminate sentence. The medical model replaced the punitive model. As a result of positivism and science, we witnessed the psychoanalytic movement (Chapter 12) and the poverty program as ways of treating crime and criminals. The positive school was attached to the classical model of justice after the fact-finding stage, that is, after guilt has been determined and sentencing and disposition were to take place. Procedural rights for criminals were not developed for the sentencing and post-sentencing phases, since the law protected the rights of those to be punished, not those to be treated. Misuses and abuses of therapies and dispositions of offenders occurred. Because of abuses of the treatment model, an antitherapy movement took place in the 1980s when we entered a new era of punishment along with the rejection of the rehabilitative ideal (Chapters 8 and 21). We found out that (1) we did not have effective treatment methods for criminals, and (2) we had a legal system designed to punish but one that did not protect the rights of those we wished to treat and rehabilitate.

Sociological Definitions of Crime

Garofalo (Chapter 5) defined crime as acts against the moral sense of the community as found in the sentiments of pity and probity, and in terms of the scientific needs of criminology rather than legal norms. Ferri (Chapter 5) stated that crime was not a legal concept but a social fact, and ''the proper subject of criminal anthropology is the antisocial individual and his activities'' (Ferri, 1917). Ferri became a fascist in Mussolini's Italy in the 1930s, and the emphasis of the positivists on the state and the defense of the state at the expense of the individual is a major issue for scientific criminology (Hall, 1945:348).

Sellin, an early historian/sociologist at the University of Pennsylvania, responded to the Michael and Adler book (discussed below) in his *Culture Conflict and Crime* (Sellin, 1938). Sellin denied the legal definition of crime as put forth by lawyers, and in its place he used the concept of social norms. Crime is the violation of a conduct norm of a group, and scientists can use definitions of crime which they find suitable for scientific research purposes. ''Ultimately, science must be able to state that when a person with certain personality elements in a certain configuration happens to be placed in a certain hypothetical life situation, he will probably react in a certain manner, whether the law punishes the response as a crime or tolerates it as unimportant'' (Sellin, 1938:44–45).

In this statement Sellin is repeating the observation made by Ferri that the antisocial person is the proper object of study for criminologists. The problem is that Sellin, like Ferri, is ignoring the fact that an explanation of behavior is not an explanation of the criminality of the behavior. Sellin states that he does not care whether the behavior is regarded as criminal or as unimportant. The purpose of criminal law is to make decisions as to whether behavior is criminal or noncriminal. This is the difference between the classical and the positive school, and Sellin's statement illustrates how whole hog positivistic American criminology is, or was, until the 1960s.

Sutherland and Cressey (1970:4–21) state that crime is a violation of criminal law, and then they go on to state: ''The legal definitions should not confine the work of the criminologist, and he (she) should be completely free to push across the barriers of legal definitions wherever he (she) sees noncriminal behavior which resembles criminal behavior.'' How do they know when they see behavior that resembles criminal behavior if behavior has not first been declared to be criminal? Sutherland and Cressey are also confusing the study of behavior with the process by which behavior is designated criminal.

Legal Definitions of Crime

In 1933, Michael and Adler (1933) published *Crime, Law and Social Science*, in which they denied the sociological definition of crime when they stated that the formal cause of crime is criminal law. They defended a legalistic view of crime while advocating the introduction of social science materials into law school curricula. They denied the scientific status of criminology since it was based on nonscientific psychology and sociology. This book had a major impact on criminology, and it will be discussed in greater detail later in the chapter.

Paul Tappan (1947), a lawyer/sociologist, defended the legal definition of crime. Tappan wrote that crime is violation of the criminal law, and the law, not social norms, sets the boundaries of criminology.

Karl Llewellyn (1949), a University of Chicago law professor, opposed the definition of crime in sociological terms. As he stated: ''When I was younger I used to hear smuggish assertions among my sociology friends such as 'I take a sociological, not a legal approach to crime,' and I suspect an inquiring reporter could still hear much of the same (perhaps with psychiatric often substituted for sociological)—though it is surely somewhat obvious that when you take 'the legal' out, you also take out 'crime.' "

Jerome Hall (1945:354–355), a law professor, defended the legal approach to criminology. "Sociology of criminal law is that division of legal sociology which deals primarily with social phenomena relevant to the norms of penal law; hence, criminology in this view is synonymous with the sociology of criminal law." By this Hall did not mean that the behavioral aspects of criminology are not also important, but he did emphasize that criminology and criminal law are very interdependent. His work in criminology and criminal law is discussed in more detail later in the chapter.

Roscoe Pound (1945), a biologist and lawyer and dean of the Harvard Law School, advocated the legal approach to crime. Pound, who was interested in law as a means of social control, wrote: "The broader usage (law as custom and norms) is common with sociologists. But certainly for jurists, and I suspect also for sociologists, it is expedient to avoid adding to the burden of the term of too many meanings, and to use 'law' for social control through the systematic application of the force of politically organized society."

In summarizing the relationship between criminology and criminal law Geis stated:

> Much of the attempt to escape from a legally-rooted concept of crime, apart from a wholesome endeavor to redefine behaviorally homogeneous criminal groups, appears to stem from the fact that sociologists are not interested because of disciplinary values in dealing with the diffuse and complicated criminal law system, a system which they neither created nor can control, and therefore prefer to ignore. . . . In conclusion, then, it may be noted that both sociology and law, despite recurrent flirtations, have been beset by some basic conflicts which often grow out of deep-seated commitments to diverse viewpoints, as well as out of more mundane items such as the status of the practitioners. Cross-fertilization between sociology and law, in either direction, has been comparatively limited (Geis, 1959:145).

The argument that legal definitions are arbitrary and change over time and place is not an issue since social norms also change over time and place and are also arbitrary. Laws are formalized social norms. The question is not whether we define crime in legal or sociological terms but whether we study law, science, and society as interrelated issues.

THE INTEGRATION OF CRIMINAL LAW AND CRIMINOLOGY

In this section I discuss the different ways in which legal and behavioral scholars have addressed the conflicting issues involving classicism and positivism. These people have made historically important statements concerning classicism and positivism, and though some favor classicism and some positivism, they all agree that the conflict must be resolved or at least acknowledged.

Leon Radzinowicz

Sir Leon Radzinowicz, now retired, was the Wolfson professor of criminology and the director of the Institute of Criminology at Cambridge University, Cambridge, England. He was a student of Ferri in Rome, and he brought to British criminology the flavor of positivism. At the same time he was aware of the need to relate positivism to classicism [Radzinowicz (1966); see also Hood (1974)].

Radzinowicz discussed the need for a proper home for criminology, an academic setting devoted to criminology as an interdisciplinary science. He wrote: "As long as there is no separate course, there will be no flow of trained criminologists to discharge the functions of teaching and research" (Radzinowicz, 1962:34). He noted that in many European countries criminology is part of the law school curriculum, as in Germany, France, and the Netherlands. In America and in England positivism flourished as a new scientific discipline and as part of sociology separate from law schools. Radzinowicz felt that it was unfortunate that criminology was absent in law schools in the United States (Radzinowicz, 1962:161).

Radzinowicz concluded with a plea for an interdisciplinary approach to criminology, involving law, psychiatry, psychology, sociology, and statistics. He also argued that criminology should have a close relationship to criminal justice and to the treatment of offenders (Radzinowicz, 1962, 1966; Hood, 1974).

In *The Need for Criminology,* Radzinowicz (1965) advocated the establishment of an institute for the study of criminology. This center would be interdisciplinary in nature and approach and would develop an integrated approach to crime and criminal behavior. Radzinowicz was also a legal historian, producing a five-volume work entitled *A History of English Criminal Law and Its Administration from 1750* (Radzinowicz, 1948–1956).

As director of the Institute of Criminology at Cambridge University, Radzinowicz established an interdisciplinary model for the study of criminology. A former colleague of mine, Paul Jeffrey Brantingham, tells the following story of his experiences at the Institute of Criminology. He arrived at Cambridge with a J.D. degree from Columbia University, and he was told that since he was trained as a lawyer, he would be assigned to Donald West, a physician and psychiatrist, so that his training would be interdisciplinary. When Brantingham arrived at West's office to introduce himself, he was handed a bucket containing a freshly exorcised human brain to carry to the next lecture on neurology and criminal behavior.

Michael and Adler

Jerome Michael (a Columbia University law professor) and Michael Adler (a University of Chicago philosophy professor) were commissioned by the Bureau of Social Hygiene of the state of New York to study the feasibility of an institute to study the relationship of law and social science. This was preliminary to a move to establish such an institute in New York City. Radzinowicz performed a similar task for the Association of the Bar of the City of New York, and his report is found in *The Need for Criminology* cited above.

Michael and Adler (1933) started by defining crime in terms of legal, not sociological, concepts. They found that criminology was lacking as a science since criminology had established no known causes or cures for crime. Michael and Adler pointed to the dependency of criminology on psychology and sociology, neither of which is a science, and they concluded that for this reason criminological research was weak and inconclusive.

In their discussion of the aims of criminal law and criminal justice, Michael and Adler reject the retributionist model, which, as put forth by Kant and Hegel, makes punitive retribution or justice the purpose of criminal law (Michael and Adler, 1933:347–349). Michael and Adler argued that retribution is an untenable justification for punishment, and they supported the utilitarian view of the protection of society, social welfare, and the common good. To quote them: "But if the criminal law is properly conceived, a crime can be defined without any reference to the concept of responsibility. There is then no need for differentiation between the responsible and the irresponsible, between individuals upon whom it is just to visit retributive punishment and individuals whom it is unjust to punish. The justifiability of treatment is determined by deference to its effects, and not by reference to the free will of a moral agent" (Michael and Adler, 1933:369). In this statement Michael and Adler go to the very foundations of criminal law in their denial of free will and moral responsibility. They stated, for example, that we should treat the child murderer as we would the insane person who has committed a crime.

Treatment should be individualized for each offender (positive school model) rather than by the offense (classical school model). However, Michael and Adler included punishment and deterrence in their concept of treatment, whereas the usual positivistic criminologist makes a real distinction between deterrence, punishment, and treatment.

Michael and Adler advocated the establishment of an institute of criminology and criminal justice in order that scientific knowledge for crime control could be developed. They emphasized the fact that knowledge must come before criminal justice policy (the reverse has been and still is the political policy of criminal justice system planning).

Karl Llewellyn responded to the Michael and Adler book by stating that "it was as stimulating, irritating, vitally wise, and hopelessly absurd a book as I have ever read" (Radzinowicz, 1965:25). Radzinowicz (1965:25–26) expressed his opinion of the book in the following manner: "They crossed the line that divides constructive reappraisal from destructive nihilism. . . . But the book had a deadly effect."

In his *Culture Conflict and Crime*, Sellin (1938) wrote a major rebuke of the Michael and Adler book for the Social Science Research Council. Sutherland at first rejected the Michael and Adler report, but later said he found it to be of some value (Sutherland, 1956).

Barbara Wootton

Barbara Wootton, Lady Baronness of Abinger, is a British magistrate who has written several provocative works on the interrelationship of law and crime. In *Social Science and Social Pathology* (Wootton, 1959), she reviewed criminological findings pertinent to the nature and causes of crime (i.e., age, sex, race, socio-economic status, psychopathy, etc.) and concluded that there were no causal relationships in criminology and would not be until criminologists became more scientific.

Crime and the Criminal Law (Wootton, 1963) focused on the nature of the criminal law and the problems involved in relating criminal law to science. Wootton reviewed the impact of science and positivism on criminal law, and she noted that sociology and psychology are not adequate for understanding criminal behavior and/or for policy purposes. She then analyzed the criminal justice system as a barbaric prescientific process devoted to retribution and punishment. Wootton pointed out that criminal law is based on the doctrine of mens rea, moral guilt, and moral responsibility, and because of its orientation, criminal law cannot address the more crucial issue of how law can be used to prevent and control crime and criminal behavior. Treatment and prevention must replace retribution as the purpose of the criminal law. "Once the criminal law is conceived of as an instrument of crime prevention, it is these facts which demand attention, and from which we can learn to improve the efficiency of the instrument; and the question [of free will] is no longer relevant" (Wootton, 1963:78).

Like Michael and Adler, Wootton highlighted the fact that legalistic criminology, based on a mind–matter dualism and nonscientific approach to behavior, cannot be integrated with science. She challenged us to address the question: Is the law for purposes of social control and social engineering, or for the purpose of moral condemnation and revenge?

Wootton has been seriously criticized for her positivistic treatment of criminal law. Hart (1968:195–209) rejected Wootton's scientific approach to criminal law and wrote that mens rea is a critical element in the criminal law.

Karl Menninger

Karl Menninger is a psychiatrist and the founder of the Menninger Clinic in Topeka, Kansas. He has written extensively in the psychiatric/mental health field (Menninger, 1938, 1942, 1945, 1972).

In *The Crime of Punishment,* Menninger (1968) attacked the criminal law and criminal justice system as an ineffective, immoral, and unjust system. He makes the comparison between the mental institutions (snake pits) of several hundred years ago and our prison system of today, and he noted that we have moved from regarding mental illness as an affliction from the devil to treating it as a psychiatric and neurological problem.

As a psychiatrist Menninger views behavior as determined, not as a product of free will. Since the criminal justice system ignores science while it pursues revenge, the crime committed is not by the criminal but by the state. The present criminal justice system does not help the offender, nor does it protect society. In its place Menninger would use a medical model based on clinics and hospitals rather than prisons. The offender would be studied as an individual and given individualized treatment based on scientific methods.

Menninger, even more than Michael and Adler and Wootton, advocates a positivistic criminology. This is the program Enrico Ferri put forth in his *Criminal Sociology* (Chapter 5). Menninger does not outline in detail the specifics of his treatment program, which one can assume would be psychiatric in nature, nor does he ever address the question of how politicians can be convinced that treatment and hospitals must replace prisons and punishment. Twenty years after the appearance of his book the criminal justice system is an even bigger failure than in 1968, yet there is little or no evidence that we are about to accept his medical model of treatment and prevention in place of a legal model of justice.

Nicholas Kittrie

Kittrie is a law professor at the Washington School of Law, American University. In *The Right to Be Different,* Kittrie (1971) outlined the theoretical difficulties found in classicism and positivism and put forth a program for integrating law and the behavioral sciences.

Within positivism there is a major theoretical problem, that is, the welfare of the individual is sacrificed to the welfare of the state for purposes of social defense. No major guidelines were developed by the positivists for their treatment model. Garofalo favored social rather than legal definitions of crime, and Ferri advocated science and scientific experts in court in place of judges to determine the disposition of criminal cases. The indeterminate sentence would replace the determinate or fixed sentence. Discretion would abound in the criminal justice system in the decisions of judges, police officers, parole officers, and therapists. The positivist was not concerned with who the experts are or with who controls the experts.

As a result of positivistic ideas the juvenile court, probation and parole, and indeterminate sentencing came into existence in the late nineteenth and early twentieth centuries. These programs operated on a ''cure rather than punish'' philosophy without legal restrictions over the power of the juvenile court or the probation officer or the psychotherapist. Therapies were made mandatory for crimes or quasi-crimes, such as alcoholism, sex offenses, drug addiction, mental illness, and sexual psychopathy.

Kittrie noted that positivism gave us the concept of *parens patriae*, the state acting on behalf of the child as a legal guardian. The therapeutic state emerged committed to treatment of the individual offender within a therapeutic model. Within this system individuals could be designated as sick and in need of treatment, and the therapeutic model placed individuals in the power of therapists and parole boards without any legal protection. The therapeutic state did not develop legal controls over treatment which the punitive state developed to control the use of punishment. This occurred historically because the therapeutic state and positivism were grafted onto the classical model of punishment without an awareness that the medical model requires its own legal structure and legal doctrine.

Kittrie reviewed the attacks on the medical model as found in efforts to rehabilitate alcoholics, delinquents, drug addictions, the mentally ill, and sex offenders, and he reviewed the attacks on the medical model by the antipsychiatry movement (Szasz), by radical criminologists (Platt), and by liberal criminal law professors (Morris). Kittrie used several basic ideas from political philosophy to resolve the conflict between positivism and classicism. First, he notes that J. S. Mill in his *On Liberty* defined the limits of state action against individual citizens in terms of the utilitarian standard of "harm to others." The liberty of an individual cannot be interfered with by the state other than where the liberty of one individual interferes with the liberty of another individual. It is obvious that my freedom to behave as I wish must be limited by the same right for other individuals. The state can take action to prevent "harm to others," but it cannot take action to prevent my doing harm to myself. The concept of the therapeutic state cannot extend to forcing individuals to care for their health and welfare. My right to behave as I wish extends only so far as it does not interfere with your right to behave.

Such a doctrine allows us to define crime and criminal acts. A crime is a public harm committed by one person against another person. The criminal law could not prohibit alcohol or drug use or homosexuality under this standard, but it could prohibit or regulate public use of alcohol and drugs, or driving while intoxicated. Your right to drive or to drink does not extend to your right to drive while drunk. In the latter case there is a possibility that I may be driving on the same road. My rights include the right not to be killed by a drunk driver. Many crimes against morality would not be crimes under the standard of "harm to others."

Kittrie did not rule out treatment; in fact, for those whose pose a clear threat to others, *compulsory rehabilitation* would be imposed (Kittrie, 1971:379). Compulsory treatment is one of the most controversial issues in criminology today, as found in discussion of preventive detention, compulsive therapies, and the prediction of future dangerousness (see Chapter 21). Kittrie stated: "As long as an individual remains dangerous, there is no way that society will tolerate his release" (Kittrie, 1971:399). Kittrie argued that the right to treatment not only means the right of an individual to treatment, but the right of the state to protect itself by compulsory treatment of those who are a danger to others. Kittrie stated his argument in the following passages:

> While the value of guilt and of the ritual of punishment cannot be readily dismissed, it is nevertheless ironic that late nineteenth-century determinism and its denial of the criminal model should be currently followed by a movement reemphasizing the requirement of individual guilt and indeed seeking to curtail the therapeutic experiment in the name of a growing concern for social controls. (Kittrie, 1971:405)

At the same time, the therapeutic state's concept of a deviant as a patient in need of a positive change (personal and environmental) continues to provide a much more effective model for behavioral change than is supplied by the criminal process' concept of a criminal as one who requires negative sanctions. There is a world of difference between the therapeutic conclusion that "you have done a terrible thing and must change before you resume your role in society" and the criminal law's pronouncement that "you are a terrible person and must be punished." (Kittrie, 1971:407)

Kittrie argued that if we are to develop treatment programs we must first be willing to experiment with new and controversial programs. Along these lines Kittrie developed the "Therapeutic Bill of Rights" for the therapeutic state.

1. No person shall be compelled to undergo treatment except for the defense of society.
2. Man's innate right to remain free of excessive forms of human modification shall remain inviolable.
3. No treatment sanction may be invoked unless the person subjected to treatment has demonstrated a clear and present danger through truly harmful behavior which is immediately forthcoming or has already occurred.
4. No person shall be subjected to involuntary incarceration or treatment on the basis of a finding of a general condition or status alone.
5. No social sanction, whether designated criminal, civil, or therapeutic, may be invoked in the absence of a previous right to a judicial or other independent hearing, appointed counsel, and an opportunity to confront those testifying about one's past conduct or therapeutic needs.
6. Dual interference by both the criminal and therapeutic process is prohibited.
7. An involuntary patient shall have the right to receive treatment.
8. Any compulsory treatment must be the least required reasonably to protect society.
9. All committed persons should have direct access to appointed counsel and the right, without any interference, to petition the courts for relief.
10. Those submitting to voluntary treatment should be guaranteed that they will not be subsequently transferred to a compulsory program through administrative action (Kittrie, 1871:402–404).

Kittrie then wrote: "So circumscribed, in order to prevent its excesses, the therapeutic state seems destined to replace the traditional criminal process" (Kittrie, 1971:404). The return to punishment, prisons, and just retribution during the 1970s and 1980s was contrary to Kittrie's conclusion that the therapeutic state should replace the punishing state (see Chapter 8).

Kittrie combined the ideas of Mill, Menninger, and Wootton into a powerful plea for positivism as found in the therapeutic state, compulsory treatment, and a therapeutic bill of rights. Kittrie did what the positivists did not do; he extended the classical idea that the individual has legal protections against punishment to legal rights for those subject to compulsory treatment. Kittrie noted that the classical school defines rights in terms of "negative rights," that is, those things the state cannot do to its citizens. He advocated a statement of "positive rights," those rights possessed by citizens requiring positive action on the part of the state. Kittrie realized the need for a legal model for treatment instead of one for punishment and prisons.

The one issue remaining to be answered, however, pertains to therapeutic right 1: Treatment shall be undertaken only for the protection of society. This means that the good of society is superior to the welfare of the individual. Any system of social control requires this. For example, we cannot allow people to drive cars in any way they want, or to behave in public in an uncontrolled manner, or to use firearms in public in a dangerous manner. We do require quarantines and the payment of taxes and military services, all of which are done in the name of the betterment of society. The threat remains, however, of a dictator requiring individual sacrifices for the good of the state as defined by the dictator. Will such a doctrine allow dictators to use people to further the personal needs of the dictator, such as putting political dissidents in mental hospitals as mentally ill? (Jeffery, Del Carmen, and White, 1985) This issue is discussed in Chapter 20.

The Future of Interdisciplinary Criminology

As we noted in Chapter 1, lawyers are not trained in psychiatry, biology, and sociology, whereas behavioral scientists are not trained in law or in other behavioral sciences. It has been suggested by a number of scholars, including Michael and Adler, Hall, Radzinowicz, and Mueller, that there is a need for an interdisciplinary institute for criminology and criminal law. This institute would have an interdisciplinary faculty, including mathematicians, geneticists, neurologists, psychiatrists, psychologists, sociologists, economists, urban planners, lawyers, and philosophers. Special institutes and seminars would be sponsored during the year for practicing lawyers and judges, as well as for behavioral scientists. Examples of some of the seminars that might be held include:

The Insanity Plea and Modern Biological Psychiatry
Alcoholism: Legal and Medical Aspects
Drug Addiction: Legal and Medical Aspects
Sociopathy: Legal and Medical Aspects
Drug Therapies, Mental Illness, and the Law
Premenstrual Syndrome: Legal and Medical Aspects
The Right to Treatment: Legal and Medical Issues

The Role of Diet and Nutrition in Antisocial Behavior
The Use of Environmental Design to Prevent Criminal Behavior

In these seminars lawyers would become familiar with CAT scans and PETT scans and the role of the biochemistry of the brain in alcoholism, drug addiction, and violent behaviors. The behavioral and medical scientists would become aware of legal doctrines concerning mens reas, guilt, insanity, retributive justice, and punishment. The impact of prisons on behavior and recidivism rates, as well as the effectiveness of police programs and diversionary programs, would be reviewed. An institute for criminology and criminal law could become a clearinghouse for new ideas and for the testing and distribution of ideas that hold promise of success.

The Future Legal Education of Lawyers

Lawyers are in charge of the criminal justice system. They are also heavily represented as state legislators, members of Congress, governors, attorneys general, and as members of crime commissions and advisory boards. Lawyers make important decisions that affect our social, political, and economic life. Lawyers decide issues concerning the right to life, the right to die, genetic engineering, the creation of new life forms, punishment, imprisonment, executions, what a crime is, what insanity is, and what the causes and cures of human social problems are.

Lawyers and judges are not trained to deal with such issues. Lawyers are not accountable to anyone but other lawyers. If I have a dispute with my government or my neighbor, I have to go to a lawyer since I am not allowed to settle the case myself. If I do not accept the decision given to me by lawyers, I must go to other lawyers who will make other decisions. I can appeal the case until it reaches the U.S. Supreme Court, in which case eight men and a woman will hand down the final decision. This then becomes the law of the land regardless of how stupid or invalid it may be.

If I manufacture bridges, I must build good bridges or they will collapse, and my reputation, as well as my profits, will be lost. If I am a football player, I must know how to play football or my teammates will not regard me as one who should be allowed to play football. If I run a business, I must do so in such a way that it is a success, for otherwise the business is no longer in existence.

Jacobs (1978:11) observed that "all persons with substantial authority in the courts come from the legal profession, and almost all decisions are made in the presence of lawyers or by them." He notes that "lawyers come from one tradition and one type of training, and lawyers assume that the presumptions of the legal culture are legitimate and appropriate."

If the Supreme Court says that punishment is the goal of the criminal justice system, or that executions are legal, how does one challenge the Court's decision? Behavioral scientists publish studies showing a lack of deterrence or a minimal amount of deterrence from just retribution and punishment and executions, yet our governors continue to execute prisoners and our state legislators continue to spend millions of dollars to build new prisons and to support the present criminal justice system. New therapies are developed by chemists and neurologists, yet these new scientific ideas are not used in the treatment and rehabilitation of criminals. We must develop a crime prevention program to supplement (and perhaps replace) the modern criminal justice system (Chapters 19 and 21).

Today, because of its narrowness and vocationalism, law school education has been under attack. Derek Bok, the former dean of the Harvard Law School and now the president of Harvard University, stated in 1983 (*Chronicles of Higher Education*, 1983) in his annual report to the trustees of the university that "we have the most expensive legal system in the world, and yet we cannot manage to protect the rights of most of our citizens." Bok notes that Japan has a total of 15,000 lawyers, whereas the United States turns out 30,000 new lawyers a year. Many bright students end up in law school, where they add little to the economy, culture, or human spirit. Bok states that law schools do little research, and he quotes a law professor who quipped: "All research corrupts, and empirical research corrupts absolutely."

Former Chief Justice Warren Burger (1980) stated that 50 percent of the lawyers are incompetent and that law schools are producing "hired guns and legal mechanics" rather than men and women trained in the ethical and social issues of the day.

The Brandeis Brief

The "Brandeis brief" is named after Louis D. Brandeis, who before his appointment to the U.S. Supreme Court included in his briefs references to social science materials. An Oregon case, Mueller v. Oregon, 208 U.S. 412 (1908), involved a state law limiting the number of hours that women could work on a job. The statute came before the U.S. Supreme Court on constitutional grounds involving the right of an employer (Mueller) to contract for the labor of women without interference from the state of Oregon. Brandeis served as counsel for the state of Oregon, and he prepared a detailed brief that used social science materials and statistics to show the impact of long working hours on the health and welfare of females. The Supreme Court upheld the right of the state of Oregon to pass special legislation to protect females. Here the issue is one of the welfare of females versus the interests of business owners (Monahan and Walker, 1985:5 ff.).

Another famous case involving the use of social science materials occurred in Brown v. Board of Education, 347 U.S. 483 (1954). This case involved the segregation of black children in classrooms in Topeka, Kansas. In an earlier decision, *Plessy* v. *Ferguson*, the Supreme Court held that facilities could be "separate but equal." In the *Brown* case the plantiffs introduced psychological evidence from the work of Kenneth Clark, a black psychologist, to show the harmful effects that segregated education had on the lives of young black children. The scientific basis for the conclusions drawn by Clark concerning the impact of education on behavior has been widely debated in the social sciences since the 1954 decision (Monahan and Walker, 1985:85 ff.). The court decision did not resolve the issues surrounding how a legal decision is implemented, and the attempt to desegregate public schools has created major social, political, economic, and educational problems. The knowledge needed to implement educational reforms is not available. We could have a court order today stating that all children must receive a high-quality education, but that would not mean that this would be achieved. As we shall see in a later chapter, a District of Columbia court ordered an alcoholic to be reformed, but the court did not say how this was to be achieved. The gap between legal rhetoric and implementation is so broad that we cannot conclude that just because a law is on the books, the law is a behavioral reality. This gap between the law on the book and the law as it really operates is what has been referred to as legal realism.

An effort must be made to integrate criminal law and social science materials. For example, a brief could be filed on behalf of a defendant in a rape or murder case showing the impact of biochemical and neurological disorders on his/her criminal behavior. Brain injuries, epileptic episodes, the premenstrual syndrome, the posttraumatic stress syndrome, and other brain disorders could be and have been introduced into criminal trials, as we shall see in Chapter 20.

Whenever major legislation is pending in Congress or state legislatures, such as spending millions of dollars to build new prisons versus spending millions of dollars on prevention and rehabilitation, or increasing the penalties for crimes, or reducing the use of parole and probation, a panel of experts from several disciples could be assembled to evaluate the consequences of the legal action and to make recommendations about the proposed action and the need for future research. Follow-up evaluations would also be made after the program is implemented.

SUMMARY

The conflict between classical legal philosophy and positivistic scientific criminology is reviewed in this chapter in terms of legal versus social definitions. Legal definitions are rejected by sociologists, who use social definitions.

The attempts of some legal scholars—Radzinowicz, Michael and Adler, Kittrie, and Wootton—to integrate law and social science issues are reviewed. The need for an interdisciplinary approach to criminology and criminal law is emphasized, with a strong plea for changes in legal education in the direction of interdisciplinary cooperation with behavioral sciences.

FURTHER STUDIES

Courses in the sociology of law and jurisprudence are offered in sociology departments, philosophy departments, and law schools.

REFERENCES

BURGER, W. E. (1980). "The Role of the Law School in Teaching of Legal Ethics and Professional Responsibility." *Cleveland State Law Review*, 29:377–395.

The Chronicles of Higher Education (1933). "Harvard's Bok Urges Changing Expensive, Inefficient Legal System: Seeks Law Curriculum Reforms." May 4.

FERRI, E. (1917). *Criminal Sociology*. Boston: Little, Brown.

GEIS, G. (1959). "Sociology, Criminology, and Criminal Law. *Social Problems* 7(1):40–47, Summer.

HALL, J. (1945). "Criminology." In *Twentieth Century Sociology,* ed. G. Gurvitch and W. E. Moore. New York: Philosophical Library.

HART, H. M. L. (1968). *Punishment and Responsibility*. New York: Oxford University Press.

HOOD, R. (1974). *Crime, Criminology, and Public Policy*. New York: Free Press.

JACOBS, H. (1978). *Justice in America*. Boston: Little, Brown.

JEFFERY, C. R. (1956). "The Structure of American Criminological Thinking." *Journal of Criminal Law, Criminology, and Police Science,* Vol. 45:5, pp. 658–672.

JEFFERY, C. R. (1970). "The Historical Development of Criminology." In *Pioneers in Criminology,* ed. H. Mannheim. Montclair, N.J.: Patterson Smith.

JEFFERY, C. R., R. V. DELCARMEN, and J.D. WHITE (1985). *Attacks on the Insanity Defense: Biological Psychiatry and New Perspectives on Criminal Behavior*. Springfield, Ill.: Charles C Thomas.

KITTRIE, N. (1971). *The Right to Be Different*. Baltimore: Johns Hopkins University Press.

LLEWELLYN, K. N. (1949). "Law and the Social Sciences: Especially Sociology." *American Sociological Review,* 14(4):451–462, April.

LOPEZ-REY, M. (1961). "Some Misconceptions in Contemporary Sociology." In *Essays in Criminal Science*, ed. G. O. W. Mueller. Littleton, Colo.: Fred B. Rothman & Co.

MANNHEIM, H. ed. (1970). *Pioneers in Criminology*. Montclair, N.J.: Patterson Smith.

MATZA, D. (1964). *Delinquency and Drift*. New York: Wiley.

MENNINGER, K. (1938). *Man against Himself*. New York: Harcourt, Brace.

MENNINGER, K. (1942). *Love against Hate*. New York: Harcourt, Brace.

MENNINGER, K. (1945). *The Human Mind*. New York: Alfred A. Knopf.

MENNINGER, K. (1968). *The Crime of Punishment*. New York: Viking.

MENNINGER, K. (1972). *A Guide to Psychiatric Books*. New York: Grune & Stratton.

MICHAEL, J., and M. ADLER (1933). *Crime, Law and Social Science*. New York: Harcourt, Brace.

MILLAR, R. W. (1970). "John Henry Wigmore." In *Pioneers in Criminology*, ed. H. Mannheim. Montclair, N. J.: Patterson Smith.

MONAHAN, J., and L. WALKER (1985). *Social Science in Law*. Mineola, N.Y.: Foundation Press.

MUELLER, G. O. W. (1968). *Crime, Law and the Scholars*. Seattle: University of Washington Press.

POUND, R. (1945). "Sociology of Law." In *Twentieth Century Sociology*, ed. G. Gurvitch and W. E. Moore. New York: Philosophical Library.

RADZINOWICZ, L. (1948–1956). *A History of English Criminal Law and Its Administration from 1750*. London: Stevens & Sons.

RADZINOWICZ, L. (1962). *In Search of Criminology*. Cambridge, Mass.: Harvard University Press.

RADZINOWICZ, L. (1965). *The Need for Criminology*. London: Heinemann.

RADZINOWICZ, L. (1966). *Ideology and Crime*. New York: Columbia University Press.

SELLIN, T. (1938). *Culture Conflict and Crime.*. New York: Social Science Research Council.

SUTHERLAND, E. H. (1956). ''The Michael–Adler Report.'' In *The Sutherland Papers*, ed. A. K. Cohen, A. Lindesmith, and K. Schuessler. Bloomington: Indiana University Press.

SUTHERLAND, E. H., and D. R. CRESSEY (1970). *Criminology*, 8th ed. Philadelphia: J. B. Lippincott.

TAPPAN, P. W. (1947). ''Who Is the Criminal.'' *American Sociological Review*, 95–96, February.

VOLD, G. (1958). *Theoretical Criminology*. New York: Oxford University Press.

WOOTTON, B. (1959). *Social Science and Social Pathology*. New York: Macmillan.

WOOTTON, B. (1963). *Crime and the Criminal Law*. London: Stevens & Sons.

QUESTIONS

1. What are the major controversies involved in legalistic versus scientific approaches to crime and criminal behavior?

2. What is the significance of the Michael and Adler treatise on crime, law, and social science?

3. What objections do lawyers have to sociological definitions of crime and criminal behavior?

4. What position did Barbara Wootton take on the purpose and structure of criminal law? What major changes would be made in criminal law if we followed her advise?

5. How did Karl Menninger appraise the criminal justice system? What changes would be made in the criminal justice system if we were to follow his recommendations?

6. How did Nicholas Kittrie resolve the conflict between scientific and legalistic criminology?

7. What changes have to be made in law schools and legal education if criminal law is to meet the challenges of modern behavioral sciences?

The Criminal Justice System: Law Enforcement and the Courts **8**

INTRODUCTION

As we stated in Chapter 1, this book is concerned with criminology, not with criminal justice per se. I have argued that there are good textbooks in criminal justice, and there is a need to recognize the separation of criminology and criminal justice. There is also a need to recognize the need to integrate criminology and criminal justice. Inciardi (1987:v) states that "criminal justice refers to the structure, functions, and decision processes of agencies that deal with the management and control of crime and criminal offenders—the police, courts, and corrections departments. It is often confused with the academic disciplines of criminology and police science."

Other textbooks discuss criminal justice in great detail, and there are also courses on law enforcement, courts, and corrections separate from criminology and criminal justice. Most universities support criminal justice programs with only slight attention paid to criminology (see Chapter 1). Even at Florida State University, which has the only program called "criminology," a major part of the program at the undergraduate level is criminal justice courses and educating people who will be police officers or correctional officers. In academic language the university educates rather than trains, and the better the academic program, the more education there is.

The purpose of this chapter is to relate the criminal justice system to some basic issues raised in contemporary criminology, such as the nature of human nature, the nature of society, the purpose of criminal law, the effectiveness of punishment and deterrence, and the effectiveness of the police–courts–corrections system as a crime control model. There are certain basic issues and assumptions concerning human behavior that run throughout discussions of criminal justice systems which must be highlighted if we are to understand these systems. The argument presented in this book and in this chapter is that criminal justice systems are hundreds of years old and are sorely-outdated models for the control of human behavior. If we are to establish a successful crime control model, we must integrate modern behavioral science within the criminal justice system.

THE CRIMINAL JUSTICE MODEL

The criminal justice system is part of the political state and criminal law (Chapters 3 and 4), which in turn are based on power, coercion, and force. The criminal justice system is therefore concerned with the use of and the limits placed on the use of punishment and force by the state as a means of social control (Chapter 15). Force, coercion, and punishment as found in the criminal law have been justified in terms of retribution, incapacitation, and deterrence (Inciardi, 1987:449 ff.; Mueller, 1966:58 ff.). Mueller classified retribution, vindication, and penitence as the nonutilitarian aspects of punishment. I regard all three as coming under the general concept of retribution. Mueller classified under the utilitarian approaches to punishment incapacitation (neutralization), rehabilitation (resocialization), and deterrence. I treat rehabilitation (and the prevention of crime) as a nonpunitive and noncriminal justice idea originating within the scientific-positivistic school of criminology (Chapter 5) and in direct competition with retribution and deterrence as philosophical and theoretical orientations for crime control models. I devote several chapters (Chapters 19 and 21) to crime prevention and rehabilitation. As was mentioned in Chapter 1, this book differs from other textbooks in criminology and criminal justice in rejecting retribution and deterrence in favor of prevention and treatment, and it argues in favor of a medical as opposed to a legal model of crime control. In this chapter I focus on retribution, incapacitation, and deterrence as traditional theoretical underpinnings for the criminal justice system.

Retribution and Revenge

Retribution is the oldest and original justification of punishment (Chapter 4). Retribution is backward looking and nonutilitarian. It does not consider the future consequences of the acts of vengeance and revenge. The crime rate can go up, but this does not refute the retributive model of criminal justice. Mueller (1966:66) has written that theories of retribution are archaic and irrational. In recent years (1970–1980 era) there has been a return to the just retribution model and to increased use of executions and prisons to control human behavior.

Deterrence

The theory of deterrence is fundamental to the classical school that developed from the works Bentham, Beccaria, Paley, and Romilly (Chapter 4). According to the classical model, the justification for punishment and the criminal law is deterrence, that is, a reduction to the crime rate in the future because pain is applied to criminal behavior. This is a hedonistic pain and pleasure model of behavior which states that the pleasure from crime must be exceeded by the pain from punishment, but the pain must not be an excess of the amount that will deter future criminal behavior. The punishment must fit the crime. Great care is taken to see that the punishment is applied only after a lengthy legal process of investigation, arrest, search and seizure, trial, conviction, and sentencing. Emphasis is placed on the legal process by which punishment is applied. A person has his or her day in court before being hanged.

Deterrence is both general and specific. General deterrence refers to the deterrence of noncriminals from future criminal activity through the punishment of known criminals; specific deterrence refers to the deterrence of criminals from future criminal activity through the punishment of these persons for their past criminal activities (Zimring and Hawkins, 1973; Andenaes, 1974). It should be noted that general deterrence depends on imitative learning, whereas specific deterrence depends on associational learning, that is, the association of a painful stimulus with a given behavioral pattern (Chapter 13).

The deterrence model of crime control is a utilitarian concept of the protection of society and the future benefits to be gained from punishment. It is also a rational-person model; that is, people can select those behaviors that maximize pleasure and minimize pain. There is no room here for emotional or irrational behaviors or mistakes in judgment. The models of behavior presented by Freud and by modern neurological evidence concerning the emotional and violent centers of the brain do not support a rational-person model of human behavior.

The ultimate justification for deterrence is that the crime rate is reduced and people no longer commit crimes. One of the major points made by the positive school is that punishment does not reduce the crime rate, and therefore punishment does not protect individuals or society. As John B. Waite, a law professor and member of the Model Penal Code Committee for the American Law Institute, observed:

> After Henry VIII had executed 16,000 male-factors and hung their bodies in chains for the world to see, still 16,000 more are said to have come undeterred down the paths of crime to his axe and gibbet. . . . When Bruno Richard Hauptmann had been executed following the Lindbergh kidnapping, the frequency of kidnappings increased. In 1950, Detroit judges, disgusted with the failure of monetary fines to check automobile traffic offenses, instituted a crack-down by way of jail sentences. At the end of six months, they had sent 2,000 drivers to jail—without any diminution in the number of violators brought before them. . . . But whatever the reason, the threat of punishment for crime committed is not an effective or satisfactory deterrent. (Waite, 1958:595–596)

Deterrence and the Economist

Cook (1980) outlines a rational-person model used by economists to analyze economic behavior. Each person, through rational calculations, seeks to maximize pleasure and minimize pain. This model is used by economists to interpret criminal behavior, that is, criminals behave rationally so as to gain pleasure. Criminal behavior can be deterred by the use of punishment. This is an extension of the Benthamite utilitarian doctrine of human behavior and deterrence theory. Cook (1986) uses economic theory to develop what he calls an ''opportunity model'' of crime, that is, the availability of targets and the interaction of criminals and potential victims over time and space. Opportunity theory is another name for crime prevention and environmental design, and I discuss crime prevention in detail in Chapter 19.

In a 1968 article, Becker, a prominent economist, stated that crime could be analyzed in economic terms as a means of gaining economic utility (pleasure) from activity. Becker (1976) noted that maximization of pleasure is a basic assumption of the economic model of crime. A student of Becker, Isaac Ehrlich (1975), developed an economic model to show that capital punishment reduced the murder rate. Ehrlich's work will be discussed below in relation to the death penalty.

Several economists have put forth economic models of deterrence based on a rational pleasure/pain model of human behavior (Votey and Phillips, 1974; Phillips and Votey, 1981; Adreano and Siegfried, 1980: Witte, 1980; Rottenberg, 1973). In a report on rehabilitation (Martin, Sechrest, and Redner, 1981:53–56), the National Academy of Sciences reviewed the economic model and concluded that it might make more sense to design treatment programs and improve job training and job opportunities rather than to use more punishment to deter crime. As we note in Chapter 13, alternative responses for a reward can be utilized to alter behavior by rewarding legal behavior rather than punishing illegal behavior.

Incapacitation

Incapacitation is the removal of the criminal from the community. As long as the criminal is not in the community, he/she is not committing crimes against the community, although he/she may be committing crimes against other inmates while in prison. Since 95 percent of all inmates are ultimately released from prison, incapacitation is not a deterrent for crime but is, at best, a delay for crime.

The National Advisory Commission on Criminal Justice Standard and Goals concluded that the protection offered by incapacitation is only temporary and does not provide for reintegration of the offender into the community upon his/her release (Inciardi, 1987:451). Inciardi notes that incapacitation works only on a death or life sentence, and this is not feasible for most crimes. Also, it requires millions of dollars worth of prisons to implement.

In a review of incapacitation, Cohen (1983) states that collective incapacitation (increased prison terms for all persons sentenced to prison) would have a low impact of 10 to 20 percent on the crime rate and a high impact on the number of prisoners in prison, which would increase four- or five-fold. Selective incapacitation (increased sentences for a few people selected for special long-term prison sentences) has been studied by both the Rand Corporation and the Carnegie–Mellon Urban Systems Institute. The Rand Corporation model, which was developed by Greenwood and others, uses the traits of criminals, such as prior convictions and convictions before age 16, to classify persons as high risk and in need of selective incapacitation. It is estimated that with the use of this model, robberies would be reduced by 20 percent, along with a slight increase in prison populations. However, the Rand Corporation model presents ethical problems concerning the use of imprisonment for future unpredictable behavior, methodological problems, and a 55 percent false positive prediction problem (Cohen, 1983; Greenwood and Abrahamse, 1982; Greenwood, 1983).

In a follow-up study by the Rand Corporation, Klein and Caggiano (1986) found that the recidivism rate for inmates released from prison was high. Of the California inmates released, 76 percent were reincarcerated; of the Texas inmates released, 60 percent; and of the Michigan inmates released, 53 percent. As far as the prediction of future criminal activity is concerned, they found that the statistical scores used to predict recidivism were only 5 to 10 percent better than chance, or in other words, almost useless.

The Carnegie–Mellon model developed by Blumstein, Cohen, Chaiken, and others uses a criminal career model which attempts to identify career offenders with high crime rates for specific crimes and long, well-developed criminal careers. Robbery and burglary are the most suitable crimes for this model. A decision to incarcerate is based on arrest rates, offense, race, age, and prior arrest history.

As Cohen notes, incarceration does not prevent the first crime, since in order to be incarcerated at least one crime must have been committed. By focusing on the serious repeat offender, the model does highlight the need to deal with the 6 or 8 percent of the population who are the major problems, a point made more than once in this book (Cohen, 1983).

The Dangerous Offender Project at Ohio State University (Van Dine, Conrad, and Dinitz, 1979:111–116) found that the arrest rate for violent offenses was around 25 percent, and the conviction rate and incarceration rate were similarly low. Violent behavior could not be predicted. Violent crimes could not be prevented; and the false positive rate (those incarcerated who would not have committed a crime if on the streets) was 90 percent. A major conclusion from the study was that a flat time sentence of five years for all felonies would reduce the felony rate by 4.7 percent at the arrest level and by 2.1 percent at the conviction level. Such a policy would increase the prison population by 500 to 600 percent in order to gain the 4.7 percent reduction in felony arrests.

Incarcerating the career criminals rather than finding out through interdisciplinary research why such people exist in our society neither prevents future crimes nor identifies the major antisocial persons in our society before they commit crimes. In Chapter 21 I suggest that we focus our research efforts on a target population of career criminals and hard-core recidivists. The research of Wolfgang, Figlio, and Sellin (1972) on birth cohorts, and the work of Cohen, Blumstein, Greenwood and others, have real meaning only when tied into a crime prevention program. Concentrating the career criminals in our prisons will not answer the problem. Incapacitation is a temporary solution, not an answer.

THE JUST RETRIBUTION MODEL; 1970–1980

The End of the Rehabilitative Ideal

Frank Allen.   During the 1890–1968 era there was a weak attempt made at rehabilitation of offenders as suggested by the positive school (Chapter 5). One attempt was by psychiatrists (Chapter 12) and another was by sociologists and the war on poverty during the 1960s (Chapter 14).

The beginning of the end of what is known as "the rehabilitative ideal" came in several articles written by Francis Allen from 1956 to 1959. Allen, a professor of law at the University of Chicago Law School at that time, and later a professor of law at the University of Michigan, heralded the end of the rehabilitative ideal and socialized justice.

Allen (1964) noted that the positivistic idea of rehabilitation had some unforeseen and unintended consequences, that is, the juvenile court and probation and parole served as social service agencies rather than as criminal justice agencies. The substitution of social services for legal procedures resulted in the corruption and weakening of both types of agencies. Juveniles and probationers were not properly protected by the legal guarantees of a court trial and a lawyer, while at the same time, social services were not provided for juveniles as required by the treatment model. Terms such as "the quiet room" and "therapy" were used in place of solitary confinement and punishment.

Allen wrote about the basic conflict between justice and rehabilitation. He argued that justice requires specific sentences based on the crime or the act, and equality of sentences rather than discretion. Justice operates on a deterrence and retribution model. On the other hand, the rehabilitative ideal requires individualized justice, discretion in sentencing, and therapeutic intervention into people's lives as needed for treatment without regard for legal protections. Allen concluded that individualized justice is at odds with criminal law doctrines of liberty, freedom, and equality.

In a 1981 book, Allen (1981) discussed the decline of the rehabilitative ideal during the 1960–1970 era. He reviewed the emergence of the just retribution doctrine, the student protests, and the emergence of radical criminology. He noted that rehabilitation failed for three reasons: (1) rehabilitation is a threat to a free society; (2) rehabilitation can be used for evil and unintended ends; and (3) treatment methods are lacking in success.

Allen pointed to the dangerousness and intrusiveness of psychosurgery and drug therapies, and he supported the view put forth by Norval Morris that treatment should be limited and voluntary. Like the other just retributionists, Allen did not point out the intrusion into the personality of executions and imprisonment, nor did he address the issue raised by Kittrie in 1971 (Chapter 7) concerning the need for the state to assume a positive right to treatment for criminals in place of punishment.

At the end of his 1981 book, Allen showed some concern for prison over-crowding and prison brutality (a direct result of the just retribution model of the 1970s), but he concluded that in the future any rehabilitative efforts must be peripheral and not central to criminal justice (Allen, 1981:75). Allen thus disagreed with the point of view expressed by Wootton, Menninger, Kittrie, and myself.

In Kent v. United States, 86 S.Ct. 1045 (1966), Justice Abe Fortas stated that "there is evidence in fact that there may be grounds for concern that the child receives the worst of both worlds: that he gets neither the protections accorded to adults nor the solicitous care and regenerative treatment postulated for children" (Jeffery, 1967; Faust and Brantingham, 1979:277). The U.S. Supreme Court in *In re* Gault, 87 S.Ct. 1428 (1967), restored to the alleged juvenile offender most of the legal rights found in the Bill of Rights and started the movement toward a due process procedure for juveniles in place of the social work concept of a socialized juvenile court (Faust and Brantingham, 1979). The court held in the *Gault* case that the juvenile justice system neither protected the constitutional rights of juveniles nor did it afford them treatment as postulated for the juvenile court movement. In a dissenting opinion in the *Gault* case, Justice Potter Stewart noted that "in the nineteenth century there were no juvenile proceedings, and a child was tried in a conventional criminal trial. So it was that a 12-year-old boy named James Guild was tried in New Jersey for killing Catherine Beakes. A jury found him guilty of murder and he was sentenced to death by hanging. The sentence was executed. It was all very constitutional." This statement summarizes the problem of a legalistic due process model of criminal justice: we end up hanging 12-year-old children and hanging the mentally ill and hanging the brain damaged. These two important cases in juvenile court law came after the articles by Allen in the 1950s, and although there is no way to know whether or not the members of the Court read or were familiar with the Allen argument, it is obvious that rehabilitation was dead by 1970.

The view expressed in the late 1950s by Allen became the dominant theme for criminal justice in the 1970s under the banner of "the justice model" or "just retribution." The major figures in this movement were David Fogel, Norval Morris, James Q. Wilson, and Andrew von Hirsch.

The Martinson Report.   In 1975 (D. Lipton, R. Martinson, and J. Wilks) a report was published, referred to as the "Martinson Report" which surveyed correctional programs over a period of years. This report found that rehabilitative efforts had little or no effect on crime rates, and the general conclusion was that "nothing works." The Martinson Report was used by Morris, Wilson, and others as a basis for a rejection of rehabilitation during the 1970s.

David Fogel.   Fogel (1975) stated the case for the justice model in terms of fairness and making punishment fit the crime. The rehabilitative ideal had introduced too much discretion and inequality into the sentencing system. Discretion in sentencing must be replaced with a more deterministic sentencing policy. Therapies are the work of technological fascists, and research into the causes of behavior are futile. Rehabilitation is no longer the purpose of the criminal justice system; rather, justice is. There are to be no involuntary cures or therapies in our prisons.

Norval Morris.   Morris (1974) also started with the observation that rehabilitation has been a failure, citing the Martinson Report along with other studies that found that prisons do not rehabilitate (prisons are not supposed to rehabilitate). For Morris, punishment is based on retribution, which is the limiting principle of punishment, and on deterrence, which is the defining principle for punishment. Just retribution means that the sentence must fit the crime, not the criminal. Discretion is removed from the system. Release from prison cannot be based on successful rehabilitation or therapy, and participation in therapy may not be used as a qualification for release. Release is based on time served, not behavior. Inmates cannot be held for future dangerousness, and they must be released when the sentence set by the court expires, regardless of how dangerous they are. The prediction of future dangerousness is not allowed; the individual must kill before he or she can be apprehended. Morris outlined a new type of institution for Butner, North Carolina, which we discuss in Chapter 21.

James Q. Wilson.   Wilson (1975), a professor of political science at Harvard University, used a conservative deterrence argument when he noted that crimes are committed because the criminal gains more from the crime than he/she loses through punishment. He rejected sociological explanations of criminal behavior, and he based his argument on the Martinson report and the failure of rehabilitation. Wilson wanted a crime control model based on strict law enforcement and strict court processing of offenders. Mandatory prison sentences must be utilized, along with more prisons, more prosecutors, and more defense attorneys. Wilson ended the book with the statement: "Wicked people exist. Nothing avails except to set them apart from innocent people" (Wilson, 1975:209).

Wilson did not advocate more behavioral science research and/or better treatment methods. Rather, like Morris, he used the failure of rehabilitation in the past as a reason for returning to a police–courts–corrections model of justice. In a 1985 book with a psychologist (Wilson and Herrnstein, 1985) Wilson discussed the biological and psychological aspects of criminal behavior, but at the end of the book he rejected a treatment model while retaining a punishment model. The rejection of treatment for punishment because treatment has failed is like the medical profession returning to witchcraft because a new cure for cancer has failed. There are other alternatives to the control of human behavior besides punishment.

American Friends Service Committee. The liberal position for the justice model is found in the American Friends Service Committee (1971) report on *The Struggle for Justice.* According to this report, treatment is based on individualized justice, treatment makes great use of discretion, treatment forces people into therapeutic programs, and treatment is a failure. The committee wanted fairness and justice; that is, the criminal must be punished for the crime without any additional restraints from the state in the form of therapies. There are to be no coercive therapies. They stated: "Even if treatment were scientifically feasible, we would object to it on moral grounds" (American Friends Service Committee, 1971:146).

Andrew von Hirsch. Andrew von Hirsch (1976) also put forth a liberal argument for punishment when he argued that treatment is a failure, discretion in the criminal justice system is dangerous, and punishment must be based on just deserts. He wrote:

> The fundamental principle of desert in punishment is that the severity of the punishment should be commensurate with the seriousness of the offender's criminal conduct. The focus of the commensurate-deserts principle is on the gravity of past conduct,not on the likelihood of future behavior; this retrospective orientation distinguishes desert from crime control goals of deterrence, incapacitation, and rehabilitation. . . . The amount of punishment therefore ought to compare, as a matter of justice, with the degree of blameworthiness of the offender's criminal conduct. (von Hirsch, 1983:211)

Graeme Newman. In a recent book, Graeme Newman (1983) suggested that we return to corporal punishment in the form of electroshocks, especially for those property offenders who do not need a lengthy prison term. Corporal punishment can be administered quickly, it can fit the severity of the offense, and it is over with quickly.

Cullen and Gilbert: Reaffirming Rehabilitation

Cullen and Gilbert (1982) explored the impact of the justice model on the criminal justice system. They found the consequences to be longer prison sentences, more discretion in the hands of the police and prosecutors, and overcrowding and brutalization of the prison system. Without rehabilitative aims there is no room for humanitarianism within the system we call "justice."

Cullen and Gilbert call for a revival of the rehabilitative ideal in place of the retributive justice model.

The Federal Crime Control Program

In 1964, Senator Barry Goldwater, the Republican candidate for president, urged a conservative "law and order" campaign to stop crime in the streets in place of liberal social welfare programs. Johnson met the Republican challenge with a "War on Poverty," which had been started by J. F. Kennedy. A War on Poverty would create an opportunity model as discussed in the Cloward and Ohlin book (Chapter 14), and crime would be controlled. As part of his anticrime effort, Johnson appointed an advisory commission called the President's Commission on Law Enforcement and the Administration of Justice, under the chairmanship of N. Katzenbach, former attorney general of the United States. Of the 19 members on the commission, 15 were lawyers. There was not a single behavioral scientist on the commission. The commission published a monograph, *The Challenge of Crime in a Free Society* (1967b), and a series of task force reports (1967a).

The basic conclusions of the commission were: (1) we did not know enough about behavior to fight crime (President's Crime Commission, 1967a:8, *Task Force Report on Juvenile Delinquency and Youth Crime*); (2) we spend only a small fraction of 1 percent of the criminal justice budget on research (President's Crime Commission, 1967b:x, *The Challenge of Crime in a Free Society*); and (3) we must improve our urban schools, combat racial segregation, and create employment opportunities for minorities (President's Crime Commission, 1967b:vi, *The Challenge of Crime in a Free Society*). From the President's Commission report came legislation from Congress in the Safe Streets and Crime Control Act of 1967. By the time the Safe Streets Act reached Congress the United States was involved in an unpopular war in Vietnam, the United States was torn by student protests and racial violence, and a sense of social injustice was widespread. Johnson did not run for reelection because of the war in Vietnam and the failure of the poverty programs. By 1969 Nixon was president of the United States, and by 1975 the school of criminology at the University of California at Berkeley had been closed because of the conflict between radical criminology and conservative politics.

The Safe Street Act created the Law Enforcement Assistance Administration (LEAA) in 1969. This legislation was passed by a conservative Republican Congress, and it was unrecognizable in the form it took. It was no longer a liberal program (Cronin, Cronin, and Milakovitch, 1981). It became a policeman's program. The original theme of social justice, social welfare, racial desegregation, and an opportunity structure as found in the commission's reports was missing. In its place was a "law and order" program of stronger law enforcement, including overriding the *Miranda* warning and an extension of a wiretapping provision. The Goldwater/Nixon concept of crime control replaced the liberal philosophy of social intervention (White and Krislov, 1977; Cronin, Cronin, and Milakovitch, 1981; Feeley and Sarat, 1980).

LEAA was set up to spend millions of dollars on law enforcement through block grants to individual states, and the states in turn would create state planning agencies (SPAs) to administer the money. No theory or research was involved; suddenly, states found themselves with millions of dollars to fight crime with no new ideas as to how to do it. The same people who had failed to solve the crime problem as law enforcement officers or judges or prosecutors were now given the task of coming up with new solutions to the crime problem. As Feeley and Sarat (1980:92–93) observe: ''It is paradoxical that the role as envisioned for those agencies whose primary commitments over the years had been to law enforcement and presumably to the reduction of crime would be to plan and implement, with the assistance of federal revenues, new ideas which in the past they had resisted.'' Millions of dollars were spent on the criminal justice system, including educational funds for criminal justice training (see Chapter 1). The behavioral sciences were left aside. If 10 percent of the LEAA monies had been placed in several major research centers for basic behavioral science research, we would be well on our way to resolving the crime problem by 1989.

The state SPAs were controlled by state politicians, sheriffs, and other political types. Local criminal justice agencies gained control of the federal monies (Feeley and Sarat, 1980:94–97). In Florida, for example, I went to the SPA for money to do research on crime prevention through environmental design, and I was told that money was allocated to three desks—police, courts, and corrections. Crime prevention was not an idea they were prepared to entertain.

The official research arm of LEAA was the National Institute of Law Enforcement and Criminal Justice. What research the institute performed was poorly conceived and executed. White and Krislov (1977) found the research of the institute to be mediocre and with few examples of successes or usefulness. They did not find that the work of the Institute built a coherent body of knowledge which is necessary for successful research.

By 1972 Congress was reevaluating the performance of LEAA, and it soon became obvious that LEAA was a major shame and tragedy. LEAA was disbanded during the Carter administration, 1976–1980. At its height in 1975, LEAA had a budget in excess of $895 million. What a beautiful research facility and program $895 million would have built.

Before the end, LEAA shifted from a ''reduce crime'' goal to an ''improve the efficiency of the justice system'' role. The leadership of LEAA changed frequently, and it included Charles Rogovin, a prosecuting attorney; Richard Velde, the son of a congressman and an aide to Senator J. Hruska; Clarence Coster, a police chief; and Jerris Leonard, an attorney from the Department of Justice and a friend of Attorney General J. Mitchell. There was not one first-rate criminologist at LEAA (Cronin, Cronin, and Milakovitch, 1981:139–145).

THE CRIMINAL JUSTICE SYSTEM

Measuring Crime and Crime Statistics

The criminal justice system is most ineffective in identifying, prosecuting, punishing, deterring, or reforming criminals. If we had a radar defense system or an emergency medical system that operated at the level found in the criminal justice system, we would not be alive for very long. Yet we continue to support the criminal justice system in its present form. One should conclude from this that we do not really want to do away with or control crime. The criminal justice system is reactive and not proactive; that is, it waits for the crime to occur before reacting, and it does not try to prevent crimes before they occur (Chapter 19).

The *Uniform Crime Report* (Federal Bureau of Investigation, 1986) consists of a compilation of crime reports filed by local police agencies throughout the nation, and it covers, among other things, eight Part I offenses: murder and nonnegligent manslaughter, forcible rape, robbery, aggravated assault, burglary, larceny-theft, motor vehicle theft, and arson. These are crimes known to the police, and usually from reports filed by a victim with the police. The UCR reflects the "official crime rate," that is, those crimes recorded by an official criminal justice agency. *Uniform Crime Report* data are shown in Figures 8–1 and 8–2, and Tables 8–1 to 8–4.

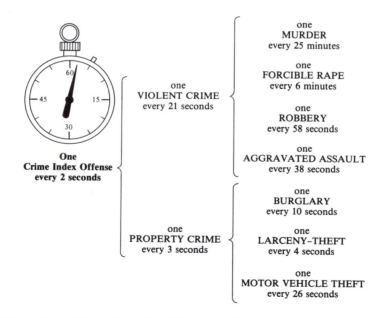

Figure 8–1 Crime Clock for 1986. From *Uniform Crime Reports*, Federal Bureau of Investigation, Washington, D.C., 1986.

TABLE 8-1 INDEX OF CRIME, UNITED STATES, 1978-1987[a,b]

Population[c]	Crime Index total[d]	Violent crime[e]	Property crime[e]	Murder and nonnegligent manslaughter	Forcible rape	Robbery	Aggravated assault	Burglary	Larceny-theft	Motor vehicle theft
Number of offenses:										
1978—218,059,000	11,209,000	1,085,550	10,123,400	19,560	67,610	426,930	571,460	3,128,300	5,991,000	1,004,100
1979—220,099,000	12,249,500	1,208,030	11,041,500	21,460	76,390	480,700	629,480	3,327,700	6,601,000	1,112,800
1980—225,349,264	13,408,300	1,344,520	12,063,700	23,040	82,990	565,840	672,650	3,795,200	7,136,900	1,131,700
1981—229,146,000	13,423,800	1,361,820	12,061,900	22,520	82,500	592,910	663,900	3,779,700	7,194,400	1,087,800
1982—231,534,000	12,974,400	1,322,390	11,652,000	21,010	78,770	553,130	669,480	3,447,100	7,142,500	1,062,400
1983—233,981,000	12,108,600	1,258,090	10,850,500	19,310	78,920	506,570	653,290	3,129,900	6,712,800	1,007,900
1984—236,158,000	11,881,800	1,273,280	10,608,500	18,690	84,230	485,010	685,350	2,984,400	6,591,900	1,032,200
1985—238,740,000	12,431,400	1,328,800	11,102,600	18,980	88,670	497,870	723,250	3,073,300	6,926,400	1,102,900
1986—241,077,000	13,211,900	1,489,170	11,722,700	20,610	91,460	542,780	834,320	3,241,400	7,257,200	1,224,100
1987—243,400,000	13,508,700	1,484,000	12,024,700	20,100	91,110	517,700	855,090	3,236,200	7,499,900	1,288,700
Percent change; number of offenses:										
1987/1986	+2.2	-.3	+2.6	-2.5	-.4	-4.6	+2.5	-.2	+3.3	+5.3
1987/1983	+11.6	+18.0	+10.8	+4.1	+15.4	+2.2	+30.9	+3.4	+11.7	+27.9
1987/1978	+20.5	+36.7	+18.8	+2.8	+34.8	+21.3	+49.6	+3.4	+25.2	+28.3

Rate per 100,000
inhabitants:

Year										
1978	5,140.3	497.8	4,642.5	9.0	31.0	195.8	262.1	1,434.6	2,747.4	460.5
1979	5,565.5	548.9	5,016.6	9.7	34.7	218.4	286.0	1,511.9	2,999.1	505.6
1980	5,950.0	596.6	5,353.3	10.2	36.8	251.1	298.5	1,684.1	3,167.0	502.2
1981	5,858.2	594.3	5,263.9	9.8	36.0	258.7	289.7	1,649.5	3,139.7	474.7
1982	5,603.6	571.1	5,032.5	9.1	34.0	238.9	289.2	1,488.8	3,084.8	458.8
1983	5,175.0	537.7	4,637.4	8.3	33.7	216.5	279.2	1,337.7	2,868.9	430.8
1984	5,031.3	539.2	4,492.1	7.9	35.7	205.4	290.2	1,263.7	2,791.3	437.1
1985	5,207.1	556.6	4,650.5	7.9	37.1	208.5	302.9	1,287.3	2,901.2	462.0
1986	5,480.4	617.7	4,862.6	8.6	37.9	225.1	346.1	1,344.6	3,010.3	507.8
1987	5,550.0	609.7	4,940.3	8.3	37.4	212.7	351.3	1,329.6	3,081.3	529.4
Percent change; rate per 100,000 inhabitants:										
1987/1986	+1.4	−1.3	+1.6	−3.5	−1.3	−5.5	+1.5	−1.1	+2.4	+4.3
1987/1983	+7.3	+13.4	+6.5		+11.0	−1.8	+25.8	−.6	+7.4	+22.9
1987/1978	+8.1	+22.5	+6.4	−7.8	+20.6	+8.6	+34.0	−7.3	+12.2	+15.0

[a]Although arson data are included in the trend and clearance tables, sufficient data are not available to estimate totals for this offense.

[b]All rates were calculated on the offenses before rounding.

[c]Populations are Bureau of the Census provisional estimates as of July 1, except April 1, 1980, preliminary census counts, and are subject to change.

[d]Because of rounding, the offenses may not add to totals.

[e]Violent crimes are offenses of murder, forcible rape, robbery, and aggravated assault. Property crimes are offenses of burglary, larceny-theft, and motor vehicle theft. Data are not included for the property crime of arson.

Source: Federal Bureau of Investigation, Uniform Crime Reports, 1987.

TABLE 8-2. INDEX OF CRIME, UNITED STATES, 1987[a]

Area	Population[b]	Crime Index total	Violent crime[c]	Property crime[c]	Murder and nonnegligent manslaughter	Forcible rape	Robbery	Aggravated assault	Burglary	Larceny-theft	Motor vehicle theft
United States Total	243,400,000	13,508,708	1,483,999	12,024,709	20,096	91,111	517,704	855,088	3,236,184	7,499,851	1,288,674
Rate per 100,000 inhabitants		5,550.0	609.7	4,940.3	8.3	37.4	212.7	351.3	1,329.6	3,081.3	529.4
Metropolitan Statistical Area	186,637,562										
Area actually reporting[d]	98.1%	11,613,326	1,333,808	10,279,518	17,028	78,454	499,116	739,210	2,738,932	6,346,964	1,193,622
Estimated totals	100.0%	11,747,875	1,343,765	10,404,110	17,132	79,264	501,347	746,022	2,771,222	6,427,814	1,205,074
Rate per 100,000 inhabitants		6,294.5	720.0	5,574.5	9.2	42.5	268.6	399.7	1,484.8	3,444.0	645.7
Other Cities	22,752,410										
Area actually reporting[d]	93.3%	1,039,689	74,045	965,644	960	5,161	10,499	57,425	220,550	702,052	43,042
Estimated totals	100.0%	1,114,517	79,814	1,034,703	1,032	5,541	11,357	61,884	237,082	751,440	46,181
Rate per 100,000 inhabitants		4,898.5	350.8	4,547.7	4.5	24.4	49.9	272.0	1,042.0	3,302.7	203.0
Rural Counties	34,009,028										
Area actually reporting[d]	89.3%	592,456	54,930	537,526	1,720	5,846	4,572	42,792	208,390	294,997	34,139
Estimated totals	100.0%	646,316	60,420	585,896	1,932	6,306	5,000	47,182	227,880	320,597	37,419
Rates per 100,000 inhabitants		1,900.4	177.7	1,722.8	5.7	18.5	14.7	138.7	670.1	942.7	110.0

[a]Although arson data are included in the trend and clearance tables, sufficient data are not available to estimate totals for this offense.

[b]Populations are Bureau of the Census provisional estimates as of July 1, 1987, and are subject to change.

[c]Violent crimes are offenses of murder, forcible rape, robbery, and aggravated assault. Property crimes are offenses of burglary, larceny-theft, and motor vehicle theft. Data are not included for the property crime of arson.

[d]The percentage representing area actually reporting will not coincide with the ratio between reported and estimated crime totals, since these data represent the sum of the calculations for individual states which have varying populations, portions reporting, and crime rates.

Source: Federal Bureau of Investigation, *Uniform Crime Reports*, 1987.

TABLE 8-3. INDEX OF CRIME, REGIONAL OFFENSE AND POPULATION DISTRIBUTION, 1987[a]

Region	Population	Crime Index total	Violent crime[b]	Property crime[b]	Murder and non-negligent manslaughter	Forcible rape	Robbery	Aggravated assault	Burglary	Larceny-theft	Motor vehicle theft
United States Total[c]	100.0	100.0	100.0	100.0	100.0	100.0	100.0	100.0	100.0	100.0	100.0
Northeastern States	20.7	18.0	21.5	17.6	17.2	16.2	27.6	18.6	16.0	17.1	24.5
Midwestern States	24.5	21.6	20.2	21.8	19.8	24.3	19.9	20.0	20.0	22.9	19.7
Southern States	34.5	36.6	34.3	36.9	41.9	36.2	31.1	35.9	40.6	36.2	31.4
Western States	20.4	23.8	23.9	23.7	21.1	23.4	21.4	25.6	23.4	23.8	24.4

[a]Although arson data are included in the trend and clearance tables, sufficient data are not available to estimate totals for this offense.

[b]Violent crimes are offenses of murder, forcible rape, robbery, and aggravated assault. Property crimes are offenses of burglary, larceny-theft, and motor vehicle theft. Data are not included for the property crime of arson.

[c]Because of rounding, percentages may not add to totals.

Source: Federal Bureau of Investigation, *Uniform Crime Reports*, 1987.

TABLE 8-4. ARRESTS, NUMBER AND RATE[a], BY REGION, 1986

Offense charged	United States total (10,743 agencies; population 198,488,000)	Northeastern states (2,157 agencies; population 39,918,000)	Midwestern states (2,618 agencies; population 43,754,000)	Southern states (4,272 agencies; population 69,890,000)	Western states (1,696 agencies; population 44,924,000)
Total	10,384,722	2,156,363	1,828,805	3,713,752	2,685,802
Rate	5,231.9	5,402.0	4,179.7	5,313.7	5,978.5
Murder and nonnegligent manslaughter	16,066	2,499	2,845	6,595	4,127
Rate	8.1	6.3	6.5	9.4	9.2
Forcible rape	31,128	6,137	6,540	11,392	7,059
Rate	15.7	15.4	14.9	16.3	15.7
Robbery	124,245	41,913	15,111	36,117	31,104
Rate	62.6	105.0	34.5	51.7	69.2
Aggravated assault	293,952	61,495	40,770	105,744	85,943
Rate	148.1	154.1	93.2	151.3	191.3
Burglary	375,544	60,304	56,725	144,441	114,074
Rate	189.2	151.1	129.6	206.7	253.9
Larceny-theft	1,182,099	190,990	246,531	412,848	331,730
Rate	595.6	478.5	563.4	590.7	738.4
Motor vehicle theft	128,514	21,864	19,010	41,962	45,678
Rate	64.7	54.8	43.4	60.0	101.7
Arson	15,523	3,187	3,377	4,993	3,966
Rate	7.8	8.0	7.7	7.1	8.8
Violent crime[b]	465,391	112,044	65,266	159,848	128,233
Rate	234.5	280.7	149.2	228.7	285.4
Property crime[c]	1,701,680	276,345	325,643	604,244	495,448
Rate	857.3	692.3	744.3	864.6	1,102.8
Crime Index total[d]	2,167,071	388,389	390,909	764,092	623,681
Rate	1,091.8	973.0	893.4	1,093.3	1,388.3
Other assaults	593,902	100,663	110,245	227,212	155,782
Rate	299.2	252.2	252.0	325.1	346.8

Forgery and counterfeiting	76,546	10,086	12,329	34,751	19,380
Rate	38.6	25.3	28.2	49.7	43.1
Fraud	284,790	51,672	32,603	178,247	22,268
Rate	143.5	129.4	74.5	255.0	49.6
Embezzlement	10,500	805	991	6,021	2,683
Rate	5.3	2.0	2.3	8.6	6.0
Stolen property; buying, receiving, possessing	114,105	30,097	21,720	27,482	34,806
Rate	57.5	75.4	49.6	39.3	77.5
Vandalism	223,231	62,751	55,372	54,405	50,703
Rate	112.5	157.2	126.6	77.8	112.9
Weapons; carrying, possessing, etc.	160,204	23,900	30,369	65,104	40,831
Rate	80.7	59.9	69.4	93.2	90.9
Prostitution and commercialized vice	96,882	28,471	11,851	23,126	33,434
Rate	48.8	71.3	27.1	33.1	74.4
Sex offenses (except forcible rape and prostitution)	83,934	12,989	15,445	24,837	30,663
Rate	42.3	32.5	35.3	35.5	68.3
Drug abuse violations	691,882	166,809	68,888	220,901	235,284
Rate	348.6	417.9	157.4	316.1	523.7
Gambling	25,839	10,712	3,383	8,674	3,070
Rate	13.0	26.8	7.7	12.4	6.8
Offenses against family and children	47,327	8,316	10,759	23,934	4,318
Rate	23.8	20.8	24.6	34.2	9.6
Driving under the influence	1,458,531	163,104	283,425	503,202	508,800
Rate	734.8	408.6	647.8	720.0	1,132.6
Liquor laws	490,436	98,907	138,534	110,112	142,883
Rate	247.1	247.8	316.6	157.5	318.1
Drunkenness	777,866	36,180	60,493	479,522	201,671
Rate	391.9	90.6	138.3	686.1	448.9
Disorderly conduct	564,882	219,170	128,548	152,685	64,479
Rate	284.6	549.0	293.8	218.5	143.5

TABLE 8-4 CONTINUED

Offense charged	United States total (10,743 agencies; population 198,488,000)	Northeastern states (2,157 agencies; population 39,918,000)	Midwestern states (2,618 agencies; population 43,754,000)	Southern states (4,272 agencies; population 69,890,000)	Western states (1,696 agencies; population 44,924,000)
Vagrancy	32,992	8,180	2,612	1,661	20,539
Rate	16.6	20.5	6.0	2.4	45.7
All other offenses (except traffic)	2,272,589	696,150	392,930	748,068	435,441
Rate	1,145.0	1,743.9	898.0	1,070.3	969.3
Suspicion (not included in totals)	7,455	1,567	2,386	3,174	328
Rate	3.8	3.9	5.5	4.5	.7
Curfew and loitering law violations	72,627	20,245	20,883	9,122	22,377
Rate	36.6	50.7	47.7	13.1	49.8
Runaways	138,586	18,767	36,516	50,594	32,709
Rate	69.8	47.0	83.5	72.4	72.8

[a]Rate: Number of arrests per 100,000 inhabitants.

[b]Violent crimes are offenses of murder, forcible rape, robbery, and aggravated assault.

[c]Property crimes are offenses of burglary, larceny-theft, motor vehicle theft, and arson.

[d]Includes arson.

Source: Federal Bureau of Investigation, *Uniform Crime Reports*, 1986.

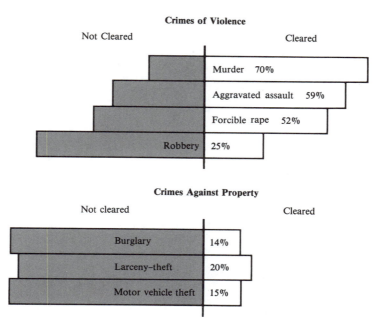

Figure 8-2 Crimes Cleared by Arrest in 1986. From *Uniform Crime Reports*, Federal Bureau of Investigation, Washington, D.C., 1986.

The official crime rate does not reflect the true crime rate for several reasons. For one, people may not know that a crime was committed; they may not report a crime out of fear or embarrassment. Rape is underreported for these reasons. The police may not maintain accurate records, their reporting systems may differ from city to city, they may measure and count crime in different ways or the legal definitions of crime may differ, or the legal category used by any given police officer may involve a great deal of discretionary behavior. The police underreport or overreport criminal statistics for political reasons (Reid, 1985; Nettler, 1984; Gibbons, 1982; Siegal, 1986).

To capture the "hidden crime" figure or "dark crime" figure, the U.S. Bureau of the Census conducts a survey of a sample of the population to determine who has been a victim of a crime during a given period of time. The National Crime Survey (NCS), as it is called, reports three times more crime than does the UCR. Here the measurement is not of police behavior but of victim behavior. In Chapter 6 I emphasized several theories of crime and criminal law, including legal realism, which focuses on the behavior of lawyers, judges, police, victims, and so on. It is important to understand that what is called crime and who is labeled a criminal (Chapter 6) depend on human behavior. People have to behave, and other people have to respond to the behavior with a label of "crime" before we have crime. That is why I have consistently talked about theories of crime and criminal law versus theories of human behavior.

NCS statistics are criticized because the victim may lie, may be mistaken, may have forgotten, or may wish to conceal or exaggerate a situation. Nettler commented in this respect that verbal behavior is not to be trusted, or as he put it: ''Never bet on an animal that talks'' [Nettler (1984:70); see also Reid (1985); Bureau of Justice Statistics (1983:23–25), and Gibbons (1982)]. A comparison of NCS victimization rates and UCR official rates records is shown in Figure 8–3.

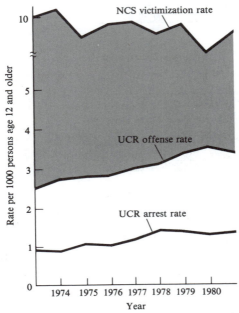

Figure 8–3 Fallout for the Crime of Aggravated Assault. From Bureau of Justice Statistics, 1987. Sources: *BJS National Crime Survey*, 1973–81; *Uniform Crime Reports*, Federal Bureau of Investigation, Washington, D.C., 1973–81.

Self-reports are also used to gather information about criminal behavior. A self-report survey will ask a sample population, often college sophomores, to fill out a questionnaire concerning crimes they have committed. This self-reporting technique has been used by a number of criminologists, including Porterfield (1943), Wallerstein and Wyle (1947), Nye and Short (1957), Dentler and Monroe (1961), Clark and Wenninger (1962), Erickson and Empey (1963), Reiss and Rhodes (1961), Gold (1966), Petersilia (1978), and Elliott and Ageton (1980). The main controversy to come out of self-report studies is the fact that many people confess to crimes for which they had not been convicted, and these are middle- and upper-class persons, whereas the usual official police records show most criminals to be members of the lower class and from minority groups. The social class/crime issue will be discussed in detail in Chapter 16.

The discrepancies between self-reports and UCR official data have been reconciled at least in part by the observation that self-reports tap the less serious offenses, whereas the official crime rate taps the most serious offenses (Hindelang, Hirschi, and Weis, 1975, 1981). As will be discussed below, the criminal justice system selectively handles or funnels cases from the police to the courts to the correctional system. It is to be expected that those offenders ending up in prison are the most serious offenders and those not picked up in the self-reporting studies.

Of the crimes known to the police, arrests are made for only one of five offenses, or 20 percent (Bureau of Justice Statistics, 1983:52–53). A Vera Institute of Justice study found a 26 percent arrest rate for violent crimes and an 11 percent arrest rate for property offenses (Gottfredson and Gottfredson, 1980:77). The rate of crimes known to the police is 33 percent of crime reported by victims, and of this 33 percent, 20 percent of the cases result in an arrest. We start the criminal justice process with only 6 percent of the crimes reported by victims. The "funnel effect" has been written about over the years, as shown in Figures 8–4 and 8–5. The exact figures and percentages do not always match because different authors use different sources of data over different periods, but the conclusions are the same.

After an arrest, the prosecutor must investigate the case and either file charges or drop the case. In 45 to 60 percent of the felony cases where an arrest is made there is a prosecution, and of those prosecuted, 90 percent are handled by plea bargaining (Bureau of Justice Statistics 1983:55; Cole, 1986:291). Only 10 percent of the guilty pleas result in a prison sentence (Cole, 1986:291).

If we start with 6 percent of the crimes reported by victims, and we prosecute 50 percent of these cases, then 3 percent of all cases are prosecuted. Of those prosecuted 10 percent result in a felony prison sentence, or 0.003, which is 3 out of 1000. As shown in Figure 8–6, 1 percent of the crimes known to the police result in a prison sentence. These figures are based on crimes reported to the police, and if we multiply by 3 to get the crime reported by victims, we are dealing with rates per 300,000, not 100,000, crimes. If 1 percent go to

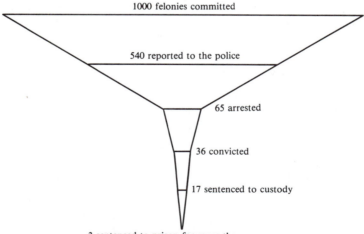

1000 felonies committed

540 reported to the police

65 arrested

36 convicted

17 sentenced to custody

3 sentenced to prison for more than one year

Figure 8–4 Funneling Effect from Committed Felonies Through Prison Sentences. From *The American System of Justice,* 4th ed., by G. F. Cole. Copyright © 1986 by Wadsworth, Inc. Reprinted by permission of Brooks/Cole Publishing Company, Pacific Grove, CA 93950.

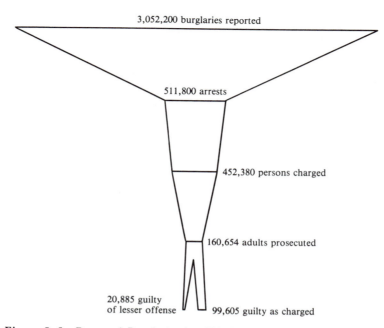

Figure 8-5 Reported Burglaries in 1977. From Blumberg, A.S. (1979). *Criminal Justice.* New York: New Viewpoints, p. 13. Source: *Uniform Crime Reports—1977,* Federal Bureau of Investigation, Washington, D.C., 1978, pp. 23-26.

prison based on crimes known to the police, then one-third of 1 percent, or 0.003, or 3/1000, go to prison on the basis of crimes reported by victims. By using data from Cole, Abadinsky, and others we come up with a figure of 3 out of 1000, which is a remarkable consistency considering the differences in crime statistics from different sources.

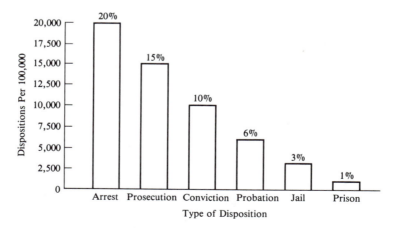

Figure 8-6 Disposition Percentages for 100,000 Crimes Reported. From Abadinsky, H. (1987). *Crime and Justice.* Chicago: Nelson Hall. p. 144.

If we use figures from Gottfredson and Gottfredson (1980:148) we start with 3 felony convictions for 100 arrests. If we multiply 100 × 5 for crimes known to the police, we have a rate of 3 felony convictions for 500 crimes known to the police; and if we multiply 500 × 3 for crimes committed but not known to the police, we have 3 felony convictions for 1500 criminal acts.

Regardless of the goals of the criminal justice system, whether it is incapacitation or deterrence, the system cannot reach these goals with imprisonment of 3 out of 1000 or 3 out of 1500 criminals.

The Police

The beginning of the criminal justice process is an investigation and/or arrest by the police. As we noted, an arrest occurs in only 20 percent of the cases known to the police, and the police know about 33 percent of those crimes reported by victims. Some of the reasons for a lack of success on the part of the police will be discussed, but this discussion is not intended as a course on law enforcement.

Very little time and effort on the part of the police is devoted to crime control. Police functions are divided into (1) service, (2) order maintenance, and (3) law enforcement. It has been estimated that 10 to 20 percent of the police effort is devoted to law enforcement (Wilson, 1968; Inciardi, 1987; Reid, 1985; Bureau of Justice Statistics, 1983).

The police are reactive, not proactive (Jeffery, 1971, 1977; Reid, 1985). They wait in their squad car until a message comes in that a crime has occurred, and then they respond. Crime cannot be prevented or controlled by waiting for it to occur (see Chapter 19). Response-time studies show that unless the call for help from the victim goes out within 3 minutes of the crime, the chances of catching the criminal are slim, or around 3 percent (Abadinsky, 1987; Bureau of Justice Statistics, 1983; Cole, 1986). It has been noted by Carl Klockers that 95 percent of all serious crimes that are solved by detectives are solved by a witness or informant talking to the police or by routine clerical procedures (Inciardi, 1987:205).

August Vollmer, the founder of the school of criminology at the University of California at Berkeley and the police chief of Berkeley for many years, stated: "I have spent my life enforcing the law. It is a stupid procedure, and it has not, nor will it ever solve the problem unless it is supplemented by preventive measures" (President's Crime Commission, 1967a:2, *The Police*).

The police use what is known as "preventive patrol," that is, cruising the streets in order to deter crime while waiting for a radio call to come in concerning a crime that has been committed. The Kansas City Patrol Study made use of an experimental design whereby preventive patrolling was increased in one area, decreased in another area, and maintained at a normal level in a third area. The Kansas City study revealed no major differences in crime rates attributable to patroling patterns (Abadinsky, 1987: 181–182; Cole, 1986; Kelling, 1974).

The police are involved in a "crime control" model of justice whereby efficiency in solving crimes, arresting criminals, and prosecuting criminals is emphasized. This is in contrast to a "due process model," which is a legalistic model based on setting up barriers at all stages and defending the rights of citizens from the police and courts (Skolnick, 1966; Packer, 1968).

Under the Warren Court (Chief Justice Earl Warren in the 1960s), a liberal U.S. Supreme Court expanded on the due process model of criminal justice (Inciardi, 1987:719). In Mapp v. Ohio, 367 U.S. 643 (1961), the Court put forth the "exclusionary rule," whereby they found that evidence gained from an illegal search and seizure is in itself contaminated and cannot be used against the defendant (Reid, 1985; Inciardi, 1987). In Miranda v. Arizona, 383 U.S. 436 (1966), the Supreme Court required that upon arrest the police read a warning to the arrestee notifying him/her of his/her rights to remain silent and the right to hire a lawyer. In United States v. Wade, 388 U.S. 218 (1967), the Court allowed a suspect to have a lawyer present during a police lineup. In Gideon v. Wainright, 372 U.S. 335 (1965), the Court established the right to legal counsel for those who could not afford counsel. In general, the Warren Court applied the Bill of Rights to the criminal law, that is, the right to be free of self-incrimination, a right to counsel, a right to a speedy trial, and prohibitions against cruel and unusual punishment (Inciardi, 1987:719 ff.; Reid, 1985:334 ff.).

During the 1970–1980 era of the Burger Court (Chief Justice Warren Burger), the U.S. Supreme Court returned to a "crime control model" of justice (Inciardi 1987:721 ff.). The Burger Court limited the *Miranda* and the *Mapp* decisions. In modifying the *Mapp* decision on illegally gained evidence the Court held that such evidence was admissible if the police officer acted in "good faith" (Reid, 1985; Inciardi, 1987). The Court has moved more and more in the direction of protection of the activities of police officers as opposed to protecting the rights of citizens and of those who are suspects in a criminal case. The Reagan administration (1980–1988) has supported the concept of a law-and-order fight on crime, with emphasis placed on a strong military state and a strong domestic police force and criminal justice system to fight crime. This is the model outlined as the "justice model" by Wilson, Morris, Fogel, and von Hirsch. One Reagan-era attorney general, Edwin Meese, a strong law-and-order man and a former prosecutor whose hobby is monitoring police calls, has been quoted as stating in 1985 that "if a person is innocent of a crime then he is not a suspect" (Inciardi, 1987:726).

There has been a major shift under the Reagan administration from a liberal to a conservative court. The resignation of Chief Justice Burger and the appointment of Justice Rehnquist as the Chief Justice (1986), the appointments of Justice O'Connor (1981) and Justice Scalia (1986), and the resignation of Justice Powell in June 1987, created for President Reagan an opportunity to establish a court more in line with his conservative political philosophy. His nomination of Robert Bork and Douglas Ginsburg to fill the Powell position on the Court in 1987 caused major opposition from moderate and liberal groups. I mentioned in Chapters 6 and 7 that the law was part of a political and behavioral process, and the idea that the Supreme court is independent of political and social pressures is nonsense. The Supreme Court makes critical decisions on all kinds of life and death issues with little restraint from outside sources.

Police discretion to arrest or not to arrest is another major factor in crime control. Goldstein (1960) pointed out that there is wide discretion in police work, and he advocated full enforcement of the law, or an arrest for every crime known to the police. Since then other studies have been made of police discretion (LaFave, 1965; Reid, 1985). It should be noted that if the police used full enforcement, police departments, courts, and prisons would be more overworked and overloaded than they are now.

Police corruption, which is prominent in areas of enforcement involving gambling, drugs, alcohol, and prostitution, as well as white-collar and professional crime, also limits police effectiveness. The Knapp Commission (1972) found that one-half of the New York City police officers were involved in police corruption (Inciardi, 1987:271–278). Frank Serpico (Maas, 1974), a New York City police officer who turned in some of his fellow police officers, was almost killed for his effort (Abadinsky, 1987:216). A movie was made of the Serpico story. Recently, four Miami police officers were arrested for murder and cocaine trafficking in connection with the Miami drug scene (Inciardi, 1987:282–283; Abadinsky, 1987:216–217).

Police brutality and violations of the civil liberties of citizens is also a major issue of concern for law enforcement (Inciardi, 1987:267 ff.). As has been noted, the police sometimes make arrests and searches which are in violation of the constitutional rights of citizens. As long as we depend on the police to protect us and to control crime, we must accept the fact that we will have police brutality and police violations. A strong argument in favor of crime prevention (Chapters 19 and 21) is that by preventing crime before it occurs, no illegal arrests or searches or interrogations will follow from police activities. There are prices we pay for ''crime control'' models and ''due process'' models of crime control.

At one point in history we used a ''policeman at his elbow'' test for legal insanity; that is, if someone committed a crime when a policeman was at his elbow, he must be insane (Chapter 20). If we think about it, however, we would realize that no amount of police protection will prevent crime. John F. Kennedy was assassinated while surrounded by a small army of police officers. Lee Harvey Oswald, the accused killer of Kennedy, was killed by Jack Ruby while surrounded by police officers. John Hinckley, Jr. shot Ronald Reagan while Reagan was surrounded by police officers.

Not only do the police fail to protect even those citizens such as presidents who are most carefully guarded and protected, but the court system also fails to respond to resolve the crime problem. When Kennedy was assassinated in 1963, President Johnson appointed the Warren Commission to investigate the assassination and make a report. The Warren Commission reported that there was a single gunman and that no conspiracy existed. A 1979 report by a House committee (U.S. House of Representatives, 1979) reported a high probability that two gunmen were involved in the assassination of Kennedy, that there was evidence of a conspiracy, and that Jack Ruby and James R. Hoffa, as part of organized crime and the Teamsters Union, were also involved in the assassination. If the highest officer in the United States, the president, cannot use his powers to solve a very major crime (the assassination of another president), how do we expect the courts to solve criminal cases of a lesser importance as a routine matter?

The Courts

The courts get approximately 20 percent of the crimes known to the police, or 6 percent of the crimes committed. Of these cases 50 percent are prosecuted, and of those prosecuted 90 percent are resolved with guilty pleas. Despite this "funnel effect" the courts are congested and unable to handle the present case load. The criminal court system operates on the number of beds available in the prison system rather than on major legal and philosophical principles.

Police investigations are often shoddy and short, prosecution of cases is often based on a desire to clear dockets and present good public records, the defense attorneys are minimally involved in the case, and negotiated justice is the overall result. Criminal justice is denied, and legal principles are lost in reality (Weinreb, 1977). Feeley (1979) has described the judicial process as punishment, with congestion, corruption, incompetent attorneys, and plea bargaining, all carried on in an expensive and very depressing environment.

Alan Stone has been quoted that stating that "The American criminal justice system is ready to collapse under its own weight. The criminals, if they ever organized themselves into a union and refused to plea bargain, could bring the whole enterprise to its knees" (Finkel, 1988:320).

The Prosecutor

The prosecutor is a political figure with political ambitions. He/she has a "prosecutor's bias" in that the job of the prosecutor is not to protect the innocent as is stated in television programs, but to gain as many convictions as possible (Weinbreb, 1977; Inciardi, 1987; Reid, 1985). Geraldine Ferrarro, the 1984 Democratic candidate for vice president on the Mondale ticket, stated: "I was a district attorney, and I put people behind bars" (*Newsweek*, July 23, 1984). She was voted the eighth most liberal person in Congress at the same time.

The prosecutor enters into a negotiated plea with the defense attorney in which the needs of the prosecutor and the court receive a high priority over the needs of the defendant. The negotiated plea is at one and the same time a part of the adversarial system and a substitute for it (Rosett and Cressey, 1976; Weinreb, 1977; Feeley, 1979).

The prosecutor has absolute discretionary power over which cases are prosecuted. He/she is also involved in the adversarial system and a trial by battle where truth is decided by legal maneuvers and tactics rather than by fact-finding efforts. Evidence is selected for presentation depending on its impact on the outcome of the case. The prosecutor starts with the need to get a guilty verdict, whereas the defense attorney starts with a need to get an acquittal (Weinreb, 1977).

Defense Counsel

The defense attorney is often not from the top of the legal profession. Criminal law is not a lucrative field of legal practice. Many defense attorneys are court appointed or are public defenders (Inciardi, 1987; Reid, 1985), and the defense attorney works on the basis of small fees because most of his/her clients are poor, and he/she cannot spend hours preparing a case.

Although the right to counsel doctrine has been put forth by the Supreme Court in Powell v. Alabama, 287 U.S. 45 (1932) and Gideon v. Wainwright, 372 U.S. 335 (1965), in practice it has not guaranteed adequate legal representation for indigent defendants in criminal trials.

The Trial Phase

The trial phase is a battle between attorneys on the basis of an adversarial legal system. Legal rules and procedures govern the battle, which is poorly designed to find facts, and appellate courts review legal doctrines rather than facts. Jerome Frank (Chapter 6) stated that the courts are not suited for this fact-finding role. Because of the domination of lawyers and legal procedures in criminal trials, behavioral science evidence bearing on a case is often neglected or introduced in such a way as to be ineffective or ignored.

The Sentencing Phase

At the sentencing phase three models are available to the judge: (1) a deterrence and incapacitation model, (2) a retribution model, and (3) a rehabilitation model (von Hirsch, Knapp, and Tonry, 1987; Gottfredson and Gottfredson, 1980, 1987; Blumstein et al., 1983). A retribution model is based on past conduct and the sentence must fit the crime. A deterrence and incapacitation model is based on an assessment of punishment on the future conduct of the criminal and/or potential criminal. The rehabilitative model is based on an assessment of the psychological and social needs of the defendant, and a suitable program of treatment for each criminal. A great deal of discretion exists in the third model, whereas the first and second models require fixed sentences and very little judicial discretion. The crime and not the criminal is the object of the sentence for the deterrence and retribution models, and the purpose of the sentence is to punish rather than reform. These models were discussed in Chapter 4 as part of legal criminology, as well as in this chapter. We review the medical treatment model for offenders in Chapters 20 and 21, and this chapter is limited to a discussion of punishment as found in deterrence and retribution arguments.

For two-thirds of this century the impact of the positive school on the administration of justice was reflected in individualized sentences, indeterminate sentences, and a great deal of discretion for judges and parole boards. Starting with the retributive justice model of the 1970s there was a major change in sentencing policy and philosophy, reflected in plea bargaining guidelines, mandatory minimum sentences, determinate sentences, sentencing guidelines, the abolition or limitation of parole and probation, and appellate review of sentences. There was a return to the classical position of fixed sentences based on the offense.

Sentencing commissions are needed to create sentencing conformity and to do away with sentencing discretion (Tonry, 1983:1483; von Hirsch, Knapp, and Tonry, 1987; Blumstein et al., 1983). If we do away with rehabilitation as a goal for criminal law, we must establish standards by which we apply the concepts of incapacitation and just retribution. Sentencing commissions have been set up in Minnesota, Washington, and Pennsylvania. A U.S. Sentencing Commission has also been established for the federal court system (von Hirsch, Knapp, and Tonry, 1987).

The Minnesota plan uses both incapacitation and just retribution as goals for the criminal justice system. For just retribution weight is given to a seriousness index for each crime, and sentences are scaled according to the seriousness of the offense. For incapacitation, an offender score is determined by the past criminal history of the offender (incapacitation). The Minnesota plan relies on the just deserts model, and as a result there has been an increase in the length of prison terms for highly serious crimes, and a decrease in prison terms for defendants with a high criminal record index but a nonserious or less serious offense (von Hirsch, Knapp, and Tonry, 1987).

It must be noted once again, in the light of the new popularity of sentencing commissions, that sentencing policy under either model, retribution or incapacitation, does not prevent crimes from occurring; nor will such a policy reduce the crime rate in the future.

The influence of legal versus extralegal influences on sentencing (sex, race, and socioeconomic class) is a major issue in sentencing. Are sentences based on legal principles such as deterrence or retribution, or are they based on extralegal factors such as age, sex, race, and socioeconomic status? Nettler (1984:275 ff.) from a review of the literature concluded that extralegal factors are not nearly as important as legal factors [see also Zenoff (1983), Feeley (1979:133), and Gottfredson and Gottfredson (1980:330)]. Gottfredson and Gottfredson (1987) listed as critical variables in the sentencing process: (1) the seriousness of the offense, (2) the prior criminal conduct of the defendant, and (3) the nature of the personal relationship between the offender and victim. They noted that there are two criminal justice systems, one for serious offenders and one for less serious offenders, where extralegal variables such as age and sex take over. A personal relationship between offender and victim will reduce the severity of the sentence. Feeley (1979:11) on the other hand argued that sentences could not be accounted for in terms of the seriousness of the offense or the prior record of the offender. Feeley explained the legal process in terms of the complexity of court organization, the values and norms of society, and the expensiveness of court procedures. Courts are characterized by confusion and decentralized authority (Feeley, 1979:13–15). The National Research Council Report (Blumstein et al., 1983) concluded that race was not a major factor in sentencing, whereas the findings concerning the impact of socioeconomic status and sex (being a female) were uncertain and preliminary since other variables do and can influence these relationships. They concluded that severity of the offense and the offender's past record emerged as the key determinants of sentences, and even with this information 66 percent of the variance in sentences is not explained (Blumstein et al., 1983:10–11). We can conclude that both legal and extralegal factors have a bearing on sentencing, but the exact relationship is yet to be worked out. A survey of the decision process in the criminal justice system by Gottfredson and Gottfredson (1987) found that the system has conflicting goals and policies where decisions made in one stage of the process conflict with and do not support decisions made at another phase. They traced the decision process from arrest to charge to trial, as well as the decision process involved in sentencing, probation, and parole. Gottfredson and Gottfredson (1987) concluded that the criminal justice process needed more rationality, or more information on which to base decisions, and better use of statistical prediction tables to predict outcome of various decision processes.

In conclusion, criminal courts try to sort the innocent from the guilty on the basis of plea bargaining and the adversarial system. As Herbert Packer (1968) stated, the courts pursue a due process model, whereas the police are involved in a crime control model. The court procedures do little or nothing (1) to prevent crimes in the future, (2) to rehabilitate offenders, or (3) to deter future criminal activites. At the end of a very expensive and technical legal procedure, very few criminals are sent to prison. The courts serve neither a deterrent nor a rehabilitative goal. At best it can be said to have some retributive value.

After a defendant is found guilty, he/she is sentenced to prison in some cases. We examine next the prison/correctional system to see what impact imprisonment has on the crime rate.

FURTHER STUDIES

Most, if not all, criminology and criminal justice programs offer courses in law enforcement and the criminal court system. Specialized courses in these areas are offered in law schools and in police science programs.

REFERENCES

ABADINSKY, H. (1987). *Crime and Justice*. Chicago: Nelson-Hall Publishers.
ADREANO, R., and J. SIEGFRIED (1980). *Economics of Crime*. New York: Halsted Press.
ALLEN, F. A. (1964). *Borderland of Criminal Justice*. Chicago: University of Chicago Press.

ALLEN, F. A. (1981). *The Decline of the Rehabilitative Ideal*. New Haven, Conn.: Yale University Press.

AMERICAN FRIENDS SERVICE COMMITTEE (1971). *The Struggle for Justice*. New York: Hill & Wang.

ANDENAES, J. (1974). *Punishment and Deterrence*. Ann Arbor: University of Michigan Press.

BECKER, G. S. (1968). *The Economic Approach to Human Behavior*. Chicago: University of Chicago Press.

BECKER, G. S. (1976). *The Economic Approach to Human Behavior*. Chicago: University of Chicago Press.

BLUMSTEIN, A., J. COHEN, S. E. MARTIN, and M. H. TONRY, eds. (1983). *Research on Sentencing: The Search for Reform*. Washington, D.C.: National Academy Press.

BUREAU OF JUSTICE STATISTICS (1983). *Report to the Nation on Crime and Justice*. Washington, D.C.: U.S. Department of Justice.

CENTER FOR ECONOMETRIC STUDIES OF THE JUSTICE SSYTEM (1979). *Research Developments*. Stanford, Calif.: Hoover Institution Press.

CLARK, J. P., and E. P. WENNINGER (1962). "Socio-economic Class and Area as Correlates of Illegal Behavior among Juveniles." *American Sociological Review*, 28:826–834.

COHEN. J. (1983). "Incapacitation as a Strategy for Crime Control: Possibilities and Pitfalls." In *Crime and Justice*, Vol. 5, ed. M. Tonry and N. Morris. Chicago: University of Chicago Press.

COLE, G. F. (1986). *The American System of Criminal Justice*. Monterey, Calif.: Brooks/Cole.

COOK, P. J. (1980). "Research in Criminal Deterrence: Laying the Groundwork for the Second Decade." In *Crime and Justice*, Vol. 2, ed. N. Morris and M. Tonry. Chicago: University of Chicago Press.

COOK, P. J. (1986). "The Demand and Supply of Criminal Opportunities." In *Crime and Justice*, Vol. 7, ed. M. Tonry and N. Morris. Chicago: University of Chicago Press.

CULLEN, F. T., and K. E. GILBERT (1982). *Reaffirming Rehabilitation*. Cincinnati, Oh.: Anderson.

CRONIN, T. E., T. Z. CRONIN, and M. E. MILAKOVITCH (1981). *U.S. v. Crime in the Streets*. Bloomington: Indiana University Press.

DENTLER, R. A., and L. J. MONROE (1961). "Social Correlates of Early Adolescent Theft." *American Sociological Review*, 26:733–743.

EHRLICH, I. (1975). "The Deterrent Effect of Capital Punishment: A Question of Life and Death." *American Economic Review*, 397–417, June.

ELLIOTT, D. S., and S. S. AGETON (1980). "Reconciling Race and Class Differences in Self-Reported and Official Estimates of Delinquency." *American Sociological Review*, 45:95–110.

ERICKSON, M. L., and L. T. EMPEY (1963). "Court Records, Undetected Delinquency and Decision-Making." *Journal of Criminal Law, Criminology, and Police Science*, 54:456–469.

FAUST, F. L., and P. J. BRANTINGHAM (1979). *Juvenile Justice Philosophy*. St. Paul, Minn.: West Publishing Co.

Federal Bureau of Investigations (1986). *Uniform Crime Reports*. Washington, D.C.: U.S. Government Printing Office.

FEELEY, M. M. (1979). *The Process Is the Punishment*. New York: Russell Sage.

FEELEY, M. M., and A. D. SARAT (1980). *The Policy Dilemma*. Minneapolis: University of Minnesota Press.

FINKEL, N. J. (1988). *Insanity on Trial*. New York: Plenum.

FOGEL, D. (1975). *We Are the Living Proof*. Cincinnati, Ohio: Anderson Publishing Co.

GIBBONS, D. C. (1982). *Society, Crime, and Criminal Behavior*. Englewood Cliffs, N.J.: Prentice Hall.

GOLD, M. (1966). "Undetected Juvenile Behavior." *Journal of Research on Crime and Delinquency*, 13:27–46.

GOLDSTEIN, J. (1960). "Police Discretion Not to Invoke the Criminal Process: Visability Decisions in the Administration of Justice." *Yale Law Journal*, 69:543–594.

GOTTFREDSON, M. R., and D. M. GOTTFREDSON (1980). *Decision Making in Criminal Justice*. Cambridge, Mass.: Ballinger.

GOTTFREDSON, M. R. and D. M. GOTTFREDSON (1987). *Decison Making in Criminal Justice*, 2nd ed. New York: Plenum.

GREENWOOD, P. W. (1983). "Controlling the Crime Rate through Imprisonment." In *Crime and Public Policy*, ed. J. Q. Wilson. San Francisco: Institute of Contemporary Studies.

GREENWOOD, P. W., and A. F. ABRAHAMSE (1982). *Selective Incapacitation*. Santa Monica, Calif.: Rand Corporation.

HALL, J., (1935). *Theft, Law and Society*. Indianapolis, Ind.: Bobbs-Merrill.

HINDELANG, M. J., T. HIRSCHI, and J. G. WEIS (1975). "Correlates of Delinquency: The Illusion of Discrepancy between Self Reports and Official Measures." *American Sociological Review*, 44:995–1014, December.

HINDELANG, M. J., T. HIRSCHI, and J. G. WEIS (1981). *Measuring Delinquency*. Beverly Hills, Calif.: Sage.

INCIARDI, J. (1987). *Criminal Justice*. Orlando, Fla.: Harcourt Brace Jovanovich.

JEFFERY, C. R. (1971, 1977). *Crime Prevention through Environmental Design*. Beverly Hills, Calif.: Sage.

KELLING, G. (1974). *The Kansas City Preventive Patrol Experiment*. Washington D.C.: Police Foundation.

KLEIN, S. P., and M. N. CAGGIANO (1986). *The Prevalence, Predictability, and Policy Implications of Recidivism*. Santa Monica, Calif.: Rand Corporation.

LAFAVE, W. R. (1965). *Arrest*. Boston: Little, Brown.

LIPTON, D., R. MARTINSON, and J. WILKS (1975). *The Effectiveness of Correctional Treatment: A Survey of Treatment Evaluation Studies*. New York: Praeger.

JEFFERY, C. R. (1967). *Criminal Responsibility and Mental Disease*. Springfield, Ill.: Charles C. Thomas.

MAAS, P. (1974). *Serpico*. New York: Bantam Books.

MARTIN, S. E., L. B. SECHREST, and R. REDNER (1981). *New Directions in the Rehabilitation of Criminal Offenders.* Washington D.C.: National Academy Press.

MORRIS, N. (1974). *The Future of Imprisonment.* Chicago: University of Chicago Press.

MUELLER, G. O. W. (1966). "Punishment, Corrections and the Law." *Nebraska Law Review*, 45:58–96, January.

NETTLER, G. (1984). *Explaining Crime.* New York: McGraw-Hill.

NEWMAN, G. (1983). *Just and Painful.* New York: Macmillan.

NYE, F. I., and J. F. SHORT (1957). "Scaling Delinquent Behavior." *American Sociological Review*, 22:326–331.

PACKER, H. (1968). *The Limits of the Criminal Sanction.* Stanford, Calif.: Stanford University Press.

PETERSILIA, J. (1978). "The Validity of Criminality Data Derived from Personal interviews." In *Quantitative Studies in Criminology*, ed. C. Wellford. Beverly Hills, Calif.: Sage.

PHILLIPS, L., and H. L. VOTEY (1981). *Economics of Crime Control.* Beverly Hills, Calif.: Sage.

PORTERFIELD, A. L. (1943). "Delinquency and Its Outcome in Court and College." *American Journal of Sociology*, 49:199–208.

President's Commission on Law Enforcement and the Administration of Justice (1967a). *Task Force Reports: The Police; The Courts; Corrections; Juvenile Delinquency and Youth Crime; Organized Crime; Science and Technology; Assessment of Crime; Narcotics and Drugs; Drunkenness.*

President's Commission on Law Enforcement and the Administration of Justice(1967b). *The Challenge of Crime in a Free Society.* Washington, D.C.: Government Printing Office.

REID, S. T. (1985). *Crime and Criminology.* New York: Holt, Rinehart and Winston.

REISS, A. J., and A. L. RHODES (1961). "The Distribution of Juvenile Delinquency in the Social Class Structure." *American Sociological Review*, 26:720–732.

ROSETT, A., and D. R. CRESSEY (1976). *Justice by Consent.* Philadelphia: J.B. Lippincott.

ROTTENBERG, S. (1973). *The Economics of Crime and Punishment.* Washington, D.C.: American Enterprise Institute for Public Policy Research.

RUBIN, L. (1986). *Quiet Rage: Bernhard Goetz in a Time of Madness.* New York: Farrar, Straus & Giroux.

SIEGAL, L. (1986). *Criminology.* St. Paul, Minn.:West Publishing Co.

SKOLNICK, J. (1966). *Justice without Trial.* New York: Wiley.

TONRY, M. (1983). "Sentencing: Sentencing Councils." In *Encyclopedia of Crime and Justice,* ed. S. H. Kadish. New York: Free Press.

U.S. House of Representatives (1979). *Report of the Select Committee on Assassinations,* House Report 95–1825, Part 2.

VAN DINE, S., J. P. CONRAD, and S. DINITZ (1979). *Restraining the Wicked.* Lexington, Mass.: D.C. Heath.

VON HIRSCH, A. (1976). *Doing Justice.* New York: Hill & Wang.

VON HIRSCH, A. (1983). "Commensurability and Crime Prevention: Evaluating Formal Sentencing Structures and Their Rationale." *Journal of Criminal Law and Criminology*, 74:209–248.

VON HIRSCH, A., K. A. KNAPP, and M. TONRY (1987). *The Sentencing Commission and Its Guidelines*. Boston: Northeastern University Press.

VOTEY, H. L., and L. PHILLIPS (1974). "The Control of Criminal Activity: An Economic Analysis." In *Handbook of Criminology*, ed. D. Glaser. Skokie, ILL.: Rand McNally.

WAITE, J. B. (1958). "The Legal Approach to Crime and Corrections." *Law and Contemporary Problems*, 23(4):594–610, Autumn.

WALLERSTEIN, J. A., and C. J. WYLE (1947). "Our Law-Abiding Law Breakers." *Federal Probation*, 25:107–112.

WEINREB, L. L. (1977). *Denial of Justice*. New York: Free Press.

WHITE, S. O., and S. KRISLOV (1977). *Understanding Crime*. Washington, D.C.: National Academy of Sciences.

WILSON, J. Q. (1968). *Varieties of Police Behavior*. Cambridge, Mass.: Harvard University Press.

WILSON, J. Q. (1975). *Thinking about Crime*. New York: Basic Books.

WILSON, J. Q., and R. J. HERRNSTEIN (1985). *Crime and Human Nature*. New York: Simon & Schuster.

WITTE, A. D. (1980). "Estimating the Economic Model of Crime and Individual Data." *Quarterly Journal of Economics*, 94:57–84, February.

WOLFGANG, M., R. FIGLIO, and T. SELLIN (1972). *Delinquency in a Birth Cohort*. Chicago: University of Chicago Press.

ZENOFF, E. H. (1983). "Sentencing: Disparity." In *Encyclopedia of Crime and Justice*, ed. S. H. Kadish. New York: Free Press.

ZIMRING, F. E., and G. J. HAWKINS (1973). *Deterrence*. Chicago: University of Chicago Press.

QUESTIONS

1. What major theoretical systems are used to support criminal law and the criminal justice system?
2. What is the basis for the deterrence theory of punishment?
3. How successful is incapacitation as a crime control model?
4. What arguments were made by legal scholars such as Allen, Morris, Wilson, and von Hirsch for retribution and the "just deserts" model of criminal law?
5. What major changes occurred in the American criminal justice system in the 1970s?
6. What aspects of crime are measured by the UCR? By the NCS? By self-reports?
7. Discuss the funnel effect of the criminal justice system.
8. What differences exist between the due process model and the crime control model of criminal justice?
9. What are the several models of sentencing that criminal courts can use?

The Criminal Justice System: Corrections

9

INTRODUCTION

The correctional system is a graded tier system composed of inmates serving long sentences in maximum security institutions, inmates serving short sentences in medium or minimum security institutions, and inmates released on suspended sentences or on probation or work release or other community programs. The history of prisons is reviewed in every correctional and criminal justice text, and I will not review it here.

The Numbers

Because of the new law-and-order movement described earlier, prison populations have increased rapidly in the past 10 years. From 1972 to 1978 the state and federal prison population increased by 28 percent, and the total figure for federal, state, and local institutions was 450,000 (National Institute of Justice, 1980:12). In 1982 there were 412,000 in federal and state institutions (excluding local). The gain in prison populations in 1981 was 37,000, or 90 percent of the gain from 1977 to 1981 (Bureau of Justice Statistics, 1983:81). By 1983 there were 439,000 prisoners in state and federal prisons (Bureau of Justice Statistics, 1984).

The law-and-order philosophy of the 1970s created a major crisis in our prison system. *Newsweek* (October 6, 1986) described the Texas prison system as the ''toughest,'' where 52 inmates were murdered in two years while in prison (Martin and Ekland-Olson, 1987). Major riots occurred at Attica State Prison in New York in 1971, and in the New Mexico State Prison in 1980, where 33 prisoners were brutally murdered by other prisoners. The Arkansas prison scandal of 1967 revealed a series of brutalities, murders, and assaults on inmates by guards and other inmates. Sexual assaults are very common in prisons (Inciardi, 1987). As a result of the Arkansas scandal a federal court declared the entire Arkansas prison system to be unconstitutional because it constituted cruel and unusual punishment (Holt v. Sarver, 309 F. Supp. 362, 1970). A number of cases followed *Holt* v. *Sarver,* defining the conditions under which people can be held in prison. These decisions included references to shelter, food, safety, medical care, overcrowding, and sanitary conditions (Gottfredson and McConville, 1987).

By 1983 the penal systems of Alabama, Florida, Mississippi, Oklahoma, Rhode Island, Tennessee, Texas, and the male facilities in Michigan were declared unconstitutional, and 21 other states were operating under court orders to eliminate overcrowding (Bureau of Justice Statistics, 1983:80; Inciardi, 1987; National Institute of Justice, 1980; Allen and Simonsen, 1986). By 1986, 46 states were under court orders or were in litigation concerning the legality of prisons within these states (Gottfredson and McConville, 1987). It is estimated by the National Council on Crime and Delinquency that by 1992 prison populations will be up by 21 percent over the 1988 figures (*USA Today,* April 14, 1988).

In a Texas case that was in the courts for 13 years, Ruiz v. Estelle, F.2d 115 (1982), the court ordered sweeping changes in the Texas prison system, including better staffing, limitations on the use of inmates as guards, better medical care, better housing, less brutality, and new prisons to alleviate overcrowding. The court order had little or no impact on the Texas system (*Newsweek,* October 6, 1987). In Alabama, in 1980, 1000 inmates were in local jails due to the overcrowding of the prison system (National Institute of Justice, 1980). A number of states are now releasing inmates prior to the end of their sentences in order to comply with court orders brought about by overcrowding. In Florida in 1987, an inmate cannot be sentenced to prison unless an inmate is first released from the prison system. Florida is now using jails, tents, and and early release of inmates to meet the problem of prison overcrowding. In the state of Arkansas 50 inmates were chained to trees because there was no room in the prison (*Tallahassee Democrat,* July 28, 1987).

The answer to the issues surrounding prison overcrowding is discussed by Gottfredson and McConville (1987) in terms of three options:

1. Build more prisons
2. Reduce the intake of prisoners
3. Accelerate the release of those already in prison

They note that these options have not worked in the past, but they state that "we do suggest, however, that this brief listing of policy options is in fact exhaustive. There is nothing more that could be done other than to build prisons, reduce intakes, or accelerate releases." Blumstein (Gottfredson and Mc-

Conville, 1987:161 ff.) stated that we can use short-range measures to alleviate prison overcrowding, such as sentencing guidelines, early release, and the use of empty schools and hospitals to hold criminals.

It should be noted that neither S. Gottfredson and McConville nor Blumstein considered options other than arresting, sentencing, imprisoning, and releasing on early release for prisoners. They reject treatment and crime prevention as alternatives to prisons, and in fact they adjust the flow of inmates into and out of prisons rather than cutting off the flow of prisoners into prisons. As I stated in an earlier chapter, this is like constructing more rape crisis centers for rape victims, or creating more emergency facilities for automobile accident victims, rather than preventing rape or automobile casualties.

Don Gottfredson (Gottfredson and McConville, 1987) came at the problem from a different perspective when he wrote that the United States imprisons more people than nearly any other country, the cost of imprisonment is high, deterrence and incapacitation do not work, and ethical reasons force us to reduce the use of imprisonment and to find new and creative alternatives to prisons.

In her discussion of the need to deescalate criminal sanctions, Harris (Gottfredson and McConville, 1987) quoted John Conrad as follows: "We live in a country where inhumanity administered by governments upon persons under total control has reached a nadir of barbarism."

The brutalities associated with our prison system are remarkably like those in Soviet prisons as described by Solzhenitsyn in *The Gulag Archipelago* (Solzhenitsyn, 1974). It is remarkable that lawyers who are very much involved in the defense of individual rights and freedoms have not raised a voice in protest over what is a major disgrace for the United States.

Treatment within Prisons

Treatment programs within prisons are almost nonexistent and are very unsuccessful, to say the least. Prisons are devoted to security and imprisonment, not to rehabilitation (Allen and Simonsen, 1986). Studies by Martinson, Bailey, Logan, and others found few if any successful therapy programs within prisons (Allen and Simonsen, 1986; National Institute of Justice, 1980). One summary of the situation (National Institute of Law Enforcement and Criminal Justice, 1979) stated that some programs show some success with some inmates, but as a whole rehabilitation does not work. There is no right to treatment doctrine for inmates (see Chapter 21).

One way of measuring the success of prisons in deterring crime is through the recidivism rate, or the rate at which prisoners return to prison after serving time and being released. This standard of success applies only to the deterrence theory since the retribution theory does not demand a decrease in the crime rate, and rehabilitation is based on therapies and outside a prison setting. Recidivism is a most difficult thing to measure (Gottfredson and Gottfredson, 1980) because of low arrest and conviction rates and because of different definitions of recidivism and success. About 66 percent of all adult inmates have been in an institution prior to their current prison term. Within three years after release, 64 percent of all parolees are back in prison (Bureau of Justice Statistics, 1983:84; Fox, 1985).

Probation is not a successful legal process either. Because of the crisis in prison overcrowding, the state of California has moved to *felony probation,* or the placement or probation of felons not usually eligible for probation. In a study of felony probation by the Rand Corporation, Petersilia et al. (1985) found that over a 40-month period, 65 percent of the sample of probationers were rearrested, 18 percent were reconvicted for serious crimes, and 34 percent were reincarcerated. The Rand Corporation study found that the prediction of success on probation was very poor, and from their study they were able to identify only 3 percent of the incoming inmate population sampled as having a 75 percent chance at success in given probation (Petersilia et al., 1985).

In a later study (Petersilia, Turner, and Peterson, 1986) the Rand group followed 511 prisoners and 511 probationers over a two-year period, and they found that 72 percent of the prisoners were rearrested and 31 percent reincarcerated, whereas 63 percent of the probationers were rearrested and 31 percent reincarcerated. They concluded that prisons neither rehabilitate nor deter. Building more prisons is very costly and will not resolve the crime problem.

PUNISHMENT AND DETERRENCE: THE EMPIRICAL EVIDENCE

The Psychology of Punishment

As we indicate in Chapter 13, punishment does not control criminal behavior for any number of reasons. We will briefly summarize the reasons here:

1. The time lag between the criminal act and the punishment is too long. Punishment is not swift.
2. Punishment is not certain. Less than 1 percent of those committing crimes receive a prison sentence. Too many decisions are made between the crime and imprisonment to make for any certainty of punishment.
3. Punishment is often not severe because of suspended sentences, probation, and plea bargaining. Where sentencing is severe, it leads to prison overcrowding and brutalization.
4. Criminal behavior is always paired with a reward or reinforcement system as well as with the threat of punishment. The potential offender must make a decision concerning the probability of rewards versus punishment for a criminal act. The odds favor the reward over punishment.
5. Punishment is successful only when alternative responses are made available for the same reward.
6. Punishment acts as a conditioned reinforcer and can reinforce certain responses. By doing so, punishment creates more behavior, not less.

7. Punishment creates escape and avoidance responses. People do not learn law-abiding behavior, but they do learn to avoid arrest, conviction, and sentencing. This is why the criminal justice system imprisons offenders for less than 1 percent of the crimes reported by victims.

8. Punishment makes those who are punished more violent. Pain creates violent responses. This is why prisons are such violent places.

9. Punishment makes negative stimuli of those who do the punishing, such as parents, teachers, police, and friends. These people are identified as agents of punishment and are avoided. The punished person comes to regard the social world as made up of punitive stimuli which are to be avoided, and this means running away from home or playing truant at school.

10. Punishment creates learned helplessness.

11. Punishment is reinforcing to the punisher; that is, people are reinforced for punishing others. This is why we continue to punish criminals even though studies show that punishment does not deter the criminal. It does reinforce lawyers, judges, legislators, and the general public. The more we punish, the more we need to punish.

12. The psychopath does not learn from punishment.

I shall not discuss these issues in detail, since they are discussed in detail in Chapter 13. Suffice it to say, from a psychological point of view, punishment is not an effective means of controlling behavior.

Deterrence Research: 1960–1980

Deterrence research gained in popularity during the 1965–1975 era due to the return to punishment and a law-and-order basis for criminal justice (Gottfredson and Gottfredson, 1980). The theory of deterrence is based on the utilitarian idea that punishment should serve some social good, and it is usually placed in opposition to the just retribution model, which denies the utilitarian aims of punishment. Deterrence theory is discussed in Chapter 4 and also earlier in this chapter.

Modern studies of deterrence have focused on certainty and severity of punishment as they affect crime rates (deterrent effect). Tittle (1969) and Tittle and Logan (1973) found a deterrent effect for certainty but not for severity except for homicide. Chiricos and Waldo (1970) and Waldo and Chiricos (1972) found no deterrent effect for severity and a slight and inconsistent negative relationship between certainty of punishment and deterrence. As we noted above, the certainty of a prison sentence is less than 1 percent for all crimes reported by victims. The certainty of punishment is very weak at best. I also mentioned the problem of overcrowding in prisons. The more we use punishment to deter criminals, the more criminals we are going to have in our prison system. The prison crisis of today is related to the belief that we can stop crime by putting more people in prison.

Deterrence: What Is It?

Gibbs (1975) observed that we can never observe deterrence since deterrence is the absence of a response. If a person does not commit a crime, how do we know that he/she was deterred by the threat of punishment, or by internalized norms or for some other reason? Gibbs asserted that the only affirmative statement we can make is that some individuals are deterred in some situations for some crimes by some punishments (Gibbs, 1975:11). He concluded that no theory of deterrence is now available (Gibbs, 1975:217). The impact of punishment on behavior will depend on the interaction of at least four different variables: (1) the nature of the offender, (2) the nature of the offense, (3) the nature of the environment in which the crime occurred, and (4) the nature of the punishment, including severity and certainty. Gibbs stated that in order to study deterrence, we must move to the concept of punishment, which can be studied empirically. He stated further that punishment can prevent crime in nine ways *other than through deterrence.*

1. Incapacitation
2. Surveillance
3. Enculturation
4. Reformation
5. Normative validation
6. Retribution
7. Stigmatization
8. Normative isolation
9. Habituation

Some of these variables have been explored by other writers. Gramick and Green (Paternoster et al., 1983a) used three variables: (1) moral commitment, (2) fear of social disapproval and reprimand, and (3) threat of punishment. They found that all three influenced crime rates in independent ways. Blumstein, Cohen, and Nagin (1978:5) concluded that three basic problems face any evaluation of punishment as a deterrent: (1) errors in the measurement of crimes, (2) the confounding effects of incapacitation and deterrence (i.e., if we imprison someone, is the impact on crime rates due to deterrence or incapacitation since both are occurring simultaneously?), and (3) the possibility of two-way causation between punishment and crime rates; that is, crime rates affect the rate of punishment and the rate of punishment influences crime rates. The simultaneous effects are negative; that is, the more crime, the more the overload on the criminal justice system. The ability of the criminal justice system to respond to crime is reduced and the certainty of punishment decreases. I discussed these issues in Chapter 8 as part of the overburdening of the police, courts, and correctional system. Geerken and Gove (1977) referred to this as system overload, and Pontell (1978) called it system capacity. There is also the other possibility not discussed by these writers; that is, as crime rates go up, punishment rates go up, since there will be more police, more arrests, more convictions, and more prison sentences. Geerken and Gove (1977) also discussed incapacitation as a way in which punishment lowers the crime rate other than by deterrence.

The statistical techniques used to study deterrence have also been challenged for not taking into account extralegal factors such as unemployment, social class, and the opportunity structure for crime. Blumstein, Cohen, and Nagin (1978:7) concluded: "In summary, therefore, we cannot yet assert that the evidence warrants an affirmative conclusion regarding deterrence." They recommended further and more valid research.

Deterrence and Perception

Gibbs (1975) noted that since deterrence cannot be studied directly, research must focus on the perception of the threat of punishment for the potential criminal. Gibbs (1977:419) concluded: "By definition no individual can be deterred unless he or she perceives the anticipated legal sanctions for crime as painful." Perception is defined as knowledge or cognition and it is that aspect which deals with the internal mental states of humankind (see Chapter 12). Terms such as "attitude," "self-concept," and "value" are used to refer to internal mental states. Like deterrence, perception is never known directly but is inferred from physical behaviors. The usual way (Waldo and Chiricos, 1972) is to ask research subjects if they know the penalties for a certain offense, such as the possession of marijuana or theft. The verbal response of the subject, which is in itself behavior, is then translated into a mental state called "perception."

Henshel and Carey (Henshel and Silverman, 1975:55) also used subjective perception to explain deterrence. Erickson, Gibbs, and Jensen (1977:307) studied the perception of the certainty of punishment by using the verbal behavior of subjects, and they stated that perception must be included in studies of deterrence. They found that extralegal factors such as the social condemnation of crime also influences behavior as well as the perceived threat of punishment. By using a questionnaire, Waldo and Chiricos (1972) found that perceived certainty of punishment appears to be related to self-confessed criminality, but the relationship is weak and varies by the crime and by the measure of certainty that is used. In some later work Waldo and Chiricos reversed their position on perception (Paternoster et al., 1982, 1983b). They found inconsistencies and methodological errors in perception research, as well as a lack of stability in perceptual reports over time. They concluded that the perceived threat of punishment may be the consequence of criminal behavior, not the cause. Behavior can cause perception, as well as perception causing behavior. It can be

$$\text{Perception} \longrightarrow \text{Behavior}$$

or

$$\text{Behavior} \longrightarrow \text{Perception}$$

(Paternoster et al., 1983b:477). They concluded that "the earlier perceptual research tells us nothing about deterrence effects . . . since little is known about how perceptions are shaped and reshaped over time" (Paternoster et al., 1983a:296–297).

An experimental psychologist with background in neurological theories of learning (Chapter 13) would state that the problem of perception as one of

Environment ⟶ Black box ⟶ Behavior

rather than

Environment ⟶ Perception ⟶ Behavior

"Perception" is a term we use for our ignorance of what is going on inside the brain. As Nettler observed (1984:95), "critical comments about verbal reports as indicators of behavior have been required because of sociologists' reliance on strangers' answers to their questions and because of the persistent quarrel among criminologists about what to conclude. My personal advice is to accept the gambler's maxim, noted previously, about the hazard of betting on talking animals."

Deterrence, Learning Theory, and the Brain

Punishment is measured in terms of the number of people in prison, or the length of sentences, or the number of arrests, and then this figure is related to changes in behavior (crime rates). Such a model assumes that the environment (punishment) affects behavior (crime rates) without going through the individual, or if the individual is considered, the individual is a "black box," that is, the stimulus becomes perception and perception in turn causes behavior. Individual differences are ignored, and punishment is viewed as affecting each individual in the same manner. It is assumed that a twenty-year sentence will affect 1000 potential criminals in exactly the same way.

Deterrence theory is based on learning theory. General deterrence is a type of learning based on modeling and imitation; that is, one learns by observing others being punished. Special deterrence is based on associational learning of a Pavlovian and Skinnerian type (Chapter 13). A potential target for crime, such as money or a female or a car, can be associated with pleasure or pain through classical or operant conditioning. Whether or not the stimulus "car" or "money" or "female" produces a criminal response or an avoidance and escape response depends on whether or not the stimulus arouses the pleasure or the pain centers of the brain. This in turn depends on the potential criminal's genetic background, past learning experiences, the present environmental setting for the behavior, and the biochemical state of the individual's brain at that moment in time. For punishment to be effective, the stimulus object (female, money) must activate specific neurons in the brain, which in turn activate the autonomic nervous system so as to produce fear and anxiety. Psychopaths show no such fear arousal because they lack autonomic nervous system arousal (Chapter 18). To understand deterrence and punishment we must understand the nature of the brain and the manner in which neuronal pathways are biochemically coded through earlier experiences with punishment. The so-called deterrent effect of punishment is a biochemical code in the brain, and whether or not the punishment acts as a deterrent depends on the manner in which the neurons are connected in the brain. This of course varies from one person to another.

The environment affects individual behavior through the brain, and this underlying fact of behavior has been emphasized throughout this book. Without major knowledge of neurology and how it applies to punishment we will never understand the reasons punishment does what it does. The reason deterrence research is so mixed and inconclusive is because it is

Environment $\longrightarrow$ Black box $\longrightarrow$ Behavior research

rather than

Environment $\longrightarrow$ Brain $\longrightarrow$ Behavior research

Professor Tittle on Sanctions and Deterrence

In his book on sanctions and deterrence Tittle (1980) raised some basic issues concerning deterrence research. Tittle was one of the pioneers in deterrence research, and his conclusions are especially enlightening as a commentary on a phase of criminological research.

Tittle noted that deterrence research suffers from three different types of problems: (1) individual differences, (2) formal versus informal social controls, and (3) psychological aspects of deviance. In his review of the literature Tittle found that age and sex are predictors of deviance, whereas socioeconomic class, marital status, race, and labor force status are not predictors. He ruled out four of six categories, and for age and sex he wrote: "Even for these categories it is clear that differences among individuals are a more compelling mystery than are status differences" (Tittle, 1980:125). Tittle found that deviance is greater in general for males than for females. However, women between the ages of 15 and 24 admit to more offenses than any category of males except males under the age of 25. Unmarried females admit to more deviance than most categories of males. Similarly, young females have a much higher rate of deviancy than older females (Tittle, 1980:82–86). The point is that age or sex by itself cannot account for behavior. Tittle concluded that since sociologists are unable to explain deviance at a social level, he felt justified in pursuing a study of deviance at the individual level (Tittle, 1980:86).

Tittle found that formal sanctions have little or no effect on deterrence, and in fact there is a reverse effect, that is, crime causes punishment, a point made earlier. Tittle concluded that informal sanctions are more important than formal sanctions in the social control of behavior (Tittle, 1980:241).

Tittle argued that we need individualistic psychological theories of deviance, and perhaps "some of the psychological variables that sociologists discount are necessary to achieve effective explanations or to account for persistent categorical differences" (Tittle, 1980:320). He repeated the assertion that age, sex, race, and socioeconomic status are inadequate and incomplete explanations of deviant behavior. Tittle argued that perception is the most important variable in deterrence research, and he stated that we must connect psychological data to sanctions and behavior (Tittle, 1980:327–328). If the criminologist is to follow Tittle's suggestion of looking at individual differences, then one must look at variables associated with genetics and brain structure, a position maintained throughout this text.

Tittle, who was an early pioneer in deterrence research (Tittle, 1969; Tittle and Logan, 1973), arrived at a point by 1980 where he totally demolished deterrence research. Gibbs (1979:672–673) reached a somewhat similar conclusion when he stated that there is little support for deterrence research. A radical restatement of deterrence research is called for, including a need to work with experimental psychologists in a collaborative effort. Tittle and Gibbs did not suggest neurology and psychobiological learning theory, but their comments and conclusions support my contention that deterrence and punishment must be studied as an aspect of neurologically based learning theory.

In the meantime penal policy in the United States changed from rehabilitation to retribution, and the argument that punishment had a deterrent effect was a major part of such a policy. As I mentioned in Chapter 7 in discussing the Brandeis brief, behavioral science materials can have and often do have unintended effects on public policy. Poor and inadequate behavioral research is no way to integrate criminal law and the behavioral sciences. Lawyers seldom listen to behavioral scientists and when they do, they are often misled. We need better behavioral research as well as better legal policy.

The Death Penalty and Deterrence

In recent years, because of the return to retribution, there has been an increase in executions in the United States. In earlier periods of history up to 80,000 people were executed a year for a great variety of offenses, many of them minor, and discretion in the system was common (Radzinowicz, 1948). Starting around 1890 there was a major decline in the use of capital punishment, and from 1972 until 1977 there was a moratorium on executions due to the *Furman* decision.

The U.S. Supreme Court has made several critical decisions recently in the area of capital punishment. In Furman v. Georgia, 408 U.S. 238 (1972), the U.S. Supreme Court held that death penalty statutes that involved arbitrary and discriminatory discretion on the part of judges or juries are unconstitutional because they constitute cruel and unusual punishment as prohibited by the Eight Amendment. In Gregg v. Georgia, 428 U.S. 153 (1976), the Court held that the death penalty in itself is not cruel and unusual punishment if it is applied in a nonarbitrary and nondiscriminatory manner. This opened the door for states to revise and reinstate their death penalty statutes in such a manner as to conform to the requirements of the *Gregg* decision. These new statutes provided for mitigating and aggravating circumstances in order to remove the arbitrariness of the death penalty (Bowers, 1984; Inciardi, 1987; Bedau, 1987). In 1977, Gary Gilmore was executed in Utah, thus breaking the moritorium. Between 1976 and January 1, 1986, 50 people were executed and there were 1649 inmates on death row on that date. The number of executions is considerably higher now since courts are allowing more and more executions to occur (Inciardi, 1987:485).

In 1987 in McClesky v. Kemp, 55 U.S. Law Week 4537 (1987), the U.S. Supreme Court heard evidence from a sociological study that the death penalty was applied more often to blacks than to whites. However, the Court refused to overturn the death penalty verdict in this case. It was held that the study did not show discrimination in this particular case, but rather a general pattern of discrimination.

The death penalty has been used against the poor and minority groups to a far greater extent than would be true by chance. Also, the death penalty has been used overwhelmingly in southern and western states, where the homicide rates are usually high (Bowers, 1984). Very few inmates who are eligible for executions were executed even during the height of the capital punishment movement, which made the application of the death penalty arbitrary and discriminatory. Hall (1935:135) found that for embezzlement, a capital offense in 1732, there were approximately 40,000 known embezzlements, 10 prosecutions, and 3 executions. Another argument against the death penalty is that there is doubt about the guilt of some of those executed, and in the past innocent people have been executed (Inciardi, 1987:490–491).

It is estimated that 2 percent of the murder cases brought to trial result in an execution (Bowers, 1984:273). This is not a deterrent, but to argue for more executions is dehumanizing and brutalizing. The legal delays before an execution are both inhumane and very expensive.

The death penalty is defended and/or criticized in terms of the same arguments used to support punishment in general, that is, retribution and deterrence. These arguments can be either ethical or scientific arguments. Moral arguments range from "Vengeance is mine sayeth the Lord" to "Only God has the right to take a life." The sanctity of life argument is used to support the death penalty, that is, murder requires the death penalty since the life of the murder victim is sacred; and the same principle can be used to oppose the death penalty, that is, the life of the murderer is sacred and the state cannot commit legalized murder by executing murderers. As Bedau (1987) noted, any moral argument can be used to support either side in the death penalty debate.

The theory of retribution is found in Kant's ethical philosophy, whereas the utilitarian view is found in the work of Bentham (see Chapter 4). These views were discussed above. The death penalty involves two contradictory views on the right-to-life issue. The right-to-life doctrine is basic to Western ethical and political philosophy. Kant used the right-to-life doctrine to defend the execution of the last murderer since the murderer had violated the right-to-life doctrine for another person, and therefore the murderer had sacrificed his/her right to life. Bentham, on the other hand, used the right-to-life doctrine to argue that the state cannot take the life of a murderer since this is in itself murder and an act that violates the sanctity of life. Bentham also believed that capital punishment did not deter crime and that punishment must be for the purpose of deterrence or not used at all. Locke argued that the murderer forfeited his/her right to life (Bedau, 1987).

An interesting debate on the death penalty took place between Ernest van den Haag and John Conrad (1983). Conrad took the antideath penalty viewpoint on the basis of a retributionist argument, whereas van den Haag defended the pro-death penalty position on the basis of a deterrence argument. This was unusual in the sense that most people supporting the death penalty do so for reasons of justice and revenge.

Conrad stated that he started out as a utilitarian and a believer in the doctrine of deterrence, but he no longer believed in rehabilitation or deterrence. He concluded that the purpose of punishment is retribution, which is achieved when prisons carry out the sentence of the court. Conrad added, however, that the death penalty is not necessary for just retribution.

Van den Haag (1975) wrote a book in support of the death penalty which became popular just at the time when the United States returned to executions as a means of controlling criminal behavior. He continued this position in the 1983 debate with Conrad, wherein he stated that the purpose of capital punishment is primarily to deter crime. Van den Haag noted that deterrence does not work every time for everyone, but that it works often enough to justify the continued use of the death penalty.

There is no way to defend the retributionist argument morally or scientifically, since retribution is based on emotions and hatred toward the criminal rather than scientific conclusions concerning the effectiveness of retribution. We can attempt to understand aggression and violence as psychobiological behavioral events, but this does not tell us whether or not we should hate or kill criminals. In *Gregg* v. *Georgia* the Court held that retribution is not forbidden as a goal of the death penalty, and the Court noted that the death penalty serves to satisfy the feelings and needs of the public for revenge (Bedau, 1987).

The evidence to support the death penalty as a deterrent is negative. An economist, I. Ehrlich (1975) concluded from his study that one execution would prevent seven or eight murders in the future. This study has since been challenged by a number of writers, including Bowers and Pierce (1975), Passell and Taylor (1976), and Passell (1975). A review of the Ehrlich paper by Klein, Forst, and Fitalov (Blumstein, Cohen, and Nagin, 1978) found the paper to contain errors in the measurement of homicide rates, errors in the time series used, and errors in the variables omitted from the study [see also Waldo (1981) and Bowers (1984)].

The Ehrlich paper was introduced as evidence in Fowler v. North Carolina, 420 U.S. 969 (1975), by Solicitor General Robert Bork in defense of the death penalty (Bowers, 1984:304). In *Gregg* v. *Georgia* the U.S. Supreme Court held that the Ehrlich study was inconclusive and did not support the claim of deterrence for the death penalty (Bowers, 1984:306).

Bowers and Pierce (Bowers and Pierce, 1975; Bowers, 1984:272 ff.) found a brutalization effect for the death penalty, that is, an increase in the murder rate after an execution. Van den Haag (van den Haag and Conrad, 1983:144) found the Bowers and Pierce article to be "silly," and he then cited a study by Phillips that showed a drop in the murder rate two weeks after an execution. In his response to van den Haag, Conrad stated that the Phillips study was based on 22 executions from 1857 to 1921 which were listed in the *London Times*. Conrad asked: "I wonder why Phillips bothered" (van den Haag and Conrad, 1983:151).

Finally, for anyone interested in a medical model for the prevention of criminal behavior, based on biochemical and neurological problems in the brain, it must be noted that many neurologically damaged individuals have been executed (Jeffery, 1985:107; Amnesty International, 1987). The state of Florida attempted to execute Alvin Ford, but the U.S. Supreme Court reversed the Florida court and remanded the case [Ford v. Wainwright, No. 85-5542 (1986)]. Dorothy Lewis (1986), a psychiatrist, examined 15 death row inmates and found that all had histories of severe head injuries, five had major neurological impairments, and seven others had less serious neurological problems. Six subjects were schizophrenic and two were manic-depressive. Four of these people had been executed at the time the article was written (Lewis, 1986). Lewis et al. (1988) discovered from a study of 14 juveniles who were on death row that (1) 14 of 14 had serious head trauma from head injuries, (2) 14 of 14 had neurological disorders and 9 of the 14 had serious major neurological impairments, (3) 12 of 14 had IQ scores below 90, and (4) 12 of 14 had been physically brutalized as children, including 5 who had been sodomized as children. Thirteen of the 14 families had a history of violence in the family, and most had a history of alcohol and drug abuse. In only five cases was there anything resembling a pretrial investigation of the case by the lawyers, and in fact the lawyers tried to ignore or hid the psychiatric findings of the Lewis study. The issue of the treatment of brain-damaged individuals will be discussed in Chapter 21.

The Death Penalty and the Brain

In Chapter 11 we emphasize the fact that the brain is in control of both rational and emotional behaviors. We have also noted that the criminal justice system is based on emotions such as anger, hatred, and revenge, emotions that we cover with the rationality of a legal process. Retribution comes from the emotional and not the rational aspects of the brain. The emotions of fear, anger, and revenge are especially obvious in the case of the death penalty.

The major reinforcement for the death penalty comes from the pleasure people derive from punishing other people and seeing other people punished (Chapter 13 and this chapter). The death penalty is perpepuated not because it deters criminals but because it makes politicans and the general public feel good. The reinforcement serves the emotional centers of the brain and does not prevent crime in the future.

At the recent execution of Ted Bundy in the state of Florida (January 24, 1989) police officers, students from Florida State University, and others gathered outside the prison to cheer and drink beer. Signs that read "burn Bundy burn" went up, and the sound of burning bacon was played over radio stations. This sort of carnival atmosphere surrounded the early executions in England that were open to the public and that attracted up to fifty thousand people. We still regard executions as carnivals. It is a sad commentary on the moral and ethical fiber of our society.

Politicians support executions because it is politically advantageous to do so. It cost $8–12 million to execute Bundy, and his execution did not protect a single citizen or prevent a single crime. Many co-eds have been murdered since January 1978, when Bundy murdered two co-eds on the Florida State University campus. If we feel we can protect society from criminals by executing them, we have a great deal to learn about human behavior. We must stop rationalizing our revenge by saying it will benefit citizens in the future, and focus instead on the fact we are paying a high price for our feelings of hatred.

The Economic Cost of the Criminal Justice System

There is no way to estimate the cost of the criminal justice system in terms of human suffering and social cost for both the defendants/criminals and for the victims. We cannot establish a price for a murdered person or a raped female. Even estimating the cost of operating the system is difficult at best. The cost of operating the system in 1979 was $26 million for the criminal justice system alone, and this does not count the cost of crime to the victims in terms of lost property, lost time at work, or the loss of a life (Bureau of Justice Statistics, 1983:88).

The cost of a felony trial is around $32,000 (Bureau of Justice Statistics, 1983:92); a murder trial with a conviction and death penalty that goes to the Supreme Court on appeal several times will cost millions of dollars. All death penalty cases are appealed, and most of them several times or more before the execution can take place. The cost of keeping an inmate in an institution for a year is $5000 to $22,000 per year, and the cost of building a prison cell for one inmate costs between $34,000 and $110,000 and this does not include upkeep in the future (Bureau of Justice Statistics, 1983:93).

The cost of criminal justice is high. Whenever I tell my students we should spend money on medical examinations for criminals, they say: "Do you know how much that would cost?" It might be $500 to $1000 per inmate. They do not know the cost of a trial and imprisonment. As has been said, it would be much cheaper to send our inmates to Harvard University for an education at a cost of $21,000 per year than to put them in prison. It costs $3.2 million for every person executed by the state of Florida (*Tallahassee Democrat,* July 17, 1988).

We are willing to spend millions of dollars a year on prison construction and prison maintenance, knowing that this will not reduce the crime rate, yet we are not willing to spend even $2 or 3 million on a major serious research project. We spent millions to put Ted Bundy to death, but we did not spend a dollar to study his brain (see Chapters 18, 20, and 21). What good does it do to put someone in prison for twenty years at the cost of $800,000? Why not spend the money on crime prevention?

SUMMARY AND CONCLUSIONS

The criminal justice system is an ineffective and inefficient way to control crime. The police are reactive and they make arrests in 20 percent of cases. Crimes reported by victims are three times the number of crimes known to police. Few cases go to trial, and of those 90 percent are handled by a plea of guilty. Few people end up in prison. The justice system waits until the crime is committed. After that everything that is done is useless—arrest, prosecution, conviction, and imprisonment. The system does not serve to protect the criminal, the victim, or the general public. If our medical system was this inefficient it would be terminated.

The criminal justice system is justified on the basis of revenge, deterrence, and incapacitation, and there is no empirical proof that any one of these theoretical justifications lowers the crime rate or controls crime. Because of the failure of prisons to rehabilitate the retribution model (just retribution or the justice model) emerged in the 1970s as the model to be pursued by criminal justice agencies, and a major federal program under LEAA attempted to create such a justice model. As a result, our prisons are now overcrowded, dangerous, and cruel and inhumane. The death penalty has been restored in an effort to allow for retribution and/or to deter crime, but without success.

We are left in the 1980–1990 era without a crime control model. What this writer will suggest is that our new knowledge of genetics, psychobiology, neurology, the psychology of learning, and the ecological aspects of crime be used to develop a crime prevention model in place of a punitive model of crime control. A crime prevention model is an extension of the scientific model of human behavior, and it is discussed in detail in Chapters 18, 20, and 21.

FURTHER STUDIES

Criminal justice schools or departments of criminal justice, law enforcement, courts, and corrections offer course work in these areas. Law schools sometimes offer courses in the administration of criminal justice and criminal law procedures.

REFERENCES

ALLEN, H. E., and C. E. SIMONSEN (1986). *Corrections in America*. New York: Macmillan.

AMNESTY INTERNATIONAL (1987). *United States of America: The Death Penalty*. London: Amnesty International Publications.

BEDAU, H. (1987). *Death Is Different.* Boston: Northeastern University Press.

BLUMSTEIN, A., J. COHEN, and D. NAGIN (1978). *Deterrence and Incapacitation: Estimating the Effects of Criminal Sanctions on Crime Rates.* Washington, D.C.: National Academy of Sciences.

BOWERS, W. (1984). *Legal Homicide.* Boston: Northeastern University Press.

BOWERS, W. J., and G. L. PIERCE (1975). ''The Illusion of Deterrence in Isaac Ehrlich's Research on Capital Punishment.'' *Yale Law Journal,* 85:December–January: 187–208.

BUREAU OF JUSTICE STATISTICS (1983). *Report to the Nation on Crime and Justice.* Washington, D.C.: U.S. Department of Justice.

BUREAU OF JUSTICE STATISTICS (1984). *Prisoners in 1983.* Washington, D.C.: U.S. Department of Justice.

CHIRICOS, T., and G. P. WALDO (1970). ''Punishment and Crime: An Examination of Some Empirical Evidence.'' *Social Problems,* 18(2):201–217, Fall.

EHRLICH, I. (1975). ''The Deterrent Effect of Capital Punishment: A Question of Life and Death.'' *American Economic Review,* 397–417, June.

ERICKSON, M. L., J. P. GIBBS, and G. F. JENSEN (1977). ''The Deterrent Doctrine and the Perceived Certainty of Legal Punishment.'' *American Sociological Review,* 42:301–317, April.

FOX, V. (1985). *Introduction to Corrections.* Englewood Cliffs, N.J.: Prentice-Hall.

GEERKEN, M., and W. R. GOVE (1977). ''Deterrence, Overload, and Incapacitation: An Empirical Evaluation.'' *Social Forces,* 56(2):424–447, Special Issue, December.

GIBBS, J. (1975). *Crime, Punishment, and Deterrence.* New York: Elsevier.

GIBBS, J. (1977). ''Social Control, Deterrence, and Perspectives on Social Order.'' *Social Forces,* 56(2):408–423, Special Issue.

GIBBS, J. (1979). ''Assessing the Deterrence Doctrine.'' *American Behavioral Scientist,* 22(6):653–677, July–August.

GOTTFREDSON, M. R., and D. M. GOTTFREDSON (1980). *Decisionmaking in Criminal Justice.* Cambridge, Mass.: Ballinger.

GOTTFREDSON, S. D., and M. S. MCCONVILLE (1987). *America's Correctional Crisis: Prison Populations and Public Policy.* Westport, Conn.: Greenwood Press.

HALL, J. (1935). *Theft, Law, and Society.* Indianapolis: Bobbs-Merrill.

HENSHEL, R., and R. A. SILVERMAN (1975). *Perception in Criminology.* New York: Columbia University Press.

INCIARDI, J. (1987). *Criminal Justice.* Orlando, Fla.: Harcourt Brace Jovanovich.

JEFFERY, C. R. (1985). *Attacks on the Insanity Defense: Biological Psychiatry and New Perspectives on Criminal Behavior.* Springfield, Ill.: Charles C Thomas.

LEWIS, D. O. (1986). ''Psychiatric, Neurological, and Psychoeducational Characteristics of 15 Death Row Inmates in the United States.'' *American Journal of Psychiatry,* 143(7):838–845, July.

LEWIS, D. O., ET AL. (1988). Neuropsychiatric, Psychoeducational, and Family Characteristics of 14 Juveniles Condemned to Death in the United States.'' *American Journal of Psychiatry,* 145(5):584–589.

MARTIN, S. J., and S. EKLAND-OLSON (1987). *Texas Prisons.* Austin: Texas Monthly Press.

NATIONAL INSTITUTE OF JUSTICE (1980). *American Prisons and Jails,* Vol. 1. Washington, D.C.: U.S. Department of Justice.

NATIONAL INSTITUTE OF LAW ENFORCEMENT AND CRIMINAL JUSTICE (1979). *How Well Does It Work?* Washington, D.C.: U.S. Government Printing Office.

NETTLER, G. (1984). *Explaining Crime.* New York: McGraw-Hill.

NYE, F. I., and J. F. SHORT (1957). "Scaling Delinquent Behavior." *American Sociological Review,* 22:326–331.

PASSELL, P. (1975). "The Deterrent Effect of the Death Penalty: Statistical Test." *Stanford Law Review,* 28:61–80.

PASSELL, P. and J. B. TAYLOR (1976). "The Deterrence Controversy: A Reconsideration of the Time Series Evidence." In *Capital Punishment in the United States,* ed. H. A. Bedau and C. M. Pierce. New York: AMS Press.

PATERNOSTER, R., ET AL. (1982). "Perceived Risk and Deterrence: Methodological Artifacts in Perceptual Deterrence Research." *Journal of Criminal Law and Criminology,* 73(3):1238–1258, Fall.

PATERNOSTER, R., ET AL. (1983a). "Estimating Perceptual Stability and Deterrent Effects: The Role of Perceived Legal Punishment in the Inhibition of Criminal Involvement." *Journal of Criminal Law and Criminology,* 74(1):270–291, Spring.

PATERNOSTER, R., ET AL. (1983b). "Perceived Risk and Social Control: Do Sanctions Really Deter?" *Law and Society Review,* 17(3):459–479.

PETERSILIA, J., S. TURNER, and J. E. PETERSON (1986). *Prison versus Probation in California: Implications for Crime and Offender Recidivism.* Santa Monica, Calif.: Rand Corporation.

PETERSILIA, J., ET AL. (1985). *Granting Felons Probation.* Santa Monica, Calif.: Rand Corporation.

PONTELL, H. (1978). "Deterrence: Theory versus Practice." *Criminology,* 16(1):3–22, May.

RADZINOWICZ, L. (1948). *A History of English Criminal Law,* Vol. 1. London: Stevens & Sons.

SOLZHENITSYN, A. I. (1974). *The Gulag Archipelago.* New York: Harper & Row.

TITTLE, C. R. (1969). "Crime Rates and Legal Sanctions." *Social Problems,* 16:409–423.

TITTLE, C. R. (1980). *Sanctions and Social Deviance.* New York: Praeger.

TITTLE, C. R., and C. H. LOGAN (1973). "Sanctions and Deviance: Evidence and Remaining Questions." *Law and Society Review,* 7(3):371–392.

VAN DEN HAAG, E. (1975). *Punishing Criminals.* New York: Basic Books.

VAN DEN HAAG, E., and J. CONRAD (1983). *The Death Penalty: A Debate.* New York: Plenum.

WALDO, G. P. (1981). "The Death Penalty and Deterrence: A Review of Recent Research." In *The Mad, the Bad, and the Different,* ed. I. L. Barak-Glantz and C. R. Huff. Lexington, Mass.: D.C. Heath.

WALDO, D. P., and T. CHIRICOS (1972). "Perceived Penal Sanctions and Self-Reported Criminality: A Neglected Approach to Deterrence Research." *Social Problems,* 19(4):522–540, Spring.

QUESTIONS

1. Why has prison overcrowding become a critical problem during the 1970–1980 era?
2. What conclusions can be drawn concerning the effectiveness of deterrence?
3. Why is it that punishment does not work in the prison system?
4. Why has the concept of ''perception'' been of little or no value in deterrence research?
5. What conclusions did Charles Tittle reach concerning the value of deterrence research?
6. Evaluate the statement that ''the death penalty is an effective deterrent to criminal behavior.''
7. Discuss as a policy issue the placement of millions of dollars into prison construction versus putting the money into major research efforts.

Biological Criminology: Genetics

10

HISTORICAL AND IDEOLOGICAL BACKGROUND

Criminology grew out of biology as found in the works of Darwin, Lombroso, Freud, and the early geneticists. Starting in the 1920s sociology developed criminology as a subspeciality of sociology, at the same time totally ignoring biology and psychology (Chapter 14). Recently, however, biology and psychology have reemerged as parts of an interdisciplinary criminology. This is reflected in *Crime and Human Nature* by Wilson and Herrnstein (1985).

A description of the role of biology in behavior must begin with a discussion of genetics, that is, the biochemical part of each cell, which determines how the cell develops and interacts with other cells to form organs and organisms. In our discussion of systems theory (Chapter 2) we presented a cell to organ to organism to society model of development. Genes control cells and help determine whether the cells become horses or snakes or human beings, or whether they possess language and a complex brain.

In this chapter I discuss the Darwinian theory of evolution and the interaction of genes and environments to produce individuals and species. The process by which individuals developed is referred to as ontogeny; the process by which species develop is referred to as phylogeny. The topics include the ways in which genes and environments interact, how gene/environment interaction is studied, and how genes influence behavior in general and criminal behavior in particular. The political and ethical issues associated with genetics are reviewed as well.

166

EVOLUTION

Darwinian Evolution

Charles Darwin (1809–1882) totally changed scientific thought about human-kind and the nature of human nature. Darwin was a naturalist who traveled around the world studying various plants and animals. He was fascinated by the fact that different species of animals adapted to different types of environments; for example, long-legged birds were wading birds, whereas short-legged birds were tree and bush climbers. He observed finches with different types of beaks on the Galapagos Islands, each designed to be used in a different way in different environments.

In his *The Origin of Species* (1859) Darwin put forth his theory of evolution. Human beings were a part of nature, evolving from other species over a long period of time. Darwin posited variation, adaptation, and natural selection as the basic processes by which evolution occurred (Volpe, 1970; Mayr, 1978). Variation was found between species and within species, and each species used these differences to adapt to the environment. Darwin did not explain variation in genetic terms as Mendel did; rather, he accepted Lamarck's notion of acquired characteristics. Lamarck believed that if a bird stretched its legs in order to eat, the legs of its offspring would be longer. If a person is exposed to the sun, he/she would pass on the darker skin to his/her offspring. We know that inheritance is through the genes and not through the environment. One can cut the tails off rats and the offspring will still be born with tails. To change the nature of inheritance, the environment must have an impact on the genes, as in the case of environmental pollution or radiation. Genetics as found in Mendel's work was united with Darwin's ideas early in the twentieth century.

Adaptation is necessary if individuals or species are to survive. Adaptation requires the ability to eat, avoid danger, and reproduce. Successful adaptation led to natural selection, that is, the survival of those who adapt and reproduce. The idea of natural selection or ''survival of the fittest'' does not mean a superior race or a group of elite individuals predestined to wealth and fame, as the social Darwinists interpreted it to be. Natural selection only means the ability to reproduce. What survives is the genetic system, not the individual. Individuals die, but genes survive. If the gene for a given trait does not survive, that trait, and perhaps the species, disappears.

It should be emphasized here that evolution is a matter of both genetics and environment in interaction. Whether or not a given genetic trait is of value in adaptation and survival depends entirely on the environment to which the individual must adapt. In fact, diversity of traits is of great help in survival since if one trait or combination of traits are not adaptable, perhaps others are. Birds with genes for both short and long legs will survive in more environments than will only short- or long-legged birds. The importance of the environment to this process must be emphasized since many social scientists view the problem as one of genes *or* environment, not genes *and* the environment.

Darwin's theory of evolution was opposed by Christian theologians, who accepted the story of genesis as the explanation of creation. Bishop Wilberforce and Thomas Huxley debated this issue of creationism versus evolutionism at Oxford University, and in 1925 a young Tennessee biology instructor was convicted of teaching evolution to his students. In 1986 the state of Louisiana required the teaching of creationism in its schools.

The facts of evolution are established, but the theory of evolution is changing; that is, natural selection is now regarded as only one of several ways in which evolution occurs. In this context it might be noted that religion and science need not conflict, since each is involved in asking different types of questions and finding different types of answers (Gould, 1987).

The Evolution of Cells

In Chapter 2 we discussed the evolution of living systems from cells to society. The earth is 4.5 billion years old, and cells are 3 million years old. Cells are combinations of 24 chemical elements, the most important of which are nitrogen, hydrogen, oxygen, phosphorus, and carbon. Biochemicals in interaction under special conditions form life, that is, cells consisting of amino acids and polypeptide protein chains. In this sense creationism and evolutionism are back to the same basic question since the creationist can ask: "Where did hydrogen and oxygen come from in the first place?" The theologian might find the answer in God; the scientist must answer: "There is no way that I can answer that type of question."

The Evolution of Organisms

Cells come together to form organisms, including one-celled organisms and invertebrates. The first vertebrates were fish, then amphibians, insects, reptiles, birds, mammals, primates, and humans. In Chapter 3 we discussed the evolution of primates, including humans, and the important features of this evolutionary history. Such basic features as upright posture, a thumb and opposing finger, and a complex brain are critical features in human evolutionary history and adaptation to the environment through cultural and technological means.

The Evolution of Behavior

The history of the evolution of behavior is the evolution of the primate brain and the human brain. As species evolved, the brain evolved from a simple to a very complex organ. The primitive brain of an ant or bee allows the organism to respond to the environment in very limited and stereotypic ways based on prewired stimulus–response patterns. Such behavior is innate rather than learned. As the complex primate brain evolved, learning assumed a very critical role in environmental adaptation. Human adaptation and survival are now based on learning and not on innate behavioral patterns.

The model we use throughout this book is an Environment × Organism = Behavior model. The brain controls behavior and the ways in which the individual adapts to his/her environment. The brain is discussed in Chapter 11.

GENETICS

Basic Mendelian Concepts

Gregor Mendel (1822–1884) discovered that when cross-fertilized, ordinary garden peas produced three times as many yellow seeds as green seeds. This 3:1 ratio also held for round versus wrinkled seeds, inflated versus pinched pods, and other characteristics of the peas. Mendel had observed a basic unit of inheritance which came to be known in later biology as the gene. The gene is that part of each cell that determines the development of the cell. The genetic structure of the cell determines whether or not the cell develops in one way or another, for example, whether the organism produced from these cells is female or male, a horse or a cat, or has a large brain or a small brain.

The fact that certain genes produce yellow seeds whereas others produce green seeds is an example of dominant versus recessive characteristics. When a gene for a yellow seed combines with a gene for a green seed the seed is yellow, because yellow is dominant and green is recessive. Only when two green seeds combine do you get a green seed as an offspring.

Yg (plant 1)		Yg (plant 2)		
Y	×	Y	=	Y
Y	×	g	=	Y
g	×	Y	=	Y
g	×	g	=	g

This pattern of inheritance is for monogenetic traits, that is, traits determined by a gene for a trait, such as eye color. Such traits are discrete; that is, brown eyes and blue eyes do not combine to produce brown–blue eyes. There is also polygenetic inheritance, that is, traits determined by the combination of several genes. Such traits are continuous, such as height, weight, intelligence, and skin color. Polygenetic traits arrange themselves in the form of a bell-shaped curve. Most people are average height or average intelligence, with a few people 5 feet or 6 feet 10 inches in height, or with an intelligence score of 60 or 160 (see Figure 10–1).

Chromosomes, Mitosis, and Meiosis

Genes, hundreds of thousands of them, are located on amino acid chains called chromosomes. Human beings have 46 chromosomes, 44 autosomes and 2 sex

1	0	0	1	5	7	7	22	25	26	27	17	11	17	4	4	1
4:10	4:11	5:0	5:1	5:2	5:3	5:4	5:5	5:6	5:7	5:8	5:9	5:10	5:11	6:0	6:1	6:2

Figure 10-1 Polygenetic Distribution of Height. From A. F. Blakeslee, "Corn and Men," *Journal of Heredity* (1914). Vol. 5, No. 11, pp. 511-17.

chromosomes (see Figure 10-2). The sex chromosomes, the sperm for males and the egg or ovum for the female, carry all of the hereditary materials. The sperm and egg unite during sexual intercourse to form a new organism.

The autosomes divide by mitosis; that is, the cell splits and the same chromosomes appear in the new cell as in the parent cell. However, in meiosis,

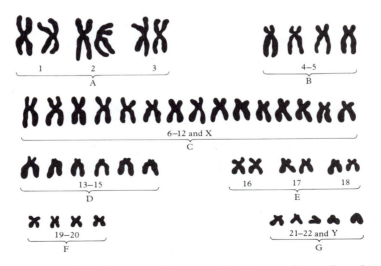

Figure 10-2 Male Karyotype (Courtesy of Dr. Margery Shaw). From Sam Singer, *Human Genetics,* 2nd ed. Copyright © 1985 W. H. Freeman and Company. Reprinted with permission.

which is limited to the sex cells (sperm and ovum), the original cell divides into four cells, each of which contains half of the chromosomes of the original cell, or 23 chromosomes. Thus the sperm and egg contain half of a complete chromosomal package. When the egg is fertilized the 23 sperm chromosomes and the 23 egg chromosomes are reunited, forming 46 chromosomes (23 pairs) for the new zygote-fetus. Inheritance by children from parents takes place only in the sex chromosomes.

The purpose of bisexual reproduction, as opposed to asexual reproduction, is diversity. As we noted in our discussion of evolution, diversity is absolutely essential for adaptation to a variety of environments. If we had only mitosis, everyone would be identical. Because of meiosis, each person, with the exception of MZ twins, is unique. Through the recombination of genes and chromosomes we inherit 50 percent of our genes from each parent on average. We are therefore only half like our parents, and half like our siblings or offspring genetically. I may inherit my hair color or intelligence or height from my father, whereas my brother or sister may not.

What traits emerge in the new infant depends not only on what genes were selected in the process of meiosis, but whether the genes inherited are dominant or recessive. If one recessive gene is present, the trait does not emerge, although a recessive gene can be passed on to children. A dominant and a recessive gene in combination will produce the trait controlled by the dominant genes. Two recessive genes in combination will produce the trait controlled by the recessive gene. I can possess a recessive gene without the phenotypic trait being manifested. Given the fact of dominant and recessive genes, and of meiosis, it is not possible to predict what traits will be inherited from which parent. A parent may be feebleminded, but I may not inherit these genes, or a given environment may be needed to trigger the emergence of the trait. As we shall see, genetic expression depends on the environment in which the genetic system is developing. Different environments have different impacts on different genetic systems (Halsey, 1977; Lindzey and Thiessen, 1970).

Sex Chromosomes

Each cell contains 46 chromosomes, including the two sex chromosomes. The female sex chromosome is called an X chromosome, the male sex chromosome is called a Y chromosome. The male sperm determines the sex of the new fetus since the sperm can carry either an X or a Y chromosome. The egg carries two X chromosomes. If the sperm carries an X chromosome, the new embryo is a female, or an XX; if the sperm carries a Y chromosome, the embryo is a male or an XY.

There are also sex chromosomal abnormalities, wherein the new embryo has more or less than the usual XY or XX combination. These possible XY combinations appear in the following list:

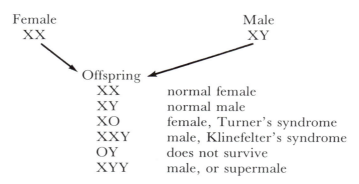

Female		Male
XX		XY

Offspring
XX	normal female
XY	normal male
XO	female, Turner's syndrome
XXY	male, Klinefelter's syndrome
OY	does not survive
XYY	male, or supermale

Several issues critical to criminology are contained in the XX–XY chromosomal pattern. The male is half female (XY) and the normal state of the egg is that of a female. When a Y chromosome is present at conception, chemical messages are sent to make this embryo into a male. The change from female to male requires a great deal of altering of the original plan. The male is more vulnerable from conception to death to birth defects, early childhood and adolescent diseases, mental illness, behavioral problems, and learning disabilities. Many of these problems are later defined as criminal behavior. The male is 5 to 10 times more criminalistic than the female. The female has a much better survival rate and fewer risks in life, including the risk of a criminal career. The importance of male and female differences and crime is discussed in Chapter 18.

Genes and Biochemistry

The most recent developments in genetics involve the joining of biochemistry and biology in the explanation of genetic processes. We discussed in Chapter 2 the emergence of interdisciplinary studies, including the joining of biology, chemistry, and psychology. In the 1950s James Watson and Francis Crick published a paper on the structure of genetic materials based on the nucleic acids DNA and RNA. These molecules are made up of adenine (A), guanine (G), thymine (T), and cytosine (C), and they form chains, called a double helix, where A and T are paired and C and G are paired.

The order in which A, T, C, and G appear on the chromosomal thread will determine the genetic message transferred to the new cell, which in turn controls the synthesis of proteins. DNA and RNA are chemical messengers that carry the information needed to create a new organism (horse, dog). If any part of the DNA–RNA code is missing or inaccurate, we have a coding error and a genetic defect. Like any information-processing system, errors in the transmission of information are possible in the genetic transmission of information. The simplest definition of a gene might be a biochemical code that carries the information needed to build new cells and new organs and new organisms.

GENETIC–ENVIRONMENT INTERACTION

The basic formula used in genetics is G × E = P, or genotype in interaction with the environment produces the phenotype. The phenotype is the organism or the observable traits produced by gene–environment interaction. What we observe are phenotypic traits, such as blue eyes or short stature; we do not observe the genes themselves unless we are looking at cell structure through a high-power microscope. Another way to express this relationship is $V_g \times V_e = V_p$, or variation in the genotype in interaction with variation in the environment will produce variation in the phenotype. In other words, everything about us is both genetic and environmental, or more properly said, is a result of the G × E interaction (Halsey, 1977; Lindzey and Thiessen, 1970; Thiessen, 1972).

It is critical to emphasize this interaction since in the past the argument has been made that behavior is either genetic or environmental. The correct argument is that behavior is a product of genetics and environment in interaction. It is not nature or nurture, but nature and nurture. As we saw in our discussion above, environmentalism has been so strong in the social and behavioral sciences that the interaction process has been ignored.

We can illustrate this interaction process by pointing out that children of Japanese parents are usually several inches taller than their parents if they are reared in the United States. This is due to a better diet, better sanitation measures, and better medical care. Another excellent example of G × E interaction is found in the way the brain develops. The brain cells need environmental stimulation in order to grow and develop. Rosenzweig and his colleagues found that rats reared in an enriched environment had more neurons, better neuronal connections, better dendrite growth, and so on, than did rats reared in a poor environment (Bloom, Lazerson, and Hofstadter, 1985:178). This topic is discussed in detail in Chapter 11.

How to Study Genetic–Environment Interaction

If everything we observe as a trait is a combination of genes and environment, how do we ever separate the influences of the two? This is a major task for behavioral genetics. Four basic methods have been used to do this: (1) family studies, (2) twin studies, (3) adoption studies, and (4) experimental studies.

Family Studies. The early work in genetics was based on family studies, such as Galton's study of the hereditary genius, and Goddard's study of Jukes and Kallikaks, with their high number of prostitutes and feebleminded individuals. A comparison was made of fathers and sons as to such traits as alcoholism, criminality, mental illness, and feeblemindedness, and then a conclusion was reached that the sons inherited the condition from the fathers.

The problem with family studies is that the family is both a biological and a social unit, or both genetics and environment. If a son is criminal and his father is criminal, is it because the son inherited genes for criminality or because he was reared in an environment with a criminal father?

Twin Studies.   A basic method used by behavioral geneticists is that of twin studies. A fertilized egg can split into two eggs and produce two identical individuals, with both possessing the same chromosomes. These twins are monozygotic (MZ) twins, and they share 100 percent of their chromosomes, which no other group of individuals do.

The other type of twins is the fraternal or dizygotic (DZ) twin. The DZ twin is a product of two eggs being fertilized at the same time, and the two being born at the same time. These twins are related as brother and brother, brother and sister, or sister and sister. MZ twins are always the same sex, whereas DZ twins can be of either sex. DZ twins share 50 percent of their chromosomes.

Nature has thus provided a natural experiment for separating genetic and environmental influences. Since MZ twins are identical for genetic structure, any differences must come from the environment. Also, since MZ twins are more alike than DZ twins, MZ twins should resemble each other more than do DZ twins, or siblings, or unrelated people.

MZ and DZ twins are compared for a given trait, such as intelligence, height, mental illness, or criminality, and the degree of similarity is called concordance. As Figure 10–3 shows, unrelated persons have low correlations for IQ scores, whereas siblings show a .40 to .60 correlation, and MZ twins show a .85 to .90 correlation. This is exactly what we would predict knowing that unrelated people share no genes, siblings share 50 percent of their genes,

Genetic and nongenetic relationships studied		0.00	0.10	0.20	0.30	0.40	0.50	0.60	0.70	0.80	0.90	Expected values
Unrelated persons	Reared apart											0.00
	Reared together											
Foster–parent–child												0.00
Parent–child												0.50
Siblings	Reared apart											0.50
	Reared together											
Twins — Two-egg	Opposite sex											0.50
	Like sex											
Twins — One-egg	Reared apart											1.00
	Reared together											

Figure 10–3 A Summary of Correlation Coefficients Concerning IQ Scores. The horizontal lines show the range of correlation coefficients for intelligence between persons who are related to various degrees either by genes or by environment. From Sam Singer, *Human Genetics,* 2nd ed. Copyright © 1985 W. H. Freeman and Company. Reprinted by permission.

and MZ twins share 100 percent of their genes (Halsey, 1977; Lindzey and Thiessen, 1970; Singer, 1985; Singer and Hilgard, 1978).

It should be noted that even in the case of MZ twins, the concordance is less than 100, which means that the environment has influenced the IQ scores as well as genetic systems. A major twin study has been under way at the University of Minnesota by Thomas Bouchard and his colleagues. They have studied twins reared apart and have found great similarities among MZ twins in physical traits, intelligence, personality characteristics, expressive behaviors, speech, movements, fears, habits, brain waves, heart patterns, and other physical and emotional characteristics (Bouchard, 1984; Bouchard et al., 1986).

Adoption Studies.   The adoption study method is regarded as superior in some ways to the twin study method. Twin studies depend on the twins being separated at birth, which is often not the case, and one finds different results for twins reared together and twins reared apart. One of the criticisms of twin studies is that they do not entirely separate heredity and environment.

Adoption studies have the advantage that the infant is usually removed from the biological mother at birth, so as to maintain complete separation of biology and environment. In the usual adoption study the adopted child (usually as an adult) is compared on a trait such as criminality or schizophrenia with both the biological and the adoptive mother. In cases of schizophrenia, criminality, IQ, and depression, the adoptive child is more likely to follow the biological parent than the adoptive parent. These behavioral disorders are discussed below.

The model for the adoption study is as follows:

Experimental Methods.   The experimental method is the most exact approach to the problem, but for moral and legal reasons it is not used on human subjects. We do selectively breed corn, wheat, dogs, race horses, hogs, sheep, cows, and so on, to increase meat or egg production, or the corn crop, or the speed of the race horses, and we have major state fairs to exhibit the best of show for plants and animals.

In laboratories species can be bred for certain traits, such as mice that are violent or gentle, or dogs that are attack dogs or family pets. Fighting fish provide another example of selective breeding. The same holds true for plants such as corn or wheat.

An example of experimental genetics would be to take hybrid corn seed from an experimental farm and plant the seed (with the same genetic components) in nine different environments: warm and dry, hot and dry, hot and wet, cold and dry, cold and wet, high nitrogen, low nitrogen, and so on. We would then measure the amount of corn produced in each environment, such as 9 bushels, 2 bushels, zero bushels, 28 bushels, and so on. We could then conclude that this specific corn seed (genetic system) does better or worse in its expression (production of corn) in different environments. Similarly, we could take nine different types of corn seed and plant them in one environment, say hot and dry. We would then measure the amount of corn produced by each seed in a constant environment. We can hold genetics constant and vary the environment, or we can hold the environment constant and vary the genetic system.

The interaction of genetics and environment is clearly seen in these examples, since the same genetic system produces different corn yields given different environments, and different environments produce different corn yields with different corn seeds. Here we see that one genotype will do better or worse in one environment than in another environment. Very bright children need a different environment than do retarded children in order for either group to maximize its genetic potential. We must match genetic potential and environmental input to maximize the human potential.

Genetics and Abnormal Behavior

We are interested in genetics as it contributes to our understanding of human behavior, especially abnormal behavior. At this point we must emphasize a crucial issue concerning the impact of genes on behavior. Genes do not cause behavior; genes influence phenotypic traits, which in turn influence behavior. The phenotype or organism is a product of genetic–environmental interaction, whereas behavior is a product of organism/environment interaction.

$$G \times E = \text{Organism (phenotype)}$$
$$O \times E = \text{Behavior}$$

Genes influence behavior through the brain, nervous system, and hormonal systems. These are called "pathway mechanisms" since they are the pathways by which genes get to behavior.

Genes ⟶ Brain ⟶ Behavior
Brain chemistry
Hormones

Schizophrenia has been found to have a high genetic component; at the same time, one of the major theories of schizophrenia emphasizes the high levels of dopamine in the brains of such persons. It is possible that the genetic system controls the neurotransmitter system and creates high levels of dopamine, which in turn influence behavior. Psychopathy has been related to genetic influences and to an underaroused autonomic nervous system.

A major study by Kety and others found that 4 percent of the nonschizophrenic adoptees in their Danish study had biological relatives who were schizophrenic, compared to 12 percent of the schizophrenic adoptees. Taken together three major studies found that the incidence of schizophrenia among the biological relatives of schizophrenics was 13 percent, compared to 1.6 percent for the nonschizophrenic group (Stine, 1977; Singer, 1985).

The environment is also critical to schizophrenia, as our $G \times E = P$ model would predict. Stress might trigger schizophrenia in a person predisposed to schizophrenia who might under other circumstances not become schizophrenic. Schizophrenia might be a product of a recessive gene, or it might be an expression of several genes in interaction, so that every person with a schizophrenic parent is not going to become schizophrenic. A summary of some of the twin studies of schizophrenia is presented in Table 10-1.

Alcoholism has a high genetic component and is very directly related to criminal behavior, a topic to be discussed in Chapter 18.

Criminal Behavior and Genetics

For general discussions of genetics, biology, and criminal behavior see Ellis (1982), Mednick and Volavka (1980), Mednick, Schulsinger, Higgins, and Bell, 1974; Vold and Bernard (1986), Shah and Roth (1974), Taylor (1984), and Mednick, Moffitt, and Stack (1987).

Several different types of studies are relevant to this discussion. We mentioned in Chapter 5 the work of Lombroso with body types. This work was carried on in the 1920–1950 era by Kretschmer, Sheldon, Hooton, and the Gluecks (Vold and Bernard, 1986; Rennie, 1978). Although such studies have been the source of controversy, they all agree that the mesomorphic type (athletic, muscular) is much more inclined to criminality than is the ectomorphic type (thin, skeletal, nervous) or endomorphic type (heavy, fatty tissue). The presence of different body types in the human population is clear, but the relationship of body type to behavior is less clear. Some sociologists would argue that it is all cultural, that is, how the culture defines the meaning of muscle

TABLE 10-1 UNCORRECTED CONCORDANCES FOR SCHIZOPHRENIA IN TWIN STUDIES REPORTED SINCE 1946

Investigator	Year	Country	MZ co-twins of schizophrenics		DZ co-twins of schizophrenics	
			Affected/total	%	Affected/total	%
Kallmann	1946	U.S.	120/174	69	53/517	10
Slater	1953	U.K.	24/37	65	10/112	9
Inouye	1961	Japan	33/55	60	2/17	12
Tienari	1963	Finland	0/16	0	2/21	10
Kringlen	1966	Norway	19/50	38	13/94	14
Gottesman and Shields	1966	U.K.	10/24	42	3/33	9
Fischer	1966	Denmark	3/10	30	0/8	0

Source: McClearn and DeFries, 1973, p. 273; after Shields et al., 1967, p. 393.

versus bone versus fat. We do know that the idea of the body beautiful varies from one culture to another.

However, the fact that there is such agreement as to the role of the mesomorphic body type in criminality, and the fact that body build is more than cultural interpretation, means that we must seek other explanations for this relationship. My own explanation is related to learning theory, which is discussed in Chapter 13. People who are muscular gain pleasure and rewards from large muscle activities, such as fishing, hunting, skiing, and football. This is a direct result of the way the brain is wired to the muscular system. The mesomorph is involved in "the Michelob weekend." In the same way people who are thin and dominated by nerve tissue are more sensitive to noise, light, and color, and they are much more likely to find art or music more rewarding and pleasurable than duck hunting at 5 A.M. in freezing waters, or trying to cast a fly on the Yellowstone River in a 50-mph wind. The endomorph is one who likes good food and "no wine before its time."

Early genetic studies support the idea that MZ twins are much more concordant for criminality than are DZ twins or unrelated persons (see Table 10-2).

A study of XYY men in Denmark by Wilkin et al. (Mednick and Christiansen, 1977) revealed that of 4139 males studied 12 were XYY cases. Of the XYY cases, five, or 41.7 percent, had a criminal record, compared to 9 percent of the XY cases. The original hypothesis was that XYY men had an additional amount of testosterone, the male hormone, which is related to violence and aggression. Further studies showed that XYY criminals were not violent offenders but were more of an inadequate personality type. The Wilkin study found low IQ to be associated with XYY, and it may be that the linking variable between XYY and crime is intelligence.

XYY ⟶ Intelligence ⟶ Crime

TABLE 10-2 CONCORDANCE WITH REGARD TO ADULT CRIMINALITY IN MONOZYGOTIC AND SAME-SEXED DIZYGOTIC TWIN PAIRS

Investigator and year		Monozygotic pairs Conc.	Disc.	Dizygotic pairs Conc.	Disc.	Concordance (%) MZ	DZ
Rosanoff, Handy and	Males:	29	9	5	18	76	22
Plesset (1941)	Females:	6	1	1	3	86	25
Lange (1929)		10	3	2	15	77	12
Le Gras (1933)		4	—	—	5	100	0
Kranz (1936)		20	11	23	20	65	53
Stumpfl (1936)		11	7	7	12	61	37
Borgstrom (1939)		3	1	2	3	75	40
Yoshimasu (1965)		14	14	—	26	50	0

Source: McClearn and DeFries, 1973, p. 301. after Slater and Cowie, 1971, p. 114.

Whether or not intelligence turns out to be a pathway mechanism for XYY cases remains to be seen. A general theoretical approach would be one that viewed the extra Y chromosome as creating a number of brain abnormalities and brain defects which render the person vulnerable to deviant and nonadaptive behaviors, and which could result in a wide spectrum of behaviors. There is no reason to believe that the extra Y chromosome produces only one type of behavior. It can be hypothesized that the extra Y can create not one but several types of brain defects, or that in interaction with different environments the Y can produce a variety of maladaptive response patterns.

A study by Hutchings and Mednick (Mednick and Volavka, 1980) using the adoption study method found that if the biological father was criminal, 22 percent of the adopted sons were criminal. If the adoptive father was criminal, 11.5 percent of the adopted sons were criminal. If both the biological and adoptive fathers were criminal, 36 percent of the adopted sons were criminal. If neither of the fathers was criminal, 10.5 percent of the adopted sons were criminal (see Table 10-3).

Several things must be pointed out concerning this study. It shows the interaction of genetics and environment (36 percent) and the absence of the influence of the environment without genetics (11.5 percent). Two other interesting questions are raised by the study. Of those sons who had criminal influences from both genetic and environmental sources, 36 percent were criminal. This means that 64 percent of those exposed to both genetic and environmental influences did not become criminals. We must explain the 64 percent as well as the 36 percent. It could be that different genetic systems were at work since only 50 percent of the genes on average are shared by father and son. It could be a matter of recessive genes, which influenced some sons but not other sons. The different environments could affect the different genotypes in different ways. The 10.5 percent also needs explaining, since these sons had *no* genetic or environmental influence toward criminality, yet they became criminals. Since everything in behavior is both genetic and environment, how do we explain this group of criminal behaviors? We must assume that our studies are missing some of the important variables that cause crime; otherwise, how can we have criminal sons with noncriminal fathers, or criminals from genetic and environmental backgrounds that do not produce criminals? Again we can assume re-

TABLE 10-3 CRIMINALITY IN MALE ADOPTEES AND THEIR BIOLOGICAL AND ADOPTIVE FATHERS[a]

Is biological father criminal?		Yes	No
Is adoptive father criminal?	Yes	$\frac{21}{58} = 36.2\%$	$\frac{6}{52} = 11.5\%$
	No	$\frac{46}{214} = 21.5\%$	$\frac{35}{333} = 10.5\%$

[a]"Cross-fostering" analysis: Table values are percentage of adoptive sons who are registered criminals.

Source: Mednick and Volavka, 1980, p. 99.

cessive genes or different genetic compositions for different sons. Similarly, what may be a noncriminal environment for a father may be a criminal environment for a son.

Another theoretical approach to this issue, and one that I have pursued throughout this book, is that of individual differences, which is one way of summarizing what we have said about genetic and environmental differences for each son. Since each person is different from every other person for both genetic and environmental factors, we are going to find great individual variation in any phenotypic trait we study, even criminality. We must design our future research with individual differences in mind.

Rowe (1986) found in his twin study of delinquents that a common or shared environment which should make the twins similar contributed nothing to their behavioral or personality development. This is consistent with adoption studies which have found that being reared together contributed nothing to personality development. Rowe found that heredity played a major role in delinquent behavior in terms of such temperamental traits as anger, impulsivity, deceitfulness, and antisocial behaviors and concluded that "delinquent behavior is not affected by common environmental influences—such as social class, religion, parental values, and parental child-rearing practices (Rowe, 1986:527).

The within-family environment which is unique to each person and which makes twins differ from one another did contribute to behavioral and personality development. Rowe explained the environmental impact on behavior as idiosyncratic, affecting each person in a totally different way from every other person. This is essentially my argument; one must look closely at individual differences since no two persons are alike (except for identical twins).

Scarr, from her studies of adoptive children, concluded that the resemblance between adoptive parents and children is practically nonexistent. From his study of twins, Loehlin could not identify any relationship between personality development and childhood environments. They both concluded that individual differences are critical to the understanding of human behavior (Research and Education Association, 1982:146).

There is a large body of literature in criminology concerning the psychopath as an antisocial person. Psychopathy has a hereditary component, and it is a central nervous system disorder resulting in a learning disability. The topic of the psychopath is discussed more fully in Chapter 18.

POLITICAL AND ETHICAL CONCERNS

The emergence of Darwinian evolutionary thought and Mendelian genetics raised serious questions concerning the nature of human nature. Religion, philosophy, and law taught a dualism of mind and body, and concepts of free will and moral responsibility.

The scientific view of humankind and the religious, philosophical, and legal views came into conflict. The impact of biology on religion and ethics is discussed in terms of eugenics, Nazism, communism, environmentalism, political ideology, and special creationism.

Eugenics

Eugenics means the improvement of the species through selective breeding. This idea is used in agricultural genetics to produce superior race horses or chickens or cows or corn, but major legal and ethics problems emerge when we attempt to create super human races through selective breeding (Kevles, 1984).

Francis Galton (1822–1911) published in 1869 his *Hereditary Genius,* in which he argued that certain family lines produce geniuses and other family lines produce idiots and degenerates. At the same time, other scientists started to look for the genetic component in mental illness, feeblemindedness, and criminality. In 1912, Henry Goddard published *The Kallikak Family: A Study in the Heredity of Feeblemindedness,* in which he claimed that delinquency was due feeblemindedness. Richard Dugdale made the same claims in his study of the Jukes family (Vold and Bernard, 1986). This eugenics movement led to the use of sterilization of feebleminded women to prevent future generations of feebleminded people. In a famous Supreme Court decision, *Buck* v. *Bell,* upholding a Virginia statute which provided for sterilization, Justice O. W. Holmes said that ''three generations of imbeciles are enough'' (Rennie, 1978).

The eugenics movement oversold genetic causes for social problems while ignoring environmental issues. The eugenics movement was also bad genetics in some respects. For example, feeblemindedness can be a result of genetic-environment interaction, lack of a proper diet, or a recessive gene that will affect only one in four children from a given family. Some very bright people produce feebleminded or defective children, and a feebleminded mother can produce a normal child.

We know today that genetics is an important factor in many social problems, such as mental illness, alcoholism, intelligence, and criminality. By putting forth claims before they were seriously researched and tested, the eugenics movement set genetic research back for many years.

Nazism and Racism

In *The Inequality of the Human Races* (1915), Count de Gobineau argued for a biological base for racial inequalities and racial inferiorities. H. S. Chamberlain in *The Foundations of the Nineteenth Century* praised the Germans as the superior race. In *Mein Kampf,* Adolph Hitler made racism and the superiority of the Germans basic to the Nazi movement of the 1930s (Simpson and Yinger, 1953; Mazur and Robertson, 1972). As a result of this movement to use genetics in a political way, the holocaust occurred in Germany, and millions of Jews were killed. This, as well as Nazi medical experimentation beyond the limits of scientific ethics, made ''genetics'' a dirty word among many social scientists.

Communism and Lysenkoism

Whereas Nazism is regarded as fascistic and elitist, communism is based on the ideology of equality and the power of the masses. The Russian czar abdicated in 1917 and in 1918 was killed by the Bosheviks (later the communists). There emerged a new political ideology based on a belief in a classless society and the equality of individuals. Part of this political ideology included total environmental determinism and a rejection of genetic factors.

Under Stalin, from 1930 to 1953, the Soviet Union was governed by a dictator who purged his enemies. A young agricultural specialist by the name of T. D. Lysenko believed in the Lamarckian doctrine of acquired characteristics, that is, that characteristics acquired by the individual from the environment would be transmitted as traits to its offspring. The food supply was always a problem in the Soviet Union, and Lysenko convinced Stalin that the Soviets could produce great wheat crops in the frozen tundra of Siberia if they would subject the wheat seed to a cold environment prior to planting the seed in order that the seed could "adapt" to the cold climate. This model became a basic part of Stalin's effort to solve the Soviet food problem, and it was a total failure. As a result the Soviets have been buying wheat from the United States, and the United States is in fact feeding the Soviet war machine while pouring billions of dollars into a military system to be used to defend the country against the Soviets.

The Lamarckian–Lysenko doctrine has been thoroughly rejected by geneticists from England and the United States. At one time the Soviets had the top geneticists in the world, but they were put into prison or exiled, and many of them came to the United States to establish genetic research programs (Plomin, DeFries, and McClearn, 1980; Joravsky, 1970).

Environmentalism

The fourth factor in the rejection of genetics is the environmentalism of American social science. American social anthropology and sociology taught cultural determinism, as found in the work of Franz Boaz, Ruth Benedict, and Margaret Mead. Anthropology is divided into social and cultural anthropology, physical anthropology, and archeology. We thus have physical anthropology versus social anthropology, as we have biological psychology versus mentalistic psychology. Social scientists assume that biology has been replaced by cultural evolution. Eckland stated that social science rejects genetics because of the strong environmentalism and the ideology that all persons are created equal. Social scientists are also opposed to reductionism and racism, which they think they find in genetics (Mazur and Robertson, 1972).

Experimental psychology as developed by John Watson and his followers was based on the idea that any type of person could be created given the right environment (McClearn and DeFries, 1973). Behaviorism is S-R psychology, the belief that response is determined by the stimulus or environment. This psychology will be discussed in detail in Chapter 13.

Equality of All

The political doctrine that "all men are created equal" runs counter to the findings of genetic research. Our Constitution states that all are equal before the law. There are several different meanings of equality. Equality can mean equality of opportunity to develop one's capabilities to their fullest. Another concept of equality is that all people are equal and should be treated alike and should reach the same position in life at the same time (Taylor, 1984).

The main lesson of genetics is the total diversity of human types and individual differences (McClearn and DeFries, 1973). No two people are alike, except for monozygotic twins. Equality cannot mean equality of outcome or goal attainment. Individuals differ greatly as to traits, abilities, and interests. A tall muscular person can become a football or basketball star much more easily than can a short and nonmuscular person. This can mean fame and fortune for the genetically predisposed athlete. The same can be said for those with exceptional talent or beauty who can become television and movie personalities and thus earn millions of dollars.

Religion and Special Creationism

A basic doctrine of fundamentalist religions is that the origins of the earth and of human beings are explained in the Book of Genesis, that is, special creationism. Evolutionary theory taught that the evolution of life forms, including the human life form, took place over billions of years and involved the emergence of the human species from other, already existing species. Evolutionism and special creationism are in direct conflict.

Genetics and the Law

The legal system rejects many of the scientific advances made in the study of human behavior because of the concepts of "mind" and "free will." Yet as Taylor (1984) wrote, the law must come to terms with genetics and the ability to predict and treat violent behaviors based on genetic variables. Taylor concluded by observing that:

> If we choose to accept cancer as being divinely caused, we are unlikely to find a cure for that disease. If we choose to believe that crime is caused by environmental conditions because that theory is socially acceptable, we are unlikely to discover ways to prevent criminal conduct or rehabilitate criminals.
>
> We are not all born equal. Insisting that we are—that we are clay at birth, waiting to be formed by the environment—accomplished nothing but a postponement of the ability to deal effectively with the problem of crime in our society. (Taylor, 1984:164)

Biology and Criminologists

As I pointed out in Chapter 2, biology has, for the most part, been rejected by criminologists. The 1978 ASC meeting in Dallas where biology was made a part of the program was subject to heavy criticism. As late as 1979, Cressey (1979: 50) stated: "Some of the theories on which interventionist policies were based turned out to be silly. . . . For example, the biological determinism theory of criminal conduct went down the tube long ago, though there are periodic attempts to revive it." The 1987 program in Montreal had several major sessions devoted to biology and crime, and the sessions were well attended and well received.

Mednick (Mednick, Moffitt, and Stack, 1987:3–4) recounted his experiences with biology and criminology, in which he noted that XYY studies were referred to as "demonism revisited." Mednick had a proposal to study serious career offenders using physiological data, and a Washington columnist stated in a newspaper article that these were "Voodoo tests." The Department of Justice promptly canceled the contract, and Congress passed legislation making it illegal for the agency to do physiological research on criminals. We can put criminals in hell-holes called prisons, and we can execute them, but we cannot do research as to the causes of criminal behavior.

SUMMARY

Human behavior, including criminal behavior, involves genetics and environment in interaction. The study of genetics has been opposed for religious, moral, and political reasons, and *environmentalism* has dominated the social and behavioral sciences for many years. In recent years major progress have been made in the biological sciences and in behavioral genetics which have major implications for criminology. Darwinian evolution and Mendelian genetics have been discussed briefly, as they contribute to our understanding of the mechanisms upon which behavior is founded.

The basic concept in genetics today is that of genes and environment in interaction. It is not nature versus nurture, but nature and nuture in interaction. The basic formula is genetics $\times$ environment = phenotype. Family studies, twin studies, adoption studies, and experimental studies have been used to study this interactional process. Genes influence behavior through pathway mechanisms such as the brain, brain chemistry, and hormonal systems, all in interaction with one another and with the environment.

The impact of genetics has been found on such abnormal behaviors as schizophrenia, depression, alcoholism, and criminal behavior. Future studies of criminal behavior must include genetic factors as well as environmental factors. Most of our studies of criminals totally ignore biology and the genetic aspects of human behavior. As Gardner Lindzey has stated: "A science of behavior that ignores genetic variations sets marked limits to the progress it can hope to make" (Manosevitz, Lindzey, and Thiessen, 1969:5).

FURTHER STUDIES

Courses in behavioral genetics and evolution are offered in biology and psychology departments. Several psychology departments—the University of Minnesota, the University of Texas, and the University of Colorado—have major programs and institutes in behavioral genetics.

REFERENCES

BLOOM, F., A. LAZERSON, and L. HOFSTADTER (1985). *Brain, Mind, and Behavior.* New York: W.H. Freeman.

BOUCHARD, T. J. (1984). "Twins Reared Together and Apart: What They Tell Us about Human Diversity." In *Individualism and Determinism: Chemical and Biological Bases,* ed. S. W. Fox. New York: Plenum.

BOUCHARD, T. J., D. T. LYKKEN, N. L. SEGAL, and K. J. WILCOX (1986). "Development in Twins Reared Apart: A Test of the Chronogenetic Hypothesis." In *Human Growth: A Multidisciplinary Review,* ed. A. Demirjian. London: Taylor & Francis.

CRESSEY, D. R. (1950). "Criminological Theory, Social Science, and the Repression of Crime." *Criminology: New Concerns.* ed., E. Sagarin pp. 39–59. Beverly Hills: Sage.

ELLIS, L. (1982). "Genetics and Criminal Behavior." *Criminology,* May, 43–66.

*FULLER, J. L., and W. R. THOMPSON (1978). *Foundations of Behavioral Genetics.* St. Louis; Mo.: C. V. Mosby.

GOULD, S. J. (1987). "Darwinism Defined: Sifting Fact from Theory." *Discover,* January, 13–26.

HALSEY, A. H. (1977). *Heredity and Environment.* New York: Free Press.

*HENDERSON, N. D. (1982). "Human Behavior Genetics." *Annual Review of Psychology,* Vol. 33. Palo Alto: Calif., Annual Reviews.

JORAVSKY, D. C. (1970). *The Lysenko Affair.* Cambridge, Mass.: Harvard University Press.

KEVLES, D. J. (1984). "Annals of Eugenics." *New Yorker,* October 8, 15, 22, 29.

LINDZEY, G., and D. D. THIESSEN (1970). *Contributions to Behavior—Genetic Analysis.* New York: Appleton-Century-Crofts.

MANOSEVITZ, M., G. LINDZEY, and D. D. THIESSEN (1969). *Behavioral Genetics.* New York: Appleton-Century-Crofts.

MAYR, E. (1978). "Evolution." *Scientific American,* September, 46–55.

MAZUR, A., and L. S. ROBERTSON (1972). *Biology and Social Behavior.* New York: Free Press.

MCCLEARN, G. E., and J. C. DEFRIES (1973). *Introduction to Behavioral Genetics.* San Francisco: W. H. Freeman.

MEDNICK, S., and K. O. CHRISTIANSEN (1977). *Biosocial Bases of Criminal Behavior.* New York: Gardner Press.

*Source of particular importance in the preparation of this chapter

MEDNICK, S., T. MOFFITT, and S. A. STACK (1987). *The Causes of Crime: New Biological Approaches.* Cambridge: Cambridge University Press.

MEDNICK, S. A., F. SCHULSINGER, J. HIGGINS, and B. BELL (1974). *Genetics, Environment, and Psychopathy.* Amsterdam: North-Holland.

MEDNICK, S. A., and J. VOLAVKA (1980). ''Biology and Crime.'' In *Crime and Justice,* Vol. 2, ed. N. Morris and M. Tonry. Chicago: University of Chicago Press.

*PLOMIN, R., J. C. DeFRIES, and G. E. McCLEARN (1980). *Behavioral Genetics.* San Francisco, W. H. Freeman.

RENNIE, Y. (1978). *The Search for Criminal Man.* Lexington, Mass.: Lexington Books.

*RESEARCH AND EDUCATION ASSOCIATION (1982). *Behavioral Genetics.* New York: Research and Education Association.

ROWE, D. C. (1986). ''Genetic and Environmental Components of Antisocial Behavior: A Study of 265 Twin Pairs.'' *Criminology,* 24(3):513–542, August.

SHAH, S., and L. ROTH (1974). ''Biological and Psychophysiological Factors in Criminality.'' In *Handbook of Criminology,* ed. D. Glaser. Skokie, Ill.: Rand McNally.

SIMPSON, G. E., and J. M. YINGER (1953). *Racial and Cultural Minorities,* 4th ed. New York: Harper & Row.

*SINGER, S. (1985). *Human Genetics.* New York: W. H. Freeman.

SINGER, S., and H. R. HILGARD (1978). *The Biology of People.* San Francisco: W. H. Freeman.

SLATER, E., and V. COWIE (1971). *The Genetics of Mental Disorders.* London: Oxford University Press.

STINE, G. (1977). *Biosocial Genetics.* New York: Macmillan.

TAYLOR, L. (1984). *Born to Crime.* Westport, Conn.: Greenwood Press.

THIESSEN, D. D. (1972). *Gene Organization and Behavior.* New York: Random House.

VOLD, G., and T. J. BERNARD (1986). *Theoretical Criminology.* New York: Oxford University Press.

VOLPE, E. P. (1970). *Understanding Evolution.* Dubuque, Iowa: Wm. C. Brown.

WILSON, J. Q., and R. J. HERRNSTEIN (1985). *Crime and Human Nature.* New York: Simon & Schuster.

QUESTIONS

1. What are the principles of Darwinian evolution?
2. Why did Mendel observe a ratio of 3:1 of yellow seeds to green seeds in his flowers?
3. What are the basic functions of mitosis and meiosis?
4. What are the functions of the sex chromosomes?
5. Explain $G \times E = P$.
6. How do geneticists study genotype–environment interaction?

*Source of particular importance in the preparation of this chapter

7. How do genes get translated into behavior?
8. What relationship exists between genetics and criminal behavior?
9. What did the study by Hutchins and Mednick indicate concerning genetics and criminality?
10. Why is there so much political and ethical controversy surrounding the study of genetics?
11. What is meant by the statement that ''except for MZ twins, no two people are alike''? What are the implications of this statement for the study of criminal behavior?

Biological Criminology: The Brain

11

INTRODUCTION

The Story of One Student

A few years back a young student, harassed and depressed, walked into my office with a green knapsack on her back to discuss criminology. She was disappointed with the police–courts–corrections materials she was being exposed to, and she was now in my CCJ 4610 class on criminal and delinquent behavior, in which I discussed biological and psychological aspects of human behavior. She wanted to inquire whether or not other people were utilizing this approach, and where she could go to pursue a psychobiological approach to criminal behavior. I pointed out to her that Florida State University had a fine psychology department that offered a number of courses in psychobiology and learning theory.

She then entered our graduate program and had my biological and psychological theories of criminal behavior course, as well as a number of courses in the psychology department. She ended up with a dissertation on hypoglycemia and antisocial behavior which immediately gained some national attention. From there she received a three-year postdoctoral fellowship to study neurology and neurometrics at the school of medicine of the University of Maryland, and now she is a research associate at the National Institute on Drug Abuse, doing very sophisticated biochemical research with some of the top scientists in the world in this field. She is now a major contributor to the literature on the biochemical aspects of antisocial behavior.

Overview

In this chapter we discuss the brain, the organ of behavior. There is probably less known about the brain than any other aspect of nature, or human nature. In the past we have left the explanation of the brain to philosophers and mentalistic psychologists and sociologists, who have either distorted the nature of the brain, or have ignored it. In recent years there has been a major revolution in the brain sciences and our understanding of the role of the brain in human behavior. This is found in the interdisciplinary work that has produced biochemistry, neurology, biological psychiatry, and psychobiology. Today, biological psychiatry and psychobiology are on the leading edges of medicine and psychology. Introductory textbooks start with the biological basis of behavior, and many major graduate programs offer specialized programs in psychobiology. For example, the University of Arizona (I use Arizona as an example only because I had a graduate catalog from Arizona in front of me while I was typing this), offers the following graduate courses in psychobiology:

Neurological Psychology
Body Chemistry and Behavior
Biopsychology
Human Brain–Behavior Relationships
Neuropsychology: Assessment and Clinical Applications

I could have used the programs at Florida State University or the University of California at Irvine, or many others as examples. The APA *Monitor* (September 1985) had a total issue devoted to the role of the brain sciences in the new psychobiology.

The brain controls our cognitive and rational behaviors, such as language, thought, decision making, and learning, as well as certain aspects of our emotional and motivational life, such as hunger, sex, thirst, anger, aggression, drug and alcohol addiction, and pleasure and pain. The brain plays a central role in mental illnesses and criminal behaviors, and treatment of these abnormal behaviors has become increasingly based on drug therapies and neurological examinations.

The Mind–Brain Problem

There are two opposing views of human nature: one based on rationalism and mentalism, the other based on empiricism, physicalism, and science (Chapters 2 and 12). The mind–body problem arises from the dualism of rationalistic philosophy, which uses a nonphysical concept of the "mind" to explain physical changes in the body. In this chapter we develop a systems model of behavior, an Environment × Brain = Behavior model. The brain replaces the mind and the empty organism.

Materialism or physicalism holds that all events or properties are physical, and what we refer to as the "mind" can be explained as activities of a physical entity called the brain. We regard simple reflex actions such as an eye blink or a knee jerk as physical action (see Chapter 4 on voluntary versus involuntary explanations of behavior as found in the law); on the other hand, we regard thought, cognition awareness, decision making, language, and memory as "mental states." The concept of free will comes from these mental states, which are free of physical constraints. In psychobiology, cognition and thinking are regarded as the most complex functioning of a complex primate brain with a large cortex. The role of the cortex is discussed in a later part of this chapter. We do not usually refer to lower animals (worms, insects, fish) as possessing a "mind" or a "soul." The differences lie in the organization and structure of the brain as found in the evolutionary history of the brain. The primate brain is much more complex, with different capabilities, than the simple brain of fish or insects or reptiles (Gilinsky, 1984; Carlson, 1984).

Mentalism, the idea of a "mind," is the first major barrier to a scientific study of behavior as a product of brain–environment interaction. As Kalat has stated:

> The brain controls behavior. This is considered common knowledge, but not everyone understands and accepts its philosophical implications. To accept it fully one must rethink one's view of the nature of mind, the nature of life, individual responsibility for behavior, and virtually all the other basic questions of human existence. (Kalat, 1984:xv)

Bloom, Lazerson, and Hofstadter (1985) argue that the central dogma of neurological psychology and biological psychiatry is that the concept of mind can be understood as the functioning of the physical brain.

Brain–Environment Interaction

The brain is a product of genetic and environmental factors and interaction. The genetic code puts down a basic "hard wiring" diagram of the brain. This hard wiring is basic to the behavior of simple organisms, and to such human responses as seeing, hearing, walking, or breathing. Each species (phylogeny) and each individual (ontogeny) have different brains, due to genetic and environmental differences.

At the same time the hard wiring can be modified and altered by experience. The development of the brain depends upon stimulation from the environment. A kitten that has a patch placed over one eye from birth will never develop sight in that eye later, even after the patch is removed. The proper nerve connections from the eye to the brain are not made if the optic nerve system is not stimulated during this critical period of development. Rats reared in an impoverished environment have fewer neurons, synaptic connections, dendrites, and other neural developments than do rats reared in an enriched environment.

A child reared in poverty on a low-protein diet will not develop a normal brain. We talk a great deal about poverty being related to criminal behavior, but we never specify the mechanisms by which poverty contributes to criminal behavior. One mechanism is the impact of poverty on the human brain. We put children in remedial education courses or in penal institutions when we should be worrying about their diet and nutritional intake.

Since the brain is sensitive to environmental input, the brain will respond to such environmental situations as isolation, maternal deprivation, environmental pollution, and nutrition and diet. Lead and cadmium are very harmful when they get into the brain, as are other toxic chemicals which come from polluted food, water, and air. The brain is the major consumer of sugar and oxygen, and a lack or excess of either will cause serious brain disorders. Hypoglycemia, low blood sugar levels, can be related to such behavioral disturbances as violent outbursts. Lack of a specific enzyme in the brain can cause violent outbursts when a small amount of alcohol is ingested and taken into the brain.

Environmentalism is the second major barrier (mentalism being the first) to a scientific study of human behavior, that is, the belief that behavior is caused by something in the environment, such as poverty, unemployment, racism, social norms, social class, or a lack of education. This is the view of behavior found in much of psychology (humanistic, clinical) and sociology, based on attitude formation, self-concepts, and social environmental determinism.

The model of behavior we use here maintains that *all environmental experiences go through the brain to be analyzed, stored, and utilized by the brain.* The eye does not "see" a tree or people in our environment. The stimulus hits the retina of the eye and is transmitted to the visual centers of the brain, where the brain interprets the stimulation as a tree or person. The pain from a broken bone in the leg is not in the leg; the nervous system transmits this information to the brain, where it is interpreted as pain. If we are under the influence of pain-killing drugs, we will not feel the pain although the leg is still broken. We can undergo serious surgery without pain because drugs can block the neural pathways from the surgery to the brain.

The brain stands between the environment and behavior in every aspect of behavior. We must accustom ourselves to thinking in terms of an

$$\text{Environment} \times \text{Brain} = \text{Behavior}$$

model rather than

$$\text{Environment} \longrightarrow \text{Behavior}$$

model. This is a radical departure from a great deal of the psychology, anthropology, and sociology that many of us were taught during our undergraduate and graduate school days.

THE NERVOUS SYSTEM

Systems Theory and the Brain

A living system has the capacity to take in information and energy from the environment, to code it and store it, and to use the information in order to respond to the environment (Chapter 2). A living system needs (1) a sensor or detector system for detecting changes in the environment and for furnishing input from the environment to the system; (2) a selector system or decision process for coding, storing, and retrieving information for future decisions and actions; and (3) an effector system or output system for responding to the environment. Such responses allow the system to survive and adapt to the environment.

The brain is a living system, where the sensor system is the sensory system; the selector system is the brain; and the effector system comprises the muscles and glands.

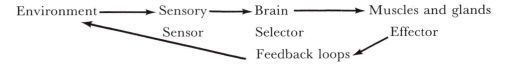

What is referred to as behavior is the effector system—muscles and glands. The function of the brain is to join the environment and the muscles; that is, the environment enters the brain and in turn the brain controls behavior.

Evolution of the Nervous System

Primitive organisms do not have specialized organs for sensing or responding to the environment. Rather, they have a few sensitive cells scattered throughout the body which respond to environmental stimuli, such as light or heat or chemicals. These cells act individually and are not integrated and organized so as to communicate with one another. The response is a generalized, uncoordinated response.

As species evolve, so do specialized organs. Sensory organs, such as eyes, ears, noses, and mouths, emerge when light-sensitive, sound-sensitive, and odor/chemical-sensitive cells migrate to one position to form a more effective and adaptive sensory organ. An eye is thus a collection of cells that come together to specialize in responding to light. At the same time vertebrates (with a spinal cord) emerged from invertebrates (without a spinal cord). For vertebrates the spinal cord became a specialized nervous system running from one end of the body to the other. At the top of the spinal cord emerged a collection of cells (ganglia) which received neural messages from and sent neural messages to the spinal cord. The spinal cord connected the arms, legs, and skin with one another and with the central ganglia. The central ganglia, in turn, developed into primitive brains.

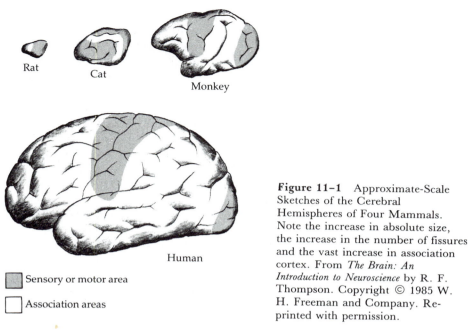

Figure 11–1 Approximate-Scale Sketches of the Cerebral Hemispheres of Four Mammals. Note the increase in absolute size, the increase in the number of fissures and the vast increase in association cortex. From *The Brain: An Introduction to Neuroscience* by R. F. Thompson. Copyright © 1985 W. H. Freeman and Company. Reprinted with permission.

Rat

Cat

Monkey

Human

☐ Sensory or motor area

☐ Association areas

The primitive brain is essentially one devoted to sensory and motor functions which are necessary to survival, such as eating, sleeping, walking, temperature regulation, mating, respiration, digestion, and heart action. As the brain developed from a primitive brain to a mammalian and primate brain the new brain or neocortex developed, which allowed the organism to learn and to adapt to the environment by means of learned responses rather than innate instinctive responses (see Figure 11–1).

The Sensory System

The five sensations can be represented as follows:

Sensory process	Sensory system	Stimulus
Vision	Eye	Light
Auditory	Ear	Sound
Taste	Tongue	Chemicals—liquid
Olfactory	Nose	Chemicals—gases
Tactile	Skin	Touch, pressure, heat, cold

Sensory neurons are sensitive to environmental stimuli, such as light, sound, liquids, odors, touch, heat, and cold. Thus our knowledge of the environment comes from experience (see John Locke and empiricism in Chapters 2 and 13). However, these stimuli must be processed by the brain since as was noted above, we see and hear with the brain, not the eye or ear. The brain organizes discrete sensory experiences into a coherent whole, thus giving support to the rationalist view (see rationalism in Chapters 2 and 12) that there is more than sensation involved in knowledge. What the rationalist referred to as innate or preexisting ideas can better be described as the brain. The brain is the center of reason and thought. Empiricism and rationalism can be merged into one major theoretical system. Both *environment* and *organism* are necessary. The mistake has been to regard human nature as innate and in the individual, or as experience and sensation and in the environment. The interactionist point of view presented in this book overcomes this either–or view of human nature.

Sensory input (light, sound, chemicals, touch) is changed to a biochemical code, which is then transmitted to the brain. This process, whereby one form of energy (light) is changed into another form (electrical or chemical), is technically called transduction. This occurs when we speak into a telephone and the sound of the voice is changed into an electrical signal to be transmitted to another phone and then changed back into a human voice. Light does not enter the brain. The brain is designed to receive bioelectrical signals, to interpret and store them, and to send out biochemical messages to the muscles and glands.

The sensory organs are connected to the brain by special nerve pathways and by specialized parts of the brain which handle visual or auditory or olfactory input. These processes are described in more detail below.

The Nervous Systems

The central nervous system (CNS) is composed of the brain and the spinal cord, to be discussed below. The peripheral nervous system (PNS) is composed of everything not included in the CNS. The PNS is divided into the *somatic* nervous system and the *autonomic* nervous system. The somatic nervous system, made up of spinal and cranial nerves, controls the large striated muscles or skeletal muscles found in the arms, legs, face, and so on. These muscles are involved in what we often refer to as "voluntary" behavior or self-initiated behavior.

The autonomic nervous system controls the smooth muscles as found in the pupil of the eye, blood vessels, lungs, intestines, bladder, and sex organs, as well as the cardiac muscle of the heart. Glands such as the salivary gland are also controlled by the autonomic nervous system. The activities of the autonomic system are often referred to as "involuntary" or beyond self-control. This is the basis for the distinction in criminal law between voluntary and involuntary behaviors, and the notion that voluntary behaviors involve free will and moral responsibility (Chapter 4). Our voluntary responses are not the product of mental states; they are the product of the nervous system and are physical in nature. The difference between voluntary and involuntary behavior is in the structure of the nervous system, and it is possible to study voluntary behavior as part of the nervous system.

The autonomic nervous system is divided into the *sympathetic* nervous system and the *parasympathetic* nervous system (Figure 11–2). The sympathetic nervous system increases the activity of the target organ (e.g., an increase in blood pressure or heart beat or perspiration rate or rate of respiration). The heart, lungs, and blood vessels work harder. On the other hand, the parasympathetic nervous system decreases the rate of activity (e.g., slows the heart rate, the rate of perspiration, the rate of respiration, and the blood pressure).

The sympathetic nervous system increases our ability to meet a crisis or to prepare the body for the ''flight-or-fight'' response. When we are angry or fearful or aggressive, the sympathetic nervous system is involved. It is involved in controlling eating and drinking behavior and sexual behavior, or behaviors basic to survival. The sympathetic nervous system also contains the centers for pleasure and pain, or the basic emotional and motivational aspects of behavior.

The parasympathetic nervous system is more involved in our calmer and quieter behaviors, such as eating and digestion, as well as slowing down the heart and respiration. That is why it is so difficult to eat when we are angry or excited or fearful. We say ''my stomach is tied in a knot,'' which is literally true since the nerves from the sympathetic nervous system will constrict the stomach and intestinal muscles while preparing the body for a flight-or-fight response. We try to relax before dinner with a glass of wine and some quiet music.

The somatic nervous system is basic to operant conditioning or learning, whereas the autonomic nervous system is basic to classical or Pavlovian learning. The manner in which we learn depends on the organization of the nervous system, as we shall see in Chapter 13.

Neurons

The nervous system is based on special cells called neurons. A neuron is sensitive to outside stimulation and it has the capacity to transmit this information to other neurons. The human brain is composed of 50 to 100 billion neurons, each with many connections with other neurons in various types of networks and interconnected systems.

Neurons are classified as receptor, motor, or interneurons. Receptor neurons are involved in the sensory organs and the transmission of sensory information to the brain or to other neurons. Motor neurons are output or efferent neurons, and they join various parts of the brain to target organs, such as muscles and glands. Motor neurons synapse with (join) muscle tissue in order to activate the muscles. What we call ''behavior'' is the motor system activating the skeletal muscles.

The associational or interneurons connect sensory and motor neurons. If a sensory neuron synapses with a motor neuron through the spinal cord, we have a reflex action, such as an eye blink or a knee jerk. Learning is not involved in a reflex action, and such reflexes are found among simple organisms without great brain development. If sensory and motor functions are separated by millions of neurons, there is room for learning and modification of behavior

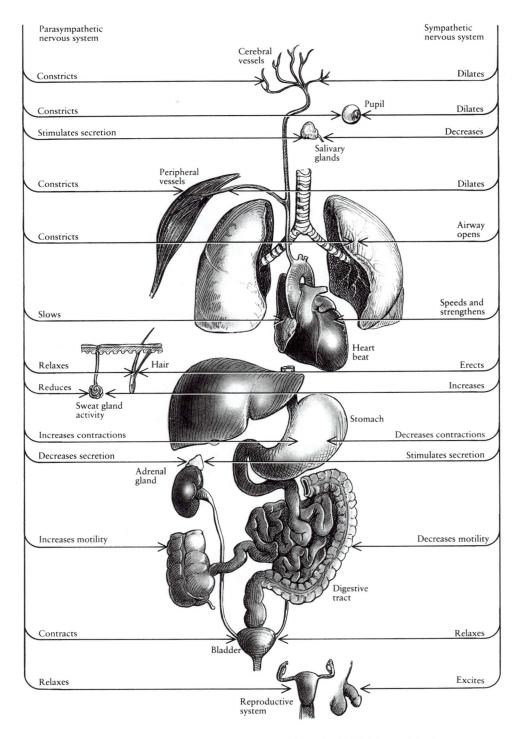

Parasympathetic
nervous system

Sympathetic
nervous system

Cerebral
vessels

Constricts — Dilates

Constricts — Pupil — Dilates

Stimulates secretion — Decreases

Salivary
glands

Peripheral
vessels

Constricts — Dilates

Constricts — Airway
opens

Slows — Speeds and
strengthens

Heart
beat

Relaxes — Hair — Erects

Reduces — Increases

Sweat gland
activity

Stomach

Increases contractions — Decreases contractions

Decreases secretion — Stimulates secretion

Adrenal
gland

Increases motility — Decreases motility

Digestive
tract

Contracts — Relaxes

Bladder

Relaxes — Excites

Reproductive
system

Figure 11–2 The Sympathetic and Parasympathetic Divisions of the Autonomic Nervous System, the Organs They Innervate, and the Effects Each
Produces.

by experience, since the motor neuron is not activated immediately by the sensory neuron, but rather is dependent on millions of other neurons in interaction. This more complex brain model is found among mammals and primates. The development of a large cortex facilitates for learning in place of innate action as a basis for environmental adaptation (see Chapter 13).

At one end of the neuron are dendrites, fingerlike projections. The core or central area is the body or the soma. From the soma is an axon that descends and joins other neurons at the soma, or axon, or dendrites (Figure 11–3).

Neurons send both electrical and biochemical messages. The axon contains potassium (K^+), and the space outside the axon contains sodium (Na^+). When the axon is activated, the sodium enters the axon and the potassium leaves the axon. The sodium–potassium pump, or exchange, creates an *action potential* or electrical activity in the neurons, which then travels the length of the axon. This electrical activity in the brain can be measured in several ways, including the electroencephelograph (EEG).

Neurons do not join directly, but are connected by a synapse or a space between the axon of one neuron and the receptor sites of other neurons. Chemicals, called neurotransmitters, are released into the synaptic cleft, where they activate or deactivate neural activity in the postsynaptic receptor sites on other neurons. The neurotransmitter system will be discussed below in more detail.

THE BRAIN

How to Study the Brain

It has been mentioned that most psychologists and sociologists do not get "inside the skin" in order to study behavior. They observe behavior and then explain such behavior on the basis of inferential mental concepts such as mind, attitude, self, or ego. The behaviorists study the stimulus–response relationship while ignoring what goes on inside the organism, which is an "empty organism" model of behavior. Bioenvironmentalism studies the brain as the critical link between environment and behavior, which means getting inside the brain (see Chapter 18).

The oldest way to study the brain is by means of introspection and verbal reports from the subject. The subject is asked by the therapist (usually on a couch) how he or she feels. This technique is basic to behavioral and social science research as found in survey research, interviews, questionnaires, personality tests, and intelligence tests. Such procedures tell us how individuals behave in answering questions, but it does not tell us why they behave as criminals. We use one set of behaviors (interviews, surveys, questionnaires) to study another set of behaviors (voting behavior, criminal behavior, racial behavior, aptitudes, etc.).

The brain sciences use direct ways of studying the brain. One of the earliest was to look at individuals who had had accidents to the brain, such as the case of Phineas Gage, who, while tamping an explosive powder into a hole,

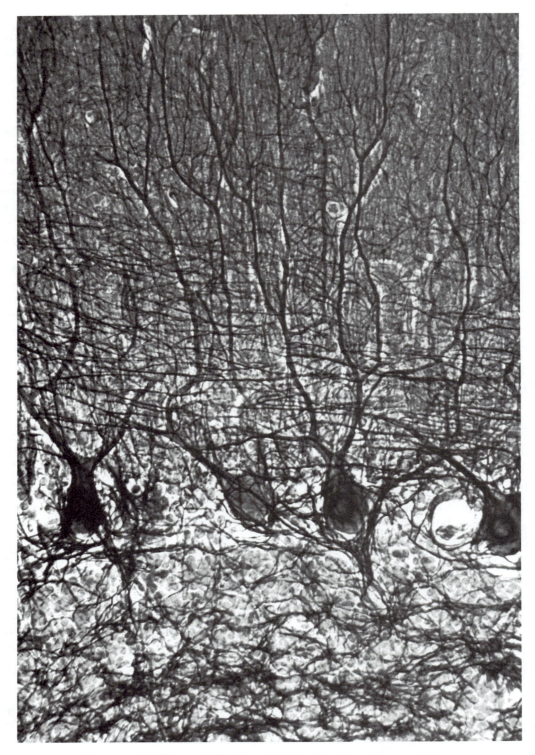

Figure 11-3 Neuron Cell Body, including Dendrites, Soma and Axon.

had the tamping steel rod blown through his brain. He survived, but he experienced great personality changes as a result of this brain damage. He became very violent and antisocial. During World War I many studies were made of soldiers who suffered from brain injuries due to bullet or shrapnel wounds.

Lesions are created experimentally in the brains of animals by means of surgery or freezing, and the impact of the destroyed tissue on behavior is then studied. Moreover, autopsies on the brains of cadavers are used to locate brain damage or brain abnormalities in patients with known neurological or psychiatric disorders.

New technologies now allow us to study the living brain. In the electroencephalograph (EEG) electrodes are placed on the skull to study the electrical activity of the brain. The evoked potential is a specialized EEG technique whereby a stimulus is presented to a subject and the resulting electrical activity of the brain is fed into a computer to separate out action due to that stimulus and action in the brain produced by other stimuli. In this way, a stimulus, say a light or sound, can be traced from the eye or ear into the various inner parts of the brain.

Electrodes can be implanted into the brain to study the electrical activity of nerve cells. Electrodes implanted into the brain are also used to stimulate a given part of the brain. The stimulation will produce movement in an arm or leg, or colors, or memories, or music, depending on what part of the brain is being stimulated. By implanting electrodes into the brain, an animal can be made to act as if it is hungry, thirsty, violent, sexually aroused, calm, happy, or fearful. The pleasure centers were discovered through electrical stimulation of the brain.

There are now machines that will scan the brain and take pictures of it, such as CAT (computerized axial tomography), PETT (positron emission tomography), NMR (nuclear magnetic resonance), and BEAM (brain electrical activity mapping). These scans reveal the structural and biochemical nature of the brain. The use of the CAT scan to find a tumor in the brain of a violent criminal will be discussed in Chapters 18 and 20.

The biochemical composition of the brain can also be studied through spinal taps, urine samples, blood samples, and hair analysis. The brain is very responsive to sugar deficits or excesses, to heavy metal contamination, and to other dietary deficiencies. These brain conditions are treatable through diet, drug therapies, and brain surgery, as discussed in Chapter 18.

The Structure of the Brain

In this section I will discuss the basic structure of the brain without going into great detail. The lower brain stem where the spinal cord joins the brain includes the medulla, the pons, and the cerebellum, which are involved in basic survival behaviors such as respiration, heart action, gastrointestinal functions, and motor coordination. Above the lower brain lie the thalamus, hypothalamus, and the limbic system. The thalamus is a sensory relay center which transmits information from the sensory organs to other parts of the brain. The

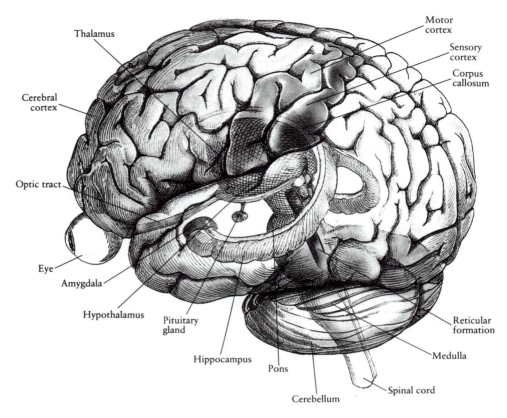

Figure 11-4   Human Brain.

hypothalamus is the control center for the autonomic nervous system through the pituitary gland. It is a control center for emotions, pleasure and pain, anger, fear, aggression, hunger, thirst, and sex. The so-called "food, sex, flight, and fight" syndrome is controlled to a great extent by the hypothalamus (Figure 11-4).

The limbic system is a name given to an interconnected system of brain structures, including the amygdala, hippocampus, limbic cortex, and the septal area. The limbic system is critical to our emotional life, to anger, fear, hatred, and aggression, and along with the hypothalamus is involved in the motivational and emotional aspects of our behavior (Figure 11-5).

The outer layer of the brain is the cortex. The cortex is divided into four subdivisions: frontal, temporal, parietal, and occipital. The cortex is also divided into two hemispheres, the left and right hemispheres, joined by the corpus collosum (see Figure 11-6).

The cortex contains major sensory and motor areas as well as associational areas. In this way the cortex processes incoming sensory information and controls outgoing motor activity from the motor centers. What we gener-

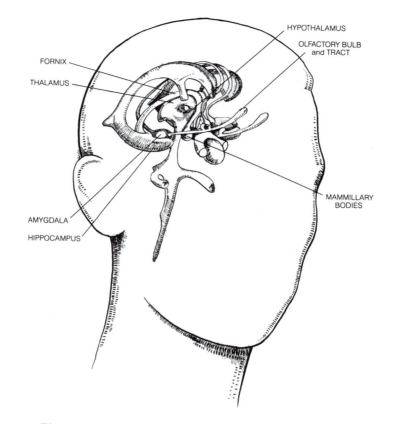

FORNIX

THALAMUS

HYPOTHALAMUS

OLFACTORY BULB
and TRACT

MAMMILLARY
BODIES

AMYGDALA

HIPPOCAMPUS

Figure 11–5   The Limbic System.

ally call human mental processes occur in the cortex (e.g., thought, rationality, decision making, consciousness, and evaluation). The cortex functions as an overall integrating system for the motor, sensory, and emotional activities of the brain.

The language areas of the brain are usually located in the left hemisphere for right-handed people and in both hemispheres for left-handed people. The left hemisphere controls the right side of the body, and the right hemisphere controls the left side of the body.

Motor functions are located in the cortex, in the pyramidal system, and in the extrapyramidal system. The extrapyramidal system includes the cerebellum, the basal ganglia, and the recticular activating system. The initiation of behavior starts in the motor centers of the cortex. Before voluntary behavior takes place there is activity in the motor cortex, as for example if one is thinking about moving one's hand, the activity shows up on a PETT scan before the actual behavior takes place. Activity initiated in the motor cortex controls the muscles or what we call "behavior." Just because it is under the control of the motor cortex does not mean that it is "voluntary" in the sense of being

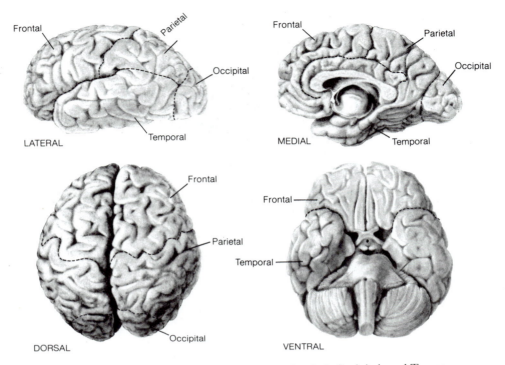

Figure 11-6 The Location of the Frontal, Pareital, Occipital, and Temporal Lobes of the Human Brain.

produced by indeterminacy, free will, and mental states. Physical activities in the brain are necessary to initiate such motor behaviors.

The brain, then, consists of three basic functions:

1. Sensory input from the sensory organs.
2. Motor output from motor centers to muscles and glands.
3. Associational processes whereby sensory and motor activities are joined and coordinated. These processes include emotional input from the limbic system and hypothalamus, as well as learning and memory.

It is now thought that higher complex cognitive functions, such as awareness, consciousness, and voluntary behavior, are related to vertical columns of neurons in the cortex. These vertical columns are involved in the identification of objects or in the formation of concepts. Certain columns are involved in the receiving and processing of information, and feature recognition and detection. These vertical columns of cells may permit higher-order learning and cognition to take place. It has been argued that we must use the ''mind'' to explain things, but it could be that the vertical columns are the answer to the mind/brain problem (Bloom, Lazerson, and Hofstadter, 1985; Winson, 1985; Gilinsky, 1984).

The Neurotransmitter System

As mentioned earlier, transmission of information along neurons is both electrical and biochemical. The important process is biochemical and it occurs at the synapses where the neurons join. These neurochemicals (called neurotransmitters) are manufactured and/or stored in the presynaptic axons, and they are released upon an electrical and biochemical impulse to the synaptic site, where they then act on postsynaptic receptors of other neurons.

Neurotransmitters can either increase (excite) or decrease (inhibit) the activity of receptor neurons. The action of specific neurotransmitters depends on (1) the nature of the neurotransmitter, (2) the amount of the neurotransmitter available for the synapse, (3) the number and condition of the postsynaptic receptors, and (4) the action of other neurotransmitters which may increase or decrease the action of the neurotransmitter under study.

The major neurotransmitters are classified as follows:

Acetylcholine (ACh)

Norepinephrine (NE)

Dopamine (DA)

Serotonin (5-HT)

GABA

The neurotransmitters and the neurotransmitter pathways in the brain are shown in Figure 11–7 and Table 11–1.

Because of the neurochemical nature of the brain, the brain is very sensitive to environmental input involving food and drugs. Diet and nutrition are extremely important to the understanding of the functioning of the brain. ACh is processed from choline, which is found in eggs, peanuts, and other amino acids. Tyrosine, an amino acid, is used by the brain to create L-dopa, dopamine, norepinephrine, and epinephrine. In other words, tyrosine is a precursor to these neurochemicals, and it comes from our diet.

Tryptophan, also an amino acid, is the precursor to serotonin. Tryptophan levels in the blood are increased by carbohydrates, which in turn release insulin into the bloodstream. Low levels of tryptophan in the blood will reduce serotonin levels, which in turn can increase violent and aggressive behaviors (Chapter 18). The level of tryptophan in hypoglycemics is low because they have exhausted their insulin supply. One treatment for violence and aggression might include increased intake of tryptophan (a health store item).

It has been suggested that an increase in epinephrine will increase fear, whereas an increase in norepinephrine levels can increase anger and aggression (Hinton, 1983). Social and psychological isolation will also increase norepinephrine levels, and in turn violence. Diet and nutrition are also closely related to the neurotransmitter functioning involved in alcoholism, drug abuse, violence, and mental illness (see Chapter 18).

The neurotransmitter system is subject to the influence and control of other chemicals in the form of enzymes and hormones. Monoamine oxidase

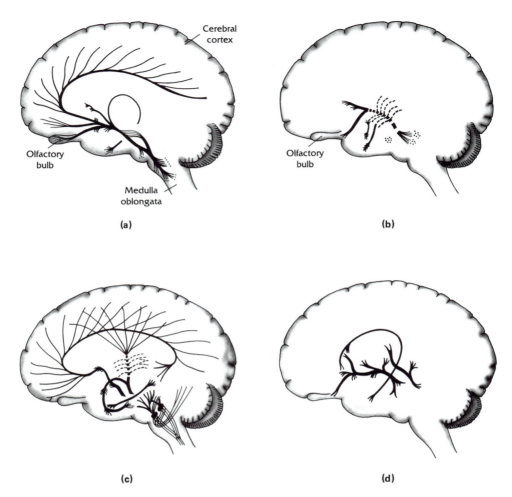

Figure 11-7 Neurotransmitter Pathways in the Brain. From *Biological Psychology,* 2nd ed. by James W. Kalat. Copyright © 1981, 1984 by Wadsworth, Inc. Reprinted by permission of the publisher.

(MAO) destroys dopamine, norepinephrine, and serotonin in the synaptic cleft. If MAO is absent, NE, DA, and 5-HT continue to stimulate the postsynaptic receptor sites. Therefore, MAO inhibitors (agents that reduce or eliminate MAO) will increase NE and DA levels in the synapses, therefore causing excitation. MAO inhibitors and tricyclic antidepressants are used in psychiatry to increase NE and DA levels as antidepressant drugs (see Chapter 18).

The Endocrine System

The endocrine system is composed of a number of glands which secrete hormones (biochemical agents) into the bloodstream. The hormones then go to target organs which they control (see Figure 11-8 and Table 11-2). The endo-

TABLE 11-1 PROBABLE TRANSMITTER SUBSTANCES

Probable transmitter substance	Location	Hypothesized effect
Acetylcholine (ACh)	Brain, spinal cord, autonomic ganglia, target organs of the parasympathetic nervous system	Excitation in brain and autonomic ganglia, excitation or inhibition in target organs
Norepinephrine (NE)	Brain, spinal cord, target organs of sympathetic nervous system	Inhibition in brain, excitation or inhibition in targert organs
Dopamine (DA)	Brain	Inhibition
Serotonin(5-hydroxytryptamine, or 5-HT)	Brain, spinal cord	Inhibition
Gamma-aminobutyric acid (GABA)	Brain (especially cerebral and cerebellar cortex), spinal cord	Inhibition
Glycine	Spinal cord interneurons	Inhibition
Glutamic acid	Brain, spinal sensory neurons	Excitation
Aspartic acid	Spinal cord interneurons, brain (?)	Excitation
Substance P	Brain, spinal sensory neurons (pain)	Excitation (and inhibition?)
Histamine, taurine, other amino acids; peptides such as oxytocin and endogenous opiates; many others	Various regions of brain, spinal cord, and peripheral nervous system	(?)

Source: Carlson, 1986, p. 69.

crine system helps regulate sexual behavior, sex hormones, the development of sperm and eggs, pregnancy and lactation, water retention, blood pressure, and glucose and insulin levels.

The brain, through the hypothalamus, controls the master gland or the pituitary gland, which in turn controls the other glands. The hypothalamus signals the pituitary to produce ACTH, which when released into the bloodstream causes the adrenal medulla (over the kidneys) to secrete norepinephrine and epinephrine. These neurotransmitters in turn control the fight-or-flight response of the autonomic nervous system. The hypothalamus–pituitary–adrenal medulla–autonomic nervous system axis is critical for survival, and it emerged as a part of our evolutionary history. This system is critical to our emotional behaviors as involved in anger, aggression, and sex.

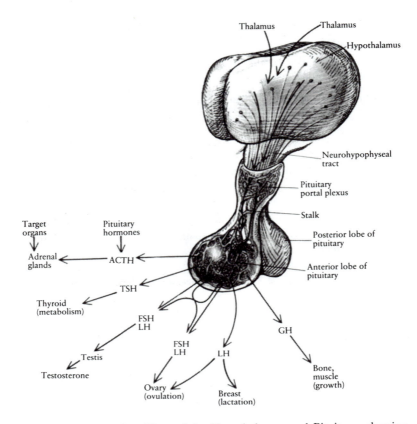

Figure 11-8 Surface View of the Hypothalamus and Pituitary, showing the Essential Cell Systems and the Hormones They Produce. Certain neurons of the hypothalamus secrete directly into the bloodstream through the posterior lobe of the pituitary, triggering the release of hormones that travel to target organs throughout the body.

Learning and Memory

The more complex the brain, that is, the larger the cerebral cortex and the associational areas, the more the organism uses learning to adapt to the environment. As has been discussed, the greater the distance from the sensory to the motor centers, the more associational neurons are involved in relaying information from sensory to motor neurons.

Learning involves modification of behavior by experience, or changes in the physical structure of the neurons due to experience. There are changes in the brain (e.g., in the neurons, synapses, dendrites, and neurotransmitter systems) as a result of input from the environment. As mentioned above, rats reared in an enriched environment will possess a more fully developed brain than rats reared in an impoverished environment. A kitten with a patch over

TABLE 11-2 THE ENDOCRINE SYSTEMS

Tissue	Hormone	Target cells	Action
Pituitary, anterior lobe	Follicle-stimulating hormone	Gonads	Ovulation, spermatogenesis
	Luteinizing hormone	Gonads	Ovarian/spermatic maturation
	Thyrotropin	Thyroid	Thyroxin secretion
	Adrenocorticotropin	Adrenal cortex	Corticosteroid secretion
	Growth hormone	Liver	Somatomedin secretion
		All cells	Protein synthesis
Pituitary, posterior lobe	Prolactin	Breasts	Growth and milk secretion
	Vasopressin	Kidney tubules	Water retention
	Oxytocin	Arterioles	Increase blood pressure
		Uterus	Contraction
Gonads	Estrogen	Many	Secondary sexual characteristics
	Testosterone	Many	Muscle, breast growth
Thyroid	Thyroxin	Many	Increases metabolic rate
Parathyroid	Calcitonin	Bone	Calcium retention
Adrenal cortex	Corticosteroids	Many	Mobilization of energy fuels
			Sensitization of vascular adrenergic receptors
			Inhibition of antibody formation and inflammation
	Aldosterone	Kidney	Sodium retention
Adrenal medulla	Epinephrine	Cardiovascular system, skin, muscle, liver, and others	Sympathetic activation
	Norepinephrine		
Pancreatic islets	Insulin	Many	Increases glucose uptake
	Glucagon	Liver, muscle	Increases glucose levels
	Somatostatin	Islets	Regulates insulin, glucagon secretion
Intestinal mucosa	Secretin	Exocrine pancreas	Digestive enzyme secretion
	Cholecystokinin	Gallbladder	Bile secretion
	Vasoactive intestinal polypeptide	Duodenum	Activates motility and secretion; increases blood flow
	Gastric, inhibitory peptide	Duodenum	Inhibits motility and secretion
	Somatostatin	Duodenum	Inhibits motility and intestinal secretion

Source: Bloom, Lazerson, and Hofstadter, 1985, p. 100.

207

the eye will never develop neural connections from the retina to the brain. Learning and memory are discussed in detail in Chapter 13.

Hemispheric Functions

The cortex is divided into left and right hemispheres, with the languages areas in the left hemisphere, whereas the right hemisphere is more involved in mathematical and spatial processing. The left hemisphere controls the right side of the body, and the right hemisphere controls the left side. Ninety percent of the population is right-handed; thus 90 percent of the right-handers have left hemisphere dominance, for left-handers (10 percent of the total population), 70 percent have left hemispheric dominance, 15 percent have right hemispheric dominance, and 15 percent have bilateral (both hemispheres) dominance.

Many behavioral problems occur as a result of hemispheric dysfunction. Dyslexia and aphasia are more common among males (4:1) than among females, and often among left-handed males. A high proportion of male criminals are left-handed (Chapter 18).

A Brain/Control Model of Criminal Behavior

In summary, I wish to put forth a basic model of behavior control based on the structure and functioning of the brain. The brain has sensory–experience input and motor–muscle output. Between the sensory input and the motor output is a vast and complex brain structure based on genetic–environment interaction, brain–environment interaction, learning and memory, and emotionality and motivation.

Human beings have essentially three brains, as Paul McClean has stated. The reptilian brain, shared with lower animals, is concerned with self-preservation and reproduction. The old mammalian brain (primarily the limbic system) is concerned with emotions, pleasure, pain, anger, fear, sex, hunger, and flight-or-fight responses. The neomammalian brain (cortex) is concerned with complex behaviors such as language, thought, rationality, and learning (Figure 11–9).

Humankind has inherited two different types of brains: one devoted to sex, hunger, anger, fear, and aggression; the other devoted to rationality, planning, and the control of emotions. Humankind has created major religions and major cultural and technological systems. The same animal is capable of violence beyond that of any other animal, as he/she engages in cruelty to children, cruelty to animals, spouse abuse, wars, rape, assaults, and murder. The human animal worships the activities controlled by the limbic system: violence on TV and movies, auto racing, sky diving, football, hockey, cock fights, pit bull fights, and the like. The human animal is the only one that will pay to watch a fight to death between a bull and a man, or two dogs, or two cocks, or who will strap a fellow man into an electric chair and electrocute him.

The response of an individual to a stimulus input from the environment will depend on (1) the genetic inheritance, and (2) the environmental input into the brain. Genetic systems can control the structure of the brain or the

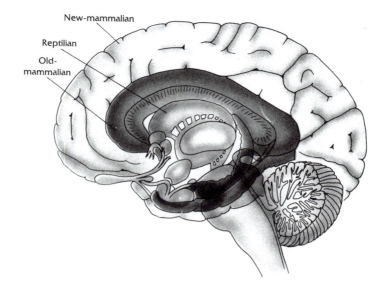

Figure 11–9 Three Parts of the Human Brain. From J. Kalat, (1988). *Biological Psychology,* 3rd ed. Copyright © 1988 by Wadsworth, Inc. Reprinted by permission of the publishers.

amount of a neurotransmitter or hormone available to the brain. Pollution of the air, water, or food can damage the brain. Drugs and alcohol can damage the brain. These topics will be discussed in later chapters.

Whether a person behaves as a criminal depends on which neurons are activated, that is, what part of the brain is stimulated. For violence, anger, and fear to be controlled, the cortex must exercise control over the neural pathways to the limbic system. Whether or not we respond to an insult by committing murder or walking away depends on how much control the cortex has over the limbic system. This control depends on learning and past experience and the present condition of the brain, that is, the impact of diet (sugar) and amino acids (protein) on the brain, or the presence of lead and cadmium in the brain.

Major neural networks descend from the cortex to the limbic system to control violence, aggression, and predatory behaviors (including robbery, burglary, and other property offenses). If these neural connections are inadequate, the person will rob or rape or murder. It is not argued here that we understand totally all these neural processes. It is argued that we can, through future research, come to understand them and use this knowledge to prevent criminal behavior. The model is not limited to personal crimes, but extends to property crimes, as will be discussed in later chapters.

The idea that humans are both rational and emotional has been expressed over and over again in religion, philosophy, and science. This is the theme of good versus evil, right versus wrong. A summary of the brain–behavior process is that humankind seeks pleasure and avoids pain. This pleasure–pain idea is basic to religion, to political philosophies (see Chapters 4 and 5), to

Freudian psychology, to behaviorism, and to biological psychology. The brain has centers for pleasure and pain (the limbic system), and it has centers for rationality and social control (the cortex). The role of pleasure and pain in learning theory, in mental illness, and in criminal behavior will be discussed in future chapters.

SUMMARY

This chapter described the role of the brain in behavior, especially human behavior. The brain stands between the environment and behavior as the organ that takes in sensory information, processes, stores, and retrieves information, and sends out information to motor centers, which in turn control behavior.

The brain has major centers for sensory input and motor output. The brain also contains centers for the control of emotional and motivational behavior, as well as for the control of rational behavior and decision making. Behavior is a product of the interaction of the millions of neurons in the brain.

The brain functions primarily as a bioelectrochemical system, which in turn produces electrical and neurochemical activity in the neurons. These neurochemical activities in the neurotransmitter systems and hormonal systems are subject to the influence of diet and nutrition, as well as environmental pollution. The most important new development in the behavioral sciences has been in the brain sciences, and the joining of psychology, biochemistry, neurology, and psychiatry into an interdisciplinary approach to a theory of human behavior.

FURTHER STUDIES

Courses in neurology and psychobiology are offered in biology and psychology departments as well as in medical schools. The school of criminology at Florida State University offers several courses in the biological and psychological aspects of criminal behavior, and some of our graduate students take courses in the department of psychology in the area of psychobiology. A great deal of research is now going on concerning the neurological foundations of criminal behavior, and this research is discussed in Chapter 18.

REFERENCES

*BLOOM, F. E., A. LAZERSON, and L. HOFSTADTER (1985). *Brain, Mind, and Behavior*. New York: W. H. Freeman.

CARLSON, N. (1984). *Psychology*. Boston: Allyn and Bacon.

*CARLSON, N. (1986). *Physiology of Behavior*, 3rd ed. Boston: Allyn and Bacon.

GILINSKY, A. S. (1984). *Mind and Brain*. New York: Plenum.

GLEITMAN, H. (1981). *Psychology*. New York: W. W. Norton.

*GROVES, P., and K. SCHLESINGER (1979). *Biological Psychology*, 2nd ed. Dubuque, Iowa: Wm. C. Brown.

HINTON, J. W. (1983). *Dangerousness: Problems of Assessment and Prediction*. London: Allen & Unwin.

*HUBEL, H. (1979). "The Brain." *Scientific American*, September, 44–53.

*KALAT, J. (1984). *Biological Psychology*, 2nd ed. Belmont, Calif.: Wadsworth.

MCCONNELL, J. V. (1980). *Understanding Human Behavior*, 3rd ed. New York: Holt, Rinehart and Winston.

*RESTAK, R. (1984). *The Brain*. New York: Bantam Books.

*RESTAK, R. (1988). *The Mind*. New York: Bantam.

*THOMPSON, R. F. (1985). *The Brain*. New York: W. H. Freeman.

WINSON, J. (1985). *Brain and Psyche*. New York: Anchor.

QUESTIONS

1. What is the "mind–body problem"?
2. Why must the brain only be studied in interaction with the physical environment?
3. What is meant by "environmentalism"?
4. How are sensations (light, color, taste, smell) conveyed from the physical environment to the brain?
5. What are the basic divisions of the nervous system?
6. How do neurons communicate with one another?
7. How is the brain studied?
8. What is the function of the hypothalamus? The limbic system? The cortex?
9. How does the neurotransmitter system work?
10. Why is the brain involved in learning and memory?
11. The brain is both rational and emotional. How is this fact related to criminal behavior?

*Source of particular importance in the preparation of this chapter.

Psychological Criminology: Freudian Psychology   12

INTRODUCTION

In the next two chapters we examine several models of human nature which have emerged from philosophy and science. There are two basic schools of psychology, one based on rationalism and one based on empiricism. Each of these philosophical positions has made certain assumptions about human nature which have become basic aspects of psychological theory. It is important to understand the several views of human nature since these views determine what we regard as crime and what we regard as criminal behavior. These ideas also determine whether we rehabilitate criminals or put them in prison to be punished.

Three Models of Behavior

Three basic models of behavior have emerged from philosophy and psychology: (1) mentalism, (2) behaviorism, and (3) bioenvironmentalism. Each position starts with an individual organism interacting with an environment, but the nature of this interaction differs for each model. For mentalism the interaction between the individual organism and environment is by means of the mind. For behaviorism the emphasis is placed on the environment, not on the organism. For bioenvironmentalism the emphasis is on the interaction of the individual organism with its environment by means of the brain. Each of these models will be discussed in more detail below.

Mentalistic and Cognitive Psychology

As was discussed in Chapter 2, rationalism as put forth by Plato and Kant placed emphasis on the individual and his/her innate ideas. People are born with certain rational, emotional, and volitional qualities, which then determine the behavior of the individual (Sahakian, 1968). In psychology this came to be known as the "Kantian" view of human nature (Rychlak, 1981).

The important element is the individual and his/her reaction to the environment. The term "cognition" is generally used to refer to the ability of individuals to interpret, know, and evaluate their sensory experiences. Cognition means the mental activities of the "mind" as opposed to the physical properties of the body. Such a psychology is based on the mind–body dualism of philosophers such as Descartes and Kant. We often make reference to these mental processes when we say "he had a mind to go into town," or "he made up his mind to buy a car," or "he has a mental illness," or "he is a strong-willed person."

The mentalistic/cognitive model of human behavior is

$$\text{Environment} \longrightarrow \text{Mind} \longrightarrow \text{Behavior}$$

In this model the mind is a nonphysical entity. Since the psychologist cannot get "inside the skin" of the subject, he/she must use the method of "introspection" by asking the subject to reflect on his/her feelings and to make reports to the psychologist on such subjective feelings. Free will and intentionality play a major role in such a psychology (Gatchel and Mears, 1982:417 ff.). This method is basic to Freudian psychiatry, clinical psychology, and sociology, where reliance is placed on verbal reports and/or interviews and questionnaires. Once the environment enters the "mind" it takes the form of attitudes, personality, ego, self, or similar concepts. Psychologists and sociologists never observe attitudes or egos or self-concepts, but they infer such concepts from the behaviors observed. Thus a criminal attitude is inferred from the fact that a person has been arrested and convicted, or the fact that the person reports having committed crimes. The attitude comes from the behavior, not the behavior from the attitude. However, the mentalistic psychologist or sociologist assumes that attitudes cause behavior. A recent book in psychology defines methodology in terms of paper and pencil questionnaires and interview methodologies (Cohen, 1988). We can never know the "mind" from direct empirical observations, only by inferences from external events such as behavior.

This view of human behavior has been diagrammed by the British criminologist Hermann Mannheim (1965:202) as follows:

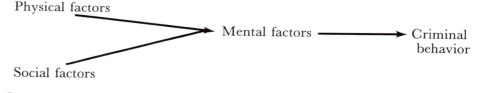

Throughout the history of philosophy there have been attempts to answer the question of how mind and body interact, or how an immaterial substance can cause changes in physical substances, but so far there is no way of demonstrating the existence of the mind or how the mind causes the body to behave. The mental processes of the mind are not known by direct observation, only by indirect observations of the behavior they cause. This methodological problem will be discussed below.

The rational view of human beings is usually represented as the "humanistic" view. Humans are in control of their behavior; they have free will and moral responsibility for their actions. The human animal is an actor, not a reactor; a creator, not a robot. Regardless of genetics, neurology, learning, and socialization, human beings are viewed in humanistic philosophy as having a small part of their mental system (soul or mind or spirit) that is not determined by the physical body. This is the position of indeterminacy, which is opposed to that of determinacy. In his book *The Idea of Man*, Matson (1976) defends the model of humanistic man against the emerging scientific ideas of man as found in "man the beast" (biological man) and "man the machine" (psychological man). Matson denies the determinacy of human behavior as found in modern biology and psychology. This idea is well expressed by Mortimer Adler (1985) when he states that intellect and will are immaterial and therefore follow humanistic laws, not scientific laws. Free will is part of the determinacy by immaterial phenomena of material events. It follows, therefore, that moral responsibility is compatible with immaterial determinism but not with material determinism.

Doctrines of rationalism, immaterialism, and moral responsibility dominate moral philosophy, law, and humanistic psychology. It is the basic model of human nature which is part of our criminal law doctrine of punishment and prisons. The idea that human beings possess a mind separate from the physical body is basic to criminal law as found in the doctrines of mens rea and actus reus (Chapter 4). People must possess an "evil mind" to be guilty of crime. Clinical psychology and psychoanalysis are also very much involved in the use of mentalistic concepts to be explained by human behavior.

A major contribution to clinical and psychoanalytic thought was that made by Sigmund Freud, and his work will be the subject of this chapter. Empirical and scientific psychology as found in behaviorism and learning theory is discussed in Chapter 13.

FREUDIAN PSYCHOANALYSIS

The Freudian model of psychology is a mixture of the Kantian and Lockean models. Freud emphasized a biological base for behavior, but he also emphasized the role of experience in creating the personality. He emphasized introspection and verbal reports rather than studies of the brain, and at the time he was writing, techniques for examining the brain such as the CAT scan and the NMR scan were not available.

Sigmund Freud (1856–1939) was a Viennese medical doctor who specialized in neurology. In the course of his medical practice he came into contact with patients who suffered from nervous disorders (e.g., hysteria, phobia, anxiety, and sexual problems). In his effort to understand these abnormal behaviors he created a theory and a method of treatment which has come to be known as psychoanalysis or psychodynamic psychology. This model became a basic approach for many M.D.'s who specialized in psychiatry (the study of abnormal behavior). The psychiatrist is a person with a M.D. degree and is trained in medicine, whereas a psychologist has a Ph.D. degree and specializes in human behavior. The subject matter of the two disciplines overlaps and is identical in many respects.

It must be noted that Freud was a biologist/M.D., as was Lombroso (Chapter 5), and the basic foundations of criminology are in biology and neurology. It must also be noted that although Freud was a neurologist, his system of treatment, called psychoanalysis, split with traditional neurology in its nonphysical approach to human problems. There was a split at that time (1910–1920) between neurology and psychiatry; however, in more recent years the split has been reduced and/or eliminated in a great deal of the work now going on as the neurological and biochemical bases of mental illness, aggression, alcoholism, drug addiction, and sexual deviancy (see Chapters 18 and 20 for a discussion of these issues).

Psychoanalysis deals primarily with the neuroses (anxiety, phobias, amnesia, sexual disorders) as opposed to psychiatry, which deals with psychoses (schizophrenia, paranoia, and manic-depression). The psychoanalyst will usually be in a private practice where he/she sees patients for an hour at a time based on talking therapy, whereas the psychiatrist is more likely to be in a state mental institution treating people who have been committed as ''mentally ill'' and who need major antipsychotic drugs (see Chapter 20).

There is also a distinction made between *organic* disorders and *functional* disorders. Organic disorders have an organic base in brain or brain chemistry, whereas functional disorders have no known physical base and are therefore regarded as mental or psychic. We use the term ''mental illness'' to refer to the sick mind. Today there is evidence that many of the so-called functional disorders have a base in brain functioning, and distinction between physical and mental illness is still a major issue in law, criminology, and psychiatry. These issues will be discussed in Chapter 20.

Freud's Theory of Personality

Freud broke with the rationalists and the idealists who viewed the human animal as totally rational (see Chapter 2). Freud emphasized that humankind was also emotional, irrational, aggressive, and vicious. Life, as Hobbes said, is ''nasty, brutish, and short.''

Humankind by nature has a need for controls over his/her biological impulses, and only through socialization does he/she learn to control basic impulses. This view of human nature is in complete opposition to the view put forth by sociologists, who hold that humans are born devoid of human nature, since human nature develops only in social interaction with other human beings in a social setting. Humans are social conformists, and deviancy must be explained in terms of social experiences (see Chapter 14).

The basic core of personality as defined by Freud is biological, the instincts and needs associated with food, thirst, sex, and survival. This complex of basic biological drives is called the *id*. The id is the survival mechanism based on the *pleasure principle*. The id seeks immediate gratification of its impulses without concern for the consequences.

Out of the id develops the *ego*, that part of the personality based on experience with the environment. The ego has an awareness of the consequences of behavior and it acts as a mechanism for guiding the id in its search for pleasure. The ego is the *reality principle*, the executive control of the personality over raw biological impulses.

The reaction of others to the behavior of the individual, especially that of the father and mother, is called the *superego*. The superego is the evaluative and moral aspect of behavior, and it represents the cultural values and social control efforts of society over individuals. This basic model emphasizes the development of social control over individuals who are not socialized and who under the best of circumstances will never be totally socialized. The concept of the superego allies Freudian psychology with anthropology and sociology, and many social scientists concentrate on the social interaction aspects of Freud's work.

The id, ego, and superego can be in conflict as to when and how biological desires, especially sexual desires, are gratified. The superego defines as acceptable or not acceptable the impulses of the id, and the ego must then act as an executive to find socially acceptable means by which the id can gratify its basic needs.

Internal psychic conflict can lead to the *repression* of desires or unpleasant memories, which in turn leads to fundamental personality problems. Repression explains another of Freud's basic concepts, that of the *unconscious*, where repressed desires and memories reside. *Anxiety* then results from these unconscious motives and drives. The person will resort to a number of different *defense mechanisms* in order to keep from facing the reality of his/her hidden desires and wishes. These defense mechanisms include displacement, reaction formation, rationalization, and projection. The person will dream about forbidden acts as a way of wish fulfillment, or he/she will have a ''slip of the tongue'' whereby unconscious feelings and desires are expressed overtly, as seen in a letter written by a young bride to her new mother-in-law in which she addressed the letter ''to my dead mother'' instead of ''my dear mother.''

Freudian psychology places a great dependency on symbolism as found in dreams or verbal behaviors. Words come to be symbolic of repressed desires, usually of a sexual nature. A long, narrow object can represent a penis, and a purse or box can represent a vagina. The job of the psychoanalyst is to penetrate the symbolism to find the true meaning of a dream or a verbal report.

Psychoanalysis as a Method of Treatment

Freud discovered that his patients (mostly neurotics) would talk about past experiences associated with their childhood and their relationship with their parents. Such memories could be relived and brought from the unconscious to the conscious part of the brain. In his early work in the treatment of hysteria Freud resorted to hypnosis as a means of uncovering unconscious desires and wishes.

Later in his career Freud would have the patient lie on a couch and recall his/her early childhood experiences. This method of reaching repressed feelings was called *free association*, wherein the patient would say whatever came into his/her mind at the time. This process looks a lot like associational learning to be discussed in Chapter 13. Because psychoanalysis is based on talking, it has been labeled "talk therapy," in contrast to drug therapies and electrical stimulation of the brain, which are physical therapies designed to alter the state of the brain. As a patient dwells on past painful experiences, he/she will develop *resistance* to the revelation of these repressed feelings, and the therapist has to help the patient overcome this resistance to revealing the sources of unconscious motivation.

As a result of the therapeutic process the patient will engage in *transference*, whereby these suppressed feelings are projected onto the therapist. If the patient hates his/her mother, these feelings will come out in reference to the therapist. In this way the patient will gain *insight* into his/her true feelings and thus understand the true reasons for his/her behavior which had been repressed before therapy.

Stages of Psychosexual Development

The sexual impulses form the id and the controls exercised by the ego and superego produce several stages of psychosexual development in the individual. Such basic needs as sex and hunger are gratified in terms of certain pleasure zones in the body.

The first stage was the *oral* stage (birth–1), which centers on the mouth and the pleasures associated with sucking or eating. An infant at birth can suck and satisfy its basic needs through the mouth, as seen in sucking on a nipple or a thumb. Even a fetus will place the thumb in the mouth. The oral stage can show up in later personality traits, such as being passive or dependent, or gaining pleasure from talking or eating or chewing gum or smoking. The mouth has nerve endings which go to the pleasure centers of the brain.

The *anal* stage, age 1–3, involves the pleasure of urination and defecation. The anal stage focuses on toilet training and learning to control the elimination process, which is a matter of learning to control the sphincter muscles which surround the rectum and urethra. The infant must learn to control the motor centers of the brain which in turn control these muscles (see Chapter 11). The anal stage leads to such personality traits as compulsiveness, stinginess, and orderliness. In this way the superego starts to develop.

The *phallic* stage, age 3–5, involves the pleasure zones associated with the genitals (penis and vulva/vagina). This is expressed in masturbation and sexual curiosity, but more important, a young boy can form an attachment for his mother and attach sexual feeling to the mother. At the same time the boy must compete with the father for the mother, and this results in a fear that the father will castrate the son. This conflict between son and father, and the desire of the son to kill his father, is labeled the Oedipus complex after a Greek tragedy in which the son kills his father. The normal son resolves this conflict by identifying with the father and obeying him. This is again a stage in the development of the superego.

The period of *sexual latency*, ages 6–13, marks the repression of sexual feeling and interest in children. Boys play with boys, and girls play with girls.

The final stage of development is the *genital* stage, age 13 on, in which the individual matures sexually into an adult male or female. In the normal course of development males and females develop an interest in each other and start to attach sexual feelings to one another. Normal heterosexual relationships develop from this point on. Problems in psychosexual development can occur, in which case the individual will experience sexual conflict and may become sexually deviant. Sexual behavior and sexual crimes are discussed in Chapter 18.

Freud's Project for a Scientific Psychology

In 1895, Freud published his notes on a Project for a Scientific Psychology, which was his "psychology for neurologists" (Pribram and Gill, 1976). Pribram and Gill conclude that Freud was an early pioneer in cognitive theory and neuropsychology. In his book *Freud: Biologist of the Mind*, Sulloway (1979:500) wrote: "To those who share Freud's goal of uniting psychology with biology, Freud must be considered with Darwin as the founding father of the psychobiological concept of man."

Freud attempted to find but never did find a neurological base for his theory of personality, primarily because the state of neurology at that time was not adequate. However, without too much imagination, we can say that the id refers to the limbic system and the emotional centers of the brain, whereas the ego and the superego refer to the cerebral cortex and to learning, memory, evaluation decision making, and rationality. As we pointed out in Chapter 11, the human being is both an emotional and a rational animal. The control of anger and aggression by the cortex is a critical issue in an understanding of the violent brain.

Although Freud is usually placed in model 1, the introspective and mentalistic model, he should be viewed as an early pioneer for model 3, the integrated systems approach to behavior wherein neurology is regarded as critical to human behavior. Biological psychiatry is very much a combination of neurology and psychiatry (see Chapter 20).

Sociocultural Theories and Freudian Psychology

A number of psychologists/psychiatrists reject Freud's concept of biological man, and look to culture and socialization as alternatives to biology. These psychologists are known collectively as "ego psychologists" since they place emphasis on the ego and superego. These people include Eric Erikson, Alfred Adler, Harry Stack Sullivan, Karen Horney, and Eric Fromm. These psychologists emphasize the cultural setting, family environment, self-concepts, and interpersonal relationships. The emphasis is on the environment rather than biology, and as we have seen, there is a major disagreement in the behavioral and social sciences as to the relative importance of each. In this book the view is taken that both are important and critical to an understanding of human behavior.

SUCCESS OF PSYCHOTHERAPIES

Evaluations of Psychotherapy

In 1952, Hans Eysenck published an evaluation of psychotherapy where he reported that 72 percent of the neurotics improved without therapy, compared to 44 percent of those in psychoanalytic therapy. Later evaluations have challenged the Eysenck findings; however, the success rate of psychotherapy for the major psychoses is very limited. Modern biological therapies are more successful than talk therapies (see Chapters 18 and 20).

Liebert and Spiegler (1982) wrote that Freudian concepts are vague, the theory is unreliable, projective techniques have low reliability and validity, psychoanalysis is not a science, and treatment outcomes are questionable. Wilson and Rachman (1983) reviewed a major study of the effectiveness of psychological therapies which had been made by Smith and Glass (1977). Smith and Glass concluded that psychotherapies are successful. Wilson and Rachman found that the Smith and Glass analysis was methodologically flawed, had omitted relevant studies, and had reached an erroneous conclusion that psychoanalysis was successful. In addition, the Smith and Glass study found that therapy success was not related to the length of the therapy, the experience of the therapist, the diagnosis of the therapist, or the type of therapy. This raises some real questions concerning the use of psychotherapy (Wilson and Rachman, 1983).

The Influence of Freud on Criminology

Freudian psychoanalysis had an immediate impact on criminology as seen in the number of books devoted to the analysis of behavior by psychoanalysts (Jeffery, 1967, 1985; Rennie, 1978; Vold and Bernard, 1986). In *Wayward Youth*, August Aichhorn (1935) described delinquency in terms of classical Freudian theory. Delinquents are caught within the conflicts of the id, ego, and superego. Some delinquents have too little love and therefore have an undeveloped superego. Other delinquents have too much love and are not restrained by their parents. Still others have criminal superegos, that is, they belong to criminal groups or identify with a delinquent father (a sociological theory of criminality).

Kate Friedlander (1947) in *The Psychoanalytical Approach to Juvenile Delinquency* argued along the same lines as did Aichhorn. The delinquent has a poorly developed superego which cannot control the antisocial impulses of the id. Kurt Eissler (1949) in *Searchlights on Delinquency* argued that delinquency is a reaction to the values of society by the ego. He classified neurotic behavior as "autoplastic" characterized by inwardly directed aggression, and criminal behavior is "alloplastic," characterized by aggression directed outwardly toward others.

In *Children Who Hate*, Fritz Redl and David Wineman (1951) interpreted delinquent aggression and frustration as a product of inadequate ego and superego development. Such delinquents have no close personal relationships with adult figures.

A number of studies have been made of the relationship between psychiatric disorders and criminal behavior. Healy and Bronner (1936) in *New Lights on Delinquency and Its Treatment* found 90 percent of the delinquents to be emotionally disturbed as a result of internal mental conflicts. Alexander and Staub (1931) classified criminals as (1) the chronic criminal, who is a product of brain damage, alcoholism, and drug addiction; (2) the neurotic criminal, who has a defective ego and superego and who acts out his/her conflicts in compulsive crimes such as kleptomania and pyromania; (3) the criminal with a criminal superego, that is, he/she is reared in a criminal home and environment; (4) the genuine criminal, who never develops a superego and who lives by id impulses alone, often known in criminology as the psychopath or sociopath; and (5) the accidental and occasional criminal.

Guttmacher and Weihofen (1952) classified criminals as follows:

Classification	Percentage
Normal	65–75
Occasional and accidental	5
Psychopaths	5–10
Neurotic	10
Organic brain lesions	5
Psychoses	1–2

Alexander and Staub (1931) discussed the case of Karl, who had a dominant father who did not allow him to eat sugar. Karl developed an oral fixation and an Oedipus complex. He felt guilty for wanting to kill his father. Karl shot and wounded his girl friend in an effort to hurt his father and to be punished for his guilty thought. Another case cited was that of a woman who shot and killed her pregnant daughter-in-law because of penis envy and an unresolved Oedipus complex. By killing her daughter-in-law she symbolically killed her mother. At the same time the unborn child represented a penis which she did not have but wanted.

Alexander and Healy (1935) cited the case of Richard, who had oral aggressive tendencies and who hated his mother because she preferred his brother to him. By stealing, Richard could find a substitute for forbidden sexual acts, could rid himself of his guilt feelings, and could show hatred toward his mother. Another case, that of Sigrid, involved a kleptomaniac (compulsive stealing). Sigrid stole pocketbooks, which were symbolic of a vagina and to satisfy her repressed sexual desires and an unresolved Oedipus complex. She hated her mother and liked her father, who was in prison, and her stealing gave her a solution to unresolved inner psychic conflicts.

Abrahamsen (1960) tells the story of a man who killed his pregnant girl-friend, to get back at his sister whom he hated. He also cites the case of a taxi driver who killed a male passenger because he resembled his father, whom he hated. Another case involved a man who shot his wife because symbolically she represented his mother, whom he hated.

Abrahamsen (1952) relates the story of Fred, a 17-year-old who stole to gain revenge against his mother. Peter stole cars as a symbolic substitute for his mother, who died when Peter was 10 years of age. John was a middle-aged businessman who became involved in embezzlement and gambling because of guilt feelings over masturbation as a child, for which he was punished by his parents.

The problems involved in the evaluation of psychoanalysis and criminal behavior are immense and beyond the scope of this chapter. There is no agreement as to the classifications that are used, and 100 different psychotherapists will give a great many classifications for the same behavior. The psychotherapist goes back in time to find the cause of behavior, and he/she picks a cause from a multitude of past experiences. There is no way to know that a particular childhood experience did or did not cause anxiety behaviors at a later date. There is no way to relate a causal variable to the effect variable. The assumption is made that one class of behaviors (neuroses, psychoses, psychopathy) causes another class of behaviors (criminal behavior). There is no reason to assume a causal relationship since both are dependent variables (behaviors) and both can and may be related either spuriously or by reason of other antecedent variables which they have in common.

The Success of Psychotherapies in the Treatment of Criminals

Criminologists who have evaluated psychoanalytic and therapeutic interventions into criminal careers have concluded that such therapies show a very low rate of success. The Judge Baker Clinic Guidance Center in Boston under the directorship of Richard Cabot and William Healy had an 88 percent recidivism rate for those delinquents at the clinic, and it was judged to be failure (Witmer and Tufts, 1954). A major evaluation of the effectiveness of delinquency prevention through psychological therapies occurred from 1936 to 1945 with the

Cambridge–Somerville Project. In that project 325 delinquents were selected for treatment by a variety of therapeutic means (the treatment group), and 325 delinquents matched for background characteristics were selected to receive no treatment (the control group). At the end of the project no differences between the treatment group and the control group could be found, and there was a 29.5 percent failure rate for the treatment group and a 28.3 failure rate for the control group (Powers and Witmer, 1951; McCord and McCord, 1959).

Guided group interaction projects (group therapies) such as Pinehills, Silverlake, and Highfields have been evaluated as failures or no better than programs not involving therapies (Riesmann, Cohen, and Pearl, 1964; McCorkle, Bixby and Elias, 1958; Kasselbaum et al., 1971; Empey and Lubeck, 1971). Clarke (1974) concluded that ''the studies reviewed present little evidence that the juvenile offender treatment programs succeeded in reducing delinquency, and there is much evidence that they failed.''

Schuessler and Cressey (1950) reviewed the outcome of 30 personality tests given to criminals, and they found that 42 percent of the studies differentiated criminals from noncriminals. From a review of 29 personality tests, Waldo and Dinitz (1967) found that 81 percent of the studies differentiated criminals and noncriminals. It must be remembered that these studies covered a wide variety of techniques and personality traits, and the results did not indicate the direction of influence of causality. The personality trait(s) could cause criminal behavior, or criminal behavior could cause the personality trait(s). Hakeem (1958), in a sociological response to the psychiatric approach to crime, stated that psychiatric testimony is unscientific, psychiatry makes crime a medical rather than a social problem, psychiatric categories are unreliable, and there is no evidence that mental disease causes criminal behavior. It must be remembered that Hakeem was critiquing the old psychoanalytic framework and not the new biological psychiatry. The implications of biological psychiatry, and the relationship between psychiatry, law, and crime, are discussed fully in Chapter 20.

In general, it can be stated that sociological criminologists have rejected Freudian psychiatry primarily because the psychological model is based on the individual and not the social environment, whereas sociological explanations of behavior are based on the social environment (see Chapter 14).

A survey by Walter Bailey (1966) of 100 individual treatment programs found that ''evidence supporting the efficacy of correctional treatment is slight, inconsistent, and of questionable reliability.'' A major survey of rehabilitation programs from 1945 to 1967 by Lipton, Martinson, and Wilks (1975), usually known as the Martinson report, found that ''the rehabilitative efforts that have been reported so far have had no appreciable effect on recidivism'' (Martinson, 1974).

A major survey by the National Academy of Sciences (Sechrest, White, and Brown, 1979:34) concluded that ''there is not now in the scientific literature any basis for any policy or recommendations regarding rehabilitation of criminal offenders.'' The panel went on to recommend that ''research on offender rehabilitation should be pursued more vigorously, more systematically, more imaginatively, and more rigorously'' (Sechrest, White, and Brown, 1979:10). The National Academy of Sciences also published a follow-up report on possible new directions in rehabilitation research (Martin, Sechrest, and Redner, 1981).

The failure of individual rehabilitation programs guided and designed by clinical psychologists and psychiatrists led to the end of the rehabilitation model in the 1970s (see Chapter 8 for a discussion of this movement). The Freudian model of behavior was the second major development to emerge in the positive/scientific school (the first being the biological school) in criminology. The psychiatrist established a scientific approach to the study of human behavior which although it failed in its initial phases, may eventually provide a means for rehabilitating offenders. In the 1980s there is a reemergence of scientific biological psychiatry which can serve as a base for the structuring of a crime prevention model. Mental disorders are now redefined as brain disorders based on neurochemistry and brain trauma, and treatment of brain chemistry by drug therapies is emerging as the model of prevention and treatment in biological psychiatry (see Chapters 18 and 21).

SUMMARY

Freudian psychology is based on an organism–environment model with behavior originating in biological urges (the id). The control of these drives by the ego and superego are fundamental aspects of the human personality.

Freud used talk therapy and free association to bring out unconscious psychic conflicts which resulted from the repression of biological drives. Because of its emphasis on introspection, Freudian psychology is regarded as mentalistic in nature, although it was originally anchored in basic neurology and brain functioning.

Psychoanalysis has not been a successful means of treating criminals; however, it did create an interest in psychological treatment which is reemerging in the 1980s in biological psychiatry.

FURTHER STUDIES

Further course work in clinical psychology or psychoanalysis can be taken in psychology departments or in departments of psychiatry in medical schools. Abnormal psychology courses cover many of the topics discussed in this chapter. Criminology courses in the treatment of offenders will also deal with psychoanalytic therapies.

REFERENCES

ABRAHAMSEN, D. (1952). *Who Are the Guilty*. New York: Grove Press.

ABRAHAMSEN, D. (1960). *The Psychology of Crime*. New York: Columbia University Press.

ADLER, M. (1985). *Ten Philosophical Mistakes*. New York: Macmillan.

AICHHORN, A. (1935). *Wayward Youth*. New York: Viking Press.

ALEXANDER, F., and W. HEALY (1935). *Roots of Crime*. New York: Alfred A. Knopf.

ALEXANDER, F., and H. STAUB (1931). *The Criminal, the Judge, and the Public*. New York: Macmillan.

BAILEY, W. C. (1966). "Correctional Outcome: An Evaluation of 100 Reports." *Journal of Criminal Law, Criminology, and Police Science*. 57:153–160, June.

*CARLSON, N. R. (1984). *Psychology*. Boston: Allyn and Bacon.

CLARKE, S. H. (1974). "Juvenile Offender Programs and Delinquency Prevention." In *Aldine Crime and Justice Annual*, ed. S. Halleck et al. Chicago: Aldine.

COHEN, L. H. (1988). *Life Events and Psychological Functioning*. Beverly Hills: Sage.

EISSLER, K. (1949). *Searchlights on Delinquency*. New York: International Universities Press.

EMPEY, L., and S. G. LUBECK (1971). *The Silverlake Experiment*. Chicago: Aldine.

*ERDELYI, M. H. (1985). *Psychoanalysis: Freud's Cognitive Psychology*. New York: W. H. Freeman.

FRIEDLANDER, K. (1947). *The Psychoanalytic Approach to Juvenile Delinquency*. New York: International Universities Press.

*GATCHEL, R. J., and F. G. MEARS (1981). *Personality*. New York: St. Martin's Press.

*GLEITMAN, H. C. (1981). *Psychology*. New York: W. W. Norton.

GUTTMACHER, M. S., and H. WEIHOFEN (1952). *Psychiatry and the Law*. New York: W. W. Norton.

HAKEEM, M. (1958). "A Critique of the Psychiatric Approach to Crime and Corrections." *Law and Contemporary Problems*, 23:650–682, Autumn.

HEALY, W., and A. BRONNER (1936). *New Light on Delinquency and Its Treatment*. New Haven, Conn.: Yale University Press.

JEFFERY, C. R. (1967). *Criminal Responsibility and Mental Disease*. Springfield, Ill.: Charles C Thomas.

JEFFERY, C. R. (1985). *Attacks on the Insanity Defense*. Springfield, Ill.: Charles C Thomas.

KASSEBAUM, G., ET AL. (1971). *Prison Treatment and Parole Survival*. New York: Wiley.

LIEBERT, R. M., and M. D. SPIEGLER (1982). *Personality*. Homewood, Ill.: Dorsey Press.

LIPTON, D., R. MARTINSON, and J. WILKS (1975). *The Effectiveness of Correctional Treatment*. New York: Praeger.

MANNHEIM, H. (1965). *Comparative Criminology*. Boston: Houghton Mifflin.

MARTIN, S. E., L. B. SECHREST, and K. REDNER (1981). *New Directions in the Rehabilitation of Criminal Offenders*. Washington, D.C.: National Academy Press.

MARTINSON, R. (1974). "What Works?: Questions and Answers about Prison Reform." *The Public Interest* 35:22–54, Spring.

MATSON, F. W. (1976). *The Idea of Man*. New York: Delta.

McCORD, J., and W. McCORD (1959). "A Followup Report on the Cambridge-Somerville Youth Study." *Annals of the American Academy of Political and Social Science*, 322:89–98, March.

*Source of particular importance in the preparation of this chapter.

McCORKLE, L. W., L. F. BIXBY, and A. ELIAS (1958). *The Highfields Story*. New York: Holt.

*NEEL, A. F. (1977). *Theories of Personality*. New York: Wiley.

POWERS, E., and H. WITMER (1951). *An Experiment in the Prevention of Delinquency: The Cambridge-Somerville Youth Study*. New York: Columbia University Press.

PRIBRAM, K. H., and M. M. GILL (1976). *Freud's Project Revisited*. New York: Basic Books.

REDL, F., and D. WINEMAN (1951). *Children Who Hate*. Glencoe, Ill.: Free Press.

RENNIE, Y. (1978). *The Search for Criminal Man*. Lexington, Mass.: D. C. Heath.

RIESMANN, F. J., J. COHEN, and A. PEARL (1964). *Mental Health and the Poor*. New York: Free Press.

*RYCHLAK, J. (1981). *Personality and Psychotherapy*. Boston: Houghton Mifflin.

SAHAKIAN, W. S. (1968). *History of Philosophy*. New York: Barnes & Noble.

SCHUESSLER, K. F., and D. R. CRESSEY (1950). ''Personality Characteristics of Criminals.'' *American Journal of Sociology*, 55:476–484.

SECHREST, L. B., S. V. WHITE, and E. D. BROWN (1979). *The Rehabilitation of Criminal Offenders: Problems and Prospects*. Washington, D.C.: National Academy of Sciences.

*SINGER, J. (1984). *The Human Personality*. San Diego, Calif.: Harcourt Brace Jovanovich.

SMITH, M. L., and G. V. GLASS (1977). ''Meta-analysis of Psychotheraphy Outcome Studies.'' *American Psychologist*, 32:752–760.

SULLOWAY, F. J. (1979). *Freud: Biologist of the Mind*. New York: Basic Books.

VOLD, G. B., and T. J. BERNARD (1986). *Theoretical Criminology*. New York: Oxford University Press.

WALDO, G. P., and S. DINITZ (1967). ''Personality Attributes of the Criminal: An Analysis of Research Studies, 1950–1965.'' *Journal of Research in Crime and Delinquency*, 4:185–202.

WILSON, G. T., and S. J. RACHMAN (1983). ''Meta-analysis and Evaluation of Psychotheraphy Outcome: Limitations and Liabilities.'' *Journal of Consulting and Clinical Psychology*, 51:55–63.

WITMER, H., and E. TUFTS (1954). *The Effectiveness of Delinquency Prevention Programs*. Washington, D.C.: Childrens Bureau, U.S. Department of Health, Education, and Welfare.

QUESTIONS

1. What is meant by ''mentalistic psychology''?
2. How is the philosophy of rationalism related to mentalistic psychology?
3. Sigmund Freud made humankind a part of nature, and he made emotionality as important an aspect of behavior as rationality. Explain.
4. What was Freud's theory of personality?

*Source of particular importance in the preparation of this chapter.

5. How does psychoanalysis treat emotional disturbances?
6. What was Freud's Project for a Scientific Psychology?
7. How successful have Freudian therapies been?
8. How do psychoanalysts explain criminal behavior?

Psychological Criminology: Behaviorism and Learning Theory

13

INTRODUCTION

The Development of Behaviorism

The second major theoretical development in psychology occurred with the emergence of behaviorism as a major school of psychology. Behaviorism denies the mentalistic and philosophical foundations of humanistic and introspective mentalistic psychology as it seeks a science of psychology based on the study of observable events. The behaviorist denies both mind and brain as unobservable events, and he/she explains behavior in terms of stimulus–response (S-R) relationships. This is environmentalism in an extreme form, and the organism (O) plays a minor role at best. The behaviorist measures the environmental input (S) and the response (R) without the use of intervening variables to connect the S and the R. As we mentioned in Chapter 12, other theoretical schools of psychology use the S-O-R model, with an organism possessing either (1) a mind, consciousness, and awareness, or (2) a brain that mediates all environmental experience and controls behavior. Behaviorism in its extreme forms denies any intervening variable(s) between the environment and the response. However, today there is a return to *cognitive psychology,* which emphasizes perception, cognition, evaluation, and awareness in the behavioral process. This is especially true of the biologically based learning theories.

Learning is the third major aspect of human behavior, the other two being genetics and brain function. Learning is at the individual or organism level, the other level of analysis being the environment. This is the O × E model based on an interdisciplinary systems approach to the analysis of behavior which we have used throughout this book. Learning is a topic that unites all of the behavioral sciences—biology, psychology, and sociology—since all disciplines contribute to our understanding of the learning process. Each scientific discipline has its own theories of learning, and in this chapter we discuss biological, psychological, and social theories of learning.

Philosophical Issues: Rationalism versus Empiricism

The field of learning theory, like those of science, law, and personality theory (Chapters 2 and 12), is dominated by rationalism versus empiricism. Rationalism, based on the philosophical traditions of Plato and Kant, placed emphasis on innate ideas, reason, and cognitive processes within the individual organism. Rationalism, or the "Kantian" concept of human nature (Chapter 12), is found in Gestalt learning theory, Freudian psychoanalysis, and modern neurological learning theory.

Empiricism emphasized observable events and the importance of sensory experience and the environment (Russell, 1945). This school is called "Lockean" psychology because of Locke's emphasis on the human being as a *tabula rasa,* an empty tablet, whose nature was determined by his/her sensory experiences. People are born empty and whatever they are is determined by the environment (Rychlak, 1981).

The behaviorist is a scientist, not philosopher. He/she depends on laboratory procedures, experimental methods, direct observations of behavior, and empirical approaches to the study of human behavior. This type of psychologist is called a behaviorist because he/she observes behavior, not mental states. The model for behaviorism is

Environment ⟶ Empty organism ⟶ Behavior

Behaviorism came to dominate American psychology from 1913 to the 1960s under such titles as a science of behavior, learning theory, behavioral therapies, experimental psychology, and token economies.

In contemporary learning theory those who place emphasis on processes within the organism are called "centralists" (mentalistic or biological learning theory), whereas those who place emphasis on behavior and the environment are called "peripheralists" (the classical behaviorists) (Bower and Hilgard, 1981; Schwartz, 1978; Fantino and Logan, 1979).

Innate versus Learned Behaviors

The nature versus nurture, or heredity versus environment, argument also emerges in learning theory since if behavior is determined by biology, the environment plays no role in the determination of behavior. Some responses are biologically determined because of the way in which the brain is prewired. These responses are such instinctive or innate responses as the sucking response or the grasping response or the knee reflex or the eye reflex. When a stimulus produces a response without prior conditioning, we call it a *reflex action*.

Innate behaviors are studied primarily by biologists interested in nonhuman animal behavior, who are known as ethologists. These persons, who are often European by birth and biologists by training, study fish and birds, using natural field observations primarily. On the other hand, learning theorists are usually American by birth and psychologists by training, and they use laboratories and experimental methods (Dewsbury, 1978).

Ethologists focus on reflex actions based on prewired stimulus–response relationships. They place emphasis on species-specific responses (behaviors unique to a species or phylogeny), stereotypic fixed action patterns (given a stimulus, a certain response will occur), and innate releasing mechanisms (activity in the central nervous system which release the fixed reaction pattern).

Three ethologists of special importance in the history of animal behavior and the development of ethology each received the Nobel Prize in Physiology and Medicine in 1973. Konrad Lorenz is known for his studies of imprinting, whereby young animals attach themselves to a moving object during the first several days of birth. Lorenz discovered that young ducklings followed him around as he moved about, or they followed a moving tire or box. The evolutionary advantage for imprinting behavior is that the young ducklings can follow the mother duck without being trained to do so. A very similar response is the grasping response of a young animal to the fur of the mother, as in the case of a young primate. A young human infant has the same response. This has been portrayed in the comic strip ''Peanuts'' as the Linus response, whereby a young boy holds onto a fuzzy blanket or animal.

Niko Tinbergen worked with the stickleback fish, native to the Netherlands. The male stickleback develops a red belly during the mating season, to attract female sticklebacks to his nesting area. If another male stickleback enters his territory the stickleback will become aggressive and attack the intruder. If a pencil with a red dot on it is placed in the pond, the male stickleback will attack the pencil. This is a *fixed action pattern* or innate stimulus–response relationship.

Karl von Frisch studied the dance of the bees. If a bee locates a source of food, it will return to the hive and do a dance consisting of rotations or waggles. This dance tells other bees the exact location and distance to the food supply, and the other bees then fly straight to the food.

Innate reaction patterns are based on the genetic and nervous system structures of a given species. Each species possesses innate response patterns which allow it to adapt to the environment without learning. The evolution of behavior is related to the evolution of the brain (Chapter 11); for example, spiders spin webs, geese fly south for the winter, salmon migrate from the ocean to small ponds in Alaska where they were hatched, and newly hatched sea turtles break their shells and head for the sea.

The basic behaviors needed for survival are innate in the lower animal forms: reproduction, rearing of the young, protection from predators, gathering food, communication, and social organization. As the brain and nervous system develops, learning becomes more and more important to the survival of the species. As we noted in Chapter 11, the simple brain consists of sensory neurons synapsing on motor neurons in a reflex action manner. A complex brain will have millions of neurons between sensory input and the motor output because of the size and organization of the neocortex.

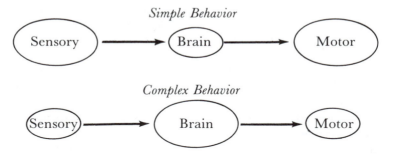

Behavior can be adaptive by being unlearned and genetically based, or by being learned through experience. For example, when a human being is warm, he/she sweats, which is an unlearned reflex action based on the sweat glands and the autonomic nervous system. Or a person can learn to build a house, or an air-conditioning system, or put on clothing when cold. This is learned behavior that becomes part of a cultural system.

ASSOCIATIVE LEARNING

Pavlovian Conditioning

Pavlovian conditioning, also known as classical conditioning, type I conditioning, and type S conditioning, was the result of the work of Ivan Pavlov (1849–1936), a Russian physiologist who won the Nobel Prize in Physiology and Medicine in 1904. Like Lombroso and Freud, Pavlov came to psychology and criminology from biology and medicine, and like Lorenz, Tinbergen, and von Frisch, he was honored with the Nobel Prize.

As a physiologist, Pavlov was interested in salivation. In his experiments Pavlov placed a dog in a harness with an apparatus in the salivary gland to measure salivation. He would present food to the dog to get the dog to salivate (an innate reaction response), and he discovered quite by chance that after an initial training period, dogs would begin to salivate at the sight of the attendant in a white coat. Pavlov could not explain anticipatory salivation in terms of a physiological model, so he redefined his laboratory research to study this phenomenon.

Pavlov presented the sound of a bell before the food, and found that the food–salivation response could be conditioned to a bell. Pavlov labeled the food as the unconditional stimulus (US), salivation was the unconditional response (UR), and the bell was the conditional stimulus (CS). If the bell was presented without the food, salivation still occurred, and it was the conditional response (CR).

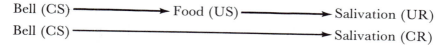

Bell (CS) ⟶ Food (US) ⟶ Salivation (UR)
Bell (CS) ⟶ Salivation (CR)

Pavlov was a European ethologist working with innate reaction patterns at the level of the food–salivation reflex. Pavlov was the father of learning theory or associative learning or conditioning. The importance of his work for psychology cannot be overstated since all learning theories are based on his original work. Pavlov demonstrated that an unlearned stimulus-response relationship based on the neural system of the organism can be modified through experience. This modification of behavior through experience is *learning*. Not only can an organism respond to food by salivation, but it can now learn to respond to food in terms of any number of neutral stimuli that do not produce salivation under normal circumstances. Food can be associated with a light or a bell or a color or a picture or a word. This ability to attach new meaning to a stimulus makes possible a great variety of responses. The organism is not limited to a simple stimulus-response relationship. Great plasticity and flexibility of behaving is now possible.

Principles of Pavlovian Conditioning. Pavlovian conditioning is based on several principles which must be mentioned at the beginning of our discussion.

1. Pavlov dealt with a reflex action, the sensory–motor relationship found in food and salivation. Such responses are under the control of the autonomic nervous system, which controls the smooth muscles and glands (Chapter 11). Classical conditioning involves such autonomic responses as salivation, eye reflex, heart beat, blood pressure, perspiration, respiration, galvanic skin response, pupil contraction, knee jerk, and leg flexion. These responses are often labeled "involuntary" responses since we do not think of ourselves as controlling our heart beat or blood pressure.
2. The conditioning or association that is important is between the US and CS, not between the CS and the UR. A CS such as a bell must signal the delivery of food, the US. The important thing is the information conveyed by the CS concerning the US.

Behaviorism

Behaviorism is an extention of John Locke's ideas of sensation and associationism. In 1914, John Watson (1878–1958) published a book on behaviorism in which he argued that to be scientific, psychology must limit its research to observable facts—and this meant behavior. Watson denied the mind and any psychology that studied mental activities, consciousness, awareness, and the like. As Kantor and Smith (1975) observed: "To a great extent behaviorism represents an attempt to overcome the difficulties of mentalistic psychology. The behaviorist declares that it is impossible for psychology to be a science as long as its subject-matter is transpatial and therefore unobservable." For many years behaviorism was the major theoretical framework in psychology, and this meant a denial of the inner processes of thought and action. Behaviorism places emphasis on the environment while minimizing species differences and individual differences in the learning process. General laws of learning that transcend species differences and individual differences are the goal of the behaviorist.

Operant Conditioning

The name most often associated with operant conditioning is that of B. F. Skinner (1904–). Skinner's behaviorism is more strict than that of most other learning theorists in that he limits psychology to direct observations and does not allow for such intervening variables as "connectionism" and "drive reductionism" as do other psychologists. Skinner is interested primarily in a rigorous methodology and a science of behavior, as indicated in his book *Science and Human Behavior* (Skinner, 1953).

Skinner looked for the conditions under which a response was strengthened by an unconditioned stimulus. He distinguished Pavlovian conditioning from another type of conditioning, which he called type II or type R conditioning. The term "operant" means a response that operates on the environment to produce or eliminate a stimulus. In Skinnerian conditioning the response comes before the stimulus, an R-S psychology.

When the organism behaves, it changes the environment around it, and the behavior produces stimuli that either strengthen and reinforce or weaken the behavior. If the stimulus increases the response rate, the R-S relationship is called "positive reinforcement." If the stimulus decreases the response rate, the R-S relationship is called "positive punishment." The terms pleasure and pain are not used, although pleasure and reinforcement, and pain and punishment, are the same. Like Bentham and Freud, Skinner made pleasure and pain basic to his theory of behavior.

Whereas classical conditioning involves the involuntary responses related to the smooth muscles, operant conditioning involves the somatic nervous system and the striated skeletal muscles. What we refer to as "behavior" are the muscular movements associated with the skeletal muscles of the arms, legs, face, and so on. We regard these as "voluntary" responses, compared to the "involuntary" responses involved in classical conditioning. This is a critical distinction because the criminal law tries to distinguish between voluntary and involuntary behaviors (Chapter 4). It must be emphasized that these concepts, which are critical to philosophical discussions of human responsibility, are based on the organization of the brain and the central nervous system.

Reinforcement and Punishment. Reinforcement is defined as an increase in the response rate. Reinforcement of behavior takes place in two ways: (1) by the presentation of a stimulus that increases the response rate, or (2) by the removal of a stimulus that increases the response rate. Punishment is defined as a decrease in a response rate. Punishment can take place in two ways: (1) by the presentation of a stimulus that weakens the response rate, or (2) the removal of a stimulus that weakens the response rate.

A stimulus that increases a response rate is labeled a reinforcing stimulus (RS), and a stimulus that decreases a response rate is labeled punishing stimulus (PS) or aversive stimulus. In other words, these stimuli create pleasurable or painful experiences within the individual. The following table illustrates these relationships:

Response rate	Stimulus[a]	Process
Up	RS +	Positive reinforcement
Up	PS −	Negative reinforcement
Down	PS +	Positive punishment
Down	RS −	Negative punishment

[a]RS +, a reinforcing stimulus is presented; PS −, a painful stimulus is removed; PS +, a painful stimulus is presented; RS −, a reinforcing stimulus is withdrawn.

Examples of these reinforcers include the following:

RS +: food, sex, water, social praise, physical comfort
PS −: removal of a headache, removal of physical discomfort, removal of anxiety, removal of an enemy
PS +: shock, a blow to the head, a beating, an injury
RS −: loss of a job, loss of money, loss of freedom, loss of contact with the opposite sex

In child rearing, if we beat a child we are using positive punishment, whereas if we tell a child he/she cannot have an ice cream cone or go to a movie or watch television, we are resorting to negative punishment. As Bentham said, we serve two masters—one is pleasure, the other is pain (Chapter 4). Punishment is a major way in which we control human behavior, especially in the criminal justice system.

Shaping Behavior. In a typical laboratory experiment the experimenter takes a naive subject (a rat that has never been in the experimental cage before) and places the rat in a cage or Skinner box. In the box is a lever attached to a food mechanism. If the lever is pressed, a pellet of food drops into a tray and the rat is able to eat. The rat is at 80 percent of body weight and is hungry, since a satiated rat will not perform. The rat does not associate the lever press (an operant response) with food (an unconditioned stimulus), but the rat comes equipped with some natural exploratory behaviors such as sniffing around and exploring the cage with its paws. Whenever the rat approaches the lever the experimenter releases food into the tray by means of a control button that activates the food mechanism. The rat hears the food mechanism and the food dropping, and it approaches the tray and finds the food. This procedure is repeated several times until the rat stays near the lever. The rat will now place a paw on the lever and food will be released. At this point the rat associates a lever press (operant response) with food (an unconditioned reinforcing stimulus). Operant conditioning has taken place.

It must be noted that the biological conditions of the organism are basic to this R-S relationship, that is, the level of hunger and satiation, the natural exploratory behaviors of a rat, and the natural or innate reaction pattern of the organism as related to food.

Conditioned Reinforcement and Punishment. In Pavlovian conditioning a neutral stimulus takes on the reinforcing or punishing qualities of an unconditioned stimulus such as food or shock. This also occurs in operant conditioning. The cage and the lever take on the properties of the reinforcing stimulus, and when the rat is placed in the cage it will run to the lever. A light can be turned on to indicate that a lever press will be followed by food, and the light now becomes a conditioned reinforcer, as the bell did in the Pavlovian experiment. The rat will now work (press a lever) to get the light to turn on, since the rat is reinforced by the presence of the light.

Many neutral stimuli can be made conditioned or secondary reinforcers. This is very important, for it allows for the *chaining* of behavior. In chaining a number of responses are reinforced with conditioned reinforcers, while the final response is rewarded with an unconditioned reinforcer (i.e., food). A rat can be conditioned to come out onto a stage, take a bow, play a horn, go up a stairway, cross a bridge, descend in an elevator, enter a room, pull a cord that plays the national anthem, and then get food for its efforts. Each stimulus becomes a conditioned stimulus for food.

A student attends college for four years to get a degree. The degree is a conditioned reinforcer attached to other reinforcers, such as marriage, a better job, higher socioeconomic status, a better house or car, medical care, vacations, and so on. A college degree is based on a number of unconditioned reinforcers, such as food, sex, and alcohol. During the college career the student is reinforced and/or punished periodically by grades, examinations, promotion, failure, new friends, parties, athletic events, and the like. Whether or not a student finishes high school or college depends on the past reinforcement history of the student and the nature of the reinforcements available in the school situation. If our education system were run along behavioral management lines, there would exist programmed reinforcements that would maintain the academic behaviors required for passing examinations and promotion to a higher level of work.

NEW DIRECTIONS IN LEARNING THEORY

Bioenvironmental Theory of Behavior

The living systems approach to human behavior is holistic in nature, based on the systems approach discussed in Chapter 2, wherein human behavior is regarded as a product of genes, brain function, learning, and social processes in interaction. The model for the bioenvironmental approach to behavior is

$$\text{Environment} \longrightarrow \text{Brain} \longrightarrow \text{Behavior}$$

The holistic approach to human behavior is a combination of the rationalist's emphasis on mental processes and the individual, and the empiricists emphasis on sensory experiences and the environment. Bioenvironmentalism places emphasis on the interaction of nature and nurture, and the interaction of the individual organism with the environment. Physicalism replaces mentalism, and the brain replaces the mind as the organ of behavior. The brain interacts with the environment through the sensory system and sensory experiences.

The bioenvironmental model of behavior has been characterized by Boss and Plomin as the interaction of the innate aspects of the individual with the environment. This view is also known as the *person × situation* model of behavior, in contrast to the *person versus situation model* of behavior (Gatchel and Mears, 1982:380 ff., 484 ff.). Rather than placing emphasis on either the person or the situation, modern psychology places emphasis on both person and situation in interaction, as found, for example, in the works of Endler and Magnusson (Gatchel and Mears, 1982:246 ff.).

Kantor and Smith (1975:21) describe the new bioenvironmental psychology, what they call interbehavioral psychology, in these terms: "Those who hold to the interbehavioral view part company from both the mentalists and the behaviorists. The interbehavioral psychologist observes that the mentalistic conception of coordinated mental and bodily functions, and the resulting division between mind and body, are not based on scientific observations. He believes that both of these conceptions are unwelcomed remnants of old intellectual traditions." The evolution of psychology from philosophy to science, and the impact of physics, chemistry, and biology on psychology, are discussed in Kantor's (1969) book on the history of psychology.

Kendler (1982:299) has written that neurophysiological interpretations of behavior will increase in popularity due to the recent developments in biology and because of the disenchantment with "black box" theories of behavior. He notes that recent developments in biochemistry, neurology, genetics, pharmacology, endocrinology, and related technological systems encourage an intimate relationship between biology and psychology (Kendler, 1982:318). "The causal basis of behavior resides within the physiology of the organism" (Kendler, 1981:316). Modern psychology is committed to the bioenvironmental model of human behavior.

The Biological Bases of Learning

We have emphasized that a latest model of behavior is one involving biology and the brain. This emphasis on the brain is also found in contemporary learning theory. Classical conditioning has a biological base in the unconditioned stimulus–response relationship, or the food–salivation reflex. Operant conditioning ignores this relationship by starting with the response; however, it must be noted that the rat is conditioned to food or water or sex or pain, all of which involve unconditioned S-R relationships. The rat comes prepared "naturally" to use its paws in search of food. This natural preparedness to learn has been investigated by Garcia, Seligman, Breland and Breland, and others (Fantino and Logan, 1979; Schwartz, 1978; Domjan and Burkhard, 1982; Seligman and Hager, 1972).

It is now recognized by learning theorists that they must return to European ethology as a basic model of the biological bases for behavior (Hinde, 1970; Hinde and Stevenson-Hinde, 1973; Dewsbury, 1978; Fantino and Logan, 1979). The extreme environmentalism of behaviorism has been replaced with an

$$\text{Environment} \longleftrightarrow \text{Organism (brain)}$$

model of behavior. The bioenvironmental model of behavior looks at such variables as the genetic history of the species and organism, past environmental influences, brain structure, and present physiological state.

Learning and the Brain

Learning involves changes in the brain, or as Domjan and Burkhard (1982:12) have stated: "Learning is an enduring change in the neural mechanisms of behavior that result from experience with environmental events." Hilgard and Bower (1981:475) observe that "nothing is more certain than that our behavior is a product of our nervous system. . . . This being the case, one may wonder why theories of learned behavior have not been more explicitly neurophysiological in their content, constructs, and referents" [see also Kupfermann (1975); Dunn (1980); Pribram (1969, 1971); Teyler (1978); and Zeiler and Harzen (1983)].

Learning involves modification of the neurons, synapses, and neurotransmitters in the brain due to experiences with the environment. As we noted in Chapter 11, rats that had experiences with an enriched environment had more dendrites and synaptic connections than did rats reared in an impoverished environment.

Learning involves the connection in the brain of a set of neurons that control the unconditioned stimulus with a set of neurons that control the conditioned stimulus (Figure 13–1). Memory is based on the ability of the brain to store past experiences in the synapses and neurotransmitters in order to use them at a later date. Memory gives a person the ability to recall images of the past and other processes which are so critical to cognitive psychology, such as consciousness, awareness, self-identity, and choice. We can recall what we were like at the age of 10, or what we would like to do next month or next year, or what we are planning to have for dinner. Such experiences are basic to "mentalism" and a belief in a mind–body dualism. However, the storage of past experiences, the ability to remember such events, and the ability to plan for the future and to make decisions concerning future goals are all functions of the brain. This gives our behavior a goal-oriented and humanistic quality found lacking in a simpler S-R model of behavior.

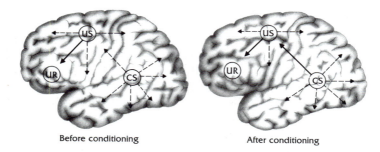

Before conditioning   After conditioning

Figure 13–1   Pavlov's View of the Physiology of Learning.

The organization of the brain also makes possible complex thought processes and complex decision-making processes that are probably contained in the vertical columns found in the cortex (Chapter 11). The hippocampus plays a very critical role in memory, as do the language areas of the left hemisphere of the brain. Today, books on the brain include major sections on the topics of learning and memory and higher thought processes (Kalat, 1984; Carlson, 1986; Bloom, Lazerson, and Hofstadter, 1985). Miller, Galanter, and Pribram (1960), in a book entitled *Plans and the Structure of Behavior,* emphasized the role of learning and the brain in complex decision processes.

If we use the brain as an explanation of how learning occurs, we can also explain one of the mysteries of learning theory: What makes a reinforcer reinforcing?

For the most part, Skinnerians ignore the biological nature of the organism and the issue of why a stimulus is reinforcing. For Skinner, reinforcement is not physiological; rather, it is an increase in a response rate following an event (Hilgard and Bower, 1981:172 ff.; Fantino and Logan, 1979:36 ff.).

For a physiological learning theorist a stimulus is reinforcing because of the evolutionary history of the species. A frog catches flies with the tongue, a trout catches flies with the mouth, a spider spins webs to catch bugs, and so on. Reinforcement occurs because of the way the brain processes a stimulus and the way the brain is wired to muscles. Reinforcement involves the pleasure and pain centers of the brain, which control the autonomic nervous system. Reinforcement involves nerve bundles that utilize neurotransmitters such as dopamine (DA) and norepinephrine (NE), as well as opiates. Drugs such as amphetamine, cocaine, and the opiates mimic the action of DA, NE, and the endorphins in the brain. Drugs and alcohol are reinforcing because of their impact on the biochemistry of the brain (Carlson, 1986:523 ff.; Domjan and Burkhard, 1982:168 ff.). Reinforcement involves the hypothalamus, median forebrain bundle, hippocampus, and the neocortex. Behaviors involving hunger, thirst, sex, and aggression are controlled by the limbic system, where the pleasure and pain centers give such behaviors the qualities of pleasure and pain. We associate pleasure and basic survival with food, sex, water, and aggression.

Social Learning Theory

An important aspect of cognitive psychology is social learning theory. Social learning theory places great emphasis on the influence of other people on the behavior of the subject, usually by means of symbolic communication within a social setting. Miller and Dollard (1941) developed social learning theory based on imitation. The idea of imitative learning has been around in social psychology for years as found in the works of Tarde, Baldwin, and G. H. Mead.

Albert Bandura (1925–   ) is a leading advocate of social learning theory as higher-order learning based on cognitive processes and vicarious experiences. Social learning theory departs from Skinnerian learning theory in that individual cognitive functions intervene between the S and the R. A person will select a social model from the environment to emulate and imitate. Role modeling, symbolic interaction, and language play major roles in social learning theory (Rychlak, 1981; Liebert and Spiegler, 1982; Hilgard and Bower, 1981).

A typical experiment by Bandura was to have a group of children watch a movie or a puppet show. The show depicted violent or nonviolent episodes, and the aggressive behaviors were reinforced, punished, or treated in a neutral manner. After watching the movie or play, the children were placed in a room with toys for one hour and a count made of the number of aggressive acts against other children or toys that occurred during the play period. The number of aggressive acts after the aggressive movie were compared to aggressive acts after the nonaggressive movie. A comparison was made between the group watching aggression being reinforced versus the group watching aggression being punished. Aggressive behavior increases after watching a movie in which aggression is shown and reinforced. Social learning maintains that the children imitate the social model from the movie who is acting violently.

Social learning theory ignores a person's biological state as well as differences among individuals due to genetic, brain, and learning differences. Not everyone imitates everything he/she sees. Different people respond differently to the same stimulus (an aggressive movie), and the same person will respond differently to the same stimulus at different times. Like the nonsocial environment, the social environment, has a different impact on different people. Give a hundred people steak to eat and you will have a hundred different brains processing the biochemicals in a hundred different ways. Show a hundred individuals an act of violence, such as a person being hanged, and you will have a hundred different responses. Many, if not most of these responses are from the autonomic nervous system (increased heart rate, increased blood pressure, nauseau, vomiting, fainting, sex orgasm) and are not learned responses.

The biological preparedness of the individual to learn, as well as the role of the brain in processing information from the social environment, are critical to learning theory, but they are ignored by social learning theory. Social reinforcement is conditioned reinforcement based on the relationship of the conditioned stimulus to an unconditioned stimulus. Sociologists use social learning theories as total explanations of learning rather than as an aspect of general learning theory that includes classical, operant, and biological learning theory. This issue is discussed in Chapter 14.

CRIMINAL BEHAVIOR AND LEARNING THEORY

Criminal Behavior as Learned Behavior

Human behavior, including criminal behavior, is learned behavior. By using the laws of classical and operant conditioning we can explain a great deal of criminal behavior. This does not mean, however, that we are going to ignore species differences or individual differences due to genetic and neurological factors. Individual differences are critical in learning theory and in criminology (Wilson and Herrnstein, 1985).

People learn to satisfy basic biological needs (food, sex, comfort, survival) by means of a primate brain and behavior. By learning stimulus–response relationships the person learns to adapt to his/her environment and to survive. Stimulus–response relationships are formed on the basis of pleasure and pain, and those behaviors that are reinforced become a part of the person's adaptation to the environment.

Criminal behavior is the manner in which a person adapts to the environment. This adaptation consists of learning to connect a given response with a reward such as food, or sex, or money, or a car. A person learns that certain stimuli are unconditioned or conditioned reinforcers, and he/she learns how to obtain certain stimuli in order to gain pleasure and avoid pain. This can include working for them and buying them, or stealing them. It should be noted that criminal behaviors are maintained by a reinforcing stimulus, such as a car or money or jewelry, and the car or money is reinforcing whether it is stolen or purchased. Property offenses are reinforced by physical objects.

In our discussions of learning theory we differentiated primary or unconditioned reinforcers from secondary or conditioned reinforcers. When a person steals a car or money or jewelry, he/she is stealing a conditioned reinforcer, but one that is associated with a primary reinforcer. Money in itself does not have any intrinsic reinforcement value, but it can be exchanged for food, sex, medical care, lodging, drugs, alcohol, and other primary reinforcers. When I presented this idea at a faculty seminar, one faculty member objected that this was rat psychology and she was not a rat working for food, but a person working for a paycheck and for social status. What she ignored was the fact that she exchanged her status and paycheck for renting a house, for purchasing food, for medical care, and for other basic comforts of life.

Another distinction we made concerning reinforcement was between positive and negative reinforcements. All the examples we have used have been of positive reinforcement with cars or money or jewelry. Someone can ask: "Where is the reinforcement for murder or rape or assault?" Crimes against the person involve negative reinforcement, that is, the removal of an aversive or painful stimulus. When a man murders a nagging wife, or a wife murders an abusive and alcoholic husband, the reinforcement for the act is the removal of the person from the environment. Humankind works to remove pain as well as to gain pleasure.

Rape is not always or even primarily an act reinforced with sexual gratification (positive reinforcement). Rape is primarily an act motivated by anger, fear, anxiety, frustration, and hatred. The act of rape is a physical assault on a female which can relieve the person of anxiety, hatred, anger, and fear.

The statement that criminal behavior involves reinforcement does not deny the role of the brain in such learning. The past experiences of the criminal are stored in the brain, and those past experiences determine whether or not the stimulus is reinforcing. Drugs and alcohol are very reinforcing, and they are very much related to criminal behavior. Stimulation of the autonomic nervous system is reinforcing, as found in behaviors involving aggression, drugs, and alcohol. It is possible that a bank robbery or a convenience store robbery or shoplifting is reinforcing because of the "thrill" it creates within the person. The thrill associated with crime is the activation of the autonomic nervous system. These topics are discussed in more detail in Chapter 18.

The Role of Punishment in Criminal Behavior

Punishment is the suppression of a response rate by the presentation of a painful stimulus or the removal of a rewarding stimulus. The impact of punishment on behavior is of central concern to criminology since punishment is the mechanism used by the criminal justice system to control criminal behavior. It is our basic crime control model as seen in the police–courts–corrections sytem.

A typical experiment in punishment is conducted as follows. A rat is trained to press a lever for food (positive reinforcement). The rat is then punished by shock (positive punishment) for the lever press. The rate of suppression of lever pressing is then measured and is called punishment. It must be noted that punishment always involves behavior that is being reinforced, for otherwise the animal will not respond. A rat does not press a lever to get a shock, nor does a criminal commit a crime to get placed in prison or in an electric chair.

The availability of an alternative response for a reinforcer will lower or eliminate a punished response. The experimenter can present a green light with a lever press that leads to food, and can present a red light with a lever press that leads to shock. The green light becomes a conditioned reinforcer for food; the red light becomes a conditioned reinforcer for shock. A rat will now press the lever in the presence of the green light, and avoid pressing the lever in the presence of the red light.

A rat can now be trained to avoid and escape punishment. A red light signals that in 10 seconds a shock will be administered. The rat is now able to escape or avoid the shock by making an operant response such as pressing a lever or running through a door, and the rat very soon learns to avoid pain through an operant response. The rat now presses the lever in the presence of the red light since the light is a signal for shock. We have labeled this negative reinforcement, the increase in a response rate due to the removal of a painful stimulus. Do not confuse negative reinforcement with punishment, for it is exactly the opposite (Fantino and Logan, 1979; Domjan and Burkhard, 1982).

Punishment and the Criminal Justice System

One of the major discrepancies between science and the criminal justice system involves punishment. In the laboratory punishment is successful in suppressing behavior, but in the criminal justice system punishment does not work. Why is this the case? The literature on punishment discusses a number of issues in relation to punishment which I shall summarize here [see Azrin and Holz (1966) and Domjan and Burkhard (1982)].

1. To be successful, the time lag between the behavior and punishment must be short. In other words, punishment must be swift. This was a basic principle of the classical school. Punishment is anything but swift with long delays between the crime, arrest, conviction, sentencing and imprisonment. Today, it may take years before a criminal is punished.

2. To be successful, punishment must be certain. In our system of criminal justice we have many unknown and unreported crimes, which can run as high as five unreported crimes for one reported crime. Of those crimes reported, few arrests are made, few convictions are made, and few criminals are sentenced to prison.

   At the sentencing stage the offender may receive a suspended sentence, probation, a fine, or a prison sentence ranging up from one year. For the same crime the sentence can vary in many ways (see Chapter 9).

3. In the typical punishment experiment the response is paired with a reinforcing stimulus such as food. To be effective, punishment must overcome positive reinforcement. A person will not respond if punishment is the sole consequence of his/her actions. Since behavior is paired with a reinforcing stimulus, the punishment may not be adequate to control the

behavior. For example, the reinforcement for smoking is strong and is rooted in physiology; therefore, it is most difficult to control smoking behavior even though some painful consequences, such as cancer or a heart attack or death, may be an eventual result. The reinforcement for smoking is immediate; the punishing consequences are in the distant future.

When a reinforcer such as money can be gotten by an illegal response, the person can weight the risk of punishment versus the monetary gain. Since the risk of punishment is low, the criminal has the odds in his/her favor as he/she commits a crime. The prospect of gaining money immediately outweights the threat of punishment in the distant future. A study by Carroll (1982) showed that criminals focus primarily on the amount and certainty of the gain from the crime, not on the severity or certainty of punishment.

4. To make punishment effective, we must provide the person with alternative means for reinforcement. If a person is offered an alternative to the punished response, the punished response will be diminished or eliminated. This implies the establishment of crime prevention programs that block the illegal opportunities structure, as well as behavioral programs that create legitimate opportunities (Chapter 19).

5. Punishment can become a conditioned stimulus for positive reinforcement. If a child is spanked and then given candy, the child will misbehave in order to get candy. If the only time a child is noticed by the parent is when the parent is punishing the child, the child will act in an antisocial manner in order to get attention. A rat can be conditioned to press a lever to get shock if the shock then results in food. In psychiatric terminology this is known as sadistic or masochistic behavior. The conditioning of pain to sexual pleasure is very common in sex crimes.

6. Punishment creates escape and avoidance behaviors. We described escape and avoidance in our discussion above. A person does not learn through punishment to obey the law; rather, he/she learns how to commit crimes and to escape punishment. A rat can learn to escape shock to its feet by lying on its back while eating (see Figure 13–2)

Criminals can avoid or escape punishment by avoiding detection and arrest; if arrested, they can give an alibi or hire lawyers; if charged, they can falsify statements, and attempt to win an acquittal; if found guilty, they can tell the social worker a story that may result in probation; if sentenced, they can try to manipulate the prison community to gain privileges and an early release.

The criminal justice system is one huge escape and avoidance conditioning system. Rather than conditioning people to legal behavior, it conditions them to escape from and avoid the law.

7. Punishment creates aggression in those who are punished. This aggression can be operant, that is, against the aggressor in order to remove the aggression, or it can be reflexive. Reflexive aggression occurs when pain is administered to a person and the person strikes out against any object

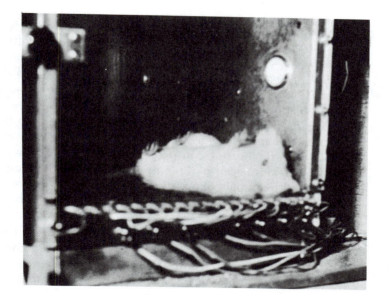

Figure 13-2 "Breakfast in Bed." A rat has learned to avoid grid shock by lying on its back while pressing the response lever with its hind foot to produce food pellets. From "Punishment," by N. H. Azrin and W. C. Holz (1966). In *Operant Behavior,* ed. by W. K. Honig. New York: Appleton-Century-Crofts.

or person in the environment. A rat that is shocked will attack a doll or another rat that happens to be in the same cage. A man who had an argument with his boss will come home angry and frustrated and strike out against his wife or children, or he will kick the cat or break down a door. When we put people in prison we make them more vicious and hateful than before. This is a major factor in the failure of our prison system to rehabilitate.

8. Any stimulus associated with punishment can become a conditioned stimulus (CS) for punishment. A parent or teacher is avoided or hated. The child may run away from home or become a truant from school. Many delinquent careers start with such behavioral problems at home or in the school. Truancy, reading problems, behavioral problems at home or in the school, a history of aggression against animals, and other such problem behaviors are associated with delinquency and with punishment. The use of punishment to control behavior creates major behavioral problems on its own.

9. Studies by Seligman (1975) and others have shown that punishment can create learned helplessness. Learned helplessness refers to the fact that if an animal is conditioned to receive unavoidable shocks (no escape or avoidance behavior is provided), the animal will not learn to avoid shock later when the shock is avoidable. Learned helplessness is also an important aspect of psychological depression. The ability to control one's environment is an important aspect of healthy adaptive behavior, and

criminal behavior can reflect learned helplessness, a trust in fate, and a loss of control over the environment [see Miller (1958) and Glueck and Glueck (1952)].

10. The punisher (lawyer, parent, teacher, police officer) may be angry or hostile toward the person punished. Aggression is rewarding for those doing the punishing. It allows for a feeling of power over others, a release of feelings of revenge and hatred, and it allows one to be aggressive in a legitimate manner. Aggression can be lawful or unlawful (Chapter 18). The reason the criminal justice system continues to punish and execute criminals is not because of the impact of punishment on the criminal but because of the impact of punishment on those doing the punishing, which includes you and me. That is why 80 percent of the public supports capital punishment.

11. The psychopath does not condition to punishment. The use of punishment against the antisocial personality does no good and it may do harm. It is necessary to understand the biological and psychological makeup of the psychopath and to design treatment measures that will halt antisocial behavior. The psychopath is discussed in detail in Chapter 18.

In conclusion, we can state that punishment is not a successful way to control behavior since it is so disruptive to other behaviors. Azrin and Holz (1966) concluded that "the disruption of social behavior constitutes the primary disadvantage to the use of punishment."

Behavior Modification and Delinquent Behavior

If behavior is learned through conditioning and reinforcement, why not use such principles to modify delinquent and antisocial behaviors? The application of learning theory to problem areas is called behavioral modification, behavioral management, token economies, and behavior therapies (Kazdin, 1978).

A typical behavior modification project involves using a reward system (money or tokens that can be exchanged for money, food, or clothing) to strengthen certain lawful behaviors that the experimenter has selected as the target behaviors. These behaviors are never criminal behaviors since the delinquent is in a special home or a school or a correctional institution, and he/she is not exhibiting criminal acts in this environment. The behaviors selected are either (1) institutional management behaviors such as getting up on time, getting to meals on time, not swearing and fighting, and cleaning one's room, or (2) academic behaviors such as studying English or math, passing an exam, and moving toward a high school diploma through a General Educational Development (GED) examination (Milan and McKee, 1974, Stumphauzer, 1986).

Two case projects were established at the National Training School in Washington, D.C. by a group of operant conditioners (Cohen and Filipczak, 1971). Within the institution these psychologists set up programmed instructional materials in order that delinquents could improve their high school academic scores. In return for good academic performance and good institutional performance the delinquents were given points or tokens which they could then exchange for food, clothing, a private room with a kitchen and television set, trips outside the institution, and so on. Since the delinquents were like the rat in the ''cage,'' they had to perform if they wanted these privileges. Real success in the modification of behavior was reported. However, three years after release the case subjects had returned to the same recidivism rate as that of persons not in the project (Cohen and Filipczak, 1971:134). Burchard and Harig (1976) concluded that the selection of case students was not representative of the general delinquent population, and those who returned to other institutional programs were not evaluated as case students. They concluded that since the project did not use experimental controls, it was not possible to make any conclusions as to the behavioral effect of the case project.

Jeffery (1971, 1977) established a project in Washington, D.C. which was an open school, not an institution. His argument with the case model was that controlling behavior in an institution would not carry over into the community environment once the delinquent was released from the institution. Up to forty hard-core delinquents 18 to 21 years of age who were high school dropouts were placed in a program set up in a rented house in Washington. Programmed instructional materials were made available, along with teachers and counselors, for completing the GED test, and the students were paid up to $40 a week for academic and institutional behaviors.

Since the subjects were not in an institution, they did not have to attend classes. The attendance rate was low and the dropout rate was high. After class the students returned to the streets of Washington to commit crimes, and many of them were arrested while in the project. They were also involved in thefts from the school of such items as typewriters, cars, fans, and so on.

Of those who took the GED examination, 13 of 22 passed, or 59 percent, which in itself is good. However, the delinquency rate of those who passed the examination was higher than for those who had not. The students in the program for a longer period were subject to a longer period of evaluation. However, the critical facts are: (1) the behaviors modified were academic and high school behaviors that had little or no bearing on changing criminal behaviors, and (2) the changes produced by the school setting did not carry over to the community environment. If one takes seriously the principles of behavioral psychology, one should not expect that changing a student's behavior as far as math or English is concerned would change his/her behavior concerning taking drugs or stealing from liquor stores. The opportunity to commit crimes is not reduced by placing delinquents in a special project either within an institution or in a school in the community. This was the beginning of Jeffery's interest in crime prevention and environmental design (Chapter 19).

Another use of behavior modification involves what has been labeled a ''social learning'' approach. Family members or foster parents are trained to act as agents for the delivery of reinforcers and punishment. Achievement Place was set up by the operant conditioners at the University of Kansas to train parents and foster parents in the proper use of behavioral principles to change the behavior of children. These children were predelinquents 8 to 12 years of age. The target behaviors were personal and institutional behaviors such as cleaning one's room, and academic behavior such as studying and passing examinations. As in other behavioral modification projects, the students were reinforced for proper behaviors.

Although there were changes in the target behaviors, there is no evidence that such changes were maintained in the community or natural environment. A National Institute of Mental Health survey of the project concluded that there was no evidence that the project altered behavior one year after release, or that it had a greater impact on behavior than that of other community projects (Burchard and Harig, 1976; Wilson and Herrnstein, 1985).

Gerald Patterson (1980) at the Social Learning Center in Oregon also used parents as agents for social control, but he used punishment rather than reinforcement as his behavioral conditioner. He observed that children who were aggressive and abused were punished more than were the control group of children. However, "stealers" (those who lied, ran around, stole, and/or set fires) were punished less by their parents. Punishment had little impact on the stealers, and Patterson concluded that the parents of stealers did not know how to punish effectively.

Several issues can be raised concerning the Patterson study and the use of punishment to change behavior. He observed that aggressive children were punished more, but he did not raise the issue of whether the child's aggression caused the parents to punish or whether parental punishment caused the child to be aggressive. We know that punishment can create aggression in the punishee. Patterson did not consider whether or not the fact that punishment had little impact on stealers was due to the fact they had been overpunished in the past and punishment had become an ineffective means of control. Perhaps the stealers were psychopaths who did not respond to conditioning through punishment. Punishment does not create conforming behavior.

In general, Patterson's conclusion that aggressive children were punished more while antisocial and predelinquent children (stealers) were punished less can be used to support an argument that punishment is a very ineffective way to shape human behavior. Patterson's conclusion that parents of delinquents do not know how to punish effectively must be questioned in terms of his own observations of what happens when children are punished.

Several major projects in behavioral modification were started in prisons using punishment; these are called aversive therapies. These are similar to the Patterson project and in contradiction to projects that use reinforcement to control behavior. Three projects were started in California, one at the Atascadero State Hospital, one at the Vacaville Rehabilitation Center, and one at the Ontario Regional Penitentiary. These projects used aversive therapy consisting of the administration of a drug that paralyses the autonomic nervous system. The ANS controls breathing and the person feels as if he is dying.

The START program at the Medical Center for Federal Prisoners and the Patuxent Institution for defective delinquents in Maryland used a graded tier system. When the inmate entered Patuxent he entered at the bottom of the system without privileges or rights, and through good behavior could advance to higher tiers with privileges. Reinforcement was built into the tier system. These programs received a great deal of negative mass media publicity, and they were halted by court order (Nietzel, 1979; Trasler and Farrington, 1979). To my knowledge, these aversive therapy programs have never been evaluated as to effectiveness in modifying criminal behavior. It is doubtful if they were successful, and even if so, they are too controversial to use.

The use of punishment for behavior change must be reevaluated, especially in terms of the extreme and unjustified ways in which it was used in these projects. The legal issues involved in punishment and treatment need to be resolved (Chapter 21).

SUMMARY

Learning is a complex process by which experience is used by the brain to organize behavior. Learning is based on pleasure and pain and the association of pleasure and pain with response patterns. Learning involves the association of stimulus–response patterns in either a Pavlovian (US-UR) or a Skinnerian (R-S) pattern.

Learning involves the interaction of biology and the environment—innate reaction patterns that are modified and extended by experience. Human behavior is very pliable because of the manner in which the human brain is constructed. Learning involves changes in the neurons and synapses of the brain. Criminal behavior is learned behavior based on reinforcement and punishment. Learning theory is critical to any discussion and understanding of criminal behavior.

FURTHER STUDIES

Courses in learning theory are offered in psychology departments. I recommend that my undergraduate and graduate students take such a course.

REFERENCES

AZRIN, N. H., and W. C. HOLZ (1966). "Punishment." In *Operant Behavior*, ed. W. K. Honig. New York: Appleton-Century-Crofts.

*BARNETT, S. A. (1981). *Modern Ethology*. New York: Oxford University Press.

BLOOM, F. E., A. LAZERSON, and L. HOFSTADTER (1985). *Brain, Mind, and Behavior*. New York: W. H. Freeman.

BOWER, G. H., and E. R. HILGARD (1981). *Theories of Learning*. 5th ed. Englewood Cliffs, N.J.: Prentice-Hall.

BURCHARD, J. D., and HARIG, P. T. (1976). "Behavior Modification and Juvenile Deliquency." In *Handbook of Behavior Modification and Behavior Therapy*, ed. H. Leitenberg. Englewood Cliffs, N. J.: Prentice-Hall.

*Source of particular importance in the preparation of this chapter

CARLSON, N. R. (1985). *Physiology of Behavior*. Boston: Allyn and Bacon.

CARROLL, J. S. (1982). "The Decision to Commit a Crime." In *The Criminal Justice System: A Social-Psychological Analysis,* ed. V. J. Komecni and E. B. Ebbesen. San Francisco: W. H. Freeman.

COHEN, H., and J. FILIPCZAK (1971). *A New Learning Environment*. San Francisco: Jossey-Bass.

*DETHIER, V. C., and E. STELLAR (1970). *Animal Behavior*, 3rd ed. Englewood Cliffs, N. J.: Prentice-Hall.

*DEWSBURY, D. (1978). *Comparative Animal Behavior*. New York: McGraw-Hill.

*DOMJAN, M., and B. BURKHARD (1982). *The Principles of Learning and Behavior*. Belmont, Calif.: Brooks/Cole.

DUNN, A. J. (1980). "Neurochemistry of Learning and Memory: An Evaluation of Recent Data." *Annual Review of Psychology*. Palo Alto, Calif.: Annual Reviews.

*FANTINO, D., and C. A. LOGAN (1979). *The Experimental Analysis of Behavior: A Biological Perspective*. San Francisco: W. H. Freeman.

GATCHEL, R. J., and F. G. MEARS (1982). *Personality: Theory, Assessment, and Research*. New York: St. Martin's Press.

GLUECK, S., and E. GLUECK (1952). *Delinquents in the Making*. New York: Harper & Row.

*HINDE, R. A. (1970). *Animal Behavior: A Synthesis of Ethology and Comparative Psychology*. New York: McGraw-Hill.

*HINDE, R. A. (1974). *Biological Bases of Human Social Behavior*. New York: McGraw-Hill.

HINDE, R. A. and J. STEPHENSON-HINDE (1973). *Constraints on Learning*. New York: Academic Press.

JEFFERY, C. R. (1971, 1977). *Crime Prevention through Environmental Design*. Beverly Hills, Calif.: Sage.

KALAT, J. W. (1984). *Biological Psychology*, 2nd ed. Belmont, Calif.: Wadsworth.

KANTOR, J. R. (1969). *The Scientific Evolution of Psychology*, Vol. 2. Chicago: Principia Press.

KANTOR, J. R., and N. W. SMITH (1975). *The Science of Psychology*. Chicago: Principia Press.

KAZDIN, A. E. (1978). *History of Behavior Modification*. Baltimore, Md.: University Park Press.

KENDLER, H. K. (1981). *Psychology: A Science in Conflict*. New York: Oxford University Press.

*KLOPER, P. H. (1974). *An Introduction to Animal Behavior*, 2nd ed. Englewood Cliffs, N. J.: Prentice-Hall.

KUPFERMANN, I. (1975). "Neurophysiology of Learning." *Annual Review of Psychology*. Palo Alto, Calif.: Annual Reviews.

LIEBERT, R. M., and M. D. SPIEGLER (1982). *Personality*. Homewood, Ill.: Dorsey Press.

*MANNINNG, A. (1972). *An Introduction to Animal Behavior*, 2nd ed. Reading, Mass.: Addison-Wesley.

*Source of particular importance in the preparation of this chapter.

MILAN, M. A., and J. M. McKEE, (1974). "Behavior Modification: Principles and Applications in Corrections." In *Handbook of Criminology*, ed. D. Glaser. Skokie, Ill.: Rand McNally.

MILLER, W. B. (1958). "Lower Class Culture as a Generating Milieu of Gang Delinquency." *Journal of Social Issues*, 3:5–19.

MILLER, G. A., E. GALANTER, and K. PRIBRAM (1960). *Plans and the Structure of Behavior*. New York: Holt, Rinehart, and Winston.

MILLER, N. E., and J. DOLLARD (1941). *Social Learning and Imitation*. New Haven, Conn.: Yale University Press.

NIETZEL, M. T. (1979). *Crime and its Modification*. Elmsford, N. Y.: Pergamon Press.

PATTERSON, G. R. (1980). "Children Who Steal." In *Understanding Crime*, ed. T. Hirschi and M. Gottfredson. Beverly Hills, Calif.: Sage.

PRIBRAM K. (1969). *On the Biology of Learning*. New York: Harcourt, Brace & World.

PRIBRAM, K. (1971). *Languages of the Brain*. Englewood Cliffs, N. J.: Prentice-Hall.

RUSSELL, B. (1945). *A History of Western Philosophy*. New York: Simon & Schuster.

RYCHLAK, J. F. (1981). *Introduction to Personality and Psychotherapy*, 2nd ed. Boston: Houghton Mifflin.

*SCHWARTZ, B. (1978). *Psychology of Learning and Behavior*. New York: W. W. Norton.

SELIGMAN, M. E. P., and J. L. HAGER (1972). *Biological Boundaries of Learning*. New York: Appleton-Century-Crofts.

SELIGMAN, M. E. P. (1975). *Helplessness*. San Francisco: W. H. Freeman.

SKINNER, B. F. (1953). *Science and Human Behavior*. New York: Macmillan.

STUMPHAUZER, J. S. (1986). *Helping Delinquents Change*. New York: Haworth Press.

SWENSON, L. C. (1980). *Theories of Learning*. Belmont, Calif.: Wadsworth.

TEYER, R. (1978). *Brain and Learning*. Stamford, Conn.: Greylock.

TRASLER, G. B., and D. P. FARRINGTON (1979). "Behavior Modification with Offenders." *British Journal of Criminology*, 19(4):314–446.

*WALLACE, R. (1979). *Animal Behavior*. Santa Monica, Calif.: Goodyear.

WILSON, J. Q., and R. J. HERNSTEIN (1985). *Crime and Human Nature*. New York: Simon & Schuster.

ZEILER, M. D., and P. HARZEN (1983). *Biological Factors in Learning*. New York: Wiley.

QUESTIONS

1. How have rationalism and empiricism influenced our views of human behavior?
2. How do European ethologists and American psychologists differ in their explanations of behavior?
3. Explain why a larger cortex means less innate and more learned behavior.
4. How was Pavlovian conditioning related to basic biological phenomena?
5. Why did the behaviorist reject the concept of mind and brain?
6. What is meant by reinforcement? By punishment?

*Source of particular importance in the preparation of this chapter.

7. What is conditioned reinforcement?
8. How does bioenvironmental (psychobiological) psychology differ from mentalistic psychology and behavioral psychology?
9. How is the brain involved in learning?
10. How does social learning theory differ from biological learning theory?
11. What learning theories are used in criminology to explain criminal behavior?
12. Why is punishment successful in changing behavior in the laboratory but not in the criminal justice system?
13. How has learning theory been applied to the rehabilitation of delinquents?

PART 4: CRIMINOLOGY: THE SOCIAL SCIENCES

Sociological Criminology **14**

INTRODUCTION

The History of Sociology

Sociology came from the social and political philosophies of the nineteenth century, especially those of Spencer, Comte, Durkheim, Weber, and Marx. Although these theorists represented somewhat different positions on social issues, they agreed on an evolutionary perspective taken from Darwinian biology and based on an organic analogy between organic evolution and social evolution. Society was an organism maturing from a simple to a complex form, or from a tribal/kinship system to a modern urban industrial society (see Chapter 3).

The emphasis was on social change and social evolution. The individual person was important only as he/she was a product of social forces and social dynamics. Sociologists rejected both biology and psychology. In his hierarchy of sciences, Comte omitted psychology as science moved from biology to sociology. Comte felt that sociology was based on biology, whereas Durkheim rejected both biology and psychology in his effort to explain behavior at the social level. Sociologists have accepted the Durkheimian rather than the Comtian view of sociology, that is, that sociology is not dependent on biology or psychology. Weber dealt with both the individual (social action theory) and social structure, whereas Marx dealt with the social and political structure (Ritzer, 1980, 1983a; Turner, 1982; Coser, 1977).

Comte's concept of science and positivism included the idea of progress through science, or the betterment of humankind through knowledge. Social reform was a central dogma in early sociology, or as H. P. Becker has noted, sociology was concerned with "sex, sin, and sewage" (Bloch and Geis, 1970:303). Such social problems as poverty, dependency, delinquency, urbanization, industrialization, and minority groups were of major concern to sociologists, and sociologists had close ties to social work and social reform movements.

The social reform orientation was joined to a Protestant work ethic and morality, whereby hard work and charity were signs of salvation and redemption in the eyes of God. Many of the early sociologists were Protestant ministers from the midwest. This Protestant reform movement combined with social Darwinism to form a basis for early sociological activity. Social Darwinism taught that certain people were favored for success and others were doomed to failure because of innate biological inferiorities or superiorities. Those predestined by God for success had to care for the poor and underprivileged class (Hinkle and Hinkle, 1954; Gibbons, 1979; Davis, 1980; Hinkle, 1980).

The ideology of the midwestern Protestant reformers was well expressed by C. Wright Mills (1943) when he argued that social reformers and social pathologists defined deviancy in terms of social norms which they assumed were rural Protestant values and norms rather than urban values and norms. The social pathologist then studies the pathologies of individuals rather than the power structure and class structure of society.

Social problems were explained as psychological and personal failures, or what Davis (1980) calls "social pathologies," although the orientation was to personal rather than social pathologies (i.e., the failures of biologically inferior people). There is also an element of social pathology present in early sociology because urbanization and industrialization disrupted the organic solidarity of society as proposed by Spencer, Comte, Durkheim, Marx, and Weber.

Although early sociologists, with the exception of Weber, ignored the nature of the individual organism, sociology has divided its subject matter between society, culture, and social organization on the one hand and the individual on the other hand. There are two sociologies: the sociology of society and the sociology of the individual, usually called social psychology (Eisentadt and Helle, 1985; Helle and Eisenstadt, 1985). Wagner (Denisoff, Callahan, and Levine, 1974:41 ff., 64 ff.) refers to these as large versus small sociological theories, or functional versus interpretative theories.

Ritzer (1983b:311) classified sociological theories as macro and micro, and as objective and subjective.

Macro objective: structure functionalism
Macro subjective: structure functionalism
Micro objective: psychological behaviorism
Micro subjective: symbolic interactionism, social psychology

By "macro" Ritzer means social structure and society; by "micro" he means the individual actor. By "objective" he means external events such as behavior; by "subjective" he means the internal mental states of individuals.

From this analysis it can be stated that all sociological theories are subjective at the individual level; that is, they depend on nonphysical mental states of individuals as the core of the individual personality.

Sociology thus had its own history, values, and traditions quite separate from those of biology, psychology, and law. There was no effort to integrate these disciplines around a common problem such as crime. At this time (1890–1920) sociology was concerned with making itself a science and finding a place for itself within the university structure, as well as divorcing itself from economics and philosophy (Hinkle and Hinkle, 1954; Gibbons, 1979). The interdisciplinary nature of criminology was lost in sociology for these historical reasons.

The Nature of Culture and Society

The term "culture" is basic to sociological thought. Culture has been defined as a system of values and meanings shared by a group or society, which would include symbols, language, values, norms, and sanctions (Popenoe, 1980); as a system of meaningful symbols that people create and share (Turner, 1985); and as human learning based on symbolic communication and conceptualization (Zeitlin, 1981). Material culture is also included in the definition, but only as a secondary aspect of culture, with the emphasis being placed on the nonmaterial aspects of culture. Cultural evolution is usually contrasted to biological evolution. The mechanism of biological evolution is genetic; the mechanism of cultural evolution is learning and symbolic communication (Gamst and Norbeck, 1976; Kessing, 1974).

Culture is divided into material and nonmaterial, the material culture consisting of technology: houses, cars, streets, buildings, radios, television, and so on. The nonmaterial aspects are the values and norms as listed above. We noted in Chapter 12 that anthropology is divided into physical anthropology and cultural anthropology; whereas psychology is divided into humanistic, experimental, and biological. Sociology does not have a division called physical sociology, primarily because it is not integrated with biology and psychology and it does not regard culture as physical (see Chapter 2).

Nettler (1984:2, fn. 1) starts his text with a statement that "society" is a vague concept, a vagueness that characterizes a great deal of sociological language. "Sociology is full of ambiguous language." It is my hope that I can remove some of the vagueness from these concepts when I try to relate sociological theories to crime and criminal behavior.

Sociology and Human Nature

American sociological criminology has been committed to finding the causes of crime in social events, but "social" has been defined as both the environment and the individual. In other chapters I have emphasized that behavior is a product of Organism × Environment interaction. Sociological theories do not differentiate the organism and environment since according to social theories the individual is a product of the social environment, not biology. Biological and psychological processes do not limit the socialization process or contribute to human behavior. As one writer of a contemporary sociology text notes (Zeitlin, 1981:88), theories of human behavior by Hobbes and Locke are in error since such theories postulate that individuals exist separate from society and actually come together as rational beings to form society. "But we have seen in the preceding chapters that the individual is a strictly social being, and that his existence is unthinkable before and outside of society." The notion that societies exist before individuals is like assuming that individuals exist before cells, and cells exist before atoms (see Chapter 2).

An introductory textbook in sociology by Hess, Markson, and Stein (1982) stated that "the sociological perspective emphasizes the importance of environmental factors in determining an individual's internal state and subsequent behavior." Sociologists look for variations in social categories such as race, sex, age, social class, and religion, rather than for variations in individuals. Behavior is not in the brain or genes (p. 19) but is in the mind (p. 56), with the mind acting as the intervening variable between the environment and behavior.

Ornstein and Sobel write

> 'Society' is often thought of as a separate, somehow incorporeal system, existing apart from the hearts and minds of real bodies. It is studied coldly in sociology treatises almost as if it had its own rules and its own realities. It has been said that to a Marxist you are born only when you apply for a job; to a Jewish mother life begins only when her son graduates from medical school; and for other theorists the world of nations, cultures, and states takes on a life of its own. But to us, human society is a group of biological organisms in its own right (Ornstein and Sobel, 1987:130).

Human nature, according to sociological theories, is dependent on the social environment and that alone. By denying or ignoring biological and psychological aspects of human nature, and the fact there is a physical organism with which the environment interacts, the sociologist has made it difficult for communication and cross fertilization with biology and psychology. The basic need in sociological criminology is to be able to integrate social and biological and psychological concepts. We need to know how social variables become behavioral variables.

Sociology, Psychology, and Biology: An Alternative

Several sociologists have criticized the social environmentalism of sociological thought. Wrong (1961) accused sociologists of ignoring psychology and biology in their "oversocialized concept of man," and he reminded them that "in the beginning there is a body." Inkeles (1959) was critical of Durkheim's famous study of suicide based on a

Society ⟶ Behavior (rate of suicide)

model. Inkeles argued that in order to explain behavior sociologists need psychological concepts, or the

$$Society \longrightarrow Personality \longrightarrow Behavior$$

model. Gove and Carpenter (1982) find "the idea that the human mind and body are separate entities is no longer a tenable position," and they advocate an interdisciplinary theory of behavior based on biology, psychology, and sociology. In his presidential address to the American Sociological Association, Homans (1964) urged sociologists to "bring man back" into sociology, by which Homans meant Skinnerian learning theory and psychology. Van den Berghe (1974) argued that sociologists must "bring beasts back into sociology," by which he meant biology and sociobiology.

American Sociological Criminology

Sociological criminology has addressed three types of issues: (1) the making of laws, (2) the breaking of laws, and (3) the reaction to the breaking of laws (Sutherland, 1947:1; Gibbons, 1979:1). Sutherland identified these as the sociology of law, the sociology of the causes of crime, and penology or the control of crime. Sutherland noted that the sociology of law received little attention in criminology (see Chapter 15), and he also noted that crime was social and not biological or psychological.

Because of the sociologist's search for the causes of crime within the confines of sociological thought, they have ignored law, biology, psychology, and history, and they have traditionally ignored the classical and positivistic schools of criminology (Gibbons, 1979:3–5). Most textbooks in criminology since 1924 have been written by sociologists [Gibbons (1979), Quinney (1975), Reckless (1970); see Chapter 1].

Like sociology, sociological criminology is divided into macro and micro criminology. Gibbons (1979:41) calls these (1) the sociology of criminality, and (2) the social psychology of the individual offender. Gibbons (1979:10) notes that sociologists deal with social attitudes, self-images, and social attributes which are "instances of the social psychology of criminal acts and careers, rather than cases of the psychological level of explanations." Social psychology replaces psychology as the explanation of individual behavior.

For the remainder of this chapter we shall discuss the sociology of the individual offender and the relationship between crime and social structure.

THE SOCIOLOGY OF THE INDIVIDUAL OFFENDER

Social Psychology and the Chicago School

Sociology was established in 1892 as an academic discipline separate from economics at the then newly established University of Chicago. The sociology program reflected the midwestern Protestant background of early sociology and social reform thought. The Chicago sociologists concentrated on social problems such as urbanization, immigration and the Americanization of the European immigrant, poverty, crime, child neglect, and prostitution (Davis, 1980; Liska, 1987). The following works are representative of the work of the early University of Chicago sociologists:

L. HENDERSON	*Introduction to the Study of the Dependent, Neglected, and Delinquent Classes* (1938)
W. I. THOMAS	*Sex and Society* (1907) *The Unadjusted Girl* (1923) *The Child in America* (1928)
W. I. THOMAS AND F. ZNANIECKI	*The Polish Peasant in Europe and America* (1918–1921)
R. PARK	*Old World Traits Transplanted* (1921) *Human Communities* (1952) *Race and Culture* (1950)
LOUIS WIRTH	*The Ghetto* (1928) "Urbanization as a Way of Life" (1938)
R. PARK, E. BURGESS, AND W. MCKENZIE	*The City* (1925)

Crime was seen as a product of urbanization, cultural conflict, immigration, poverty, ecology, and socialization. One of the major focuses of the University of Chicago school of sociology was symbolic interactionism or social psychology. Thomas and Znaniecki (1918–1921) in their book *The Polish Peasant in Europe and America* discussed immigration and Americanization in terms of attitudes and values. Attitudes are internalized and are subjective, whereas values are externalized and are found in cultural norms. To Thomas social psychology is the subjective side of culture, the means by which the individual is made part of the environment (Coser, 1977:514 ff.).

In his later writings Thomas used the phrase "definition of the situation" to refer to the subjective evaluations of meanings given to social situations by social actors. Mentalism in sociology is found in such concepts as the definition of the situation (Thomas), Verstehen and understanding (Weber), sympathetic introspection (Cooley), and dynamic assessment (MacIver). In his discussion of action theory, Weber (1974:88) defined social action in these terms: "Action is social in so far as, by virtue of the subjective meaning attached to it by the acting individual, it takes account of the behavior of others and is thereby oriented in its course." Weber used the German word "Verstehen," meaning to understand, to explain this psychological process (Coser, 1977:220). Another important figure in social psychology was Charles H. Cooley with his concept of the "looking-glass self." Cooley emphasized the impact of the primary group on the individual's self-concepts, and he placed emphasis on "sympathetic understanding and empathy." For Cooley the self was a reflection of society (Coser, 1977:305 ff.).

The Chicago school of social psychology or symbolic interactionism came to be the sociologist/criminologist's theory of human nature, with its emphasis on social learning, language, role playing, and symbolic communication. Ritzer (1978) refers to this as the "social definitionist" school of sociology. Although the Chicago sociologists dealt with social organization and social structure (crime, poverty, unemployment, dependency, human ecology, migrants), they explained social processes at the individual level of sympathetic understanding of definitions of the situation. Social psychology came to be a base for social organization.

The important figure in symbolic interactionism was George H. Mead, a philosopher at the University of Chicago who influenced many young sociology graduate students. Mead never produced a major work, but his class notes were published after his death as *Mind, Self, and Society* (Mead, 1934). Mead placed emphasis on language as a means of communicating meaning and definitions of social situations which are critical aspects of socialization. The individual internalizes the meaning of a social situation and the expectations of others, and he/she then develops an ability to play appropriate social roles as they are defined by others. "Taking the role" of others is critical in social interaction, and shared social symbols form the basis of human communication and interaction (Coser, 1977).

Although social psychology would logically seem to be a place for sociology and psychology to join, this has not been the case. A sociological social psychology (SSP) developed in sociology around the works of Mead, Herbert Blumer, and Manford Kuhn (Stryker, 1977; House, 1977; Liska, 1977; Archibald, 1976; Boutilier, Roed, and Svendsen, 1980). Sociologists are trained in different theories than are psychologists, with emphasis on symbols, roles, and social processes.

Psychological social psychology (PSP) developed out of the work of Kurt Lewin and field theory, located primarily at the University of Michigan. Lewin's work involved cognitive processes by which the individual defines his/her field of activity. PSP has also developed a behavioral and a neobehavioral branch based on Skinnerian learning theory (Gergen and Gergen, 1981; Goldstein, 1980; Hollander, 1981).

The Handbook of Social Psychology (Lindzey and Aronson, 1968) was written from the perspective of psychology, including genetics and learning theory. Lindzey has been a major figure in the development of behavioral genetics as an aspect of psychology. Most PSP psychologists have training in genetics and brain–behavior relationships as well as in social psychology. *The Handbook* was not received warmly by SPS sociologists (Stryker, 1971; Volkart, 1971).

In 1981 the Social Psychology Section of the American Sociological Association published *Social Psychology* (Rosenberg and Turner, 1981), and this book was devoted to Mead "as the single most important influence shaping symbolic interactionism." Psychologists produced *Retrospections on Social Psychology* (Festinger, 1980) as a Festschrift to Lewin by his former students. Only one sociologist was represented in this book. There is still a large gap between SSP and PSP, a gap that cannot be justified and which would not exist within a more interdisciplinary framework. Sociology and psychology do not interact with one another even within the field of social psychology.

Symbolic Interactionism and Biology

It is of historic interest to note how the social psychology of G. H. Mead became separated from biology and psychology. As stated above, Mead is regarded as the central figure in SSP, but in recent years the exact nature of Mead's social psychology has been seriously challenged. Mead referred to himself as a "social behaviorist," not a symbolic interactionist. The term "symbolic interactionism" belongs to Herbert Blumer, not Mead (Turner, 1982:322 ff.; Coser, 1977:575). In an article on "Mead versus Blumer," McPhail and Rexroat (1979) represented Mead as a behaviorist who used the methodologies of the physical and biological sciences, rather than as a symbolic interactionist as he is now regarded in sociology. Lewis (1979) also drew a distinction between social behaviorism and symbolic interactionism. According to Lewis, Mead was a behaviorist who saw a vital link between social psychology and physiological psychology.

Lewis and Smith (1980) traced the historical roots of Mead's work to realism and behaviorism, as distinct from the nominalism of James and Dewey. According to Lewis and Smith, Mead had very little impact on sociology at the University of Chicago, and was not the founder of symbolic interactionism. Symbolic interactionism was developed by Blumer and his followers following the death of Mead in 1931. It is of some interest that the controversy surrounding Mead, as found in McPhail, Rexroat, Lewis, and Smith, is mentioned only superficially in the Rosenberg and Turner book, in which Mead is still referred to as the father of symbolic interactionism.

Mead (Strauss, 1956:124–148) himself stated that he was a behaviorist, but one opposed to Watsonian behaviorism, which ignored internal cognitive processes. Mead's behaviorism was based on a study of neural processes. "What takes place in consciousness runs parallel with what takes place in the central nervous system. It is necessary to study the content of the form as physiological and also as psychological. . . . Such a psychology was called, naturally, a physiological psychology" (Strauss, 1956:146–147).

In his book on sociological theory, Abrahamson (1981) traces Mead's work to biology and Charles Darwin. L. S. Cottrell (1980), a student of Mead, argues that Mead was a physiological behaviorist, not a subjective nominalist and symbolic interactionist. W. I. Thomas, a sociologist identified with the Chicago school of social psychology, was very biological in his earlier years, with a dissertation on the biological factors in criminal behavior of males and females (Abrahamson, 1981; Lewis and Smith, 1980).

SSP, as found in symbolic interactionism, is not a true representation of its founding fathers, nor is it a theoretical application of psychology to the understanding of social behavior. Symbolic interactionism effectively cuts social psychology from biology, psychobiology, and general learning theory. Attitude formation and self-concepts are a product of the brain, probably the associational and language areas of the brain. It is known that language acquisition plays a major role in self-development, socialization, and normative behaviors, and the language areas of the brain are critical to language. As was noted in Chapter 11, the evolution of the human brain allowed for this development. Social psychology and the brain sciences can contribute to one another (Chadwick-Jones et al., 1979).

However, the symbolic interactionist does not define symbols as physical, but as mental and not empirically verifiable. As Rose (Denisoff, Callahan, and Levine, 1974:139) states: "A response to a symbol is in terms of its meaning and value rather than in terms of its physical stimulation of the sense organs." He notes that although a symbol is also physical, it stimulates behavior in a different way than does a physical stimulus. Thus, by definition, symbolic interactionism deals with mental processes and not the physical processes of the brain.

Symbolic interactionism, as found in Sutherland, Cressey, and other sociological criminologists, is based on the principle that "ideas cause action," or the mind causes behavior. This is a nonphysical and nonscientific view of human behavior. As Le Mar Empey, a sociologist, has noted, "the use of the physical and natural sciences as a model for research in criminology is inappropriate. These models stress the importance of measuring observable facts. But since human thought and consciousness cannot be readily observed, other models must be sought by which to study these phenomena." (Empey, 1982:292). Nettler notes that "the symbolic interactionist perspective is weak medicine." (Nettler, 1989:46). Symbolic interactionism and mentalism cut sociological theories off from scientific explanations of behavior as found in biology and psychology, and make integration of sociology, psychology, and biology impossible. The lack of recognition of any individual differences in sociological thought is also a barrier to an integrated science of human behavior (Nettler, 1989:1; Wilson and Herrnstein, 1985).

Edwin H. Sutherland (1883–1950)

Sutherland fits perfectly the description of the early University of Chicago sociologist. He was born and reared in Nebraska, and his father was a Baptist minister and college president (Sutherland, 1974). Sutherland's career was devoted entirely to the midwest: Ph.D., 1913, University of Chicago, University of Illinois, University of Minnesota, University of Chicago, and Indiana University. Sutherland was turned down for tenure at Chicago when he moved to Indiana as chairman (Gibbons, 1979:135).

To Indiana Sutherland brought the University of Chicago perspective, especially symbolic interactionism. Lindesmith and Strauss were there at the time as symbolic interactionists. Only two professors, A. B. Hollingshead (Nebraska) and J. S. Schneider (California), deviated from the Chicago model of sociology.

Sutherland was trained by W. I. Thomas and Park and Burgess, and the idea of the definition of the situation had a great impact on Sutherland (Sutherland, 1974:13). He also worked with Henderson, who wrote a book on dependent, neglected, and delinquent classes. Sutherland approached criminology as a midwestern moral philosopher and social reformer trained in symbolic interactionism.

In 1924, Sutherland published the first edition of *Criminology* (Sutherland, 1924). In his book Sutherland broke with the European tradition based on Lombroso and with the psychological tradition as found in Freud, as he remade criminology into sociology. Geis (1976) reexamined the textbook in 1976 and found the 1924 edition still to be an adequate text. The strengths of the Sutherland years, that of introducing social variables into criminology, was also its great weakness, with a lack of any appreciation of or understanding of biology and psychology and law. "Sutherland was consistently sociological in his analysis of crime and did not broaden his theoretical model to accommodate biological and psychological factors" (Sutherland, 1974:iii).

The Sutherland book has been revised since his death in 1950 by a former student, D. R. Cressey, and the book is now in its tenth edition. As I pointed out above, the book is half criminology and half criminal justice, a model that is still followed by criminology textbook writers.

Sutherland's work was based on three issues from the University of Chicago approach to sociology:

1. The idea of culture conflict, or social disorganization, which was based on Durkheim's idea of social solidarity around normative structures. When conflicting norms are introduced, culture conflict is the result. Thomas and Znaniecki (1918–1921) published *The Polish Peasant in Europe and America,* in which they examined the Americanization of the immigrant coming to Chicago in terms of attitudes and values (Coser, 1977:513). The cultural values of the migrants conflicted with those of native Americans (Sellin, 1938; Wolfgang, 1968). Davis (1980) places Sutherland and differential association in the chapter on value conflict rather than in a chapter on social psychology and learning theory.

2. The development of an ecological school at the University of Chicago. The work of Park and Burgess was used by Shaw and McKay to study the ecology of crime (see Chapter 19). Shaw and McKay found that delinquents lived more frequently in slum areas than in middle-class areas, and high-delinquency areas were inhabited by immigrants from Europe and Asia whose values conflicted with those of native Americans.

3. The development of social psychology at the University of Chicago as found in the work of Thomas. Sutherland borrowed from social psychology in his theory of differential association (Nettler, 1984:254–256). The theory of differential association appeared in the 1939 (third) edition of the Sutherland text. Shaw had pointed out that the second edition of the book (1934) referred to cultural areas with certain attitudes and values that are passed on to the next generation.

The Theory of Differential Association

The theory of differential association states that criminals learn criminal attitudes and values from associations with the attitudes and values of their cultural system. According to the theory (Sutherland, 1947:6), "a person becomes delinquent because of an excess of definitions favorable to violation of law over definitions unfavorable to violation of law." Sutherland also included variation in frequency, duration, priority, and intensity. Sutherland made it clear that the association was with attitudes and values, not necessarily with criminals, and that general needs and values did not explain criminal behavior. He also focused on primary or intimate group associations (from Cooley), not on secondary group associations such as the mass media.

The theory is basically a social learning theory, but it does not specify how learning takes place. The theory denies the biological and psychological bases of learning, and is based on internal mentalistic concepts as found in the model I theory of behavior (see Chapter 12). As Nettler comments (1984:256), the theory assumes that "cognition causes behavior" or the mind causes behavior in the form of attitudes and values. Nettler points out how difficult it is to demonstrate that thought causes action, since thought and action are not known independently but rather are one and the same thing. We know thoughts and action motives only because of the behavior by which they are expressed. This is basically the reason the behaviorists gave up studying the "mind" and moved to studying observable behaviors (see Chapter 13).

Hirschi and Gottfredson (1980:7 ff.) argue that Sutherland denied the basic tenets of science and positivism when he stated the theory of differential association in such a form that it could not be disproven. Sutherland argued that delinquency cannot be predicted from childhood characteristics, whereas the Gluecks, the McCords, and Farrington and West demonstrated that it could be. Theories of social learning that follow the Sutherland tradition are thus protected from scientific evaluation. "Since the theory of differential association neither predicts nor explains criminal behavior, its continuous dominance cannot be explained on grounds of scientific adequacy. . . . The fact that differential association was a *sociological* theory also guaranteed the continued domination of a single discipline over the field" (Hirschi and Gottfredson, 1980:9–10). Geis and Goff (1982) stated: "It is significant that the theory itself (differential association) has never been taken as seriously in other branches of sociological or psychological research as it has in criminology."

Several major defects are found in the theory of differential association.

1. The theory ignores individual differences. This is a point made repeatedly in this book, and I would say that by ignoring biology and psychology the sociologist must ignore individual differences [see Wilson and Herrnstein (1985) for a discussion of this topic].

2. The theory ignores the role of opportunity for crimes to occur, which I call opportunity structure and environmental design (see Chapter 19).

3. The theory cannot explain crimes of passion such as murder, rape, and assault. Crimes of passion are a product of the limbic system of the brain, and learning involves controlling basic biological impulses rather than learning an attitude toward the behavior.

4. The theory is impossible to falsify since it is stated in terms of subjective mental states, and lacks clarity and precision. There is no way by which I can know what a person's attitude is since I cannot get inside his/her mind. However, if I restate the problem in terms of getting inside the brain to discover what is going on in the brain, I can establish an experimental procedure for doing this. I can take a PETT scan or CAT scan or NMR scan to prove or disprove my hypothesis. Scientific propositions must be stated in such a way as to be falsifiable. Even Cressey, the co-author of the book, stated that differential association is not precise enough to be subjected to a rigorous empirical test (Gibbons, 1979:60; Nettler, 1984:257).

5. Differential association gives poor advice on how to control crime (Nettler, 1984:257).

There are three other issues I would raise in respect to Sutherland's theory. First, the causal relationship between association and delinquency has never been established. Glueck (1956) argues that delinquency comes first and then the associational patterns follow as delinquents seek out other delinquents for companionship. He calls this the "birds of a feather flock together" syndrome. Hirschi (1969:150–155) found the same thing in his study of delinquency. According to Hirschi, the more a boy respects his delinquent friends, the lower the delinquency rate, or the more the boy is attached to family and peer groups, the lower the rate of delinquency. Hirschi's control theory denies the relevancy of differential association theory, as well as anomie and strain theories, and these issues will be discussed below.

Second, differential association does not differentiate criminal from non-criminal behavior, although Sutherland (1974:4) stated that "the problem in criminology is to explain the criminality of behavior, not the behavior as such." The explanation of crime is different from the explanation of the behavior of individual criminals. The explanation of crime lies in criminal law and the sociology of criminal law. Although Sutherland listed the making of laws and the reaction to the breaking of laws as basic aspects of criminology, he also noted that the sociology of law was a neglected aspect of criminology. It has been argued that Sutherland was aware of the legal aspects of crime, and a letter he wrote to Jerome Hall (a legal scholar at Indiana University at that time) is used to support this contention (Sutherland, 1974:xxxi). I never detected any of Hall's influence on Sutherland, and Sutherland's discussion of the classical school in three paragraphs in his 1947 text (Sutherland, 1947:51) does not support the argument. When I read Hall's article on "Criminology" (Hall, 1945) after I had Sutherland's criminology course, I was amazed to discover that there was a major orientation toward crime called the legalistic or classical school, and that Hall was extremely critical of the sociological positivism of Sutherland and others (Jeffery, 1970).

Third, the theory of differential association is represented as a learning theory; however, it never attempts to integrate biological and psychological theories of learning into criminology.

In 1965 (Jeffery, 1965) I published an article entitled "Criminal Behavior and Learning Theory," wherein I argued that Skinnerian psychology should replace sociological learning theory and Sutherland's theory of differential association. Special reference was made to the nature of reinforcers as physical and not social, and I argued that the reinforcement for criminal behavior was money, cars, jewelry, or other physical objects, and that social reinforcement such as social acceptance and social approval was very secondary. If food controlled a rat's behavior, and if we did not need to look at how the rat "thought about the food," we could explain criminal behavior in behavioristic terms as well, that is, the stimulus *car* and the response *stealing a car*. This was a straightforward S-R model of criminal behavior. This was in my pre-biosocial learning theory days. I then attempted to apply Skinner's learning theory to the rehabilitation of delinquents in Washington, D.C., a project that failed (see Chapter 13). A year after my article appeared, Burgess and Akers (1966) wrote a response in which they stated: "This statement [by Jeffery] bears no obvious or direct relationship to Sutherland's differential association, and nowhere does Jeffery make it clear how differential reinforcement is a reformulation of differential association." Burgess and Akers failed to see the inconsistencies between the mentalism of Sutherland (attitudes and values) and the physicalism of my position (food, sex, shock). What is not appreciated by Burgess and Akers is that social learning theory is not behaviorism and is not Skinnerian psychology. Skinner went beyond metalism [see Williams and McShane (1988:121–124) for an excellent discussion of the differences between psychological and sociological learning theory].

Akers (1985) in his book once again denies the basic tenets of behaviorism when he states that deviant behavior is a result of social interaction. He identifies his approach as the "soft determinism" of Rotter and Bandura, not the hard determinism of Skinner. For Akers, learning means learning "definitions favorable to the behavior" based on social learning theory (Gibbons and Krohn, 1986:162 ff.). Akers et al. (1979) argue that social learning involves "interaction with significant group definitions, norms, and attitudes, and the principal behavioral effects come from those groups which control the individual's major source of reinforcement and punishment and expose them to behavioral models and normative definitions." This is a statement from cognitive psychology and is consistent with symbolic interactionism as found in Thomas, Mead, and Cooley. In fact, "definitions favorable to behavior" is identical to Thomas's famous "definitions of the situation." This is consistent with the observation that Sutherland's work is based on W. I. Thomas and his social psychology. It certainly is not behaviorism. The consequence of the Burgess and Akers article was to allow criminology to ignore behaviorism for another twenty or thirty years. The same thing happened to symbolic interactionism, exchange theory, and behaviorism. Behaviorism was adapted into a mentalistic framework by the sociologist.

Adams (1973) reexamined the propositions put forth by Burgess and Akers, and concluded that they were misinterpreting behavioral principles. Adams found that physical reinforcers were much more significant than social reinforcers, and he noted that Cressey quoted the Burgess and Akers article as positive proof of differential association. The sociologist has consistently rejected behaviorism, which is consistent with Sutherland's antibiological and antipsychological position.

A critique of social learning theory (Gibbons and Krohn, 1986:164–165) concluded that it is not possible to prove the nature of reinforcement involved in this type of learning since social reinforcement is defined in terms of behavioral responses. The authors concluded that differential reinforcement theory is not stated in such a form as to make it testable. It can be noted that biopsychological learning theory is stated in such a way that the reinforcement occurs in the brain and is measurable independent of the behavioral response.

Conger (1976, 1978) has noted the similarities between social learning theory, social control theory, and exchange theory. He regards attachment to friends and bonding to society as social learning based on social reinforcement from others. For Conger, as for Akers, modeling, peer reinforcement, and group processes are critical. Conger writes (1978:96): "Criminality is maintained by social reinforcement." In a 1980 article, Conger (1980) mentioned the work of Eysenck, Hirschi and Hindelang, Mednick and Christiansen, and West and Farrington, and noted that individual biological and psychological differences may be important to learning theory. This statement is consistent with the learning theory presented in Chapter 13 in this book.

Sutherland successfully rooted all biology and psychology out of criminology, and this accounts for his popularity in sociological criminology. This left sociological criminology without a basic theory of human nature. Sutherland wrote damning reviews of the work of others, such as Hooton and Sheldon (Sutherland, 1974), and he referred to Sheldon's work as "crap" (Gibbons, 1979:135).

Verification of Differential Association

Several attempts have been made to verify the theory of differential association. Short (1957, 1958) attempted to operationalize the frequency, duration, intensity, and priority statement by looking at associational patterns of delinquents. Although Short admitted that he could not operationalize and verify the heart of the theory as stated in "an excess of definitions favorable to the violation of law," he found that delinquents reported that their friends were often delinquent and that the factors of intensity and frequency were more critical than those of duration and priority. The Short study provides two valuable clues and methodological insights into the theory of differential association.

1. The theory is subjective and mentalistic, phrased in terms of attitudes and value, and one cannot measure attitudes, only behavior. Short settled

for measurements of associational patterns, not contacts with criminal attitudes. This is not a valid study of differential association, since the theory was formulated in terms of associations with attitudes.

2. Short's findings do not indicate if the associational patterns are a result of delinquency or if delinquency is a result of associational patterns. To state that delinquents associate with other delinquents is a descriptive statement of covariation, not an explanatory statement of causation.

Voss (1964) replicated the Short study in Honolulu, and he found that "adolescents who associate with delinquent friends report more delinquent behavior than those whose contact with delinquent peers in minimal." Voss found duration, not intensity, to be the most critical factor.

Reiss and Rhodes (1964), using friendship triads and actual rather than the friend's definition of delinquency, found that their subjects tended to select friends whose behavior was the same as their own; that is, law-abiding selected law-abiding, delinquents selected delinquents. This finding held for lower-class subjects but not for middle-class subjects. Such findings have the same problems as discussed in connection with the Short study. Reiss and Rhodes concluded that the findings "may be disappointing to proponents of differential association theory. The association of boys with the same kind of delinquent behavior in close friendship triads while somewhat greater than chance is well below what one would expect from . . . differential association theory."

Hindelang (1971) found that delinquency was a solitary activity with little or no social reinforcement. Jensen and Rojek (1980) found attachments to peers unrelated to delinquent careers. In general, these studies do not support the theory of differential association (Shoemaker, 1984:142 ff.). In the last paragraph of her book, Kornhauser (1978:253) summarizes differential association by stating that "cultural deviance models are without foundation in fact."

Behavioral Sociology: Skinnerian Sociology

Behaviorism and learning theory (Chapter 13), although rejected by sociological criminologists, did have a major impact on sociology in the forms of behavioral sociology. Homans was an early advocate of Skinnerian learning theory in sociology, as expressed in his book *Social Behavior: Its Elementary Forms* (Homans, 1961). Here Homans argued for a psychological basis for the study of human behavior. He was criticized by sociologists as a "psychological reductionist." Other authors have pursued the topic under the general title of "behavioral sociology" (Hamblin and Kunkel, 1977; Burgess and Bushell, 1969). However, in the long run, behavioral psychology did not survive in the academic environment of sociology.

Labeling Theory

Labeling theory emerged in the 1960s as an extension of symbolic interactionism, and follows the introspective interpretive psychology of the University of

Chicago school. Labeling was designed to answer the question of why the societal reaction to breaking the law, but it moved instead to focusing on the individual actor and not the social control system. By the 1960s sociologists were referring to normative violations as deviance rather than crime in order to include within the concept of deviance violations of norms other than legal norms. This move further weakened the link between criminology and criminal law. Sociologists started to publish books on social deviance rather than criminology, such as:

Deviants: Voluntary Actors in the Hostile World, Sargarin and Montanino
Interpreting Deviance: A Sociological Introduction, Schur
Social Deviance: Farrell and Swigert
Deviance: Action/Reaction/Interaction, Scarpetti and McFarlane
Deviant Behavior, Akers
Deviant Behavior, Goode
The Sociology of Deviance, Douglas Waksler

Sociology moved from social pathology to social disorganization to social problems to social deviancy. Becker (1963) defined the deviant as ''one to whom the label has been applied,'' and he referred to them as *outsiders.* The basic foundation of labeling theory is that groups create deviance; behavior is not deviant in and of itself. Deviancy is a group process or a process of social interaction, and labeling is referred to as the ''interactionist perspective'' (Rubington and Weinberg, 1968).

Lemert (1951) published a book entitled *Social Pathology* in which he distinguished between primary and secondary deviancy. Primary deviancy referred to the original act before it was labeled, and secondary deviancy was the deviancy produced by the label and the societal reaction. It is obvious that the original act was not produced by the label since it had to occur before it could be labeled. However, once deviancy had been labeled, deviancy itself could be encouraged and fostered by the group response. In this way the person comes to be identified as, and to identify himself as, a deviant and an outsider. Secondary deviance focuses on the actor and his/her internalized subjective evaluations of self and society, and in this way deviant labels and concepts are derived from the societal response (Davis, 1980; Gibbons, 1979; Nettler, 1984).

Labeling theory is a product of the social unrest of the 1960s: the Vietnam war, racial strife, student unrest, and social protests over social injustices. Goffman combined labeling with ethnomethodology in *The Presentation of the Self in Everyday Life* (Goffman, 1959), as well as in his works *Asylums* (1961) and *Stigma* (1963). In these works Goffman analyzed individual behavior in terms of the individual's concept of self as projected onto others in social interaction, or the impact of stigmatization and total institutions on the self-concepts of those subjected to stigma and total institutions. Other works in labeling theory include Douglas (1970), Erikson (1962), Kitsuse (1964), and Scheff (1966) [see Davis (1980), Gibbons (1979), Nettler (1984), and Schur (1981)].

Labeling theory involves taking the side of the powerless and the underdog. This includes "taking the role" of the deviant and seeing the world as he/she interprets the world. Everyone commits deviant acts, but only the poor and the powerless are labeled deviants by social control agencies and rulemakers. Labeling theory turns the issues in criminology upside down by focusing on the label applied to the act by others rather than on the actor. Society is to blame, not individuals who are deviant.

Evaluations of Labeling Theory

Nettler (1984:267 ff.) and Shoemaker (1984:185 ff.) have written that labeling theory puts forth two different types of propositions: First, deviants are labeled as deviants because they are minorities who are powerless (e.g., homosexuals, minorities, blacks, females, young people, etc.). Thus sociology is the underdog, and the argument is concerned with unjust justice. Second, the labels affect self-perceptions, social roles, and the development of delinquent and deviant careers. The criminal justice system by its labels creates crime and deviancy. There is little or no proof of either of these propositions.

As for proposition 1, the major question raised is whether sentencing practices are governed by the act or the actor. This proposition is based on the sociological argument that characteristics of the actor, such as age, sex, race, and socioeconomic status, determine sentencing practices rather than the act or the legal offense. Study after study has demonstrated that this is not true (see Chapter 8). Nettler (1984:276 ff.) concluded that legal factors (seriousness of offense, prior criminal record of the defendant, and relationship between offender and victim) outweigh sociological factors, and he cites studies by Hindelang, Meade, Pope, the Vera Foundation, Burke and Turk, Konecni and Ebbesen, Hagan, and Gottfredson and Gottfredson in support of this conclusion. In an evaluation of labeling theory Wellford (1975), argued that some acts, such as murder, rape, and robbery, are intrinsically repulsive and therefore elicit a negative social response.

As to proposition 2, that the label affects deviant behavior, Davis (1980:215) writes that labeling deals with "the inner world of the deviant," which is impossible to study and must be approached through Verstehen and interpretive interaction, symbolic interactionism, and the ethnomethodology of Goffman and Garfinkel.

Shoemaker (1984:192–194) asks why delinquents mature out of delinquent careers at the age of 18 if the label determines future deviant acts. He notes that the conclusions reached in labeling theory are questionable and oversimplified. Is the label the cause of the behavior, or is the behavior the cause of the label? Is the delinquent act prior to the label, or does it follow the label? Gove (1980) found little support for labeling theory.

Nettler (1984:271 ff.) raises a number of issues concerning label theory. Like Shoemaker, he suggests that the act could cause the label. This is the same argument that Glueck made against Sutherland and differential associa-tion when he (Glueck) argued that delinquency comes first, the associational pattern follows. The deviant act comes first, and then the label. Nettler states that deviant labels do not always affect behavior in the same ways, and since labeling theory cannot explain behavior, it denies the causes of behavior. La-beling does not help us to predict future behavior, and the usefulness of labels is very questionable. The model of causation is backwards since it assumes that the causes of deviancy are in society, not in the individual offender. As Nettler notes, mental hospitals do not cause mental illness, and the police do not cause crime. It might be noted that all sociological theories assume that the causes of behavior reside in society and not in the individual.

An unfortunate aspect of labeling theory is that it has resulted in deinsti-tutionalization (the release of individuals from prisons and mental hospitals) because of the desire of some not to treat such individuals since treatment implies a label, stigma, and perhaps a total institution or asylum. This issue is a critical one in contemporary criminology and is discussed in detail in Chapter 21).

Further Comments

The comments above were made within the sociological community. From the point of view of biological psychology and learning theory, a basic comment could be made that all sociological theories of behavior ignore the role of the brain in behavior. All environmental experiences, including experiences with other people, with cultural definitions, and with race and social class, must be taken into and processed by the brain before they are seen as behaviors. The environment does not cause behavior; the environment enters the brain and is therein transformed into a biochemical code which in turn controls behavior (Chapter 11).

CRIME AND SOCIAL STRUCTURE

Structural-Functionalism and Criminology

As was noted above, sociology is divided into the sociology of the individual and the sociology of society. We have discussed the individual sociological theo-ries in terms of social psychology, symbolic interactionism, and labeling the-ory. Next I discuss theories whose basic unit of analysis is society or culture, not the individual. Sociological theories address the issue of social structure and social organization rather than the social psychology of the individual. In turn, these theories can be classified as (1) theories that attempt to explain how social structures affect individuals in terms of criminality and deviance, theo-ries known as strain theories or anomie theories, and (2) theories that ask how social structure explains the legal structure and social control mechanisms of society. These theories are known as social control theories, conflict theories, and the sociology of law. Social control theories are discussed in Chapter 15.

Structural-functionalism grew out of the pioneering work of Spencer and Comte and the organic model of society and social evolutionism, and its basic form was put forth by the French social philospher Emile Durkheim (1858–1917). Durkheim is best known for his concept of the social fact or the belief that the social level is real. The reality of the social meant for Durkheim that biology and psychology were ignored. Ritzer called this the ''social factist'' school of sociology (Ritzer, 1980, 1983a, 1983b; Turner, 1982; Coser, 1977). Whereas the social psychologist and the labeling theorist concentrated on the psychology of the individual, structural-functionalism concentrated on social reality and society.

By ''social reality'' Durkheim meant the normative order that existed outside and independent of the individual, and which was coercive on the individual. Individuals are born with biological needs and dispositions which must in turn be controlled by society, and the control mechanisms are in the form of norms and values, or what most sociologists refer to as cultural systems. Culture is both material and nonmaterial, but it is the nonmaterial that is emphasized, especially in Durkheim's work, with its references to collective consciousness, collective representations, and symbolic systems (Davis, 1980:87 ff.).

Although Durkheim was preoccupied with the cultural level of reality, he did recognize that the cultural norms and values must penetrate or ''get into'' the individual through socialization and moral education. The individual was a product of the culture. Though Durkheim started with a concept of human nature rooted in biology, he moved to the position of social realism and the constraints of social norms over individual behavior.

Durkeim used the concept of ''anomie'' to describe a state of normlessness or a situation in which norms do not control behavior. The concept of anomie has been used to mean the strain produced by the conflicting demands of society on the individual members of society.

The work of the structural-functionalists was made the heart of the sociology of the east, or the sociology established at Harvard University and Columbia University in the 1930s. As we noted above, the sociology of the individual was located in the midwest at the University of Chicago. The sociology of society was a development related primarily to the work of Talcott Parsons, first seen in his *The Structure of Social Action* [Parsons (1937); see also Hinkle and Hinkle (1954) and Davis, (1980)].

Parsons attempted to build a unified system theory of society, and major components of his system were the biological organism, personality, culture, and society. Although most of his work was at the social and cultural levels, Parsons did recognize the need for biology and psychology, and he borrowed liberally from Freud, for example, in his theory building (Turner, 1982; Ritzer, 1983a, 1983b).

In 1955, A. K. Cohen (1955) published *Delinquent Boys*, which introduced Parsons and structural-functionalism into American criminology. Cohen had been a student of Sutherland at Indiana University, and he studied with Parsons at Harvard University, where he took his Ph.D. in sociology. In his book, which was his dissertation, Cohen tried to combine Sutherland and Parsons and he asked: "How is it that delinquent subcultures exist?" If delinquents learn from subcultural groups, then subcultural groups must exist prior to differential association. Using a functionalist approach, Cohen assumed that subcultural groups must perform a function, and the function of delinquent subcultural groups is to help manage the *status frustration* of lower-class males. According to Cohen, lower-class males are judged by middle-class standards while in school, and they soon realize they are not successful when judged by such middle-class values as long-range planning, respect for property and the rights of others, money, education, and social responsibility.

Since the lower-class male cannot make it in the middle-class world, he turns things upside down by rejecting middle-class values through a process (to be found in Freudian psychology) called *reaction formation*, or the rejection of middle-class values and the substitution of lower-class values for middle-class values. The delinquent develops a lower-class subculture around such values as negativism, nonutilitarianism, and maliciousness. The delinquent does not steal because he wants an automobile but because he wants to destroy property and thus show his rejection of middle-class values. It must be noted that although sociologists reject psychology, they often use such psychological concepts as learning, or in the case of Cohen, "reaction formation." Even the concept of "frustration" must be dealt with at the individual psychological level.

In 1957, Merton (1957) published a famous article, "Social Structure and Anomie," in which he stated that the causes of deviancy are in the social structure, not in the individual actor. Merton modified Durkheim's idea of anomie as a lack of normative consensus to one of a lack of integration of institutional goals and means (Davis, 1980:135; Liska, 1987). Merton found that lower-class delinquents accept middle-class values, but that they cannot attain these values (mostly wealth and security) because they lack the means (e.g., education, status, and behavioral prerequisites). Since the lower class cannot attain these values they adapted to middle-class values in several different ways (see Figure 14-1).

In Figure 14-1 (+) signifies acceptance, (−) signifies rejection, and (±) signifies a rejection of old values and substitution of new values. *Conformity* or consensus occurred when both the goals and the means exist. *Innovation* (or illegal activities) occur when the goals are present but the legitimate means are lacking. In this case the youths would innovate by stealing money or cars. The goal is attained by illegal means. When the means are retained after the goals are no longer accessible, *ritualism*, stereotypic and compulsive behavior, occurs. If both the goals and means are absent, *retreatism* occurs through the rejection

Modes of Adaptation	Culture Goals	Institutionalized Means
I. Conformity	+	+
II. Innovation	+	−
III. Ritualism	−	+
IV. Retreatism	−	−
V. Rebellion	±	±

Figure 14-1 A Typology of Modes of Individual Adaptation.

of both goals and means. The fifth form of adaption is *rebellion*, where both goals and means are rejected and placed by a new set of institutionalized goals and means. The adaptive modes of concern in criminological theory are the *innovative* or illegal mode and the *retreatist* mode.

Cloward and Ohlin (1960) published *Delinquency and Opportunity*, which they dedicated to Sutherland and Merton. In the cases of Cohen and of Cloward and Ohlin, the Chicago School and the Harvard School of sociology were joined. Cloward had been a student of Merton at Columbia University, and Ohlin had been a student of Sutherland at Indiana University. In this sense the functional school did not produce a pure functionalist theory of delinquency but a symbolic interactionism-functional theory.

In their book, Cloward and Ohlin state that Cohen was in error when he notes that lower-class delinquents reject middle-class values. Cloward and Ohlin argued that the lower class accepts middle-class values, but because of the disjunction of means and goals that Merton postulates, they cannot legitimately attain middle-class values and goals. Unlike Merton, Cloward and Ohlin hypothesized that not only are *legitimate means* to goals institutionalized, but also the *illegitimate means* to social goals are institutionalized in social structures. The presence of illegitimate criminal activities in a community leads to organized criminal gangs. The illegitimate gang activities, consisting of theft for profit, are found mostly in well-organized slum areas. Two other types of subcultural activities also emerge. *Conflict gangs* are involved in fighting other gangs in order to maintain reputation and territory. *Retreatist gangs* emerge from those individuals who resort to drugs and alcohol as a psychological means of coping with their lower-class status. These are labeled "double failures" since they fail in both illegal careers and legal careers. The ability of a person to become a criminal involved in illegitimate subcultural activities depends in turn on differential association, that is, he has to live in a neighborhood where such an opportunity structure exists; otherwise, he has to join a fighting gang or the drug and alcoholic subcultural systems.

The work of Merton, Cohen, and Cloward and Ohlin shifted American sociological criminology from the individual offender as represented by Sutherland to delinquent subcultural systems that support delinquent activities. A number of criticisms have been made of the structural-functional approach.

Davis (1980:96 ff.) argued that Merton assumed that deviancy is a lower-class phenomenon and a product of the acceptance of middle-class values. Such a view of the delinquent makes use of official police data while ignoring the role of the upper class in defining what is deviant. It also ignores the deviant's definition of the situation. Merton's view of the lower class is one of pathology. Davis noted that there is no simple correspondence between the social situation and the individual's response to that situation; therefore, not all lower-class individuals are deviants, nor are all lower-class individuals alienated and isolated from society. Deviance may be a cause of failure rather than a result of failure.

Short and Strodtbeck (1965) failed to find the three types of gangs hypothesized by Cloward and Ohlin, nor did they find the rejection of middle-class values hypothesized by Cohen. Cohen found delinquents to be negativistic and destructive of property, whereas others have found them to be pursuing middle-class values for the attainment of cars and money. Differences in aspirations and expectations do not seem to result in high rates of delinquency as opportunity theory suggests. The basic issue of the extent to which lower-class delinquency is a product of gang activity is itself subject to a great deal of debate (Gibbons, 1979:103–104; Davis, 1980:141–144; Shoemaker, 1984:107–118). Shoemaker concluded that the Cloward–Ohlin hypothesis might explain the content of gang delinquency but not the delinquent act itself. "To attribute to social class factors an overriding influence on behavior in any complex, modern Western society is unrealistic" [Shoemaker (1984:127); see Chapter 16].

Nettler (1984:208–211) states that the Cloward and Ohlin hypothesis is lacking in clarity of concepts, it confuses perceived and real opportunity structures, it is not adequate to describe persistent offenders, and it does not make effective recommendations for crime control policy. Nettler notes that the literature on opportunity structures as they relate to family structure, schools, and education does not support the opportunity thesis as put forth by Cloward and Ohlin.

The point raised by Nettler about the policy implications of the Cloward–Ohlin thesis was supported by the use of opportunity theory to eliminate delinquency in the 1960s as part of the War on Poverty. The Mobilization for Youth project based on the opportunity model was a failure (Davis, 1980:148; Shoemaker, 1948:118–119). The issue of prevention and poverty programs is discussed in more detail in Chapters 18, 19, and 21.

Integrated Sociological Theories

Several recent attempts have been made to integrate sociological theories of criminal behavior. Gibbs (1985; 1988) has noted the need for the construction of social theories which are testable and verifiable, and which have a basis in scientific fact. He finds that social theories are lacking such theoretical standing. Elliott (1985) has attempted to integrate social learning, social strain, and social control theories, but this attempt at integration has occurred at the social level only, with no integration at the biological or psychological levels. Short (1985) has emphasized the need to integrate theories across the individual, micro, and macro levels with bridging concepts, but he does not develop such an integrated theory.

A systems approach to human behavior is not found at one level of analysis, such as the social level. A systems theory demands an integration of biological, psychological, and social levels. The view sociologists have of human nature, that is, no individual differences and mentalism in place of the brain, has made an integrated approach to human behavior impossible. As Lewis Coser stated in his presidential address to the American Sociological Association, sociology lacks a theoretical base, is caught up in a statistical methodology, and is engaged in mentalism as it tries to find out what is going on in the mind of the social actor (Coser, 1975).

Grimshaw (1979), as editor of *The American Sociologist,* devoted the May 1979 issue to the topic of "What ought sociology to be doing? and why aren't we doing it?" He noted that the responses from leading sociologists included such things as a lack of relevance, public skepticism, and a failure to seek new perspectives or to abandon old perspectives. Gibbs stated that sociology has not been useful to policy makers, and "that all of us could die tomorrow and the world would not wobble an inch . . . the simple reason being that sociology is not useful" (Gibbs, 1979:81). These conclusions were reached by some of the best sociologists in the business. Sociology has a major contribution to make to criminology, but if and only if it becomes a part of an interdisciplinary effort to join biology, psychology, and law as a part of criminology. Sociological criminology, separate from other disciplines, is not a viable enterprise.

Theories of Social Control

As stated above, social structure theories encompass theories of social control, including social bonding theory, conflict theory, and the sociology of law. These theories are discussed in Chapter 15.

SUMMARY AND CONCLUSIONS

As has been noted above, sociological theories of criminality are based on social determinism and social environmentalism. The concept of human nature excludes biology and psychology, since human nature is a product of social environment. Society exists prior to human nature.

Sociological theories are divided into individualistic theories (differential association and labeling), and structural-functional theories (strain or anomie). These theories are based on socialization, the internalization of norms, self-concepts, and other mentalistic concepts. There is no physical organism interacting with a physical environment. There is no way for the environment to "get inside" the organism. Norms, labels, and values are not viewed as physical stimuli that excite sensory neurons and motor neurons, and no attempt is made to integrate biology, psychology, and sociology in these theories.

Sociological theories assume a uniformity of humankind while individual differences are minimized or neglected. The assumption is made that the environment affects each person in the same way, regardless of differences in genetics and brain structure. Because of individual differences, there are many exceptions to any statement made about the causes of criminal behavior (Nettler, 1989). For example, some poor people commit crimes, some do not; some males commit crimes, some do not. There is no way to predict or control human behavior on the basis of these theories. Sociologists use broad gross categories such as social class, poverty, gangs, and/or subcultural systems to explain individual behavior. These concepts are ill defined or vaguely conceptualized, and the mechanisms by which they explain individual behavior are not spelled out (Chapter 16).

We still do not have social theories that explain the differences between male and female criminality, or lower-class criminality, or upper-class criminality. We need to know how the social environment affects the physical organism. We can even ask a basic question concerning the nature of the social environment. Is the social environment physical, and if not, where does it exist? Are values and norms and attitudes physical behaviors or mental states? Sociology is caught in the mind–matter, mental–physical dualism of philosophy, which makes it difficult to discuss lower-class delinquency in terms of the structure of the physical environment or the structure of the brain. Perhaps the links between poverty and lower-class delinquency and crime are nutrition, pollution, the impact of a physical environment on the brain, and the actual structure of the brain itself. We know, as mentioned in Chapter 11, that rats reared in impoverished environments have a different brain structure from those reared in an enriched environment. Why not delinquents? This could be the next step in the integration of biology, psychology, and sociology.

FURTHER STUDIES

Courses in criminology, juvenile delinquency, and sociological theories of deviance are taught in most sociology departments. Such courses are also offered in schools of criminology and/or criminal justice.

REFERENCES

ABRAHAMSON, M. (1981). *Sociological Theory.* Englewood Cliffs, N.J.: Prentice-Hall.

ADAMS, R. (1973). "Differential Association and Learning Principles Revisited." *Social Problems,* 20:447–458, Spring.

AKERS, R. (1985). *Deviant Behavior.* Belmont, Calif.: Wadsworth.

AKERS, R., ET AL. (1979). "Social Learning and Deviant Behavior: A Special Test of a General Theory." *American Sociological Review,* 44:636–655, August.

ARCHIBALD, W. P. (1976). "Psychology, Sociology, and Social Psychology: Bad Fences Make Bad Neighbors." *British Journal of Sociology,* 27:115–124.

BECKER, H. S. (1963). *Outsiders.* New York: Free Press.

BLOCK, H. A., and G. GEIS (1970). *Man, Crime, and Society.* New York: Random House.

BOUTILIER, R., J. C. ROED, and A. SVENDSEN (1980). "Crisis in the Two Social Psychologies: A Critical Comparison." *Social Psychology Quarterly,* 43:5–15.

BURGESS, R. L., and R. N. AKERS (1966). "A Differential Association-Reinforcement Theory of Criminal Behavior." *Social Problems,* 14:128–147, Fall.

BURGESS, R. L., and D. BUSHELL (1969). *Behavioral Sociology.* New York: Columbia University Press.

CHADWICK-JONES, J. K., ET AL. (1979). *Brain, Environment, and Social Psychology.* Baltimore: University Park Press.

CLOWARD, R. A., and L. E. OHLIN (1960). *Delinquency and Opportunity*. Glencoe, Ill.: Free Press.

COHEN, A. K. (1955). *Delinquent Boys*. New York: Free Press.

CONGER, R. D. (1976). "Social Control and Social Learning Models of Delinquent Behavior: A Synthesis." *Criminology*, 14:17–40.

CONGER, R. D. (1978). "From Social Learning to Criminal Behavior." In *Crime, Law, and Sanctions*, ed. M. D. Krohn and R. Akers. Beverly Hills, Calif.: Sage.

CONGER, R. D. (1980). "Juvenile Delinquency: Behavior Restraint or Behavior Facilitation?" In *Understanding Crime*, ed. T. Hirschi and M. Gottfredson. Beverly Hills, Calif.: Sage.

COSER, L. (1975). "Two Methods in Search of a Substance." *American Sociological Review*, 40:691–700.

COSER, L. (1977). *Masters of Sociological Thought*. New York: Harcourt Brace Jovanovich.

COTTRELL, L. S., JR. (1980). "George Herbert Mead: The Legacy of Social Behaviorism." In *Sociological Traditions from Generation to Generation*, ed. R. Merton and M. Riley. Norwood, N.J.: Ablex.

DAVIS, N. J. (1980). *Sociological Constructions of Deviance*. Dubuque, Iowa: Wm. C. Brown.

DENISOFF, R. S., O. CALLAHAN, and M. H. LEVINE (1974). *Theories and Paradigms in Contemporary Sociology*. Itasca, Ill.: F.E. Peacock.

DOUGLAS, J. D. (1970). *Understanding Everyday Life*. Chicago: Aldine.

EISENSTADT, S. N., and H. J. HELLE, eds. (1985). *Macro-Sociological Theory*. Beverly Hills, Calif.: Sage.

ELLIOTT, D. S. (1985). "The Assumptions that Theories Can Be Combined with Increased Explanatory Power: Theoretical Integrations." *Theoretical Methods in Criminology*, ed. R.F. Meier. Beverly Hills, Calif.: Sage, 123–150.

ERIKSON, K. (1962). "Notes on the Sociology of Deviance." *Social Problems*, 9:307–314, Spring.

FESTINGER, L., ed. (1980). *Retrospections on Social Psychology*. New York: Oxford University Press.

GAMST, F. C., and E. NORBECK (1976). *Ideas of Culture*. New York: Holt, Rinehart and Winston.

GEIS, G. (1976). "Revisiting Sutherland's Criminology (1924)." *Criminology*, 14:303–306, November..

GEIS, G., and C. GOFF (1982). "Edwin H. Sutherland: A Biographical and Analytical Commentary." In *White-Collar and Economic Crime*, ed. P. Wickman and T. Dailey. Lexington, Mass.: D.C. Health.

GERGEN, K. J., and M. M. GERGEN (1981). *Social Psychology*. New York: Harcourt Brace Jovanovich.

GIBBONS, D. C. (1979). *The Criminological Enterprise*. Englewood Cliffs, N.J.: Prentice Hall.

GIBBONS, D. C., and M. KROHN (1986). *Delinquent Behavior*, 4th ed. Englewood Cliffs, N.J.: Prentice Hall.

GIBBS, J. (1979). "The elites can do without us." *The American Sociologist*, 14:2, 79–84.

GIBBS, J. (1985). "The Methodology of Theory Construction in Criminology." *Theoretical Methods in Criminology,* ed. R.M. Meier. Beverly Hills, Calif.: Sage, 23–50.

GIBBS, J. (1988). "The State of Criminological Theory." *Criminology,* Vol. 25:4, 821–840.

GLUECK, S. (1956). "Theory and Fact in Criminology." *British Journal of Delinquency,* 92–109, October.

GOFFMAN, E. (1959). *The Presentation of Self in Everyday Life.* New York: Anchor.

GOFFMAN, E. (1961). *Asylums.* New York: Doubleday.

GOFFMAN, E. (1963). *Stigma.* Englewood Cliffs, N.J.: Prentice Hall.

GOLDSTEIN, J. (1980). *Social Psychology.* New York: Academic Press.

GOVE, W. R., ed. (1980). *Labeling Deviant Behavior.* Beverly Hills, Calif.: Sage.

GOVE, W. R., and G. R. CARPENTER (1982). *The Fundamental Connection between Nature and Nurture.* Lexington, Mass.: Lexington Books.

GRIMSHAW, A. (1979). "What ought sociology to be doing? and why aren't we doing it?" *The American Sociologist,* 14:2, 68–69.

HALL, J. (1945). "Criminology." In *Twentieth Century Sociology,* ed. G. Gurvitch and W. E. Moore. New York: Philosophical Library.

HAMBLIN, R. L., and J. H. KUNKEL (1977). *Behavioral Theory in Sociology: Essays in Honor of G. C. Homans.* New Brunswick, N.J.: Transaction Books.

HELLE, H. J., and S. N. EISENSTADT, eds. (1985). *Micro-sociological Theory.* Beverly Hills, Calif.: Sage.

HESS, B. B., E. W. MARKSON, and P. J. STEIN (1982). *Sociology.* New York: Macmillan.

HINDELANG, M. J. (1971). "The Social versus Solitary Nature of Delinquent Involvements." *British Journal of Criminology, Delinquency, and Deviant Behavior,* 11:167–175.

HINKLE, R. C. (1980). *Founding Theory of American Sociology.* Boston: Routledge & Kegan Paul.

HINKLE, R. C., and G. M. HINKLE (1954). *The Development of Modern Sociology.* New York: Doubleday.

HIRSCHI, T. (1969). *The Causes of Delinquency.* Berkeley: University of California Press.

HIRSCHI, T., and M. GOTTFREDSON (1980). *Understanding Crime.* Beverly Hills, Calif.: Sage

HOLLANDER, E. B. (1981). *Principles and Methods of Social Psychology.* 4th ed. New York: Oxford University Press.

HOMANS, G. C. (1961). *Social Behavior: Its Elementary Forms.* New York: Harcourt Brace & World.

HOMANS, G. C. (1964). "Bringing Men Back In." *American Sociological Review,* 29:809–818.

HOUSE, J. S. (1977). "The Three Faces of Social Psychology." *Sociometry,* 40:161–177.

INKELES, A. (1959). "Personality and Social Structure." In *Sociology Today,* ed. R. K. Merton, L. Broom, and L. S. Cottrell, Jr. New York: Basic Books.

JEFFERY, C. R. (1965). "Criminal Behavior and Learning Theory." *Journal of Criminal Law, Criminology, and Police Science,* 56:294–300, September.

JEFFERY, C. R. (1970). "The Historical Development of Criminology." In *Pioneers in Criminology,* ed. H. Mannheim. Montclair, N.J.: Patterson-Smith.

JENSEN, G. F., and D. G. ROJEK (1980). *Delinquency.* Lexington, Mass.: D.C. Heath.

KESSING, R. M. (1974). "Theories of Culture." In *Annual Review of Anthropology,* Vol. 3, ed. B. J. Siegal, A. R. Beals, and S. A. Tyler. Palo Alto, Calif.: Annual Reviews.

KITSUSE, J. L. (1964). "Societal Reactions to Deviant Behavior: Problems of Theory and Method." In *The Other Side,* ed. H. S. Becker. New York: Free Press.

KORNHAUSER, R. R. (1978). *Social Sources of Delinquency.* Chicago: University of Chicago Press.

LE MAR, E. (1982). *American Deliquency: Its Meaning and Construction.* Chicago, Ill: Dorsey.

LEMERT, E. M. (1951). *Social Pathology.* New York: McGraw-Hill.

LEWIS, J. D. (1979). "A Social Behaviorist Interpretation of the Meadian 'I.' " *American Journal of Sociology,* 85:261–287.

LEWIS, J. D., and R. L. SMITH (1980). *American Sociology and Pragmatism.* Chicago: University of Chicago Press.

LINDZEY, G., and E. ARONSON, eds. (1968). *The Handbook of Social Psychology,* 2nd ed., Vol. 1. Reading, Mass.: Addison-Wesley.

LISKA, A. (1977). "The Dissipation of Sociological Social Psychology." *American Sociologist,* 12:2–23.

LISKA, A. (1987). *Perspectives on Deviance,* 2nd ed. Englewood Cliffs, N.J.: Prentice Hall.

MCPHAIL, C., and C. REXROAT (1979). "Mead vs. Blumer: The Divergent Methodological Perspectives of Social Behaviorism and Symbolic Interactionism." *American Sociological Review,* 3:449–467.

MEAD, G. H. (1934). *Mind, Self, and Society.* Chicago: University of Chicago Press.

MERTON, R. K. (1957). "Social Structure and Anomie." In *Social Theory and Social Structure,* R. K. Merton. Glencoe, Ill.: Free Press.

MILLS, C. W. (1943). "The Professional Ideology of Social Pathologists." *American Journal of Sociology,* 49:165–180, September.

NETTLER, G. (1984). *Explaining Crime,* 3rd ed. New York: McGraw-Hill.

NETTLER, G. (1989) *Criminology Lessons.* Cincinnati, Oh.: Anderson.

ORNSTEIN, R., and D. SOBEL (1987). *The Healing Brain.* New York: Simon & Schuster.

PARSONS, T. (1937). *The Structure of Social Action.* New York: McGraw-Hill.

POPENOE, D. (1980). *Sociology.* Englewood Cliffs, N.J.: Prentice Hall.

QUINNEY, R. (1975). *Criminology.* Boston: Little, Brown.

RECKLESS, W. C. (1970). "American Criminology." *Criminology,* 8:4–20, May.

REISS, A. J., and L. RHODES (1964). "An Empirical Test of Differential Association Theory." *Journal of Research in Crime and Delinquency,* 5–18, January.

RITZER, G. (1978). *Sociology: A Multiple Paradigm Science.* Boston: Allyn and Bacon.

RITZER, G. (1980). *Sociology: A Multiple Paradigm Science,* rev. ed. Boston: Allyn and Bacon.

RITZER, G. (1983a). *Sociological Theory.* New York: Alfred A. Knopf.

RITZER, G. (1983b). *Contemporary Sociological Theory.* New York: Alfred A. Knopf.

ROSENBERG, M. and R. TURNER, eds. (1981). *Social Psychology: Sociological Perspectives.* New York: Basic Books.

RUBINGTON, E., and M. WEINBERG, eds. (1968). *Deviance: The Interactionist Perspective.* New York: Macmillan.

SCHEFF, T. J. (1966). *Being Mentally Ill.* Chicago: Aldine.

SCHUR, E. (1981). *Labeling Delinquent Behavior.* New York: Harper & Row.

SELLIN, T. (1938). *Culture Conflict and Crime.* New York: Social Science Research Council.

SHOEMAKER, D. J. (1984). *Theories of Delinquency.* New York: Oxford University Press.

SHORT, J. (1957). "Differential Association and Delinquency." *Social Problems,* 233–239, January.

SHORT, J. (1958). "Differential Association with Delinquent Friends and Delinquent Behavior." *Pacific Sociological Review.* (1):22–25.

SHORT, J. F. (1985). "The Level of Explanation Problem in Criminology." *Theoretical Methods in Criminology.* Ed. R. F. Meier. Beverly Hills, Calif.: Sage, 51–74.

SHORT, J. F., and F. L. STRODTBECK (1965). *Group Process and Gang Deliquency.* Chicago: University of Chicago Press.

STRAUSS, A. (1956). *The Social Psychology of George Herbert Mead.* Chicago: University of Chicago Press.

STRYKER, S. (1971). "Review of the Handbook of Social Psychology." *American Sociological Review,* 36:894–898.

STRYKER, S. (1977). "Developments in 'Two Social Psychologies': Toward an Appreciation of Mutual Relevance." *Sociometry,* 40:145–160.

SUTHERLAND, E. H. (1924). *Criminology.* Philadelphia: J. B. Lippincott.

SUTHERLAND, E. H. (1947). *Principles of Criminology.* Philadelphia: J. B. Lippincott.

SUTHERLAND, E. H. (1974). *On Analyzing Crime.* Bloomington: Indiana University Press.

THOMAS, W. I., and F. ZNANIECKI (1918–1921). *The Polish Peasant in Europe and America.* New York: Alfred A. Knopf.

TURNER, J. (1982). *The Structure of Sociological Theory.* Homewood, Ill.: Dorsey.

TURNER, J. (1985). *Sociology.* Chicago: Nelson-Hall Publishers.

VAN DEN BERGHE, P. (1974). "Bringing Beasts Back In: Toward A Biosocial Theory of Aggression." *American Sociological Review,* 39:777–788.

VOLKART, E. H. (1971). "Review of the Handbook of Social Psychology." *American Sociological Review,* 36:898–902.

VOSS, H. L. (1964). "Differential Association and Reported Delinquent Behavior." *Social Problems,* 78–85, Summer.

WEBER, M. (1974). *The Theory of Social and Economic Organization,* trans. A. M. Henderson and T. Parsons. New York: Free Press.

WELLFORD, C. (1975). "Labeling Theory and Criminology: An Assessment" *Social Problems,* 22:332–345, February.

WILLIAMS, F. P., and M. D. MCSHANE (1988). *Criminological Theory.* Englewood Cliffs, N.J.: Prentice Hall.

WILSON, J. Q., and R. HERRNSTEIN (1985). *Crime and Human Nature.* New York: Simon & Schuster.

WOLFGANG, M. (1968). *Crime and Culture: Essays in Honor of Thorsten Sellin.* New York: Wiley.

WRONG, D. (1961). "The Oversocialized Conception of Man." *American Sociological Review,* 26:183–192.

ZEITLIN, I. M. (1981). *The Social Condition of Humanity.* New York: Oxford University Press.

QUESTIONS

1. What was the historical and social background of sociology?
2. What assumptions are made by sociologists about human nature?
3. What are the major theoretical aspects of the sociology of the individual offender? Why do we have a sociology of the individual and a sociology of society?
4. What was Sutherland's contribution to the sociology of the individual offender?
5. How does social learning theory explain criminal behavior?
6. What was Durkheim's contribution to the analysis of crime and criminal behavior?
7. How did Cohen and Cloward and Ohlin extend the work of Sutherland and Durkheim?

Sociology, Law, and Social Control

15

HISTORICAL ASPECTS OF SOCIAL CONTROL

The history of social control represents the movement from decentralized societies to centralized, from kinship and tribe to the nation-state, from custom to law, from informal to formal, and from status to contract (Chapter 3). The tribal system disintegrated in the Western world, to be replaced with the agricultural and industrial revolutions and great population growth. It is within this historical setting that the problem of social control emerged as we know it today.

Models of Social Control

Three basic models of social control are used by political scientists and sociologists: (1) control based on the acceptance of the normative standards and customs of the culture, (2) control based on the exchange of goods and services involving pain and pleasure, and (3) control based on the use of fear, force, and coercion (Ellis, 1971; Yinger, 1977).

The first model of social control depends on norms and values. Through socialization, individuals internalize cultural norms which they then view as "right" and a part of their conscience. The normative theory of social control is found in Durkheim's concept of the social reality of norms and the coercive power of norms over the behavior of individuals. The answer to the problem of social order is found in shared norms and values. This theory assumes consensus around shared norms. It also assumes that individuals have no basic biological or psychological nature that will oppose these collective norms (Ellis, 1971). Parsons represents this view in contemporary sociology (Chapter 14).

The doctrine of the internalization of norms as an explanation of behavior is difficult to support. If a person conforms, we say it was because of norms, but we do not know if it was the norm or some combination of factors that lead to conformity. From conformity we assume the internalization of norms. We do not know what variables were influencing the brain at the time the behavior occurred. Coser (1982:13 ff.) has pointed out that the sociologist has placed too much reliance on norms as means of social control, since the internalization of norms is by no means automatic. Gibbs (1982:86–88) defines social control as the effort of a first party to control the behavior of the second party through a third party. Such a definition has the advantage of defining social control *without* reference to norms or deviancy. Gibb's definition is much more behavioral and empirical and testable than a definition or explanation of social control based on internalized norms that cannot be seen or measured.

The normative approach is found in W. G. Sumner's *Folkways* (1906), where social order is based on folkways and mores. Modern sociology textbooks still present this view of social control. Spencer (1976:2) notes that "most of us do not conform to cultural norms simply because they are backed by sanctions. We obey the law because we believe it is the proper thing to do." Popenoe (1980:230) states that "the successful internalization of social norms causes people to refrain from stealing someone else's money, for example, not because they are afraid of being arrested and sent to jail, but because they believe stealing is wrong. The unconscience acts as an internal social control mechanism."

The exchange theory of social control is based on utilitarianism and self-seeking persons who wish to maximize pleasure and minimize pain. This view is found in the work of Bentham, the father of the classical school of criminology, in Adam Smith, J. S. Mill, and other utilitarians (Smart, 1967).

John Locke's concept of the state of nature was a state of peace and tranquility broken only by a few evil persons who must be restrained. The role of the state was to protect "life, liberty, and property," and otherwise to maintain a hands-off or laissez-faire approach to control. If each person pursued his/her self-interests, the "greatest happiness for the greatest number" would occur (Cranston, 1967; Sprague, 1967; Benn, 1967).

Malinowski (1926) rejected the "cake of custom" idea whereby anthropologists assumed that primitives automatically obeyed custom. Malinowski put "reciprocity and exchange" above custom. Social norms are enforced by reciprocity where if I do something for you, you will do something for me (Chapter 3).

Exchange theory (or social behaviorism as it is also known) is a major aspect of social psychological theory based on Skinnerian psychology and on the principles of reinforcement and punishment. George C. Homans (1961) is the principal figure in exchange theory as found in sociological social psychology, whereas Thibaut and Kelley (1959, 1978) represent this position in psychological social psychology. Behavior is learned on the basis of operant principles, and social interaction is governed by the exchange of pleasure and pain, or rewards and punishments (Turner, 1982; Gergen and Gergen, 1981; Goldstein, 1980).

The third form of social control is by force and violence as part of the political state (Chapters 3 and 4). Hobbes described life in the state of nature as "nasty, brutish, and short." According to Hobbes, human beings are marked by violent passions that must be controlled, and humankind entered into a social contract whereby certain rights and freedoms are surrendered in exchange for protection from the crimes and assaults of others. Both exchange theory and the force and coercion theory are based on the anatomy of the brain, with its pleasure and pain centers. Normative theory is not based on a theory of human nature.

The Need for Social Control

Why do human beings need such extensive, expensive, and oppressive social control measures? Everywhere we find that the folkways, mores, and laws are broken at a very high rate. Why is it that norms and custom and reciprocity are not strong enough to control human behavior?

In Chapters 12, 13, and 14 we discussed two basic theories of human behavior. (1) Humans are antisocial by nature and must be controlled by society. This view is found in Hobbes and in Freud. (2) Humans are basically social because they internalize norms which they obey and which limit the selfish desires and impulses of men and women. Human beings conform unless there is cultural conflict or social disorganization. This is the sociological view presented in Chapter 14. The first theory assumes deviancy, the second conformity. The interdisciplinary bioenvironmental theory of behavior presented in this book is an extension of the first view of human nature.

In Chapters 10 and 11 we presented humankind as being born with innate needs, urges, and propensities. Human beings have two brains, a rational brain and a violent brain. Humankind does not need to be motivated to commit crimes; motivation comes from the brain and the biological nature of behavior. We do have to learn to control our emotions and impulses, and these controls are neurological in nature; that is, neural connections must be formed between the cerebral cortex and the limbic system before the limbic system is brought under rational control (Chapter 11).

To survive, a person must adapt to the environment and to his/her biological needs, which include food, shelter, protection, sex, and other basic needs. These impulses and emotions are controlled in the brain by the pain and pleasure centers. Modern learning theory is based on pleasure and pain, as is Freudian psychology. We must assume that people violate norms and laws in order to gain pleasure and avoid pain. Both exchange theory and force and coercion theory are based on a pleasure–pain theory of human behavior.

One possible clue to the nature of social control can be found in sociobiology. In discussing animal societies, Wilson (1975:379 ff.) wrote that the four major stages of social evolution are (1) colonial invertebrates, (2) social insects, (3) mammals, and (4) the human primate. Evolution moves from invertebrates to humans, from no individual differences to great individual differences, and from greater dependency to lesser dependency. Men and women are far more different as individuals than are ants or coral colonies, and they are less dependent on the colony or society. At the same time, there is a decline in cohesiveness, altruism, and cooperative efforts. Wilson notes that this decline in cooperation was reversed by humans, which is "the great mystery in biology."

In respect to the social insects (ants, bees), we should note that the social behavior is genetically based. Cooperation among ants is founded on innate unlearned behaviors [Wilson (1975), Wheeler (1928); see Chapters 10 and 13]. As evolution occurred, a larger brain and learned behavior assumed a more critical role, that is, individuals behave more on the basis of learning and less as ants in a colony or bees in a beehive. Whereas genes furnish the basis for social order in insect societies, laws and norms replace genes in primate societies, especially human primate societies.

Human beings have great behavioral plasticity, so they can respond to environmental stimuli in a great many different ways. Some individuals will obey the norms and laws, others will not. Some individuals will obey some norms and not other norms. Some individuals will obey a norm at time A but not at time B or C. As we move from ants to bees to human beings, we move from biological control to social control.

The sociologist assumes this plasticity of response patterns without recognizing the biological basis for such plasticity. Even though the human infant can learn a great many responses, learning is limited by biology (see Chapter 13). Sociology assumes socialization without biology. Bioenvironmental theory assumes both biology and learning.

Why Do Human Beings Need a Society?

A basic issue in social control is why individuals submit to social control. Why must one give up freedom to live as one wants in order to live in society? Certainly, the murderer or burglar or rapist is better off without law and restraints. Hobbes said that we give up liberty to escape from the war of all against all. Locke said that we join the state to protect "life, liberty, and property."

Human beings must cooperate to survive. Human evolution depended on cooperation as well as conflict. Cooperation and competition go together. The Darwinian view of nature places great emphasis on conflict at the individual level; however, cooperation is also vital to the evolutionary process. Some sort of social order is advantageous, if not absolutely necessary, for the survival of the human species, and the complex human brain permits great variation in the forms that such social order may take. The works of Kropotkin (1902) and Allee (1951), among others, emphasize the role of mutual aid and cooperation in species evolution and development.

As we noted in Chapter 8, there is a conflict between the rights of the state and the rights of individuals. Individuals want state control but do not want to be limited by state control. All attempts to control the human animal are resisted by those being controlled; at the same time, some system of social control is necessary.

THE SOCIOLOGY OF LAW

Social control involves folkways, mores, norms, customs, traditions, beliefs, public opinion, and law. Crime involves the nation-state and the legal system, so criminology and criminal law are closely interrelated.

In Chapter 6 law was analyzed in terms of: (1) philosophy, morality, and ethics; (2) power, coercion, and the state; (3) society, history, and social evolution; and (4) science and technology. In this chapter we discuss the interaction of law and science, especially sociology and psychology, and the major efforts of legal scholars and behavioral scientists to understand law and to make use of scientific principles within the legal system. This is referred to in jurisprudence as legal realism and in sociology as "the sociology of law" (see Chapter 6). For discussions of the sociology of law, see Pound (1945), Timasheff (1939), Gurvitch (1942), Skolnick (1965), and Selznick (1967).

Auguste Comte (1798–1857)

Comte is noted for coining the term "sociology." He is also known as a great positivist who believed in using the methods of physics to study social organization. Comte saw the evolution of science in a hierarchy from mathematics and physics to chemistry to biology to sociology (Chapters 2 and 14).

Comte envisioned human knowledge as progressing through three stages: (1) the *theological* stage, dominated by priests and the military; (2) the *metaphysical* stage, dominated by priests and lawyers; and (3) the *scientific* stage, dominated by scientists. The theological and metaphysical stages are marked by supernatural causes and abstract forces, whereas the scientific stage is marked by natural laws and scientific discoveries (Coser, 1977; Martindale, 1981).

Comte's positivism and science included the idea that through science human social problems could be resolved. The idea of progress through science and technology was basic to early American sociology as developed at the University of Chicago (Chapter 14).

The theory of social control emerging from Comte's philosophy is one based on science and scholarship. The resolution of social problems is a scientific, not a religious or philosophical or legal issue. This implies that experts such as psychiatrists and sociologists intervene in the lives of people. It also calls on experts to determine how people who commit crimes should be treated, or what behaviors should be called crimes. As I have emphasized from Chapter 1 on, there is a major conflict between science and law as found in criminology and criminal justice on the issue of how we control crime. One point of view says "rehabilitation, treatment, and prevention"; the other says "revenge, deterrence, and punishment.'' One policy leads to more hospitals and medical clinics, the other leads to more prisons and electric chairs.

I will argue that in the future, science must play a much larger role in the control of crime and criminal behavior. This does not mean that scientists and experts will replace lawyers; it does mean a major interdisciplinary effort between law and science (Chapter 21).

Emile Durkheim (1858–1917)

Durkheim believed in the reality of social facts to explain human behavior at the social level. Biology and psychology were excluded from his work (Chapter 12). Durkheim taught that the cohesiveness of society comes from a collective conscience or a shared consensus about norms, which in turn act as restraints on human behavior. Human beings are possessed of biological needs that must be controlled by society, but once the individual is socialized, the role of biology in behavior disappears as norms take over. The norms that are internalized in individuals create moral obligations and commitments. Norms are obeyed because they are right. We discussed the normative approach to social control above, and we quoted sociologists who state that we obey the law because we believe it is right. The problem with the normative approach is that people disobey norms and laws, and we must explain why norms and laws are violated (Martindale, 1981; Coser, 1977; Ritzer, 1980).

Durkheim himself recognized the limitations of the normative organic model of society. In the *Division of Labor and Society* (1893), he noted that simple societies have *mechanical solidarity* as a basis for social order; that is, the members share norms and values without major individual differences. This type of society resembles E. O. Wilsons' description of an ant colony or beehive. However, as societies become complex, diffuse, and differentiated due to a division of labor, *organic solidarity* replaces mechanical solidarity. Organic solidarity is based on specialization and the exchange of goods and services. Individual differences, not similarities, are important. In specialized societies individuals develop and exchange specialized goods and services in order to survive, and such societies are held together by mutual dependency.

Durkheim regarded social disorganization as a result of anomie or normlessness. This theory came to be social strain theory in American criminology (Chapter 14). However, if individuals are held together by exchange and reciprocity in a complex society with organic solidarity, individual self-interests and differences exist which can disrupt social order. A person can cheat on an obligation or refuse to fulfill an obligation, and when conflict breaks out, the social order is disrupted. The rules of reciprocity and exchange based on pleasure and pain now govern human behavior, not moral obligations to social norms.

Although sociologists regard Durkheim's model of social control to be one of shared values and norms (Ellis, 1971), the problem of social order takes on a new meaning in advanced urban societies. I may have missed something in the literature, but I am not aware of any discussion in sociology or criminology of Durkheim's model of social control for urban societies as one based on an exchange–reciprocity model and not on a normative consensus model. If we regard Durkheim's organic solidarity as a model of control at the individual level based on pleasure and pain, then pleasure and pain and not norms govern behavior. We would then look to theories of pleasure and pain as found in Freudian theory and modern learning theory to explain criminal behavior. This is consistent with social control–bonding theory and interdisciplinary bio-environmental theory. The important thing is that if the social environment made up of norms is not adequate to control human behavior, we must move to the psychological level for our explanation of social control and human behavior. Exchange theory and coercion theory both operate on a pleasure-and-pain principle at the personal level.

Following Durkheim's argument, law takes the form of *repressive* law or criminal law in societies held together by mechanical solidarity. The purpose of law is to react against the lawbreaker and to reestablish a moral order based on consensus. Crime is normal in society since criminal sanctions reinforce the normative structure and arouse the collective conscience (Martindale, 1981: 101).

In societies held together by organic solidarity, law takes the form of *restitutive* law or tort law. Restitution and the payment of damages for an injury are the critical issues in tort law (Martindale, 1981:101).

Contracts are enforced and injuries are compensated on the basis of exchange theory and reciprocity. If obligations are to be kept, they must be enforced through tort law. This is similar to Sir Henry Maine's idea of law as involving a transition from kinship law to state law (Chapter 3). Early tribal law had punishment and revenge as aspects of social control, and it had compensation or tort law. It had both the blood feud and the payment of the wergild. As state law replaced tribal law, wrongs were once again divided into public and private. Public wrongs involved the interests of the king (society), whereas private wrongs involved the interests of private citizens. Criminal law developed out of the law of public wrongs. Both private and public wrongs belonged to the emerging legal system but were handled in different courts with different legal concepts and procedures (Chapter 3).

However, Durkheim's concept of restitutive law does not convey the role of criminal law in modern society. In the shift from mechanical to organic solidarity Durkheim ignored the fact that organic solidarity is not based solely or primarily on exchange and reciprocity. Force and coercion are used as a basis for social control when norms and reciprocity are not adequate. Durkheim's concept of organic solidarity is incomplete as a description of modern urban society. Durkheim included norms and reciprocity in his discussion, but he ignored force and coercion largely because he misconstrued norms as "social facts" rather than as individual response patterns to a social environment.

Max Weber (1864–1920)

Weber was a German sociologist whose influence on American sociology started with Talcott Parsons. He represented both the subjective individualism and the structure functionalism aspects of sociology (Coser, 1977; Ritzer, 1980; Martindale, 1981). Weber put forth a "theory of social action" based on subjective meanings and interpretations called "Verstehen," or understanding (Chapter 14). Like Cooley, Mead, and Thomas, Weber dealt with "voluntaristic nominalism," the subjective interpretations given to experiences within social settings (Coser, 1977; Ritzer, 1980).

Weber rejected the scientific positivism of Comte. He argued for the German social science philosophy represented by Dilthey, Windeband, and Rickert, where meaning is found in cultural history and in introspection rather than in science. This mentalistic and introspective philosophy is found in German psychology as represented by W. Wundt and Gestalt psychology. Weber supported an effort to create separate methodologies for the natural and social sciences, one based on physicialism and one based on mentalism. As noted in Chapter 14, there is a major conflict in sociology between the natural science methods and the social sciences methods as they apply to the study of human behavior.

Subjective social action takes four forms according to Weber (Coser, 1977):

1. Purposive rationality, goal-oriented behavior where both goals and means are rationally selected
2. Value-oriented rationality, where means are selected rationally but goals are irrational
3. Emotionally oriented goals, where behavior is based on emotionality and not rationality
4. Traditionally oriented goals, where behavior is guided not by reason or emotion but by custom and tradition

Weber thus recognized both rationality and irrationality in his theory, as did Freud, in contrast to most sociological theories, which deny emotionality. He also gave weight to tradition as well as rationality and emotionality. The split between rationality and emotionality can be traced to the division of the brain into a rational brain (cerebral cortex) and an emotional brain (limbic system).

In his discussion of social structure and the legitimacy of authority, Weber also put forth a theory of law. Authority is legitimate (regarded as proper or acceptable by those subjected to the authority) when some people claim power and control over the lives of others, and those who are the object of this control accept the right of the ruler to rule. Weber distinguished three types of legitimate authority:

1. Rational legal authority, authority based on rational grounds with impersonal formal rules codified within a bureaucratic structure. This is the authority of the president of the United States or the president of a university or corporation. In a bureaucratic hierarchy there is one head (one president, one Pope, one chief executive officer) and under him/her those

subject to the rules of the system. This type of authority characterizes our legal and political systems.

2. Traditional authority, authority based on the right of a father to rule because by tradition the father rules. A tribal leader or a hereditary monarch exemplify a traditional authority model.

3. Charismatic authority, authority to rule based on charm, appeal, and personal leadership qualities. Charisma is found in the historic figures of Christ, Joan of Arc, Hitler, Martin Luther King, and Gandhi.

These authority types are pure types which are not pure in reality. A president of the United States or of a university may have great charisma as well as being located in a formal bureaucratic structure. The point is that we obey the president whether we like him/her or not. We "salute the office, not the man/woman." We follow a charismatic leader because of belief and faith.

Weber's analysis of authority is useful in understanding the transition from tribal law (traditional) to state law (legal-rational). Rationalism and bureaucracies are characteristics of modern complex societies, and they bear a close resemblance to Durkheim's organic solidarity.

Weber divided social position into class, status, and power. Social class represents life chances and material wealth. Status represents prestige, lifestyle, and rank. Power represents the ability of someone to control the lives of others. Weber saw class, status, and power as different, though interrelated aspects of political and social life, and he denied that predictions can be made of behaviors from one without the other since a person might rank high on one and medium on two. A pluralism of forces is thus introduced into social analysis. Weber's concept of social class was much more complex than the concept of class put forth by Marx (Coser, 1977).

Karl Marx (1818–1883)

Marx was a late-nineteenth-century political and economic philosopher who attempted to interpret the growth and development of capitalism and state nationalism. Marx took Darwin's theory of evolution and conflict and applied it to economic history. If Darwin was correct in his theory that evolution occurred from simple to complex organization on the basis of conflict and competition, then Marx reasoned that human history had to be explained in terms of Darwinian principles. In the *Communist Manifesto* (1848) and *Das Kapital* (1867), Marx outlined his basic philosophy of history (Coser, 1977; Ritzer, 1983).

Marx rejected the consensus view of social order as found in Comte and Durkheim, a consensus based on a normative social order. Society was not held together by consensus and cooperation but was torn by internal conflict and competition. What better example of Darwinian conflict could Marx find than the "struggle for survival and death for the losers" as found in capitalism and the class struggle?

An earlier political philosopher, Jean-Jacques Rousseau (1712–1778), had put forth the theory that in a state of nature, humans are happy and in an ideal state of existence. In contrast to Hobbes, Rousseau taught that people were basically good. With the coming of private property came social inequality and social conflict, and the problems of humankind originated not in people but in society and the state system. "Man is born free and everywhere he is in chains" is the way Rousseau expressed it (Grimsley, 1967; Masters, 1978; Cole, 1950).

The basic structure of Marx's political thought parallels that of Rousseau in many basic respects. Marxian historical analysis starts with the observation that in simple hunting and fishing economies property is held communally. Private property did not exist. As specialization and a division of labor occurred, the means of production fell into private hands and private property came into existence. With the emergence of capitalism power came to be centralized in the state, which represents the vested interests of the upper class, who own the means of production. Because of capitalism and the private ownership of property, a two-class system emerged, property owners (bourgeoisie) and propertyless (proletariates). Capitalism has built into it the seeds of its own destruction—class conflict.

The emergence of private property and an upper class separated the worker from the means of production; workers became alienated from production as well as from work and from themselves. This new powerless and propertyless class of workers sold its labor to the propertied class. According to the "labor theory of value," goods and services have no value other than the value of the labor put into them. Since property owners pay workers less than the full value of their labor, capitalists gain wealth from the labor while the working masses are exploited by the owners of production.

The basic material foundation of society is economic, that is, the means of production. The superstructure of society—law, politics, religion, and ideologies—is a product of the economic system. This is "historical materialism" or economic determinism. The behavior of individuals is determined by social class and economic arrangements found in society. The ideology of the upper class is determined by economic interests, as is the ideology of the working class. On the basis of this assumption we can ask how much of Marxist philosophy and doctrine is a product of the economic position of Marx and his followers? The legal system, including criminal law, represents the interests of the ruling propertied class. Criminal law is used to repress, suppress, and control the lower class. Law is not just or blind, but is designed with a definite class bias. A basic assumption of Marxian doctrine which runs throughout contemporary discussions of social control is that *any form of social control is evil and must be avoided*. This led to a total rejection of therapies and medical intervention into deviance, or what is now called "the medicalization of deviance" (Chapters 20 and 21).

To control and exploit the lower class, the upper class had to create a strong centralized state system. (In Chapter 3 evidence was introduced from anthropology that the state system emerged prior to social classes rather than the other way around.) Conflict and power are central to a Marxian analysis of law. Social control is not normative and consensual, nor is it exchange and reciprocity. Law is pure coercive force and power. Social control is imposed on the weak (poor, females, minorities, children) against their wishes. Consent of the governed is not part of the political arrangement. Criminal laws do not serve to protect the interests of the lower class.

Crime is thus created in two ways by capitalism:

1. Workers are exploited by capitalism, and in an effort to survive, they commit crimes. Crimes against property can be explained in terms of unemployment and poverty, but even crimes against the person, such as murder and rape, are viewed as a response to domination and control by the upper class.

2. Laws are designed to label the lower class as criminal and to outlaw the behaviors of the lower class, whereas the behaviors of the upper class are not so labeled. Politicians and business owners commit crimes but are not prosecuted or sent to prison. The criminal justice system works in favor of the rich, and that is why there are so many poor and unemployed people in prison (Gibbons, 1979; Nettler, 1984; Shoemaker, 1984).

According to Marx, the internal inconsistencies in capitalism create crises in the system which eventually are resolved by a revolution and by a transition from capitalism to socialism. Under a socialist system the means of production are owned by the workers, the state withers away, and crime disappears since the conditions creating crime (i.e., oppressive criminal law, poverty, and unemployment) will have disappeared.

Evaluation of Marx

Marx occupies a critical place in social philosophy because of his focus on the political/economic system that emerged with capitalism and the industrial revolution. Marx made power and coercion central to his work, instead of the internalization of norms or reciprocity and exchange (McInnes, 1967a, 1967b; Cole, 1967).

Marxian ideology has been associated with the development and growth of communism and socialism in the Soviet Union, China, and elsewhere throughout the world. As third world countries and undeveloped countries moved from agrarianism to urbanization and industrialization, the problems dealt with by Marx came to be central to these social changes.

Gibbs (1982:102–103) has stated that there is little evidence to support the Marxian contention of upper-class control of criminal law. Hagan found that the influence of social class on legislation is widespread and not only to the advantage of the upper class. Also, studies have demonstrated a great deal of consensus around the criminal law, in place of the conflict that the Marxists propose (Gibbs, 1982:102–103). As a prophet, Marx fell short of predicting the twentieth century, since he was wrong in all his major assumptions. The following comments can be made concerning his predictions.

1. Marx focused on conflict at the social level (i.e., two social classes). Much more important forms of conflict occur at the biological and psychological levels. Interspecies conflict involving predators and prey is one major example. The human animal has exterminated many species from the earth, and thousands of species have disappeared as a result of biological competition and conflict.

   Intraspecies conflict also occurs. Competition among males for sex, food, and jobs is among the most prominent. Male/female competition is also great. Male aggression is a most prominent aspect of aggression in general.

   The Marxists have placed the emphasis on the wrong aspects of conflict. The important aspects of conflict are at the *biological* level, not the *social* level. Conflict at the social level is a reflection of basic conflict over food, sex, and survival, and at this level each individual is in competition for survival with every other individual. Individuals come together into groups because as groups they can compete more successfully for scarce resources than as individuals.

2. Marx based his theory on a two-class system. Such a system is typical of a feudal system with a landlord–peasant or priest–follower relationship. Capitalism is characterized by a multiclass system based on a large middle class which separates the upper and lower classes (Gilbert and Kahl, 1982; Lipset and Bendix, 1959; Kerbo, 1983; Krauss, 1976; Blau and Duncan, 1967). Class conflict is moderated by social mobility. Lower-class individuals identify with the value system of America, including Miller beer and the Chicago Bears; they do not identify with the peasants from the Soviet Union or China. Labor unions, political parties, and special-interest groups further reduce class conflict. Upper-, middle-, and lower-class persons belong to the same associations and to associations that interact with other associations that cut across class lines. Some writers [i.e., Dahl (1961, 1967) and Mills (1956)] found pluralistic centers of power in government, the military, and the corporation rather than one monolithic power structure. Pluralistic models of control are more realistic than are monolithic models.

   It could be argued that intraclass differences are greater than interclass differences; that is, people from different socioeconomic groups have more in common with each other than they have differences. The difference between driving a Ford and driving a Cadillac is small compared to being part of the aristocracy or being a peasant in a Latin American country. Whether one eats a steak or eats a hamburger is not too significant; not eating at all is significant.

3. Social class differences have not withered away; in fact, if anything, they are more prominent now than ever before. Social hierarchies are found among insects, fish, reptiles, and mammals, and to think that a human society could emerge as classless runs counter to all biological evidence. In fact, in the so-called communist countries such as the Soviet Union

and China, new elitist classes emerged after each revolution. The rulers of these countries live in more splendor, wealth, and power than do their counterparts in Great Britain or the United States.

4. The state has not withered away, and if anything, is more powerful today than it was in 1900. The trend has been from hundreds of states to a dozen states to two major powers (Chapter 3). Before World War I (1914) there were at least ten or twelve major powers; now there are the United States and the Soviet Union. The growth of the centralized state is related to a major economic depression and two major world wars between 1914 and 1946. State control over personal and business affairs is greater today than ever, since technological advancements, population growth, urbanization, and the general complexity of life have increased the need for centralized control. As noted in Chapter 3, the state evolved as a coordinator of social affairs at a time when agricultural practices demanded more control than the local tribal group could furnish. Centralization of control and coordination of affairs are interrelated aspects of a strong state system.

5. After the state withers away, what form does social control assume? The usual Marxian interpretation is that a socialist life in small rural communities will replace urban societies. The ideal situation is for all social control to disappear. The assumption is made that social control is evil and that humankind can live free in a pre-state Rousseauian society if only the evil state would wither away. Society and the nation state were big mistakes for humankind according to Marxian doctrine. People are good and the state is evil, and without the state, people can live in perfect harmony. This view holds that social deviance is caused by society, not by people. The view proposed in this book is that people are born with basic biological needs, drives, and urges related to food, sex, aggression, anger, and violence. The idea of a state of nature without biology contradicts everything known about biology and human nature. The state does not cause violence and conflict. By nature people are violent and aggressive. The state exists because people are violent; people are not violent because the state exists. Human beings organized themselves into social units to carry out raids and warfare on neighboring tribes or states, and it is through the mechanism of state action that individuals compete for the resources needed for survival.

6. Observing human conflict does not explain it. If we see two people fighting or killing one another, or if we see social classes and groups in conflict with one another, to explain the behavior as caused by social conflict is erroneous since the behavior and the conflict are the same thing. Fighting is behavior that is labeled conflict. Behavior is what we want to explain, and we cannot explain behavior by labeling it. We must have independent variables such as brain structure and environmental conditions which can be related to violence and aggression. Why individuals are competitive and aggressive is the question to be answered, and to observe that people are in conflict is no answer.

7. Since he ignored biological and psychological issues, Marx had no theory of individual behavior or individual human nature. Individual differences are ignored or minimized in a Marxian analysis of crime. The fact that genetics was outlawed in the Soviet Union under Stalin, as part of Lysenko's teachings (Chapter 10), indicates the inability of a Marxian economic environmentalism argument to include concepts of biology and psychology. There is no attempt to explain how the environment gets inside the individual organism, nor is there an explanation of how different individuals react to the same or a similar environment. Given a thousand unemployed males, you can expect a thousand different responses. Unemployment and crime are related, but first we must understand the mechanisms by which the environment impacts on human behavior (see Chapter 16).

8. Marx based his economics on the value of labor alone. Modern economics placed emphasis on four factors as aspects of economic systems: land, labor, capital, and management. Land, capital, and management are totally ignored in Marxian economic analysis.

Conflict and Radical Theory

Cultural conflict was a major orientation of the Chicago School, as demonstrated in the works of Sellin and Sutherland (Chapter 14). In the 1940–1980 era Vold and Turk pursued conflict theory based on competing interest groups and conflict among pluralistic power systems. Authority and power are basic to conflict theory. Conflict, rather than the consensus theory found in Durkheim, Merton, and Parsons, was the principal social process (Shoemaker, 1984; Gibbons, 1979; Siegal, 1986).

In the early 1970s a new version of conflict theory emerged based on Marxist doctrine. Sociologists identified as conflict theorists became radical theorists. In *The Child Savers*, Platt (1969) put forth a conflict interpretation of the juvenile court movement, whereas in 1974 his view had shifted to a Marxist position (Klockars, 1980). Quinney (1970) in his *Social Reality of Crime* put forth a pluralistic interest-group statement on crime, to be followed in 1974 by his *Critique of the Legal Order*, which was a Marxist radical statement on crime (Klockars, 1980; Gibbons, 1979). Similarly, in *Crime and the Legal Process*, Chambliss (1969) interpreted the vagrancy laws of England in terms of invested interest groups, whereas in a reprint of these statements in *Criminal Law in Action* (Chambliss, 1975), Chambliss changes certain passages so as to make them more in tune with Marxist doctrine (Klockars, 1980; Gibbons, 1979).

Radical criminology is an attack on capitalism and a program of major social and political upheaval. Power and social control are central issues within radical criminology, and there is a dramatic shift in radical criminology from an interest in the offender to an interest in the societal reaction to crime. Labeling theory started in that direction but then returned to the issue of why individuals become criminals. Radical criminology offers the same explanations for both legal definitions of crime and criminal careers, that is, capitalism.

As we stated above, Marxian theory is based on the evolution of the means of production and the development of a two-class system. Conflict between classes was of paramount importance in understanding criminal law and the criminal justice system. Criminal laws are to support the upper class and protect their interests in the exploitation and social control of the working class.

Radical theorists rejected positivism and science as a basic for criminology (Taylor, Walton, and Young, 1973; Quinney, 1974). Quinney (1974) wrote that LEAA and federal governmental policies fostered scientific research, which was then used to control the lower class. The real enemies of the people and the real criminals were government officials such as President Richard Nixon and Attorney General John Mitchell. This was the historical period of the Vietnam war, student protests, urban riots, racial unrest, and a general social injustices movement (Sykes, 1974; Gibbons, 1979). The radical movement was fired by and in turn fired antigovernment feelings and demonstrations. The demonstrations surrounding the trials of the "Boston Five," the "Chicago Eight," the "Oakland Seven," and the "Harrisburg Seven" came to symbolize the "underdogs" as the heroes of the movement. As mentioned in Chapter 14, labeling theory is "underdog theory," and this theme was picked up by radical criminology.

Racism, sexism, and social injustice are central to radical criminology. The Schwendingers would have criminologists study all violations of basic human rights, that is, "basic rights guaranteeing food, shelter, clothing, medical services, work, recreation, and security" (Gibbons, 1979:167).

In *Class, State, and Crime*, Quinney (1977) furthered his Marxian analysis of crime and criminals. He found rehabilitation to be a capitalistic means of controlling the masses, and he interpreted the return to deterrence, punishment, and prisons in the 1970s as a product of new crises in the capitalist system. Quinney castigates the work on deterrence, punishment, and the "justice model" as found in James Q. Wilson, Norval Morris, and Ernest van den Haag. [These works should be rejected—but for reasons other than those given by Quinney (see Chapter 8).]

Criticism of Radical Theory

Most of the criticisms of radical theory were mentioned above in our discussion of Marxian doctrine. Conflict is broader than social class conflict, there are more than two classes in industrial societies, social classes and the state system have not withered away, and radical theory is based on dogma and ideology rather than science. The focus of radical theory on social class has distorted the meaning of social class while ignoring other critical variables (Toby, 1980; Sparks, 1980; Klockars, 1980; Siegal, 1986). A major work, *Radical Criminology: The Coming Crisis* (Inciardi, 1980), reviews this material in great detail.

Klockars (1980) in his critique presented the most outspoken criticism of radical theory. He noted that there is a poverty of scholarship in radical criminology, the dogma of class conflict is a gross misunderstanding of social class, the pluralistic nature of society is ignored, and the use of state control by communist states such as the Soviet Union and China is ignored and is not subject to the same treatment as state control in the United States. The consensus around the law as found in several studies is ignored, and the Marxists present a theory of history that is ideological and moralistic rather than scientific. The radical theorists are the new prophets rather than scientists.

Marxism and science were in conflict from the very beginning of the scientific movement. Marxists rejected science and in its place put their faith in the equality of human beings and environmental determinism, and they attacked the positivists and biology (Rennie, 1978:99 ff.).

This conflict between Marxian and positivism–science is found in an article by Beirne (1979) in which he argued that radical theory needs to be judged not by scientific standards but by standards established by radical theorists. In a response to Beirne, David Greenberg (1980) refers to the Beirne concept as ''immaculate conception'' based on the idea that certain persons are privy to certain pure ideas that others do not have. Greenberg pointed out a need for empirical work in radical theory to give it more of a scientific base. This is an interesting exchange of comments, especially when one considers that Greenberg is identified with radical criminology (Greenberg, 1981).

Greenberg (1981:18) has written that Marxists believe in history and not science, and any findings must apply to a given historical period and are not universal in nature. There are no principles of criminology that apply across the various modes of production.

Crime Control Implications

The crime control implications of radical theory are obvious: Do away with social classes and the state system and crime will disappear. Criminal laws will disappear, as will the motivation to commit crimes. Under a socialist government, definitions of crime are no longer needed, since social control is no longer needed. We are asked to envision a society without control, often referred as anarchy.

One of the more unfortunate aspects of Marxian–radical criminology is the view that the state is bad, and therefore control is bad. Treatment is defined as dangerous since it is a means of controlling deserters and radicals. Drug treatments and other therapies must be outlawed since they are oppressive measures by the state to control its citizens (Cohen, 1985). Davis (1980:2) states: ''I no longer believe that the new criminology offers a viable research program.'' She then develops a sociology of social control based on removing control by the state over human behavior as found in prisons, mental institutions, and psychiatric therapies. She is opposed to diversion programs and the medicalization of deviance (making deviance a medical rather than a legal problem).

The analysis of the brain and deviant behavior (Chapters 11 and 21) makes it obvious that medical treatment of criminals is needed if we are to prevent crime. In opposition to the view I have expressed in this book, that behavior is a product of biological, psychological, and environmental forces in interaction, the radical criminologist says that the social environment alone causes crime. The radical insists on changing the social structure, whereas Jeffery says: "Both the individual and the environment must be of concern to those who wish to control crime." Greenberg (1981:18) states the radical case perfectly: "Even when individuals can be helped, the larger problem remains. To deal with crime by 'treating' individuals is like trying to empty the ocean with a bucket."

Radicals, liberals, and conservatives joined in the 1970–1980 era in opposition to research, to treatment, and to the prevention of crime. What this means is that we can stick a needle into an inmate's arm to execute him, but we cannot take blood from the inmate to see if he is suffering from a biochemical imbalance in the brain. This issue is critical to our discussions of punishment versus treatment and prevention in Chapters 18, 19, and 21.

THE STATE AND SOCIAL CONTROL

Liberalism versus Conservatism

There are basically two views of the state and its role in social control. One view holds that state control and interference should be at a minimum and that the rights of individuals are supreme; the other view holds that state control of individuals is necessary, and that the need for control takes precedent over individual needs and rights.

The utilitarians, Bentham, Locke, Mill, and Adam Smith, felt that human beings were governed by pleasure and pain, and that the purpose of government was to guarantee the innate rights of life, liberty, and property. Self-seeking individuals would maximize pleasure and minimize pain if left alone and free of government interference. Although Locke had a social contract theory, he utilized the government for as little control as necessary. The individual is good, and too much state control is bad. This is known as a laissez-faire or "let alone" policy of state intervention into private affairs. This philosophy came to be known as liberalism, or freedom of individuals from state interference whenever possible. Individual rights were important, not the rights of the state. The liberal position is based on legal definitions of crime and punishment, due process procedures, the right to a jury trial, the right not to testify against oneself, and the right to be free of ex post facto laws [see Chapter 4; also Radzinowicz (1966), Jenkins (1984), Cranston (1967), Clapp (1967), Munroe (1967), and Sprague (1967)].

As mentioned, Marxian doctrine carries the rejection of state power one step further and completely denied the need for state control. Crime and deviancy are products not of individual traits and biological tendencies but of the state system. The individual does not need control; he/she needs total freedom from state control. A stateless society is without laws, without prisons, without social control.

The other position holds that the individual in a state of nature is bad, and the state is good. Hobbes represented this theory of control when he noted that in a state of nature there was "a war of all against all," and humankind entered into a social contract to escape from a brutal state of nature. For Hobbes, the causes of deviancy are in the individual, not the state. Social control by the state is necessary for social order (Peters, 1967).

This view of human nature and the state came to be known as conservatism. Conservatism, as found in Edmund Burke and Thomas Hobbes, places great faith in state control through custom and tradition. The purpose of the state is to be guided by past tradition and to protect the status quo from sudden social changes. Whereas liberals emphasize the rights of individuals, conservatives emphasize the duties of citizen, along with discipline, authority, stability, and order (Minoque, 1967).

In terms of crime control policy, the modern position is one of advocating a strong role for the state in economic regulations, promotion of welfare, health, and education, and state intervention in the lives of individuals where the intervention is to help the poor and handicapped (in opposition to eighteenth-century liberalism, which did not use state intervention for welfare purposes). The role of the state is to provide employment and education and health care for the poor, and to provide poverty programs and social welfare programs that will reduce crime and delinquency (Jenkins, 1984; Jeffery, 1977). On the other hand, a conservative approach to crime control policy today advocates a strong central government to suppress wars and crimes, with large expenditures for military and criminal justice programs, but with less emphasis on health, education, and welfare spending. The model of crime control is "law and order." Crime control focuses on police and prisons, not on rehabilitation and social reform projects (see Chapter 8).

In the twentieth century a powerful centralized state is a given fact. The argument is not over a laissez-faire state versus an authoritative state as in the eighteenth century; the argument now is whether a strong state exists for the benefit of the upper class with low taxation, few economic regulations on business, and a powerful military and police force, or whether the state exists for the benefit of the poor with high taxes on property owners to pay for major welfare and health programs for the poor.

I discuss next several early British and American sociologists who put forth different views on social control, which have in turn influenced the manner in which sociologists and criminologists view the problem of social control and criminal law.

Herbert Spencer (1820–1903)

Spencer was an early British social philosopher who rejected Comte's organic model for an individualistic model based on Darwinian competition for survival. The laws of nature required that competition among individuals take place without interference from the state. In his *Social Statics,* Spencer (1851) stated that if people were starving to death, the state should not interfere, for otherwise the poor would live to reproduce and create even more mouths to feed in the future. Individual competition uncontrolled by the state guarantees a healthy society.

In a famous constitutional decision, Lochner v. New York (198 U.S. 45), the U.S. Supreme Court held that regulating the number of hours that an employee can work was unconstitutional since it violated the right to property and to contract for one's labor. In his famous dissenting opinion, Justice O. W. Holmes noted that "the Court need not establish Spencer's *Social Statics* as law" (Coser, 1977; Rossides, 1978).

Although Spencer and Marx both agreed that state interference is bad, they did so from opposite sides of the issue. Spencer supported a "social Darwinist" explanation of upper-class dominance for those who were superior by nature. It was through competition that the upper class gained its position. The state is not to interfere in this competitive process with artificial governmental aid in order to help the lower-class compete. Marx took the position that the state is an agency of the upper class used to control the lower class, and the state should not be allowed to protect the upper class to the disadvantage of the lower class. Since classes are based on economic forces and do not represent ability groupings, and since individuals are essentially the same in endowment, the state system and the class system will wither away.

Although Spencer did not support state interference to help the poor, he probably would have supported state control of the poor through the criminal law in order to protect competition and the rights to private property.

William Graham Sumner (1840–1910)

Sumner was a professor of sociology at Yale University, where he introduced Spencer to American audiences. Sumner was a positivist who pursued sociology as a science. Like Spencer, he was very much influenced by Darwin and the struggle for existence. He believed that humankind had basic biological drives related to sex, hunger, and fear, which motivate human behavior. In early sociology we witness a biological basis for behavior, as found in Comte and Darwin, which disappeared from sociology by the 1920s.

Sumner in *Folkways* (1906) discussed social control in terms of folkways, mores, and law. Folkways are behavioral responses to environmental situations which become customary ways of behaving, whereas mores have more of an element of right and wrong, or a basis in morality. Folkways and mores form the normative system that controls humankind, which emerges out of the struggle for survival.

Like Spencer, Sumner believed that conflict and inequality are natural, and that society cannot protect the unfit. In his book *What Social Classes Owe to Each Other* (1920), Sumner found the answer to be "nothing." He entitled one one of his essays "The Absurd Effort to Make the World Over" (Martindale, 1981).

Lester Ward (1841–1913)

Ward was a professional biologist and geologist who became involved in sociology at a late age as a result of his work in biology. Here is another example of sociology coming from biology and contradicting the mainstream of American sociology, which started with Durkheim's rejection of biology and psychology (Rossides, 1978; Martindale, 1981).

Ward found natural evolution to be based on pleasure and pain. Biological forces were blind, guided only by pleasure and pain in their attempt to survive in the struggle for existence. Ward used the example of a frog that lays 10,000 eggs, only one of which survives to adulthood.

In this struggle for survival, energy is released. Ward put forth the concept of *synergy*, or energy harnessed and guided in its use. In order to guide and direct the blind evolutionary forces of nature, humankind must use *social telesis*, whereby social science is used to improve social evolution. Telesis is the conscious control of social change. Here Ward is clearly under the influence of Comte and Comte's idea of social progress through positivism. Intervention by the state is a necessary part of social telesis. Human affairs need control by state action.

Gabriel Tarde (1843–1904)

According to Tarde, following the ideas of Baldwin, LeBon, and the social learning theorists, imitation was the basic process by which behavior is learned and controlled. In his *The Laws of Imitation* (1890/1903), Tarde related imitative behavior to close social contact, from the upper to the lower class, and from the substitution of one habit for another habit.

In his book *Penal Philosophy* (1890/1912), Tarde presented a social learning approach to social control and criminal behavior, in opposition to the biological theories of Lombroso and the geneticists, and the psychoanalytic theories of Freud (Vold and Bernard, 1985; Wilson, 1980; Martindale, 1981).

Tarde's penal philosophy was positivistic in nature; that is, sociological and psychological experts would decide on the treatment needed for each case on an individualized basis. Prisoners would be segregated from other prisoners so that they would not learn criminal behavior from one another. This idea is identical to Sutherland's theory of differential association, and Cressey (1955) made the same recommendation concerning associating criminals with non-criminals in order to produce differential association in favor of noncriminal behavior.

Edward Ross (1866–1951)

Ross, a midwestern sociologist, made the relationship of the individual to society the key issue in his writings. How are individuals socialized so that people's biological nature is controlled? Ross's best known works are *Social Control* (1901) and *Social Psychology* (1908).

Ross followed the idea of imitation as put forth by Tarde. The pillars of social control are sympathy, sociability, a sense of justice, and resentment of those who injure others. These sentiments are developed in social interaction, where imitation and suggestibility play important roles (Borgatta and Meyer, 1959; Martindale, 1982).

Methods of social control range from ridicule and public opinion to education, religion, and law. Beliefs, ceremony, symbols, and art also play critical roles in social control. Roscoe Pound, an important figure in sociological jurisprudence, used Ross's concept of social control when he (Pound) stated that law is a tool for social control and social engineering (Geis, 1964). Ross dedicated his book *Principles of Sociology* (1924) to Roscoe Pound (Gurvitch, 1945), and Pound presented these ideas on law and social control in his book *Social Control through Law* (1942).

Social Control/Bonding Theory

A contemporary version of social control theory is called social control or social bonding theory. To avoid any misunderstanding between the term "social control" as a general term and "social control theory" as a reference to a specific sociological theory called social control theory, I will use the term "social control/social bonding theory" to refer to the works of Reckless, Hirschi, and others.

Kornhauser (1978:253) concluded her survey of theories of delinquency with the statement that symbolic interactionism, anomie, and conflict theory are inadequate as theoretical perspectives, and she stated that social control/bonding theory is the best theoretical perspective now available.

Nettler (1984:313) writes: "Control theories have an advantage over the more strictly sociological explanations of crime causation in that they allow for individual differences in reaction to an environment. It is not assumed that 'culture' or 'class' or 'the family' is a huge stamping mill producing stereotyped images on the human materials." Nettler includes as aspects of social control/bonding theory, learning theory, patterns of child rearing, and social isolation.

Sociological theories of crime and delinquency as found in strain/anomie theory and cultural conflict theory assume that human beings are socialized and conformist, and the problem becomes one of explaining deviancy (Hirschi, 1969). Sociologists who assume conformity to normative standards use culture conflict or strain and anomie to explain crime and delinquency (Chapter 14). Social control/bonding theory starts with the assumption that humans are antisocial and deviant; the problem then becomes one of explaining conformity (Hirschi, 1969). For many sociologists the origin of motivation is in the environment and in the socialization process. For social control/bonding theorists the origin of motivation is in the nature of the individual (Nettler, 1984). Freud's theory of personality is such a social control theory. The interdisciplinary bioenvironmental theory of behavior presented in this book is a biosocial form of social control/bonding theory.

Walter Reckless (1973) asked the basic question: "Why are there good boys in delinquent areas?" He reverses the question from "why criminals?"

to "why honest people?" Sociological theories cannot explain individual differences, such as why some males are criminals and some are not, or why some poor people are criminals and some are not.

Reckless put forth containment theory, a form of social control/bonding theory, in which he explained criminal behavior in terms of "pushes" from within the individual and "pulls" from the environment. Pressures from within (self-concepts of a good or bad boy, goal directedness, realistic levels of aspiration), and pressures from without (peer groups, neighborhood, school) can isolate a person from a criminal career or force him/her into a criminal career.

Hirschi (1969) presented the most developed form of social control/bonding theory. He argued that individuals are deviants unless and until they are bonded to society by attachment, commitment, involvement, and belief. A person who is attached to parents, peer group, school, church, or job will not become a delinquent. Hirschi reversed the theory of differential association (Chapter 14). Whereas Sutherland stated that associations and attachments to criminal groups and families caused delinquency, Hirschi stated that attachment to family or peer group, even those that are criminal, will lead to social bonding and to conformity (Hirschi, 1969:152–155). Delinquency is a product of an absence of bonding to legitimate society, not bonding to a delinquent family or subculture. Hirschi found, for example, that the closer the tie between a boy and his father, the less he is likely to become a delinquent, regardless of class, race, or criminal background (Hirschi, 1969:95–98).

In his statement Hirschi denied the basic foundation of sociological theories of crime and delinquency, based on culture conflict and strain/anomie, a challenge that has yet to be answered twenty years later. Perhaps this is why Shoemaker and Nettler find social control/bonding theory to be of importance in the coming years.

One aspect of social control theory must be emphasized, however. Hirschi (Gottfredson and Hirschi, 1986:231) assumes that all people carry around within them the same motivations and susceptibilities to criminal behavior, and it is only the external social controls that prevent criminal behavior. Such a view of behavior makes the organism a zero, that is, no individual differences. The great lesson of modern psychology is that of individual differences (Wilson and Herrnstein, 1985). As discussed in Chapter 18, there are tremendous differences between violent career criminals, nonviolent occasional offenders, and nonoffenders.

An Integrated Theory of Social Control

In Chapters 11 and 13 I presented a learning theory of criminal behavior based on the organization of the brain and on pleasure and pain. I want to expand on this statement and to relate an interdisciplinary bioenvironmental theory of behavior to social control/bonding theory.

Social control/bonding theory starts with individual differences, pleasure and pain, and an antisocial person who needs to be bonded to society. Bentham's theory of pleasure and pain and Hobbes's theory of the nature of human nature are illustrative of this approach to social control. Freud's analysis of how pleasure in the id is controlled by the ego and superego is also a form of social control theory. Skinner's theory of learning based on reinforcement and punishment (pleasure and pain) is another example of this view of human nature.

Hirschi suggested that pleasure and pain play a major role in human behavior, but he never developed the biological or psychological bases for a pleasure-and-pain psychology. Some writers, such as Conger (1976, 1978), have suggested a close relationship between social learning theory, social exchange theory, and social control theory.

The theory of human nature presented in this book, one based on genetics, brain function, and learning in interaction with the environment, is a theory of antisocial persons who must be socialized through social control. Bentham, Hobbes, Freud, and Skinner have outlined in detail the several factors found in such a theory of human nature. Each organism interacts with the environment by means of the brain and learning. People survive through mechanisms of pleasure and pain since the pleasure and pain centers of the brain control motivation, and therefore, responses to the environment. The problem of social order as introduced at the beginning of this chapter is based on the absence of a genetic code for innate and stereotypic responses in human beings. In place of genes, human beings create norms, exchange rewards and punishments, and have laws backed by force and coercion. Norms are not self-enforcing through internalization as is often assumed by sociologists. Norms must be enforced; they must be backed by sanctions of pleasure and pain. Norms involved both exchange and reciprocity and physical force and coercion. Every social group or institution, from the peer group to the family to the economy to the school to the state, uses rewards and punishments to control behavior. If norms were self-enforcing, we would not need the police and armies, nor would we need to punish people for their behavior on the job or while in school. We pay those who work and not those who do not work. We give passing grades and degrees to those who follow the normative structure of the educational system. We make failures and dropouts of those who do not obey the rules.

The connecting link between individual psychology and social control is pleasure and pain. If we had a specie of animal that did not respond to pleasure and pain, we would have to control the animal by means other than pleasure and pain. All known species are controlled through pleasure and pain; cats and dogs and horses and lions want to be fed and to escape pain. This is why the procedures of operant conditioning are so powerful in behavioral control (Chapter 13).

The structure of the organism and social control are like a lock and key. To put it another way, the term "social control" means controlling the environmental contingencies for behavior in such a way as to control the pleasure and pain available to the individual. Those who control rewards and punishments control human behavior.

SUMMARY AND CONCLUSIONS

Social control theory deals with two different types of problems: (1) the nature of human nature, and (2) the nature of the state. These issues are interrelated in the sense that the nature of human nature determines the nature of the state. One theoretical orientation holds that people are good and the state is bad; the other holds that the state is good and the individual is bad. Sociologists and criminologists accept or reject social control by the state depending on their views of human nature.

Social control has been analyzed in terms of (1) normative structures, (2) exchange and reciprocity, and (3) force and coercion. Each of these systems of control can in turn be viewed as social control through pleasure and pain. Norms are not self-enforcing; they must be enforced by sanctions. Exchange theory views pleasure and pain as basic to human behavior. Law that is based on force and coercion also uses pleasure and pain as sanctions.

The relationship of sociology to law was reviewed in terms of the work of Comte, Durkheim, Weber, and Marx. Sociological theories of social control were summarized. Two basic sociological theories of deviance developed from the analysis of social control, the conflict and radical theory of deviance as found in Marxian writings, and the social control/bonding theory of deviance as found in the works of Reckless and Hirschi.

Social control ultimately resides in the brain of each person, since it is the brain that controls response patterns. Whatever control mechanisms are set up in society must be processed by the brain. Since the brain works on a pleasure/pain basis, the types of social controls used by society must ultimately be based on pleasure and pain. This is consistent with our pleasure-and-pain theory of criminal behavior as presented in Chapter 13.

FURTHER STUDIES

Courses in the sociology of law and social control are offered in sociology departments. Related courses may be found in schools of criminology and criminal justice.

REFERENCES

ALLEE, W. C. (1951). *Cooperation among Animals*. New York: Henry Schuman.
BEIRNE, P. (1979). ''Empiricism and the Critique of Marxism on Law and Crime.'' *Social Problems*, 26(4):373–385, April.

BENN, S. (1967). "State." In *Encyclopedia of Philosophy*, Vol. 8, ed. P. Edwards. New York: Macmillan.

BLAU, P., and O. D. DUNCAN (1967). *The American Occupational Structure*. New York: Wiley.

BORGATTA, E. F., and H. J. Meyer (1959). *Social Control and the Foundations of Sociology*. Boston: Beacon Press.

CHAMBLISS, W. (1969). *Crime and the Legal Process*. New York: McGraw-Hill.

CHAMBLISS, W. (1975). *Criminal Law in Action*. Santa Barbara, Calif.: Hamilton.

CLAPP, J. G. (1967). "Locke, John." In *Encyclopedia of Philosophy*, Vol. 4, ed. P. Edwards. New York: Macmillan.

COHEN, S. (1985). *Visions of Social Control*. Cambridge: Polity Press.

COLE, G. D. H. (1950). *The Social Contract*. New York: E. P. Dutton.

COLE, M. (1967). "Socialism." In *Encyclopedia of Philosophy*, Vol. 8, ed. P. Edwards. New York: Macmillan.

CONGER, R. D. (1976). "Social Control and Social Learning Models of Delinquent Behavior: A Synthesis." *Criminology*, 14:17–40.

CONGER, R. D. (1978). "From Social Learning to Criminal Behavior." In *Crime, Law, and Sanctions*, ed. M. D. Krohn and R. Akers. Beverly Hills, Calif.: Sage.

COSER, L. (1977). *Masters of Sociological Thought*. New York: Harcourt Brace Jovanovich.

COSER, L. A. (1982). "The Notion of Control in Sociological Theory." In *Social Control*, ed. J. P. Gibbs. Beverly Hills, Calif.: Sage.

CRANSTON, M. (1967). "Liberalism." In *Encyclopedia of Philosophy*, Vol. 4, ed. P. Edwards. New York: Macmillan.

CRESSEY, D. R. (1955). "Changing Criminals: The Application of the Theory of Differential Association." *American Journal of Sociology*, 61:116–120.

DAHL, R. (1961). *Who Governs*. New Haven, Conn.: Yale University Press.

DAHL, R. (1967). *Pluralistic Democracy in the United States*. Skokie, Ill.: Rand McNally.

DAVIS, N. J. (1980). *Sociological Constructions of Deviance*. Dubuque, Iowa: Wm. C. Brown.

DURKHEIM, E. (1893/1956). *The Division of Labor in Society*. New York: Free Press.

ELLIS, D. P. (1971). "The Hobbesian Problem of Order: A Critical Appraisal of the Normative Solution." *American Sociological Review*, 36(4):692–699, August.

GEIS, G. (1964). "Sociology and Jurisprudence: Admixture of Lore and Law." *Kentucky Law Journal*, 52:267–293, Winter.

GERGEN, R. J., and M. M. Gergen (1981). *Social Psychology*. New York: Harcourt Brace Jovanovich.

GIBBONS, D. (1979). *The Criminological Enterprise*. Englewood Cliffs, N.J.: Prentice-Hall.

GIBBS, J. P. (1982). *Social Control*. Beverly Hills, Calif.: Sage.

GILBERT, D., and J. A. KAHL, (1982). *The American Class Structure*. Homewood, Ill.: Dorsey Press.

GOLDSTEIN, J. H. (1980). *Social Psychology*. New York: Academic Press.

GOTTFREDSON, M., and T. HIRSCHI (1986). "The True Value of Lambda Would Appear to Be Zero: An Essay on Career Animals, Criminal Careers, Selective Incapacitation, Cohort Studies, and Related Topics." *Criminology*, 24(2):213–234.

GREENBERG, D. (1980). "A Critique of the Immaculate Conception: A Comment on Beirne." *Social Problems*, 27(4):476–77, April.

GREENBERG, D. (1981). *Crime and Capitalism*. Palo Alto, Calif.: Mayfield Publishing Company.

GRIMSLEY, K. (1967). "Rousseau, Jean-Jacques." In *Encyclopedia of Philosophy*, Vol. 7, ed. P. Edwards. New York: Macmillan.

GURVITCH, G. (1942). *Sociology of Law*. New York: Philosophical Library.

GURVITCH, G. (1945). "Social Control." In *Twentieth Century Sociology*, ed. G. Gurvitch and W. E. Moore. New York: Philosophical Library.

GURVITCH, G., and W. E. Moore (1945). *Twentieth Century Sociology*. New York: Philosophical Library.

HIRSCHI, T. (1969). *Causes of Delinquency*. Berkeley: University of California Press.

HOMANS, G. C. (1961). *Social Behavior: Its Elementary Forms*. New York: Harcourt Brace Jovanovich.

INCIARDI, J. (1980). *Radical Criminology: The Coming Crisis*. Beverly Hills, Calif.: Sage.

JEFFERY, C. R. (1977). *Crime Prevention through Environmental Design*. Beverly Hills, Calif.: Sage.

JENKINS, P. (1984). *Crime and Justice*. Monterey, Calif.: Brooks/Cole.

KEBRO, H. R. (1983). *Social Stratification and Inequality*. New York: McGraw-Hill.

KLOCKARS, C. (1980). "The Contemporary Crisis of Marxist Criminology." In *Radical Criminology: The Coming Crisis*, ed. J. Inciardi. Beverly Hills, Calif.: Sage.

KORNHAUSER, R. (1978). *Social Sources of Delinquency*. Chicago: University of Chicago Press.

KRAUSS, I. C. (1976). *Stratification and Inequality*. New York: Free Press.

KROPOTKIN, P. (1902/1955). *Mutual Aid*. Boston: Extending Horizons Books.

LIPSET, S. and R. BENDIX (1959). *Social Mobility in Industrial Society*. Berkeley: University of California Press.

MALINOWSKI, B. (1926). *Crime and Custom in Savage Society*. London: Kegan Paul, Trench, Trubner & Co.

MARTINDALE, D. (1981). *The Nature and Types of Sociological Theory*, 2nd ed. Boston: Houghton Mifflin.

MASTERS, R. D. (1978). *Rousseau: On the Social Contract*. New York: St. Martin's Press.

MCINNES, N. (1967a). "Marx, Karl." In *Encyclopedia of Philosophy*, Vol. 5, ed. P. Edwards. New York: Macmillan.

MCINNES, M. (1967b). "Marxist Philosophy." In *Encyclopedia of Philosophy*, Vol. 5, ed. P. Edwards. New York: Macmillan.

MILLS, C.W. (1956). *The Power Elite*. New York: Oxford University Press.

MINOQUE, K. (1967). "Conservatism." In *Encyclopedia of Philosophy*, Vol. 2, ed. P. Edwards. New York: Macmillan.

MONRO, D. H. (1967). "Bentham, Jeremy." In *Encyclopedia of Philosophy*, Vol. 1, ed. P. Edwards. New York: Macmillan.

NETTLER, G. (1984). *Explaining Crime*, 3rd ed. New York: McGraw-Hill.

PETERS, R. S. (1967). "Hobbes, Thomas." In *Encyclopedia of Philosophy*, Vol. 4, ed. P. Edwards. New York: Macmillan.

PLATT, A. M. (1969). *The Child Savers*. Chicago: University of Chicago Press.

POPENOE, D. (1980). *Sociology*, 4th ed. Englewood Cliffs, N.J.: Prentice Hall.

POUND, R. (1942). *Social Control through Law*. New Haven, Conn.: Yale University Press.

POUND, R. (1945). "Sociology of Law." In *Twentieth Century Sociology*, ed. G. Gurvitch and W. E. Moore. New York: Philosophical Library.

QUINNEY, R. (1970). *The Social Reality of Crime*. Boston: Little, Brown.

QUINNEY, R. (1974). *Critique of Legal Order*. Boston: Little, Brown.

QUINNEY, R. (1977). *Class, State, and Crime*. New York: David McKay.

RADZINOWICZ, L. (1966). *Ideology and Crime*. New York: Columbia University Press.

RECKLESS, W. C. (1973). *The Crime Problem*, 5th ed. Englewood Cliffs, N.J.: Prentice Hall.

RENNIE, Y. (1978). *The Search for Criminal Man*. Lexington, Mass.: Lexington Books.

RITZER, G. (1980). *Sociology: A Multiple Paradigm Science*. Boston: Allyn and Bacon.

RITZER, G. (1983). *Sociological Theory*. New York: Alfred A. Knopf.

ROSS, E. A. (1901). *Social Control*. New York: Macmillan.

ROSS, E. A. (1908). *Social Psychology*. New York: Macmillan.

ROSS, E. A. (1924). *Principles of Sociology*. New York: Century.

ROSSIDES, D. W. (1978). *The History and Nature of Sociological Theory*. Boston: Houghton Mifflin.

SELZNICK, P. (1967). "Sociology of Law." In *Encyclopedia of Philosophy*, Vol. 7; ed., P. Edwards. New York: Macmillan, pp. 478–480.

SHOEMAKER, D. (1984). *Theories of Delinquency*. New York: Oxford University Press.

SIEGAL, L. (1986). *Criminology*, 2nd ed. St. Paul, Minn.: West Publishing Co.

SKOLNICK, J. (1965). "Trends in American Sociology of Law." *Social Problems*, 13(1):1–56, Law and Society Supplement, Summer.

SMART, J. J. C. (1967). "Utilitarianism." In *Encyclopedia of Philosophy*, Vol. 8, ed. P. Edwards. New York: Macmillan.

SPARKS, R. F. (1980). "A Critique of Marxist Criminology." In *Crime and Justice*, Vol. 2, ed. N. Morris and M. Tonry. Chicago: University of Chicago Press.

SPENCER, H. (1851). *Social Statics*. London: Chapman.

SPENCER, M. (1976). *Foundations of Modern Sociology*. Englewood Cliffs, N.J.: Prentice Hall.

SPRAGUE, E. (1967). "Smith, Adam." In *Encyclopedia of Philosophy*, Vol. 7, ed. P. Edwards. New York: Macmillan.

SUMNER, W. G. (1906). *Folkways*. Boston: Ginn & Company.

SUMNER, W. G. (1920). *What Social Classes Owe to Each Other*. New York: Harper.

SYKES, G. M. (1974). "The Rise of Critical Criminology." *Journal of Criminal Law and Criminology*, 65:211, June.

TARDE, G. (1890/1903). *The Laws of Imitation*. New York: Holt.

TARDE, G. (1890/1912). *Penal Philosophy*. Boston: Little, Brown (translation).

TAYLOR, I., P. WALTON, and J. YOUNG, (1973). *The New Criminology*. London: Routledge & Kegan Paul.

THIBAUT, J. W., and H. H. KELLEY (1959). *The Social Psychology of Groups*. New York: Wiley.

THIBAUT, J. W., and H. H. KELLEY (1978). *Interpersonal Relations*. New York: Wiley.

TIMASHEFF, N. S. (1939). *An Introduction to the Sociology of Law*. Cambridge, Mass.: Harvard University Press.

TOBY, J. (1980). "The New Criminology Is the Old Balony." In *Radical Criminology: The Coming Crisis*, ed. J. Inciardi. Beverly Hills, Calif.: Sage.

TURNER, J. H. (1982). *The Structure of Sociological Theory*. Homewood, Ill.: Dorsey Press.

VOLD, G. B., and T. J. BERNARD (1986). *Theoretical Criminology*, 3rd ed. New York: Oxford University Press.

WHEELER, W. M. (1928). *The Social Insects*. New York: Harcourt, Brace.

WILSON, E. O. (1975). *Sociobiology*. Cambridge, Mass.: Harvard University Press.

WILSON, J. Q., and R. HERRNSTEIN (1985). *Crime and Human Nature*. New York: Simon & Schuster.

YINGER, M. (1977). "Countercultures." *American Sociological Review*, 42(6):833–853, December.

QUESTIONS

1. What basic models exist for social control?
2. Why does the human animal need social control?
3. What was Comte's contribution to the sociology of law?
4. How did Durkheim explain the emergence of criminal law? Of tort law?
5. Discuss Weber's concept of legitimate authority.
6. What was Marx's explanation of criminal law?
7. What are the implications for crime control of Marxian and radical criminology?
8. Compare and contrast the positions taken on social control by Spencer, Ward, and Tarde.
9. What is meant by "social control/bonding theory"?

Biosocial and Demographic Variables   **16**

INTRODUCTION

Biosocial and demographic variables include those variables associated with age, social class, race, education, the economic system, the family, and the mass media. These variables represent biological, psychological, and social variables in interaction. Age, for example, is biological, psychological, and social. These variables also interact with one another, and it is difficult to measure the contribution of any one variable to criminal behavior because of the interaction process.

Sociological criminology regards these variables as the cornerstone for theorizing about criminal behavior (see Chapter 14). For years it has been observed that the typical criminal is a young adult male, 15 to 21 years of age, lower socioeconomic status, and from a minority group, usually black. He was undereducated, unemployed or underemployed, and from a broken home.

These conclusions are based on aggregate data: how many males are criminal, or how many blacks are criminal. Such data reflect the *prevalence* rate, or the number of persons in a population who have committed crimes. The *incidence* rate consists of individual-level data, and gives the rate at which individual offenders commit crimes (Farrington, Ohlin, and Wilson, 1986). There is a great difference in aggregate-level data and individual data. Nettler (1984:100–104) has labeled aggregate data the "aggregative fallacy," that is, drawing conclusions about individuals from aggregate data. This is also known in the literature as the "ecological fallacy" (Robinson, 1950; Alker, 1969). "The assumption that correlations among aggregates describe associations between events among individuals is sometimes true, sometimes false, and at all times to be questioned. We do learn things about individuals by studying groups; this is the value of epidemiological research. But it is recommended that the study of aggregates be complemented by the study of individuals'' (Nettler, 1984:101).

The reason for the aggregative or ecological fallacy was discussed earlier in this book. Behavior is a product of the brain, not the environment. For behavior to occur, the environment, including social class, education, and age as a social role, must enter the brain and be processed:

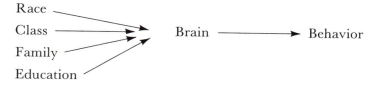

The model of behavior used in this chapter to understand how these variables affect criminal behavior is the Environment × Organism (brain) × Environment model of behavior developed in earlier chapters.

AGE

Age: Biological, Psychological, or Social?

Age is often treated as a social variable (i.e., social roles and social expectations); however, age is obviously a biological and a psychological variable as well. The social meanings attached to age by various cultures are part of the socialization process. Every society, even the most primitive, has age and sex differentiations in its division of labor. The young are treated differently from adults, as are the elderly.

Age involves maturation from infancy and helplessness to adulthood and independence. Many biological and physiological changes occur in the individual as he/she matures from infancy to adolescence. These include major sexual and/or hormonal changes during adolescence. Age and sex obviously interact, since males and females mature differently and are treated differently in social situations.

Age and Crime

The typical age curve for crime is a rapid increase in crime from age 12 on, with peaking during years 15 to 21, followed by a sharp decline after age 25. Those 15 to 16 years old have a high rate of arrest for burglary, larceny, and motor vehicle theft, and those 17 to 21 have a high arrest rate for homicide, rape, robbery, and drug violations. Although the overall crime rate declines after age 21, there is an increase in embezzlement, fraud, gambling, and driving under the influence of alcohol in later years (Greenberg, 1983; Wilson and Herrnstein, 1985).

Rowe and Tittle (1977) found that the effect of age on crime rates was robust and independent of other variables, such as education, occupation, and family. Greenberg (1977, 1985) argued that the usual sociological theories do not explain the criminal behavior and age relationship, and he introduced strain and control as variables to explain the age and crime relationship. Strain occurs for adolescent males due to the fact they are excluded from the means of production and suffer from material deprivation and masculine identity anxiety. Control over adolescent behavior increases with age, since the legal penalties increase and the male is integrated into society as he grows older.

Hirschi and Gottfredson (1983) argued that sociological theories, such as those put forth by Cohen, Sutherland, Cloward and Ohlin, and Greenberg, are not adequate to explain the age/crime relationship. They noted that the age curve in relationship to crime is one in which the crime rate increases after 12 years of age, peaks at 18 to 21, and then takes a dramatic decline after 21. This age–crime curve is consistent over time and space, that is, in the eighteenth century, and in England, France, and Germany as well as the United States.

Since age in its relationship to crime is constant and invariant over time and cultures, Hirschi and Gottfredson concluded that age has a direct effect on crime rates rather than being an intervening variable or having an impact on other intervening variables so as to influence or cause criminal behavior. Age is a variable independent of all other variables. The causes of crime are the same for any age group, and there is no interaction effect from other variables, such as social class, education, or sex. Hirschi and Gottfredson condemn longitudinal studies which distort the variables related to criminal behavior, such as age.

Farrington (1986) questioned the conclusion that the age curve shows a peak at age 17 and then sharply declines. He noted that such statistics are aggregate, based on prevalence rates, not incidence rates. If one looks at age and crime in terms of incidence data, that is, the rate at which individual offenders commit crimes, one finds an entirely different age–crime curve. Longitudinal studies by Blumstein, Cohen, and others on career criminals showed quite conclusively that individual crime rates for career criminals do not peak and decrease after age 18; rather, the incidence rate is constant from onset to cessation. Farrington, using his own data, based on longitudinal data and incidence data, showed that the worst offenders at one age are the worst offenders at another age. He noted that age is not an isolated variable, but that it interacts with sex and type of crime committed. If one looks only at prevalence data, the typical age peak at 15 to 17 occurs; if one looks at the rate of offending among individuals (incidence data), the rate of offending does not decrease with age for the serious offender. Age has an impact on crime rates starting with early adolescence, but the pattern and duration of offending beyond the age of 21 vary tremendously between career offenders and occasional offenders.

Two basic points must be made concerning the age–crime relationship. First, even with prevalence data and the peaking of crime rates at 15 to 17, not everyone in that age group is criminalistic. Individual differences must still be explained. Second, the sudden and dramatic drop in crime rates after age 18 has been attributed to maturity, marriage, employment, social control, and other social variables. This sharp decline disappears when we use longitudinal studies and incidence data. Why is it that social controls, maturation, marriage, and employment are not effective for the career criminal? Again, the answer must be individual differences. Blumstein and others (1986:76) stated that ''in contrast to the patterns observed in aggregate data on population arrest rates, individual frequency rates for active offenders do not vary substantially with the demographic attributes of sex, age, or race.'' From this we must conclude that variables other than age, sex, or race are responsible for criminal behavior. Again, the answer must be individual differences. Age is a combination of biological, psychological, and environmental variables in interaction, and the impact of age on behavior will vary for each individual. Nettler (1984:104) concluded that ''to explain the 'age effect' one has to abandon sociological and sociopsychological theories of crime causation and revert to physiology, to the ways organisms differentially function with age.''

SOCIOECONOMIC STATUS

What Is Social Class?

Class has been measured in different ways: education, occupation, wealth, political power, life chances, and class consciousness. Weber referred to social position in terms of class, status, and power (Chapter 15). Marx referred to class in terms of class consciousness and one's position in respect to the means of production (Chapter 15).

Sociologists generally refer to three social classes: upper, middle, and lower. Warner and Lunt (1941) divided social classes in America into six classes: upper upper, lower upper, upper middle, lower middle, upper lower, and lower lower. Coleman and Rainwater (1978) used three classes but with divisions within each class. In their classic study, *Middletown*, Robert and Helen Lynd (1937) described six social classes.

Like age, socioeconomic status is a combination of biological, psychological, and social variables. One's position in a society can be ascribed (age and sex), that is, given at birth; or status can be achieved through achievement (education, income, occupation) after birth (Linton, 1936:115).

The way in which one behaves as a male or female, young person or old person, poor person or wealthy person, depends on the interaction of biological, psychological, and social variables. One can attain wealth and status through age and sex: a young male adult who is a tremendous athlete or musician, or a young female who is physically attractive and a successful actress or model or television personality.

Social class also interacts with family, education, occupation, and income. A wealthy family can furnish a son or daughter with a stimulating environment, a good education, a higher IQ, and a good income. These factors, in turn, allow for more education, more income, and a better occupation. A higher income can lead to a higher IQ, a better education, and a better occupation; and a higher IQ can lead to a better education, a higher income, and a better occupation. These variables are interactive and interrelated.

Socioeconomic Status and Crime

Sociological criminologists have studied the impact of socioeconomic status on crime rates in attempting to explain criminal behavior; in fact, SES is the major variable in most sociological theories of criminality (Chapter 14). Class position is usually measured objectively in terms of education, occupation, income, and residency. For youthful offenders, the class status of the parents is used.

Sociological criminologists have utilized an ecological approach to crime, looking at the number of criminals living in each area of a city (Nettler, 1984:112). The Warner and Lunt study (1941) found that 25 percent of the population was in the lower lower class, and that the lower lower class committed 65 percent of the crimes. This finding over many years and many studies has led sociologists to explain crime in terms of unemployment, poverty, and lower-class status.

The high correlation between SES and crime is based on official crime statistics, usually UCR data (Chapter 8). As was pointed out, there is a big difference between UCR data and self-report data or NCS data. UCR data, based on official police statistics, reveal high crime rates for the lower class. When self-report data are used, the relationship between SES and crime disappears or is greatly diminished. Self-report data have been interpreted to mean that SES is not critical to criminal behavior.

Tittle, Villemez, and Smith (1978) started a major controversy when they observed that official data reveal a bias against the lower class; however, if one uses self-report data, the correlation between class and crime is low. They labeled the social class and crime theory "a myth."

Hindelang, Hirschi, and Weis (1979) compared UCR official report data and self-report data and concluded that there is no discrepancy between the two measures of crime rates. Self-report studies tap less serious offenses, whereas UCR data tap more serious criminal activities. One finds class differences in favor of the lower class for serious offense but not for minor offenses. Hindelang et al. therefore concluded that there is no social or racial bias in the courts in sentencing a larger proportion of lower-class black defendants than white defendants to prison, thus creating a large number of poor blacks in the criminal justice system. Rather, UCR statistics are based on more serious offenses, and poor blacks commit more serious offenses than do middle-class whites.

Elliott and Ageton (1980), using National Youth Survey data, found class differences for serious crimes against the person and against property, but not for victimless crimes. These figures were based on incidence and not prevalence data. Braithwaite (1981) reexamined the Tittle et al. conclusions, and he came to his own conclusion that class differences do exist for official crime since lower-class people commit serious interpersonal crimes for which they are arrested and sent to prison.

Thornberry and Farnsworth (1982) found no relationship between social class and self-reported crime or official crime for juveniles, but did find a relationship between SES and crime for adult offenders. They concluded that the impact of social class on behavior varies with age.

Hindelang, Hirschi, and Weis (1981) found an absent to weak inverse relationship (the lower the class standing, the higher the crime rate) for *both* self-reported and official data. Weis (1987:74) concluded from these studies that "there is not the kind of robust relationship between social class and either self-reported or official juvenile crime that most contemporary theories of crime propose should exist."

From a review of the social class and crime literature, Hindelang (1983:180) concluded that there was a small inverse relationship between class and crime when official data are used. "No other sociological variable in the study of crime causation has been able to muster so much allegiance over so long a period with so little empirical data on individuals to sustain it" (Hindelang, 1983:180). Hindelang concluded that other variables, such as age, sex, and race, account for far more crime than does social class. He noted that Hirschi did not use social class in his theoretical work (Hindelang, 1983:180).

A summary of self-reported crimes and social class revealed that 22 studies found no relationship, 18 studies found a relationship, and 7 studies cited evidence for both a relationship and the lack of a relationship (Hagan, 1985:116).

The Seattle Youth Study (Weis, 1987:74) carried forward the study by Hindelang et al. (1981). The SYS replicated the Elliott and Ageton study using the measurements and scoring procedures of the Elliott–Ageton study. The SYS could not duplicate the Elliott and Ageton study, and the SYS study found no relationship between social class and crime. Weis (1987:90) summarized his finding by stating: "Perhaps social class as a correlate of crime is not so elusive after all—it may simply not exist as proposed or assumed by criminological theorists and researchers." The SYS also analyzed the impact of ecological areas on crime rates and found a very inconsistent weak relationship when individual-level data were used (Weis, 1987:89).

There are several reasons for this confusion over the possible impact of social class on crime rates and criminal behavior: The ecological fallacy is involved in some of the studies; the measures used of behavior (official records and self reports) are questionable; and social class involves so many different variables, such as income, education, status, residency, and occupation. It is not possible to know which variable or variables are involved in any specific behavioral pattern. Different crimes (murder, robbery, burglary) may involve different variables.

The major defect in the social class studies, as in other sociological studies, is that they do not specify the mechanisms by which social class influences behavior. Social class is an environmental variable or combination of variables, and these environmental variable(s) must affect the brain and the physical organism. Income, place of residency, education, and occupation determine the physical surroundings of individuals through such mechanisms as diet, health, medical care, quality of the air and water, the nature of diseases and injuries, and so on. For example, lower-class youths have a poor diet, have a high rate of exposure to lead and cadmium, which then enters the brain, and have a very high rate of brain trauma from accidents, fighting, and child abuse (Chapter 18). Social class has an impact on behavior through the brain. None of the social class and crime studies cited above has attempted to measure this relationship. Until we have a better understanding of human behavior and the role of the brain in human behavior, we will have fuzzy and inconsistent findings concerning the social class and crime relationship.

RACE

Race and Criminality

All official measures of crime rates show that blacks commit a higher proportion of crime than would be consistent with the number of blacks in the general population. According to the UCR, blacks commit 49 percent of murder, 48 percent of rapes, and 60 percent of robberies (Willie and Edwards, 1983; Sheley, 1985; Siegal, 1986). Blacks make up around 11 percent of the population. Using UCR data, Hindelang (1978, 1981) found blacks to have a much higher rate of crimes against the person.

Race and Crime: A Causal Relationship?

When we try to explain the high crime rate for blacks, and it must be noted that blacks are the victims of crime to a much greater extent than are whites, there is no clear consensus as to how race and crime are related. It has been noted in criminology since the early days of the University of Chicago school of sociology that certain minority groups have high rates of crime, whereas other groups have low rates of crime. Sutherland (1947) pointed out years ago that some immigrant groups have high crime rates among the second-generation youths, whereas other groups have a low rate. He noted that oriental groups have a very low crime rate in the United States, and he interpreted this in terms of urbanization, Americanization of immigrants, and the influence of social ecological areas on the learning of social norms. This is in keeping with the University of Chicago approach to sociology and social problems in terms of urbanization, Americanization, and ecological areas [Chapter 12; Wilson and Herrnstein (1985:459 ff.)].

One interpretation of black crime rates is associated with racism, discrimination, poverty, unemployment, low socioeconomic status, and criminal justice prejudice. However, the high association between being blacks and high crime rates remains, even when age, sex, and socioeconomic status are held constant. In other words, the relationship between being black and high crime rates is due to something other than these variables (Nettler, 1984:139). It has been argued that the true relationship between race and crime is confused by economic differences, personality differences, biological characteristics, and racism (Sample and Phillips, 1984; Siegal, 1986:90).

Watts and Watts (Byrne and Sampson, 1986:64) found that crime rates influence the percentage of blacks living in an area rather than the percentage of blacks living in the area influencing the crime rate. The direction of causality is turned around if this explanation is accepted. In high-crime-rate areas, non-blacks leave the area because of crime, leaving nonwhites in a high-crime-rate area. The interpretation is then made that areas with a high percentage of blacks are high-crime-rate areas, which may not be the case at all.

Wilson and Herrnstein (1985:459 ff.) observed that differences within racial groups are greater than between racial groups. Blacks are more mesomorphic, score higher on most scales of the MMPI test, and score 15 points lower on IQ tests. Wilson and Herrnstein discuss four theoretical approaches to race and crime: (1) physical and genetic differences, (2) economic opportunities and poverty, (3) inadequate socialization, and (4) the subculture of poverty. They concluded that there is no support for any of the four theories. They noted that in the 1960s the Moynihan report referred to the black family as a "tangle of pathology" because 40 percent of black families were single-parent, female-headed households living in poverty and/or on the welfare system.

Poverty and unemployment by themselves are not explanations of the black crime rate since other minority groups react to poverty in other ways. As Silverman pointed out, the war on poverty and the civil rights movement improved the condition of blacks while the black crime rate increased (Sheley, 1985:158; Wilson and Herrnstein, 1985:472 ff.). This could be due to a general increase in prosperity and therefore an increase in the number of available targets. Environmental opportunities for crime are discussed in Chapter 19. We know from many studies that the relationship between being black and crime is not due to prejudice in the criminal justice system [Nettler (1984:138), Sheley (1985:157), Siegal (1986:89); see also Chapter 8].

Finally, it can once again be observed that a socioeconomic variable such as race does not explain individual behavior. This can be viewed as an aspect of the aggregative or ecological fallacy. Studies of race and crime ignore how the environment "gets into" the individual so as to cause behavior. Individual differences are of great importance, and they have been ignored in most criminological writings, as Herrnstein and Wilson observed in their book. I can also repeat the findings on career criminals which stated that "individual frequency rates for active offenders do not vary substantially with the demographic attributes of age, sex, or race" (Blumstein et al., 1986:76). In fact, the career criminals study found that the black/white ratio was nearly 1:1 when viewed in terms of individual frequency rates rather than aggregate data (Blumstein et al., 1986:2, 70).

SCHOOLS AND EDUCATION

For years it has been observed that delinquents often come from poor educational backgrounds, including dropping out of high school before graduation. A delinquent career is often marked by truancy, behavioral problems in school, poor reading and academic abilities, and related academic problems (Wilson and Herrnstein, 1985:266 ff.; Gottfredson, 1981:424 ff.; Schafer and Polk, 1967; Office of Education, 1967:278 ff.).

Two major theoretical approaches have been used to explain how schools and education are related to crime and delinquency. One approach deals with delinquency as a characteristic of the individual; the other deals with delinquency as a characteristic of a social institution—in other words, the same two approaches to behavior that have been discussed throughout this book: the individual and the environment. It was noted in Chapter 14 that sociological criminology is divided between theories of the individual and theories of society.

The social institution approach views the school as the cause of delinquency and criminal behavior. The educational system is a failure for lower-class youths who are ill prepared by their socioeconomic background to succeed in high school. Middle-class teachers do not understand or help lower-class students. This approach is consistent with the theoretical work done by A. K. Cohen, R. Cloward, and L. Ohlin in the 1955–1960 era. Schafer and Polk (1967) and Polk and Schafer (1972) put forth this argument for the President's Commission on Law Enforcement and the Administration of Justice. They blamed the schools for delinquency, especially when schools place lower-class students in ability tracks and identify them as noncollege material. Labeling theory is used to explain the link between school failures and delinquency.

In a 1983 article, Polk (1983) again repeated the argument that schools are failures, and the tracking system and the labeling process are ways in which the educational system produces delinquents. Polk (1983:693) denied that individual biological or psychological traits of students have anything to do with the grades the students receive, with school performance, or with antisocial behaviors. He cites D. Gibbons to the effect that there is no relationship between the characteristics of individuals and school performance. Polk (1983:693) argued that low grades predict delinquency; then he argued that low grades are a result of the school system, not the individual student. The Polk approach is pure environmentalism, with the individual contributing nothing to his/her behavior. There are no genetic differences, IQ differences, ability differences, personality differences, or learning ability differences among students, according to Polk.

The individual-level approach to the school-delinquency link assumes that individual students brings something with them to the school situation which in turn influences school performance, such as genetic background, brain structure, IQ, past experiences, language and mathematical skills, and so on. A student's response to the school environment is a response to the environment; it involves the biological and psychological background of the person who is responding to the environment. Individual differences are critical.

Wilson and Herrnstein (1985:264 ff.) discuss the individual-level approach in terms of two different causal models. The *common cause* model uses the individual personality as causing both poor school performance and delinquency; the *intervening variable* model views personality as causing poor school performance, and poor school performance then causes delinquency.

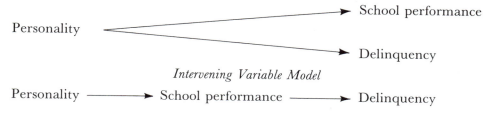

Common Cause Model

Personality → School performance

Personality → Delinquency

Intervening Variable Model

Personality → School performance → Delinquency

Hirschi (1969) and Hirschi and Hindelang (1977) came to the conclusion that low IQ influences school performance, which in turn influences delinquency:

IQ → School performance → Delinquency

When intervening variables are introduced into the explanatory model, the relationship between education and delinquency becomes blurred. School performance and education are influenced by socioeconomic status, IQ, income, occupation, and family background. In turn, education influences socioeconomic class, income, IQ, and occupation. These variables are interdependent rather than independent variables, and they influence one another through interaction. At the same time, biological and psychological variables are interacting with the social–environmental variables. The direction of causality is impossible to determine unless we use longitudinal and experimental data, and I will discuss these variables in terms of interaction rather than causation.

A major issue that has arisen in the literature pertains to the relationship between dropping out of school and delinquency. A common interpretation of the fact that delinquents are often high school dropouts is to state that the youth drops out of school, is unemployed, and then becomes a delinquent. Elliott and Voss (1974) and Bachman et al. (1978) found a strong positive relationship between delinquency and dropping out of school, except that the temporal relationship was one of delinquency and then dropping out of school. This model suggests that delinquency involves biological and psychological problems which contribute to many other behavioral problems related to dropping out of school and unemployment. Personality may contribute to both delinquency and dropping out of school. Criminologists are reluctant to regard criminal behavior as a causal or contributing factor to the social variables which they use to explain criminality (i.e., socioeconomic class, unemployment, and poverty). Class position and unemployment can be a result of as well as a cause of delinquent behavior. The causal order of the variables has not been established in criminological research.

Education and the school system can also influence delinquency rates through the usual channels hypothesized by sociologists, such as differential association, gang membership, lack of opportunity structure, status frustration and aggression, low self-esteem, income, and employment. A learning theorist would note that youths drop out of school and pursue illegal activities because of lack of reinforcement for legitimate activities. Academic behaviors are not heavily reinforced in our society, compared to sports activities, theft, gambling, and drug and alcohol consumption. A logical solution to this problem is to reinforce high school students with money, or driver's licenses, or status, for good academic performance. However, as pointed out in Chapter 13, behavioral modification programs have been failures. We can preach all we want about how desirable it is to educate and find careers for our youths, but the truth is that education is a behavioral task and we do not have the behavioral techniques necessary to turn a high school failure into a high school graduate. We must be more aware of the biological and psychological nature of the student, his/her abilities and limitations, and the role that individual differences play in the educational process.

Several successful projects have been reported in the popular media. Several millionaires, including George Kettle and Eugene Lang, have guaranteed inner-school students a college education if they finish high school. Success has been reported for such programs (William Raspberry column, *Tallahassee Democrat*, July 21, 1987). The National Alliance of Business in Boston has agreements with local high schools to provide jobs for students who show improvement in test scores and class attendance. Boston-area colleges are cooperating in admitting these students to college programs upon graduation (*USA Today*, December 24, 1987). In Rochester, New York, the school board has announced plans to select and pay a special group of teachers $45,000 to 70,000 annually to work with hard-to-reach students. The teachers would work long hours, would be concerned with the potential dropout, and would be judged on performance and not seniority (*Tallahassee Democrat*, November 8, 1987).

Greenwood (Greenwood and Zimring, 1985; Greenwood, 1986) has noted that special education programs, such as wilderness training and special schools for problem children, can be utilized in an effort to help chronic offenders. At the same time, Greenwood and Zimring (1985:60) state that studies by Coleman, Jencks, and others have shown that school background plays a minor role in educational success. What is important is the family and personality background of the student. One of the programs highly regarded by Greenwood was the Vision Quest program, an outdoor cowboy type of setting located in Tucson, Arizona. An evaluation of the program by CBS News (1988) revealed that the program had overcharged the agencies using the facility and had taken in $126 million for its former football player owner. An evaluation of the program by the San Diego probation department revealed that 92 percent of the Vision Quest boys had been rearrested within three years of release from the program. Solid evaluation of programs that are supposed to work is critical.

School systems should place more emphasis on setting up programs for the early identification of children with behavioral problems. Such programs should focus on preschool and elementary school students, and should involve routine screening for major neurological and learning defects. The types of programs that could be established are discussed in Chapter 21.

Toby (1983a, 1983b) advocated dropping compulsory attendance laws since a high compulsory attendance age creates a high rate of violence in the schools. A student who is failing in high school will often be dismissed to go to the streets faced with unemployment and frustration. If he/she remains in school, he/she will be an unhappy student.

THE FAMILY

The Family: Biological, Psychological, or Social?

The influence of the family on criminal behavior is a difficult thing to determine for the simple reason that the family is a biological, psychological, and social unit. The biological family determines the genetic background of the individual. If both the biological and social family are the same, the parents contribute both in terms of genetics and environment. For this reason, twin studies and adoption studies are used to separate out the genetic and environmental influences (Chapter 10).

Besides the direct biological relationship between parents and child, the family provides the physical and social environment within which the infant and child is nurtured. The growth and maturation of the organism is a response to the physical environment. Nutrition, the quality of life, the quality of the air and water, the pollution level are all established by the family environment. A rat reared in an impoverished environment will have a smaller and less complete brain than that of a rat reared in an enriched environment (see Chapter 11).

One critical aspect of human growth and development is related to parental care, especially maternal care. Spitz observed that children reared in hospitals and orphanages, and thus isolated from normal social contacts, suffered from a lack of normal physical and social development. Harry Harlow reared infant monkeys in isolation, which were then incapable of normal adult behaviors. John Bowlby, a British psychologist, has written extensively on maternal deprivation and its impact on human behavior. Bowlby found that maternal deprivation was one of the major factors in juvenile delinquency (Hinde, 1974:208 ff.; Feldman, 1977:38–40). A condition known as ''deprivation dwarfism'' occurs in some cases of severe neglect and deprivation where physical growth is actually stunted. Growth is dependent on the stimulation of the hypothalamus and pituitary gland, which in turn control the growth hormones

(Zimbardo and Ruch, 1975:6–7). This is an extreme example of parent–child interaction at the biological level. Psychopathy is a possible result of early child abuse and neglect (Wilson and Herrnstein, 1985:222–223).

Psychological Aspects of the Family

The family provides the basic setting for love, hatred, and learning for the developing child. Any theoretical scheme, from classical and operant conditioning to social learning theory to Freudian psychoanalysis, places great emphasis on early childhood experiences and family environment. The satisfaction of basic biological and psychological needs as expressed in Freudian psychology, and the basic pattern of reinforcement and punishment as found in classical and operant conditioning, can be used to explain the impact of the family on a child's behavior. Morality, socialization, and personality development are a product of experiences within the family.

Sheldon and Eleanor Glueck used an interdisciplinary approach to delinquency in their longitudinal studies of delinquent careers. They found that delinquents were more mesomorphic (muscular, athletic) than were the general population (Glueck and Glueck, 1956, 1962, 1974). They also found that delinquents came from family backgrounds in which the supervision of the boy by the mother was unsuitable, the discipline by the mother was lax, the cohesiveness of the family was rated low, affection for the boy by the mother was indifferent or hostile, the discipline of the boy by the father was overstrict or erratic, and the affection of the father for the boy was indifferent or hostile.

McCord (1979) found that delinquents came from families that showed poor parental supervision, lack of affection from the mother, alcoholism and a criminal career for the father, and parental conflict and aggression. West and Farrington (1973; Farrington, Ohlin, and Wilson, 1986) found that delinquents came from families in which there was low income, large family size, parents who were criminals, low IQ, neglect, harsh and erratic discipline, and parental conflict and aggression.

The lack of adequate control over the child has been emphasized by Patterson at the Oregon Social Learning Center, which was discussed in Chapter 13. According to Patterson, the families of delinquents were unskillful and unsuccessful in their use of punishment. Patterson stated that delinquent behavior will disappear if punishment is properly utilized by the parents. Behavioral control that uses punishment was reviewed critically in Chapter 13. The use of punishment is most ineffective as a behavioral control measure, especially if it is excessive and abusive. Child abuse is a major characteristic of families of delinquents (Wilson and Herrnstein, 1985:253).

Sociological Aspects of the Family

Sociologists emphasize social learning theory, role models, imitative learning, and social norms. Sutherland's theory of differential association placed importance on the learning of attitudes and values within the family and peer group context. Hirschi's social control theory is based on attachment, commitment, belief, and involvement in the bonding of the individual to society. Bonding to the family is a critical aspect of social control theory.

A structural-functional approach to delinquency as found in social opportunity theory (Cohen, Cloward, Ohlin) or in Marxist conflict theory looks at the role of the family as an aspect of the opportunity structure for youths. If a family is lower class, the youth will suffer from deprivation, a lack of opportunity, status frustration, and economic and political conflict with the class system. The importance of the family is determined by the theoretical framework used by the sociologist to explain behavior.

The Family and Criminal Behavior

In summary, the family contributes to the biological, psychological, and sociological variables involved in human behavior in various combinations and interactional patterns. The family contributes both to the organism and to the environment in interaction.

A general tentative conclusion can be reached that any weakness or defect in the genes, in brain structure, in learning and socialization patterns, in interpersonal dynamics, and in any other variable(s) related to behavior are part of the relationship between the family and criminal careers. Poor family background is a contributor to poor physical and social development. However, despite poor family backgrounds, many individuals develop into mature, well-adjusted, law-abiding citizens. A study by Werner and Smith (Wilson and Herrnstein, 1985:262) of children who survived poverty, birth defects, prenatal complications, parental discord, unemployed fathers, siblings with behavioral problems, and poor relationships with parents were a group who were "vulnerable but invincible." They did not succumb to these biological and social pressures. These children were firstborn, cuddly, active, and affectionate; they had few health problems, had close bonds with the mother during the first two years of life, and had high IQs. Individual differences are very critical in the analysis of human behavior. It is important to recognize that some people are "invincible."

Another way of looking at the impact of the family on children is to compare the occupational and social status of fathers and sons. A child inherits his/her biological nature from the family, and also inherits a social nature from the family. Blau and Duncan (Nettler, 1984:210) found that 16 percent of the son's social status is accounted for by the father's status. Jencks (Nettler, 1984:210) concluded from his study that "more than 60 percent of variation in men's school attainment is completely unaccounted for by any background characteristics." White (Nettler, 1984:211) found that less than 5 percent of the variance in individual's academic achievement is accounted for by measures of socioeconomic status; however, when aggregate data are used, the correlation between socioeconomic status and academic achievement moves to +.73, showing the fallacy of aggregate data.

THE ECONOMY

Crime and Economic Conditions

Poverty and unemployment have been major explanations of crime and criminal behavior since the early days of sociological criminology. The ecological studies of the Chicago School found that delinquents lived in slum areas and were from the lower class. The Marxist or conflict approach to criminology has argued that poverty and unemployment, as caused by the capitalistic system, are major factors in criminal behavior (Chapter 15).

The relationship between crime and economic conditions is unclear because of the many variables that are involved. The level-of-analysis problem is a major issue. Most studies of crime and the economy are at the aggregate data level, and the aggregative or ecological fallacy emerges. Aggregate data generally show a positive relationship between unemployment and crime (as unemployment increases, crime increases), whereas individual or incidence rate data do not reveal such a relationship (Nettler, 1984:128–130). Sutherland (1947:173–178) noted that the relationship between crime rates and major economic trends (periods of prosperity and depression over time) was not related to changes in crime rates, whereas crime rates were highly correlated with lower-class economic status and ecological areas; that is, people living in slum areas commit a great many crimes. Sutherland argued that where one lives and one's socioeconomic class influence one's associations with criminal and noncriminal attitudes and values, whereas major periods of prosperity or depression do not influence these associational patterns.

Glaser and Rice (1959; Glaser, 1983) found that an increase in unemployment would increase crime among 20- to 25-year-old males, whereas a period of prosperity and high employment would decrease adult crime but increase juvenile crime. They interpreted the increase in juvenile crime as related to the fact that the parents were working and were away from the home for long periods. Studies of offenders by Glaser and Pownell (Glaser, 1983) showed that offenders were often unemployed before they committed a crime, and unemployment after release from prison greatly increased the probability of recidivism and parole violations. Chaiken and Chaiken (1982) and Greenwood (1982) also found unemployment to be highly predictive of a criminal career pattern. They also found early antisocial behavior (before the usual age of employment) and heavy drug and alcohol use to be predictors of later criminal careers.

These studies raise the basic issue of whether unemployment causes criminal behavior, or whether unemployment is in itself a result of early neurological, behavioral, and/or psychological disturbances, poor school performance, heavy drug and alcohol use, and related psychological and social liabilities. Are individuals criminals because they are unemployed, or are they unemployed and criminal because of other variables related to both unemployment and criminal behavior?

West and Farrington (1977) found that delinquents are more likely to be employed than are nondelinquents. However, these delinquents were also involved in sex, gambling, alcohol, and drug addiction, indicating that delinquency is related to physiological factors associated with gambling, drugs, and alcohol abuse. Hirschi (1983:58) concluded from these studies that "delinquency predicts socioeconomic status better than socioeconomic status predicts delinquency."

Wilson and Herrnstein (1985:312 ff.) list four ways in which crime and the economy might be interrelated:

1. Unemployment can cause criminal behavior.
2. Crime and unemployment might have a common cause.
3. Affluence and not poverty might cause crime by increasing the number of goods available to be stolen or by increasing the value of criminal behavior compared to noncriminal behavior.
4. A person might be envious of another person's wealth and status, and he/she might therefore commit crimes to increase his/her social and economic status.

Farrington, Ohlin, and Wilson (1986) list the following five relationships between crime and unemployment:

1. People who are unemployed turn to crime as a means of livelihood.
2. Certain personality traits may cause both crime and unemployment.
3. People who find crime rewarding will reject legitimate employment even if it is available.
4. Affluent criminals may set role models for others for not working in legitimate businesses.
5. People who are in poverty may assume that jobs are not available, and they do not look for employment.

Freeman (1983:89 ff.) found that crime rates and economic conditions are not related over time. Ecological studies show a positive relationship but one that involves the ecological or aggregative fallacy. Where crime and unemployment are related, the relationship goes both ways: Crime causes unemployment, and unemployment causes crime.

Unemployment and the Individual Offender

Unemployment and criminal behavior are related, but the relationship is weak at best, and the mechanisms by which unemployment influences criminal behavior are not spelled out in these studies. Wilson and Herrnstein (1985:335) argue that individual factors must be taken into account. Farrington, Ohlin, and Wilson (1986:13) also argue that individual differences are critical to any criminological research effort.

An observation of a correlation between aggregate unemployment data and aggregate crime rates does not give us an explanation of the relationship. Several possible mechanisms by which unemployment influences criminal behavior can be suggested. Unemployment creates a certain physical environment for the human body, such as nutrition, lead pollution, overcrowding, physical diseases and defects, brain damage, and other neurological and medical problems associated with a poor environment. Whatever impact poverty and unemployment have on behavior, it must be by way of the brain. We noted in Chapter 11 that the brains of rats reared in an impoverished environment are small and defective. We also know that malnutrition can affect the structure and operation of the human brain (Scrimshaw and Gordon, 1968; Kolb and Whishaw, 1985:604 ff.; Dhopeshearkar, 1983).

We must focus on individual or incidence data rather than on aggregate data. Chiricos (1987) found that the most significant relationship between unemployment and crime occurred at the intracity level, the lowest level of aggregation used in his study. The closer we are to the individual level, the more confidence we can have in the findings. Chiricos used aggregate-level data rather than individual-level data, and his conclusions must be taken within the framework of the aggregative or ecological fallacy.

Grainger (Nettler, 1984:129) concluded that studies based on aggregate data give misleading results and should be abandoned. Nettler (1984:129) stated that studies using individual-level data are not available. He cited a study by Paez (Nettler, 1984:130) as an anomaly because Paez found that 66 percent of the inmates studied were working the month prior to the crime for which they were arrested, whereas 12 percent were looking for work. Orsagh (Nettler, 1984:131) summarized his review of the literature by stating: "Unemployment may effect the crime rate, but even if it does, its general effect is too slight to be measured."

Cantor and Land (1986) distinguish between the opportunity effect of unemployment and the motivational effect. When the unemployment rate is high, the amount of goods and people in circulation is decreased so that the opportunity for crime is reduced. When the unemployment rate is high, the motivation for crime is high, thus increasing the crime rate. They found that the relationship between unemployment and crime is negative; that is, the higher the one, the lower the other. They also found that this relationship was due to the opportunity effect and not the motivational effect. In other words, unemployment changes the environment within which crimes occur and not the individual who is unemployed. The opportunity theory of crime is presented in greater detail in Chapter 19.

Projects to Reduce Poverty and Unemployment

A common sociological response to unemployment and poverty is "reduce unemployment and you will reduce crime" (Nettler, 1984:131). Many attempts have been made to reduce criminal behavior through poverty programs, usually consisting of remedial education, job training, and unemployment benefits. The antipoverty, educational, and job training programs of the 1960s were marked with failure, political controversy, and corruption (Jeffery, 1977:143 ff.). We do not have the knowledge at the present time to reduce unemployment or to educate those with academic and social deficiencies.

I reviewed in Chapter 13 the difficulties with behavioral modification and delinquency prevention. The case projects established during the 1960s, and the Washington D.C. project that I established at the same time were not successful in the education or rehabilitation of delinquents. The Transitional Aid Research Project (TARP) conducted by Rossi, Berk, and Lenihan (1980; Wilson, and Herrnstein, 1985; Farrington, Ohlin, and Wilson, 1986) provided unemployment benefits for six months for a group of ex-offenders to determine if such aid would reduce the recidivism rate. Compared to a control group that did not receive the payments, the experimental group showed no significant difference in arrest rates one year later, and took much longer to find a job, and were less likely to hold a job. The project actually delayed lawful employment and may in this way have contributed to a higher crime rate.

The Manpower Demonstration Research Corporation (MDRC) Project provided job training and work experience for ex-offenders and dropouts in a carefully controlled environment. The results showed that the project did not help ex-offenders or dropouts to lead a more legitimate lifestyle (Wilson and Herrnstein, 1985:323). As has been suggested repeatedly in this book, new knowledge concerning the biological and psychological foundations of behavior must be used to analyze and change behavior that is antisocial. We must start with 2 to 6 year olds, not wait until the person is 15 or 18 to start crime prevention efforts (see Chapter 21).

THE MASS MEDIA

Imitative Learning and the Media

Social learning theory maintains that individuals learn by observing others and imitating how others behave (see Chapter 13). This is the major approach used to study the impact of the mass media (television and movies primarily) on aggressive behaviors in children. The usual study is to have a group of children watch a violent film or play and then see if the rate of violence increases. Such an interpretation of behavior (1) assumes total environmental determinism, (2) assumes that learning is an imitative process rather than a neurological process, (3) ignores types of learning other than imitation, and (4) ignores individual differences in responses to environmental stimuli.

Ball-Rokeach and DeFleur (1983) argued that the influence of the mass media on behavior does not exist in reality, and they made the observation that different people respond differently to the mass media. They also noted that individuals are much more influenced by peer groups, families, and friends than by the mass media.

Television and Violence

A major interpretation of violent behavior has been that violence is a product in part of the mass media because of the large amount of violence shown in movies and on television. With the increase in viewing of television by children, and the increase in the depiction of violence and television, there is concern that television watching can cause violence.

A report by Baker and Ball (1969) and a report by the Surgeon General's Scientific Advisory Committee on Television and Social Behavior (1972) found a link between television viewing and violence in children. Many other studies during the 1970s supported the hypothesis that such a link did in fact exist. A report in 1982 by the National Institute of Mental Health based on a survey of the literature concluded that violence as found in family conflicts, delinquency, and assaults was related to heavy television viewing of violent programs (National Institute of Mental Health, 1982; Comstock, 1982).

Huesmann (1982) analyzed the impact of television on behavior in terms of five variables:

1. Observational and imitative behavior
2. Catharsis, or the release of pent-up anger and hostility
3. Emotional and physiological arousal
4. Attitude change
5. Rationalization and justification of violence by the subject

Of the five processes, Huesmann found that observational learning and attitude change were related to aggressive behaviors, justification and physiological arousal were not proven, and catharthis as a process in aggression was disproved. It should be noted that Huesmann was classifying different forms of behavior at different levels of analysis into one explanatory scheme. Nowhere did he consider operant conditioning or classical conditioning as possible explanations of learning and aggression. He found no basis for physiological arousal, although we know that the television set has to arouse the neurons in the brain in order for behavior to occur. Imitation and attitude change are labels for neurological changes in the brain that result in aggressive behavior.

Zillman (1982) addressed the issue of physiological arousal and television watching. He noted that cortical arousal had never been measured as part of the television and violence studies. He suggested that autonomic nervous system arousal is an important aspect of violence and that this issue has never been satisfactorily explored, and he recommended research in this area.

A study by the National Broadcasting Corporation (NBC) research team (Milavsky et al., 1982) used a longitudinal panel study (interviewing a group of children over a period of time) to investigate the link between television and violence, and they concluded that there was no long-term effect by television on violent behavior. This study focused on long-term changes in behavior rather than short-term changes that might occur immediately after watching a television program.

The National Institute of Mental Health (1982) report concluded that there is no evidence for the long-term impact of television on violent behavior in children, and that some children are receptive whereas others are not. Individual differences are critical. The Report concluded: "No single study unequivocally confirms the conclusion that televised violence leads to aggressive behavior. Similarly, no single study unequivocally refutes that conclusion" (National Institute of Mental Health, 1982, Vol. 1, 89).

Conclusions

The mass media are a part of the physical environment of the individual. As such, the environment enters a person's sensory system and central nervous system, is processed by the brain, and in turn, the motor system of the brain controls the response pattern to the environment. Individual differences in brain structure, in past learning, and in the person's present state of receptivity will make for differences in responses to environmental input (see Chapter 13).

There has been some discussion in criminology of "copycat crime"; that is, a given television program will produce violence of a similar sort in persons who have watched the program. The movie *Taxi Driver* with Jodi Foster has been implicated in the attempted assassination of Ronald Reagan by John Hinckley, Jr. Other films, such as *The Wild Ones, The Deer Hunter, Doomsday Flight,* and *Born Innocent* have also been imitated by others (Hagan, 1986; Nettler, 1989). A recent example of copycat crime is *The Burning Bed,* a movie in which an abused wife kills her husband by burning him while he is asleep in bed.

The best conclusion we can reach is that a few persons who are susceptible to violence may react violently to a television program, whereas the vast majority will not. We must have a basic theory of human behavior that we use, one that recognizes the neurological basis of violence and learning, before we can fully understand the impact of television on human behavior.

SUMMARY

Although age, class, education, race, family, and the mass media are used by sociological criminologists to explain crime rates, there is an absence of significant relationships between crime rates and all these variables. Age is significant if one uses aggregate data; age is not a significant variable if individual incidence data are used. There is no agreement in sociology as to the impact of social class on crime rates. Some studies find a significant relationship; other studies find no relationship. Again, if one uses individual data, the relationship disappears.

The school system is blamed for delinquency by sociologists, who point to the failure of schools to educate lower-class youths. However, this is a pure environmentalistic approach to behavior which denies and ignores the nature of the individual and his/her personality based on genetic makeup, brain structure, personality development, and past learned experiences. Although delinquency is related to dropping out of high school, delinquency occurs before dropping out, suggesting that personality variables probably cause both dropping out of school and engaging in antisocial behaviors.

Race is related to crime on an aggregate data basis, but not on an individual data basis. The relationship of race to crime rates is not clear because of the many other variables that are related to race and crime, such as income, education, socioeconomic, class, and area of residency.

The family contributes to the genetic, psychological, and sociological makeup of an individual. It is clear that any defect in any of these processes can lead to behavioral problems. However, even with all these problems, there are children who are ''invincible''—who do not succumb to the bad events in their lives.

Unemployment is related to crime rates if aggregate data are used; it is not if individual data are used. It is not clear whether unemployment is a dependent variable, an intervening variable, or an independent variable. Unemployment can cause criminal behavior and criminal behavior can cause crime. The relationship between unemployment and crime rates is weak at best.

For career criminals, criminal activities start at the ages of 10 or 12, long before the person is employable. It is obvious that for a criminal career that starts before unemployment, unemployment did not cause, or affect, the person's criminal career.

Studies of the mass media and violence show that there is a positive relationship between media violence and violent behavior. How the media (the environment) influence behavior has never been explained. One of the major problems is that neurological learning theory and the role of the brain in behavior are ignored by these studies. The environment can affect behavior only through the brain. The same criticism can be made of studies of age, race, family, education, and unemployment. All such theories ignore the neurological foundations of learning. At present, the scientific status of all of these variables is questionable.

FURTHER STUDIES

The biosocial variables are usually discussed in criminology courses, or in sociology courses devoted to deviant behavior, social class, or race and ethnic relations. Such variables are also discussed in courses devoted to social theories of crime and criminal behavior.

REFERENCES

ALKER, H. R. (1969). ''A Typology of Ecological Fallacies.'' In *Quantitative Ecological Analysis in the Social Sciences,* ed. M. Dogan and S. Rokkan. Cambridge, Mass.: MIT Press.

BACHMAN, J. G., P. M. O'MALLEY, and J. JOHNSTON (1978). *Adolescence to Adulthood: Changes and Stability in the Lives of Young Men.* Ann Arbor: University of Michigan Institute for Social Research.

BAKER, R. K., and S. J. BALL , eds. (1969). *Violence and the Media: A Staff Report to the National Commission on the Causes and Prevention of Violence.* Washington, D.C.: U.S. Government Printing Office.

BALL-ROKEACH, S. J., and L. B. DeFLEUR (1983). "Mass Media and Crime." In *Encyclopedia of Crime and Justice,* ed. S. H. Kadish. New York: Free Press.

BLUMSTEIN, A., J. COHEN, J. A. ROTH, and C. A. VISHER, eds. (1986). *Criminal Careers and Career Criminals,* Vols. 1 and 2. Washington, D.C.: National Academy Press.

BRAITHWAITE, J. (1981). "The Myth of Social Class and Criminality Reconsidered." *American Sociological Review,* 46:35–58.

BYRNE, J. M., and R. J. SAMPSON (1986). *The Social Ecology of Crime.* New York: Springer-Verlag.

CBS NEWS (1988). "*60 Minutes: Vision Quest,*" Vol. 20, No. 43.

CANTOR, D. I., and K. C. LAND (1986). "Unemployment and Crime Rates in the Post-War II United States: A Theoretical and Empirical Analysis." *American Sociological Review* 50: 317–332.

CHAIKEN, J. M., and M. CHAIKEN (1982). *Varieties of Criminal Behavior.* Santa Monica, Calif.: Rand Corporation.

CHIRICOS, T. G. (1987). "Rates of Crime and Unemployment: An Analysis of Aggregate Research Evidence." *Social Problems,* 34:187–211.

COLEMAN, R. P., and L. RAINWATER (1978). *Social Standing in America.* New York: Basic Books.

COMSTOCK, G. (1982). "Violence in Television Content: An Overview." In *Television and Behavior: Ten Years of Scientific Progress and Implications for the Eighties,* Vol. 2. Rockville, Md.: National Institute of Mental Health.

DHOPESHEARKAR, D. (1983). *Nutrition and Brain Development.* New York: Plenum.

ELLIOTT, D., and S. AGETON (1980). "Reconciling Race and Class Differences in Self-Reported and Official Estimates of Delinquency." *American Sociological Review,* 45:95–110.

ELLIOTT, D., and H. VOSS (1974). *Delinquency and Dropout.* Lexington, Mass.: Lexington Books.

FARRINGTON, D. (1986). "Age and Crime." In *Crime and Justice,* Vol. 7, ed. M. Tonry and N. Morris. Chicago: University of Chicago Press.

FARRINGTON, D., L. OHLIN, and J. Q. WILSON (1986). *Understanding and Controlling Crime.* New York: Springer-Verlag.

FELDMAN, M. P. (1977). *Criminal Behavior: A Psychological Analysis.* London: Wiley.

FREEMAN, R. B. (1983). "Crime and Unemployment." In *Crime and Public Policy,* ed. J. Q. Wilson. San Francisco: ICS Press.

GLASER, D. (1983). "Unemployment and Crime." In *Encyclopedia of Crime and Justice,* ed. S. H. Kadish. New York: Free Press.

GLASER, D., and K. RICE (1959). "Crime, Age, and Employment." *American Sociological Review,* 24:676–686.

GLUECK, S., and E. GLUECK (1956). *Physique and Delinquency.* New York: Harper.

GLUECK, S., and E. GLUECK (1962). *Family Environment and Delinquency.* Boston: Houghton Mifflin.

GLUECK, S., and E. GLUECK (1974). *Of Delinquency and Crime.* Springfield, Ill.: Charles C Thomas.

GOTTFREDSON, G. (1981). "Schooling and Delinquency." In *New Directions in the Rehabilitation of Criminal Offender,* ed. S. E. Martin, L. B. Sechrest, and R. Redner. Washington, D.C.: National Academy Press.

GREENBERG, D. (1977). "Delinquency and the Age Structure of Society." In *Criminology Review Yearbook,* Vol. 1, ed. S. L. Messinger and E. Bittner. Beverly Hills, Calif.: Sage.

GREENBERG, D. (1983). "Age and Crime." In *Encyclopedia of Crime and Justice,* ed. S. H. Kadish. New York: Free Press.

GREENBERG, D. (1985). "Age, Crime, and Social Explanations." *American Journal of Sociology,* 91:1–21.

GREENWOOD, P. (1982). *Selective Incapacitation.* Santa Monica, Calif.: Rand Corporation.

GREENWOOD, P. (1986). *Intervention Strategies for Chronic Juvenile Offenders.* Westport, Conn.: Greenwood Press.

GREENWOOD, P., and F. ZIMRING (1985). *One More Chance.* Santa Monica, Calif.: Rand Corporation.

HAGAN, J. (1985). *Modern Criminology.* New York: McGraw-Hill.

HAGAN, F. E. (1986). *Criminology.* Chicago: Nelson-Hall Publishers.

HINDE, R. (1974). *Biological Basis of Human Behavior.* New York: McGraw-Hill.

HINDELANG, M. J. (1978). "Race and Involvement in Common Law Personal Crimes." *American Sociological Review,* 43:93–109.

HINDELANG, M. J. (1981). "Variations in Sex–Race–Age Specific Incidence Rates of Offending." *American Sociological Review,* 46:461–474.

HINDELANG, M. (1983). "Class and Crime." In *Encyclopedia of Crime and Justice,* ed. S. H. Kadish. New York: Free Press.

HINDELANG, M., T. HIRSCHI, and J. WEIS (1979). "Correlates of Delinquency: The Illusion of Discrepancy between Self-Report and Official Measures." *American Sociological Review,* 44:995–1014.

HINDELANG, M., T. HIRSCHI, and J. WEIS (1981). *Measuring Delinquency.* Beverly Hills, Calif.: Sage.

HIRSCHI, T. (1969). *Causes of Delinquency.* Berkeley: University of California Press.

HIRSCHI, T. (1983). "Crime and the Family." In *Crime and Public Policy,* ed. J. Q. Wilson. San Francisco: Institute for Contemporary Studies.

HIRSCHI, T., and M. GOTTFREDSON (1983). "Age and the Explanation of Crime." *American Journal of Sociology,* 89:552–584.

HIRSCHI, T., and M. HINDELANG (1977). "Intelligence and Delinquency: A Revisionist Review." *American Sociological Review,* 42:571–587.

HUESMANN, L. R. (1982). "Television Violence and Aggressive Behavior." In *Television and Behavior: Ten Years of Scientific Progress and Implications for the Eighties,* Vol. 2. Rockville, Md.: National Institute of Mental Health.

JEFFERY, C. R. (1977). *Crime Prevention through Environmental Design.* Beverly Hills, Calif.: Sage.

KOLB, B., and I. Q. WHISHAW (1985). *Fundamentals of Human Neuropsychology.* New York: W. H. Freeman.

LINTON, R. (1936). *The Study of Man*. New York: Appleton-Century.

LYND, R. S., and H. M. LYND (1937). *Middletown in Transition*. New York: Harcourt Brace Jovanovich.

McCORD, J. (1979). "Some Child-Rearing Antecedents of Criminal Behavior in Adult Men." *Journal of Personality and Social Psychology*, 37:1477–1486.

MILAVSKY, J. R., R. KESSLER, H. STIPP, and W. S. RUBENS (1982). "Television and Aggression: Results of a Panel Study." In *Television and Behavior: Ten Years of Scientific Progress and Implications for the Eighties*, Vol. 2. Rockville, Md.: National Institute of Mental Health.

NATIONAL INSTITUTE OF MENTAL HEALTH (1982). *Television and Behavior: Ten Years of Scientific Progress and Implications for the Eighties*. Rockville, Md.: National Institute of Mental Health.

NETTLER, G. (1984). *Explaining Crime*. New York: McGraw-Hill.

NETTLER, G. (1989). *Criminology Lessons*. Cincinnati, Oh.: Anderson.

OFFICE OF EDUCATION (1967). "Delinquency and the Schools." In *Task Force Report: Juvenile Delinquency and Youth Crime*. President's Commission on Law Enforcement and the Administration of Justice. Washington, D.C.: U.S. Government Printing Office.

POLK, K. (1983). "Education and Crime." In *Encyclopedia of Crime and Justice*, ed. S. H. Kadish. New York: Free Press.

POLK, K., and W. E. SCHAFER (1972). *Schools and Delinquency*. Englewood Cliffs, N.J.: Prentice Hall.

ROBINSON, W. S. (1950). "Ecological Correlations and Behavior of Individuals." *American Sociological Review*, 15:351–357.

ROSSI, P. H., R. A. BERK, and K. L. LENIHAN (1980). *Money, Work, and Crime*. New York: Academic Press.

ROWE, A. R., and C. TITTLE (1977). "Life Cycle Changes and Criminal Propensity." *Sociological Quarterly*, 18:223–236.

SAMPLE, B., and M. PHILLIPS (1984). "Perspectives on Race and Crime in Research and Planning." In *Criminal Justice System and Blacks*, ed. D. E. George-Abeyie. New York: Clark Boardman.

SCHAFER, W., and K. POLK (1967). "Delinquency and the Schools." In *Task Force Report: Juvenile Delinquency and Youth Crime*. President's Commission on Law Enforcement and the Administration of Justice. Washington, D.C.: U.S. Government Printing Office.

SCRIMSHAW, N., and J. E. GORDON, eds. (1968). *Malnutrition, Learning, and Behavior*. Cambridge, Mass.: MIT Press.

SHELEY, J. E. (1985). "Exploring Crime." In *America's Crime Problem*. Belmont, Calif.: Wadsworth.

SIEGAL, L. J. (1986). *Criminology*. St. Paul, Minn.: West Publishing Co.

SURGEON GENERAL'S SCIENTIFIC ADVISORY COMMITTEE ON TELEVISION AND SOCIAL BEHAVIOR (1972). *Television and Growing Up: The Impact of Televised Violence*. Washington, D.C.: U.S. Government Printing Office.

SUTHERLAND, E. H. (1947). *Principles of Criminology*. Philadelphia: J. B. Lippincott.

THORNBERRY, T., and M. FARNSWORTH (1982). "Social Correlates of Criminal Involvement." *American Sociological Review*, 47:505–518.

TITTLE, C., W. VILLEMEZ, and D. SMITH (1978). "The Myth of Social Class and Criminality: An Empirical Assessment of the Empirical Evidence." *American Sociological Review*, 43:643–656.

TOBY, J. (1983a). "Crime in the Schools." In *Crime and Public Policy*, ed. J. Q. Wilson. San Francisco: ICS Press.

TOBY, J. (1983b). "Crime in the Schools." In *Encyclopedia of Crime and Justice*, ed. S. H. Kadish. New York: Free Press.

WARNER, L., and P. S. LUNT (1941). *The Social Life of a Modern Community.* New Haven, Conn.: Yale University Press.

WEIS, J. (1987). "Social Class and Crime." In *Positive Criminology*, ed. M. R. Gottfredson and T. Hirschi. Newbury Park, Calif.: Sage.

WEST, D. J., and D. P. FARRINGTON (1973). *Who Becomes Delinquent?* London: Heinemann.

WEST, D. J., and D. P. FARRINGTON (1977). *The Delinquent Way of Life.* London: Heinemann.

WILLIE, C. V., and O. L. EDWARDS (1983). "Race and Crime." In *Encyclopedia of Crime and Justice*, ed. S. H. Kadish. New York: Free Press.

WISON, J. Q., and R. HERRNSTEIN (1985). *Crime and Human Nature.* New York: Simon & Schuster.

ZILLMAN, D. (1982). "Television Viewing and Arousal." In *Television and Behavior: Ten Years of Scientific Progress and Implications for the Eighties*, Vol. 2. Rockville, Md.: National Institute of Mental Health.

ZIMBARDO, P., and F. L. RUCH (1975). *Psychology and Life.* Glenview, Ill.: Scott, Foresman.

QUESTIONS

1. What are the differences between prevalence rates and incidence rates of criminal behavior? What is the "aggregative fallacy"?

2. What relationship does age have to crime rates as measured by aggregative data? By incidence data?

3. Socioeconomic status is measured in terms of age, sex, education, income, and occupation. How are these variables interrelated to or interactive with one another?

4. Sociologists have found a positive relationship between socioeconomic status and crime. Why have studies found this relationship, and what is the current status of the belief that SES causes crime?

5. How do sociologists explain the relationship between race and crime?

6. Is poverty an explanation of the high crime rate among blacks?

7. How does the educational system affect crime and delinquency rates?

8. Poor schools cause delinquency. Comment.

9. Does the family affect criminal and delinquent behavior through biological variables? Through social variables? Comment.

10. Unemployment causes crime. Comment.

11. How does a bioenvironmental theory of behavior explain the impact on human behavior of age, sex, race, family, schooling, and the economy?

Economic and Political Crimes 17

INTRODUCTION

In this chapter I look at crimes that have a political or economic base; that is, they involve corporations that are committing crimes or are having crimes committed against them by employees; governmental systems that are committing crimes or having crimes committed against them by citizens; and large-scale organizations organized for the purpose of illegal activities. The crimes included in this discussion are often referred to as ''white-collar crimes,'' ''political crimes,'' and ''organized or syndicate crime.''

As these types of crime are discussed it will become apparent that many of the theoretical issues discussed above are most relevant for this chapter. Two issues are especially critical: (1) whether or not the theoretical structure of criminology deals with the individual offender or the structure of society and organizations, and (2) whether or not white-collar crime, political crime, and organized crime are defined and dealt with as crime.

BUSINESS CRIMES: WHITE-COLLAR CRIME AND OCCUPATIONAL CRIME

Definitions

As discussed earlier in several chapters, legal versus social definitions of crime have been used in criminology. The concept of white-collar crime is plagued by such definitional issues. In his original work on white-collar crime, Sutherland (1940, 1945, 1949) defined it as a breach of trust by an upper-class person.

Later he included in his definition a socially injurious harm for which there was a penalty. These definitions included violations of criminal law, civil law, and administrative tribunals (Geis, 1968, 1984; Hochstedler, 1984).

In his original study Sutherland looked at the records of 70 large corporations related to violations of restraint of trade laws, misadvertising, patent and copyright infringements, rebate violations, unfair labor practices, and fraud. Of the 980 decisions against corporations, 159 or 16 percent were criminal; the rest were civil trials or administrative hearings. According to Sutherland, 90 percent of the corporations were habitual criminals and 97 percent were recidivists.

There have been many criticisms of Sutherland's concept of white-collar crime. As I indicated in Chapters 14 and 15, Sutherland rejected a legal definition of crime in order to use a social definition. Geis and Goff (Wickman and Daily, 1982) found that Sutherland used a moralistic approach to crime. He was regarded by some as a muckraker. He was an agrarian populist with socialist leanings.

Tappan, a lawyer/sociologist who defined crime in terms of legal processes (Chapter 15), argued that Sutherland did not satisfactorily differentiate crime from noncrime. Sutherland was dealing with harmful and morally objectionable behavior and not criminal behavior, and Tappan concluded that "our definition of crime cannot be rooted in epithets, in minority value judgements or prejudice, or in loose abstractions" (Tappan, 1947; Geis, 1968; Geis and Goff, 1982).

Jerome Hall (1982:275 ff.) argued for a legal definition of crime, and he found Sutherland's social definition to be inadequate. He noted that Sutherland's concept of crime covered embezzlement, fraud, larceny, bribery, restraint of trade, antitrust violations, gambling, and prostitution. Some of these acts are defined by criminal codes, some by civil procedures, and some by administrative procedures.

Hall pointed out that criminal liability is based on the concept of criminal intent (mens rea), and since a corporation is a legal entity and not a biological entity, a corporation does not possess mental processes or intent. The use of a strict liability doctrine (where intent is not required for criminal liability) is not acceptable to Hall, and he concluded that corporations cannot commit crimes. Robert G. Caldwell (1958; Geis, 1968), another lawyer/sociologist, also argued for a legal rather than a social definition of crime.

Cressey (1953) redefined crime by grouping into one social category those crimes involving "a violation of trust," and he concluded that a "nonshareable problem was the cause of violations of trust." Kitch (1983) defined economic crime as "criminal activity with significant similarity to the economic activity of normal non-criminal business," and he included in this definition both white-collar crime and organized crime.

Criminological Theory and White-Collar Crime

As I have discussed above, criminologists focus on the study of the individual offender as found in criminological positivism (Chapter 5). Sutherland himself focused on the individual offender in his theory of differential association (Chapter 14).

This same confusion exists in the area of white-collar crime. Is the focus on the individual offender or on the organization (Wheeler, 1983)? Crimes such as fraud, embezzlement, larceny, and conspiracy are committed by individuals and not corporations, and they are committed against corporations by individuals. The argument contained within the concept of white-collar crime is that powerful corporations are criminals, while at the same time corporations are the victims of crime. One of the ways out of this confusion is to differentiate occupational crime from corporate crime, as did Clinard and Quinney (1973). Occupational crime would include fraud, embezzlement, credit card fraud, and other crimes committed by people with professional status in the course of their occupational duties. It would not include crimes such as murder, rape, and robbery committed by middle- or upper-class individuals. It must also be noted that all the offenses committed by individuals are crimes within the common-law definition of crime; that is, larceny, fraud, embezzlement, and other such ''business crimes'' are property crimes within the usual definition of crime. Hall's work (1935) on theft showed how legal definitions of larceny could change to include larceny by trick and fraud (Chapter 7) as economic conditions changed.

Hirschi and Gottfredson (1987) argue that the concept of white-collar crime is a product of sociological thinking in the sense that sociologists argue that poverty causes crime and criminological theories are based on a lower class criminal. If upper class individuals are criminals, then a new theory has to be invented. They argue that criminologists do not need a different theory of crime in order to explain white-collar crime.

It would serve the field of criminology to limit white-collar crime to corporate crime, and to regard crimes committed by individuals as common-law property offenses. It serves no good theoretical purpose to differentiate the upper-class criminal from the lower-class criminal from a legal definitional point of view. The criminologist can engage in research and speculation as to why upper-class individuals are criminals, but this must be done within a legal definition of crime. If criminologists accept a social definition, they are stuck with every antisocial act that someone wants to call a crime. If we limit the term ''white-collar crime'' to corporate crime, we must determine if corporations can commit crimes, which is the next issue to be discussed.

Corporations as Criminals

When I entered Sutherland's criminology class as a graduate student, I had a degree in economics and graduate work in economics. I was surprised to hear Sutherland discussing corporate crime as white-collar crime that could be explained by differential association, since in courses in corporate finance, political and economic theory, and government regulation of business, white-collar crime was analyzed as an aspect of political and economic history, as Hall (1935) had analyzed the law of theft.

In previous chapters we discussed the evolution of the state, the growth and development of industrialization and urbanization, and the emergence of several theories of social control. The Spencerian view was that the state should not regulate business in order to help the poor since the laws of economic competition should control economic events. The Marxian position is that the state will wither away when the ruling class is no longer in power. The state did not wither away, and in fact became more powerful than ever in the twentieth century. Corporate crime is a direct result of the growth of centralized bureaucratic structures to govern economic life (corporations) and centralized structures to govern political and social life (the state system). The growth of large corporations and large government, along with the development of large powerful labor unions, was the setting within which government regulation of business occurred after the Civil War.

Federal laws were passed to regulate corporations because the growth of large corporations threatened free competition. An economic model of individual competition (which was taken from Darwin) was used to judge an economy based on corporate organization. It was automatically assumed that corporations should behave as individuals, that is, in terms of free competition in the open marketplace. I do not believe that a theory of free competition can be used in the analysis of corporate affairs, and I do not wish to use my ancient knowledge of economics to settle the issue, so I will leave it to economists to discuss the theory of free competition as applied to corporations. I will only note that laws were passed to regulate corporate activities, and these laws created what we now refer to as "corporate crime." A study of corporate crime as an aspect of the study of the sociology of law (Chapter 15) would involve an analysis of the political and economic history of the 1890–1935 era that produced this body of legislation.

During the 1880–1935 era many laws were passed regulating corporations, along with laws regulating working conditions for women and children and minimum hour and wage laws. The Sherman Antitrust Act (1890) and the Clayton Act (1914) prohibited monopolistic competition, price fixing, and price discrimination. The Federal Trade Act (1914) further outlawed unfair trade practices, and the National Labor Relations Act (1935) granted workers the right to organize and collectively bargain, and defined unfair labor practices (Kitch, 1983; Russell, 1983). This was a period of labor violence and strikes. What Sutherland labeled "white-collar crime" was a product of this legislation, and white-collar crime did not exist before the Sherman Antitrust Act.

The legislation governing corporations is of a mixed type, including criminal, civil, and administrative legal procedures. The use of criminal procedures against corporations is a very special use of the concept of crime and criminal law. Can a corporation be guilty of a crime? A corporation is a legal person, not a biological person. The criminal law requires a mind with mens rea and intent. Where does the intent exist in corporate crime? Corporations do not behave, only individuals behave. A corporation is composed of individuals. Are all employees of a corporation guilty of crime, or only the board of directors or the chief executive officer? What sanctions do we use, civil or criminal? If we use criminal sanctions, who goes to prison? We cannot put a corporation in prison, yet the purpose of criminal law is to punish and imprison. If prisons do not deter or reform criminals, and if prisons are in such a mess today, why do we wish to use prisons to help us solve the problem of corporate crime?

The concept of criminal liability for corporations must be based on some concept of corporate liability for the acts of its agents, since only individuals act, corporations do not. The concept of corporate criminal responsibility has been founded on the legal doctrine of superior orders or *respondent superior*. A corporation is responsible for the acts of agents that are (1) committed within the scope of their employment, and (2) are intended for the benefit of the corporation (Coffee, 1983). This involves an imputation of intent from an individual to a legal entity, and it downgrades the intent and blameworthiness required by the criminal law. A corporation operates under incorporation papers issued by a state and is not legally empowered to commit a crime (Coffee, 1983).

The Model Penal Code, section 2.07, defines corporate liability for a crime in three different ways. The first applies to crimes of intent where no legislative purpose to impose liability on corporations plainly appears. A corporation can be held liable for these crimes only if the offense was performed, authorized, or recklessly tolerated by the board of directors or a high corporate officer. The second applies to crimes where the legislature intended to impose corporate criminal liability. A corporation is liable for these crimes if the act falls within the master–servant rules (from tort law). The third applies to strict liability crimes where the corporation is liable without regard to whether there was any intent to benefit the corporation (Kitch, 1983:675).

Mueller (1957) pointed out the difficulties with the concept of corporate criminal liability as it developed over the past fifty years, and he emphasized that there is no such concept in civil law countries. He argued that we should not extend criminal liability where it is not needed or where we can use concepts of civil liability. He recommended that we focus on high corporate management, or "the brain center which moves the hand."

Coffee (1983) concluded his discussion of corporate liability with the observation that the issue involves an "uneasy marriage of civil and criminal concepts of responsibility that has long proved troubling to legal scholars" (Coffee, 1983:253). "The case for corporate criminal liability is problematic and, as civil enforcement procedures are formalized and enhanced, it may diminish significantly" (Coffee, 1983:263).

Frank (1984) traced the concept of corporate liability as it took place in the development of health and safety legislation in the United States. The doctrine of strict liability was used which required no mens rea, but this blurred the distinction between civil and criminal liability. The U.S. Senate also used the concept of strict liability in defining corporate responsibility for criminal activities.

Parisi (1984) wrote that corporate liability is based on the doctrine of mens rea, and the transfer of liability from individuals to corporations is based on two different theories: (1) the theory of identification by which the act of an individual is viewed as the act of the corporation, and (2) the theory of imputation, by which a corporation is viewed as liable for the acts of individual officials, and the intent of the individual transfers to the corporation. Parisi did not accept either of these legal fictions and she concluded: "Corporations don't commit crimes, but people do. There can be no justification for corporate criminal liability" (Parisi, 1984:63–64). As Cressey points out, "It is time for criminologists to eradicate this embarrassment by acknowledging that corporation crimes and organizational crimes are phantom phenomena" (Cressey, 1989:48).

Seriousness of White-Collar Crime

One line of reasoning for labeling white-collar crime as crime is that it is serious and does more damage than street crime. At the same time it is not punished as seriously as is street crime. It was estimated that in 1976 the cost of white-collar crime in the United States was $44 billion, compared to $5.1 billion for common crimes against property. There were 14,200 deaths from occupational hazards and 30,000 deaths from defective consumer products (Wickman and Dailey, 1982:xii; Hochstedler, 1984:19–20).

The position pursued by criminologists since Sutherland's time states that the high status of the white-collar criminal protects him/her from criminal prosecution. The emergence of radical theory in criminology has reinforced this viewpoint (Wickman and Dailey, 1982:259 ff.). The criminologist sympathizes with the lower-class criminal, but not with the white-collar criminal, whom he/she wants in prison (Geis, 1984:153).

The belief that white-collar criminals are treated leniently has been seriously challenged by empirical work in the past few years. Wolfgang, Short and Schrager, and Cullen, found that white-collar crime is taken as seriously as street crime (Geis, 1984:147–150). Wheeler, Weisburd, and Bode (1982) found a "very strong positive relationship between one's socioeconomic status . . . and the probability of incarceration," and that high-status white-collar offenders have been more harshly punished than have lower-class criminals (Wheeler et al., 1982:650–657). The higher the status, the more likely the person will receive a prison term. From these studies we must conclude that Sutherland was wrong about leniency and high-status offenders.

Hagan, Nagel, and Albonetti (1982) found that white-collar criminals are given more lenient sentences due to the organization of the court. The prosecutor in white-collar crime cases must have cooperation from the defendant in order to get a conviction, and this means less serious charges and more plea bargaining.

We are thus back to the original question: "Why do we use the label of crime for occupational or corporate crimes when the end result is a prison term?" "Why send white-collar criminals to prison if prisons are not good for people?" If one takes the position of defending the underdog, as many sociological theories do (Chapter 14), one can say that it is all right to put upper-class people in prison. But if prisons and deterrence and punishment are as I have described them (Chapters 8 and 9), prisons are not the answer to white-collar criminality. Block, Nold, and Sidak (1981) found that the deterrent impact of the heavy electrical equipment antitrust suit came not from criminal sanctions but from civil sanctions.

Explanations of Occupational and Corporate Crime

A major issue raised by the concept of white-collar crime is that of behavior and its causes. Why are crimes committed by individuals and/or corporations? As noted above, the concept of white-collar crime is used to refer to both individual crimes and corporate crimes.

Sutherland was a sociological positivist who wanted to explain criminal behavior in social psychological terms (Chapter 14). In his book *White Collar Crime,* Sutherland (1949:5–10), stated that the purpose of the study of white-collar crime was to prove that criminal behavior is not caused by biological or psychological pathologies, as Freud and others had suggested. He also stated that crime is not caused by poverty since white-collar criminals are from the middle and upper classes. Sutherland used his social psychological learning theory of differential association to explain white-collar crime. He used examples of a used-car salesman and a shoe salesman (thought by some to have been Sutherland himself) as examples of how individuals learn crime through differential association with criminal attitudes and values. These examples seem somewhat naive in light of the fact that the major thrust of white-collar crime analysis has been the large corporation and activities involving millions of dollars. Sutherland's own original research dealt with 70 giant corporations, not individual shoe salesmen.

Cressey (1989) argued that Sutherland treated corporations as individuals rather than as legal entities. ''Sutherland neglected to show how differential association or any other social psychological process might possibly work to produce criminal conduct in the fictitious persons called corporations'' (Cressey, 1989:39).

Sutherland was in error even when he tried to reduce white-collar crime to the level of individual behavior. There have been no major studies of the biological and psychological makeup of white-collar criminals, and we certainly do not know the biochemical and neurological functioning of these persons. Are white-collar criminals left-handed or left-brained? Are they more psychopathic than are noncriminals? Do they suffer from biochemical disorders of the brain? Is the brain of the white-collar offender as much involved in crime as is the brain of the serial murderer? How the brain is involved is the research task ahead.

It was pointed out in Chapter 13 that people are conditioned to reinforcement from the environment, such as status and money, and that such reinforcement is ultimately tied to the pleasure and pain centers of the brain.

Individual behavior is based on adaptation to the environment and survival through adaptation. The white-collar criminal seeks the same reinforcement that we all seek, as found in money and status. The corporate environment may be conducive to some types of property offenses, just as the street environment is conducive to other types of property offenses. Different environments exhibit different types of potential targets (Chapter 19). The rewards for crimes against the corporation or for crimes committed by officers of the corporation are great and the risks are small. As far as the poverty argument is concerned, money is as or more reinforcing for the rich as for the poor. Money is a powerful generalized reinforcer (Chapter 13). I have argued in this book that human beings are selfish, pleasure-seeking animals seeking pleasure over pain. The white-collar criminal is no exception to the bioenvironmental model of behavior outlined above for criminal behavior, and for behavior in general.

There is an alternative to individualistic theories of white-collar crime. Corporations are formalistic large-scale organizations, and organizational theory can be used to understand and explain corporate crime. Smith (1982:23 ff.) has argued that there is a crisis in criminological theory concerning individualistic versus organizational theories of corporate crimes. The size and position of the corporation in the competitive marketplace has a great deal to do with whether or not the officers of a corporation violate regulatory laws. The competitive position of the corporation will determine the environment within which corporate officials respond. Individuals commit crimes; the corporate structure furnishes the environment for such crimes. Smith concluded that "organized crimes . . . are the result of the process by which political restraints are placed on economic activity" (Smith, 1982:33).

Kramer (1982:79) wrote that "corporate crime is organizational crime, and its explanation calls for an organizational level of analysis." Gross (1980:52 ff.) stated that a corporation is an organization, not a person, and we need organizational theory to understand white-collar crime, not individualistic theories. The legal and economic environments within which corporations operate must be studied and understood. Gross (1980:73) ends by noting: "Clearly our ability to understand, let alone control, organizational crime requires going beyond theories of individual deterrence and punishment. We shall have to study organizations themselves and the organizational world they have created."

From her study of Medicare billing violations by Revco Drug Stores, Vaughan (1980:77) concluded that corporate violations of this type are a product of characteristics of organizations, such as size, wealth, leadership, and market position. She noted that "certain social structure arrangements exist which contribute to crime between organizations" (Vaughan, 1980:85). She recommended that criminologists study the organizational characteristics and environmental conditions of corporations, which include the conflict between free competition and profit maximization, organizational straticiation, and a normative system that supports profit maximization.

Hopkins (1980) was also very critical of Sutherland's view of white-collar crime because Sutherland focused on the criminal. He noted that there was a dearth of research on organizational behavior and corporations. Hopkins studied the Australian Government's Trade Practices Act of 1974 in terms of organization deficits rather than individual deficits, and he found such organization deficits as the flow of information from one division of the corporation to another, or the failure of management to give sales personnel adequate facts about a product.

Studies of organizational structure would be at the macro rather than micro level. I discussed in Chapter 14 the split in sociology and criminology between macro and micro studies, or social structure versus individualistic theories of crime and criminal behavior. Also, in Chapter 2 I developed a systems approach to the study of behavior, and this included social, legal, and economic levels. When we discuss white-collar crime or corporate crime we must integrate the biological, psychological, social, and legal levels of analysis. As I indicated above, the individual white-collar offender is still a biological and psychological individual, but the context within which his/her behavior occurs is the organizational structure of the corporation. To compete within the corporate structure, a person must behave so as to maximize his/her position, which in turn is related to pleasure and pain as found in basic biological and psychological needs.

Selected Corporate Crime Cases

Geis (1968:105 ff.) studied the Heavy Electrical Equipment Antitrust Case of 1961, involving several corporations, but primarily Westinghouse Corporation and General Electric Corporation. These corporations had engaged in restraint of trade practices as defined by the Sherman Antitrust Act by rigging bids on the prices of electrical equipment. Seven of the defendants, as individuals, received 30-day sentences. The court found individual liability for corporate action.

One of the major corporate criminal liability cases to emerge was the Ford Pinto case (Cullen, Maakestad, and Cavender, 1984). Ford Motor Company produced the Pinto in an attempt to compete with foreign imports from Germany and Japan, and in an effort to increase profits. The Pinto had a defect in the location of the gas tank, which could explode on impact in a rear-end collision. Ford Motor Company knew about this defect and knew it could be repaired for $11 a car, but they chose not to undergo the expense. Safety was not a concern at Ford at that time (Kramer, 1982; Cullen, Maakestad, and Cavender, 1984).

In 1978 near Elkhart, Indiana, a Ford Pinto was struck from the rear by a van, and it burst into flames, killing the three teenage girls riding in the car. Indiana criminal statutes defined homicide to include any reckless killing of another human being by a person. A corporation was defined as a person by the Indiana penal code. The prosecuting attorney brought criminal charges of reckless homicide against the Ford Motor Company rather than against individual corporate officials.

The Ford Motor Company poured a great deal of money into defending itself against the criminal charges, whereas the state of Indiana had very limited resources. At the conclusion of the trial Ford Motor Company was acquitted, mainly because there was uncertainty as to whether the Pinto car had stopped on the highway prior to being struck, and some jurors felt that any small car was hazardous. Whether or not recklessness had been established was also an issue (Cullen et al., 1984).

A Marxist/conflict interpretation of the Ford Pinto case was presented by Cubbernuss and Thompson (1983). They cited Quinney, Chambliss, and Platt to the effect that law is controlled and used by the upper class to control the lower class (Chapter 15), and therefore criminal law cannot be used successful against corporations that commit crimes. They noted that Ford Motor Company made contributions to political organizations and therefore helped to control legislation regulating automobile safety.

Cubbernuss and Thompson (1983:132–133) interpret the legal trial of Ford Motor Company as ''formal rationality of the legal system as a means of determining corporate responsibility.'' According to Cubbernuss and Thompson, the lawyers for Ford Motor Company defined corporate liability in terms of the letter of the law, and the judge acted within the letter of the law while ignoring the complexities of the case. ''The formal rationality of both the law and Ford, a complex organization, functioned to create a definition of corporate responsibility that was largely ahistorical and very narrow'' (Cubbernuss and Thompson, 1983:135). They go on to argue that we need a broad view of corporate responsibility based on social justice and social responsibility, not on narrow legal definitions.

The Marxist/conflict approach to criminal law was discussed in Chapter 15. It has been noted that nonlegal definitions of crime based on social ideologies pose serious problems for criminologists, as Hall, Tappan, Caldwell, Jeffery, and others have observed. It is difficult to frame a concept of corporate legal responsibility based on broad concepts of social justice, especially since there are many definitions of social justice and social responsibility.

Starting in May 1986, a number of arrests and charges of insider trading on the New York Stock Exchange were made. Those charged include a number of prominent Wall Street brokers, such as Dennis Levine of Drexel, Burnham Lambert; Martin Siegal of Kidder, Peabody and Company; and Ivan Boesky, a Wall Street arbitrageur. Boesky paid a fine of $100 million (*USA Today*, February 16, 1987, February 17, 1987).

In April 1987, federal drug agents arrested 19 stockbrokers on charges of exchanging stocks, customer lists, and tips on the stock market for cocaine (*The Miami Herald*, April 17, 1987). In June 1987, Chrysler Corporation and two of its executives were indicted for fraud and conspiracy on charges of disconnecting the odometers on cars and then selling these cars as new cars. It was a routine practice to disconnect the odometers on cars driven by Chrysler executives (*Tallahassee Democrat*, June 25, 1987).

ORGANIZED CRIME

Historical Background: Urban America

Organized crime is even more difficult to define and delimit than white-collar crime and corporate crime since it involves legitimate and illegitimate business activities as well as political activities. The same historical variables present for the emergence of white-collar crime existed for organized crime, and they emerged in the same period (1880–1920).

As discussed in Chapter 3, the state emerged as a major form of social control when other social units, such as the family and church, could no longer coordinate the efforts of an emerging agricultural and industrial society. American sociology and criminology (Chapter 14) developed as a part of the social transition from rural to urban, and from Protestant to Catholic and Jewish. The rural Protestant ethnic and religious social structure, based on a fundamentalist religion, morality, and individualism, was challenged by the urban Catholic/Jewish setting which emerged in the United States after the Civil War (Callow, 1976; Banfield and Wilson, 1963).

Both white-collar crime and organized crime emerged out of this historical period. White-collar crime emerged from the Sherman Antitrust Act and other legislation based on rural Protestant American value systems. Organized crime was the product of two major pieces of federal legislation; the 18th amendment to the Constitution (1920), which prohibited the manufacture, sale, or transportation of liquors; and the Harrison Act (1914), which required that a special tax be paid to the Treasury Department for the importation, manufacture, and sale of cocaine and opiate drugs. These two major pieces of legislation came within six years of one another, and they outlawed or restricted the use of alcohol and other drugs (alcohol is a drug) which were in heavy demand by the general public. Drug use is based biologically, in the structure of the brain (Chapter 18). The main point is that a primary source of biopsychological reinforcement was made illegal for millions of people.

The major pressure for prohibition came from rural Protestant America, where drugs and alcohol were viewed as immoral and sinful (Abadinsky, 1985:91). It is critical to understand that criminal law can create crime, not only in the sense of defining the limits of criminal behavior (Chapters 4 and 15), but also in the sense of organizing human behavior for purposes of violating the law. Because of the legal regulations on drugs, illegal activities developed to satisfy the demand for these substances.

To understand organized crime we must understand the political and social organization of urban America after 1870. These new urban areas were populated by eastern and southern Europeans (Polish, Jewish, Italian, Greek), as opposed to earlier migrations from northern Europe (England, Ireland, Germany, Norway, Sweden). The Jewish and Italian immigrants formed the basis for urban America with their ghettoes in Chicago and New York City.

Early immigrant life, such as the Irish who emigrated from Ireland to Boston and New York City during the Irish potato famine in the 1840s, revolved around the saloon or tavern, which was a place for males to gather for recreation (male bonding is very common among primates). These saloons also acted as a center for local politics, and many of the Irish entered political life as policemen.

Political machines dominated by ward bosses emerged in the city. These political machines were made up of a coalition of Irish, Jewish, Italian, Polish, and other urban immigrant ethnic groups. These groups, along with the South, formed the heart of the Democratic party, which supported F. D. Roosevelt for president in 1932 (Abadinsky, 1985; Stedman, 1972; Callow, 1976; Banfield and Wilson, 1963). The role of the ward boss was to control votes for the Democratic party in return for favors, such as turkeys on Thanksgiving Day, jobs, help in getting welfare payments, help in getting garbage picked up, and so on.

Notable political machines were the Pendergrast machine in Kansas City, which produced Harry Truman; Big Bill Thompson and Tony Cermak in Chicago; William (Boss) Tweed, head of Tammany Hall in New York City; Carmen DeSapio of New York City; Frank Hague of Jersey City; Richard Daley of Chicago; and James M. Curley of Boston (Banfield and Wilson, 1963; Callow, 1976; Stedman, 1972; Gardiner and Olson, 1974). Boston produced John F. Kennedy and Thomas (Tip) O'Neil as prominent politicians in the 1960–1980 era.

The ethnic political machines that were organized to rule local urban political life gave ethnic groups control over the political and business activities of the city, including gambling, liquor, and prostitution. Jewish organized crime leaders emerged in New York City around Arnold Rothstein, Louis Buchalter, Meyer Lansky, and Ben Siegal. The Italian crime figures included Lucky Luciano, Frank Costello, Vito Genovese, Albert Anastasia, Carlo Gambino, and Joseph Bonanno. These groups were often at war with one another and many of these leaders were killed in "gangland wars." After prohibition the O'Banion gang (Irish) and the Bugs Moran gang vied with the Al Capone (Italian) gang for control of Chicago (Abadinsky, 1985).

Definition of Organized Crime

Cressey, in his report for the Task Force on Organized Crime (President's Commission on Law Enforcement and the Administration of Justice, 1967:58–59), defined organized crime in terms of a business venture or organization based on corruption and the use of physical force for enforcement. The core of organized crime is the supplying of illegal goods and services, such as gambling, narcotics, racketeering, prostitution, and theft to the general public, which demands these services (Abadinsky, 1985).

The popular view of organized crime is the "ethnic conspiracy" view. This theory holds that there is a national organization called the Mafia which controls major criminal activities in the United States. The Mafia is composed of families that moved from Sicily to the United States after 1870 and settled in the urban areas of the United States. There are 24 families that rule organized crime as a national syndicate governed by a commission of crime lords or bosses, referred to in movies and popular books as the "Godfather" (Abadinsky, 1985; Morash, 1984; Ianni and Reuss-Ianni, 1983).

The Mafia is portrayed as having a corporate structure and a bureaucratic system, from a boss to lieutenants to soldiers. The organized crime syndicate is based on conspiracies; violence; discipline; political graft and corruption; monopolistic control of gambling, vice, and liquor; and a code of rules based on honor (the movie *Prizzi's Honor* had this theme).

This Italian confederation conspiracy argument was put forth by U.S. Senate Investigating Committees headed by Senator Kefauver (1951) and Senator McClellan (1962). A minor crime figure, Joseph Valachi, testified before the McClellan Committee that organized crime was in the hands of a national conspiracy called the Cosa Nostra. The argument for the existence of a Mafia or national conspiracy controlled by Italian crime lords was accepted by the *Task Force Report: Organized Crime*, especially in the consultant's report by D. R. Cressey. Cressey (1969) also used the Valachi story as a basis for his book on organized crime. Law enforcement agencies such as the Federal Bureau of Investigation also used the concept of a national conspiracy in fighting organized crime.

There has been a shortage of scholarly studies of organized crime. Block (1980), Smith (1975), and Hawkins (1969) found no evidence to support the ethnic conspiracy theory of a Mafia and organized crime (Albanese, 1983; Morash, 1984). Ianni and Reuss-Ianni (1972, 1983) found a kinship system based on ethnic and cultural values in place of the Mafia.

An alternative view is that many ethnic groups besides the Italians are involved in organized criminal activities, including Jews, blacks, Irish, and Hispanics. Daniel Bell refers to this as "ethnic succession," with one ethnic group taking the place of other ethnic groups. Lupsha (1983) questioned the "ethnic succession" thesis, and in its place he found that black and Hispanic groups entered organized crime along with Italians and other ethnic groups. Blacks and Hispanics entered the drug trafficking field after World War II, especially in New York City and Miami (Abadinsky, 1985). These ethnic groups emerged out of the migration patterns to the cities and out of the entrance of blacks and Hispanics into the power struggle of urban communities.

Organized crime can best be viewed as a relationship on a local level between politics, business, and the ethnic communities. This model views organized crime as a product of the political, social, and economic history of American urban centers. Market conditions and organizational factors are critical, as they are for the interpretation and understanding of white-collar crime (Morash, 1984; Albanese, 1983; Ianni and Reuss-Ianni, 1972, 1983). American urban centers provided the political and economic environment necessary for criminals involved in organized crime. This observation is consistent with the Environment × Organism × Environment model used in this book.

The Activities of Organized Crime

As has been noted, organized crime is in those businesses that are illegal because of the Harrison Act of 1914 and the Volstead Act of 1920 as related to drugs and alcohol. Other activities closely related to the distribution of drugs and alcohol involve gambling, racketeering, and prostitution.

Gambling and Bookmaking. Skolnick (1978, 1983) started his discussion of gambling by observing that gambling is generally regarded as a victimless crime or an act that should be ignored by the criminal law. Eighty percent of the population believes that gambling should be legalized.

Gambling is both legal and illegal in the United States. Twenty-one of the states have legalized on-track racehorse betting, 16 states have legal lotteries, 13 have legal dog racing, and 4 have legal jai alai (Skolnick, 1983). Clubs and charitable organizations, such as church groups, have weekly bingo games which are, in many instances, illegal. Private card and dice games occur in homes and in the backrooms of restaurants and pool halls. A number of states are turning to lotteries as a means of supplementing state budgets.

Casino gambling emerged in Europe as a pastime for the rich. In the United States the centers for casino gambling are Atlantic City, New Jersey, and Las Vegas, Nevada. Gambling is associated with large hotels, often national chains, which operate casinos on the premises. This ties gambling into the hotel restaurant and bar business. Prostitution also becomes a part of the entertainment package. In 1946, Bugsy Siegal helped organized crime move into Las Vegas, and until 1966 organized crime controlled Las Vegas. In 1966, Howard Hughes purchased seven casinos, after which the role of organized crime in Las Vegas casino life was cut. The Nevada State Gambling Control Board also started to monitor the ownership and activities of the casinos (Skolnick, 1978, 1983).

One of the arguments against legalized gambling is that it encourages illegal activities such as theft, assault, murder, rape, robbery, and prostitution. There was a 25 percent increase in crime in Atlantic City following the legalization of casinos (Skolnick, 1983). On the other hand, it can be argued that by legalizing gambling, as well as the use of alcohol, these activities can be monitored and controlled. Since gambling will occur even when outlawed, it is better to control it and tax it rather than spending money trying to enforce unenforceable laws against it.

In his study of police records from New York City, Reuter (1983) found no Mafia-type control over bookmaking, the numbers game, or loansharking (lending money at very high rates of interest). Individual dealers are able to enter and leave the market with relative ease, and there is little or no violence connected with these illegal activities. There is an element of cooperation among those engaged in these activities, as there is among persons in legitimate activities. It is not a tightly knit Mafia-type operation. Reuter noted that organizational theory and marketplace determinants are the critical variables in understanding these activities.

Alcohol Distribution. With the passage of the Eighteenth Amendment and the Volstead Act, alcohol production and distribution were outlawed. The prohibition era produced Al Capone and other figures associated with organized crime (Abadinsky, 1985). With the repeal of prohibition with the Twenty-First Amendment, the manufacture and distribution of alcohol passed into the hands of legitimate businesses that are in competition with one another. There also emerged state control over alcoholic beverages in the form of taxation and regulation.

Drug Distribution. In his book on organized crime, Abadinsky (1985) noted that there is no monopoly over drug trafficking and the market is easy to enter. He mentioned the emergence of blacks and Hispanics after World War II in heroin and cocaine trafficking. Reuter (1983:183–184) stated that the Mafia is not involved in drug trafficking to any extent.

The international distribution of drugs comes primarily from the Golden Crescent (Turkey, Syria, Iran, Pakistan) and the Golden Triangle (Burma, Thailand, Laos), which produce heroin and some marijuana. Mexico also produces a supply of heroin and marijuana. Columbia, Equador, and Peru act as major sources for cocaine (Inciardi, 1986). Countries producing drugs are well organized for this purpose, sometimes with the support of the government and the army, since cocaine, marijuana, and heroin are a major part of the economy. The international trafficking in drugs is not controlled by one group but involves the coordinated effort of many people. Each political state has its own structure for drug trafficking and production.

The control of drug use has been by means of the crime control model rather than by a medical–scientific model of treatment and prevention of addiction. The crime control model requires that more and more police be involved in the enforcement of drug laws. Under the Reagan administration the law enforcement policy has extended to include the military (Hamowy, 1987; Treback, 1987). Also, the drug trafficking problem has extended to high-level politicians. General Noriega, the dictator of Panama, has been involved in the control of drug trafficking through many Central American nations, and he has been connected to political alliances with high-level U.S. politicians (*Newsweek*, February 15, 1988).

Labor Racketeering. Organized crime has been involved in the labor movement for many years. As noted above, labor unions developed at the same time that urban areas and corporations developed, and labor unions are the organizational counterpart to the corporation. The control of wealth and business by corporations forced laborers to organize in an effort to negotiate with ownership. There were many bitter battles between labor and management, and persons with Mafia backgrounds were hired by corporations as strike breakers. At the same time, labor unions found organized crime helpful in fighting big business (Abadinsky, 1985).

The story of Jimmy Hoffa illustrates the labor union–organized crime relationship. Hoffa was a small-time labor organizer who rose to become the head of the International Brotherhood of Teamsters. Hoffa was investigated by the McClellan Committee in 1957 for having organized crime connections. Robert Kennedy was a staff member for the McClellan committee and became attorney general of the United States in 1961 when his brother, John F. Kennedy, became president of the United States. Robert Kennedy pursued the prosecution of Hoffa, and Hoffa did serve a term in prison. Upon his release he disappeared, and it is thought that he was killed by a rival group (Abadinsky, 1985). A congressional investigation of the assassination of John F. Kennedy in 1963 (U.S. House of Representatives, 1979) involved both Hoffa and Jack Ruby, the man who shot Lee Harvey Oswald, in the assassination plot.

Legitimate Business. Organized crime has in many instances infiltrated legitimate businesses such as restaurants, hotels, beer distribution, construction work, garbage disposal, and other small businesses (Morash, 1984; Abadinsky, 1985). The relationship between organized crime and legitimate business can be one of investments of illegally gained monies in legitimate business. If I had stolen $100,000 and bought IBM stock with the money, I would have invested illegal money in a legitimate enterprise. The line between legal and illegal business practices is not always that clear.

A case in point is the story of hazardous waste disposal in northern New Jersey and southern New York. According to Block and Scarpetti (1983), regulation of the removal of hazardous waste materials involved two different and competing governmental agencies, the Department of Environmental Protection and the New York State Task Force on Organized Crime. The Department of Environmental Protection defined the problem as one of white-collar crime, that is, haulers who were in violation of regulatory legislation as put forth and enforced by the Department of Environmental Protection. On the other hand, the Task Force on Organized Crime found organized crime involvement in the disposal industries themselves, and the problem was with the industries, not with the haulers.

The regulations and controls used will vary depending on the definition of the problem by a governmental agency. The one major difficulty I had with the Block and Scarpetti argument is that they never defined organized crime and white-collar crime. Perhaps one can conclude that the distinction between the two is an arbitrary matter since organized crime is based on business, politics, and labor in various organizational configurations.

WAR CRIMES AND TERRORISM

War crimes are quite different from other crimes in that in the case of war crimes the legitimacy and authority of the state system itself is challenged. Most crimes involve injuries to individuals by other individuals, and although the law regards rape and murder as crimes against the state, the injured party in reality is an individual. In the case of terrorism and war crimes the state itself is the victim; that is, the authority of those in power is challenged.

As noted in Chapter 3, the nation-state was established on the basis of power and sovereignty of groups over territory. As long as this power and sovereignty are not challenged, the legitimacy of the state system is recognized. This power can be challenged and threatened by a group from within the state system (civil disobedience, riots, civil war, terrorism), or from outside the state system (warfare with another state system). If the revolutionaries win, they become the new rulers and they then dispose of the old ruling class. We can cite some real examples of postrevolutionary political conditions. After the French Revolution (1789) a reign of terrorism existed in which wealthy persons, including Queen Marie Antoinette and King Louis XVI, were executed by the revolutionaries. The guillotine was used during the Reign of Terror, a period of history made famous by Charles Dickens in *A Tale of Two Cities*. The Russian Revolution occurred in 1917 following World War I. Germany had invaded Russia and the Russian leadership was so weak by 1917 that the czar abdicated in 1917. The czar and his family were executed by the victorious Boksheviks in 1918. The invasion of China by Japan in the 1930s so weakened the Chinese regime that Mao Tse-tung and the communists were able to take control of China after World War II. After the communist takeover there was a purge of all evidence of elitism and class differences, and well-educated lawyers and doctors were forced to go into the fields to work as peasants. Under the Mao regime attacks on individual rights and freedom were made and many people were executed or moved to communal farms.

On the other hand, if revolutionaries lose, they are tried as criminals and executed or imprisoned. The final basis for law and authority is therefore an ability of individuals to exercise force and coercion over other individuals residing on a given piece of land (Chapter 3). In well-developed Western democracies the transition in authority is orderly and fairly peaceful, through the mechanism of democratic elections. In the United States, Great Britain, and the European democracies, elections are held periodically to decide issues of authority and power. In less-well-developed nations, as in Africa, Asia, and South America, revolutions occur with great frequency and new power structures are created by military revolutions and guerrilla activities. Recent events in Nicaragua, the Dominican Republic, Panama, and the Philippines illustrate the political unrest that exists. The governments are not powerful enough to control through legitimate means (elections, socialization, nonviolent social control measures), so that constant struggles for power and leadership exist.

The concept of war crimes raises another interesting issue. Warfare is legalized violence by a state against another state and/or against its citizens.

The use of violence by the state is regarded as legitimate under certain conditions, such as a declaration of war, the use of the police force and violence to maintain peace, and the imprisonment or execution of citizens. The state can be the victim of crime, while at the same time the state can be the criminal. Once the state is established, there remains the issue of whether the acts of the state are lawful and must be obeyed. According to Hobbes, once the social contract is entered into, citizens cannot rebel against the state. On the other hand, according to John Locke the citizens retain the right to rebel against unjust laws even after the social contract is entered into. The right to rebel or the right to civil disobedience as a political concept was put forth by many political philosophers, including Henry David Thoreau in his treatise on "Civil Disobedience" in 1849, in which he argued that the individual should refuse to obey unjust laws. There is always a basic conflict between the rights of individuals and the rights of the state. Criminal law is constantly redefining the boundaries of these relationships and rights (Chapter 4).

Riots, social protests, rebellions, and the like are usually framed within a political argument that the state is illegal and the officials of the state are violating the basic social rights of some of the citizens. When this happens, citizens have a right and a duty to rebel. Whether or not a law is legal or illegal becomes a major issue in war crimes and terrorism. Since different groups have different opinions on such issues, these differences can be resolved either peacefully through the political process, or through violence, rebellion, and warfare.

Political Terrorism and Political Crime

Political crime is defined by Georges-Abeyie (1980:314) as "a criminal act that challenges the collective administrative authority of the nation-state." Turk (1984:120) defined political crime as "whatever is recognized or anticipated by authorities to be resistance threatening the established structure of differential resources and opportunities." Roebuck (Turk, 1984:121) noted that political crime can involve acts by citizens against the government and by the government against citizens. Usually, we regard the government as the victim, not as the criminal. Kerstetter (1983) also emphasizes that terrorism can be violence by state officials as well as violence against state officials.

Political terrorism has been differentiated into rural terrorism versus urban terrorism. Rural or guerrilla terrorism occurs mostly in developing nations, as in Africa, Asia, and South America. Urban terrorism occurs in well-developed nations such as Syria, Lebanon, Japan, Germany, United States, and Great Britain (Bassiouni, 1975; Georges-Abeyie, 1980; Kerstetter, 1983).

Terrorism can also be differentiated in terms of (1) violence against foreigners, and (2) violence against one's countrymen. The objects of terrorist attacks may be public officials, such as the assassination of Sadat of Egypt, or attacks on innocent civilians carried out by planting bombs in cars or hijacking an airliner. The establishment of the state of Israel among the Arab nations has created a political situation where terrorism is used to gain support for a political cause. For example, in October 1985, four Palestinians seized the Italian cruiseship *Achille Lauro* and killed an elderly American. In December 1986, Arab terrorists attacked the airports in Vienna and Rome, killing nineteen people.

Simon Dinitz pointed out to me that the issue of terrorism is very complex, involving as it does over 350 ethnic and racial groups worldwide. We have terrorism in the Middle East involving Jews versus Arabs, Arabs versus Arabs, and Moslems versus Christians. We are witnessing major terrorism in Ireland involving Catholics versus Protestants and Catholics versus the British government. International terrorist groups trained in Syria come from and go back to Germany, Japan, Nicaragua, and elsewhere. Most if not all of the major political and religious conflicts of the day involve terrorist groups using terrorism as a major political weapon.

War Crimes

Crimes against or by the state are usually classified as follows:

1. War crimes
2. Crimes against peace
3. Crimes against humanity

The concept of a war crime is taken from custom and the history of international law based on treaties and international agreements among nations. Although violence is the nature of warfare, it has generally been recognized that violence and bloodshed must be limited to military personnel and military targets (Bassiouni, 1983, 1975; Ferencz, 1983; Friedman, 1983). Friedman (1983:1645) defined war crimes as (1) acts of violence against civilian populations, prisoners of war, or in some cases enemy soldiers in the field; (2) acts committed primarily by military personnel; (3) acts in violation of the laws and customs of war; (4) acts not justified by military necessity; (5) acts involving weapons or military methods of unusual cruelty or devastation.

Crimes against peace involve the concept of "just" and "unjust" wars as put forth in international law over the centuries and as stated in the Kellogg-Briand peace pact of 1928, which condemned "a recourse to war for the solution of international controversies" (Friedman, 1983; Bassiouni, 1983; Ferencz, 1983). Crimes against the peace are based on the distinction between offensive and defensive warfare. Offensive wars are illegal, but wars in defense of one's country and sovereignty are legal. This distinction then raises the further issue of who is the aggressor in any conflict. For example, in the Vietnam war (discussed below), both the South and North Vietnamese claimed that the other side was the aggressor nation.

Crimes against humanity involve acts that violate concepts of natural law and natural rights of human beings as human beings. Crimes against humanity often occur within a nation as acts of state officials against citizens, as in the case of Nazi Germany in the 1930s with the extermination of Jewish populations and others through genocide during the holocaust (Friedman, 1983; Bassiouni, 1983, 1985; Ferencz, 1983).

The concept ''crime'' involves the enforcement of the law by state officials through a police force and criminal justice system. One major difference between domestic criminal law and international law is that in the case of international law there is no enforcement machinery. Nations enforce international agreements, and sovereignty exists at the national but not at the international level. Domestic criminal law involves concepts of sovereignty, jurisdiction, territoriality, and mens rea not found in international law (Wise, 1975).

Since international criminal law depends on voluntary compliance, there is no direct enforcement of such law. Bassiouni (1986) observed that international criminal law depends on national crime law for its enforcement, and this has created an enforcement crisis in international criminal law. ''The creation of an international criminal court would entail the development of a new international system of justice. . . . The creation of an international criminal court is unlikely given modern economic and political realities. . . . International criminal law is presently in a state of crisis'' (Bassiouni, 1983:907). Mueller and Besharov (1986) also observed this enforcement crisis in international criminal law. Crime law evolved in a hierarchical manner from clan to tribe to kingdom to international law (Chapter 3), and the international level is still developing. This means that national law must enforce international law at this point in history.

War crimes are acts defined at the international level, and they must be distinguished from military crimes committed by U.S. service personnel while in uniform. A soldier can commit rape, robbery, or murder while serving in the armed forces. In the United States the Uniform Code of Military Justice defines the crimes and procedures used to try military personnel accused of military crimes. These crimes can include acts against other military personnel, against civilians, and even against soldiers and civilians of the enemy nation (Bryant, 1983).

The Nuremberg Trials

After the defeat of Germany and Japan in World War II, the Allied nations (United States, Great Britain, France, and Russia) met in London in 1945 to form the International Military Tribunal and adopted the London Charter. The International Military Tribunal under the charter was to prosecute German and Japanese military and civilian officers for war crimes and crimes against humanity.

Under the London Charter, trials were held in Nuremberg, Germany, called the Nuremberg trials, in which 24 German leaders were indicted and 12 were sentenced to death and hanged. They were all found guilty of crimes against humanity (Taylor, 1970; Baird, 1972; Woetzel, 1960; Benton and Grimm, 1955; Appleman, 1954).

The trial and execution of German leaders raised serious legal problems concerning crime and criminal law (Baird, 1972; Taylor, 1970; Woetzel, 1962;

Benton and Grimm, 1955). Baird (1972:x) summarized these arguments in the following way:

1. The International Military Tribunal operated without legal precedent, as it was formed by the victors to punish the vanquished after World War II. If Germany had won, one can assume that the German military system would have charged United States and British leaders with war crimes and crimes against humanity.
2. The trials were military trials, not civilian trials, and they did not follow civilian criminal law.
3. The International Military Tribunal served as a source of new law as well as prosecutor, judge, and jury.
4. The International Military Tribunal created law after the fact, that is, for acts that occurred before the law was stated. This is ex post facto law, which violates the principle of legality as found in *nullum crimen sine lege*.
5. The Nuremberg trials violated German sovereignty.
6. The war crime trials found persons guilty of acts committed while carrying out the orders of their superiors.

The issue of ex post facto laws was a critical issue raised by the defendants in the Nuremberg trials. Sheldon Glueck, a Harvard University criminologist, argued that the illegality of aggression was implicit in international law before 1945 even though there was no international agreement forbidding it. Glueck also argued that individuals can be held responsible for acts carried out while obeying the orders of superiors (Baird, 1972:91 ff.). On the other hand, Robert Taft, a U.S. Senator from Ohio, argued that the Nuremberg trials violated the ex post facto doctrine and were therefore illegal (Baird, 1972:107 ff.).

The other major issue raised at the Nuremberg trials was the "superior order" defense; that is, is a soldier guilty of a war crime or a crime against humanity if he/she kills another human being on orders from a superior officer? A soldier is trained to kill and must obey a lawful order of a superior officer or is subject to disciplinary action through a court martial. A soldier is thus put into a Catch-22 situation. If he/she obeys the order and is subsequently captured, the soldier is subject to being tried by the enemy nation as a war criminal. If the soldier refuses to obey the order, the person is shot by his/her own troops.

The Nuremberg defendants raised the defense of superior orders, but the military tribunal ruled that a superior order does not relieve a soldier of legal responsibility under international law if a moral choice was in fact possible (Taylor, 1970; Duke, 1983). The Nuremberg defense raised the moral and legal issue of orders given to soldiers during wartime. How does a soldier know if an order is legal? An assumption is made that individuals have an innate sense of what is right and legal which transcends social learning and conditioning. Otherwise, individuals will do what they have been trained to do, that is, obey orders and kill. As Taylor (1970:83) noted: "Individuals have international duties which transcend the national obligations of obedience imposed by the individual states. . . . From a psychological point-of-view a soldier is conditioned to obey.''

To summarize the Nuremberg trials, the concept of crime was based on international law and an international military tribunal, not on the concept of state sovereignty; the law used was questionable from the point of view of the doctrine of *nullum poene sine lege* and has been regarded by some critics as ex post facto; the defendants did not need to possess mens rea; and the defendants could not use the defense of superior orders. The concept of war crimes as put forth at Nuremberg violated several basic principles of criminal law as found in domestic criminal law.

The Eichmann Trial

In May 1960, Adolph Eichmann was kidnapped in Argentina and taken to Israel for trial as a war criminal. Eichmann had been a member of Hitler's S.S. and the Gestapo. He held an important position in the government as part of the program to exterminate Jews. Eichmann was charged with genocide, crimes against humanity, and war crimes. He was convicted and executed by the Israeli officials (Papadatos, 1964; Woetzel, 1960).

Many of the issues raised by this trial were also raised at the Nuremberg trials, although Eichmann was tried under Israeli law, not under international law. Eichmann might have been tried under an international law system, but the Israelis decided to use their own legal system.

Eichmann had been illegally kidnapped and taken from Argentina to Israel. Although the sovereignty of Argentina had been violated, this was not viewed by the court as a bar to jurisdiction by the court over the case. In other American and British cases, courts had ruled that such illegal kidnappings did not interfere with the jurisdiction of the court over the case. The doctrine of territoriality holds that if a defendant is before the court, the court has jurisdiction (Papadatos, 1964; Woetzel, 1960). Although the acts of Israeli agents were illegal, this did not bar the Israeli court from trying Eichmann. I personally do not think that illegal acts by governmental officials should be sanctioned, as is the case for illegally gained evidence which is not admissible in court (Chapter 8). However, the Eichmann trial was surrounded by emotional and ethical issues that overshadowed the legal issues.

The jurisdiction of the Israeli court was an issue for another reason. The state of Israel did not exist at the time the crimes were committed. After its foundation after World War II, Israel passed legislation, entitled the Nazis and Nazi Collaborators Law 5710 (1950), which made war crimes crimes against Israel. This law was based on the principles of Nuremberg and was used in the trial of Eichmann. This law was ex post facto and violated the principle of *nullum crimen sine lege*. However, the Israeli court argued that such a law is legitimate because of the universality of these crimes; that is, they are crimes against natural law and against humanity as such. The argument is also developed, as in the Nuremberg trials, that international criminal law is in its infancy and cannot be expected to respect well-established legal principles (Papadatos, 1964; Woetzel, 1960).

Eichmann's defense counsel argued that the doctrine of superior orders applied in his case since the policy of exterminating Jews was a national policy of the Nazi regime and not his own policy. The court held that superior orders do not free a person of legal responsibility. In Eichmann's case there was also the issue of whether his position in the Hitler regime was such as to make him part of the policymaking process. At what level does taking an order from a superior become one of giving an order to a subordinate?

Eichmann was executed despite the fact that the Israeli government opposed capital punishment. The argument for his execution was the moral and ethical nature of the crimes he committed (Papadatos, 1964; Woetzel, 1960). I remember feeling at the time of his execution in 1962 that the Israelis had merely perpetuated the view that the only way to control violence is with more violence, and I wished they had used the occasion to express a need for a more humane and rational penal policy than that of hanging people. The Israelis missed a beautiful opportunity for a moral lesson for the world community. The hanging of Eichmann was not the right message to come out of the gas chambers or concentration camps of Nazi Germany.

The main lesson I absorbed from the Eichmann trial is that state systems are based on power and coercion. The establishment of the state of Israel put the Jewish immigrants at war with the Arab world. The Israelis are now involved in accusations of atrocities against Arabs in refugee camps that the Israelis had set up in Lebanon. In 1982, Israel invaded Lebanon. Lebanese Christians under the military control of the Israeli army attacked and massacred Palestinians who were being held in refugee camps in Beruit. At the present time (1988) the Israeli government is involved in violent encounters with the Palestinians, and many Palestinians have been killed as a result.

Legal concepts such as mens rea, *nullum crimen sine lege*, ex post facto, territoriality, and jurisdiction have been forged out of a long history of political struggle, and they are very fragile in the face of emotional trials such as the Eichmann trial. If such concepts are important within the context of our political philosophy, they should be important enough to guide us in those most critical trials and issues that occur in our legal system. If they do not, they are not serving the purpose for which they were designed.

Vietnam and War Crimes

In the 1960s the United States sent troops to South Vietnam to aid the South Vietnamese in their battle against North Vietnam. Vietnam had been divided in a civil war involving the communists from North Vietnam and the South Vietnamese. War was never officially declared against North Vietnam, and the president was at odds with Congress over American involvement in the Vietnam war. Serious questions were raised at the time concerning the legality of the war. The 1960s were a time of political and social unrest, with racial riots and student protests, and this made the Vietnam war a most unpopular war from the point of view of the United States (Taylor, 1970; Baird, 1972).

Support for the position that the United States should be involved militarily in the war was based on the following arguments. The United States was justified for being in Vietnam because North Vietnam had invaded South Vietnam, and therefore under the concept of crimes against peace North Vietnam was an aggressor nation. Under the United Nations Charter the United States could go to the defense of South Vietnam under the concept of defensive warfare (Baird, 1972; Taylor, 1970).

Those who argued against the participation of the United States in the Vietnam war did so from the following positions. The United States was in an illegal war and was guilty of war crimes under the rules established at the Nuremberg trials. The bombing of North Vietnam was illegal and constituted crimes against citizens and crimes against humanity. The Vietnam war was a civil war, not an international war as defined by international treaties and United Nations resolutions (Baird, 1972; Taylor, 1970).

The issue of war crimes by the United States in Vietnam became a major controversy because of the massacre of women, children, and elderly men at My Lai, a province of Son My. U.S. troops destroyed the village and killed civilians. The defense used to justify the My Lai massacre was that the Vietcong (North Vietnamese) waged guerrilla warfare in which women and children were part of the warfare, and in such a conflict it is not possible to distinguish between military troops and civilians. Lieutenant Calley was found guilty of military offenses under U.S. military law for his actions at My Lai. There was no international military tribunal after the Vietnam war as after World War II, for the simple reason that the United States was not defeated by North Vietnam, and the sovereignty of the United States remained intact after the war. However, the issues raised at the Nuremberg trials were extended to Vietnam. Did the United States commit war crimes and crimes against humanity? Did the Nuremberg defense of not obeying an unlawful order from the superior apply to American soldiers who argued that the war in Vietnam was an illegal war? (Baird, 1972; Taylor, 1970). Taylor (1970:207) concluded his book by stating: "We have failed to learn the lessons we undertook to teach at Nuremberg, and that failure is today's American tragedy."

SUMMARY

Several basic themes run throughout the discussion of economic, political, and war crimes. One theme is that the definitions of these crimes are most controversial in terms of what a crime is. White-collar crime is often defined in social rather than legal terms. The definition and existence of the Mafia has been questioned. War crimes, crimes against humanity, and crimes against peace are defined outside the bounds of domestic criminal law.

The second theme is that the unit of analysis is questionable. Is the individual offender the unit of analysis, or the corporation, or the criminal syndicate, or the nation-state? Only individuals can behave and commit crimes. A corporation or a syndicate or a state system can act only through its agents or officials who have brains and can behave.

The third theme is that we use the same concepts found in the criminal justice system for street crime to deal with major social, economic, and political issues. We use the police, we arrest, we convict, and we put these offenders into prisons. We witnessed the failure of this approach to the control of alcoholism during prohibition, but we still pursue this policy. We do not see white-collar crime as a problem in economic organization. We do not see organized crime as a problem in urban politics and social control. We do not see war crimes as a problem in the use of force and coercion to settle international disputes. In each case the response has been one of using state force to solve a problem rather than using knowledge of the political, economic, and social systems involved. As Mueller and Besharov (1986:80) point out, we must show less reliance on criminal law and more reliance on civil and urbane approaches to law enforcement. The criminal justice system is not adequate to handle major social and economic problems. Criminology does not have an adequate theoretical framework for dealing with such issues. Different theoretical frameworks must be developed.

FURTHER STUDIES

Courses in economic crime, political crime, and organized crime are often offered in programs in criminal justice or criminology, or in law schools.

REFERENCES

ABADINSKY, H. (1985). *Organized Crime.* Chicago: Nelson-Hall Publishers.

ALBANESE, J. S. (1983). "God and the Mafia Revisited." In *Career Criminals,* ed. G. P. Waldo. Beverly Hills, Calif.: Sage.

APPLEMAN, J. A. (1954). *Military Tribunals and International Crimes.* Indianapolis, Ind.: Bobbs-Merrill.

BAIRD, J. W. (1972). *From Nuremberg to My Lai.* Lexington, Mass.: D. C. Heath.

BANFIELD, E. C., and J. Q. WILSON (1963). *City Politics.* New York: Vintage Books.

BASSIOUNI, M. C. (1975). *International Terrorism and Political Crimes.* Springfield, Ill.: Charles C Thomas.

BASSIOUNI, M. C. (1983). "International Criminal Law." In *Encyclopedia of Crime and Justice,* ed. S. H. Kadish. New York: Free Press.

BASSIOUNI, M. C. (1986). *International Criminal Law,* Vol. 1: *Crimes.* Ardsley-on-Hudson, N.Y.: Transnational Publishers.

BENTON, W. E. and G. GRIMM (1955). *Nuremberg.* Dallas, Tex.: Southern Methodist University Press.

BLOCK, A. A. (1980). *East Side, West Side: Organized Crime in New York, 1930–1950.* Cardiff, Great Britain: University College Cardiff Press.

BLOCK, M. D., F. C. NOLD, and J. G. SIDAK (1981). "The Deterrent Effect of Antitrust Enforcement." *Journal of Political Economy,* 76:745–756, June.

BLOCK, A., and F. SCARPETTI (1983). "Defining Illegal Hazardous Waste Disposal: White Collar or Organized Crime." In *Career Criminals,* ed. G. P. Waldo. Beverly Hills, Calif.: Sage.

BRYANT, C. D. (1983). "Military Justice." In *Encyclopedia of Crime and Justice,* ed. S. H. Kadish. New York: Free Press.

CALDWELL, R. G. (1958). "A Re-examination of the Concept of White-Collar Crime." *Federal Probation*, 30–36, March.

CALLOW, A. B. (1976). *The City Boss in America.* New York: Oxford University Press.

CLINARD, R., and R. QUINNEY. (1973). *Criminal Behavior Systems: A Typology.* New York: Holt, Rinehart and Winston.

COFFEE, J. C. (1983). "Corporate Criminal Responsibility." In *Encyclopedia of Crime and Justice*, ed. S. H. Kadish, New York: Free Press.

CRESSEY, D. R. (1953). *Other People's Money.* New York: Free Press.

CRESSEY, D. R. (1969). *Theft of the Nation.* New York: Harper & Row.

CRESSEY, D. R. (1989). "The Poverty of Theory in Corporate Crime Research." *Advances in Criminological Theory*, eds. W. S. Laufer and F. Adler. New Brunswick, N.J.: Transaction.

CUBBERNUSS, D., and B. THOMPSON (1983). "Corporate Responsibility: Some Implications of the Ford Pinto Case." In *Career Criminals*, ed. G. P. Waldo. Beverly Hills, Calif.: Sage.

CULLEN, F. T., W. J. MAAKESTAD, and G. CAVENDER (1984). "The Ford Pinto Case and Beyond: Corporate Crime, Moral Boundaries, and the Criminal Sanction." In *Corporations as Criminals*, ed. E. Hochstedler. Beverly Hills, Calif.: Sage.

DUKE, S. (1983). "Excuses: Superior Orders." In *Encyclopedia of Crime and Justice*, ed. S. H. Kadish. New York: Free Press.

FERENCZ, B. B. (1983). "International Crimes against the Peace." In *Encyclopedia of Crime and Justice*, ed. S. H. Kadish, New York: Free Press.

FRANK, N. (1984). "Choosing between Criminal and Civil Sanctions for Corporate Wrongs." In *Corporations as Criminals*, ed. E. Hochstedler. Beverly Hills, Calif.: Sage.

FRIEDMAN, L. (1983). "War Crimes." In *Encyclopedia of Crime and Justice*, ed. S. H. Kadish. New York: Free Press.

GARDINER, J. A., and D. J. OLSON (1974). *Theft of the City.* Bloomington: Indiana University Press.

GEIS, G. (1968). *White-Collar Criminal.* New York: Atherton Press.

GEIS, G. (1984). "White-Collar and Corporate Crime." In *Major Forms of Crime*, ed. R. F. Meier. Beverly Hills, Calif.: Sage.

GEIS, G., and C. GOFF (1982). "Edwin H. Sutherland: A Biographical and Analytical Commentary." In *White-Collar and Economic Crime*, ed. P. Wickman and T. Dailey. Lexington, Mass.: Lexington Books.

GEORGES-ABEYIE, D. E. (1980). "Political Crime and Terrorism." In *Crime and Deviance*, ed. G. Newman. Beverly Hills, Calif.: Sage.

GROSS, E. (1980). "Organization Structure and Organizational Crime:" In *White-Collar Crime*, ed. G. Geis and E. Stotland. Beverly Hills, Calif.: Sage.

HAGAN, J., I. NAGEL, and C. ALBONETTI (1982). "The Social Organization of White-Collar Sanctions: A Study of Prosecution and Punishment in the Federal

Courts." In *White-Collar and Economic Crime*, ed. P. Wickman and R. T. Dailey. Lexington, Mass.: Lexington Books.

HALL, J. (1935). *Theft, Law and Society*. Indianapolis, Ind.: Bobbs-Merrill.

HALL, J. (1982). *Law, Social Science and Criminal Theory*. Littleton, Colo.: Rothman.

HAMOWY, R. (1987). *Dealing with Drugs*. San Francisco: Pacific Research Institute for Public Policy.

HAWKINS, G. (1969). "Organized Crime and God." In *The Honest Politician's Guide to Politics*, ed. N. Morris and G. Hawkins. Chicago: University of Chicago Press.

HIRSCHI, T., and M. GOTTFRESON (1987). "Causes of White-Collar Crime." *Criminology* 25:4, 949–974.

HOCHSTEDLER, E. (1984). *Corporations as Criminals*. Beverly Hills, Calif.: Sage.

HOPKINS, A. (1980). "Controlling Corporate Deviance." *Criminology*, 18(2):198–214.

IANNI, F. A. J., and E. REUSS-IANNI (1972). *A Family Business: Kinship and Social Control in Organized Crime*. New York: Russell Sage.

IANNI, F. A. J., and E. REUSS-IANNI (1983). "Organized Crime." In *Encyclopedia of Crime and Justice*, ed. S. H. Kadish. New York: Free Press.

INCIARDI, J. (1986). *The War on Drugs*. Palo Alto, Calif.: Mayfield Publishing Company.

KITCH, E. W. (1983). "Economic Crime: Theory." In *Encyclopedia of Crime and Justice*, ed. S. H. Kadish. New York: Free Press.

KRAMER, R. C. (1982). "Corporate Crime: An Organizational Perspective." In *White-Collar and Economic Crime*, ed. P. Wickman and T. Dailey. Lexington, Mass.: Lexington Books.

LUPSHA, P. A. (1983). "Networks and Networking: Analysis of an Organized Crime Group." In *Career Criminals*, ed. G. P. Waldo. Beverly Hills, Calif.: Sage.

MORASH, M. (1984). "Organized Crime." In *Major Forms of Crime*, ed. R. F. Meier. Beverly Hills, Calif.: Sage.

MUELLER, G. O. W. (1957). "Mens Rea and the Corporation." *University of Pittsburgh Law Review*, 19:21–46.

MUELLER, G. O. W., and D. J. BESHAROV (1986). "Evolution and Enforcement of International Criminal Law." In *International Criminal Law*, Vol. 1: *Crimes*, ed. M. C. Bassiouni. Ardsley-on-Hudson, N.Y.: Transnational Publishers.

PAPADATOS, P. (1964). *The Eichmann Trial*. New York: Praeger.

PARISI, N. (1984). "Theories of Corporate Criminal Liability." In *Corporations as Criminals*, ed. E. Hochstedler. Beverly Hills, Calif.: Sage.

PRESIDENT'S COMMISSION ON LAW ENFORCEMENT AND THE ADMINISTRATION OF JUSTICE (1967). *Task Force Report: Organized Crime*. Washington, D. C.: U.S. Government Printing Office.

REUTER, P. (1983). *Disorganized Crime*. Cambridge, Mass.: MIT Press.

RUSSELL, K. A. (1983). "Economic Crimes: Antitrust Offenses." In *Encyclopedia of Crime and Justice*, ed. S. H. Kadish. New York: Free Press.

SKOLNICK, J. H. (1978). *House of Cards: Legalization and Control of Casino Gambling*. Boston: Little, Brown.

SKOLNICK, J. H. (1983). "Gambling." In *Encyclopedia of Crime and Justice*, ed. S. H. Kadish. New York: Free Press.

SMITH, D. C. (1975). *The Mafia Mystique*. New York: Basic Books.

SMITH, D. C. (1982). "White-Collar Crime, Organized Crime, and the Business Establishment: Resolving a Crisis in Criminological Theory." In *White-Collar and Economic Crime*, ed. P. Wickman and T. Dailey. Lexington, Mass.: Lexington Books.

STEDMAN, M. S. (1972). *Urban Politics*. Cambridge, Mass.: Winthrop.

SUTHERLAND, E. H. (1940). "White-Collar Criminality." *American Sociological Review*, 5:1–12, February.

SUTHERLAND, E. H. (1945). "Is White-Collar Crime Crime?" *American Sociological Review*, 10:132–139, April.

SUTHERLAND, E. H. (1949). *White Collar Crime*. New York: Holt, Rinehart and Winston.

TAPPAN, P. (1947). "Who Is the Criminal?" *American Sociological Review*, 12:96–102, February.

TAYLOR, T. (1970). *Nuremberg and Vietnam*. Chicago: Quadrangle Books.

TREBACK, A. (1987). *The Great Drug War*. New York: Macmillan.

TURK, A. (1984). "Political Political Crime." In *Major Forms of Crime*, ed. R. F. Meier. Beverly Hills, Calif.: Sage.

U.S. HOUSE OF REPRESENTATIVES (1979). *Report of the Select Committee on Assassinations*, House Report 95–1825, Part 2.

VAUGHN, D. (1980). "Crime between Organizations: Implications for Victimology." In *White-Collar Crime*, ed. G. Geis and E. Stotland. Beverly Hills, Calif.: Sage.

WHEELER, S. (1983). "White Collar Crime: History of an Idea." In *Encyclopedia of Crime and Justice*, ed. S. H. Kadish. New York: Free Press.

WHEELER, S., D. WEISBURD, and N. BODE (1982). "Sentencing the White-Collar Offender: Rhetoric and Reality." *American Sociological Review*, 47:641–659, October.

WICKMAN, P., and T. DAILEY, (1982). *White-Collar and Economic Crime*. Lexington, Mass.: Lexington Books.

WISE, E. M. (1975). "War Crimes and Criminal Law." In *Studies in Comparative Criminal Law*, ed. E. M. Wise and G. O. W. Mueller. Springfield, Ill.: Charles C Thomas.

WOETZEL, R. K. (1960). *The Nuremberg Trials in International Law*. London: Stevens & Sons.

QUESTIONS

1. What is meant by white-collar crime as a legal concept? As a sociological concept?
2. Are white-collar crimes committed by individuals or by corporations, or both?
3. Are corporations capable of being criminals?
4. What arguments are put forth for studying white-collar crime from the corporate level rather than the individual level of analysis?
5. What socioeconomic background factors account for the emergence of organized crime in America?
6. Discuss the argument that organized crime is controlled by an international syndicate. Discuss the argument that the concept of organized crime is a creation of sociologists.

7. How has the legal and political structure of the United States influenced the development of organized crime?

8. How does the role of the state differ in the case of war crimes and political crimes from that of ordinary common-law crimes?

9. How do war crimes differ from crimes against peace? Against humanity?

10. What major legal issues emerged from the Nuremberg trials?

11. Did the United States commit war crimes as a result of the Vietnam war?

Recent Research on the Individual Offender   18

A BASIC OBSERVATION

All environmental influences, including experiences that are labeled learning, socioeconomic class, poverty, and race, must enter the brain in order to influence behavior. Whatever there is that is involved in criminal behavior is therefore in the brain. Wheresoever we start with our analysis of behavior (e.g., genetic influences, psychological influences, or socioeconomic and political influences), we must ultimately look for these influences in the neural patterns of the brain.

Great advances have been made in recent years in the brain sciences; in fact, the greatest advances in the behavioral sciences and in science in general have occurred in the brain sciences. However, since the brain is the most complex organ in the human body, there is still a great deal about it that we do not know. For that reason, much of what is discussed in this chapter is experimental, controversial, and subject to change at any moment. This chapter must be read as one that will be out of date by the time it is printed, and a year from now it will be even more out of date if scientists working in the area are doing their job.

The brain is the product of genetic–environmental interaction. As noted in Chapter 11, an impoverished environment creates an impoverished brain. Gentetic defects, such as the XYY syndrome, and hormonal defects also influence the brain. The impact of genes and the environment on the brain can take many forms, but the most common ones can be classified as (1) the general structure of the brain, (2) brain trauma and injuries, (3) the neurotransmitter system, (4) nutrition and pollution, and (5) hormones, especially those associated with male/female differences in brain structure.

THE BRAIN AND CRIMINAL BEHAVIOR

The Autonomic Nervous System

The brain controls all basic bodily functions, including motor activities, eating, sleeping, digestion, sex and reproduction, learning, and social behavior. As noted in Chapter 11, the hypothalamus controls the pituitary gland, which in turn controls other glands, such as the adrenal glands, the ovaries, and the testes. The adrenal glands secrete epinephrine and norepinephrine, which as neurotransmitters act to stimulate and inhibit neural activity in the autonomic nervous system (Chapter 11). The autonomic nervous system (ANS) is composed of the sympathetic nervous system (SNS) and the parasympathetic nervous system (PNS). The SNS is an arousal system which increases heart beat, blood pressure, respiration rate, and perspiration rate, slows down digestion, and controls orgasms in the sex organs. The hypothalamus–pituitary–autonomic nervous system connection is central to the basic survival behaviors involved in feeding, fighting, fleeing, and sex. The PNS, on the other hand, has a calming and quieting effect on the internal organs.

Our emotional and motivational life is associated with the SNS, that is, the arousal of pleasure and the avoidance of pain associated with drinking, eating, sex, alcohol, drugs, and the avoidance of danger.

The Autonomic Nervous System and the Psychopath

According to Pavlovian classical conditioning, an animal can learn to associate a conditioned stimulus with an unconditioned stimulus (bell—food—salivation; see Chapter 13). Some stimuli excite and arouse the autonomic nervous system; some stimuli inhibit the system.

Hans Eysenck (Eysenck and Wilson, 1976; Gatchel and Mears, 1982) developed a theory of personality based on the Pavlovian concepts of excitation (SNS) and inhibition (PNS) of the central nervous system. According to Eysenck, one dimension of personality is a neuroticism-psychoticism dimension. Neuroticism is characterized by a high level of physiological arousal, which leads to anxiety states. Psychoticism is an impaired sense of reality as seen in hallucination and delusions. Schizophrenics and manic-depressives are psychotic. Eysenck also relates psychoticism to psychopathy. The psychopath is an asocial, antisocial person who lacks feelings and is unable to relate to other people.

The other personality dimension is that of introversion–extroversion. Introverts are loners, less sociable, and very inhibited; whereas extroverts are less inhibited, very sociable on a superficial level, and are impulsive and thrill-seekers.

Persons high on the introversion scale are high in sympathetic nervous system excitation. Since they are overstimulated, they become introverts to escape from sensory input. People high on the extroversion scale are low in sympathetic nervous system excitation. They are understimulated, so they must seek stimulation (Eysenck and Wilson, 1976).

Introverts are easily conditioned by environmental experiences, whereas extroverts are extremely difficult to condition to pain because they are understimulated and underaroused by such stimuli. Extroverts have a difficult time making stimulus–response connections and therefore are unable to learn from painful experiences. Criminals and psychopaths are high on the extroversion scale and are therefore difficult to socialize and to condition (Eysenck and Wilson, 1976; Gatchel and Mears, 1982). Drugs that increase stimulation of the CNS (stimulants) increase the ability to learn, whereas drugs that decrease stimulation of the CNS (depressants) decrease the ability to learn, according to Eysenck's theory (Eysenck and Wilson, 1976).

The Psychopath

The psychopath is defined by Cleckley and others as antisocial, superficial, a liar, and a deceiver. Such a person lacks a sense of guilt or empathy, is promiscuous in sexual relationships, is impulsive, lacks meaningful social relationships, and fails to learn from experience (Hare and Connally, 1987; Mednick et al., 1982; Hare and Schalling, 1978; Reid et al., 1986). The psychopath by definition is antisocial, so the label "psychopath" is of little help in understanding criminal behavior. When the term "psychopath" is used to indicate antisocial behavior without any other theoretical framework, it is a meaningless term. The term has been used carelessly in psychiatry to refer to any behavior that is not clearly psychotic or neurotic, and as such is a wastebasket term without real meaning. The term "psychopath" is also used to refer to a constellation of behaviors which originate in a certain biological foundation (Farrington and Gunn, 1985).

Mednick and others (Mednick et al., 1982; Mednick et al., 1987; Venables, 1987) explain psychopathy in terms of underarousal of the autonomic nervous system. The psychopath does not develop anxiety or fear in the presence of punishment or danger because the autonomic nervous system is not aroused by danger. To learn to avoid danger there must be an arousal of the sympathetic nervous system. The psychopath does not respond to cues of potential danger. His/her low autonomic response rate to punishment and danger is in the form of a low heart rate or a low galvanic skin response. (The galvanic skin response measures the conductivity of the skin to electricity, which increases when one sweats. Since sweat and a high heart rate depend on the arousal of the SNS, a low autonomic response is a sign of an underaroused ANS.)

Improper functioning of the ANS in psychopaths results in poor avoidance conditioning for psychopaths. Avoidance conditioning is negative reinforcement based on an escape or avoidance response, that is, the ability of the individual to anticipate the consequences of his/her action in order to avoid punishment and pain (Chapter 13). In a typical avoidance conditioning experiment a rat learns to associate the appearance of a conditioned stimulus (a red light) with the delivery of an unconditioned stimulus (shock or pain). The rat is then given an opportunity to learn a response (pressing a lever or running from the room) by which the shock can be avoided or escaped. This is diagrammed as follows:

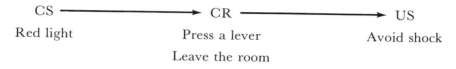

CS ——————————→ CR ——————————→ US

Red light   Press a lever   Avoid shock

Leave the room

One theory as put forth by Mowrer is that the red light creates fear through arousal of the autonomic nervous system, and the conditioned escape or avoidance response reduces or eliminates the fear and anxiety. Another theory is that the avoidance of pain in itself is reinforcement for the conditioned avoidance response (Chapter 13). In either case, since the psychopath does not experience fear or anxiety, he/she does not condition easily to avoidance responses, which is necessary to avoid conflicts with the legal system (Mednick et al., 1982).

Hare (Mednick et al., 1982) found psychopaths to be among the most dangerous of the recidivists in a prison population. A British study by Hinton (Mednick et al., 1982; Hinton, 1983) found two types of violent offenders. One type commits violent crimes against strangers for gain (robbery or murder for gain), whereas the second type commits acts of violence against friends and family members without any property gain. The former group makes up the recidivist and career criminal group, and this group is characterized by an underaroused autonomic nervous system. The latter group is characterized by brain damage and mental illness. Mednick et al. (1982) suggest that we distinguish those offenders who are violent against strangers from those offenders who are violent within a friendship group. This distinction also makes sense in terms of two different types of aggression: (1) *predatory* aggression or aggression for gain, and (2) *affective* or emotional aggression—aggression growing out of hatred, anger, and fear. This issue is discussed below.

Brain Laterality and Criminal Behavior

As noted in Chapter 11, the brain is divided from left to right into two hemispheres, connected by the corpus callosum. Each hemisphere has its own specific functions, but in a normal brain the two parts of the brain interact and communicate with one another. Asymmetry of the two hemispheres, that is, unequal functioning, can lead to major behavioral problems.

The left hemisphere is the dominant hemisphere for right-handed people (which is about 90 percent of the population), since the left hemisphere controls the right side of the body. Seventy percent of left-handers are left-hemisphere dominant, whereas the other 30 percent are either right-hemisphere dominant or bilateral. The langauge areas of the brain are in the left hemisphere in the frontal and temporal lobes for left-hemisphere-dominant people. Left-hemisphere activity involves language, memory, thought, and planning, whereas the right hemisphere involves spatial and tactual skills as well as nonverbal skills.

There are two critical aspects to hemispheric specialization, one related to sex and one related to handedness. Females are generally regarded as more left-hemisphere dominant, whereas males are more right-hemisphere dominant. This issue is discussed below (Kalat, 1988; Kolb and Whishaw, 1985).

Left-handed people have a much higher rate of mental, social, and behavioral disturbances and illnesses (Kalat, 1988; Herron, 1980; Porac and Coren, 1981). It has been noted in the criminological literature that criminals are more likely than noncriminals to be left-handed. A study by Gabrielli and Mednick (Nachshon and Denno, 1987) found that 64 percent of left-handers had been arrested once, compared to 29 percent of the right-handers. On the other hand, a study by Nachshon and Denno (1987) revealed that left-handedness was greater among nonoffenders than among offenders. However, 60 percent of the violent offenders had left-eye preference (not left-hand preference), which they related to left-hemispheric dysfunction, as discussed by Yeudall and others. Nachshon and Denno concluded that more research is needed on the issue of handedness and criminality.

Hare (1987:218 ff.) has looked at psychopathy as a function of hemispheric dysfunction. The left hemisphere processes language for most people. Hare found that psychopaths have less hemispheric lateralization, and the left hemisphere is less capable of processing verbal information in psychopaths. This means that psychopaths are less attuned to the social definitions and norms of society, which depend on language and symbolic interaction. Social psychologists (Chapter 14) have placed great emphasis on language skills as a basis for socialization and social control.

The Frontal and Temporal Lobes

Two areas of the brain critical to the emotional and motivational aspects of behavior are the frontal and temporal lobes (see Figure 11–6). These two lobes are located at the front or anterior part of the brain, and they are located in both the left and right hemispheres.

The temporal lobes include the hippocampus, the amygdala, the auditory cortex, and the limbic cortex, and they have rich connections with the hypothalamus. This interrelated group of areas of the brain is often referred to as the limbic system, although it is more of an interaction of several critical parts of the brain rather than an integrated system (Kolb and Whishaw, 1985; Kalat, 1988).

The temporal lobes are involved in auditory and visual sensory processing, in long-term memory (especially in the hippocampus and the amygdala), and in the emotions of anger, fear, hate, and love. Language is also partially contained in the temporal lobes (Kalat, 1988; Kolb and Whishaw, 1985). Temporal lobe damage is often found in temporal lobe epilepsy or temporal lobe lesions. Such conditions can lead to violence and rage (Mark and Ervin, 1970; Kalat, 1988).

Electrical stimulation of the amygdala area will produce either violent rages or calmness, depending on which area is stimulated. The amygdala is involved in feeding, drinking, and sexual behavior as well as aggression. The close connection in the brain between sexual behavior and violence is important in understanding sexual violence, which will be discussed below.

The frontal lobe includes the motor cortex, Broca's language area, and the prefrontal cortex. The frontal lobes are involved especially in motor coordination, memory, long-range planning, and spatial orientation. Damage to the frontal lobes results in severe personality changes, as seen in the case of Phineas Gage, who had an iron bar pass through the frontal lobe as a result of an industrial accident. He became a violent and moody person after the accident. Individuals with frontal lobe damage become nasty, psychopathic, and antisocial, with abnormal sexual behavior and an inability to plan ahead or to see the future consequences of their actions (Kolb and Whishaw, 1985).

In summary, the temporal and frontal lobes are involved in perception, planning, and memory, as well as aggression, sex, and hunger. The integration of basic biological instincts and learned patterns of behavior occurs in these parts of the brain.

Yeudall et al. (1985; Nachshon and Denno, 1987) have developed a three-dimensional model of the brain to explain criminality and violence. There is a left–right dimension involving the left and right hemispheres; there is a top–bottom dimension involving the neocortex and the limbic system; and there is a front–back dimension involving the temporal and frontal lobes (front or anterior), and the parietal and occipital lobes (back or posterior). Yeudall and his associates found from many years of studying the brains of criminals that they have frontal and temporal lobe damage, which is located in the left or dominant hemisphere. Seventy-six percent of the aggressive criminals studied showed evidence of left-hemisphere dysfunction in the frontal and temporal lobes. Yeudall et al. (1985) found that 91 percent of the psychopaths examined had dominant hemisphere dysfunction in the temporal and frontal lobes. Sexual offenders also showed this pattern of brain defect.

Research with juveniles (Yeudall et al., 1982) found the opposite pattern, that is, juveniles had greater nondominant or right-hemisphere dysfunction in the temporal and frontal lobes. They explained this finding in terms of (1) the low number of violent offenders in the youthful offender group, and (2) the presence of depression and mood disorders in the youthful group. Depressed patients have non-dominant-hemispheric disorders. This is consistent with a position I will take that few offenders are career offenders and/or dangerous offenders. It is also consistent with Mednick's statement that violent offenders can be classified into two groups, those who attack strangers for monetary gain, and those who attack family members because of fear, hate, or anger. Yeudall et al. (1982) found a clustering of drug and alcohol abuse along with depression among the delinquent population. They used a power spectral EEG to map the brain, and this enabled them to differentiate violent criminals from other populations in situations where a normal EEG would not.

Brain Injuries and Trauma

A very high rate of brain injuries has been reported for delinquents (Lewis, 1981; Lewis and Balla, 1976; Yeudall et al. 1985). This can be the result of child abuse, the violent environment of the delinquent, or the lack of adequate medical attention when head injuries occur. D. Lewis (1986) found that 14 of 14 juveniles sentenced to death for violent crimes had major neurological defects. Lawyers paid no attention to such defects during the trials of these juveniles. Abnormal EEG readings have been found in criminal populations as a result of head injuries, and epileptic seizures are also a result of head trauma. Violent repeat offenders have four times the number of abnormal EEG readings as those of offenders with only one offense. In one study 60 percent of the violent offenders had abnormal EEG readings. Yeudall found that 70 percent of the violent offenders he examined had suffered from head injuries (Volavka, 1987; Mednick et al., 1982).

Slow alpha-wave activity has been found among criminal populations. The slow-alpha-wave syndrome has been interpreted as a sign of a low level of autonomic nervous system responsiveness, associated with difficulty in learning avoidance responses (Mednick et al., 1982; Volavka, 1987).

The Neurotransmitter System and Violence

As stated in Chapter 11, the transmission of nerve impulses is both electric and biochemical. The chemicals that act in the synapses (spaces between neurons) to transmit impulses to other neurons are called neurotransmitters. To review, the major neurotransmitters are:

Acetylcholine (ACh)
Norepinephrine (NE)
Dopamine (DA)
Serotonin (5-HT)

Acetylcholine will increase all types of aggression: *affective* (aggression with emotion, anger, fear); *predatory* (aggression used to kill and feed on other animals); and *sexual* (aggression as part of sexual behavior). Dopamine and norepinephrine increase affective and sexual aggression and decrease predatory aggression. Epinephrine decreases all three types of aggression. Serotonin decreases all three types of aggression (Moyer, 1976; Cloninger, 1987). One way of summarizing these relationships is to note that predatory aggression, which involves eating and basic survival mechanisms of the brain, is increased by acetylcholine, dopamine, and norepinephrine; serotonin, and to a lesser extent epinephrine, decrease all three types of aggression. In other words, different neurotransmitter systems are involved in different types of aggressive behavior.

Nutrition, Pollution, and the Brain

Any chemical substance that enters the body can potentially affect the brain, including the food we eat, the water we drink, and the air we breathe. In this way the environment in which we live enters our brain and influences our behavior.

The major neurotransmitter systems use food products as precursors (substances or amino acid chains which are converted into neurotransmitters). Choline is converted into acetylcholine; tyrosine is converted into dopamine, norepinephrine, and epinephrine; tryptophan is converted into serotonin (Kalat, 1988:57).

A dietary condition related to behavioral disorders is hypoglycemia, a low blood sugar level. Insulin, secreted by the pancreas, removes sugar from the bloodstream, converts sugar into fats, and stores it in the liver. The fat is then reconverted into sugar when the body needs it. For people who are hypoglycemic, the body produces abnormally low amounts of insulin, and the blood sugar level is low. Hypoglycemia can also be produced in people prone to the condition by a diet heavy in refined sugars. The sugar exhausts the insulin supply, and without insulin the blood sugar level becomes too low. People become very anxious, excitable, confused, dizzy, and sometimes even violent while hypoglycemic (Virkkunen, 1987; Moyer, 1987; Valzelli, 1981). It should be noted the alcohol is rich in sugar and can produce hypoglycemia. Hypoglycemia is also a major characteristic of the premenstrual syndrome. I noted in Chapter 13 in connection with the Washington, D.C. delinquency prevention project that the delinquents would arrive at the project with a 32-ounce coke and a moon pie. In the famous trial of Dan White, who killed the mayor and city commissioner of San Francisco, the "Twinkee defense" was introduced because White had consumed 40 Twinkees just before the killings. He was given a reduced sentence (see Chapter 20).

Fishbein (1981) took a group of subjects from a young adult institution in Florida who had been rated high on a hypoglycemia symptoms test, and by placing these inmates on a low-refined-sugar diet for one month, was able to reduce the number of maladaptive behaviors reported for the group.

An excess of lead and cadmium in the brain can lead to a 50- to 75-point deficit in IQ scores (Fishbein and Thatcher, 1982). The widespread pollution of the air by gasoline fumes from automobiles has caused a great increase in the lead contamination of the environment (National Academy of Sciences, 1980). The role of nutrition and pollution in the functioning of the brain can be expected to become even more important in the future as new research is carried on (Nutrition Foundation, 1984).

Walsh did a hair analysis of Henry Lee Lucas, a drifter who has confessed to more than 300 murders. The exact number is unknown, but it is probably well above 12. The hair analysis showed high levels of lead and cadmium and low levels of zinc and magnesium. An analysis of the hair of James Q. Huberty, the man who killed 21 persons in a McDonald's restaurant in San Diego, revealed cadmium concentrations over 30 times that of the normal level, and lead concentrations over 8 times the normal level (Walsh, 1984, 1985). Pihl et al. (1982) also found elevated levels of lead and cadmium in hair samples from violent offenders.

Sociologists have discussed unemployment and poverty as causes of criminal behavior. One of the most obvious links is between diet, environmental pollution, the brain, and poverty. Poor people are much more likely to suffer brain damage from pollution and a poor diet than are wealthy people.

We know that there is a high rate of brain cancer in the Houston–Galveston area, which has a concentration of petrochemical industries and pollutants. An interesting study would be to evaluate and compare the impact of pollutants on the brain with changes in the rate of violent crimes in the area over the years. An even better research project would be to measure the lead and cadmium levels of violent recidivists in the Texas Prison System.

A review of nutrition, corrections, and criminology can be found in Fishbein and Pease (1988).

Hyperactivity and Attention Deficit Disorders

There are serious behavioral problems referred to as "learning disabilities," "hyperactivity," "attention-deficit disorders," and "minimal brain dysfunction." I will treat these disorders as a common group of disorders related to minimal brain damage.

Hyperactivity has been related to head injuries, malnutrition, child abuse, exposure to toxins, and infections. The hyperactive child has behavioral problems, has a short attention span, is impulsive, and he/she is likely to be a school failure. Males are five times more likely to be hyperactive than females. These individuals often are in trouble with the law (Kalat, 1988; Kolb and Whishaw, 1985; Satterfield, 1987; Freier, 1986).

Satterfield (1987:163) reported that 64 percent of the admissions to the California Youth Authority had attention-deficit disorders. These subjects suffered from low cortical arousal (as do the psychopaths discussed above). Stimulants have been shown to be useful in the treatment of hyperactivity. Since the hyperactive child suffers from low cortical arousal, hyperactive behavior is a way of compensating for the low level of arousal. The child needs stimulation and excitement. The observation is often made that psychopaths need excitement and thrills, which is why they commit crimes. It may be that hyperactivity is an extension or aspect of the underaroused autonomic nervous system syndrome.

Moffitt et al. (1987) found that attention-deficit disorders (ADD) were higher among delinquents than among nondelinquents. A diagnosis of ADD was present in 18 percent of the delinquent group compared to 2 percent of the nondelinquent group. ADD/delinquent subjects (both ADD and delinquency in same subject) showed a greater level of cognitive defects than did non-ADD/delinquent subjects, and nondelinquent/ADD subjects had better cognitive functioning and verbal skills than did the ADD/delinquency group. There is a special subgroup of ADD children who have neurological problems, are aggressive and antisocial, and who are at high risk for later delinquent careers. Moffitt et al. concluded that we need to focus on the ADD plus delinquency syndrome, which is part of a more general neurological basis for antisocial behavior, along with psychopathy, the underaroused autonomic nervous system, and the hemispheric dysfunctions.

Fishbein et al. (1987) in a National Institute of Drug Abuse study reported that antisocial personalities could and should be differentiated from violent and aggressive persons. Aggressive subjects had low alpha and high delta waves as shown on a brainstem-evoked potential examination. Aggressive subjects showed low arousal levels and frontal lobe dysfunction, which is consistent with the work of Mednick, Yeudall, and others cited above. It was possible in this study to differentiate antisocial and aggressive persons. This is a critical step in early diagnosis and treatment. The report also noted a high level of drug and alcohol use among both antisocial and aggressive individuals, and the authors suggested that both an antisocial personality and an aggressive personality contributed independently to drug and alcohol abuse.

Farrington et al. (1987), on the basis of a British study of adolescent boys, concluded that boys with hyperactivity–impulsivity–attention deficits (HIA) could be distinguished from youths with conduct problems (CP), even though the two groups overlapped by some 60 percent. The HIA group were charged with a first offense at an earlier age, they became chronic offenders, they had low IQ scores, and they came from families with criminal fathers. CP boys had more convictions for the first offense as adults, and they came from families characterized by poor parenting and poor supervision. Both HIA and CP were predictive of later delinquency independent of one another, with CP as a better predictor, but they were additive in their influence on later delinquent careers. This type of study supports the growing notion that there may be subgroups of delinquents who are (1) hyperactive or neurologically defective, (2) antisocial, or (3) some combination or interaction of both.

SEX AND CRIMINAL BEHAVIOR

Sexual Differences

Male and female differences start with genetic differences, which are in turn influenced by environmental experiences. At conception the male is an XY and the female is an XX (Chapter 10). All newly fertilized eggs (zygotes) are female until about the second or third week after conception. If there is a Y chromosome present, the embryo starts to send out male sex hormones (androgens, of which testosterone is the best known). The embryo then develops male sex organs and a male brain. In some instances the fetus may be an XO, XXY, or XYY (Chapter 10). At puberty major sex changes occur in the body that differentiates the typical male body from the female body.

The XX and XY chromosomal systems affect the brain. The hypothalamus controls the pituitary gland, which in turn contols the adrenal glands, the testes (male sex organ), and the ovaries (female sex organ). In the presence of a Y chromosome, the testes produce androgens; in the presence of the X chromosome, the ovaries produce estrogen and progesterone. Since the male carries both a Y and an X chromosome, the male produces male and female sex hormones, and the female produces testosterone as well as estrogen. The male production of testosterone is about 10 times that of the normal female, but it is testosterone and not estrogen that controls the female sex drive and sex behavior (Kalat, 1988; Carlson, 1986; Parsons, 1980).

There are two conditions under which the impact of androgens can create abnormal male/female characteristics. In the case of the *androgenized female*, the female fetus is exposed to excess testosterone because the mother has a high level of circulating testosterone which reaches the fetus through the shared blood supply between mother and fetus. The same thing can happen after birth if the female produces excess testosterone because of the malfunctioning of her adrenal glands (Kalat, 1988; Carlson, 1986; Parsons, 1980; Carlson, 1980). Androgenized females are more masculine in appearance and behavior. They have been described by Money and Ehrhardt (1972) as tomboyish, with interests in masculine clothes, toys, and behavioral pursuits (Parsons, 1980).

In the male there is a condition called *androgen insensitivity*, whereby during the fetal stage the brain does not develop receptor sites for androgen. Regardless of the testosterone level, these males will look and behave like females because the brain is not receiving testosterone.

The *activational effect* of sex hormones is in terms of the brain. The male brain develops differently from the female brain, and as a consequence there are different behaviors associated with being a male and a female. The brain, not the sex organs, control behavior (this may be difficult for some college males to accept). During the fetal stage right-hemispheric development is more prominent than left in males (see the discussion of laterality above). One theory, put forth by Geschwind and Galaburda, is that testosterone delays the development of the left hemispheres in males, thus giving males a larger and more prominent right hemisphere. Males are more prone to left-handedness and language dysfunctions such as dyslexia and stuttering. Males are better than females in mathematics and worse in language skills (Kalat, 1988; Parsons, 1980). Males suffer more left-hemisphere dysfunction as found in the frontal and temporal lobes (see the discussion above).

Behavioral Differences in Males and Females

Maccoby and Jacklin (1974) identify four major and important differences between males and females:

1. Females are more verbal (left hemisphere).
2. Males are more visual, audio, and spatial (right hemisphere).

3. Males are better in science and mathematics.
4. Males are more aggressive, dominant, and curious.

The conclusions are framed in terms of general statements rather than statements about specific individuals. Some females are great mathematicians, and many males have verbal abilities. In general, males are better athletes than females, although there are great female athletes. For criminologists the important differences relate to aggression and antisocial behaviors.

There are two ways of accounting for behavioral differences between the sexes. The first is based on biological differences; the second is based on social differences and the ways in which males and females are socialized. Starting at birth a male is differentiated from a female by name and color of booties. In most cultures boys are expected to be tough and dominant, whereas females are to be quiet, submissive, and gentle.

Sociologists and anthropologists emphasize socialization and social roles (Chapter 14). Mead (1935) as an anthropologist discussed three different societies; in one society males and females were gentle and submissive; in one society males and females were dominant and aggressive; and in one society males behaved as females are supposed to, and females behaved as males are supposed to. Freeman (1983) published a different account of the findings put forth by Margaret Mead. Freeman argued that Mead overemphasized the cultural aspects of personality while ignoring the biological foundations of human behavior. The ''nurture over nature'' picture painted by Mead was very popular in the 1940–1960 era, as has been noted several times in this book. The more usual interpretation of male/female differences is to view these differences as an interaction of biological, psychological, and sociological variables (Parsons, 1980). This is certainly the view taken in this book.

It is known that historically the male has played an important role in the political and economic life of communities. In hunting and fishing economies the male is the hunter and the dominant person, whereas in agricultural communities the female plays a more dominant role (Parsons, 1980). Sex roles are limited by biology, such as the woman as the mother, but they are most flexible, as we can see in modern urban industrial societies, where females act as lawyers, medical doctors, police officers, and soldiers (Rossi, 1985).

A study cited to show the impact of socialization on sexual behavior is one from the Dominican Republic (Kalat, 1988). Due to a genetic defect the young boys do not have penis development until adolescence. They are reared as girls until puberty, at which time they develop male sexual characteristics and are then treated as males. They assume adequate male gender identification at adolescence. It must be remembered that these boys, though reared as girls, were genetically and biologically males; they had male testosterone levels and a male-organized brain. The loss of a penis or incomplete development of a penis does not determine hormonal levels or brain organization. Another study involves a male infant who lost the penis shortly after birth due to an accident during circumcision. He was reared as a female and adapted to the female role. However, another study of the same individual reported that she had a difficult time as a female, looked like a male, and was not accepted as a female. There is also evidence that she had been castrated and had received estrogen therapy (Carlson, 1986:394; Bell et al., 1981:215; Carlson, 1980).

Males have more mathematical ability than do females. At the same time, males are encouraged by society to take math and science courses, whereas females are encouraged to take English and foreign languages. Are mathematical abilities biological or social? Benbow (1986) did a major study of mathematically and verbally precocious students (top 1 in 10,000). In this study it was hypothesized that verbal reasoning, like math, was in the right hemisphere, not in the left hemisphere as are verbal abilities. She found that this group was high in left-handedness, asthma and allergies, and myopia. These dysfunctions have all been traced by Geschwind to right-hemisphere development, due to the impact of testosterone on the left hemisphere in males. Thus she found males to be superior in mathematics because of the way the male brain is organized in response to testosterone.

The observation that males are violent and are mathematically inclined can be interpreted as depending on social reinforcement. However, if males are naturally inclined toward violence and math, it is possible that society reinforces those behaviors that are already present. The social reinforcement of violence does not mean that violence grows out of social reinforcement. Both biology and social reinforcement are involved in any behavior, as we have noted repeatedly in this book.

Human Sexual Behavior

Human sexual behavior is characterized by several basic biological conditions:

1. Along with other mammals, the human female carries the egg inside the body, where it is fertilized. A mother-infant relationship is established during pregnancy and after the birth of the infant is continued with nursing and caring for the infant after the birth. A breach of the mother–child bond can result in serious behavioral problems for the child in later life.

2. The human sexual cycle is a 12-month cycle that is independent of the menstrual cycle. Other species, including primates, have a very definite mating cycle when the female is sexually attractive to and receptive to the male. Such mating cycles are governed by changes in climate and physiological changes in both the male and female.

   One theory put forth by evolutionary biologists and sociobiologists is that the male/female bond at the human level depends on a constant sexual bond between male and female (Washburn and McCown, 1978; Lockard, 1980; Barash, 1977; Symons, 1979).

   In many species after the mating cycle the male leaves and the female is left alone to rear and care for the offspring. The long period of dependency for human childhood requires the presence of a male in the family. We use social and legal pressures, such as the law of marriage and divorce, to strengthen the male/female bond, which is evidence that the biological/sexual bond between male and female is in itself not enough to sustain the bond.

3. The human male produces millions of sperm cells every several days, whereas the female produces one egg per month. In some species millions of eggs are produced, and only one or two reach maturity (called the ''r'' strategy). In the human species one egg is produced and fertilized with the expectation that it will reach maturity (called the ''K'' strategy) (Barash, 1977). In the case of the K strategy the female has a major investment in one egg, one mate, and one offspring, and the mate must remain around until the child is mature.

Human sexual behavior is learned behavior, based on biology, as is all human behavior (Chapter 13). The brain controls sexual behavior as well as all other behavior. For a sexual response to occur, the proper area of the brain must be stimulated, either by internal or external stimuli. Much of the control of sexual behavior is in the hypothalamus and areas related to the limbic system.

Nonhuman species respond to stimuli on the basis of unlearned or innate reaction patterns; that is, given a stimulus, a response occurs (Chapter 13). These responses are controlled by basic biological stimuli, such as songs by males, or dances and strutting, or odors from the female, or feathers and horns on the male.

In the case of human sexual behavior the male comes prepared at maturity to respond sexually to the female, and the female to the male. The usual attraction at puberty is male/female, and at that time couples pair off for courtship and sex. On the basis of brain organization (different for males and females) classical and operant conditioning occurs. As in the case of Pavlovian conditioning of the bell and food, conditioning can occur in the case of sexual behavior. A bell or buzzer can act as a conditioned stimulus for an unconditioned stimulus (female) and an unconditioned response (male sexual behavior). Sexual arousal can be associated with flowers, music, clothing, food, and most of the stimuli in our environment. That is why sexy young females sell toothpaste and underarm deodorants in TV advertisements. When a male responds to a female sexually, the arousing stimulus may be any one of many stimuli in the external environment, plus the past conditioning history of the person and his own hormonal levels at the time.

Sexual Deviancy

The usual forms of sexual deviancy are:

Transsexualism: a physical change of a male into a female

Transvestism: a male who dresses as a female

Fetishism: attachment of sexual desires and feelings to stimulus objects such as shoes or dresses or hair or undergarments

Voyeurism: observing others in the nude or while engaged in sexual activities without the knowledge of those being observed

Exhibitionism: practice of males exhibiting their sex organs to females in public places and against the wishes of the female

Sadism:gaining of sexual pleasure from the infliction of pain on others

Masochism: gaining of sexual pleasure from the administration of pain by others to oneself

Pedophilia: refers to sexual activities with children

Homosexuality: refers to sexual activities with someone of the same sex (i.e., male/male or female/female)

Bestiality: refers to sexual activities with animals

Necrophilia: sexual activities with a corpse

The explanations of sexual deviancy involve all the topics discussed above as aspects of human sexuality. Brain organization and hormonal levels are involved, since the brain controls sexual behavior. Learning is involved. Individuals are conditioned to associate sexual feelings with clothing or music or children or observing others. This is classical and operant conditioning. A male can be predisposed to homosexuality by his brain organization and hormonal systems, and he can be conditioned to reject females as sex objects while accepting males as sex objects. A person can be conditioned in childhood to associate pain with sexual pleasure through the punishment of sexual activities of children by parents. The brain mechanisms controlling sex and pain are very closely related to one another. Punishment can act as a conditioned reinforcer for other behaviors, such as sexual behaviors (Coleman et al., 1984; Drzazga, 1960; Gebbard et al., 1965; Karpman, 1954; de River, 1958; Money and Ehrhardt, 1972; Carlson, 1986; Bell et al., 1981).

Sexual behavior and sexual deviancy involve all the mechanisms of behavior discussed herein, including the brain and nervous system and the environment and learned experiences with the environment.

Sex and Criminal Behavior

As noted in Chapter 16, males are much more criminalistic than females, being convicted and sentenced 5 to 10 times as often as females. Simon (1983) reported that 11 percent of those arrested for violent crimes were females, whereas 23 percent of those arrested for property crimes were females. Warren (1986) cited lower figures, that is, 7 percent of the robberies and 5 percent of the burglaries were by females.

The discrepancy between male and female crime rates has several important implications for criminology. There are no sociological theories that explain these differences. If social opportunity theory or differential association or labeling or social bonding explain human behavior, females should be as criminalistic as males (Harris, 1977; Sheley, 1985). The second point is that among career criminals the sex ratio is 2:1, not 10:1. Blumstein et al. (1986:67–76) found less than a 2:1 male/female ration for career criminals.

Female criminality has been explained within the framework of major criminological theories. Lombroso and Freud placed emphasis on biological factors and the innate inferiorities and weaknesses of females. In a 1950 book, Pollack argued that females were more deadly and more criminalistic than males, but that female criminality was kept hidden (Sheley, 1985; Simon, 1983; Warren, 1986). In the 1970s a new view of and interest in female criminality emerged in American criminology, put forth by female criminologists. Adler (1975) published *Sisters in Crime,* in which she argued from a sociological perspective that females had been gaining equality with males in socioeconomic roles because of the feminist movement, and this new equality and freedom created more opportunities for females to commit crimes. The liberating influence of the feminist movement was critical to Adler's argument.

Simon (1975) argued that the women's liberation movement had little to do with female criminality. She also found little support for the argument that the criminal justice system discriminates against females by either being too harsh or too lenient. "Data do not indicate how significant a factor the sex of the defendant may be in determining guilt or imposing sentence" (Simon, 1983:1667).

Although there has been an increase in female criminality as measured by official records over the past twenty years, it has occured in fraud, forgery, and embezzlement. There has been no increase in violent crimes by females (Simon, 1975, 1983; Warren, 1986). This is a critical factor in terms of what was stated above about male/female differences in brain organization and aggressive behavior.

Several writers, notably Steffensmeier and Steffensmeier, Weis, Smart, Box, and Hale, have denied the "female liberation" approach to female criminality. They noted that female criminality cannot be explained in terms of male/female sex roles since socially males and females still play quite different roles in our society (Siegel, 1986; Nettler, 1984; Sheley, 1985).

VIOLENCE AND AGGRESSION

Biological and Psychological Variables

Violent behavior involves the biological variables we discussed earlier, that is, genetic structure and brain structure. The brain, hormones, and the neurotransmitter system are critical to an understanding of violent behavior (Wolfgang and Weiner, 1982).

Psychological variables related to violent behavior include classical and operant conditioning as well as social learning theory (Chapter 13). In our discussions of learning theory we indicated how violence and aggression can be related to the principles of learning.

Social Variables

Sociologists have studied violence and aggression as aspects of age, sex, and race; for example, young black males are involved in violence both as perpetrators and as victims (Newman, 1979; Wolfgang, 1958). Sociologists have also studied violence as an aspect of culture, that is, as a subculture of violence based on social norms, customs, and a way of life (Wolfgang and Ferracutti, 1967). The idea that violence is a product of cultural norms has all the problems associated with any theory that explains behavior in terms of the social environment (Chapter 14). The environment influences the brain; the brain, not the social environemnt, controls behavior.

It has also been observed that certain countries have high murder rates, whereas other countries have low murder rates. The United States has a high murder rate compared to those of England, Sweden, Denmark, and Japan (Newman, 1979; Archer and Gartner, 1984; Barlow, 1987). The southeastern part of the United States has had a high rate of violence over the years. Gastil found that the high homicide rate in the south was due to the southern culture, based on mob violence, a frontier mentality, vengeance, and possession of guns. Loftin and Hill, on the other hand, found that economic variables, not cultural differences, explained the high murder rate in the south (Siegel, 1986; Barlow, 1987). The issue of southern violence is far from settled at this time.

It has been stated that since some countries at some times have high crime rates, and other countries at other times have low crime rates, this must prove that violence is cultural and not biological or psychological, since people with the same biological and psychological traits are violent in some cultures and not in others. The "culture causes violence" theme is found in the work of Montagu (1968). On the other hand, Lorenz (1966) and Ardrey (1966) argue for a basic biological model of aggression.

Several comments are in order concerning broad cultural interpretations of violence and aggression. All behavior involves the organism in interaction with the environment. All persons are capable of violence given a proper set of environmental conditions. Each person responds to the environment in a different way. More people will be violent in one cultural setting (Friday night in a bar, or after a major football game) than in other settings (Christmas Eve in a Catholic Church). James Huberty walked into a McDonald's in San Diego and killed a number of people on a very quiet morning. The brain responds to environmental stimuli in many different ways. The "culture causes violence" argument assumes that the environment causes behavior, rather than looking at behavior as an

$$\text{Environment} \longrightarrow \text{Brain} \longrightarrow \text{Behavior}$$

process involving the interaction of many variables. Such an argument also contains an ecological or aggregative fallacy, since it assumes that we can know something about individual behavior from aggregate group data. In the same environment most people will be nonviolent; a few will be violent. We have to know more about Organism–Environment interaction to handle such an observation.

The Violent Offender

The Violent Offender Project at Ohio State University under the directorship of John Conrad and Simon Dinitz (1977) found that 61 percent of violent offenses were committed by chronic offenders (Hamparian et al., 1978:6). They also found that most chronic offenders start their criminal careers at an early age, a finding that was also true of the works of the Gluecks, Mannheim and Wilkins, and Wolfgang et al. (Hamparian et al., 1978:8). Sixty-five percent of the violent offenders had five offenses or more. Of the group containing murderers, assaulters, and rapists, 57 percent had five offenses, whereas 76 percent of the robbers had five offenses (Miller et al., 1982:216). Once an offender was arrested, there was an 85 percent probability that he/she would be arrested again, and 5 percent of the offenders with five or more arrests accounted for 15 percent of the violent crimes for which arrests were made (Miller et al., 1982:81). The study showed that robbers were not like murderers, assaulters, and rapists (Miller er al., 1982:106 ff.).

The project concluded that the criminal justice system was ineffective in controlling violent crimes. The more severe the punishment after the first arrest, the shorter the time span until the second arrest; in other words, arrests accelerated the criminal career pattern (Hamparian et al., 1978:119). A Project report estimated that if those committing violent crimes were given a flat-time sentence of 5 years (this in response to the just retribution argument put forth by J. Q. Wilson and others; see Chapter 8) the violent crime rate would be reduced by 25 percent, whereas the prison population would increase by over 500 percent (Van Dine et al., 1979:122–125).

The study of the violent offender found little specialization, that is, these offenders committed nonviolent offenses as well. The study also indicated that one is unable to predict future crimes from past crimes (Miller et al., 1982:215). The report concluded that violent offenders will continue in a career of crime after the first arrest, the criminal justice system is ineffective and does not deter, incapacitation will not reduce the rate of violent crimes, the criminal justice system in unpredictable, and a large proportion of violent crimes are not cleared by the police (Miller et al., 1982:223).

The Sexually Violent Offender

Most deviant sex acts do not involve violence. The serious sex offenses involve either violence and force or an offense involving a child. Rape or sexual assault is defined as a sexual act involving force or the threat of force against the will of the victim.

In his study of rape in Philadelphia, Amir (1971) found that 80 percent of the victims of rape were black, 77 percent of the rapes were black attacker-black victim, 16 percent were white–white, 4 percent were white–black, and 3 percent were black–white. Rape is an intraracial affair, with blacks being both the rapists and the victims. The belief that black males attack white females is a myth.

Rape is an underreported crime due to the nature of the crime and the difficulties that female victims have with the police and with lawyers (Barlow, 1987; Siegel, 1986). Earlier studies of rape showed that 50 percent involved strangers, and 50 percent involved friends and acquaintances. More recent studies have placed the figure of stranger-to-stranger rape at 80 percent (Barlow, 1987; Siegel, 1986).

Testosterone not only affects the development of the male brain, but is also related to sexual violence. The exact relationship between testosterone levels and violence is not clear since testosterone activates violence under some circumstances and not others (Prentsky, 1985). The impact of testosterone on male sexual behavior will depend on brain organization and the way in which the male brain was influenced by testosterone during the prenatal period of development. The environmental situation and learning also enter into the response of the male to sexual stimulation.

All the factors involved in any human behavior are involved in rape: genetic, hormonal, brain functioning, and learning variables. Any abnormality of the frontal and temporal lobes can result in abnormal sexual behavior. The brain has capacities for both the arousal and the control of sex responses. When socially acceptable sex behavior occurs, the rational part of the brain is in control of the emotional part. When deviant sexual behavior occurs, it is because the emotional part of the brain is in control.

Rape involves violence as a part of the sex act. As was noted above, sex and pain are closely related in the brain. Rapists are conditioned to associate pain with sexual gratification, just as fetishists associate shoes with sexual arousal.

Groth and Birnbaum (1979) have classified rapists into three categories: (1) rape growing out of anger and anxiety, or rape motivatied by emotional feelings; (2) rape for power, or the use of rape as a means of dominating and humiliating females; and (3) sadistic rape, or the association of sexual arousal with the pain and torture of another person. Rape is not an act motivated by sexual feeling, but rather, is an act of violence. It has been estimated that 80 percent of rapists have themselves been sexually abused as children (Groth, 1983). Several feminist authors, notably Brownmiller (1975) and Russell (1975), interpret rape as a manifestation of male dominance over females and an expression of the view that females are the property of males.

Acquaintance rape often involves family members or persons involved in a dating relationship. The line between necking, petting, and sexual intercourse is not clearly defined in our society, and what is viewed as rape by the female may be viewed as an invitation by the male. One of the most helpful moves that could be made would be to teach couples to discuss their sexual expectations openly prior to a potential physical encounter. Often, the female is unable to control the situation after heavy petting occurs.

Recent studies of rapists have focused on the stimulus situation to which the rapist responds sexually. A nonrapist will respond sexually to movies depicting sex between a male and a female on a consensual basis. Rapists respond to sex scenes depicting violence and nonconsensual situations. Rapists often view women as objects to be used (Malamuth and Donnerstein, 1984).

Research projects on sex offenders are using a penile plethsmograph to measure penile erections. The subject is shown a variety of sex scenes: normal male–female, male–male, female–female, child–adult, and sadistic and violent. The responses of the subjects to these scenes are then measured in terms of sexual arousal (*Psychology Today*, March 1986). If such a technique is perfected and works, it will be possible to distinguish the rapist from the violent sadist from the child molester from the homosexual. The way in which the human brain responds to such stimulus situations will depend on genetic endowment, the organization of the brain, the endocrine and hormonal levels, and the past conditioning history of the individual. By using sexual stimuli to test sexual responses of males the S-R pattern of any person can be determined. Such research is consistent with the stimulus–brain–response model of behavior presented in this book.

Premenstrual Syndrome

Some women, perhaps 5 to 10 percent of menstruating women, suffer from premenstrual syndrome (PMS). The levels of estrogen and progesterone are low at the end of the menstrual cycle, and these levels increase just prior to ovulation (release of the egg 14 days after the last menstrual cycle). After ovulation the levels of both estrogen and progesterone drop rapidly, and just prior to the next menstrual cycle, PMS symptoms occur, including bloating, irritability, mood swings, breast tenderness, and tension (Ginsburg and Carter, 1987).

There is no satisfactory definition of PMS. Some social psychologists and sociologists (Bell, Erickson, Ruble) state that the symptoms of PMS are social definitions of how women are supposed to respond to menstruation, that is, behave as weak, neurotic creatures. PMS so defined becomes a part of a culture where females are taught that they are expected to be sick during the menstrual cycle. If we are content to define PMS in terms of what females tell us about PMS, then by definition PMS is what females define as PMS (Ginsburg and Carter, 1987).

The only acceptable definition of and approach to PMS is a medical-biological one. Changes in the hormonal levels must be related to changes in the brain of the female and these changes then traced to changes in female behavior (Bird, 1987). The general conclusion of an interdisciplinary group studying PMS was that more good research is needed (Ginsburg and Carter, 1987). It must be recognized that PMS is a real biological issue with some females, and it is not a figment of the imagination nor is it a social definition of illness. Treatment can vary from drug therapy (usually progesterone) to psychotherapy to counseling.

A few women have committed murder or serious assaults while suffering from PMS. In such cases PMS has been introduced as a legal defense in a few criminal cases (see Chapter 20). It is important to understand that females as well as males respond to sex hormones. The female brain is responsive to these hormones. To understand the behavior, we must understand the neurological processes.

Family Violence

A great deal of the violence that occurs in our society occurs within the family setting, involving spouses and/or parents and children. According to Straus, Gelles, and Steinmetz (1980), 48 million couples were involved in spouse abuse in 1976. The same level of violence is found against the husband by the wife as by the husband against the wife (Nagi, 1983).

Violence within the family is usually emotional violence motivated by anger, fear, and frustration. The day-to-day interaction of individuals within a family setting can cause tension and anxiety. A crying baby does not usually trigger a deadly response on the part of a parent, but if it occurs after years of family strife, unemployment, alcoholism, financial problems, sexual problems, and the like, a baby crying at 2 A.M. can trigger a violent response. A level of anger and hostility is present in the brain of the parent, so that any small incident can trigger a major response.

Spouse and child abuse are part of a general pattern of family conflict and stress. Gelles (1987) has discussed the violent family in terms of the place of the family in the social structure. The violent family is often at the bottom of the socioeconomic ladder, is marked by stress and frustration, has less income and education than the average family, and the parents were often subjected to child abuse and violence when they were children. A recent book on women who kill their husbands (Browne, 1987) found that such women had husbands who were violent, alcoholic, and assaultive. These women lived in fear, with feelings of helplessness. Many women feel that they cannot leave abusive husbands for financial or psychological reasons. The sad thing about child abuse is that children cannot leave the home. The head of a psychiatric hospital in Florida for troubled boys was recently arrested and convicted of sodomizing youths in his charge. These activities had been going on for forty years; officials knew about the abuse but did nothing to stop it for that period of time (*Tallahassee Democrat*, April 17, 1988). A recent letter to a newspaper by an abused child (made into a popular song) expressed the problem in this way: ''Dear Jesus, when will the hurt stop?''

The Murderer

The murderer is often a person who commits one murder out of anger or fear and never commits another offense. On the other hand, the murder may be a biologically and psychologically sick person who kills a great number of people at one time (mass murderer) or who kills over and over again (serial murderer).

The legal term "murder" is a broad term that covers a wide spectrum of behavioral acts.

Most murders are committed by acquaintances and family members in homes or in bars (Siegel, 1986; Barlow, 1987; Lester, 1986). Wolfgang (1958) found that 63 percent of the murders he studied involved alcohol. These murders occur in bedrooms and kitchens and are motivated by anger and frustration. Such acts represent both emotional aggression and instrumental aggression as defined above.

Most murders are intraracial affairs. Ninety-four percent of the blacks murdered were murdered by blacks; 88 percent of the whites murdered were murdered by whites. The murderer and the victim are usually young black males from the slum areas of urban cities (Siegel, 1986). One of the leading causes of death among young black males is murder. It was noted above that the Center for Disease Control has now classified violence as a disease that should be studied as part of an ecological and epidemiological approach to disease control.

The high rate of male–male murder gives credence to the belief put forward by Moyer and animal behaviorists concerning intermale aggression and competition. Competition and conflict among males are high in many mammalian and primate species.

A most important and unanswered question is the extent to which violent criminals are also property offenders. Some studies have found specialization; that is, violent criminals do not commit nonviolent property offenses. Other studies have found that violent criminals also commit nonviolent offenses (Lester, 1986). This issue is addressed further below in the discussion of career criminals.

As indicated above, many offenders, especially antisocial and psychopathic types, have major brain dysfunctions. The sociological literature on murder looks primarily at age, sex, and race as variables used to explain murder and violence, and it ignores the biological factors. For example, in a book on mass murderers, Levin and Fox (1985) discuss the topic in terms of normal people who are evil and not crazy. As mentioned above, Walsh (1984, 1985) and Pihl et al. (1982) through hair analysis found elevated levels of lead and cadmium in violent offenders and serial murderers. Studies of the brains of violent offenders are not mentioned in the Levin and Fox book.

ALCOHOL AND DRUG ABUSE

Drugs and the Neurotransmitter System

Drugs act on the brain and behavior through the neurotransmitter systems. Drugs are classified as follows:

> *Sedatives/depressants*, which reduce neural activities: barbiturates, antianxiety agents, alcohol

Stimulants and antidepressants, which increase neural activity: amphetamines, cocaine, antidepressant drugs (MAO inhibitors, tricyclic compounds), caffeine, nicotine

Antipsychotic drugs for schizophrenia and depression: chlorpromazine, reserpine, lithium

Opiates: heroin, morphine, codeine

Psychedelics: LSD, mescaline, psilosybin, phencyclidine (angel's dust) cannabis, marijuana (Julien, 1985; Kolb and Whishaw, 1985)

The sedative/depressant drugs decrease the amount of norepinephrine in the brain. Stimulants and antidepressants, on the other hand, increase norepinephrine and serotonin levels in the brain, which in turn stimulate the central nervous system. Alcohol is a depressant; it decreases the amount of norepinephrine in the brain (Restak, 1988; Stephens, 1987).

Drugs have a very reinforcing quality on behavior. Norepinephrine and dopamine stimulate the pleasure centers of the brain. Opiates are also pleasurable because they kill pain and activate the dopamine receptors in the brain. The reinforcement areas are in the hippocampus, the hypothalamus, and the thalamus areas of the brain, areas involved in the temporal and frontal lobes (Carlson, 1986).

Drugs are used extensively today to treat behavioral problems or what is called mental illness. The sedatives are used for anxiety and hysteria disorders. The antipsychotic drugs are used for schizophrenia since they decrease the dopamine levels of the brain. This has led to the theory that schizophrenics have an excess of dopamine and/or dopamine receptors in the brain. Drugs that increase the level of dopamine in the brain (cocaine, amphetamines, and L-dopa) increase the schizophrenic symptoms in patients (Kolb and Whishaw, 1985; Kalat, 1988). Schizophrenics also have evidence of brain damage as found by CAT and PETT scans. The ventricles of the brain (fluid-filled spaces) are much larger in schizophrenics than in nonschizophrenics. It was a CAT scan of the brain of John Hinckley, Jr. (the man who shot Ronald Reagan) that resulted in the verdict of not guilty by reason of insanity in this case (Chapter 20). Lithium is especially useful in the treatment of manic depression, or the bipolar disorders. The psychedelic drugs induce disturbances in cognition and perception, as well as some major emotional disorders (Kolb and Whishaw, 1985; Julian, 1985; Kalat, 1988).

The opiates kill pain by increasing the endorphins in the brain. The word "endorphin" means endogenous morphine, or morphine produced by the body itself as a natural defense against pain. The endorphins can create feelings of pleasure and a real opiate-type "high," as is experienced by runners who experience the release of endorphines in the body. The endorphins are also involved in the pleasure felt from food. On the other hand, the endorphins can dampen sex excitement and feeling. The natural action of the endorphins on the brain creates a new way of dealing with drug addiction by means of the biochemistry of the brain (Levinthal, 1988; *Psychology Today*, July 1988).

Pepinsky (1982:12) made the following comment about the discovery of endorphins in the body:

Human beings produce their own opiates, called "endorphins," and Harrison speculates that marathon runners are more heavily addicted than many veteran mainliners of heroin. People's survival rests in part on habitual opiate production and use. By the time his analysis is finished, principled narcotics enforcement has become a contradiction in terms. I must admit to feeling sheepish after reading Harrison's analysis. I am among those who have called upon criminologists to address higher levels of abstraction about social structure and to ignore biological sources of criminality. Just as Braithwaite perverts Marxist criminology by calling for revolution within the system, so Harrison perverts social science by calling for initial focus on biological processes within individuals.

Some of the most important work on serotonin levels and violence has come from the research of Linnoila and his associates. They found low levels of 5HIAA (a by-product of the metabolization of serotonin by the brain) in impulsive but not in nonimpulsive violent offenders. The same pattern, that is, low serotonin levels, existed in alcoholics. The same pattern also held for arsonists. Most of the impulsive violent offenders and arsonists were also alcoholics. They concluded that there is a need for research as to the interaction of impulsivity, violent behavior, alcoholism, and low glucose tolerance levels (Linnoila, 1983; Virkkunen et al., 1987). In a paper (Virkkunen et al., 1988), M. Linnoila and his associates concluded that they could accurately predict 84 percent of the violent offenders from low serotonin and lower glucose tolerance tests. Such tests could have major implications for the prevention of violent behavior.

Drug Treatment for Aggressive Behaviors

The use of antipsychotic drugs, antidepressant drugs, and anticonvulsant drugs (dilantin) has been successful in the control of violent and aggressive behaviors (Valzelli, 1981; Moyer ,1987; Rubin, 1987; Cloninger, 1987). Low levels of serotonin have been related to high levels of aggression. Tryptophan, the precursor of serotonin, can be used to increase the serotonin level in the brain and thereby reduce the level of aggression (Rubin, 1987; Valzelli, 1981).

On the other hand, drugs that increase norepinephrine levels in the brain and decrease serotonin levels increase aggression. These drugs include amphetamines, caffeine, and alcohol (Valzelli, 1981).

Alcoholism as a Genetic Disease

Many studies have been made of alcoholism as a disease with a strong genetic component. An adoption study done in Denmark found that sons with alcoholic biological fathers were four times as likely to become alcoholics as sons from nonalcoholic families, although both lived in the environment of an adoptive home. Cloninger and others found not only a strong genetic link, but they found that there were two types of alcoholism, one very responsive to environmental factors, and one not at all responsive to environmental factors (Galanter, 1985; National Institue of Alcohol Abuse and Alcoholism, 1985; Goodwin, 1988). One type of alcoholism is *milieu-limited* alcoholism, or alcoholism that occurs in both males and females. It is marked by a family history of moderate and not severe alcoholism, mild alcohol abuse by the sons and daughters, and there are no major problems by either the parents or the children with the law. Milieu-limited alcoholism is carried in the genes, but it depends on an environment in which there is stress and low socioeconomic status in order for the genes to be expressed. This is a very clear expression of gene–environment interaction, as discussed in Chapter 10.

Male-limited alcoholism is the second type of alcoholism. It occurs only in males, it is found in families where the father had severe alcoholism problems but the mother was not an alcoholic, it has a history of early onset in the vulnerable sons, and it occurs in people who know no signs of other psychopathologies (National Institute on Alcohol Abuse and Alcoholism, 1985; Galanter, 1985; Goodwin, 1988). The male-limited alcoholic has serious problems with the criminal law. Twenty-five percent of the alcoholics studied were male-limited alcoholics, and in families with male-limited alcoholism, alcohol abuse was nine times greater for the sons adopted out regardless of the environment than for other families. Wereas milieu-limited alcoholism depends on environmental factors, male-limited alcoholism occurs in most of the environments studied. It appears as if male-limited alcoholism might be carried on the Y chromosome or involve other chromosomes in interaction with the Y chromosome, since only males carry the Y chromosome and only males have this type of alcoholism.

Alcohol and the Brain

Alcohol is a depressant on the central nervous system. It is classified as a depressant drug, along with the barbiturates and antianxiety drugs (Julian, 1985). The behavioral symptoms of alcohol ingestion are disorientation, amnesia, impaired judgment, poor motor control, and violent behavior. Alcohol destroys brain cells, which can lead to serious neurological disorders. If a pregnant female is using alcohol during the course of the pregnancy, the fetus may suffer from a "fetal alcohol syndrome," wherein the fetus is born deformed and brain damaged. Fetal damage also occurs from the use of drugs other than alcohol (Julian, 1985; Rydberg et al., 1985).

Alcohol acts on the brain by interfering with the release of norepinephrine and dopamine. Alcohol and the opiates (narcotics) use the same receptor sites in the brain, and this suggests that alcohol and drug addiction may have common mechanisms (National Institute on Alcohol Abuse and Alcoholism, 1985).

Once in the body, alcohol is converted to *acetaldehyde* by enzymes in the liver. In turn, acetaldehyde has to be converted into another chemical form and then into carbon dioxide and water. If acetaldehyde is allowed to accumulate in the body, the person suffers from nausea and vomiting illness. Individuals who retain acetaldehyde in the blood system do not become alcoholics because they are made ill by alcohol consumption (Julian, 1985; Kalat, 1988). The born alcoholic, the male-limited alcoholic, does not process alcohol normally, and this may be a function of the lack of acetaldehyde in the system (or other enzymes from the liver), which allows the person to engage in excessive drinking. Orientals process acetaldehyde in a different fashion, and they are usually unable to drink; therefore, alcoholism is not a problem for most Orientals (Galanter, 1983; Goodwin, 1988).

Criminality, Violence, and Alcoholism

As mentioned above, male-limited alcoholics commit a high number of crimes. Fifty percent of the crimes involve alcohol either on the part of the offender or the victim (Julian, 1985; Collins, 1981). Nineteen to 39 percent of those arrested report heavy drinking just prior to the offense for which they were arrested. Alcohol is highly correlated with murder, rape, family violence, and traffic accidents. Sixty-three percent of the murders involved alcohol (Wolfgang, 1958). Hypoglycemia is also related to alcoholism, leading to depression, confusion, anxiety, and violence (Pihl and Ross, 1987; Winick, 1986; Collins, 1981).

It is estimated that 56 percent or better of all crimes involve drug use. In Orange County, FL, 84 percent of those arrested were drug users (Florida Department of Law Enforcement, n.d.). Before the crime problem can be solved there must be means for preventing alcohol and drug addiction.

Alcoholism, Crime, and Culture

It has been noted over the years that certain ethnic groups (i.e., Italians and Jews) have a very low rate of alcoholism, whereas other ethnic groups (i.e., Irish) have a very high rate of alcoholism (Winick, 1986; Goodwin, 1988). The explanation given is in cultural terms. The Jews and Italians drink at home and use alcohol as part of a family and religious tradition, so alcoholism is not associated with violence or intoxication. With the Irish, drinking is carried on by males in pubs away from the family, and it is part of a male-dominated social and political group. Heavy drinking is thus encouraged. Room (1983) goes so far as to state that alcoholism is social and not pharmacological.

From the evidence presented above, it is obvious that genetic and neurochemical factors play a major role in alcoholism. For many Orientals, it is a matter of too much acetaldehyde, which is an inherited condition. In the case of milieu-limited alcoholism it is a matter of gene–environment interaction. The individual comes to any environmental situation prepared to learn or not learn a given response. We are born vulnerable to certain environmental situations (Galanter, 1983; National Institute on Alcohol Abuse and Alcoholism, 1985). Gordon (1984) argues from an anthropological/ecological perspective that in rural agrarian societies alcohol is used in a ceremonial and ritualistic way, and it creates integration and social cohesion. In urban societies drinking becomes individualized, asocial, and pathological. It leads to violence and criminal behavior. Jews and Italians exemplify the first pattern, and many Irish, the second pattern. Social factors are involved in alcoholism as in all behavior; however, social factors must enter the brain and change the neural structure of the brain in order to alter behavior. Culture affects the brain, which in turn impacts on behavior.

Alcoholism as a Disease

In his book *The Disease Concept of Alcoholicm* Jellinek (1960) focused on alcoholism as a disease and a medical problem and not a legal problem. He removed alcoholism from the legal category of behavior based on free will and moral responsibility, and he emphasized the biological, psychological, and social causes of alcoholism. If alcoholism is a disease, it should be treated and not punished. The medical versus legal view of alcoholism is discussed in Chapter 21.

Drug and Alcohol Addiction

Drug addiction (including alcohol) is physiological and psychological. Drugs change the neurochemistry of the brain. Drugs reach the reinforcement centers of the brain, or the pleasure and pain areas of the brain. Drugs control behavior by increasing pleasure and decreasing pain. Some drugs (alcohol, barbiturates, opiates) kill pain. Other drugs (stimulants, antidepressants) increase pleasure. Individuals learn through classical and operant conditioning to associate drugs with pleasure and pain (Restak, 1988). Neutral stimuli, such as a needle or a room or a person, can be associated with alcohol or heroin or cocaine. The movie *The Days of Wine and Roses* has as its theme a husband and wife who reinforced the alcoholism in each other. The physiological need and dependency come to be associated with objects in the social world. Akers (1977:135 ff.) interprets alcoholism in terms of social learning theory, social norms, and social definitions of behavior. Alcoholism is not social learning, but learning involving the brain as found in bioenvironmental learning theory (Chapter 13).

The Treatment of Drug and Alcohol Addictions

There are many psychotherapeutic approaches to the treatment of addictions. I will discuss the most recent ones based on psychopharmacology and the chemistry of the brain.

Cocaine use decreases the neurotransmitters in the brain (norepinephrine, dopamine, and serotonin). By increasing the tyrosine and tryptophan levels in the brain (precursors for the neurotransmitters), or by using agonists (drugs which increase the dopamine levels in the brain), or by using tricyclic antidepressants (which increase dopamine levels in the brain) the craving for cocaine can be reduced. Similar drug therapies have been used for the treatment of alcoholism (Zweben and Smith, 1988).

THE CAREER CRIMINAL: THE CONCEPT

For years criminologists have noted that a small number of offenders commit many of the more serious crimes. This observation has been made by the McCords (1959), West and Farrington (1973, 1977), the Gluecks (1950, 1968) Wolfgang et al. (1972), and Farrington, Ohlin, and Wilson (1986). These studies are longitudinal in design and they use incidence rather than prevalence data; that is, they look at the career of a given person over a long period rather than using aggregate data for a specific time frame.

From her study of delinquents, Robins (1966) found a small group of psychopathic children characterized by genetic defects, brain effects, childhood trauma and neglect, and families where alcoholism and unemployment were common. She observed that childhood antisocial behavior was a very good predictor of adult antisocial behavior. She also found that popular sociological theories of delinquency, such as differential association, lower class status, and subcultural systems, were not supported by these findings. Robins (1966:199) concluded that this group is evidence of a psychiatric disease, not lower-class membership. Wolfgang et al. (1972) found that 6 percent of the cohort group studied committed 52 percent of the offenses. Farrington (Farrington, Ohlin, and Wilson, 1986:51) found that 6 percent of the delinquents studied had 49 percent of the convictions.

In recent years focus has been placed on this small group of offenders under the general title of "career criminals." An early study by the Rand Corporation (Petersilia et al., 1977) revealed two types of offenders, the intensive offender and the intermittent offender. The intensive offenders made up 33 percent of the criminal population, and the intermittent offenders made up 66 percent of the offenders. The intensive group committed more violent and serious crimes and were involved in drug use or drug and alcohol use, their criminal careers started at or before age 13, and the intensives committed 10 times as many crimes as the intermittents. The intermittents were involved in less serious crimes, committed fewer crimes, were involved in alcohol use but not drug use, and had better school and employment records.

A study by Chaiken and Chaiken (1982) classified offenders into a hierarchy based on the seriousness of the offense, with the *violent predator* as the most serious category. Violent predators were robbers, assaulters, and drug dealers, with the assaulter category including homicide arising out of a robbery or assault, but not homicide occurring as a result of a domestic disturbance or an argument in a bar.

The violent offenders also committed burglary (81 percent of them) and theft (71 percent of them). The burglars and thieves did not commit violent offenses to any great extent. The violent predators started their criminal careers at an earlier age, had more arrests for more serious offenses, 83 percent of them had a history of multiple drug use plus alcohol use, and most of them had a history of unemployment. The report (Chaiken and Chaiken, 1982:18) noted that the violent predators were "different in kind," although the report does not go on to detail how they are different in kind. I will argue that they are different in kind in terms of the neurological and psychological variables discussed above.

The report (Chaiken and Chaiken, 1982:19–20) listed the following as basic indicators of a violent criminal career:

1. A violent crime before the age of 18
2. An early career in juvenile crime, especially violent crime
3. A number of adult robbery convictions
4. Young
5. Unmarried
6. Unemployed
7. Mixed drug and alcohol use

Another criminal career project has been ongoing at Carnegie–Mellon University by Albert Blumstein and others (Blumstein et al., 1986). This project was also based on longitudinal and not cross-sectional data, and it used incidence and not prevalence data. As is discussed in Chapter 16, prevalence data look at the distribution of crime throughout the total population, whereas incidence data look at the distribution of crime among individual offenders. Longitudinal data tell you whether or not an offender has committed two offenses or twelve offenses over a one-year period.

The incidence data used by Blumstein and his colleagues revealed that the career criminal did not stop offending at the age of 18; rather, they continue to offend into the 30s and 40s. The ratio of males to females was close to 2:1, not 8:1 as found in prevalence data for the occasional offender. The ratio of black to white was 1:1, not 4:1 as usually reported in criminology textbooks (Blumstein et al., 1986). The career offender is marked by (1) drug use, (2) unemployment, (3) prior criminal record, (4) a criminal career that started before the age of 13, and (5) a high frequency of offending. Ten percent of the offenders interviewed were classified as career criminals (Blumstein et al., 1986:76).

It is now possible to summarize a great deal of information concerning the violent career offender. There is a small group of habitual offenders, 6 to 10 percent of the offender population, who commit 50 percent of more of the offenses and who persist in criminality beyond the age of 18. Social variables, such as age, sex, race, and socioeconomic status (Chapter 16), are very weakly related to criminal behavior. The work on the career offender reinforces this finding. Official criminal statistical data reveal a few people who commit a great many crimes. Self-report data show a high number of people involved in committing a variety of offenses. Mednick found two types of violent offenders, those who murder for gain and those who murder out of anger and fear. The Violent Offender Project differentiated the murderer from the robber. Studies of alcoholics differentiate milieu-limited alcoholism from male-limited alcoholism. Throughout criminological literature is a finding of a special group of offenders who are recidivists, violent, have an early entry into a criminal career, continue in crime beyond the age of 18, are unemployed and unemployable, are into hard drugs and alcohol use, and have a high offense rate are measured by frequency data.

There is now a need to look at individual differences in the analysis of criminal behavior (Farrington, Ohlin, and Wilson, 1986; Wilson and Herrnstein, 1985). It is my argument that these serious violent offenders differ from the less serious offenders and the nonoffenders in terms of the genetic, neurological, and psychological variables discussed throughout this book. The work of Petersilia, the Chaikens, and Blumstein and others has not touched on this aspect of criminal careers. What is needed is a major research project focused on the violent career criminal from an interdisciplinary approach. The emphasis must be on prevention programs, not on punishment and prisons (Chapter 21).

SUMMARY

Violent offenders differ from occasional offenders in terms of brain structure. Serious offenders have autonomic nervous system disorders, have more right-hemispheric dominance, have temporal and frontal lobe damage, have brain injuries, have high lead and cadmium concentrations in the brain, and have attention-deficit disorders.

Male/female differences in behavior, including criminal behavior, are a result of sex hormones and the changes they produce in the organization of the brain. Human sexual behavior, including sexual deviancy, is a product of genetics, brain structure, and learning in interaction. The brain controls sexual behavior as well as other behavior.

Violence and aggression are a product of genetic, neurological, and environmental factors. Aggression can be predatory or emotional, as well as involving territoriality, sexual behavior, and intermale aggression. Certain neurotransmitters increase violence; others decrease violence.

Drugs (including alcohol) act on the neurotransmitter system. They depress or stimulate neural activity in the brain. Drugs are now used to treat mental illness and violent behavior. Alcoholism is a disease involving genetic and biochemical factors.

The career criminal is a serious offender who has a history of offenses, starts his/her career at an early age, is into heavy drug and alcohol use, and is unemployed and unemployable. Prevention programs of the future must focus on the career criminal.

REFERENCES

ADLER, F. (1975). *Sisters in Crime*. New York: McGraw-Hill.

AKERS, R. (1977). *Deviant Behavior: A Social Learning Approach*. Belmont, Calif.: Wadsworth.

AMIR, M. (1971). *Patterns in Forcible Rape*. Chicago: University of Chicago Press.

ARCHER, D., and R. GARTNER (1984). *Violence and Crime in Cross-National Perspective*. New Haven, Conn.: Yale University Press.

ARDREY, R. C. (1966). *The Territorial Imperative*. New York: Atheneum.

BARASH, D. C. (1977). *Sociobiology and Behavior*. New York: Elsevier.

BARLOW, H. D. (1987). *Introduction to Criminology*. Boston: Little, Brown.

BELL, A. P., ET AL. (1981). *Sexual Preference*. Bloomington: Indiana University Press.

BENBOW, C. P. (1986). "Physiological Correlates of Extreme Intellectual Precocity." *Neuropsychologia*, 24(5):719–725.

BIRD, S. J. (1987). "Neuroscience Research and Premenstrual Syndrome: Scientific and Ethical Concerns." In *Premenstrual Syndrome*, ed. B. E. Ginsburg and B. F. Carter. New York: Plenum.

BLUMSTEIN, A., ET AL. (1986). *Criminal Careers and Career Criminals*, Vol. 1. Washington, D.C.: National Academy Press.

BROWNE, A. (1987). *When Battered Women Kill*. New York: Free Press.

BROWNMILLER, S. (1975). *Against Our Will: Men, Women, and Rape*. New York: Simon & Schuster.

CARLSON, J. E. (1980). *The Psychobiology of Sex Differences and Sex Roles*. New York: Hemisphere Publishing Corporation.

CARLSON, N. R. (1986). *Physiology of Behavior*. Boston: Allyn and Bacon.

CHAIKEN, J. M., and M. R. CHAIKEN (1982). *Varieties of Criminal Behavior*. Santa Monica, Calif.: Rand Corporation.

CLONINGER, D. (1987). "Pharmocological Approaches to the Treatment of Antisocial Behavior." In *The Causes of Crime: New Biological Approaches*, ed. S. A. Mednick et al. Cambridge: Cambridge University Press.

COLEMAN, J. C., ET AL. (1984). *Abnormal Psychology and Modern Life*. Glenview, Ill.: Scott, Foresman.

COLLINS, J. J. (1981). *Drinking and Crime*. New York: Guilford Press.

CONRAD, J., and S. DINITZ (1977). *In Fear of Each Other*. Lexington, Mass.: Lexington Books.

DE RIVER, J. P. (1958). *Crime and the Sexual Psychopath*. Springfield, Ill.: Charles C Thomas.

DRZAZGA, J. (1960). *Sex Crimes*. Springfield, Ill.: Charles C Thomas.

EYSENCK, H., and G. D. WILSON (1976). *Human Psychology*. Baltimore, Md.: University Park Press.

FARRINGTON, D., and J. GUNN (1985). *Aggression and Dangerousness*. New York: Wiley.

FARRINGTON, D. P., L. OHLIN, and J. Q. WILSON (1986). *Understanding and Controlling Crime*. New York: Springer-Verlag.

FARRINGTON, D., ET AL. (1987). "Long-Term Criminal Outcomes of Hyperactivity-Impulsivity-Attention Deficit and Conduct Problems in Childhood." Paper presented at the annual meeting of the Society for Life History Research, St. Louis.

FISHBEIN, D. (1981). "The Contribution of Refined Carbohydrate Consumption to Maladaptive Behaviors." Paper presented at the annual meeting of the American Society of Criminology, Washington, D.C.

FISHBEIN D., and K. PEASE (1988). "The Effect of Diet on Behavior: Implications for Criminology and Corrections." *Research in Corrections.* Boulder, Colo.: National Institute on Corrections.

FISHBEIN, D., and R. THATCHER (1982). "Nutritional and Electrophysiological Indices of Maladaptive Behavior." In *Proceedings of the Center for Brain Sciences and Metabolism,* ed. R. Wurtman and H. Lieberman. Cambridge, Mass.: Massachusetts Institute of Technology.

FISHBEIN, D., ET AL. (1987). "Brainstem Evoked Response Potentials in Adult Male Drug Abusers with Self-Reported Histories of Aggressive Behavior." Paper presented at the annual meeting of the American Society of Criminology, Montreal, Canada.

Florida Department of Law Enforcement (n.d.). *Drug Abuse in Florida.* Tallahassee, Fla.: Florida Department of Law Enforcement.

FREEMAN, D. (1983). *Margaret Mead and Samoa.* Cambridge, Mass.: Harvard University Press.

FREIER. M. (1986). "The Biological Bases of Criminal Behavior." In *Intervention Strategies for Chronic Juvenile Offenders,* ed. P. Greenwood. Westport, Conn.: Greenwood Press.

GALANTER, M., ed. (1983). *Recent Developments in Alcoholism,* Vol. 1. New York: Plenum.

GALANTER, M., ed. (1985). *Recent Developments in Alcoholism,* Vol. 3. New York: Plenum.

GATCHEL, R. J., and F. G. MEARS (1982). *Personality.* New York: St. Martin's Press.

GEBBARD, P., ET AL. (1965). *Sex Offenders.* New York: Harper & Row.

GELLES, R. J. (1987). *The Violent Home.* Newbury Park, Calif.: Sage.

GINSBURG, B. E., and B. F. CARTER (1987). *Premenstrual Syndrome.* New York: Plenum.

GLUECK, S., and E. T. GLUECK (1950). *Unraveling Juvenile Delinquency.* Cambridge, Mass.: Harvard University Press.

GLUECK, S., and E. T. GLUECK (1986). *Delinquents and Nondelinquents in Perspective.* Cambridge, Mass.: Harvard University Press.

GOODWIN, D. W. (1988). *Is Alcoholism Heriditary?* New York: Ballantine.

GORDON, A. J. (1984). "Alcohol Use in the Perspective of Cultural Ecology." In *Recent Developments in Alcoholism,* Vol. 2., ed. M. Galanter. New York: Plenum.

GROTH, A. N. (1983). "Rape." In *Encyclopedia of Crime and Justice,* ed. S. H. Kadish. New York: Free Press.

GROTH, A. N., and H. J. BIRNBAUM (1979). *Men Who Rape: The Psychology of the Offender.* New York: Plenum.

HAMPARIAN, D. M., ET AL. (1978). *The Violent Few.* Lexington, Mass.: Lexington Books.

HARE, R., and J. F. CONNALLY (1987). "Perceptual Asymmetries in Information Processing in Psychopaths." In *The Causes of Crime: New Biological Approaches,* ed. S. A. Mednick et al. Cambridge: Cambridge University Press.

HARE, R. D., and D. SCHALLING (1978). *Psychopathic Behavior.* New York: Wiley.

HARRIS, A. R. (1977). "Sex and Theories of Deviance: Toward a Functional Theory of Deviant Type-Scripts." *American Sociological Review*, 42(3):3–16.

HERRON, J. (1980). *Neuropsychology of Left Handedness*. New York: Academic Press.

HINTON, J. W. (1983). *Dangerousness: Problems of Assessment and Prediction*. London: Allen & Unwin.

JELLINEK, E. M. (1960). *The Disease Concept of Alcoholism*. New Haven, Conn.: Hillhouse Press.

JULIAN, R. M. (1985). *A Primer of Drug Action*. New York: W.H. Freeman.

KALAT, J. W. (1988). *Biological Psychology*. Belmont, Calif.: Wadsworth.

KARPMAN, B. (1954). *The Sexual Offender and His Offense*. New York: Julian Press.

KOLB, B., and I. Q. WHISHAW (1985). *Fundamentals of Neuropsychology*. New York: W.H. Freeman.

LESTER, D. (1986). "The Violent Offender." In *Psychology of Crime and Criminal Justice*, ed. H. Toch. Prospect Heights, Ill.: Waveland Press.

LEVIN, J., and J. A. FOX (1985). *Mass Murder*. New York: Plenum.

LEVINTHAL, C. F. (1988). *Messengers of Paradise*. New York: Doubleday.

LEWIS, D. (1981). *Vulnerabilities to Delinquency*. Jamaica, N.Y.: SP Medical and Scientific Books.

LEWIS, D., and D. A. BALLA (1976). *Delinquency and Psychopathology*. New York: Grune & Stratton.

LEWIS, D., ET AL. (1986). "Neuropsychiatric, Psychoeducational, and Family Characteristics of 14 Juveniles Condemned to Death in the United States." *American Journal of Psychiatry*, 45:5, 584-589.

LINNOILA, M. (1983). "Low Cerebrofluid 5HIAA Acid Concentration Differentiates Impulsive from Nonimpulsive Violent Behavior." *Life Sciences*, 33:2609–2614.

LOCKARD, J. (1980). *The Evolution of Human Social Behavior*. New York: Elsevier.

LORENZ, K. (1966). *On Aggression*. New York: Harcourt Brace Jovanovich.

MACCOBY, E. E., and C. N. JACKLIN (1974). *The Psychology of Sex Differences*. Stanford, Calif.: Stanford University Press.

MALAMUTH, N. M., and E. DONNERSTEIN (1984). *Pornography and Sexual Aggression*. New York: Academic Press.

MARK, V., and F. R. ERVIN (1970). *Violence and the Brain*. New York: Harper & Row.

McCORD, W. J., and J. McCORD (1959). *Origins of Crime*. New York: Columbia University Press.

MEAD, M. (1935). *Sex and Temperament in Three Primitive Societies*. New York: William Morrow.

MEDNICK, S. A., ET AL. (1982). "Biology and Violence." In *Criminal Violence*, ed. M. Wolfgang and N. Weiner. Bererly Hills, Calif.: Sage.

MEDNICK, S. A., ET AL. (1987). *The Causes of Crime: New Biological Approaches*. Cambridge: Cambridge University Press.

MILLER, S. J., ET AL. (1982). *Careers of the Violent*. Lexington, Mass.: Lexington Books.

MOFFITT, R. E., R. McGEE, and P. SILVA (1987). "Self-Reported Delinquency, Neuropsychological Deficit, and History of Attention Deficit Disorder." Paper presented at the annual meeting of the American Society of Criminology, Montreal, Canada.

MONEY, J., and A. A. EHRHARDT (1972). *Man and Woman, Boy and Girl*. Baltimore, Md.: Johns Hopkins University Press.

MONTAGU, M. F. A. (1968). *Man and Aggression*. New York: Oxford University Press.

MOYER, K. (1976). *The Psychobiology of Aggression*. New York: Harper & Row.

MOYER, K. (1987). *Violence and Aggression*. New York: Paragon.

NACHSHON, S., and D. DENNO (1987). "Violent Behavior and Cerebral Hemisphere Function." In *The Causes of Crime: New Biological Approaches*, ed. S. A. Mednick et al. Cambridge: Cambridge University Press.

NAGI, S. Z. (1983). "Violence in the Family: Child Abuse." In *Encyclopedia of Crime and Justice*, ed. S. H. Kadish. New York: Free Press.

NATIONAL ACADEMY OF SCIENCES (1980). *Lead in the Human Environment*. Washington, D.C.: National Academy Press.

NATIONAL INSTITUTE ON ALCOHOL ABUSE AND ALCOHOLISM (1985). *Alcoholism: An Inherited Disease*. Washington, D.C.: U.S. Government Printing Office.

NETTLER, G. (1984). *Explaining Crime*. New York: McGraw-Hill.

NEWMAN, G. (1979). *Understanding Violence*. Philadelphia: J. B. Lippincott.

NUTRITION FOUNDATION (1984). *Present Knowledge in Nutrition*. Washington, D.C.: Nutrition Foundation.

PARSONS, J. E. (1980). *The Psychobiology of Sex Differences*. New York: Hemisphere Publishing Corporation.

PEPINSKY, H. E. (1982). *Rethinking Criminology*. Beverly Hills, Calif.: Sage.

PETERSILIA, J., ET AL. (1977). *Criminal Careers of Habitual Felons*. Santa Monica, Calif.: Rand Corporation.

PIHL, R. O., and D. ROSS (1987). "Research on Alcohol Related Aggression: A Review and Implications for Understanding Aggression." In *Drug Use and Psychological Theory*, ed. S. W. Sadava. New York: Haworth Press.

PIHL, R. O., ET AL. (1982). "Hair Element Content of Violent Criminals." *Canadian Journal of Psychiatry*, 7(6):533–534.

PORAC, C., and S. COREN (1981). *Lateral Preferences and Human Behavior*. New York: Springer-Verlag.

PRENTSKY, R. (1985). "The Neurochemistry of Sexual Aggression." In *Aggression and Dangerousness*, ed. D. Farrington and J. Gunn. New York: Wiley.

REID, W. H., ET AL. (1986). *Unmasking the Psychopath*. New York: W. W. Norton.

RESTAK, R. M. (1988). *The Mind*. New York: Bantam.

ROBINS, L. N. (1966). *Deviant Children Grown Up*. Baltimore, Md.: Williams & Wilkins.

ROOM, R. (1983). "Alcoholism and Crime: Behavioral Aspects." In *Encyclopedia of Crime and Justice*, ed. S. H. Kadish. New York: Free Press.

ROSSI, A. (1985). *Gender and the Life Course*. New York: Aldine.

RUBIN, R. (1987). The Neuroendocrinology and Neurochemistry of Antisocial Behavior." In *The Causes of Crime: New Biological Approaches*, ed. S. A. Mednick et al. Cambridge: Cambridge University Press.

RUSSELL, D. (1975). *The Politics of Rape.* Briarcliff Manor, N.Y.: Stein & Day.

RYDBERG, U., ET AL. (1985). *Alcohol and the Developing Brain.* New York: Raven Press.

SATTERFIELD, J. H. (1987). "Childhood Diagnosis and Neurophysiological Predictors of Teenage Arrest Rates: An Eight-Year Prospective Study." In *The Causes of Crime: New Biological Approaches,* ed. S. A. Mednick et al. Cambridge: Cambridge University Press.

SHELEY, J. F. (1985). *America's Crime Problem.* Belmont, Calif.: Wadsworth.

SIEGEL, L. (1986). *Criminology.* St. Paul, Minn.: West Publishing Co.

SIMON, R. J. (1975). *Women and Crime.* Lexington, Mass.: D.C. Heath.

SIMON, R. J. (1983). "Women and Crime." In *Encyclopedia of Crime and Justice,* ed. S. H. Kadish. New York: Free Press.

STEPHENS, R. (1987). *Mind-Altering Drugs.* Newbury Park, Calif.: Sage.

STRAUS, R., R. GELLES, and S. STEINMETZ (1980). *Behind Closed Doors: Violence in the American Family.* New York: Doubleday.

SYMONS, D. (1979). *The Evolution of Human Sexuality.* New York: Oxford University Press.

VALZELLI, L. (1981). *Psychobiology of Violence and Aggression.* New York: Raven Press.

VAN DINE, S., ET AL. (1979). *Restraining the Wicked.* Lexington, Mass.: Lexington Books.

VENABLES, P. (1987). "Autonomic Nervous System Factors in Criminal Behavior." In *The Causes of Crime: New Biological Approaches,* ed. S. A. Mednick et al. Cambridge: Cambridge University Press.

VIRKKUNEN, M. (1987). "Metabolic Dysfunctions among Habitually Violent Offenders: Reactive Hypoglycemia and Cholesterol Levels." In *The Causes of Crime: New Biological Approaches,* ed. S. A. Mednick et al. Cambridge: Cambridge University Press.

VIRKKUNUN, M., ET AL. (1987). "Cerebrospinal Fluid Monoamine Metabolite Levels in Males Arsonists." *Archives of General Psychiatry,* 44:241–247.

VIRKKUNEN, M., ET AL. (1988). "Relationship of Psychobiological Variables to Recidivism in Violent Offenders and Impulsive Fire Setters: A Follow Up Study."

VOLAVKA, J. (1987). "Electroencephalogram among Criminals." In *The Causes of Crime: New Biological Approaches,* ed. S. A. Mednick et al. Cambridge: Cambridge University Press.

WALSH, W. J. (1984). "Trace Metal Concentrations in the Hair of Henry Lee Lucas." Unpublished manuscript.

WALSH, W. J. (1985). "Elemental Concentrations in the Hair of James Oliver Huberty." Report to the Coroner, San Diego County, Calif.

WARREN, M. Q. (1986). "The Female Offender." In *Psychology and the Criminal Justice System,* ed. H. Toch. Prospect Heights, Ill.: Waveland Press.

WASHBURN, S. L., and E. R. McCOWN (1978). *Human Evolution Biosocial Perspectives.* Menlo Park, Calif.: Benjamin-Cummings.

WEST, D. J., and D. P. FARRINGTON (1973). *Who Becomes Delinquent.* London: Heinemann.

WEST, D. J., and D. P. FARRINGTON (1977). *The Delinquent Way of Life.* London: Heinemann.

WILSON, J. Q., and R. J. HERRNSTEIN (1985). *Crime and Human Nature*. New York: Simon & Schuster.

WINICK, C. (1986). "The Alcohol Offenders." In *Psychology of Crime and Criminal Justice*, ed. H. Toch. Prospect Heights, Ill.: Waveland Press.

WOLFGANG, M. (1958). *Patterns in Criminal Homicide*. New York: Wiley.

WOLFGANG, M., and F. FERRACUTI (1967). *The Subculture of Violence*. London: Tavistock.

WOLFGANG, M., and N. A. WEINER (1982). *Criminal Violence*. Beverly Hills, Calif.: Sage.

WOLFGANG, M., ET AL. (1972). *Delinquency in a Birth Cohort*. Chicago: University of Chicago Press.

YEUDALL, L., ET AL. (1982). "Neuropsychological Impairment of Persistent Delinquency." *The Journal of Nervous and Mental Disease*, 170:257–265, May.

YEUDALL, L., ET AL. (1985). "A Neuropsychological Theory of Persistent Criminality: Implications for Assessment and Treatment." In *Advances in Forensic Psychology and Psychiatry*, Vol. 2, ed. R. Rieber. Norwood, N.J.: Ablex.

ZWEBEN, J. E., and D. E. SMITH (1988). "Pharmocological Adjuncts and Nutritional Supplements in the Treatment of Drug Dependence." *Journal of Psychoactive Drugs*, 20:3, 229–329.

QUESTIONS

1. How is the autonomic nervous system related to criminal behavior? How is the concept of a psychopath related to the autonomic nervous system?

2. How is brain laterality related to criminal behavior?

3. What evidence exists that brain injuries are related to criminal and delinquent behavior?

4. How does the neurotransmitter system affect criminal behavior?

5. Why are males more criminalistic than females? How does testosterone affect male behavior?

6. What conclusions can we reach from the studies made of violent behavior? Studies of the violent offender?

7. Drug and alcohol abuse are located in the brain. Explain.

8. What are the essential characteristics of the career offender?

9. What crime control model is available for the violent career offender?

Crime Prevention: Ecology, the Physical Environment, and Crime

19

A great physician prevents disease
A mediocre physican treats disease in its early stages
An incompetent physican treats disease in its full-blown stages

A Chinese Proverb

INTRODUCTION

Crime prevention means the use of measures before the crime occurs that will reduce the possibility of the crime occurring. Crime prevention efforts are directed at both the environment in which crime occurs and at high-risk individuals who will commit crimes in the future if no prevention action is taken.

Crime prevention rejects retribution, deterrence, incapacitation, and rehabilitation as crime control models. Efforts to deter, incapacitate, and rehabilitate occur after the crime has taken place, and as such are futile. As discussed in Chapter 15, the criminal justice system reacts after the crime has taken place in order that future crimes do not occur. One does not control crime by waiting for it to occur anymore than one can control automobile accidents or heart attacks by waiting for such events to take place. The criminal justice model is one of

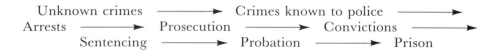

Unknown crimes ⟶ Crimes known to police ⟶
Arrests ⟶ Prosecution ⟶ Convictions ⟶
Sentencing ⟶ Probation ⟶ Prison

As stated in Chapter 8, less than 1 percent of the crimes known to the police result in a prison sentence, and of those 60 to 70 percent are rearrested upon release from prison. At the same time, new crimes are being committed every day. How can such a crime control model control crime?

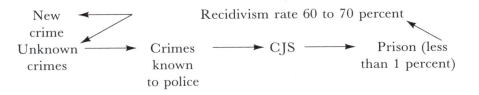

As stated in Chapter 8, this is a reactive and most unsuccessful model of crime control. It does not deter or rehabilitate; it is a cruel and inhumane system based on prisons and executions; prisons do not resolve the crime problem; the criminal justice system leads to many civil liberties violations; and the criminal justice system is a very expensive way to deal with behavioral problems.

The prevention model has been developed over the years in the public health area. Emphasis is placed on the prevention and early diagnosis of heart disease, cancer, and AIDS. Rather than waiting for a person to have a heart attack, preventive action is taken in the form of diet, exercise, control of smoking, weight loss, low cholesterol levels, and periodic stress tests of the heart. Cancer prevention includes a complete genetic history, control of smoking, control of carcinogenic substances in food, and periodic examinations for suspicious lumps or signs. This is in contrast to waiting until a person has cancer or a major heart attack.

A beautiful example of the public health prevention model is found in the discussion Burke (1985) gives of the control of cholera in nineteenth-century London. Public officials observed that cases of cholera usually occurred in very specific areas along the Thames River, and research revealed that the river was polluted with human waste and garbage, which in turn polluted the wells along the river from which the citizens of London drew their drinking water. Once the contamination of the Thames was eliminated, the cholera epidemic was brought under control. My idea of crime prevention is based on such an observation. Crimes occur in very specific parts of the city and not in other parts, just like cholera in nineteenth-century London. What are the characteristics of urban areas which result in a very high crime rate?

Brantingham and Faust (1976) divided prevention efforts into primary, secondary, and tertiary. Primary prevention prevents the appearance of the disease in a given population; secondary prevention refers to early detection and diagnosis for a population that is at risk; tertiary prevention is intervention, not prevention, since the disease has appeared in its final stages. The treatment of a heart patient in an emergency ward would be an example of tertiary prevention. Within the criminal justice system, putting people in prison after a long history of behavioral and neurological disorders is an example of tertiary prevention (or intervention, which is what it really is). Testing students who are hyperactive, who are failing in school, who are violent, or who have family problems is secondary prevention. Designing an environment that is crime-free, or developing a school system that is efficient, or training youths to be employable is primary prevention. The position taken in this book is one of primary prevention, with some emphasis on secondary prevention.

Prevention can be aimed at the environment or at the individual. The model used in this book is one of environment/organism interaction. In most instances, however, we have one or the other, that is, we have offenders who are in prison but we have no crime site; or we have a crime site, a store that has been robbed, but no criminal. The ideal theoretical model is the criminal interacting with his/her environment. At that moment we have all the elements relevant to the crime and criminal behavior. There is not a single study cited in this book or in any other criminology textbook that studied the individual criminal committing a crime at a specific crime site. This is like a physician studying heart disease without knowing both the patient and the environment in which the patient lived.

Crime prevention through environmental design is based on a simple law of behavior as derived from operant learning theory. A person will respond to the environment to gain pleasure and/or avoid pain (Chapter 13). To alter behavior and prevent criminal behavior, we must either (1) remove the reinforcement for criminal behavior, or (2) punish the response after the reinforcement (crime) has been gained. As we discussed in Chapter 13, punishment is a most ineffective way to control human behavior, since it creates escape and avoidance behaviors as well as other undesirable behaviors. Crime prevention is based on removing the reinforcement for criminal behavior. Without reinforcement, a person will not respond to an environmental stimulus.

This model of crime prevention is not based on a rational-person model of behavior as put forth by economists (Chapter 8) since behavior is a product of a brain that is both rational and emotional. The pleasure and pain centers of the brain (Chapter 11) control the motivation for responses. The limbic system is an emotional brain, not a rational brain. A neurological model of behavior control views the motivation for behavior as originating the limbic system, whereas the control of such biological impulses comes from the cortex or the rational brain. The economist equates the search for pleasure and pain with rationality; the neurologist equates the search for pain and pleasure with the interaction of several quite different parts of the brain. Individuals commit crimes for emotional as well as rational reasons.

As mentioned in Chapter 13, crimes against the person (e.g., murder, sexual assault, and assault) are based on negative reinforcement, that is, the removal of a painful or aversive stimulus such as anger, fear, or hatred. In crime prevention planning we must distinguish between property offenses where a target can be protected by security devices and street designs, and personal crimes, where security devices do not work because such crimes often occur in the home, or apartment, or in a bar, or in other places where people are by invitation. You cannot prevent the rape of a female by a friend or family member by putting locks on the doors and windows, nor can you prevent the murder of a husband by a wife in a kitchen or bedroom by locking the door. The prevention of most violent crimes against the person must take place through programs focusing on the individual offender or potential offender (Chapter 21). Environmental changes are important, such as the amount of alcohol or drugs or chemical pollution found in the environment which reaches the individual's brain, but at the same time we must deal with the person, his brain, his learned responses, and his potential for violence.

Crime prevention is based on the behavioral sciences, as found in genetics, the brain sciences, and psychological learning theory, as well as sociology, human ecology, and urban design. Neurology, psychopharmacology, psychological learning theory, environmental psychology, geography, and urban studies are all critical to the development of crime prevention programs.

THE HISTORY OF CRIME AND ECOLOGY

The Early Years

Some of the early research in crime statistics was done in France by Quetelet and Guerry (Brantingham and Brantingham, 1981; Rennie, 1978). They found that some police precincts had high crime rates, others had low crime rates. Crime varied tremendously when analyzed spatially. They found, for example, that property offenses were highest in industrialized urban areas, whereas violent crime were highest in rural areas. Spatial differences in crime rates held over time as well as over political and geographical barriers.

British ecologists also studied the variations in crime rates with England. Some of these studies were at the macro level, dealing with data from nations or provinces. Other studies were made of local areas within a city. Henry Mayhew found that there were high-crime-rate areas within London called "rookeries" where criminals lived, and he was able to show the spatial advantage to the criminal for such "rookeries" in terms of potential targets and protection from the police (Brantingham and Brantingham, 1981:11 ff.). Tobias (1972) used the Mayhew data to map the high-crime-rate areas of London.

These early ecological studies made several assumptions still found in the ecological analysis of crime: that (1) the level of analysis varies from inner-city data to national-level data; and (2) the unit of analysis is most often the individual criminal and where he/she lives, not the individual crime sites. These assumptions appear repeatedly in American criminology and are discussed in detail below.

The Chicago School of Social Ecology

As noted in Chapter 14, sociology at the University of Chicago developed around studies of migration patterns and city growth patterns. Burgess (Brantingham and Brantingham, 1981:13 ff., 229 ff.) outlined an ecological theory for city growth based on the pre-automobile pattern of Chicago, that is, growth from the center of the city outward. The inner core of the city is the business district, surrounded by a slum area or a ''zone of transition.'' This zone 2 area is in transition from residential to business use, and it is a deteriorating area that surrounds the central business district. It is an area inhabited by poor recent immigrants to the city, such as the Italian-American and the Jewish-American.

Shaw and McKay, using the Burgess model of concentric circles, plotted the residents of delinquents and found the high rate to be in the business district and in the slum area, with a progressive lower rate as one moved to the middle-class and suburban areas. The zone of transition also had a high rate of social disorganization, poverty, disease, broken homes, and population mobility. Shaw and McKay also studied Philadelphia, Cleveland, Birmingham, Denver, and Seattle, and they found the same gradient from the center of the city to the suburbs (Brantingham and Brantingham, 1981:13–14; Baldwin and Bottoms, 1976; Baldwin, 1979; Morris, 1957).

The ecological work of Shaw and McKay was basic to later developments in criminological theory. Sutherland based his theory of differential association on data from the Shaw–McKay studies (Cohen, Lindesmith, and Schuessler, 1956:13–28; Brantingham and Brantingham, 1981:14). The sociologist turned human ecology into social ecology, looking at such variables as social disorganization, poverty, race, socioeconomic status, occupation, and education. The theories that followed were based on these social variables [Chapter 14; Byrne and Sampson (1986)].

Criticisms of Shaw and McKay

Several criticisms of the work of Shaw and McKay can be noted.

1. They dealt with the criminal, not with crime sites. This is in keeping with the positivistic doctrine of studying individual offenders in order to determine why people commit crimes (Brantingham and Brantingham, 1981:227 ff.).
2. The social ecology approach ignores the basic structure of ecology, that is, the biotic relationship between human beings and the physical environment. Ecology is a subdiscipline of biology, and the real meaning of ecology is ignored or misinterpreted by the social ecologist (Baldwin, 1979).
3. The ''ecological'' or ''aggregative'' fallacy (Chapter 16) is involved in these studies, that is, going from aggregate-level data to explanations of individual behaviors (Brantingham and Brantingham, 1981:17, 1984; Baldwin, 1979; Davidson, 1981).
4. The level of analysis has been from the national to the state to the regional to the city and intracity level. The closer one comes to the actual crime site, the better the conclusions one can draw concerning the variables

involved in crime. Brantingham and Brantingham (1981; Brantingham, Dyerson, and Brantingham, 1976) refer to this as the "cone of resolution," that is, moving from national to regional to state to local to block-level data.

In summary, the social ecological approach to crime is focused on the individual criminal, not the crime site, and on the social, not the physical, environment.

Social Area Analysis

Later studies in the 1960s and 1970s by sociologists focused on aggregate data, usually census tract data which are readily accessible and can be put into a computer for analysis and instant interpretation. Statistical analysis of crime areas was done in terms of such social variables as income, education, housing, and racial composition.

Landers (1954) looked at education, rent, number of persons per room, substandard housing, and the percentage of nonwhites in the area. He combined these variables through factor analysis and came up with a variable called "anomie," which referred to a lack of social integration and cohesiveness, as an explanation of crime. Landers also found that crime was not related to the socioeconomic status of the area (Baldwin, 1979: 46 ff.). In contradiction to the Landers study, Bordua (1958) and Chilton (1964) found that socioeconomic variables were critical to crime rates.

A second type of social ecological study was social area analysis. Shevsky and Bell (1955) used three social variables, social rank, urbanization, and ethnic segregation, to explain crime rates in specific social areas. The approach produces correlations between crime rates, rank, urbanization, and segregation, but without any causal meaning. We do not know if crime causes low rank or high urbanization, or the other way around, or if all three are related to another variable.

The ecological fallacy is most obvious in the Shevsky–Bell analysis, and the approach was severely criticized by Baldwin (1974) and Gordon (1967). Brantingham and Brantingham (1984:315) stated that social area analysis "led to the complete abandonment of space and location as variables in ecological analysis; instead, ecological analysts spent a number of years trying to assess the pattern of urban crime in social space." "Very little in the way of either solid empirical description or theoretical development flowed from these studies" (Brantingham and Brantingham, 1981:16). Baldwin (1979:53) wrote that "to return to the discussion of the criminological applications of social area analysis and factorial analysis, we must, it seems, stress the sterility of each approach. Neither has yielded many new insights, and despite the immense effort expended, our knowledge of delinquency areas has been scarcely advanced."

The effort in social ecology has been identical to the effort by sociologists to relate crime rates to poverty, race, and socioeconomic status. In a recent book on social ecology, Byrne and Sampson (1986:vi) wrote that social ecology is not environmental criminology as Harries and the Brantinghams have outlined environmental criminology. Byrne and Sampson distinguish geography from social ecology, and they note that "social structure has consequences for crime that transcends geographical space" (p. 5), and "the effects of racial composition and poverty/inequality seem to be the major focus of current research on the social ecology of crime" (p. 6).

Kornhauser (1978:82, 118–119) noted that by using age, sex, race, socio-economic status, and size of the community to analyze delinquency the sociologist/criminologist ignored the intervening variables between ecology and delinquency. For this reason there are no causal variables between ecology and delinquency. Kornhauser (1978:104) also stated that area differences are due to aggregate characteristics of the communities, not the characteristics of individuals.

Bursik (Byrne and Sampson, 1986:63–74) studied the causal relationship between crime and ecological change and concluded that delinquency rates are not a product of ecological change, whereas delinquency rates do affect ecological processes. In other words, delinquency rates produce ecological changes, whereas ecological changes do not produce delinquency rates. This is a reversal of the usual interpretation given the data by sociologists. Bursik found that the number of blacks in an area did not affect the crime rate, whereas the crime rate affected the number of blacks in the area. Similarly, socioeconomic status does not influence crime rates, whereas crime rates influence socioeconomic status.

Gottfredson and Taylor (Byrne and Sampson, 1986:153) admit to both the methodological problems of social ecology and the separation of the physical from the social environment. They state that they measured observable physical characteristics of the environment. (How does one measure nonphysical characteristics?) "Variables assessed here stand only as crude proxies for things that one would prefer to measure more directly, such as the nature and extent of local social networks, social cohesion, and attachment." In other words, they measured the physical, but prefer the social.

Some major conclusions can be reached from these studies of social ecology and crime rates:

1. Aggregate data at the national, state, county, and local levels have been used. Most of these data involve addresses of criminals officially reported to police departments in UCR. Individual crime site data are seldom collected.
2. Causal relationships between variables have not been established.
3. The social ecologist uses area studies to relate such variables as poverty, unemployment, and racial composition to crime rates. They separate ecology from social ecology, and they ignore geography, the physical environment, and the spatial aspects of crime and criminal behavior.

ECOLOGY: A SYSTEMS APPROACH

Ecology is defined as "the interrelationship between organisms and their environments" (Michelson, 1976:5). Ecology is an overarching concept that unites biology, psychology, sociology, geography, and urban planning. It is basic to the study of the adaptation of organisms to their environments by both genetic and learned response patterns.

Ecology encompassed *Ecodynamics* (Boulding, 1978), the evolution of species and societies from simple to complex. The process of adaptation by the human species to the environment has resulted in great modification of the ways in which the environment is structured for survival purposes. The technological systems changed from hunting and fishing economies to urban industrial economies (Chapter 3).

Ecology integrates the various levels of organization from cells to society. It represents an integrated and holistic systems approach to knowledge [Chapter 2; Odum (1975); Ehrlich, Ehrlich, and Holdren (1973)]. The move in human ecology is toward an integrated science of human beings and the environment, with emphasis on biology and the physical environment. Duncan and Schnore (1959:134) observed that "one searches the literature in vain for more than a superficial reference to the brute fact that men live in a physical environment and they employ material technology in adapting to it." Duncan and Schnore analyze human ecology in terms of population, organization, environment, and technology (POET). They denied the need to use subjective cultural values to understand human behavior, and in the place of nonmaterial variables they used the physical environment and physical human activities. This position is the one taken throughout this book.

The POET model emphasized the interaction of population growth, organized human behavior, the physical environment, and physical technology. The importance of population growth for crime rates has seldom, if ever, been discussed in criminology, but it is obvious that the rural-to-urban transition, the creation of large urban centers, and the increase in the number of young adult males in the population bear directly on the growth of crime over the past several centuries.

Michelson (1976:7–32) wrote that the sociologist looked on ecology as a branch of sociology, not as an interdisciplinary field. The social ecologist studies the social environment to the neglect of the physical environment, and he has treated the variables studied at the aggregate level (the aggregative or ecological fallacy). Michelson recommended studying the impact of the physical environment on human behavior. Micklin (1973, 1983) has also written about the separation of social ecology from human ecology, and the separation of the social environment from the physical environment. He advocated the integration of social and physical variables into a basic model of human ecology.

Crime prevention will emphasize technology and the built environment. The increase in burglary, robbery, and larceny is a direct result of the increase in crime targets, as explained below. The growth and design of cities, the types and patterns of streets, the location of parks and terminals, and the design of building all affect crime patterns.

Environmental psychology has studied the impact of the physical environment on human behavior (Stokols, 1977; Ittelson et al., 1974; Esser, 1971; Hemstra and McFarling, 1974; Altman, 1975; Porteous, 1977). The major difference between most environmental psychology explanations and this book is that environmental psychology uses mentalistic connections between the environment and behavior, called perceptions and cognitions, rather than the brain (Porteous, 1977; Ittelson et al., 1974). The work of Kevin Lynch is cited in which he refers to the "images of the city," the cognitive maps that people carry around inside their heads (Stokols, 1978:259-261; Ittelson et al., 1977:288). The Brantinghams (1981:28-29) refer to these images as "templates," maps of the environment that people carry around with them.

Environmental sociology has also developed over the past twenty years. Dunlap (1980) wrote that social ecology has ignored the biophysical environment in its interpretations of human behavior in terms of the social and cultural environment. "Environmental sociology involves recognition of the fact that physical environments can influence (and are in turn influenced by) human societies and behavior" (Dunlap and Catton, 1979; Dunlap, 1980:244). Environmental sociology is another attempt to bring the physical environment back into sociology (Catton and Dunlap, 1978, 1980; Dunlap and Catton, 1979).

The growth of technology, populations, and urban areas is basic to our high crime rates today. In 1985, 258 cities on planet Earth had a population of over one million. The high rate of urbanization has resulted in unemployment; inadequate housing; health and nutritional problems; air, water, and noise pollution; rising crime rates; and the deterioration of the quality of life (Dogan and Kasarda, 1988). *Time* magazine, in place of the annual "Man of the Year Award," had an issue devoted to "Planet of the Year: Endangered Earth" (January 2, 1989).

CRIME PREVENTION THROUGH ENVIRONMENTAL DESIGN

A Model for Crime Prevention

The model outlined by Jeffery (1971, 1977) is based on operant conditioning, psychobiology, and the physical environment. There are two critical elements to crime prevention: (1) the place where the crime occurs (i.e., the crime site itself), and (2) the person who committed the crime. We know that high crime rates are concentrated in very few parts of the city, and we know that 6 percent of a birth cohort commit 50 percent of the crimes (Wolfgang, Figlio, and Sellin, 1972; Farrington, Ohlin, and Wilson, 1986). In this chapter we deal with the physical environment and crime rates; in Chapter 21 we deal with the nature of the individual offender and crime prevention.

Ecology and epidemiology are especially critical to crime prevention. Epidemiology, which studies the incidence, distribution, and control of diseases, is the medical model used in crime prevention. The Centers for Disease Control in Atlanta, Georgia, established a violence epidemiology branch wherein violence is studied as a disease. Since murder is one of the major causes of death among black teenage males, murder must be viewed as a disease within a medical model.

Crime prevention is interested in why certain blocks have a high or low crime rate, or why certain convenience stores are robbed and others not, or why certain apartments are burglarized or are the site of a rape and others are not. In other words, what types of environments experience what types of crimes?

There is a major difference between offense areas and offenders areas. Boggs (1965) noted that there was a difference between studying areas where offenders lived and areas where offenses were committed. By studying offender areas, as did Shaw and McKay and the social area people, the sociologist is looking for correlates between criminal behavior and poverty, unemployment, ethnicity, and socioeconomic status. Baldwin and Bottoms (1976) wrote: "The second point which is plain at first glance is that the offense and offender areas of the city are by no means the same." Morris (1957:20) also advocated studying crime sites rather than the residential areas of criminals.

A number of geographers and environmental criminologists interested in the spatial analysis of crime have emerged in recent years, including Harries (1974, 1980), Georges-Abeyie and Harries (1980), Pyle (1974), Brantingham and Brantingham (1981), Clarke and Mayhew (1980), Poyner (1983), Davidson (1981), and Herbert (1982).

The Brantinghams (1981, 1984) have outlined a crime prevention model that involves (1) a control agent, the criminal law and police; (2) a potential offender; (3) a potential target; and (4) a time and place. The offender and the control agents are discussed in other parts of this book. In this chapter we focus on the targets for criminals.

Brantingham and Brantingham (1981) created models to represent the interaction of criminals and targets, using home, work, shopping, and entertainment as the major daily activities of individuals. Criminals are at home, at work, or in shopping and entertainment centers, and crimes are committed along these paths of human activities (Figure 19–1).

The Brantinghams (1981) stated that the following urban patterns are critical to crime rates:

1. Old cities have a concentric circle pattern, as found by Shaw and McKay.
2. New cities have a dispersed crime pattern along shopping and commercial strips, with a high rate of property crime.
3. Major transportation centers and highways have a concentration of criminal events, especially at major intersections.

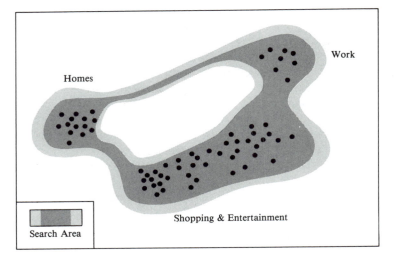

Figure 19-1 Complex Search Area for Cluster of Offenders: From P. J. Brantingham and P. L. Brantingham (1981). *Environmental Criminology.* Beverly Hills: Sage.

4. Areas with grid networks and through streets have a high crime rate compared to areas with cul-de-sacs and one-way streets.

5. As work areas and shopping areas move into the suburbs, crime moves into the suburbs.

6. Entertainment complexes, such as sports arenas, gambling centers, or theaters, have high crime rates, especially property crimes, drugs, and prostitution. Entertainment cities, such as Las Vegas, Reno, and Atlantic City, have high crime rates.

7. Certain areas of the city, the "red light" district, have high rates for prostitution, gambling, cheap bars, and cheap rooming houses. These areas often adjoin the business district (Brantingham and Brantingham, 1981:21–23).

Brantingham and Brantingham (1981:21) discuss the levels of analysis problem in terms of *macro* level (nations, states, cities), *meso* level (subareas of the city), and *micro* level (specific crime sites), types of buildings, interior design of a building, placement on a street, and so on. My own preference is for *micro*-level data, or individual crime site data, discussed in detail below.

The Social Control Model: Newman and Defensible Space

An architect, O. Newman (1972), published *Defensible Space,* in which he reported on crime rates in low-cost housing projects in New York City. He found that high-rise apartment buildings had a much higher crime rate than those of three- or five-story buildings in comparable social settings. In high-rise buildings the crimes were committed 55 percent of the time in interior public space (i.e., lobbies, elevators, stairwells, rooftops, and basements). In contrast, in the low-rise apartment buildings 17 percent of the crimes were in interior public space.

Newman explained his concept of defensible space in terms of territoriality, surveillance, image, and safe zones. Territoriality is the feeling of possessiveness and belonging that the inhabitants have for the building. Surveillance is the ability of the inhabitants to observe the territorial areas. Image is the stigma or lack of stigma associated with the building. Safe zones refers to the general location of the building in respect to streets, parks, and other physical features of the neighboring environment.

Newman recommended creating barriers between public, semipublic, and private space to increase private space and make it defensible space. Newman found, for example, that the Riverbend Project in Harlem had a low crime rate. The construction of the project is that of a two-story complex with a common lobby and common playground. The entrances are semiprivate rather than public. Thefts that did occur took place in the parking lot, which is in an isolated area. In a later report Newman and Franck (Rubenstein et al., 1980; Reiss and Tonry, 1986:399) stated that building size, accessibility, low income, teenage/adult ratios, fear of crime, and instability of residential occupancy are critical to crime rates.

The Newman social control model was found to be inaccurate by Mawby (1977). From his study Mawby determined that in London high-rise projects did not have a higher crime rate than that in low-rise housing projects. Mayhew (1979) found that the principles of defensible space did not hold up in England. Tyler, Gottfredson, and Brower (1980) stated that defensible space is based on several untested and erroneous assumptions. The defensible space modifications were not successful in deterring crime. Taylor et al. also noted that Newman assumed that residents will exercise a policing function and make use of surveillance. In his later work Newman looked more at social control and social defense by the residents themselves as part of a social network. This also did not prove to be effective (Tyler, Gottfredson, and Brower, 1980). Mayhew et al. (1979) confirmed the lack of surveillance on the part of the average citizen. Only people charged with surveillance, such as the police, guards, and employees, paid any attention to reporting crimes to the police.

In an empirical test of the ''social control model'' (Newman) versus the ''target and opportunity model'' (Jeffery and Brantingham), Greenberg and Rohe (1984) found a great deal of support for the opportunity model and little support for the social control model. They used the distribution of targets in relation to major streets, vacant lots, multiple-family units, commercial use, and parking lots, where the crime rates were high. In areas with minor streets, single-family residences, few parking lots, and few vacant lots, the crime rates were low.

Although Greenberg supported the opportunity model in her 1984 article, in 1986 (Greenberg, 1986) she reversed her position to support a social control and fear reduction model of crime prevention. From her studies she found that the character of the neighborhood had to be filtered through a perception of disorder which produced fear. She concluded that fear reduction was therefore less than optimal. It is unclear to me why she supports a fear reduction and social control model when she found so little evidence for it.

Murray (1983:107–122) defended the Newman model of crime control, although he noted that defensible space may have the least effect in places with the worst crime rate problems, whereas defensible space will work in neighborhoods where people are already allied (Murray, 1983:121–122).

In a later article Taylor and Gottfredson (1986) looked at the issue of how a potential offender selects a target site. They analyzed the decision process of the offender in terms of three levels: (1) neighborhood, (2) street or block, and (3) individual crime site. At each level the offender selects a particular environment in which to commit a crime based on opportunity factors, risk factors, and convenience factors. The offender could thus focus his/her attention on a specific neighborhood, specific block in the neighborhood, and a specific house or store within the block. Taylor and Gottfredson (1986:404) also supported the social control or Newman model of crime prevention when they cite the Wilson and Kelling model:

$$\text{Disorder} \longrightarrow \begin{array}{c} \text{Physical and} \\ \text{social incivilities} \end{array} \longrightarrow \begin{array}{c} \text{Less informal} \\ \text{social control} \end{array} \longrightarrow \begin{array}{c} \text{More} \\ \text{crime} \end{array} \longrightarrow \begin{array}{c} \text{More} \\ \text{Fear} \end{array}$$

The Opportunity Model

The availability and distribution of targets for criminal activity have been labeled the ''opportunity model'' theory by sociologists and economists (Cook, 1986). Gould (1979) observed that an increase in money in circulation and automobiles in circulation between 1921 and 1965 was somehow related to an increase in bank robberies and auto thefts. Cohen and Felson (1979; Cohen, Felson, and Land, 1980; Felson, 1983) used the variables of offenders, targets, and social control agents to analyze crime rates (same as Brantingham and Jeffery, as discussed above). They noted that a change in ''routine activities,'' such as where people go to shop, women leaving home during the day to work, and the items that are kept in stores and homes, had an impact on crime rates, the type of crimes committed, and where crimes are committed. Items stolen included radios, hi-fi sets, and television sets. There has been an increase in the availability of durable goods, which then become targets for criminal activities.

CRIME PREVENTION: SPECIFIC TOPICS

Streets and Crime

Jacobs (1961) noted in her book *The Death and Life of Great American Cities* that certain streets were safe streets and other streets were very unsafe. Those areas with ''eyes on the street'' (i.e., surveillance by others) were safe. Areas that were used by people for a variety of legitimate activities were regarded as safe, and Jacobs recommended a variety of uses for an area in order that it be a safe area (Jeffery, 1971, 1977). Streets that are major streets, with major business activities, attract more crime than other areas. Convenience stores, malls, shopping malls, and industrial parks located along major highways are high-crime-rate areas.

Transportation and Crime

As the Brantinghams stated, transportation systems, especially major highways and major intersections, are also major-crime-rate areas. Human activity creates and follows major transportation routes. Where major transportation routes intersect, cities and urban development occur. In the Middle Ages the king's highways were major sites for highway robbery. When ships were used for transportation, sea piracy came into existence. When horses were used, horse thievery developed, and it was punished by hanging since it was a very serious crime. Train robbers, such as Jesse and Frank James, came into existence with the appearance of trains. Automobiles not only led to auto theft, but to new means of committing crimes through the use of the automobile, and new means of combating crimes through putting the police in automobiles for police patrols. With the coming of the airplane came skijackings and the use of airplanes as a means of murder and suicide. (On December 10, 1987, a frustrated employee of Pacific South West Airline boarded a plane and shot and killed his former boss and the crew of the airliner. The plane crashed, killing 43 people.)

Some of the most crime-ridden areas in the history of crime have been seaports (Shanghai, Singapore, San Francisco) and rivers (the river pirates of the Thames River in London). Mueller and Adler (1985) studied the crimes occurring on the high seas, such as piracy, drug smuggling, person smuggling, arms smuggling, illegal pollution, and unlawful fishing. As Mueller and Adler report, the oceans are a unique environment for crime.

Several aspects of transportation can be singled out. Subway systems exist in major metropolitan areas, such as London, Paris, Moscow, Montreal, Toronto, New York City, Washington, D.C., and San Francisco. The subway system in New York City is dangerous (the Goetz case). I do not know how safe the relatively new systems in Washington, D.C., and San Francisco are. The systems in London, Paris, Montreal, Toronto, and Moscow are very safe and clean. I know of no study that has been made to determine why certain subways are safe and certain subways are dangerous. It is certainly a worthy research project.

Bus terminals and airports are also high-crime-rate areas, especially for the theft of cargo and baggage. The New York City bus terminal is described in detail by Jeffery (1977).

The major interstate highways (e.g., I-95 north and south from northeastern Canada through New York, Boston, Washington D.C., to Jacksonville, Tampa, and Miami; I-10 east and west from Jacksonville through New Orleans, Houston, Tucson, Phoenix, and Los Angeles; I-5 north and south from Vancouver, Canada to Seattle, Portland, San Francisco, Los Angeles, San

Diego, and Mexico) join north and south and east and west. Many high-crime-rate cities are on or near these major interstate highways. Of the ten highest cities for violent crimes, seven were in the south and west. Of the ten highest cities for property crimes, all were in the south and west (Table 19–1).

Serial murderers often follow the interstate system. Ted Bundy traveled I-75 to I-10 to Tallahassee, where he killed two coeds at Florida State University and another girl in a nearby town. Henry Lee Lucas and Otis Toole traveled I-10 from Texas through Louisiana to Florida killing women. Charles Wilder traveled I-75 to I-10 to Tallahassee, where he kidnapped a coed from the Governor's Square Mall, after which he traveled west on I-10 and I-40. The hillside strangler, Kenneth Bianchi, used the freeways of Los Angeles for disposing of the bodies of the women he killed.

The Westinghouse Project

The federal government, through the Law Enforcement Assistance Administration, put millions of dollars into the Newman "defensible space" model, calling it the Crime Prevention Through Environmental Design (CPTED)

TABLE 19-1 TEN CITIES WITH HIGHEST CRIME RATES

City	Crime rate
Violent crime (murder, forcible rape, robbery, aggravated assault)	
Miami, Fla.	1791
New York City, N.Y.	1754
Flint, Mich.	1490
Los Angeles, Calif.	1392
Baton Rouge, La.	1203
Memphis, Tenn.	1197
Jacksonville, Fla.	1170
Bradenton, Fla.	1156
Raton/Delray Beach, Fla.	1139
Baltimore, Md.	1101
Property offenses (burglary, larceny-theft, auto vehicle theft)	
Miami, Fla.	9958
Dallas, Tex.	9796
Fort Worth, Tex.	9632
Raton/Delray Beach, Fla.	9145
San Antonio, Tex.	8993
Lubbock, Tex.	8671
Bradenton, Fla.	8669
Oklahoma City, Okla.	8644
Austin, Tex.	8425
Portland, Oreg.	8279

Source: Federal Bureau of Investigation, *Uniform Crime Reports* July 1987.

project. Westinghouse established three projects: one for commercial areas, one for residential areas, and one for schools (National Crime Prevention Institute, 1986; Taylor et al., 1980).

In Portland, Oregon, a commercial area was redesigned according to the ideas of territorial defense. Changes were made in outdoor lighting, emergency phones, landscaping, special bus shelters, security surveys, neighborhood watch programs, traffic patterns and one-way streets, and the amount of cash carried or kept in stores. A general conclusion was reached that there were problems with the program, but there was success in altering citizens' fear of crime as well as improving the economy of the area (National Crime Prevention Institute, 1986:127; Taylor et al., 1980:61–62).

In Broward County, Florida, a demonstration project was established for a school environment. This project used Newman's concept of natural surveillance and an increased sense of responsibility on the part of students for crime prevention. The report stated that the techniques used ''are practical and at least somewhat effective'' (National Crime Prevention Institute, 1986:128).

In Hartford, Connecticut, a Housing and Urban Development residential housing project was used as a demonstration project for reducing residential burglary and robbery, as well as for reducing fear of crime. Streets were closed or narrowed, some streets were made one-way streets, community anti-crime groups were formed, and police–community relations were improved. An evaluation of the Hartford project found that the physical changes were less effective than the social changes. The mediating variables (residents walking in the neighborhood; residents being more observant) could not be related to the changes in crime rates (National Crime Prevention Institute, 1986:128; Taylor et al., 1980:62).

A summary statement of the link between crime and the built environment by the National Institute of Justice (Rubenstein et al., 1980) concluded that although the link between the built environment and crime had been established, the nature of the relationship had not been established. They stated that such concepts as territoriality, social control, social cohesiveness, and fear of crime are loose and fuzzy variables that do not link behavioral changes to environmental design. The report noted that three types of behavior–environment links had been studied: (1) environment–crime, (2) environment–intervening variable, and (3) intervening–variable crime. The weakness of the model is the intervening variable between the environment and behavior. Concepts such as social control, social cohesiveness, social belonging, territoriality, image, and surveillance are used as intervening variables. We have no direct measures of such intervening variables.

The link between the environment and behavior used in the Jeffery crime prevention through environmental design model is

$$\text{Environment} \longleftrightarrow \text{Brain}$$

model as developed in this book. The physical environment affects the brain; the brain codes and stores the information from the environment; and on the basis of this information, the person's past experiences, the general structure of the brain, and the present condition of the brain, the person will or will not respond to the environment by committing a crime. We need to develop a better model of organism–environment interaction based on the new brain sciences before we can develop crime prevention projects based on environmental design.

It must be noted that many of the programs established under the title of "crime prevention" deal with either the fear of crime or with making the individual citizen responsible for crime prevention. Neither of these is designed to reduce the crime rate. Such efforts are politically popular because it then appears that the elected public officials are doing something about the crime rate.

The Tallahassee Convenience Store Project

In 1985, several students in my graduate class in crime prevention undertook to study convenience store robberies in Tallahassee (Jeffery, Hunter, and Griswold, 1986). Included among the students were Jeffrey Griswold, who was a graduate student in geography as well as criminology, and Ronald Hunter, a graduate student and a police officer with the Tallahassee Police Department.

All the convenience stores in Tallahassee were surveyed (34). The robberies from January 1, 1981, to July 1, 1985 were researched. The highest number of robberies at one store was 18, the lowest was zero. Of the stores robbed in Tallahassee, 14 of the top 17 were Majik Markets. There must be some reason for this. One reason is that they used one clerk. The stores were divided into:

High (8 to 18 robberies)	$N = 8$
Medium high (4 to 7 robberies)	$N = 8$
Medium low (1 to 3 robberies)	$N = 10$
Low (zero robberies)	$N = 8$

Each store was surveyed for the presence or absence of both *internal and external* variables. The *internal variables* were: location of the cashier, number of clerks, number of mirrors, number of blind corners, phones visible from the inside of the store, hours open, and windows clear of obstructions. The *external variables* were: location on a major street, access to the store, number of exterior lights, number of gas pumps in front of store, presence of vacant lots, presence of woods, presence of shrubbery, presence of commercial buildings, presence of single-family dwellings, presence of multiple-family dwellings, presence of parking lots, vehicular traffic in front of store, and pedestrian traffic in front of store.

The variables found to be most significant were:

1. *Location of clerk:* in center of store for low-crime-rate stores; on side of store for high-crime-rate stores
2. *Number of clerks:* two or more for low-crime-rate stores; one for high-crime-rate stores

3. *Gas pumps in front of store:* yes for low-crime-rate stores, no for high-crime-rate stores

4. *Presence of single-family dwellings:* no for low-crime-rate stores; three or four dwellings for high-crime-rate stores

The surveillance of the store by the clerk or clerks, and the inability of the criminal to control the situation where two clerks or customers were involved, are obvious from the study. The impact of single-family dwellings on convenience store robberies is less obvious. It means that dwellings in the area did not have a surveillance or deterrent effect. (On July 8, 1988, a Tallahassee police officer was killed in a gun battle at the convenience store on Lake Bradford Road, ranked number 3 in the survey as to number of robberies.)

The Gainesville Project

The Gainesville Police Department, under the direction of Wayland Clifton, chief, started a convenience store project in 1985 similar to the one we were doing in Tallahassee (Clifton, 1987). The two projects were independent and unknown to one another until the results were released in 1986.

The Gainesville group observed that Kent, Ohio, had a two-clerk ordinance, which had resulted in a 74 percent reduction in convenience store robberies over a three-year period. Coral Springs, Florida, reduced convenience store robberies from three to zero by passing a two-clerk ordinance, but the small numbers make the experience suggestive and not definitive.

There were 47 convenience stores in Gainesville. Convenience store robberies represented 50 percent of all business robberies in Gainesville, which included gas stations (12 percent), fast foods (10 percent), retail sales (8 percent), hotels and motels (5 percent), and banks and saving companies (4 percent). It is obvious from both the Tallahassee study and the Gainesville study that convenience stores are the most popular business site to rob and the obvious question is: Why are convenience stores the site of so many crimes? This is the type of question that does not occur to those using defensible space or social control or social area analysis.

Ninety-six percent of the convenience stores had been robbed, compared to 36 percent of the fast-food stores. Ninety-two percent of the convenience store robberies occurred when one clerk was present. The Lil Champ Food Store had two or more clerks on duty 47 percent of the time. Of the 20 Lil Champ stores, 70 robberies occurred between 1981 and 1986, with three of the robberies occurring when two clerks were on duty. That is, 90 percent of the robberies occurred when one clerk was on duty.

The Sprint Food Store chain uses two clerks, brightly lit lots, clearly visible windows, robbery detection cameras, and drop safes. Not one of these stores had been robbed during the time of the study. The Sprint stores were located in the same areas where other stores were located that had been robbed. In one location, a competitor's store was located within 100 yards of the Sprint store, and that store had been robbed 11 times, whereas the Sprint store was never robbed.

The Southland Corporation (owner of 7-11 stores) established a crime prevention program for its stores on a nationwide basis using clear windows, limited cash, drop safes, employee training in crime prevention, and well-lit parking lots. They did not have two clerks, however. The rate of robberies at the 7-11 stores after the crime prevention program was put into effect was high; in fact, 7-11 stores had the second-highest robbery rate in Gainesville.

In 1986 the city of Gainesville passed the Gainesville Convenience Store Ordinance, which provided for:

1. Clear windows.
2. Location of clerk in a visible area.
3. A sign saying that no more than $50 is kept on the premises, along with a drop safe.
4. Parking lots to be well lit.
5. A security camera to be installed.
6. Mandatory robbery prevention training for all clerks working between the hours of 8 P.M. and 4 A.M.

A two-clerk provision was not included in the ordinance as originally passed because of opposition from store owners and operators. With the new crime prevention ordinance in place, the robbery rate increased by 130 percent. In February 1987 the two-clerk provision was added to the ordinance. The two-clerk provision was challenged in federal district court by the Southland Corporation; however, the court held that the city of Gainesville had a right to use crime prevention measures in order to protect citizens (Clifton, 1987).

After the two-clerk provision went into effect, there was a 64 percent reduction in convenience store robberies. Since the robbery rate increased after the initial ordinance and decreased 64 percent after the two-clerk provision was put into place, it can be assumed that the two-clerk provision was responsible for the decrease in robberies. This was a natural and unplanned control over the two-clerk variable. If the two-clerk provision had been part of the original ordinance, the effect of two clerks as compared to the other provisions could not have been established. In many of the crime prevention projects of the Westinghouse Corporation and other local community crime prevention efforts, everything that can be thought of is changed, and then they try to measure the impact of the program. (The 7-11 employees at Tidewater, Virginia, voted to walk out unless management agreed to two clerks in every store. The two-clerk provision was accepted. *Newsweek*, July 4, 1988.)

The Atlanta Project

In 1986, the crime prevention seminar at Florida State University looked at the distribution of residential burglaries in Fulton County, Georgia (surrounds Atlanta) (Jeffery and Gibson, 1986). Morris Gibson, the administrator for the

Fulton County Police Department, had been recording crime on a computer and locating each crime site on a one-mile-square grid. By looking at the grid map, one could locate the high- and low-crime-rate areas in Fulton County. We used residential burglary for this study.

The students, knowing the exact address of each burglary, located the crime sites on the Atlanta Aerial Atlas, which is a most comprehensive map of the area. The students took measurements from each crime site to the geographical features within 2 miles of the crime site. The features used were the Hartfield International Aiport, major highways, major shopping centers, major industrial areas, major residential areas, and so on. The three grids that had the highest residential burglary rates were located near Hartfield International Airport and near major interstate and state highways (I-285, I-75, I-85, and highway I20) which intersect in this area. There were two major industrial areas and two major shopping plazas in this area.

This is a rapidly growing area of south Atlanta and south Fulton County, and the high crime rate in this area reflects the ecological changes occurring in the area, as well as the human activities of the area. This included the extension of the MARTA system (metropolitan rapid transit system) to this area of south Atlanta. It was not possible to survey the individual crime sites, due to the distance between Tallahassee and Atlanta. When they were in Atlanta for the 1986 American Society of Criminology meeting in November, several of the students did survey three apartment complexes in the area that had the highest burglary rates. They found that the apartments most often burglarized were the end apartments, especially the end upstairs apartments. Not every apartment in an apartment complex has an equal chance of being burglarized. This information could be used for crime prevention measures.

The Atlanta project was not pursued further, although the initial results were extremely encouraging. Funding was not gained from either the National Institute of Justice or from an Atlanta foundation devoted to the improvement of living conditions in Atlanta.

Other Crime Prevention Projects

The Home Office in London has been very active in crime prevention and environmental design. One study showed that the use of locks on steering columns in Germany greatly reduced auto thefts in that country. Bus vandalism on London buses occurred on the upper decks of two-decker buses and on buses with a driver only as compared to buses with a driver and a conductor (Clarke and Mayhew, 1980).

A great deal of attention has been paid in crime prevention to ''target hardening,'' the use of locks, bolts, and alarm systems (National Crime Prevention Institute, 1986). Another approach to crime prevention has been through the organization of neighborhood groups, such as Neighborhood Watch projects. Such projects organize the citizens for local crime prevention efforts. The effectiveness of such projects has never been evaluated (National Crime Prevention Institute, 1986; Johnson, 1986).

Citizen projects and alarms and locks have their place in crime prevention, but they only stop those crimes that are simplest to stop. What is needed is a major effort to establish crime prevention projects based on a research effort rather than a political effort that appeals to the local citizens.

Future Research Efforts

Future research into crime prevention must be interdisciplinary in nature. It must be based on neurology, psychology, sociology, geography, and urban design. It must be based on an Organism × Environment model of behavior. Behavior, including criminal behavior, is a response to the environment by the organism. To prevent crime we must (1) alter the organism, or (2) alter the environment.

The model developed in this chapter places emphasis on the physical site of the crime, not on the social relationships or social control variables associated with social areas. Individual crime site data rather than aggregate data are also emphasized. We need to know why one store is robbed 18 times and another store is never robbed.

One basic research design I would like to see carried out would follow up on the Tallahassee, Gainesville, and Atlanta research projects. Police departments now have a major computer capacity which they utilize as file cabinets to store names, addresses, aliases, license plate numbers, and other information previously kept on 3 × 5 index cards.

A project could be established that would use computers for drawing maps and analyzing geographical data. These capabilities are already in use by geographers and urban planners. Each crime site would be individually located on a map, and the relationship between crime sites and major geographical features would be determined. The major geographical features would include major highways, major residential areas, major shopping centers, major industrial plazas, parks, vacant lots, and so on. This is a much more imaginative use of computers.

As each crime occurred, a special research team would visit the site within a week to gather data on the physical features of the site. High crime sites would be compared to low crime sites in an attempt to determine the critical differences in the crime sites. From such research, recommendations would be made as to changes needed in the physical design of the crime site to prevent crimes. The presence of a second clerk in convenience stores is a good example from projects already undertaken in Tallahassee and Gainesville, Florida.

An evaluation of the effectiveness of the measures taken would be made. In those instances where crimes were committed after crime prevention measures were undertaken, a follow-up study would be made to determine why in those cases crime prevention had failed. New measures would then be used, depending on the results of the research. In this way the failure of a crime prevention measure would lead to a reevaluation and new research.

As effective crime prevention measures were developed through careful research, these measures would be made available to communities in general through workshops and conferences. The critical feature, however, is to start with well-financed small projects before moving to general demonstration and implementation of crime control prevention. We must know how to prevent crime before we spend money on demonstration projects. The Westinghouse CPTED projects were not successful despite political support and millions of dollars poured into them because basic research was not done prior to demonstration. Research must be prior to application.

Urbanization, Social Change, and Crime

It was pointed out in Chapter 3 that the evolution of society was from hunting and fishing economies to urban and industrial economies. Population growth, demographic changes, and technological changes occurred which were described above as POET (population, organization, environment, and technology). These major changes in the social and physical environment had a strong impact on crime rates and on the geography of crime. Population changes, demographic changes, and urbanization are critical to the growth pattern of crime rates and to the spatial patterns of crime, as discussed above. So far our discussion has been of micro aspects of crime distribution in space. However, there is also a broad historical and macro aspect to urbanization and industrialization, which should be viewed as a critical part of the changes that occurred in crime rates over the centuries.

Shelley (1981) has undertaken to develop a model of social change and crime rates based on the concepts of modernization and urbanization. She noted that historically, as urban areas developed, high crime rates emerged in these areas.

Rural areas are characterized by more violent crimes than property crimes, but as urbanization takes place, property offenses become more prevalent than violent crimes. The high peak for property crimes is for developing nations (rural to urban transition) at the point of transition from rural to urban. In developed nations (urbanized) there is a stabilization of property offenses, with violent offenses much less frequent and often part of property offenses (robbery, for example). "In all three countries [France, England, and Germany] the mature years of industrialization were characterized by fewer violent offenses and more frequent though less threatening crimes against property" (Shelley, 1981:33).

In developed nations females are more involved in property offenses than they are in developing nations. Male youths are also greatly involved in crime in developing nations. These urban areas are characterized by immigrants, racial grouping, and slum areas with high crime rates (see Chapter 14 and the discussion in this chapter).

Shelley found no major differences between capitalistic and socialistic countries in the response of crime rates to urbanization. The socialist countries were classified as developed. "Under socialism, as under capitalism, crime is one of the major costs of modernization" (Shelley, 1981:134).

Socialism did not wipe out the state system, or state control, or crime as is argued would happen by Marxist criminologists (Chapter 13). Shelley did mention that Switzerland and Japan, which were highly industrialized nations, have not experienced high crime rates as did other capitalist nations, perhaps due to their small size, homogeneous population and culture, and their heavy reliance on personal social controls and traditional family and community values.

Clinard (1978) studied Switzerland as a country with little crime. He noted that Switzerland was industrialized, wealthy, and urbanized, and therefore Switzerland should have the high crime rates of other industrialized nations, but it did not. Why? Clinard related the low crime rate of the Swiss to the smallness of the country, their lack of centralized government, and their reliance on local citizens for social control, self-help, and solidarity. He recommended for the United States more decentralization of power and less centralized control of criminal justice policy.

Adler (1983) picked out ten low-crime countries (Algeria, Saudi Arabia, Costa Rica, Peru, Bulgaria, German Democratic Republic, Ireland, Switzerland, Nepal, and Japan) and compared these countries on the basis of demographic, economic, social, legal, and political variables to determine why they had so little crime. This is the same technique at the macro level that Reckless used as the micro level in asking why good boys are good and do not become delinquents (Chapter 15).

Adler found that these countries differed in rural–urban development, social welfare systems, type of government, and economic and unemployment conditions. What they had in common was strong informal social control systems outside the formal criminal justice system. Social control is found in the family and in the community. She reviewed the theoretical work of Comte, Durkheim, Spencer, Weber, and Marx, and she noted that Durkheim's theory of anomie or alienation and normlessness has been used as a framework for explaining crime within sociology (see Chapters 14 and 15). She also noted that Durkheim put forth a theory of social cohesiveness and solidarity in his concepts of mechanical and organic solidarity. In place of Durkheim's concept of anomie and alienation, Adler used the term ''synnomie'' to express social cohesiveness around collectively shared norms and values.

Fishman and Dinitz (1989) point out that Japan is a country with safe streets. It is also a country without a due process model, where the police are known in local communities, in which punishment is light and certain, and where there is a social cohesiveness and homogeneity of the population.

It was pointed out in Chapter 3 that social control shifted from the family-tribe to the state, and from decentralized to centralized political control. This is also a basic doctrine in the work of Comte, Durkheim, Spencer, Weber, and Marx. The work of Shelley, Clinard, and Adler is consistent with and carries on the nineteenth-century efforts to establish a broad historical base for understanding social control.

The broad social changes in social structure, organization, population and demographics, and urbanization totally changed people's ecological relationship to their environment. These changes produced the state as the agent of social control. As stated in Chapter 3, the state developed out of the disintegrating tribal units, which could no longer coordinate the tribal hunts, the distribution of food resources, the management of irrigation and water resources, and other issues critical to the ecology of survival. The coming of the agricultural revolution, the growth of towns and populations, and the industrial revolution further resulted in even greater population growth and urbanization. More centralized and powerful means of social control were required in the form of a centralized state system. In Chapter 21 we return to the issue of how much state control over human activities is needed. This is a major issue in contemporary criminology.

SUMMARY

Crime prevention involves taking action that will prevent a crime from occurring in the first place. It stands in stark contrast to the criminal justice model, which waits for the crime to occur.

Crime prevention can be either (1) physical design and the physical environment (e.g. CPTED), or (2) social control and social surveillance as proposed in the defensible space model put forth by Newman.

The crime prevention through environmental design model is based on an ecological model of the physical environment in interaction with the physical organism. The human-made environment becomes important in this model. The characteristics of individual crime sites, such as the type of building, the location of the streets, the location of parking lots, vacant lots, and parks, and the location of shopping malls and industrial plazas, are critical to this type of cime prevention analysis.

Defensible space projects have not been successful. Several crime prevention through environmental design projects have been successful, especially the convenience store robbery projects in Tallahassee and Gainesville. However, these projects were small projects with no major funding. The field of crime prevention must go beyond this in the future.

As we discuss in Chapter 21, the future of crime control in the United States depends on crime prevention technologies, not more prisons or criminal laws. Prevention must replace punishment and revenge as the basis for crime control.

REFERENCES

ADLER, F. (1983). *Nations Not Obsessed with Crime.* Littleton, Colo.: Fred B. Rothman & Co.

ALTMAN, I. (1975). *The Environment and Social Behavior.* Monterey, Calif.: Brooks/Cole.

BALDWIN, J. (1974). "Problem Housing Estates—Perceptions of Tenants, City Officials, and Criminologists." *Social and Economic Administration,* 8:116–135.

BALDWIN, J. (1979). "Ecological and Areal Studies in Great Britain and the United States." In *Crime and Justice,* Vol. 1, ed. N. Morris and M. Tonry. Chicago: University of Chicago Press.

BALDWIN, J., and A. E. BOTTOMS (1976). *The Urban Criminal.* London: Tavistock.

BOGGS, S. L. (1965). "Urban Crime Patterns." *American Sociological Review,* 30: 899–908.

BORDUA, D. (1958). "Juvenile Delinquency and Anomie: An Attempt at Replication." *Social Problems,* 6:230–238.

BOULDING, K. E. (1978). *Ecodynamics: A New Theory of Societal Evolution.* Beverly Hills, Calif.: Sage.

BRANTINGHAM, P. J., and P. L. BRANTINGHAM (1981). *Environmental Criminology.* Beverly Hills, Calif.: Sage.

BRANTINGHAM, P. J., and P. L. BRANTINGHAM (1984). *Patterns in Crime.* New York: Macmillan.

BRANTINGHAM, P. J., D. A. DYERSON, and P. L. BRANTINGHAM (1976). "Crime as Seen through a Cone of Resolution." *American Behavioral Scientist,* 20:261–273.

BRANTINGHAM, P. J., and F. L. FAUST (1976). "A Conceptual Model of Crime Prevention." *Crime and Delinquency,* 22:284–296.

BYRNE, J., and R. SAMPSON (1986). *The Social Ecology of Crime.* New York: Springer-Verlag.

CATTON, W. R., and R. E. DUNLAP (1978). "Environmental Sociology: A New Paradigm." *The American Sociologist,* 13:41–49.

CATTON, W. R., and R. E. DUNLAP (1980). "A New Ecological Paradigm for Postexuberant Sociology." *American Behavioral Scientist,* 24:15–47.

CHILTON, R. (1964). "Continuity in Area Research: A Comparison of Studies for Baltimore, Detroit, and Indianapolis." *American Sociological Review,* 29:71–83.

CLARKE, R. V. G., and P. MAYHEW (1980). *Designing Out Crime.* London: Her Majesty's Stationery Office.

CLIFTON, W. (1987). "Convenience Store Robberies in Gainesville, Florida." Paper presented at the annual meeting of the American Society of Criminology, Montreal, Quebec, November 1987.

CLINARD, M. B. (1978). *Crime and Modernization.* Carbondale: Southern Illinois University Press.

COHEN, A., A. LINDESMITH, and K. SCHUESSLER (1956). *The Sutherland Papers.* Bloomington: Indiana University Press.

COHEN, L. E., and M. FELSON (1979). "Social Change and Crime Rate Trends: A Routine Activity Approach." *American Sociological Review,* 44:588–608.

COHEN, L. E., M. FELSON, and K. C. LAND (1980). "Property Crime Rates in the United States: A Macro-dynamic Analysis, 1947–1977; with Ex Ante Forecasts to the Mid-1980's." *American Journal of Sociology,* 86:90–118.

COOK, P. (1986). "The Demand and Supply of Criminal Opportunities." In *Crime and Justice,* Vol. 7, ed. M. Tonry and N. Morris. Chicago: University of Chicago Press.

DAVIDSON, R. N. (1981). *Crime and Environment.* London: Croom Helm.

DOGAN M., and J. D. KASANDRA (1988). *The Metropolis Era,* Vols. 1 and 2. Newbury Park, Calif.: Sage.

DUNCAN, O. D., and L. SCHNORE (1959). "Cultural, Behavioral, and Ecological Perspectives in the Study of Social Organization." *American Journal of Sociology,* 65:132–146.

DUNLAP, R. E. (1980). "Paradigmatic Change in Social Science." *American Behavioral Scientist,* 24:15–47.

DUNLAP, R. E., and W. R. CATTON (1979). "Environmental Sociology." *Annual Review of Sociology,* 5:243–273.

EHRLICH, P. R., A. H. EHRLICH, and J. P. HOLDREN (1973). *Human Ecology.* San Francisco: W. H. Freeman.

ESSER, A. H. (1971). *Behavior and Environment.* New York: Plenum.

FARRINGTON, D. P., L. OHLIN,, and J. Q. WILSON (1986). *Understanding and Controlling Crime.* New York: Springer-Verlag.

FELSON, M. (1983). "Ecology of Crime." In *Encyclopedia of Crime and Justice,* ed. S. H. Kadish. New York: Free Press.

FISHMAN, G., and S. DINITZ (1989). "Japan: A Country with Safe Streets." *Advances in Criminological Theory,* Vol. 1, ed. W. F. Laufer and F. Adler. New Brunswick, N.J.: Transaction Press.

GEORGES-ABEYIE, G., and K. HARRIES (1980). *Crime: A Spatial Perspective.* New York: Columbia University Press.

GORDON, R. A. (1967). "Issues in the Ecological Study of Delinquency." *American Sociological Review,* 32:927–944.

GOULD, L. (1979). "The Changing Structure of Property Crime in an Affluent Society." *Social Forces,* 48:50–59.

GREENBERG, S. (1986). "Fear and Its Relationship to Crime, Neighborhood Deterioration, and Informal Social Control." In *The Social Ecology of Crime,* ed. J. M. Byrne, and R. J. Sampson. New York: Springer-Verlag.

GREENBERG, S., and W. M. ROHE (1984). "Neighborhood Design and Crime." *Journal of the American Planning Association,* 50:48–61.

HARRIES, K. (1974). *The Geography of Crime and Justice.* New York: McGraw-Hill.

HARRIES, K. (1980). *Crime and the Environment.* Springfield, Ill.: Charles C Thomas.

HEMSTRA, N. W., and L. H. McFARLING (1974). *Environmental Psychology.* Monterey, Calif.: Brooks/Cole.

HERBERT, D. (1982). *The Geography of Urban Crime.* Harlow, Essex, England: Longman.

ITTELSON, W. H., H. PROSHANSKY, L. RIVLEN, and G. WINKEL (1974). *An Introduction to Environmental Psychology.* New York: Holt, Rinehart and Winston.

JACOBS, J. (1961). *The Death and Life of Great American Cities.* New York: Random House.

JEFFERY, C. R. (1971, 1977). *Crime Prevention through Environmental Design.* Beverly Hills, Calif.: Sage.

JEFFERY, C. R., and M. GIBSON (1986). "Computer Analysis of Residential Burglary in Fulton (Atlanta) County, Georgia." Paper presented at the annual meeting of the American Society of Criminology, Atlanta. November 1986.

JEFFERY, C. R., R. HUNTER, and J. GRISWOLD (1986). "Crime Prevention and Computer Analysis of Convenience Store Robberies in Tallahassee, Florida." Paper presented at the annual meeting of the Academy of Criminal Justice Sciences. Orlando, Fl., March 1986.

JOHNSON, E. H. (1986). *Handbook on Crime and Delinquency Prevention.* Westport, Conn.: Greenwood Press.

KORNHAUSER, R. R. (1978). *Social Sources of Delinquency.* Chicago: University of Chicago Press.

LANDERS, B. (1954). *Towards an Understanding of Juvenile Delinquency.* New York: Columbia University Press.

MAWBY, R. I. (1977). "Defensible Space: A Theoretical and Empirical Appraisal." *Urban Studies,* 14:169–179.

MAYHEW, P. (1979). "Defensible Space: The Current Status of a Crime Prevention Theory." *Howard Journal,* 17:150–159.

MAYHEW, P., ET AL. (1979). *Crime in Public View,* Home Office Research Study No. 49. London: Her Majesty's Stationery Office.

MICHELSON, W. H. (1976). *Man and His Urban Environment.* Reading, Mass.: Addison-Wesley.

MICKLIN, M. (1973). "Introduction: A Framework for the Study of Human Ecology." In *Current Issues in Human Ecology,* ed. M. Micklin. Hinsdale, Ill.: Dryden Press.

MICKLIN, M. (1983). "Whatever Happened to Human Ecology? A Theoretical Autopsy." Paper presented at the Southwestern Social Science Association, Houston, Tex., March 16–19, 1983.

MORRIS, T. (1957). *The Criminal Area.* London: Routledge & Kegan Paul.

MUELLER, G. O. W., and F. ADLER (1985). *Outlaws of the Ocean.* New York: Hearst Marine Books.

MURRAY, C. (1983). "The Physical Environment and Community Control of Crime." In *Crime and Public Policy,* ed. J. Q. Wilson. San Francisco: ICS Press.

NATIONAL CRIME PREVENTION INSTITUTE (1986). *Understanding Crime Prevention.* Stoneham, Mass.: Butterworth.

NEWMAN, O. (1972). *Defensible Space.* New York: Macmillan.

ODUM, E. P. (1975). *Ecology: The Link between the Natural and Social Sciences.* New York: Holt, Rinehart and Winston.

PORTEOUS, J. D. (1977). *Environment and Behavior.* Reading, Mass.: Addison-Wesley.

POYNER, B. (1983). *Design against Crime.* London: Butterworth.

PYLE, G. (1974). *The Spatial Dynamics of Crime,* Research Paper No. 159. Department of Geography, University of Chicago.

RENNIE, Y. (1978). *The Search for Criminal Man.* Lexington, Mass.: Lexington Books.

REISS, A. J., and M. TONRY, eds. (1986). *Communities and Crime,* Vol. 8, Crime and Justice Series. Chicago: University of Chicago Press.

RUBENSTEIN, H. C., ET AL. (1980). *The Link between Crime and the Built Environment.* Washington, D.C.: National Institute of Justice.

SHELLEY, L. I. (1981). *Crime and Modernization.* Carbondale: Southern Illinois University Press.

SHEVSKY, E., and W. BELL (1955). *Social Area Analysis: Theory, Illustrative Application and Computational Procedures.* Stanford, Calif.: Stanford University Press.

STOKOLS, D. (1977). *Perspectives on Environment and Behavior.* New York: Plenum.

STOKOLS, D. (1978). "Environmental Psychology." In *Annual Review of Psychology.* Palo alto, Calif.: Annual Reviews, pp. 253–296.

TAYLOR, R. B., and S. GOTTFREDSON (1986). "Environmental Design, Crime Prevention: An Examination of Community Dynamics." In *Communities and Crime*, Vol. 8, Crime and Justice Series, ed. A. J. Reiss and M. Tonry, Chicago: University of Chicago Press.

TOBIAS, J. J. (1972). *Urban Crime in Victorian England.* New York: Schocken Books.

TYLER, R. B., S. D. GOTTFREDSON, and S. BROWER (1980). "The Defensibility of Defensible Space: A Critical Review and a Synthetic Framework for Future Research." In *Understanding Crime*, ed. T. Hirschi and M. Gottfredson. Beverly Hills, Calif.: Sage.

WOLFGANG, W. E., R. M. FIGLIO, and T. SELLIN (1972). *Delinquency in a Birth Cohort.* Chicago: University of Chicago Press.

QUESTIONS

1. What are the essential characteristics of crime prevention programs?
2. How did the Chicago school of social ecology explain delinquency rates?
3. How does a bioenvironmental approach to human ecology differ from a social ecological approach to human behavior?
4. What view of human behavior is basic to a bioenvironmental crime prevention program?
5. What role does the physical environment play in crime prevention?
6. Discuss the Jeffrey–Brantingham model of crime prevention. The Newman social control model of crime prevention.
7. How are crime rates related to our interstate highway system?
8. How come cities in the "sunshine belt" have such a high crime rate?
9. How did Gainsville, Florida reduce its convenience store robbery rate by 64 percent?
10. How could computers be utilized in crime prevention programs?

Criminal Law and the Insanity Defense

20

LEGAL ISSUES

Criminal Law and Voluntary Behavior

The law assumes free will, moral responsibility, and mens rea (Chapter 4). If a person does not possess free will and mens rea, there can be no moral or legal guilt. This was expressed very well in Durham v. United States, 214 F.2d 862 (1954).

> The legal and moral traditions of the Western world require that those who, of their own free will and evil intent or mens rea commit acts which violate the law, shall be criminally responsible for those acts. Our traditions also require that where such acts stem from and are a product of mental disease or defect as those terms are used herein, moral blame shall not attach, and hence there will not be criminal responsibility.

The criminal law is careful to differentiate involuntary behavior from voluntary behavior. Involuntary behavior includes coerced movements, reflex movements, convulsions, and unconsciousness (Chapter 4). The voluntariness of behavior is to be found in mens rea, the ability of the actor to form an intent to commit the crime. From the point of view of modern psychology, involuntary behavior is a product of the autonomic nervous system, whereas voluntary behavior is the product of the somatic nervous system. The differences between voluntary and involuntary depend on the organization of the brain and the types of learning involved (Chapters 11 and 13). The autonomic nervous system controls such action as heart beats and digestion, which we call involuntary behaviors. The somatic nervous system controls the arms and legs, what we call voluntary behaviors. The frontal and temporal lobes are involved in complex thought, planning, rationality, and decision making. We cannot avoid a scientific analysis of behavior by classifying some behavior as voluntary and some as involuntary. All behavior is controlled by the brain, and to understand behavior, we must first understand the brain.

The brain is not separated into tight compartments of rationality and irrationality, or voluntary and involuntary behaviors. The legal view is that involuntary behavior involves the "brain" or the physical structure, such as a convulsion or epileptic seizure; whereas voluntary behavior involves the "mind," which is not influenced by physical causation. If we view behavior as a product of brain/environment interaction, it is more profitable to talk about behavior and its relationship to the brain, rather than talking about voluntary versus involuntary behaviors.

The criminal law recognizes that although the philosophy of voluntary behavior and mens rea are posited as basic to the definition of crimes and to be found in all adult human beings, there are situations in which people are not free to behave as they want. The doctrine of special defenses includes infancy, ignorance, coercion, and insanity. The classic example used in criminal law classes of free will and responsibility is the case of Regina v. Dudley and Stephens (Q.B. 1884), 14 B.D. 273. This case involved two sailors who were shipwrecked and on a life boat with a young boy. Rather than starve to death, they killed the young boy and ate his body. They were eventually saved and afterward charged and convicted of murder, but the court sentenced them to only six months in prison. The court held that the need to survive did not justify murdering someone else, but that under the circumstances the sentence should be light.

The insanity defense is a legal defense because of the legal doctrine that people possess free will and mens rea but are not capable of exercising this free will and mens rea if they are insane. The relationship of the insantiy defense to modern biological psychiatry will be examined next.

Insanity and the Insanity Defense

The insanity defense goes to the heart of the criminal law in that it examines the issue of the ability of the defendant to form the necessary intent or mens rea. In 1843 a man by the name of M'Naghten shot and killed a man named Drummond, mistaking Drummond for Sir Robert Peel, the prime minister of Great Britain. M'Naghten was under the psychotic delusion that Peel was persecuting him (a delusion of persecution is a symptom of schizophrenia). The court found M'Naghten not guilty by reason of insanity, and the decision was highly criticized, as was the Hinckley decision, discussed below. In defending the decision the court put forth the legal bases for insanity, which are known as the "M'Naghten rules." The rules state that the defendant is not guilty if "the accused was laboring under such a defect of reason, from a disease of the mind, as not to know the nature and quality of his act, and if he did know it, that he did not know that what he was doing was wrong." This has come to be known as "the right and wrong test," although a more accurate appraisal would be to call it the "test of rationality"; that is, was the defendant rational at the time of the crime? (Robinson, 1980; Bromberg, 1979; Brooks and Winick, 1987; Brooks, 1974; Finkel, 1988).

The M'Naghten test of right and wrong forces the court to focus on rationality or cognition, rather than volition and emotionality. This is a legal, not a medical or scientific definition. There is no such thing medically as insanity. The psychiatrist must translate the term "insanity" into the term "mental illness," and in this translation there is room for misinterpretation and disagreement. The usual procedure is to classify psychoses as those mental illnesses that qualify under the law as insanity.

A major criticism of the right and wrong test is that it does not allow the psychiatrist to testify in medical terms. In an attempt to address this criticism, the court in United States v. Durham, 214 F.2d 862 (1954), led by Judge David Bazelon, declared that the "accused is not criminally responsible if his unlawful act was a product of mental disease or mental defect."

The Durham case did not define the terms "mental disease and mental defect" other than to state that a mental disease is a condition capable of improving or deteriorating, and a mental defect is a condition incapable of improving or deteriorating. Such a definition is absolutely useless. Under the Durham rule, alcoholism, drug addiction, neuroses, and psychopathy have been included as mental illnesses. In Blocker v. United States, 288 F.2d 853 (1961), the court held that the defendant was a psychopath, but psychopathy was not a mental disease. After the decision, the staff of St. Elizabeth's Hospital in Washington, D.C., changed their opinion and stated that psychopathy was a mental illness, a disease. In United States v. Currens, 290 F.2d 751 (1961), the court ruled that psychopathy was a mental disease.

The Durham decision also required that the criminal behavior be a "product of" the mental disease or mental defect. The "product of" rule is usually interpreted to mean that a condition called schizophrenia or alcoholism or psychopathy be found in the defendant who is charged with a criminal act. This means the presence of two labels for one person, one label "mentally diseased" and one label "a criminal." There is no causal relationship between mental illness and criminal behavior. In fact, mental illness and criminal behavior might be the product of a third variable, or might be the result of a spurious relationship, or criminal behavior might cause mental illness (Jeffery, 1967, 1985).

In response to the Durham decision, especially the Currens decision, Bernard Diamond (1962), a forensic psychiatrist, stated that the law must go beyond M'Naghten and Durham in light of the new emerging biological psychiatry, which has destroyed the meaning of mental illness and insanity. He noted that schizophrenia and manic-depression are not the same diseases they were twenty years ago since it is now possible to prove the presence or absence of schizophrenia or manic-depression through neurological tests of the brain. Diamond predicted that in ten years (which would have been 1972) biochemical tests would demonstrate that a number of our vicious criminals are sick. We have ritualized judicial murder for the helpless victims of diseases of the brain (Diamond, 1962:118).

The Durham decision, which applied only to the District of Columbia, was abandoned in United States v. Brawner, 471 F.2d 969 (1972). In this case the court adopted the American Law Institute (ALI) Model Penal Code definition of the insanity defense. The cognitive test of insanity as found in the M'Naghten rules was supplemented throughout the years with an irresistible impulse test as developed in New Hampshire in 1871 (Jeffery, 1985; Bromberg, 1979; Finkel, 1988; Simon and Aaronson, 1988). The irresistible impulse test states that a defendant is not legally responsible if he/she cannot control his/her behavior. This is known as the *volition* test, which addresses the issue of volition rather than rationality. The ALI test states that "a person is not responsible for criminal conduct if at the time of such conduct as a result of mental disease or defect he lacks substantial capacity either to appreciate the criminality of his conduct or to conform his conduct to the requirements of the law" (Section 4:01 of the Model Penal Code).

The ALI rule on insanity combines both rationality and volition into one rule. As noted in our discussion of the brain, the brain has a capacity for both rationality and emotionality, and the two must interact properly for lawful behavior to occur. In states that use the M'Naghten rule the defendant can be a violent serial murderer with major brain defects and still be legally sane since he/she knew "right from wrong" by demonstrating rationality in the courtroom. The prosecutor will introduce evidence that the defendant planned the crime, bought a gun, and then tracked the victim over a period of time before shooting him/her. This is to show that the defendant was not insane but rather was rational at the time. In the trial of John Hinckley, Jr. for the shooting of President Reagan, the government introduced this type of testimony in an effort to show that Hinckley was sane when he shot the president. Hinckley bought a gun, tracked the president, left newspaper clippings of Reagan's activities in his hotel room, and wrote to Jodie Foster, the movie star, of his love for her because of *Taxi Driver* and his plans to assassinate the president (Caplan, 1984; Low, Jeffries, and Bonnie, 1986). In a recent competency hearing for Ted Bundy, the serial murderer who killed a number of women, including two coeds at Florida State University, evidence was introduced by the government that Bundy was sane since he had acted as his own attorney and had cooperated with the lawyers and the court in his trial. This evidence was introduced by lawyers and judges and police officers. The one psychiatrist who testified at the hearing, Dorothy Lewis, maintained that Bundy was neurologically ill and should be given a complete medical examination (*Tallahassee Democrat,* December 12, 1987). No CAT scan or PETT scan was ever done on Bundy, and the insanity defense was never raised at the original trial. At this time we have no idea what the medical status of Bundy was, but it is of little value to have police officers and judges talking about whether Bundy is competent to stand trial on the basis of his behavior in a courtroom.

The Hinckley Trial and Changes in the Insanity Defense

On March 3, 1981, John Hinckley, Jr. shot and wounded President Reagan in Washington, D.C. This was while Reagan was surrounded by police officers. (An old test of insanity is whether or not the defendant would have committed the act if a policeman had been at his side. Perhaps the defense should have used the "policeman at the side" defense. Also, this knocks the theory that by hiring more police, we will be able to control crime.) In May 1982, Hinckley was tried in Washington, D.C. and was found to be not guilty by reason of insanity (Low, Jeffries, and Bonnie, 1986; Jeffery, 1985; Finkel, 1988; Simon and Aaronson, 1988). In the District of Columbia the ALI rule is used, which provided that both rationality and volition are to be grounds for an insanity decision. If Hinckley had been tried in a M'Naghten state, such as Florida, he would have been found guilty because he was rational and knew right from wrong.

The defense psychiatrists introduced evidence that Hinckley was schizophrenic or suffered from a borderline personality disorder. The government psychiatrists found him to have a mood disorder or a narcissistic personality disorder or a schizoid disorder (Low, Jeffries, and Bonnie, 1986). None of these diagnoses were based on neurological examiniations. The government paid great attention, as was mentioned above, to the fact that Hinckley had planned his actions over a period of months.

The most interesting twist to the Hinckley case, and one totally missing from the Low, Jeffries, and Bonnie (1986) discussion of the Hinckley decision, involved the testimony of a young biological psychiatrist named David Bear from Harvard Medical Center (Caplan, 1984:75). Bear attempted to introduce into the discussion evidence from a CAT scan which showed that Hinckley had an abnormal brain structure. The judge ruled that the CAT scan evidence could not be introduced. A major argument between Bear and the judge occurred, and Bear indicated that he would not testify as an expert witness unless he was allowed to present what he considered to be the most crucial bit of evidence he had as to Hinckley's psychiatric and medical condition. The judge later allowed the CAT scan to be introduced as evidence. I do not know why the jury brought in a verdict of not guilty by reason of insanity, but I would bet it was because the evidence on the CAT scan introduced by David Bear was in contrast to the psychobabble about borderline personalities and mood disorders, and they wanted to follow the leads of modern biological psychiatry.

Since the Hinckley trial a number of changes have been made in the insanity defense due to the overwhelming public reaction to the fact that Hinckley was put in a mental hospital rather than the electric chair (Caplan, 1984). Bonnie, a law professor (Low, Jeffries, and Bonnie, 1986:127), advocated elimination of the volitional aspect of the ALI rule, and in its place, use of the "appreciate the wrongfulness of his conduct" standard as a test of insanity. This would be a return to the M'Naghten rule and the cognitive test of insanity. It is hard to imagine why anyone would advocate in 1986 a standard of evaluation of criminal defendants based on an "appreciate the wrongfulness of his conduct" standard, especially in the light of what we know today about the brain. The American Bar Association and the American Psychiatric Association also recommended a return to the M'Naghten rule (Jeffery, 1985; Low, Jeffries, and Bonnie, 1896; Brooks and Winick, 1987; Caplan, 1984).

Morris (1982) rejected the insanity defense in favor of the mens rea rule, which repeats the criminal law requirement that if the defendant possesses mens rea, he/she is responsible for his/her acts. Morris does not feel that an insanity defense is necessary in light of the mens rea requirement. Morris reasserts the basic propositions of mentalism, mens rea, and moral guilt as basic to the criminal law and criminal justice. Like Professor Bonnie, he does not consider neurological evidence as a part of modern criminal law.

Some eight or nine states, including Michigan and Illinois, have passed legislation creating a special verdict called "guilty but mentally ill." Under this verdict a defendant can be found mentally ill but sent to a prison as a guilty criminal. The legislation does not require hospitalization or treatment of the criminal after he has been found mentally ill (Jeffery, 1985; Brooks and Winick, 1987; Low, Jeffries, and Bonnie, 1986; Simon and Aaronson, 1988).

The "guilty but mentally ill" verdict is a horrible contradiction in terms. The legal requirement of mens rea and moral responsibility is basic to the criminal law, yet it is ignored in this verdict since to be guilty but mentally ill means to be without mens rea and guilty intent. A person cannot be mentally ill and responsible for his/her conduct at one and the same time. The extent to which the general public, the political system, and the legal system will go to punish rather than rehabilitate criminals is revealed in the post-Hinckley development in the insanity defense. It should be kept in mind that these developments were part of the return to revenge and the "law and order with justice" movement of the 1970s that I discussed in Chapter 8.

Problems with the Insanity Defense

Three concepts are confused in the insanity defense. The concept of insanity is a legal term; the concept of mental illness is a psychiatric term; and the concept of a brain disorder is a neurological concept. In the past psychiatrists and lawyers have tried to force psychiatric testimony into legal concepts of right and wrong or cognition. This led to the "battle of the experts" (Low, Jeffries, and Bonnie, 1986). There is no way to establish insanity or mental illness as scientific verifiable concepts.

Gaylin (1982), a psychiatrist, in *The Killing of Bonnie Garland* told about the murder of a 17-year-old girl from a prominent family in New England by her boyfriend, a poor Mexican-American student at Yale University. Gaylin describes the adversarial system between lawyers and psychiatrist as one devoted to revenge and not truth. Psychiatric testimony is "the faith of the story teller." "Freud's concept of determinism and the law's demand for moral responsibility have made a mess of the insanity defense." As Gaylin pointed out, the psychiatrist has no definition of mental illness and must answer questions concerning right and wrong and irresistible impulses.

Justice B. Cardozo stated that "everyone contends that the present legal definition of insantiy has little relation to the truth of mental life." Justice F. Frankfurter stated: "I do not see why the rules of law should be arrested at the state of psychiatric knowledge at the time when they were formulated. . . . I think the M'Naghten rules are in a large measure shams" (Brooks, 1974:139–140). Philip Roche (1958:14), a psychiatrist, has noted that there is no legal or medical definition of insanity or mental disease. "Two of the most frequently encountered terms in psychiatry are 'psychosis' and 'neurosis,' and it might appear that in such currency their meaning would be settled in universal agreement. . . . Not only is there confusion as to the precise meaning of each term, but there is often as much confusion as to the existence of the pathological process to which either or both terms can be applied" (Roche, 1958:24–25).

Low, Jeffries, and Bonnie summarize the problems with the insantiy defense when they state:

> The insanity defense is a difficult subject. In large measure this is because the causal link between mind and behavior continues to defy scientific understanding. Most of the clinician's operating assumptions about mental abnormality are not susceptible to empirical validation. Moreover, the prevailing clinical understanding is not easily translated into concepts of interest to the criminal law, mainly because scientific study of the human mind is fundamentally unconcerned with questions of blameworthiness and responsibility. (Low, Jeffries, and Bonnie, 1982:651–652)

PSYCHIATRIC ISSUES

Psychiatry and Mental Illness

Psychiatry, the branch of medicine devoted to the treatment of mental illness and behavioral disorders, is divided into two general approaches, psychoanalysis and talk therapy based on Freudian psychology (Chapter 12), and biological psychiatry based on brain function and drug therapy. Mental hospitals for the insane (schizophrenic and manic-depressives) are usually run on the basis of physical therapies; the treatment of neuroses and hysterias are usually left to therapists who use couch therapies. Freud himself attempted in his *Project for Scientific Psychology* to relate behavior to neurological disorders, but he was never able to do so (Pribram and Gill, 1976; Rychlak, 1981; Sulloway, 1979).

The concept of "mental illness" is by definition a sickness in the mind, not the brain. The way we explore mental illness is to talk to the patient and ask him/her questions about past experiences and recollections. Free association is used to bring out repressed feelings and events (Chapter 12). Paper-and-pencil tests, such as the Bender-Gestalt, TAT, Rorschach, and MMPI, are used to produce these hidden emotions (Jeffery, 1985).

The typical psychiatric testimony offered in court for the insantiy defense is based on a psychiatric interview with the client/criminal for 20 minutes to an hour, perhaps with a test or two administered by a psychologist. Since the brain is never examined, the explanations of behavior are based on verbal interviews and nonphysical concepts of causation of behavior as found in psychoanalytic psychiatry. This procedure produces contradictory opinions from psychiatrists concerning the correct diagnosis of the defendant's condition. One psychiatrist will testify that the defendant is schizophrenic and another psychiatrist will testify that he/she is not schizophrenic. The usual situation in a criminal trial is for the government to hire psychiatrists who testify that the defendant is sane, whereas the defense lawyer hires psychiatrists who testify that the defendant is insane. This is the famous "battle of psychiatrists" that takes place in criminal trials (Jeffery, 1967, 1985).

There is little reliability or validity for psychiatric testimony (Ziskin, 1975). Ziskin and Faust (1988) and Faust and Ziskin (1988) concluded that clinical psychiatrists are unable to make accurate clinical judgments as to diagnosis and treatment of mental illnesses. There is in clinical psychiatry no standard of expertise or scientific knowledge. It must be remembered that this type of evidence is from couch interviews and pencil-and-paper tests, not from CAT scans or MRI scans. Robinson (1980) has written that psychiatric testimony is opinion unless backed by biochemical and neurological findings. In Washington v. United States, 390 U.S. F.2d 444 (1967), the court held that psychiatric testimony is filled with unexplained labels and unscientific procedures. The failure of psychoanalytic psychiatry to rehabilitate offenders was discussed in some detail in Chapter 12.

The Rise of Biological Psychiatry

Over the past thirty years the behavioral sciences have shifted from an introspective "mind-oriented" psychology to a scientific "brain-oriented" psychology. This is seen in behavioral genetics, in brain/behavior models of behavior, and in learning theory, which now has a biological base (Jeffery, 1985; Restak, 1988; Wender and Klein, 1981; Lickey and Gordon, 1983). Mental disorders, such as schizophrenia and depression, are now regarded as biochemical disorders of the brain to be treated by drug therapies. We listed in Chapter 19 the major classes of drugs: antidepressants, anticonvulsants, antianxiety, and antipsychotic drugs. The major emphasis today is on the neurotransmitter systems and the biochemistry of the brain (Snyder, 1980; Reinis and Goldman, 1983; Jacobs and Gelperin, 1981; Curzon, 1980; Meltzer, 1979). The development of a pysychiatry based on neurology fulfilled Freud's dream of a scientific psychology.

Psychiatry now uses CAT scans, PETT scans, EEF readings, evoked potentials, and hair analyses for establishing brain abnormalities. The organ of behavior is physical and can be studied by the same means as the heart or kidneys or liver. We have moved from mentalism and the mind to physicalism and the brain.

Biological Psychiatry and the Law

In the past the law–psychiatry relationship has involved Freudian psychoanalysis and criminal law. The lawyer accepted the Freudian model of behavior as an accurate and correct model of human behavior, and this theory was supported in the courtroom. This model was neither scientific or effective, and as a result the battle between law and psychiatry has raged over the years within the context of the adversarial system.

Today we are witnessing a new biological psychiatry based on the new sciences of behavioral genetics, neurology, biochemistry, and psychopharmacology. The interaction of law and biological psychiatry is just starting to develop, and I will discuss a few examples of how this is taking place.

One of the major issues that is emerging concerns the admissibility of neurological evidence into a criminal trial where the issue is insanity. If the defendant has a diseased brain, of what relevance is this fact for determining whether or not he is insane? Insanity is not a broken brain, but rather, not knowing right from wrong. We saw that in the Hinckley trial a CAT scan examination was introduced into the courtroom as evidence. The modern psychiatrist may use the CAT scan, PETT scan, EEG, NMR, or hair analysis to explore the human brain. Rather than talking about the mind of the defendant, the modern psychiatrist is involved in direct physical examinations of the human brain. How can such evidence be made admissible under the present rules and concepts of the legal system? How does a lawyer introduce evidence of brain dysfunction if the court wants to ask whether the defendant knew right from wrong? The courts can either reject such medical evidence based on scientific procedures, or they can relabel an XYY syndrome or hypoglycemia or epilepsy as a mental disease or as insanity.

Automatism is a defense under the doctrine of involuntary behavior. Yet courts have held that epilepsy is not insanity. On the other hand, other courts have found that epilepsy does qualify as insanity (Feldman, 1981; Jeffery, 1985; Fairall, 1981a, 1981b; McKay, 1980). It is a violation of common sense to label epilepsy as insanity or not insanity. Epilepsy is a disease of the brain, and it cannot be forced into the legal category of insanity.

The premenstrual syndrome (PMS; see Chapter 18) has been used as a defense in several trials in Britain, Canada, France, and the United States (Ginsburg and Carter, 1987; Jeffery, 1985; Brahams, 1981; Mulligan, 1983; Dalton, 1964, 1980; Carly-Thomas, 1982). Rather than finding the defendant insane, the court will find the defendant guilty and sane, but then introduce PMS as a mitigating circumstance. The court will then reduce the sentence and place the defendant on probation and require medical treatment for PMS.

Hypoglycemia was introduced in the case of Dan White, a former councilman in San Francisco who shot and killed the mayor and another councilman after eating over 40 Twinkees. The jury rejected the insanity defense, but they did reduce the sentence to eight years. This is known as the "Twinkee defense." Again the court used the neurological condition as a mitigating circumstance rather than as evidence that medical treatment was required. As far as I know, Dan White never did receive medical treatment for hypoglycemia. In Louisiana v. Parker, 416 So.2d 545 (1982), the Supreme Court of Louisiana rejected hypoglycemia as a mental condition even though an endocrinologist had testified on behalf of the defendant.

Posttraumatic stress disorder (PTSD) has been very common among Vietnam veterans, and there has been a high rate of criminal activity among former Vietnam veterans. Under the M'Naghten rules, PTSD is not a defense, but it may be introduced as a mitigating circumstance in order to reduce the sentence. Under the ALI rule, PTSD is a defense (Brotherton, 1981; Jeffery, 1985). Duane Samples, who graduated with honors from Stanford University, after his return from a tour of duty in Vietnam became disorganized, was filthy, felt guilty about those he had killed, and was a heavy drug user (CBS, "60 Minutes," August 2, 1983). Samples killed two women and was sentenced to prison for life. The sentence was commuted and then reinstated due to a public outcry for blood. As far as I know, Samples is now in prison. In the state of Florida the Supreme Court upheld a murder conviction and the death sentence for a Vietnam veteran when it rejected PTSD as a mitigating circumstance or as insanity (*Tallahassee Democrat,* September 17, 1983).

As noted above, psychopathy was rejected as a mental disease under the Durham rule and later reclassified as a mental disease. Under the ALI rule, a mental disease cannot be demonstrated by repeated antisocial acts. Antisocial behavior is not in itself evidence of a psychopathic condition because psychopathy is defined as antisocial behavior.

The definition of psychopathy found in the Diagnostic and Statistical Manual III (American Psychiatric Association, 1980) is based on a case history of truancy, antisocial behavior, delinquency, casual sex, drunkenness, drug use, family problems, a failure to accept social norms, and aggressive and assaultive behavior. Uelman (1980) argues that we should reject the DSM III definition of psychopathy in favor of the ALI position. If we accept Uelman's position, we reject the evidence that psychopathy is a brain disorder.

However, if we define psychopathy as a defect in the autonomic nervous system, the evidence of psychopathy is neurological, and not derived from a case history of antisocial behavior. The cause of psychopathy is in the nervous system. Psychopathy is not caused by antisocial behavior; psychopathy is antisocial behavior. I accet the ALI rule as far as it excludes psychopathy as a mental disease, but I also want a new definition of what constitutes psychopathy beyond that stated in the DSM III.

Alcoholism is very strongly related to criminal behavior. But intoxication is not a defense to a criminal charge. Voluntary intoxication may be introduced as evidence that the special mens rea required for certain specific crimes was lacking. The law once again is involved in dividing behavior into voluntary and involuntary. A person who becomes an alcoholic or is drunk is assumed to be acting in a voluntary manner and to be in control of his/her behavior. From the discussion of alcoholism in Chapter 18, we know that there is a genetic and brain chemistry basis for alcoholism. It is not voluntary behavior.

In an unusual decision the U.S. Supreme Court held in California v.

Robinson, 370 U.S. 660 (1962), that alcoholism is a disease to be treated, not a criminal act to be punished. In Driver v. Hinnant, 356 F.2d 761 (1966), the court of the District of Columbia held that alcoholism is a disease involving involuntary behavior; therefore, alcoholics must be put in treatment programs rather than in prisons. In Easter v. District of Columbia, 361 F.2d 50 (1966), the court held that an alcoholic is a sick person in need of treatment and rehabilitation. However, in Powell v. Texas, 392 U.S. 514 (1968), the U.S. Supreme Court held that alcoholics have some control over their behavior, and punishment is a proper response to the alcoholic.

An unusual case involving a crime is told by Mayer and Wheeler (1982) in *The Crocodile Man*. A young college student, a male, after taking a small amount of beer, attacked and almost killed two females. He was charged with attempted murder. The defendant's father happened to be a prominent biochemist at an eastern university, and he felt that there was a biochemical defect in his son's brain that was responsible for the violent behavior. He was able to convince the court that his son should be evaluated medically, which the court agreed to. After months of research they discovered a defect in the liver enzyme system used to control the conversion of alcohol in the brain. The defendant was released for medical treatment of a medical problem. *The Crocodile Man* is a classic in legal–medical jurisprudence. The term ''crocodile'' is taken from the concept of the reptilian brain, although as noted above, the limbic system that controls violence and aggression is mammalian, not reptilian.

One of the arguments against the insanity defense is that dangerous people are released back into the community to kill and rape again rather than being sent to a prison. The argument is fallacious for two reasons. The insanity defense carries with it a mandatory treatment commitment to a mental hospital before the defendant is released back into the streets. If the patient is not cured, at least he/she was in a treatment setting for a period of time. Those sent to prison are also released back into the streets to rape and kill once again, usually in a more vicious condition than when they entered the prison system. They are put in prisons, where they receive no treatment. We do not prevent crime by sending people to prison rather than to treatment centers. If treatment centers do not successfully treat criminals, it is a matter of putting our resources into building successful therapeutic programs through research and evaluation. That is what this book has been about.

The practice of using a physical condition as a mitigating circumstance means that the defendant spends less time in prison without treatment. This is the worst of all possible worlds. If we are going to introduce into the criminal trial such issues as hypoglycemia, PMS, brain dysfunctioning, CAT scans, and PETT scans, we must be prepared to assure that treatment will be carried out. We cannot allow courts to find that people are brain damaged and then have lawyers releasing such people back onto the street without treatment. Mitigation of the sentence without treatment is a common practice, but it is not good for the defendant, the victim, or the public. It is not the intent of the treatment model to put untreated and dangerous persons back on the streets untreated and dangerous (Jeffery, 1985). The medical model must be a treatment model, not a legal model for reducing punishment so as to place the criminal back on the streets without treatment.

A Psychobiological Definition of Mental Illness

Given the conflict between law and biological psychiatry, it is essential that a new definition of mental illness be put forth based on modern scientific knowledge about behavior. Such a definition would be based on neurological examinations of the brain, as discussed above.

The legal definitions of insanity go to the issues of cognition and volition. A lack of cognition (M'Naghten) or volition and cognition (ALI rule) are regarded as insanity and a bar to prosecution for a criminal act. The new definition of insanity would state that "any evidence introduced from neurological examinations as to damage to or dysfunction of the brain, which damage or dysfunction impairs the rational cognitive functions of the brain and interferes with the ability of the cognitive brain to control the emotional and volitional aspects of brain, is grounds for a legal finding that the defendant is medically unfit for a criminal trial and is in need of medical treatment rather than punishment."

This definition would tie the criminal law directly into scientific psychology and psychiatry. The "battle of the experts" would be eliminated and psychiatrists and psychologists would appear as expert witness for the court rather than as hired help for one side or the other (government or defense). Only physical evidence obtained from CAT scans and EEG readings and other such neurological examinations would be admitted. This would eliminate the controversial testimony of psychiatrists who present any number of contradictory opinions concerning any given defendant.

This position I am taking on a neurological definition of insanity is supported by the work of D. N. Robinson (1980), a psychologist. Robinson notes that the insanity defense is based on testimony from psychologists and psychiatrists which is not scientific and which is based on opinion rather than science. Robinson lists among his recommendations the following:

1. All statements regarding the mental state of the accused or of any party to litigation are to be treated as statements of belief or opinion. They are not to be accorded the status of evidence, and juries are to be instructed not to take them as evidence.

2. In all cases in which psychiatric or psychological testimony is to the effect that the party at issue is diseased, the testimony must be accompanied by relevant biochemical or neurological findings. For purposes of justice, the term *disease* refers to a discernable pathological process in the tissues or organs of the body. The term "mental disease" is to be taken as a metaphor, not as a diagnostic specification. (Robinson, 1980:206).

Finkel (1988) rejects the position taken by Robinson and myself, and he argues that psychologists must be allowed to testify as to the mental status of the defendant in terms of perception, awareness, and memory. Finkel does not want to reduce the concept of "mind" to the brain. Simon and Aaronson (1988) discuss in their book the Hinckley case and the Dan White case (the Twinkee defense) without mentioning either the CAT scan performed on Hinckley or the issue of hypoglycemia as raised in the White case. They totally ignore the issue of mental disease versus brain disease.

SUMMARY

The insanity defense is an excellent example of the conflict between law and science. The mens rea and free-will arguments of the law conflict with the deterministic view of science.

The insanity defense is based on mentalistic concepts of the rational mind (M'Naghten rule) and/or the emotional mind (the ALI rule). An inability of the mind to form a criminal intent or to control the emotional mind is regarded as insanity and a defense of criminal charges.

The psychiatric concept of mental illness is also mentalistic, but it is based on determinism and Freudian psychoanalysis. There is little reliability or validity to psychiatric testimony based on psychiatric interviews and paper-and-pencil tests.

Biological psychiatry is putting forth the concept of brain damage and brain defects in place of either the concept of insanity or the concept of mental illness. A biological concept of brain disorder is based on neurological damage as found in a CAT scan or a PETT scan or some other type of medical examination. The concept of brain damage should replace the concepts of insanity and mental illness. Currently, evidence of brain damage is being introduced into criminal trials, as in the trial of John Hinckley, Jr., where a CAT scan was introduced as evidence.

Lawyers do not want to consider neurological evidence in cases involving murder, rape, assault, or drug use, but they routinely consider such evidence in cases involving brain damage due to birth trauma, automobile accidents, or assaults. CAT and PET scans are part of any trial procedure where damage to the brain is at issue. There is no reason that the same neurological evidence cannot be introduced in a criminal trial.

REFERENCES

AMERICAN PSYCHIATRIC ASSOCIATION (1980). *Diagnostic and Statistical Manual,* 3rd ed. Washington, D.C.: American Psychiatric Association.

BRAHAMS, D. (1981). "Premenstrual Syndrome: A Disease of the Mind?" *Lancet,* 1238–1240, November 28.

BROMBERG, W. (1979). *The Use of Psychiatry in the Law.* Westport, Conn.: Quorum Books.

BROOKS, A. D. (1974). *Law, Psychiatry, and the Mental Health System.* Boston: Little, Brown.

BROOKS, A. D., and B. J. WINICK, eds. (1987). "Current Issues in Mental Disability Law." *Rutgers Law Review,* 39(2–3):1–244.

BROTHERTON, G. L. (1981). "Post-Traumatic Stress Disorder—Opening Pandora's Box?" *New England Law Review,* 17:91–117.

CAPLAN, L. (1984). *The Insanity Defense and the Trial of John W. Hinckley, Jr.* Boston: David R. Godine.

CARLY-THOMAS, E. (1982). "Premenstrual Defense—Whither Defense." *Criminal Law Review,* 531–532, August.

CURZON, G., ed. (1980). *Biochemistry of Psychiatric Disturbances.* New York: Wiley.

DALTON, K. (1964). *The Premenstrual Syndrome.* London: Heinemann.

DALTON, K. (1980). "Cyclical Criminal Acts in the Premenstrual Syndrome." *Lancet,* 10:1070–1071, November.

DIAMOND, B. (1962). "From M'Naghten to Currens and Beyond." *California Law Review,* 50:189–205.

FAIRALL, P. (1981a). "Irresistible Impulse, Automatism, and Mental Disease." *British Journal of Criminal Law,* 5:136–155.

FAIRALL, P. (1981b). "Automatism." *British Criminal Law Journal,* 5:335–345.

FAUST, D., and J. ZISKIN (1988). "The Expert Witness in Psychology and Psychiatry." *Science,* 241: 31–34, July.

FELDMAN, W. S. (1981). "Episodic Cerebral Dysfunction: A Defense in Legal Limbo." *Journal of Psychiatry and Law,* 9:193–201.

FINKEL, N. J. (1988). *Insanity on Trial.* New York: Plenum.

GAYLIN, W. (1982). *The Killing of Bonnie Garland.* New York: Simon and Schuster.

GINSBURG, B. E., and B. F. CARTER (1987). *Premenstrual Syndrome.* New York: Plenum.

JACOBS, B. L., and P. GELPERIN (1981). *Serotonin, Neurotransmission, and Behavior.* Cambridge, Mass.: MIT Press.

JEFFERY, C. R. (1967). *Criminal Responsibility and Mental Disease.* Springfield, Ill.: Charles C Thomas.

JEFFERY, C. R. (1985). *Attacks on the Insanity Defense.* Springfield, Ill.: Charles C Thomas.

LICKEY, M. E., and B. GORDON (1983). *Drugs for Mental Illness.* San Francisco: W. H. Freeman.

LOW, P. W., J. C. JEFFRIES, and R. J. BONNIE (1982). *Criminal Law.* Mineola, N.Y.: Foundation Press.

LOW, P. W., J. C. JEFFRIES, and R. J. BONNIE (1986). *The Trial of John W. Hinckley, Jr.* Mineola, N.Y.: Foundation Press.

MAYER, A., and M. WHEELER (1982). *The Crocodile Man.* Boston: Houghton Mifflin.

McKAY, R. D. (1980). "Non-organic Automatism: Some Recent Developments." *British Criminal Law Review,* 350–361, June.

MELTZER, H. L. (1979). *The Chemistry of Human Behavior.* Chicago: Nelson-Hall Publishers.

MORRIS, N. (1982). *Madness and the Criminal Law.* Chicago: University of Chicago Press.

MULLIGAN, N. (1983). "Premenstrual Stress Syndrome as a Defense in Criminal Cases." *Duke Law Journal,* 1:176–195.

PRIBRAM, K. H., and M. M. GILL (1976). *Freud's "Project" Reassessed.* New York: Basic Books.

REINIS, S., and J. M. GOLDMAN (1983). *The Chemistry of Behavior.* New York: Plenum.

RESTAK, R. (1988). *The Mind.* New York: Bantam.

ROBINSON, D. N. (1980). *Psychology and Law.* New York: Oxford University Press.

ROCHE, P. Q. (1958). *the Criminal Mind.* New York: Farrar, Straus & Cudahy.

RYCHLAK, J. F. (1981). *Introduction to Personality and Psychotherapy.* Boston: Houghton Mifflin.

SIMON, R., and D. E. AARONSON (1988). *The Insanity Defense.* New York: Praeger.

SNYDER, S. H. (1980). *Biological Aspects of Mental Disorders.* New York: Oxford University Press.

SULLOWAY, F. (1979). *Freud: Biologist of the Mind.* New York: Basic Books.

UELMAN, G. F. (1980). "The Psychiatrist, the Sociopath, and the Courts: New Lines for the Old Battle." *Loyola Law Review,* 14:1–23.

WENDER, P. W., and D. F. KLEIN (1981). *Mind, Mood, and Medicine.* New York: Farrar, Straus, and Giroux.

ZISKIN, J. (1975). *Coping with Psychiatric and Psychological Testimony.* Beverly Hills, Calif.: Law and Psychology Press.

ZISKIN, J., and D. FAUST (1988). *Coping with Psychiatric and Psychological Testimony.* Venice, Calif.: Law and Psychology Press.

QUESTIONS

1. What is meant by insanity? How is the concept related to mentalistic psychology?
2. What is the "right and wrong" test for insanity? The "irrestible impulse" test?
3. It is stated that the insanity tests are based on the rational and emotional structures of the brain. Explain.
4. In the Hinckley trial a CAT scan was introduced as evidence of a brain defect or disorder. What is so important about this piece of evidence?
5. How is biological psychiatry being used by our criminal courts in the evaluation of the state of a defendant's mind at the time of a crime?
6. What might the insanity defense look like in the future? What would happen to legal concepts of free will and mens rea?

Crime Prevention: Scientific versus Legalistic Models 21

OVERVIEW

The Conflict between Law and Science

As has been noted throughout this book, there is a basic and unresolved conflict between law and science, between the classical school and the positive school of criminology. The legal position assumes a mind–body dualism, mentalism, mens rea, free will, and moral responsibility (Chapters 4 and 6). Scientific criminology assumes determinism and causation as far as human behavior is concerned, and it utilizes a brain–body model wherein behavior is caused by the brain and not the mind (Chapters 5, 11, and 12). Human behavior is the product of the interaction of the individual organism and the environment, and the organism is a product of genetic/environment interaction.

The legal approach is based on punishment and is justified in terms of retributive justice, deterrence, and/or incapacitation. Punishment has not resolved the crime problem, but it has resulted in a high crime rate, many criminals, many victims, and overcrowded and shameful prisons. The scientific position is based on treatment and prevention. The use of prevention strategies based on environmental design, ecology, and urban planning is discussed in Chapter 19. In this chapter we discuss the use of modern scientific procedures, such as human genetics, the brain sciences, and learning theory, to control criminal behavior at the individual level.

This conflict between law and science is found most prominently in the Wilson and Herrnstein (1985) book *Crime and Human Nature*. In this book they discuss modern biology, psychology, and sociology as applied to the concept of human nature, and they conclude the book with the statement that "we know that crime, like all human behavior, has causes, and that science has made progress—and will make more progress—in identifying them, but the very process by which we learn to avoid crime requires that the courts act as if crime were wholly the result of free choice" (p. 528). One must ask "why have psychology and a science of human behavior if we must assume free will and no determinism for human behavior?" We do not need a science of criminology to support a legal system based on free will and moral guilt.

The major need today is to integrate criminal law and science as found in modern psychobiology. Attempts to put forth a treatment/prevention model of crime control are discussed in terms of the works of Kittrie, Menninger, Michael and Adler, and Wootton (Chapter 7). These researchers argued that we must move from a mens rea and guilt-finding process to a scientific process for preventing criminal conduct. Kittrie argued that we need a therapeutic bill of rights for our treatment model.

The legal model of retributive justice and punishments has made impossible the treatment of criminals and the prevention of crime. In this chapter we address the issues involved in the production of a treatment/prevention model for criminal behavior, including the legal hurdles that the law has established against treatment and prevention.

Crime Prevention and the Individual Offender

In Chapter 19 I discussed the issue of crime prevention from the point of view of environmental design, an idea primarily related to property offenses (e.g., robbery, burglary, theft, and larceny). Crimes against the person (e.g., murder, rape, and assault) cannot be prevented by redesigning the physical environment. Two exceptions to these general rules are rape by strangers and robbery, which we will classify as both a property and a personal offense.

The reason that environment design does not work well in the case of personal offenses is that the criminal is in the environment by invitation. How do we prevent murder when the wife kills her husband in the kitchen or bedroom of their home, or a female is raped by a relative or a boyfriend on a date? Rape by a stranger who attacks in a public place, as a park or street, or who commits trespass to enter a home or apartment can be significantly prevented by the usual design measures, such as locks, bolts, and secure doors and windows. We can design apartments in relation to other apartments, streets, and parks so as to prevent crime. Similarly, many robberies can be prevented by environmental design, as in the case of convenience store robberies in Tallahassee and Gainesville (Chapter 19).

Crimes of a personal nature must be prevented by intervening at the level of the susceptible individual offender, not at the level of the crime site. People who are violent (and personal crimes are violent crimes) can be detected and their violent behavior can be reduced or eliminated. It is my intent to use the materials from Chapter 18 on the violent career criminal and his/her characteristics to build a crime prevention model for the violent career criminal.

The argument developed by Brantingham and Faust [1976; Chapter 19] is that "primary prevention" applies only to those efforts that are devoted to the environment and which are for the general social and physical well-being of everyone. Once we resort to early identification, screening, and early treatment, we are into what they call "secondary prevention." Using this classification of prevention measures, we are left with only environmental changes as primary prevention, and by definition all intervention at the individual level becomes secondary prevention.

Brantingham and Faust want to prevent the emergence, not of criminal behavior, but of those variables that might lead to criminal behavior, such as pollution, poor nutrition, and city design. In this chapter I am concerned with those measures that can be taken at the individual level to prevent the emergence of criminal behavior in some individuals. To do this we must be able to identify those variables at the individual level that are associated with criminal behavior. We must identify and treat or prevent such variables by identification, screening, and early intervention. It may well be that those variables that appear in 12- to 14-year-old career criminals can be prevented in some manner at the age of 6 months or 3 years. If so, why should we not deal with the young population? We should not limit crime prevention to the environment only, or to measures that apply equally to all individuals.

In an unpublished paper Faust has made a differentiation between treatment and rehabilitation. Treatment implies a cure for a condition, that is, the disease is no longer present; whereas rehabilitation implies measures taken to support on a long-term basis a disability that can be helped but not cured. Insulin treatment for diabetics or eyeglasses for the nearsighted are examples. It must be recognized at the outset that many of the behavioral disabilities that come to the attention of criminal courts will never be cured but can be aided through rehabilitative efforts. We can design special environments for hyperactive children or those suffering from brain trauma or nutritional defects, or we can use long-term drug therapy and behavioral therapy for those with certain brain disorders.

The Career Criminal

As discussed in Chapter 18, the violent career offender commits 50 percent of the crimes and makes up 5 to 7 percent of the criminal population. If one adds to this the fact that a few criminals suffer from serious brain defects and from male-limited alcoholism, we have an obvious small but very dangerous population upon which to focus our prevention and treatment programs. In Chapter 18 we discussed the fact that violent offenders suffer from brain trauma, nutritional and pollution damage, underarousal of the autonomic nervous system, left-hemisphere damage in the frontal and temporal lobes, hyperactivity, and attention-deficit disorders.

The purpose of crime prevention is to focus on high-crime-rate areas (Chapter 19) and on high-crime-rate individuals (violent career criminals). The 90 to 95 percent of the criminal population who commit the other and less serious 50 percent of the crimes would be handled by diversion from the criminal justice system. They would be placed in probation programs, in work release and community action programs, in special school programs, in military-type boot camps, and in wilderness training camps. Many individuals who mature out of crime by age 21 need not be sent to prison or to major neurological and psychiatric clinics. However, a 12-year-old with a major brain problem is not going to benefit from a wilderness training camp or a special education program. By age 18 he will be a serious violent offender.

The concept of a career criminal has been vigorously denied by Gottfredson and Hirschi. They assume that longitudinal studies are faulty, and they advocate cross-sectional research in criminology (Gottfredson and Hirschi, 1986, 1987). The issue of longitudinal versus cross-sectional research is not an issue I will attempt to resolve in this book.

I will cite two issues they raise in their rejection of the concept of a career criminal. One argument presented in the Gottfredson and Hirschi (1986) article is that to prevent crime, we must be able to predict the criminal career before it occurs. This means intervening in the lives of individuals at a predelinquent period, such as age 6 or age 10. They argue that there are no legal means to treat people until they are criminals, and they further argue that we do not have the means to identify and predict the behavior of the career criminal at this time. The view put forth in this chapter is that we can prevent crime by intervening before the behavior occurs if we frame the intervention in a prevention and treatment model rather than in a punishment and criminal justice model.

The other assumption made by Gottfredson and Hirschi (1986:231) is that there are no individual differences in the susceptibility of individuals to criminality. They argue that the state prevents crime through legal penalties (the deterrence argument). ''The theories of crime implicit in this strategy tend to reject the notion of a career criminal . . . because they accept the idea that the criminal propensity is lodged in the great bulk of the population. Whether advanced by economists (the rational choice theory) or by sociologists (social control theory), these explanations of crime share the view that crime occurs naturally in the absence of restraint. Crime, then, is merely natural, unskilled, unrestrained activity'' (Gottfredson and Hirschi, 1986:231). To accept the Gottfredson and Hirschi position, one must reject all the evidence presented throughout this book and in the literature on the career criminal concerning individual differences as found at the biological and psychological levels of analysis.

Early Identification of High-Risk Individuals

Crime prevention at the individual level must depend on the early identification of the high-risk individual, for otherwise the individual will be engaged in a life of crime and will be arrested and placed within the criminal justice system. The purpose of prevention is to keep individuals out of the criminal justice system.

Early identification of the individual at risk is based on the observation that individual differences are critical and a few individuals are highly susceptible to drug addiction, alcoholism, and violence. As Ornstein and Sobel (1987:31) write, it is not what disease the patient has, but what patient has the disease. Why are some people susceptible to certain diseases and others are not? Eighty percent of the individuals with high cholesterol levels do not have heart disease. Reducing the cholesterol levels for 80 percent of the population will not reduce the risk of heart attacks for this specific population. Most criminals are men. We do no want to know why some criminals are men, but why some men are criminals. Eighty percent of the criminals may be men, but 10 percent of the men are criminals. Individual differences and susceptibilities are critical in the early identification of the potential offender.

The first stage in the treatment/prevention process is that of diagnosis and identification. The potentially serious offender must be separated from the minor offender by the age of 10 to 12. For the serious offender there must be special diagnostic procedures based on modern medical science and neurology. Brain disorders and learning disabilities would be discovered through a complete medical examination.

Once a diagnosis is made, the next stage would involve treatment for an experimental group, with a control group that would not receive treatment. The control group would be selected from the pool of violent offenders as well as from nonviolent offenders and from a noncriminal population. The treatments would vary from surgery for a brain tumor to drug therapies for brain chemistry disorders, dietary and nutritional programs, including tryptophan therapy, and chelation therapy to remove lead and cadmium from the body and brain. Depo-Provera therapy is a drug therapy that could be used with certain sex offenders.

Male-limited alcoholics would be identified and treatment initiated in terms of the liver enzymes. Drug and alcohol abuse would be regarded as a neurological problem and treated by psychopharmacological means. Our present state of knowledge of the neurotransmitter system and the impact of drugs on the brain permits us to formulate drug therapies for alcoholics and addicts.

The focus of any such research project must be on the interaction of violence, hyperactivity, alcohol use, and drug abuse. It can be hypothesized that these personality disorders have a common origin in brain dysfunctioning. The challenge is to find what these disorders have in common.

People with a history of infant or childhood brain injuries and trauma should be examined periodically for brain dysfunctioning and a history of epilepsy. Any signs of neurological dysfunctioning should be taken seriously (Lewis and Balla, 1976; Lewis, 1981). Pediatricians and family practice physicians should be trained and encouraged to look for early signs of brain damage and nutritional defects. Attentional deficit disorders would be picked up as well by elementary school teachers and counselors and referred to the proper medical facilities for diagnosis and treatment. Any behavioral problems involving the family or school system should be investigated, especially those involving learning difficulties, dyslexia, or attention deficit disorders (Freier, 1986; Van

Dusen, 1986). It should not be assumed, as Polk assumed (Chapter 16), that school behavioral problems are a product of social class sytems and the educational system.

A major attempt should be made to deal with childhood behavioral disorders as possible indicators of later violent behavior. Male children of known alcoholics should be watched carefully for symptoms of male-limited alcoholism. Early signs of alcohol and drug abuse must be regarded as evidence that serious behavioral disorders are possible. We all know high school students who are emotionally in trouble and are drug and alcohol abusers, but we can do nothing to intervene. In most instances such persons do not wish to be helped and will refuse help. On February 12, 1988, a high school student in the St. Petersburg, Florida, area entered the school with a gun and shot three teachers, wounding one critically before he was wounded by the police. The suspect had been in a mental hospital several months before, and he was described as strange and "off in another world" by his mother and classmates (*St. Petersburg Times*, February 13, 1988). A program must be established that will encourage families and young people with problems to seek help without feeling that there is something wrong with helping those with problems.

Miller (1986) has pointed out the many legal constraints found in school systems where the early identification of problem children is attempted. As he noted, special intervention programs for delinquents are faced with numerous legal challenges.

Recently, a female, Laurie Dann of Winnetka, Illinois, opened fire on a second-grade class, killing one student and wounding six other students before shooting a college student and killing herself. A review of her life history revealed a long history of disturbed behavior: stabbing her husband, hiding in a closet with a paper bag over her head, making threatening phone calls to neighbors, riding all night on an elevator at her apartment complex, and setting fire to a house where she was baby sitting. A federal prosecutor from Tucson who refused to pursue the case before the fatal day stated that Dann had rights and these rights prevented him from removing her from the streets although she was a danger to self and others (*USA Today*, May 22, May 23, May 25, 1988).

A Research/Treatment Center for Tertiary Crime Prevention

In 1950, James Bennett, then Director of the Bureau of Prisons, called for the establishment of the Eastern Psychiatric Institute to be built at Butner, North Carolina. The purpose of the Institute was to do research on the mentally disturbed offender. Butner was selected because of its proximity to Duke University Medical Center, the University of North Carolina, and the Research Triangle. The plan was never carried out (U.S. Department of Justice, 1981). In the late 1960s the unit was renamed the Behavioral Research Center. This plan was also scrapped at the time of the furor about psychosurgery, XYY research, and behavioral modification in federal prisons (see the discussion below). The final version of the research center was the Federal Center for

Correctional Research. The center used the model of imprisonment put forth by Morris in his *The Future of Imprisonment* (see Chapter 8).

The Morris model is based on a humane secure environment where prisoners are aware of the release date when they enter the prison. They are not forced into therapy, and the release date is not dependent on therapeutic success while in prison. Butner has individual cells, the inmates wear street clothes, and it is a more humane setting than most prisons.

An evaluation of the Butner model by Witte et al. (1983; McCord, 1986) revealed that the Butner group had a higher arrest rate after release than the control group from other federal institutions. The Butner group (experimental group) had a longer period between release and arrest than the control group, and the Butner group had higher earnings at legitimate employment than the control group. Overall, the report concluded that there was no evidence of effectiveness in controlling crime by use of the Butner model.

It is a shame that federal authorities were scared away from the establishment of a major research facility at Butner devoted to modern neurological and psychopharmacological research. This would be an ideal location, with Duke University, the University of North Carolina, and the Research Triangle in the vicinity. Once again we must conclude that we would rather imprison and execute criminals under the philosophy of law, order, and justice than find out why people become violent (Jeffery, 1985).

To prevent criminal behavior, or treat it after it has occurred, we must establish a major research center(s), preferably associated with a major medical research center(s). Such a center would be interdisciplinary in nature, involving genetics, biochemistry, neurology, psychobiology, and psychopharmacology as well as criminology, law, and ethics.

A person admitted to such a research center would be given a total medical examination, plus a complete social case history. The center would focus on the 5 percent hard-core recidivists with violent careers. Diagnostic and treatment procedures would follow the procedures outlined in Chapter 18 and would be dictated by modern medical practices. Evaluation of the outcome would be carefully monitored.

The types of persons who would be placed in such a major research facility would include the well-known mass murderers and serial murderers of the past, such as Charles Manson, Gary Gilmore, Charles Starkweather, Frank DeSalvo, David Berkowitz, Juan Corona, Elmer Hensley, Charles Whitman, John Gacy, Henry Lee Lucas, Otis Toole, Kenneth Bianci, Ted Bundy, and Christopher Wilder (Jeffery, 1985:158 ff.). I will discuss several of these cases just to illustrate the types of behavioral problems involved in major criminal careers.

The Case of Charles Whitman

Charles Whitman was a young University of Texas student who one day climbed to the top of the University of Texas library tower and shot and killed 16 people. Before the tower incident Whitman killed his wife and mother (Restak, 1984; Jeffery, 1985).

Whitman had complained for several years of severe headaches, compulsive and violent feelings, irrational feelings, and other behavioral problems. He had been to the university clinic on several occasions but had never received a complete medical examination or any real medical help. This man was begging for help and reminds us of the William Heirens case (Freeman, 1955), the University of Chicago student who killed women and then wrote on the walls "Stop Me Before I Kill More."

Whitman was killed by the police during the shooting spree, and an autopsy on his brain revealed a malignant tumor in the amygdala area of the brain, the area of the brain controlling violence and aggression. Let us assume the following scenario for this case, using the Whitman case as an example of the problems facing the legal criminal justice system.

1. Whitman goes to a medical clinic and is referred to a psychiatrist, who recommends verbal therapy for his migraine headaches. Whitman refused to cooperate and did not return to the clinic.

2. Whitman is referred to the neurological clinic of the University of Texas Medical Center for a complete neurological examination and evaluation. A malignant tumor was found by a CAT scan and other neurological tests. The presence of the tumor was related to his violent behavior.

3. The tumor is found to be operable. The surgeon recommends surgery, and Whitman consents. Can surgery be done? Yes, since Whitman has not committed a crime and is not under any legal hold. This is a private matter between surgeon and patient.

4. The tumor is found to be inoperable. Is Whitman released, since there has been no crime committed, or is he referred to a court for a hearing and commitment as a potentially dangerous person? Is he placed in an institution for the rest of his life even though he has not committed a crime? Under what authority does the court commit him to an institution for life when he has not committed a crime? Is he a false positive or a false negative? If we release him, will he kill himself or others?

5. Whitman kills his wife and mother and 16 people on the University of Texas campus, but he is captured alive by the police. The Texas courts try Whitman for murder and he is convicted. Do we execute him, put him in prison for life, or refer him to a special medical unit established for research and treatment of violent offenders? I doubt if Texas has such a unit, or would use it if they had it, and remember that the attempt of the University of California at Los Angeles to establish such a center for the study of violence was killed because it was too inhumane and dangerous. We now have many men on our death rows with the same kind of behavioral history as Whitman, including Ted Bundy in the state of Florida.

6. Whitman is serving a life sentence or is sentenced to be executed by lethal injection (used in more advanced penal systems). He dies shortly after his arrival at prison, or he dies the day before his scheduled execution. The

students from Sam Houston State University who gathered outside the prison to cheer his execution and drink beer are very unhappy, as are the politicians of the state of Texas.

7. Whitman is sent to a diagnostic unit of the Texas prison system and is found to have headaches brought on by nervous tension. He is given aspirin and sent to a maximum security prison unit.

8. Whitman is transferred by the court to a special medical facility, where the malignant tumor is found. Do we operate on the tumor or send Whitman to a psychiatric unit for verbal therapy?

9. The tumor is operable. The medical staff recommends brain surgery. Can the state of Texas operate on Whitman? With his consent? Without his consent? Does Whitman have a right under Ruiz v. Estelle (a Texas case, see below) to medical treatment for this tumor? Does he have a right to refuse treatment?

10. The tumor is inoperable. Does Whitman have a right to release under the right to treatment doctrine? Is he sane, insane, mentally ill, or physically ill? What if by some chance Whitman lives long enough to be eligible for release from prison? Do we release him with the tumor in his brain, or do we have a right to predict future dangerousness and thus hold him in prison (or a mental hospital) for life for something he has not done but might do in the future?

Jeffrey MacDonald was a medical officer with the Green Berets. While stationed at Fort Bragg, North Carolina, his wife and two children were brutally murdered, and MacDonald was charged and convicted of the crimes (McGinnis, 1983). The trial involved conflicting testimony concerning the evidence available to convict MacDonald. The issue of a speedy trial occupied the attention of the U.S. Supreme Court rather than issues surrounding the nature of the person who committed the crimes (Jeffery, 1985).

MacDonald was described as a playboy who liked women, cars, and the good life. He had a degree of artificial charm, thrill seeking, and careless abandon. The psychiatric evidence that was introduced was very superficial and it found that MacDonald was normal. No CAT or PETT scans or EEG measure was taken. It was suggested that MacDonald was on drugs, but this was never made part of the trial proceedings (McGinnis, 1983). A lot of money was spent convicting MacDonald, and it is obvious that neurological examinations would have been of great help in the resolution of this case.

Kenneth Bianchi, the Hillside Strangler (Schwartz, 1981; *The Mind of a Murderer*, PBS film shown March 1984 on PBS stations) was arrested for the murders of a number of women whose nude bodies were left along the freeways of Los Angeles. During the trial several psychiatrists and psychologists testified that under hypnosis Bianchi revealed a split personality, and that his other personality, "Steven," not Kenneth, had murdered the women. A psychiatrist hired by the government tricked Bianchi into thinking that under hypnosis a third personality would emerge, one named "Billy." Once the manipulation of testimony by the psychiatrist was revealed to the court the judge became furious and stated that this was another classic case where psychiatrists were naive and did not know what was going on. Bianchi then pleaded guilty and was sentenced to a term in the California prison system.

Again, a crisis was created between law and psychiatry by the Bianchi case. The judge commented on the naiveté of the psychiatrists, but he did not comment on the naiveté of judges who use the "right and wrong" test for insanity, and for his own actions in not ordering a neurological examination in place of hypnosis. No neurological evidence was introduced, nor was a hair sample taken and analyzed.

I would like to see the day when any major trial of a violent person automatically involves a complete neurological examination. Walsh has done hair analysis on Lucas, Huberty, and several other mass or serial murderers, and he has found significant differences in the lead and cadmium levels of such individuals (Chapter 18). The state of California spent millions to imprison Bianchi, and the state of Florida has spent $8 to 10 million to execute Ted Bundy. Most people are convinced that if Bundy is executed, they will be safe, but in reality there are hundreds of Bundys out there waiting for an opportunity to kill again. The current criminal justice model will not help the next victims of the violent offenders.

CRIMINAL LAW AND THE MEDICAL MODEL

Prevention versus Punishment

As emphasized at the beginning of this chapter, criminal law is in conflict with science and the medical model of treatment and crime prevention. As Kittrie noted (Chapter 7), the criminal law protects the citizen from unjustifiable punishment, but it does not protect him/her from unjustifiable treatment. The medical model provides treatment but often without adequate legal safeguards for those being treated. As a result we have created three different types of institutions for medical–behavioral problems: (1) the hospital for the physically ill, (2) the mental or psychiatric hospital for the mentally ill, and (3) the prison for the bad and evil. This can be characterized as the "bad versus the mad" (Barak-Glantz and Huff, 1981). It is my argument that it is a bad mistake to regard physical disease as different from mental disease as different from criminal behavior. If we were to take individuals from each of these institutions and test them neurologically, it would be difficult to tell on the basis of medical histories which ones came from hospitals, which came from mental institutions, and which came from prisons.

The reason we classify individuals as sick, or insane, or criminals is because of our belief in mind–body dualism and the belief that some people have free will and other people do not. The medical model is based on several legal doctrines that must be dealt with before we can establish a prevention–treatment model as a crime control model.

The Right to Treatment Doctrine

As part of the insanity defense and the Durham rule, a defendant found NGI is placed back on the streets. To avoid releasing dangerous persons onto the streets, the District of Columbia passed an ordinance requiring a civil commitment and medical evaluation of all NGI cases (Jeffery, 1967; American Bar Association, 1983). In Rouse v. Cameron, 373 F.2d 451 (D.C. Cir. 1966), the court held that an NGI decision meant that a person sent to St. Elizabeths Hospital must receive treatment or be released. This decision made treatment of the criminally insane mandatory and involuntary.

Wyatt v. Stickney, 344 F. Supp. 373 (1971), is a major case in mental health law in establishing standards for treatment of the mentally ill. The court reaffirmed the treatment goal of mental institutions, and it added a list of restrictions to treatment, such as the right to privacy, a right to the least restrictive conditions possible, freedom from excessive medication, freedom from unnecessary physical restraints, and the right not to be subjected to experimental research, lobotomies, electroconvulsive therapy, and aversive therapy without informed consent. Many of the ideas put forth by Kittrie (1971) are incorporated in the decision. Also, many of the problems in administering treatment are found in the restrictions placed on experimental research.

In Donaldson v. O'Connor, 493 F.2d 507 (1974), the court held that Donaldson was deprived of basic constitutional rights when he was held in a mental hospital without treatment. He had to be released unless he was dangerous to self or others (Brooks, 1974; Miller et al., 1976).

Brooks (1974:399) has commented that it is strange that the right to treatment doctrine has not been raised in the case of criminals. The father of the right to treatment doctrine, Morton Birnbaum (1982), has asked that the doctrine be expanded to all areas where individuals are in need of treatment. If the right to treatment doctrine were expanded to include criminals, alcoholics, drug addicts, psychopaths, neurologically damaged individuals, and so on, it would mean the creation of a criminal justice system based on a therapeutic model.

In Holt v. Sarver, 309 F. Supp. 362 (1970), the court found that the Arkansas State Penitentiary system constituted cruel and unusual punishment because of isolation cells, overcrowding, assaults and rapes, brutalities, and a lack of medical treatment. The court stated that an absence of programs for reform and rehabilitation constituted cruel and unusual punishment. In James v. Wallace, 382 F. Supp, 1177 (1974), the court reaffirmed the Holt v. Sarver decision, stating that "not only is it cruel and unusual punishment to confine a person in an institution under circumstances which increase the likelihood of future confinement, but these conditions defeat the goals of rehabilitation which prison officials have set for their institutions" (Jeffery, 1985; Krantz, 1981:377). If the courts were to hold that a lack of rehabilitative facilities constitutes cruel and unusual punishment, our prisons would be closed immediately.

The Right to Medical Treatment Doctrine

The right to medical treatment is by now a well-established doctrine, if not a practice carried out by our prison officials (Krantz, 1981). The broadest interpretation of the doctrine is found in Ruiz v. Estelle, 503 F. Supp. 1265 (1980), wherein the court held in a Texas case that that Department of Corrections had violated the constitutional rights of prisoners through overcrowding, lack of physical safety from rape and assault, indifference to inmate health care, inadequate health care, and a lack of screening and evaluation of psychiatric patients.

The major issue for us under the right to medical treatment doctrine is: Does the right to medical treatment extend to neurological examinations and diseases of the brain? It is generally recognized that an inmate has a right to treatment for heart disease or cancer, but does he have the right to demand a CAT scan or PETT scan or EEG analysis? Does an alcoholic or drug addict have a right to drug therapies? Does a hypoglycemic have a right to a special low-sugar or low-starch diet? When I was teaching at Sam Houston State University for a semester I had occasion to visit the maximum security hospital, Rusk State Hospital, where the criminally insane were housed. I was told that the administration of the hospital refused to place hypoglycemics on a special diet at this institution (personal communication).

Medical care is a sham in many prison systems. The state of Florida has faced a major crisis in its prison system for years due to overcrowding and brutality. The medical services for inmates has been under increasing attack in recent years because of a high number of deaths among inmates, attributed to a lack of adequate health care and to a neglect of the inmates. A private corporation was removed from that position after a five-member medical review board appointed by the court found neglect and inadequate medical care (*Tallahassee Democrat*, September 4, 1985; September 21, 1985; October 2, 1985; October 6, 1985). Between April 1983 and April 1984, 17 inmates died from a lack of adequate medical care. These persons had a long history of mental health, addiction, and alcohol-related problems. In December 1987, the secretary of corrections admitted in federal court that the state of Florida was in contempt of court because of the medical care given to inmates (*Tallahassee Democrat*, March 1, 1987; August 5, 1987; December 20, 1987).

The Right to Refuse Treatment

The right to refuse treatment doctrine developed out of a philosophical controversy between the Kantian view and the utilitarian view of ethics (Macklin, 1982; Gaylin et al., 1978). The utilitarian view (Chapter 5) states that research and treatment can be done on individuals if it is for the general welfare of society; that is, we can require research and treatment on people with AIDS to protect others from catching AIDS. The Kantian view (Chapter 4) is that the individual can never be used for the good of others; that is, we cannot force a citizen to be treated for AIDS to protect other persons. The issue of compulsory treatment goes to the heart of our current legal/ethical dilemmas concerning the right to life (abortions) and the right to death (Shapiro and Spice, 1984; Shapiro, 1982).

The right to refuse treatment has occurred especially in cases involving drug therapies for the mentally ill, lobotomies, electroconvulsive shock therapy, behavior modification therapy, and psychosurgery (Chapter 13; Martin, 1975; Geiser, 1976; Krantz, 1981). In Knecht v. Gillman, 488 F.2d 1136 (1974), the court found that the use of an aversive drug therapy was cruel and unusual punishment. Electroconvulsive therapy (ECT) has also been challenged, although it is one of the most successful treatments for depression.

Two recent cases have addressed the rights of mental patients to refuse psychotropic drugs. In Rennie v. Klein, 462 F. Supp. 1131 (1978), the court held that there must be informed consent before a patient is given drugs, and in Rogers v. Okin, 478 F. Supp. 1342 (1979), the court held that a patient had a right to refuse nonemergency medical drug therapies (Brooks and Winick, 1987). Brooks (Brooks and Winick, 1987) has stated that control over the use of drugs is necessary especially when drugs are overadministered in order to keep patients in a stupor. There must be a review of the quality of treatment given mental patients. Brooks emphasized the quality of treatment rather than the absolute right to refuse treatment. Stancer, Garfinkel, and Rakoff (1984) published a *Guideline for the Use of Psychotropic Drugs* in which they outlined procedures for using drugs in a manner that protects the rights of the patient.

The use of surgery on the brain to change behavior, called psychosurgery, has been the most controversial therapeutic technique used in the treatment of behavioral disorders. We should be careful to differentiate neurological surgery to remove a tumor or to correct a defective blood supply to the brain from surgery to alter behavior. The case of Kaimowitz v. Michigan Department of Mental Health (Wayne County Cir. Court, 1973) (Krantz, 1981:395), involved a patient who had been on a back ward of a Michigan mental hospital for 17 years because of episodic violence due to temporal lobe epilepsy. A medical team from Harvard Medical Center agreed to perform surgery for the control of the epileptic seizures, and the consent of the patient was secured. However, before the surgery could be undertaken, the legal aid society filed suit on behalf of the patient. The court held that surgery could not be performed since the patient could not give consent to experimental surgery where the risks were unknown. It is unfortunate that this case was decided without the benefit of a major conference of medical and legal experts in order to outline the procedures for neurosurgery. It is also unfortunate that the surgery was referred to as "psychosurgery." It was neurosurgery that followed the procedures for any neurosurgery, and it was to be performed by some of the best neurosurgeons in the nation. The surgery was no more experimental than any neurosurgery performed every day in the private sector of medical practice. When we do surgery on the heart or for cancer we control behavior, but we do not refer to the surgery as "surgery to control behavior." In the field of neurosurgery we do not make a careful distinction between surgery to correct a brain defect and surgery to control behavior.

The idea of psychosurgery created a major controversy in the behavior control area (London, 1969; Valenstein, 1980; National Institute of Mental Health, 1973; Institute of Society, Ethics, and Life Sciences, 1973; Gaylin, Meister, and Neville, 1975). As a result of this political controversy, XYY research, behavioral modification in the federal prison system, and the Center for the Study of Violence at the University of California at Los Angeles were killed (Gaylin, Macklin, and Powledge, 1981). We are not allowed to do research on violent offenders or to use behavior modification or other therapies to treat the criminals. We are not allowed to draw blood to see if the inmate is hypoglycemic, but we can stick a needle in his arm to execute him. Lawyers argue that we cannot force individuals into coercive therapy because it interferes with their free will and their mentation. Mind control is wrong (Shapiro, 1982). The autonomy of the individual is protected even if it means that the person has a right to be mad and to be violent. This is defined as the justice model.

Judge David Bazelon, in U.S. v. Alexander, 471 F.2d. 923 (1973), wrote that we allow only those therapies that are guaranteed to fail; we do not allow those therapies that might work.

Informed Consent

As we saw in the cases cited above, informed consent is required before treatment is given. Informed consent consists of (1) information as to the procedures and risks of the treatment, (2) voluntary consent on the part of the patient to the procedures, and (3) the competency of the patient to make an informed decision (Horan and Milligan, 1983; Valenstein, 1980; Brooks and Winick, 1987).

The doctrine of informed consent originated in the civil law area in regard to the consent of a patient to medical treatment. A much more difficult decision is involved in the use of the concept for criminal cases. We recognize the right of individuals to refuse treatment for cancer or heart disease. In fact, as Kittrie noted (Chapter 7), the doctrine of harm put forth by J. S. Mill stated that a person cannot be prohibited from harming himself. The Mill standard of liberty says that only acts which are harmful to others can be prohibited. The criminal law is based on a "harm to others" standard.

If we are to have a treatment program for criminals, we must use Mill's concept of liberty; that is, we must prevent people from doing harm to others. This means involuntary treatment. The lawyer opposes compulsory treatment, whereas he/she does not oppose compulsory punishment. We do not ask the criminal if he wants to be executed or placed in prison, yet we ask him if he/she wants treatment. As Gary Gilmore, the man executed in Utah, said; "The state of Utah sentenced me to die. I did not know I had a choice." We use the idea of informed consent for treatment but not for the punishment of criminals.

J. S. Mill made the standard of liberty "a harm to others." There is a critical difference between the treatment of an individual for an illness harmful to him/herself, and the treatment of illness harmful to others. If I have a heart condition, I do not have to treat it; I am not required to do so, for it is of no harm to others. I may not be allowed to fly a commercial aircraft in the event that I have a heart attack and endanger hundreds of people. However, we require health examinations and immunizations for certain diseases to protect others. We refuse to allow diseased people to work in the food industries, for example. We are now struggling with the issue of compulsory identification and segregation of AIDS patients so that they will not infect others. Several people have been charged with manslaughter for having sex with others without telling them they had AIDS. In Sweden there is a prison for AIDS victims to keep them segregated from the general population (*Weekly Worldly News*, January 26, 1988).

Criminal law is based on force and coercion. People are put into prisons without consent. This is the only way the criminal law works. If we are to use treatment and prevention as goals of the criminal law, we must have compulsory treatment. We can treat for the same reasons given for punishment: retribution, justice, deterrence, prevention, rehabilitation. If we can punish to deter or rehabilitate, we can treat to deter or rehabilitate. If we do not use involuntary treatment, we will never reach those who refuse treatment, and we therefore lack a treatment program.

There are three possible answers to the treatment issue: (1) establish a compulsory treatment program based on Kittrie's "therapeutic bill of rights"; (2) establish a voluntary treatment program based on a choice given the criminal of treatment in a medical facility or punishment in a prison; or (3) use prevention measures at an early stage of human development so as to prevent the development of criminal behavior. If criminal behavior never occurs, we need not be concerned with treatment or punishment. The third model would be used regardless of which of the other two alternatives we decided to use.

An overall observation can be made to the effect that the reasoning involved in the use of punishment as opposed to treatment leaves something to be desired. We execute people, we put them in overcrowded prisons which are brutal, we deny them rehabilitation and medical care, yet we say we cannot make these individuals well-adjusted citizens who can contribute to the welfare of themselves and society. The goal of treatment is to make the person better able to make decisions and perform as a rational person. People who are now not in charge of their lives would be made responsible through successful treatment. The legal idea of a responsible person must include the concept that some people are responsible only through medical care and treatment.

The Prediction of Future Dangerousness

To prevent criminal behavior before it occurs, we must be able to predict future dangerousness. The punishment model is past-oriented; the prediction model is future-oriented. The law does not allow for interference with the freedom of the individual on the basis of what he/she might do in the future, only for what they have done in the past. One cannot prevent crime by using the legal model, for the crime has occurred before the legal system takes action.

The medical model requires a CAT scan or heart surgery before the problem arises. The justice model as advocated by Morris and von Hirsch (Chapter 8) blocks any legal action based on potential future dangerousness. Dangerous behavior is regarded as criminal behavior to be punished rather than illness to be prevented or treated (Monahan, 1981:31). If we used this model in medicine, we would allow polluted air and water to injure people before we took corrective measures.

Bottoms and Brownsword (Hinton, 1983:9 ff.) present the legalistic viewpoint when they argue that the state cannot detain people on the basis of a prediction of future dangerousness, since the prediction is wrong in two out of three cases. Gross (1979:41 ff.) argued that we cannot treat a disease before the disease occurs because we cannot predict disease. Whether or not we can predict disease depends on the type of psychiatry and psychology we are using to make our predictions. Walker (Hinton, 1983:23 ff.) presents the utilitarian point of view that we can prevent a harm to others in the name of general welfare. Walker argues that two people can be restrained and given medical treatment to prevent a third person from doing harm. We control epileptics, the mentally ill, and those with typhoid and smallpox (Hinton, 1983:23 ff.)

Prediction studies of violence have been notorious for being wrong. Kozol et al. (1972) found that his prediction studies produced 35 percent true positives (predicted to be violent and they were violent); 65 percent were false positives (predicted to be violent but they were not violent); 92 percent were true negatives (predicted not to be violent and they were not violent); and 8 percent were false negatives (predicted not to be violent but they were violent). Cocozza and Steadman (1974) and Monahan (1981) found that 86 percent of their predictions produced false positives and 16 percent false negatives [see Table 21–1]. Steadman (1977) found that 31 percent of those predicted not to be violent were rearrested after release for violent crimes, whereas 41 percent of those predicted to be violent were arrested for violent crimes upon release.

Steadman and Cocozza (1974) found that few of the mental patients released from a maximum security hospital for the criminally insane on a court order committed violent offenses after their release. It must be pointed out in connection with this finding that a person can be sent to a criminal psychiatric unit for many reasons other than dangerousness. The problem lies in the fact that the law allows legal control over the mentally ill on the basis of a ''dangerous to self or to others'' standard. It is not possible to know from the psychiatric status how dangerous an offender was or what his future dangerousness might be.

By looking at the figures in Table 21–1 we can observe that the real problems are the false positives, which are around 65 to 80 percent. From these figures Monahan (1981:77) concluded that psychiatric predictions of future dangerousness are wrong two out of three times. The seriousness of the false positive case depends on what happens to such cases. If they are placed in an institution without treatment, it is serious. If they are tested and monitored with a little restriction on freedom as possible, but not identified or interfered with beyond that, it is not serious interference. We think of interference as

TABLE 21-1 VALIDITY STUDIES OF THE CLINICAL PREDICTION OF VIOLENT BEHAVIOR

Study	Percent true positive	Percent false positive	Percent true negative	Percent false negative	Number predicted violent	Number predicted nonviolent	Follow-up years
Kozol et al. (1972)	34.7	65.3	92.0	8.0	49	386	5
Steadman and Cocozza (1974)	20.0	80.0	—	—	967	—	4
Cocozza and Steadman (1976)	14.0	86.0	84.0	16.0	154	103	3
Steadman (1977)	41.3	58.7	68.8	31.2	46	106	3
Thornberry and Jacoby (1979)	14.0	86.0	—	—	438	—	4

Source: Monahan, 1981, p. 79.

punishment, not as treatment for the potential good of the person and of society at large.

The more serious problem is the false negative, the 8 to 16 percent predicted to be nonviolent who become violent and kill and rape in the future. These are the people we must pick up with our prediction instruments, but do not. One of the problems is that our tests to predict violence do not predict violence (Megargee, 1970). These tests are pencil-and-paper tests which do not measure the neurological basis for violent behavior. CAT scans and EEG readings were not used in any of the prediction studies cited above. One conclusion we can arrive at from prediction research is that we cannot predict violent behavior by using sloppy prediction instruments. We cannot predict what people will do in the community if we test them in prison or a hospital (Monahan, 1981:89). Another major issue in statistical prediction is that it applies to group data and not to the individual. As Gordon Allport noted, for any one person the chances of criminality are zero or 100 percent, not 50 or 70 percent (Monahan, 1981:99).

From what has been stated in this book concerning violent behavior, we can conclude that we must predict for individuals only, and we must use the neurological measures related to violence. Charles Whitman had a 100 percent probability of being violent as long as he had a tumor on the brain. We must focus on the 5 to 10 percent of the criminal population who are violent career criminals and find out if we can predict with some accuracy the violent behavior of a select population.

A number of studies have shown success at prediction by using neurological measures. Tong (Hinton, 1983:59) was able to predict 95 percent of the recidivists from a group of mentally ill offenders by the use of autonomic conditioning. The recidivists had an underaroused autonomic nervous system (Chapter 18). Perkins (Hinton, 1983:71 ff.) found that the best predictor of the dangerous sex offender is a physiological measure of a penile response to pictures depicting violent sex acts. Woodman (Hinton, 1983:103 ff.) found that aggressive individuals can be diagnosed from high norepinephrine levels. Virkkunen et al. (1988) found that they could accurately predict violence in violent offenders by measuring blood sugar content and serotonin levels in the brain. The violent offenders had low blood sugar and low serotonin levels.

It is interesting to note that lawyers and judges are constantly making predictions about future dangerousness when they make decisions concerning bail, sentences, work release, early release, probation, parole, and so on (Monahan, 1981:22). In other words, most decisions in the criminal justice system involve predictions of future dangerousness based not on science but on what a judge or prosecutor happens to think. In Barefoot v. Estelle, 1035 S.Ct. 3383 (1983), the court held that psychiatrists could make predictions about future dangerousness when such predictions were part of a decision concerning the death penalty. In June 1984, the U.S. Supreme Court held that juveniles can be placed in jail if the judge predicts that the juvenile is likely to commit a crime in the future. Justice Rehnquist stated that "from the legal point of view there is nothing inherently unattainable about the prediction of future criminal conduct'' (*Newsweek*, June 18, 1984:84). Prediction of future dangerousness is okay as long as the lawyer and not the scientist does it.

Science, Research, and Politics

As I have emphasized throughout the book, there is a need to integrate policy with research by means of interdisciplinary criminology and research institutes (Chapters 1 and 7). We must replace criminal justice based on retribution with a system based on treatment and prevention. This requires that criminal justice policy be based on an ongoing research and evaluation process. Criminal justice policy must be based on empirical results.

Criminology must be more scientific in its approach to behavior. It must make better use of experimental and case study data to supplement statistical studies. The ability to predict and control individual human behavior is the object of a science of behavior, and experimental controls are necessary for prediction and control.

In Chapter 6 I discussed legal realism, that is, the study of law as behavior. It was suggested that legal realism could act as a theoretical framework for integrating science and law. A science of behavior could be applied to legal issues to help guide and direct the criminal law. A related legal position is that of social control or sociological jurisprudence, which could also be utilized as a means of interrelating law and science (Chapter 15).

Criminological research must be more independent of state and federal funding. When state or federal agencies fund projects they do so on the basis of the politics of the moment. A request for a proposal is put forth in which the research priorities and assumptions about human behavior are set out by politicians rather than scientists. University professors take such monies under the guise of research projects, whereas in fact most of the projects are designed to show that the agency granting the money is doing something significant about the crime problem. Scientists and not politicians must establish the research agenda for criminology in the future. Police officials run the National Institute of Justice, and lawyers run the Department of Justice as well as local courts and prosecutorial offices. As this book has argued throughout, there is a need for an integration of law and science, knowledge and policy.

In the war against crime many positions have been taken: eliminate poverty, use psychotherapies, build more prisons, execute more criminals, and use longer prison sentences. The only thing that has not been used is a scientific theory of human behavior. Before the politicians and lawyers can control crime, they must have a scientific theory of human behavior based on an interdisciplinary approach.

The present political scene is not one that encourages optimism as to the future of our crime control efforts. The president-elect, George Bush, followed in the footsteps of the Republican party in his campaign, emphasizing ''law and order,'' including the use of military forces to fight drug smugglers, and long mandatory prison sentences even though our prisons are overcrowded.

The Democratic candidate, Michael Dukakis, who had been accused of being soft on crime, adopted a ''get tough on crime'' stance (*Tallahassee Democrat*, June 18, 1988). His campaign manager, Susan Estrich, a Harvard University law professor, stated that criminals must be punished for their crimes (*Newsweek*, June 27, 1988). As the victim of rape (Estrich, 1987), she wants changes in the criminal law as it relates to rape (e.g., the rules of evidence for establishing consent on the part of the female, and the rules concerning the amount of force needed to establish the crime of rape). This legalistic position is based on the assumptions that (1) there will be a defendant in the courtroom, when in fact most rapists do not end up in court or in prison; and (2) by going through the motions of a legal trial and sending the rapist to prison, other women will be made safe from rape. There is no evidence that punishment and prisons have reduced the rape rate or made women safe from rape. We have never attempted to prevent rape through environmental design, or to treat rapists through medical and neurological means, as discussed in this chapter. We must assume that there will be no major shift in our crime control policies under the Bush administration. As far as the future of crime is concerned, the election of 1988 may not really matter.

Science, Politics, and Social Control

As noted in Chapter 15, there is a major debate in criminology concerning the use of power and coercion by the state system. The Marxist position is that the state should not control human behavior, or the control should be minimal at best. The view of others, including the view expressed in this book, is that strong social control measures are necessary for two basic reasons: (1) the nature of human nature, that is, humans by biological nature are violent and vicious due to the structure of the human brain; and (2) the growth of population, urbanization, and technology has made necessary the centralization of power and control (Chapters 3 and 16). The idea that we can live in a large complex industrial society without centralized control is a myth. It is not supported in any way by the history of social control measures.

The problem is to design social control measures that are consistent with human freedom and dignity rather than to deny that social control is needed. When we undergo open-heart surgery we put our lives in the hands of a surgical team. We want the surgical team to have total control over the outcome of the surgery; otherwise, we would not undergo surgery. When we fly on a jet aircraft we want the pilot to have total control over the situation.

Opposition to the medical treatment model has come from those who argue that medical treatment is an unjustifiable form of social control over individual behavior. This position is seen in the antipsychiatry movement. Szasz (1961, 1963) argued that mental illness is a myth and a political label placed on behavior by psychiatrists. Laing (1969, 1971) has led an antipsychiatry movement by arguing that schizophrenia is a valuable ethical and religious experience. The role of psychiatry, according to Laing, is to impose political control over those we label as mentally ill.

Gove and others (Gove et al., 1982) in the book *Deviance and Mental Illness* found that the belief that mental illness is nothing more than a social label is a false belief. Mental illness is a real physical disease as defined today by biological psychiatry and psychopharmacology. Sedgwick (1982a, 1982b) criticized the views of Laing and Sasz when he noted that mental illness is a real physical disease, not a label. He argued that the legal profession has overemphasized the civil liberty issues at the expense of developing a collective responsibility for the care of the mentally ill.

Of the major movements in mental health and corrections, deinstitutionalization has been a prominent one, that is, the movement of patients and inmates from mental hospitals and prisons to community-based programs (Warren, 1981, 1982; Gove et al., 1982; Torrey, 1988). As a result, many mentally ill persons are on the streets, or are housed in rundown urban hotels, and are without medical care. Many of these former mental patients are now in prison (Gove et al., 1982; Warren, 1981, 1982; Farrington and Gunn, 1985). Warren stated that she was surprised to discover a biological reality to the concept of mental illness. Jack Zusman, a psychiatrist, stated: "It is inhumane and dangerous to leave such persons on their own in order to protect their freedom. To protect freedom we must remove part of it" (Warren, 1982:128 ff.).

Arvanites (1988) from his study concluded that deinstitutionalization of the mentally ill has led to an increase in the criminalization of the mentally ill. The mentally ill were not only being handled by the criminal justice system rather than the mental health system, but they were being arrested for more serious offenses.

In October 1987, Joyce Brown, who lived on the streets of New York City over an open grate, was placed in Bellevue Psychiatric Unit for observation under the Project Help program, designed to provide medical care for street people (*USA Today*, January 22, 1988; CBS News, "60 Minutes," January 24, 1988; June 12, 1988). The case of Joyce Brown was taken to court, and the court held that street people could not be placed in mental hospitals even though they were found to be urinating and defecating on the streets, and in need of medical care. We are caught between lawyers telling us we cannot treat criminals, and sociologists telling us mental illness is a myth.

Another aspect of the argument against early identification and intervention is the position taken in labeling theory, which states that if a person is labeled a deviant or mentally ill person, he/she will become that sort of person. The notion that a label can determine behavior has never been demonstrated, and labeling theory has been under attack in recent years (Chapter 14).

In his analysis of decarceration, Scull (1977) wrote that such an analysis must involve the power structure and social class structure of society. He listed (1) the growth of centralized state power, (2) the use of institutions for criminals and the mentally ill, and (3) the use of experts to classify individuals as basic to modern social control efforts. The overcrowding of prisons and mental hospitals, and the growing expense of running such institutions, have created a major crisis in welfare capitalism. He also noted that we are resorting more and more to the use of drug therapies in the management of behavioral problems.

Cohen (1985) has characterized the control of deviancy in the 1980s as an extension of control techniques beyond institutions through the use of community programs, decarceration programs, and house arrest programs. Individuals are released from institutions, and offenses are decriminalized, but social control is now in the community program, not the institution. There is an antipsychiatry movement, but at the same time there is more reliance on professionals to classify deviants and to control deviant behavior through control of the mind by means of psychotherapies and psychotropic drugs.

Cohen is concerned about these new social control measures, especially as found in behavioral psychology, psychiatry, and crime prevention through environmental design. Cohen argued that the high cost of institutions plus the crisis in welfare capitalism have forced the state to find new means of social control.

Blomberg and his colleagues (Blomberg, 1983, 1984, 1987; Blomberg and Reed, 1987; Blomberg et al., 1986) have traced the diversionary programs over the years and have found a "net widening" effect; that is, as community control measures are extended, the prison population does not decrease. Rather, the people absorbed by community control measures are those who in an earlier period of history would have escaped the social control mechanisms and would have remained outside the system. They found no evidence that these programs are having any effect on prison populations or crime rates in general. New strategies for community control include home confinement and electronic handcuffing (Blomberg, Waldo, and Burcroff, in press; Blomberg and Reed, 1987; Blomberg, 1987).

Related to the diversionary programs are programs established for victims, such as rape crisis centers and victim compensation programs. We develop programs that deal with the victim *after the crime* has occurred rather than developing crime prevention programs for rape and robbery and murder. Again, it is a matter of allowing a woman to be raped, and then we take action by treating her for her injuries. It is like allowing a heart attack to occur before we call the medical emergency squad to the scene.

The abuses of psychiatric treatment and mental hospitals cannot be denied. Mental hospitals are depressing and awful places. Psychiatry has been used in the Soviet Union as a way of placing political dissidents in mental hospitals (Stover and Nightingale, 1985; Lynch, 1987). The political misuse of science, as in the case of genetics (Chapter 10), is all too common. All I can say is that a dictator need not be scientific to throw people into prison or boil them in oil or torture them on a rack. Totalitarian systems do not need CAT scans or behavior modification or psychotropic drugs in order to control citizens.

The use of science to control human behavior is very well illustrated by recent advancements in hair analysis and DNA analysis. Hair analysis has been used to identify individuals with abnormal body and brain chemistry so as to afford such people with early diagnosis and treatment before they become violent. The National Institute of Justice is now developing hair analysis (the RIAH method) as a means of identifying drug users so as to put such persons in prison or out of a job. The same scientific technique can be used to help the person or to punish him/her (Gropper, 1988; Baumgartner, 1988; Henderson, 1988). DNA fingerprinting is now used with sperm or tissue samples taken from rape or murder victims to identify the criminal. This is an effective way to identify the rapist. Several problems remain, such as, is the DNA test used to identify the violent person and then assure that he/she receives major medical treatment, or is it used to put the rapist in prison for life? I was recently asked by a public defender how she could challenge the DNA fingerprinting test so as to get her client free of a rape charge. She was not concerned with whether he committed the crime and if release would be a danger to society, but only that she thought her job was to see that the rapist was freed from criminal charges. As I stated in Chapter 20, lawyers will introduce evidence of mental illness in order to get a reduced sentence for their client rather than compulsory treatment. When we use biological psychiatry to reduce sentences rather than to require successful treatment, we are allowing lawyers to play games with science in order to win criminal cases. The law should be used to remove dangerous persons from society and to guarantee that they receive successful treatment. Similarly, we use criminal career studies not to treat such individuals but to see that they are prosecuted under special laws for career offenders (Sherman, n.d.; Trager et al., 1988).

SUMMARY

The conflict between legalistic and scientific criminology is highlighted in this chapter. The classical school, based on free will, moral responsibility, and punishment, is pitted against the positive school based on determinism and treatment.

The focus of the chapter is on crime prevention at the individual level (murder, rape, assault). This involves a psychobiological analysis of the career offender. Early diagnosis and intervention into behavioral problems are necessary. This means a combination of primary and secondary prevention techniques, as well as a combination of treatment and prevention techniques.

The medical/treatment model is not accepted by the legal system for the reason that the right to treatment doctrine is extended only to mental patients and not criminals. The right to medical treatment doctrine has not been extended to the right to have brain defects treated. The right to refuse treatment and the informed consent doctrine are used by lawyers to block the treatment of criminals.

The law does not allow intervention before the crime is committed. To prevent criminal behavior, we must take action before the crime is committed. A prevention technology based on accurate predictions must be developed before the crime occurs; otherwise, we do not prevent crimes from being committed.

Social control is a fact of political life, yet we reject social control as a concept for many valid reasons. We must build a model of social control consistent with human freedom and dignity. We must recognize that concepts of ethics and justice require that we treat and prevent crime rather than punish it through brutal and ineffective means. Criminology must develop a new approach to the understanding and control of human behavior.

AN AFTERTHOUGHT

As I spent the hours in recent months putting this manuscript together, it occurred to me how fragile ideas are. I was concerned about this fact until it also occurred to me that of all the things we deal with in our everyday life, ideas are the only things that survive.

Criminology needs new ideas, new ventures, and new approaches, and the courage and vision to look beyond past solutions that have failed. We find in the criminal justice system a false sense of security. As Bertrand Russell stated so admirably: "We need the creation of a school of men with scientific training and philosophical interests, unhampered by the traditions of the past" (Cousins, 1981). As Albert Schweitzer reminded us: "If you have something important to do, don't expect people to roll stones out of your way" (Cousins, 1981).

REFERENCES

AMERICAN BAR ASSOCIATION (1983). *Criminal Justice Mental Health Standards*. Chicago: American Bar Association.

ARVANITES, T. M. (1988). "The Impact of State Mental Hospital Deinstitutionalization on Commitments for Incompetency to Stand Trial. *Criminology*, 26(2):307–320.

BARAK-GLANTZ, I., and C. R. HUFF (1981). *The Mad, the Bad, and the Different*. Lexington, Mass.: Lexington Books.

BAUMGARTNER, W. (1988). Comparing Hair Testing to Urinalysis for Monitoring Criminal Justice Populations." Paper presented at the American Society of Criminology, Chicago, Ill., November 1988.

BIRNBAUM, M. (1982). "The Right to Treatment." In *Critical Issues in American Psychiatry and the Law*, ed. R. Rosner. Springfield, Ill.: Charles C Thomas.

BLOMBERG, T. (1983). "Diversion's Disparate Results and Unresolved Questions: An Integrative Evaluation Perspective." *Journal of Research in Crime and Delinquency*, 24–38, January.

BLOMBERG, T. (1984). "Community Control: An Assessment of an Alternative to Prison." Paper presented at the annual meeting of the American Society of Criminology, Cincinnati, Ohio, November 1984.

BLOMBERG, T. (1987). "Criminal Justice Reform and Social Control: Are We Becoming a Minimum Security Society?" In *Essays in the Sociology of Social Control*, ed. J. Lowman et al. Aldershot, Hampshire, United Kingdom: Gower Press.

BLOMBERG, T., and K. REED (1987). "Home Confinement in Florida: An Assessment." Paper presented at the annual meeting of the American Society of Criminology, Montreal, Canada, November 1987.

BLOMBERG, T., G. WALDO, and L. BURCROFF (in press). In *Intermediate Punishments: Electronic Surveillance and Intensive Supervision*, ed. B. McCarthy. New York: Willowtree.

BLOMBERG, T., ET AL. (1986). "Diversion and Net Widening." *Evaluation Review*, 10:1, 45–64.

BRANTINGHAM, P. J., and F. L. FAUST (1976). "A Conceptual Model of Crime Prevention." *Crime and Delinquency*, 22:284–296.

BROOKS, A. D. (1974). *Law, Psychiatry, and the Mental Health System*. Boston: Little, Brown.

BROOKS, A. D., and B. J. Winick, eds. (1987). "Current Issues in Mental Disability Law." *Rutgers Law Review*, 39(2–3):1–244.

CBS NEWS (1988). "60 Minutes, Brown v. Koch," January 24, 1988 and June 12, 1988.

COCOZZA, J., and H. STEADMAN (1974). "Some Refinements in the Measurement and Prediction of Dangerous Behavior." *American Journal of Psychiatry*, 131:1012–1020.

COHEN, S. (1985). *Visions of Social Control*. Cambridge: Polity Press.

COUSINS, N. (1981). *Human Options*. New York: W. W. Norton.

ESTRICH, S. (1987). *Real Rape*. Cambridge, Mass.: Harvard University Press.

FARRINGTON, D. A., and J. Gunn (1985). *Aggression and Dangerousness*. New York: Wiley.

FREEMAN, L. (1955). *Before I Kill More*. New York: Crown.

FREIER, M. (1986). "The Biological Bases of Criminal Behavior." In *Intervention Strategies for Chronic Juvenile Offenders*, ed. P. Greenwood. Westport, Conn.: Greenwood Press.

GAYLIN, W., R. MACKLIN, and T. M. POWLEDGE, eds. (1981). *Violence and the Politics of Research*. New York: Plenum.

GAYLIN, W., J. S. MEISTER, and R. C. NEVILLE, eds. (1975). *Operating on the Mind*. New York: Basic Books.

GAYLIN, W., ET AL. (1978). *Doing Good: The Limits of Benevolence*. New York: Pantheon.

GEISER, R. L. (1976). *Behavior Modification and the Managed Society*. Boston: Beacon Press.

GOTTFREDSON, M., and T. HIRSCHI (1986). "The True Value of Lambda Would Be Zero: An Essay on Career Criminals, Criminal Careers, Selective Incapacitation, Cohort Studies, and Related Topics." *Criminology*, 24(2):213–234.

GOTTFREDSON, M., and T. HIRSCHI (1987). "The Methodological Adequacies of Longitudinal Research on Crime." *Criminology*, 25(3):581–614.

GOVE, W., ET AL. (1982). *Deviance and Mental Illness*. Beverly Hills, Calif.: Sage.

GROPPER, B. (1988). "Advances in the State-of-the-Art in Drug Testing." Paper presented at the American Society of Criminology, Chicago, Ill., November, 1988.

GROSS, H., (1979). *A Theory of Criminal Justice*. New York: Oxford University Press.

HENDERSON, G. (1988). "Critical Review of Technology in Hair Analysis for Drug Abuse." Paper presented at the American Society of Criminology, Chicago, Ill., November, 1988.

HINTON, J. W. (1983). *Dangerousness: Problems of Assessment and Prediction*. London: Allen & Unwin.

HORAN, D. J., and R. J. MILLIGAN (1983). "Recent Developments in Psychiatric Malpractice. *Behavioral Sciences and the Law*, 1:23–28.

INSTITUTE OF SOCIETY, ETHICS, AND LIFE SCIENCES (1973). *Physical Manipulation of the Brain*. Hastings-on-the Hudson, N.Y.: Hastings Center.

JEFFERY, C. R. (1967). *Criminal Responsibility and Mental Disease*. Springfield, Ill.: Charles C Thomas.

JEFFERY, C. R. (1985). *Attacks on the Insanity Defense*. Springfield, Ill: Charles C Thomas.

KITTRIE, N. (1971). *The Right to Be Different*. Baltimore, Md.: Johns Hopkins University Press.

KOZOL, H., et al. (1972). "The Diagnosis and Treatment of Dangerousness." *Crime and Delinquency*, 18:371–392.

KRANTZ, S. (1981). *The Law of Corrections and Prisoner's Rights*. St. Paul, Minn.: West Publishing Co.

LAING, R. D. (1969). *Self and Others*. London: Tavistock.

LAING, R. D. (1971). *The Politics of Experience*. London: Penguin Books.

LEWIS, D. O., ed. (1981). *Vulnerability to Delinquency*. New York: Spectrum Publications.

LEWIS D. O., and D. A. BALLA (1976). *Delinquency and Psychopathology*. New York: Grune & Stratton.

LONDON, P. (1969). *Behavior Control*. New York: Harper & Row.

LYNCH, G. W. (1987). "Political Psychiatry in the U.S.S.R." In *Advances in Forensic Psychology and Psychiatry*, ed. R. W. Rieber. Norwood, N.J.: Ablex.

MACKIN, R. (1982). *Man, Mind, and Morality: The Ethics of Behavior Control*. Englewood Cliffs, N.J.: Prentice Hall.

MARTIN, R. (1975). *Legal Challenges to Behavior Modification*. Champaign, Ill.: Research Press.

McCORD, J. (1986). "Review of Understanding and Controlling Crime, by Farrington, Ohlin, and Wilson." *Criminology*, 24(4):799–808, November.

McGINNIS, J. (1983). *Fatal Vision*. New York: Putnam.

MEGARGEE, E. (1970). "The Prediction of Violence with Psychological Tests." In *Current Topics in Clinical and Community Psychology*, ed. C. Spielberger, New York: Academic Press.

MILLER, F. W., ET AL. (1976). *The Mental Health Process*. Mineola, N.Y.: Foundation Press.

MILLER, M. (1986). "Legal Constraints on Intervention Programs in Public Schools." In *Intervention Strategies for Chronic Juvenile Offenders*, ed. P. Greenwood. Westport, Conn.: Greenwood Press.

MONAHAN, J. (1981). *Predicting Violent Behavior*. Beverly Hills, Calif.: Sage.

NATIONAL INSTITUTE OF MENTAL HEALTH (1973). *Psychosurgery*. Washington, D.C.: National Institute of Mental Health.

ORNSTEIN, R., and D. SOBEL (1987). *The Healing Brain*. New York: Simon & Schuster.

RESTAK, R. M. (1983). "Psychiatry in America." *The Wilson Quarterly*, Fall.

RESTAK, R. (1984). *The Brain*. New York: Bantam Books.

SCHWARTZ, T. (1981). *The Hillside Strangler*. New York: Doubleday.

SCULL, A. T. (1977). *Decarceration*. Englewood Cliffs, N.J.: Prentice Hall.

SEDGWICK, P. (1982a). "Antipsychiatry from the Sixties to the Eighties." In *Deviance and Mental Illness*, ed. W. Gove et al. Beverly Hills, Calif.: Sage.

SEDGWICK, P. (1982b). *Psycho Politics*. New York: Harper & Row.

SHAPIRO, M. H. (1982). *Biological and Behavioral Technologies and the Law*. New York: Praeger.

SHAPIRO, M. H., and R. G. SPICE (1984). *Bioethics and Law*. St. Paul, Minn.: West Publishing Co.

SHERMAN, L. (n.d.). "Repeat Offenders." In *Crime File*. Washington, D.C.: National Institute of Justice.

STANCER, H. C., P. E. GARFINKEL, and V. M. RAKOFF, eds. (1984). *Guidelines for the Use of Psychotropic Drugs*. Jamaica, N.Y.: SP Medical and Scientific Books.

STEADMAN, H. A. (1977). "A New Look at Recidivism among Patuxent Inmates." *The Bulletin of the American Academy of Psychiatry and the Law*, 1977:5, 200–209.

STEADMAN, H., and J. COCOZZA (1974). *Careers of the Criminally Insane*. Lexington, Mass.: Lexington Books.

STOVER, E., and E. O. NIGHTINGALE (1985). *The Breaking of Bodies and Minds*. New York: W. H. Freeman.

SZASZ, T. (1961). *The Myth of Mental Illness*. New York: Hoeber-Harper.

SZASZ, T. (1963). *Law, Liberty and Psychiatry*. New York: Macmillan.

TORREY, E. F. (1988). *Nowhere to Go: the Tragic Odyssey of the Homeless Mentally Ill*. New York: Harper & Row.

TRAGER, K., ET AL. (1988). *The Impact of Career Criminals on Florida's Criminal Justice System*. Tallahassee, FL: Florida Department of Law Enforcement.

U.S. DEPARTMENT OF JUSTICE (1981). *Butner*. Washington, D.C.: Federal Bureau of Prisons.

VALENSTEIN, E. S. (1980). *The Psychosurgery Debate*. San Francisco: W. H. Freeman.

VAN DUSEN, K. T. (1986). "Treatment Interventions Implied by Biological Factors." In *Intervention Strategies for Chronic Juvenile Offenders*, ed. P. Greenwood. Westport, Conn.: Greenwood Press.

VIRKKUNEN, M., ET AL. (1988). "Relationship of Psychobiological Variables to Recidivism in Violent Offenders and Impulsive Fire Setters: A Follow-Up Study." Submitted for publication.

WARREN, C. (1981). "New Forms of Social Control." *American Behavioral Scientist*, 24(6):724–809.

WARREN, C. A. B. (1982). *The Court of Last Resort*. Chicago, IL: The University of Chicago Press.

WILSON, J. Q., and R. J. HERRNSTEIN (1985). *Crime and Human Nature*. New York: Simon & Schuster.

WITTE, A. D., ET AL. (1983). "The Effects of a Less Coercive Internal Prison Environment and Gradual Reintegration on Post-Release Performance: An Evaluation of Morris' Model of Imprisonment as Implemented at the Federal Correctional Institution at Butner, N.C." Report to the Federal Bureau of Prisons.

QUESTIONS

1. How does the prevention of personal crimes differ from prevention of property crimes?
2. What crime prevention projects could be used for the violent career offender?
3. What does the Charles Whitman case tell us about crime prevention?
4. What legal barriers exist to prevent the treatment of offenders?
5. How can the "right to treatment" doctrine and the "right to medical treatment" doctrine be used to create a medical model for the treatment of offenders?
6. What arguments are presented for the compulsory treatment of offenders? Against the compulsory treatment of offenders?
7. Since we cannot predict future violence, we cannot prevent future violence. Comment.
8. The legal system does not act until a crime has been committed. Does this mean that crime prevention programs are impossible in the future?
9. What legal barriers exist to research on violent offenders?
10. What concepts of social control are involved in our crime control policies?
11. What major changes would you make in criminology within the next twenty years to improve our crime prevention and crime control programs?

Index

AUTHORS

Index

Yeudall, L., 367, 368
Yinger, M. J., 181, 280
Young, J., 294
Young, P., 21

Zalman, M., 11
Zeigler, L. E., 57, 93
Zeiler, M. D., 236
Zeitlin, I. M., 253, 254
Zenoff, E., 142
Zillman, D., 326
Zimbardo, P., 320
Zimring, F., 116, 318
Ziskin, J., 433
Znaniecki, F., 256

SUBJECT

Butner Federal Correctional Institution, 446

Index

Index   **481**